How to Think in Medicine

Reasoning, Decision Making, and Communication
in Health Sciences and Professions

How to Think in Medicine

Reasoning, Decision Making, and Communication
in Health Sciences and Professions

Milos Jenicek

Routledge
Taylor & Francis Group

LONDON AND NEW YORK

First published 2018
by Routledge
2 Park Square, Milton Park, Abingdon, Oxon OX14 4RN

and by Routledge
605 Third Avenue, New York, NY 10017

First issued in paperback2021

Routledge is an imprint of the Taylor & Francis Group, an informa business

British Library Cataloguing in Publication Data
A catalogue record for this book is available from the British Library

ISBN 13: 978-1-03-209542-4 (pbk)
ISBN 13: 978-1-138-05246-8 (hbk)

Publisher's Note
The publisher has gone to great lengths to ensure the quality of this reprint but points out that some imperfections in the original copies may be apparent.

Contents

A Word from the Author: What Will You Read in This Book? vii
About the Author xvii

SECTION I FOUNDATION OF TODAY'S MEDICAL THINKING: PHILOSOPHY, MEDICINE ITSELF, QUANTITATIVE AND QUALITATIVE RESEARCH

1 Interactive Domains of Medical Thinking Today: Understanding Our Own
   Reasoning from a Broader Historical Experience 3

2 Philosophy for Medicine: Key Contributions of Philosophy to Medical
   Thinking Today—A Short Reminder and Refresher...21

3 Medicine's Own Contribution to Today's Thinking in Health Sciences
   and Professions: Not Only Philosophy, But Also Art, Craft, Scientific Method,
   and Evidence...37

SECTION II ESSENTIALS OF REASONING AND CRITICAL THINKING IN HEALTH SCIENCES

4 Then, How Do Physicians and Other Health Professionals Really (or Should)
   Think 75

5 About What to Think in Step-by-Step Clinical Work and Care: Risk, Diagnosis,
   Treatment, Prognosis 123

SECTION III MAJOR SUBJECTS AND CHALLENGES IN MEDICAL THINKING NOT TO BE MISSED: CHOOSING WHAT WE WANT TO DO, DEFINING WHAT WE ARE DOING, CAUSE-EFFECT RELATIONSHIPS, MEDICAL ERROR AND HARM

6 Thinking about What We Intend to Do: Thesis and Its Seven Cornerstones—
   "What Is on Our Mind before Talking about Anything Else? About What
   Exactly Are We Talking?" 171

7 Definitions: Thinking about What We Are Thinking, Specifying More What
   We Intend to Do—*"What Do You Mean by That?"*...191

8 How to Think about Cause-Effect Relationships: Multiple and Single
   Observations..213

9 Thinking about Medical Error and Harm: Flaws in an Operator's Reasoning
   and Decision-Making among Others 251

10 Thinking to Decide in Clinical and Community Medicine: Subjects, Thinking
   Tools, and Vehicles for the Best Possible Decisions in Practice and Research 287

SECTION IV SHARING OUR THOUGHTS ON ORAL AND WRITTEN
COMMUNICATION WITH PEERS, PATIENTS, AND COMMUNITIES

11 Communicating Our Thoughts with Peers and Patients—Mostly Oral Clinical
   Communication, Its Content, Objectives, and Vehicles.............................325

12 Sharing Our Thinking about Clinical Cases: Clinical Case Reporting—
   "Getting the Best Information from Just One Case or from a Fistful of Cases
   or Events?" 373

13 Sharing Our Thoughts in Written Essays, Research-Based Articles, and Other
   Types of Written Medical Communication: "Should We Not Think about
   and Communicate Our Research, as Well as How We Have Done It?"....................393

An Epilogue: What Did You Read in This Book?...429

Glossary: Preferred Terms and Their Definitions in the Context of This Book................437

Appendix A: List of Cognitive Biases...493

Appendix B: List of Fallacies...523

Index 537

A Word from the Author: What Will You Read in This Book?

Thoughts, Thinkers, and Things to Think About

I think the author who speaks about his own book is almost as bad as a mother who talks about her own children.
Benjamin Disraeli
1st Earl of Beaconsfield
(1804–1881)
Do I have a choice, Sir Benjamin?

The ideas I stand for are not mine. I borrowed them from Socrates, I stole them from Jesus. And I put them in a book. If you don't like their rules, whose would you use?
Dale Carnegie
(1888–1955)
The author of this book, inspired by others, has done the same!

When I want to read a good book, I write one.
Benjamin Disraeli
1st Earl of Beaconsfield
(1804–1881)
Writing comes first for any author!

*Writing comes more easily if you have
something to say.*
Sholem Asch
New York Herald Tribune
November 6, 1955
**Yes, it certainly helps, especially
for the author of this book.**

The pen is mightier than the sword.
E.G. Bulwer-Lytton
(1803–1873)
Richelieu (1839, 2.2)
**And carrying a pen does not require a
permit. Only a friendly and interested
publisher is needed!**

*Never write a textbook; If it is a failure, it is
time thrown away and worse than wasted;
if it is a success, it is a milestone around
your neck for the rest of your life.*
Michael Foster
(1836–1907)
in 1932 H.D. Rolleston's
*The Cambridge Medical School:
A Biographical History*
In this case, it is too late!

*It took me fifteen years to discover
that I had no talent for writing, but
I couldn't give it up because by that time
I was too famous.*
Robert Benchley
(1889–1945)
in 1955 by Nathaniel Benchley
**After fifteen years, that is
understandable!**

*One always tends to overpraise a long book,
because one has got through it.*
E.M. Forster
(1879–1970)
in Abinger Harvest
("T.E. Lawrence"), 1936
This is a shorter one!

A bad book is as much of labour to write as a good one, it comes sincerely from the author's soul.
Aldous Huxley
(1894–1963), 1928
This book certainly does come from the author's soul!

Writing books is the closest men ever come to childbearing.
Norman Mailer
(1923–2007), 1988
Think of a growing and shrinking organ (brain), all sorts of (mental) contractions, and losing (intellectual) waters!

When you publish a book, it's the world's book. The world edits it.
Philip Roth
New York Times
September 2, 1979
Do not hesitate to edit mine!

A book is a version of the world. If you do not like it, ignore it; or offer your own version in return.
Salman Rushdie
Imaginary Homelands (1992)
That isn't as easy to do as it may seem!

When the emperor Domitian was bored, he mangled flies with a bodkin. I write a book.
Edward Dahlberg
(1900–1977)
The Confessions of Edward Dahlberg (1971)
No, the author of this book was neither bored, nor mangled flies with a bodkin!

*I find television very educational. Every
time someone turns it on, I go in the other
room and read a book.*
Groucho Marx
(1895–1989)
Why not try this one?

*Still, the E-book is not a passing thing, it is here
to stay as it becomes cheaper and improved.
Nonetheless, it is really no more than a screen
upon which to read, and it is clear that when
enough people start reading them, electronic
books will do for the ophthalmologists, what
taffy and caramels did for dentists.*
Martin Arnoldin
New York Times
January 7, 1999
**Will this book provide the reader with
a better vision?
Dear reader, please let me know!**

*I must follow the people.
Am I not their leader?*
Benjamin Disraeli
1st Earl of Beaconsfield
(1804–1881)
**I must follow my readers.
Am I not their author?
I must follow my students.
Am I not their teacher?**

*The profession of book-writing makes a horse
racing seem like a solid, stable business.*
John Steinbeck
(1902–1968)
**The author knows; he lives on a
horse farm!**

*Preface: The part of a book
which is never read.*
Gerald F. Lieberman
(1925–1999), 1983
Why not change things up and read this one?

A person who publishes a book appears willfully in public with his pants down.
Edna St. Vincent Millay
(1892–1950)
In this era of gender equality, with HER pants too!

If we try to envisage an "average Canadian writer." we can see him living near a campus, teaching at least part time at the university level, mingling too much for his work's good with academics, doing as much writing as he can for the CBC, and always hoping for a Canada Council Fellowship.
George Woodcock
(1912–1995)
Definitely applies to the author of this book!

Writing is easy: all you do is sit starring at the blank sheet of paper until the drops of blood form on your head.
Gene Fowler
(1890–1960)
Staring at the monitor and hitting the keyboard today is even worse!

Your manuscript is both good and original; but the parts that are good are not original, and the parts that are original are not good.
Samuel Johnson
(1709–1784)
The author apologies for this!

The best way to become a successful writer is to read good writing, remember it, and then forget where you remember it from.
Gene Fowler
(1890–1960)
Our references may help!

Welcome readers from all health professions and specialties in clinical and preventive care of both individual patients and their communities! This book provides a summary of experiences to help you think, reason, make decisions, and share experiences with patients, other health professionals, and the community at large. It briefly outlines how to communicate such experiences in the health sciences, and presents recommendations regarding the *right* ways of what to do, and not do, now and in the future.

Is This Book Entirely New?

Not quite! This book is preceded by two recent titles from the same author and publisher: *A Primer on Clinical Experience in Medicine: Reasoning, Decision Making, and Communication in Health Sciences* (2013) and *Writing, Reading, and Understanding in Modern Health Sciences: Medical Articles and Other Forms of Communication* (2014). They not only paved the way for this work, but also showed that medical thinking is a topic worthy of special attention as one of the basic arts and sciences in medicine.

In fact, this book is a second edition of the two titles mentioned above, merged together, but with a different orientation, context, concept, and content. Consequently, this book has a new title (*How to Think in Medicine*) and in the subtitle, uses a part of an already published subtitle (*Reasoning, Decision Making, and Communication in Health Sciences and Professions*). We believe that the message is relevant both for scientists and practitioners as well.

Content adapted from previously published titles has been reviewed, updated, and reoriented within the new context of this monograph. Wherever this was done, the original source has been identified at the bottom of the chapter's first page of text.

What Role Does This Book Play in Current Trends in Medicine?

Medical thinking today reflects, integrates, and expands classical domains of thinking such as logic, modern argumentation, reasoning, and decision-making in philosophy in general, well beyond the traditional health and disease domain. It also provides an invaluable methodological heritage and essential experiences in fundamental, field, and clinical epidemiology; biostatistics; psychology; and other cognitive sciences.

There are three main reasons for referring to the subject matter of this book as "philosophy for physicians":

1. Since the author's student years, and until recently, philosophy as "thinking about thinking" has been considered an academic domain and the purview of brilliant minds alone. Such minds produce remarkable new concepts, innovations, and interpretations which are not necessarily followed by action. However, medicine *is* focused on action, and for good reason. The practice of medicine frequently requires action. Nonetheless, experienced clinicians know all too well that "doing nothing" is often a more challenging justification and decision than "doing something." Both "doing something" and "doing nothing" are supported by reasoning and critical thinking of common nature, structure, and content. This is mostly a qualitative approach for health professions.
2. For decades and over the course of several newer generations, medical thinking has been developed by many remarkable minds who have not been career philosophers. Now, they

increasingly include in their ranks career physicians, biostatisticians, epidemiologists, psychologists, health economists, sociologists, and health management professionals. All this health domain–related thinking, decision-making, and experience sharing (communication) has common ground anchored in the broad framework of "general" philosophy. Today, career philosophers are more involved in health sciences than ever. This approach is traditionally mostly quantitative for health professions.

3. Considering numerous recent initiatives in health professions, these experiences, and present ways of thinking in medicine are becoming common to most health sciences (with the exception of some alternative and complementary medicines). The message of this book may be helpful for many in medicine, veterinary medicine, dentistry, nursing, physiotherapy, clinical psychology, chiropractic, some other alternative and complementary medicines, and elsewhere.

Medicine is an increasingly integrated mosaic of "thinking" and "acting" skills that includes various branches of philosophy such as logic, argumentation, arts, crafts, and scientific methodology. Currently, we teach and learn this subject matter in the history of medicine, philosophy, epidemiology, biostatistics, clinical specialties, health program management in preventive and community medicine, and public health across clinical specialties. However, there is no formal course (so far) on how to think in medicine using all the above. Perhaps these pages could be a starting point of sorts.

Another Challenge: The Context and Architecture of This Book

Medicine as a biological art and science is a matter of probability and uncertainty, with missing or incomplete information, perfect, or imperfect. Within this context, situations must be understood and best possible decisions must be made and shared with patients, other health professionals, and the community.

There are two ways of tackling health problems related to the role of philosophy in health sciences. The first is to consider applying metaphysics, logic, epistemology, or aesthetics to medicine. The other approach is to combine offerings from various branches of philosophy and apply them based on the specific nature of the problems to solve, and the methodology to follow, at various gnostic steps interfacing with steps of curative and preventive care of patients and their communities. We will try to cover the latter process in these pages.

Our ways of thinking in research and practice have many common traits. Besides the scientific method used in the study of new problems, each patient in our practice is "new." We hypothesize about their health problems, about the best manner to treat them, what their future will be in terms of prognosis, and what their care should be over an extended period. All these elements are supported by "secondhand evidence," generated by scientific research and the accumulation of individual and group past and present experience. We believe there is a common way of thinking in this given context provided by philosophy, research, and practice.

Succinct repetitions in some chapters are intentional because some readers may only read specific chapters. The message of each chapter should then be complete in its essentials and thorough enough for a basic understanding without having to read other chapters. The repetitions also illustrate how essential components of modern critical thinking and argumentation apply, and are fundamental and valid in more than one domain, as Toulmin's argumentation is across the broad medical experience.

The overall Table of Contents introduces the book, and each chapter has its own Table of contents (In This Chapter). The Table of Contents are followed by an introduction to the reader by *A Word from the Author: What Will You Read in This Book?* and summarized in concluding remarks as *An Epilogue: What Did You Read in This Book?*

Four sections comprise the main content of the book. They follow a logical order:

In **Section I—Foundation of Today's Medical Thinking: Philosophy, Medicine Itself, Quantitative and Qualitative Research** (Chapters 1–3), we review interactive current domains of medical thinking, which constitute a common basis for the intellectual management of special topics and applications. This includes in Chapter 1, epidemiology, biostatistics, evidence-based medicine, and qualitative research. Chapter 2 covers the contribution of philosophy and Chapter 3 those of medicine itself. This section provides the conceptual background for what will follow.

In **Section II—Essentials of Reasoning and Critical Thinking in Health Sciences** (Chapters 4 and 5), we briefly examine the rudiments of modern reasoning, argumentation, and critical thinking (Chapter 4), and how they are reflected in a step-by-step approach to clinical work and care (Chapter 5). Basic methodological challenges of thinking adapted for health sciences and professions are proposed here to the reader.

In **Section III—Major Subjects and Challenges in Medical Thinking Not to Be Missed: Choosing What We Want to Do, Defining What We Are Doing, Cause-Effect Relationships, Medical Error and Harm** (Chapters 6–10), special chapters are devoted to subjects and problems related to thinking and solving in medical cognitive processes. Chapter 6 provides an overview of the development of a thesis for medical thinking in research and practice. Chapter 7 offers definitions of our thoughts and a path leading to any research and activity and new experience. Cause-effect relationships between desirable and undesirable phenomena are the subject of Chapter 8; and detecting, explaining, solving, and preventing medical error and harm is the subject of Chapter 9. Medical decision-making in Chapter 10 is an important thinking domain which concludes this section. It outlines how physicians think, make, and should make, decisions in research and practice.

In **Section IV—Sharing Our Thoughts on Oral and Written Communication with Peers, Patients, and Communities** (Chapters 11–13), both written and oral communication with peers, patients, and the professional and laic communities are discussed. Experiences, recommendations, and other results of thinking must be correctly shared and evaluated in oral, verbal, and nonverbal communication (Chapter 11). Written essays, scientific papers, clinical case reporting, and case series reporting (Chapter 12), as well as oral and written communication in clinical and community practice are highlighted (Chapter 13).

An Epilogue summarizes and again clarifies the most important elements and domains of medical thinking and what we might consider to do next and think about.
The **Glossary** to this book was a challenge because it must bring together a world of terms and meanings, sometimes varying, sometimes complementary, from philosophy, psychology, logic and critical thinking, fundamental and clinical epidemiologies, biostatistics, and clinical domains. Definitions presented here apply primarily to this book's message and content. These definitions offer the best possible understanding of the pages which follow.

Often, more than one definition of a given entity is offered. Some of them provide a slightly different perspective by key authors, others offer complementary concepts. The reader is encouraged to also verify them in a domain of his or her specific interest.

Relevant **References** are provided in each chapter. The **Bibliography** in most chapters also includes several online references. Many novice readers look to them first in today's electronic world. Sometimes, they are unique to the topic of interest.

Some very elementary notions, entities, and terms from epidemiology, biostatistics, medicine, and philosophy are defined in several chapters. Is this needed? It was done for two main reasons:

1. Among the readers of this monograph, there may be neophytes or novices in health sciences or medicine, or, readers from domains other than health sciences and professions who need to understand fundamental and relevant concepts. This book does not replace other fundamental references. They should, however, make this book independent from other reading which might come later.
2. Some entities are defined differently from one domain to another like rate, risk, or effectiveness, and so on. The Glossary at the end of this monograph is meant to clarify these terms and what they mean strictly for the purposes of the topics explored in this book and within this context.

How Is Each Chapter Organized?

1. Each chapter is introduced by an **Executive Summary**.
2. A table of contents (**In This Chapter**) follows. This provides easy access to understanding what follows.
3. Intentionally, a **list** (of variable length) **of historical and contemporary quotations** from health sciences and elsewhere to stimulate thoughts is offered to the reader. These sayings, some serious, some much less, are included not only to present the topic and flavour the message, but also to reflect the essence of thought, reason, and meaning of the pages that follow in each chapter. They also show that many thoughts in medicine are not as new as they might appear. Medical reflections about our matters of interest are sometimes older than many realize. They often make us humble. Some sayings quoted and enriched with our comments are meant to not only be illustrative and complementary to the following main body of the text, but also to entertain, at least more than the structured message which follows. Less formal and academic **language** is used at times to convey real-life significance to the message. This style of writing and the repetitions in this book are intentional given the content and topic. They spare the reader from moving backward and forward in the book to see each topic of interest in a specific context.
4. The **body of the chapter**, followed by **Conclusions** and **References**, covers the essentials of the selected topic. This message is not exhaustive, additional reading from the suggested references is mandatory for many.

Throughout the text, several sections are highlighted in a special way to visualize the best possible, and hopefully even better, understanding of important considerations related to the topic (subject, its enumeration, and/or classification) of interest and to support the structure and organization of the message:

1. Important definitions and other formulations are framed in a textbox as basic concepts required for the section and its understanding.
2. Series, sets, or lists of entities within a particular topic as a whole are presented on a shaded background, for example, sets of fallacies, other ordered lists, or flowcharts about a given topic, and the like.
3. Important conclusions, ensuing messages, and vital guidelines for further thought and which should be further explored, are both framed and shaded.

Let us hope that the reader will find this message and book useful and clear to follow.

So Many Well-Deserved Acknowledgments by the Author

The appreciation of the author is more than mandatory and deserved to all those without whom this book would never appear:

To Mrs. **Kristine Mednansky**, Senior Commissioning Editor at Taylor & Francis for her guidance, confidence in the author, and experience over so many years of working together.

To Mr. **Noel Fraser**, Manager of the Health Research Methods, Evidence, and Impact (HEI), formerly the Department of Clinical Epidemiology & Biostatistics, Faculty of Health Sciences, McMaster University, for his visionary support and guidance in the development of this project.

To Mr. **Steve Janzen**, Senior Graphic Designer at Media Production Services, McMaster University, for the whole artwork and directions to the best presentation of this book and message.

To Mrs. **Annamaria Feltracco**, from Feltracco Consulting, for her invaluable detailed review of the language and style of the whole text. Also, as the author's guide, she put herself masterfully in the position of a first-time reader and recipient of the message.

The author remains obliged and grateful to several authorities and organizations to which he belongs, without which it would have been impossible to offer these pages to the reader.

How all this could all be done without all of those above? If only the gratitude of the author could measure encouragements to you all!

Let us conclude then, that by reading the pages that follow, our reader can tell us how much have we succeeded in conveying this message with all the aforementioned on our mind!

To beginners, those more experienced, and all those in between from…

Milos Jenicek
Rockwood, Ontario,
Canada

REFERENCES

Jenicek M. *A Primer on Clinical Experience in Medicine. Reasoning, Decision Making, and Communication in Health Sciences.* Boca Raton/London/New York: CRC Press/Taylor & Francis/Productivity Press, 2013.

Jenicek M. *Writing, Reading, and Understanding in Modern Health Sciences. Medical Articles and Other Forms of Communication.* Boca Raton/London/New York: CRC Press/Taylor & Francis/Productivity Press, 2014.

About the Author

Milos Jenicek, MD, PhD, LMCC, FRCPC, CSPQ, is currently Professor (part time) in the Department of Clinical Epidemiology and Biostatistics, Faculty of Health Sciences, McMaster University, Hamilton, Ontario, Canada. He is also Professor Emeritus at the Université de Montréal, Montréal, Québec, Canada. In 2009, he was elected Fellow of The Royal Society of Medicine, London, United Kingdom.

Dr. Jenicek has contributed to the evolution of epidemiology as a general method of reasoning and decision-making in medicine. Supported by the Université de Montréal, he undertook short sabbaticals and study visits in the 1970s to the universities of Harvard, Johns Hopkins, Yale, Tufts, North Carolina at Chapel Hill, and Uniformed Services University of Health Sciences at Bethesda to further enhance his teaching and research. Academic, governmental, and professional institutions in Western Europe (France, Spain, Italy, Switzerland, Portugal), North Africa (Algeria, Tunisia, Morocco), and on the Pacific Rim (Japan, Korea) have also benefited from his lecturing, professional expertise, visiting professorships, and other professional initiatives.

During his term as Acting Chairman of the Department of Social and Preventive Medicine, Université de Montréal (1988–1989), he established a Clinical Epidemiology teaching program at the graduate level. The core course of this program, taught by Dr. Jenicek, was also part of a similar program at McGill University, where he was also an Adjunct Professor at that time. Until 1991, he was also a member of the Board of Examiners of the Medical Council of Canada (Committee on Preventive Medicine). In 2000, he was invited by Kuwait University to act as an External Examiner of their graduating medical students.

In addition to numerous scientific papers and other collaborations with leading medical journals, Dr. Jenicek has published 15 textbooks to date that reflect his national and international initiatives.

1. *Introduction to Epidemiology* (in French, *Introduction à l'épidémiologie*, 1975)
2. *Epidemiology: Principles, Techniques, Applications* (in French with R. Cléroux, *Épidémiologie: Principes, Techniques, Applications*, 1982, and in Spanish, 1987)
3. *Clinical Epidemiology, Clinimetrics* (in French with R. Cléroux, *Épidémiologi Clinique. Clinimétrie*, 1985); and *Meta-Analysis in Medicine: Evaluation and Synthesis of Clinical and Epidemiological Information* (in French, 1987), recognized by the James Lind Library as the first textbook on meta-analysis and systematic reviews in medicine
4. *Métanalyse en Médecine: Évaluation et Synthèse de l'Information Clinique et Épidémiologiqe* (*Meta-Analysis in Medicine: Evaluation and Synthesis of Clinical and Epidemiological Information*), EDISEM/Maloine, 1987, considered to be the first book on meta-analysis in medicine

5. *Epidemiology: The Logic of Modern Medicine* (EPIMED International, 1995), also published in Spanish (1996) and Japanese (1998)
6. *Medical Casuistics: Correctly Reporting Clinical Cases* (in French, *Casuistique Médicale: Bien Présenter un Cas Clinique*, 1997), jointly produced by Canadian (EDISEM) and French (Maloine) publishers
7. *Clinical Case Reporting in Evidence-Based Medicine* (Butterworth Heinemann, 1999), which also appears as an expanded second edition in English (Arnold, 2001), Italian (2001), Korean (2002), and Japanese (2002)
8. *Foundations of Evidence-Based Medicine,* published in 2003 by Parthenon Publishing/CRC Press/Taylor & Francis
9. *Evidence-Based Practice. Logic and Critical Thinking in Medicine* (with D.L. Hitchcock), published by the American Medical Association in 2005
10. *A Physician's Self-Paced Guide to Critical Thinking* (AMA Press, 2006)
11. *Fallacy-Free Reasoning in Medicine: Improving Communication and Decision Making in Research and Practice* (AMA Press, 2009)
12. *Medical Error and Harm: Understanding, Prevention, and Control* was published by CRC Press/Taylor & Francis in 2011
13. *A Primer on Clinical Experience in Medicine: Reasoning, Decision Making, and Communication in Health Sciences* (CRC Press/Taylor & Francis), written in 2012, proposes critical thinking as a part of clinical propedeutics for health professions
14. *Writing, Reading, and Understanding in Modern Health Sciences: Medical Articles and Other Forms of Communication* (CRC Press/Taylor & Francis, 2014)

This monograph, which follows directly from the prior two monographs, is Milos Jenicek's sixteenth.

Milos Jenicek's current interests include the development of methodologies and applications of logic, critical thinking, decision-making, and communication in health sciences, well beyond epidemiology, biostatistics, and clinical propedeutics. Enhancement of evidence-based medicine and evidence-based public health, health policies and program evaluations, and decision-oriented (bedside) clinical research are in focus.

Contact by e-mail: jenicekm@mcmaster.ca
Contact by telephone/fax: (519) 856-1324

FOUNDATION OF TODAY'S MEDICAL THINKING: PHILOSOPHY, MEDICINE ITSELF, QUANTITATIVE AND QUALITATIVE RESEARCH

1

Chapter 1

Interactive Domains of Medical Thinking Today: Understanding Our Own Reasoning from a Broader Historical Experience*

Executive Summary

At its very basis, medicine is a series of decisions made based on a combination of theory and practice derived from experience and/or evidence. But today, medicine is more. It is grounded in the scientific method, but also uses structured and focused logic and critical thinking to both understand health problems and know what to do with them. Hence, medicine today is not only experience and/or evidence-based theory and practice. Scientific method, structured and focused logic, and critical thinking lead our understanding of health problems and what to do with them. All decisions are products of rational thought and must be properly communicated and shared with all interested parties, including health professionals, patients, and other laics.

Medical thinking and experience has evolved from the thinking processes of physicians over the millennia, and contributions from Classical Greek and other philosophies. Invaluable work from many different branches within medicine, including epidemiology, biostatistics, and a broad range of experience and methodological developments in medical and surgical specialties have been vital in the development of today's critical thinking in medicine. Parallel advances in modern philosophy such as informal logic,

---

* This chapter is a humbling experience about what we have inherited not only from ourselves but so much more from the others.

argumentation, ethics, and critical thinking lead to an even clearer understanding of decision-making grounded in medicine. Medical thinking is now a better known, and understood, cognitive process.

The most recent contributions in medical thinking stem from largely quantitative to clinical epidemiology and evidence-based medicine, and also from case studies, which are becoming increasingly structured and ready for further pragmatic use. Much of this progress will come from further developments in the domains of philosophy *in* medicine, philosophy *of* medicine, theoretical surgery, theoretical medicine, argumentation-based medicine, lathology (inquiry into error and harm), or orismology (inquiry on definitions of health phenomena). Developments in these domains are under way, and will make important progress in our understanding of medicine as a cognitive science.

The chapters that follow will improve our understanding of how medicine works today. Such views and understandings apply not only to medicine but to all health sciences and professions, be it dentistry, nursing, clinical psychology, optometry, rehabilitation professions, chiropractic, or other alternative and complementary medicines like homeopathy, patient-centered medicine, and others. If not, let us be told why.

In This Chapter

Executive Summary 3
Thoughts, Thinkers, and Things to Think About 5
1.1   What Is Medical Thinking as a Cognitive Process? 8
1.2   Are There Any Parallels between Recent Developments in Medicine and across
      a Broad Spectrum of the Humanities? 9
1.3   Developments in General Epidemiology and Biostatistics 9
1.4   Developments in Clinical Epidemiology and Evidence-Based Medicine 10
1.5   Developments in Qualitative Research 10
1.6   Concurrent Developments in Arts and Sciences, and Logic and Critical Thinking
      in General 10
1.7   More Recent Development of the Health Sciences–Humanities Interface in the Theory,
      Philosophy, Logic, Decision-Making, and Communication in, and of, Medicine 11
1.8   In a Given Situation, Do We Need Another Discipline for Medicine and Other
      Health Sciences? 12
Let Us Conclude by Raising Some Questions and Proposals 15
References 16

Thoughts, Thinkers, and Things to Think About

In medicine, you don't understand things.
You just get used to them.
Paraphrasing John von Neumann
(1903–1957)
Gary Zukav
The Dancing Wu Li Masters (1979)
You shouldn't! Just try to see things
from various complementary angles.

We haven't got the money, so we have got
to think!
Baron Ernest Rutherford
(1871–1937)
in the *Bulletin of The Institute of Physics*
(1962, Vol. 13)
We didn't have enough either, so we are
getting to think, Sir Rutherford!

If I have been able to see farther than others,
it was because I stood on the shoulders
of giants.
Sir Isaac Newton
(1642–1726/27)
And of giants from more than one
domain!
Aren't we all, Sir Isaac?

Whether you want to make money, run
a streetcar, or write a book, or build a
bridge—or do anything successfully—you'll do
well to remember that in all the world there
is no word more important than "Think"!
Edwin Baird
(1886–1957)
Is there another way, Edwin?

*The little girl had the making of a poet
in her who, being told to be sure of her
meaning before she spoke, said, "How can I
know what I think till I see what I say?"*
Graham Wallas
(1858–1932)
British Political Scientist
The Art of Thought (1926)
**And what about what the author of
this book has to say?**

*Facts mean nothing unless they are rightly
understood, rightly related and rightly
interpreted.*
R.L. Long
(undated)
**Not "evidence" in medicine either—
but shouldn't we at least try?**

*What is the hardest task in the world?
To think.*
Ralph Waldo Emerson
(1803–1882)
Journals (1993)
**Let us not be discouraged, though!
Shouldn't we at least try the best
possible way?**

*Every action must be due to one or other
Of seven causes: Chance, nature, compulsion,
habit, reasoning, anger, or appetite.*
Aristotle
(384–3222 BC)
Rhetoric, 1.10
translated by W. Rhys Roberts (1954)
**And more, the venerable one!
Isn't reasoning a part of thinking?**

First learn much, and then seek to
understand it profoundly.
Talmud (1st–6th Century AD)
Rabbinical Writings in
Louis I. Newman, comp.
The Talmudic Anthology (1945, 387)
Why not to start learning thinking
itself?

Let us never forget, that how we think in medicine
today is the heritage of well more than one
millennium of experience and contributions of
thinkers and scholars well beyond the domain of
health sciences.

What kind of medicine shall we see, practice, and further develop in this millennium? Do we need a new dimension for it, an additional basic science, or simply a new discipline called "medical thinking"? We may strongly believe so, since we wish to practice a medicine that is not only effective, patient-oriented, ethical, and human, but that is also sensible, thought out, and rational.

New paradigms and their associated methodologies and wide applications and uses, are developing in increasing numbers. Where are we today? A series of questions and answers may further clarify whether we are doing our best presently, and whether this was the case in the past, and will be again in the future.

In this spirit, let us argue that:

■ Today, medicine is not only based in experience and the scientific method, but also grounded in structured, focused thinking and decision-making. All remarkable initiatives and contributions of evidence-based medicine do not bring answers and solutions to all major challenges in the health professions. However, as essential as it is, producing and evaluating (grading) the best evidence is not enough. We must also learn how to use it in the best and most effective way possible.

■ Advancements in modern philosophy, and especially within formal and informal logic and argumentation, offer operational and usable methodology to support understanding and decision-making in health professions, including medicine. These developments, together with invaluable historical developments and contributions of epidemiology and biostatistics, rationalize both understanding and decision-making in medicine. Ethics, another vital element of decision-making, is already more established and cultured in medicine than other branches of philosophy. Modern concepts of understanding and making decisions about health phenomena and their management will only benefit from these developments, provided that they are mastered and used in an integrated manner with basic sciences, clinical experience and skills, clinical and fundamental epidemiology, biostatistics, management, and decision-making methodology.

■ The attitude and skill required to think, make decisions, and communicate in health sciences and professions is a learned knowledge, as is learning how to calculate a sample size for clinical trials, or how to translate observational research of disease occurrence as incidence rates, and its causes in terms of relative risks, odds ratios, attributable risks, and etiological fractions.

■ These considerations share major traits not only with medicine, but also with all other health professions and sciences, especially where increasing use and experience support such a paradigm extension.

■ Reasoning, critical thinking, and decision-making are, and must be, a learned experience at the core of clinical and community medicine. To use them optimally, and expand such an experience, we need a new, integrated, fundamental discipline to be taught and mastered by all health sciences students from the undergraduate level onward.

The sections that follow support these five considerations.

1.1 What Is Medical Thinking as a Cognitive Process?

Medical thinking, as the intellectual process of medicine, contains several interfacing and completing components. Gnostic (knowledge-related) or epistemological (ways of acquiring knowledge) processes apply both to clinical practice and patient care, and to research based on the scientific method.

Triggers of the gnostic process include:

■ perception, information, observation, requests, orders, ideas;
■ communicating by formulating problems and raising questions, the cornerstones for tackling a problem;
■ assessing and evaluating past and present evidence;
■ making observations, their visualizations, measurements, and quantifications;
■ analyzing what was observed (epidemiology, biostatistics, qualitative research) and reasoning about what has been observed through argumentation and critical thinking (evidence-based argumentation and management ensue);
■ making claims (recommendations and conclusions) based on the above processes;
■ making medical decisions in practice and research and communicating them based on such claims (diagnosis, treatment, prognosis, and others);
■ acting or doing nothing;
■ analyzing and evaluating actions or inactions stemming from such claims (closing gnostic processes);
■ forecasting; and
■ communicating recommendations for further work (medical articles, clinical guidelines, etc.).

Currently, gnostic or epistemological processes are used across epidemiology, biostatistics, medical specialties, health management, and general philosophy, as well as a wide spectrum of broadly defined humanities.

1.2 Are There Any Parallels between Recent Developments in Medicine and across a Broad Spectrum of the Humanities?

Several distinct periods of recent study in medicine, in concert with development in the arts and sciences, further enhance our understanding of the development of medical thinking. This development is reflected across the chronology of medical articles, and even more so through the sequence of selected illustrative titles in clinical research. The books and articles quoted in Section 1.3 are not in chronological order, nor are they thematically exhaustive. They are presented here to illustrate and highlight how ideas have progressed among several remarkable medical thinkers.

1.3 Developments in General Epidemiology and Biostatistics

Prior to their current state, general epidemiology and biostatistics focused primarily on rates of illness and infection related to infectious disease within specific populations. More recently, epidemiology and biostatistics have been used to understand non-infectious diseases at the community level, and expanded to include understanding how non-infectious health phenomena were affected by health services and policies.

This is reflected in an evolving number of experiences captured in various publications in English, French, and Spanish cultures,[1–6] and subsequently summarized and overviewed in an ongoing manner.[7,8]

In these cases, crucial contributions in biostatistics have been paired with those in both the clinical and community medicine domains.[9–11] The occurrence, control, and cause-effect relationships of specific diseases are examined through an ever-more refined methodology, adopted from a larger framework of causal inference.[12,13] In essence, probability, inference, uncertainty, representativity, and comparability as well as webs of causes and webs of consequences were, and remain, a main focus not only in epidemiology and biostatistics, but also in other, 'less-clinical' domains such as philosophy in general, and philosophy of medicine in particular.[14]

Biostatistics and medical statistics are still sometimes confounded across the literature today. To be more precise:

Let us remember that **biostatistics** is a broad domain within biology. It encompasses the design of biological experiments, not only in medicine but also in pharmacy, agriculture, fishery, and elsewhere in the biology domain.[15] It also includes the collection, summarization, and analysis of data from experiments, and their interpretation and inference based on results of experimental and other approaches to biological inquiry.

Medical statistics is one of the subdomains of biostatistics.[16] It deals with applications of statistics to medicine and other health sciences, including epidemiology, public health, forensic medicine, clinical research, and other subdomains in health research and professions.

High quality monographs cover both biostatistics and medical statistics for novices and others as well. Since 1937, Austin Bradford Hill's,[17] Alvan R. Feinstein's,[9] or B. Rosner's,[18] and others[19,20] monographs, to name just a few, illustrate well past and present trends, in the often blended in title and content, biostatistics, medical statistics, clinical biostatistics, and medicine itself domains.

1.4 Developments in Clinical Epidemiology and Evidence-Based Medicine

Health phenomena in clinical medicine and in the clinical setting first appeared as the subject of possible epidemiological study and management as what was first experienced at a community level.[21] A real wave of new paradigms in clinical epidemiology followed in the 1980s,[22-27] including, at least in their title, other related entities such as clinical judgment[28-33] or clinimetrics (measurement and classification).[34] Meta-analysis and systematic reviews of health information[35,36] as 'epidemiology of research evidence and other observations, experience, and findings' followed later.

Both fundamental and clinical epidemiologies and their uses remain at the core of the current state of evidence-based medicine. This optimizes various levels of decision-making and of prevention in both clinical and community health sciences and professions settings. A better understanding of health phenomena through basic and clinical epidemiology leads to better decision-making in medicine and health management through decision analysis, implementation, and evaluation of decisions.[37-43] For example, the development, uses, and evaluation of clinical guidelines and health policies depend considerably on evidence-based medicine[44,45] and evidence-based public health.[46]

1.5 Developments in Qualitative Research

Qualitative research,[47,48] especially in health sciences, today encompasses any kind of research of a person's (health professional or patient) lived health experience that produces findings not arrived at by means of biostatistical and other quantitative methods. Clinical case reporting and some case series studies,[49] so ubiquitous and pedestrian for some researchers, are refined through qualitative research and their results reported accordingly. Single cases, or those with small sample sizes, do not usually meet satisfactory requirements for inferential and etiological research; alternative causal considerations are of interest today. Unconvincing causal considerations in some cases are solely imputable to authors on a case by case basis.

1.6 Concurrent Developments in Arts and Sciences, and Logic and Critical Thinking in General

Since Dewey's *How We Think*,[50] published in 1910, philosophers have made remarkable progress in rationalizing, structuring, and operationalizing our way of thinking. We now have a choice between the broadest domain of "***thinking***" (*mental actions which, if verbalized, are a matter of combining words in propositions*), or narrower "***reasoning***" (*thinking leading to a conclusion*) or "***critical thinking***" (*reasonable reflective thinking about 'what to do'*), based and focused on understandings, stemming from belief, proof or conviction, evidence-based or not. Other titles covering fundamental critical thinking in general[51-53] have followed Dewey.[50] More recently, several other practical publications develop and summarize the methodology of reasoning, informal logic, argumentation, and ensuing claims in more than one sense.

These early works in critical thinking have evolved into still others which explore *orismology (the domain of definitions)*.[52,54] This includes the knowledge of fallacies and ways of preventing and correcting them,[55,56] the formulation of increasingly precise questions,[57] the arguments, from those that are unsubstantiated, enthymemes, and categorical syllogisms. Most important for health sciences is Toulmin's approach to argumentation.[58–60] Toulmin's approach outlines six components: claim(s), grounds (fundamental data and information), backing (body of experience and evidence), warrant(s) or understanding of the nature of the problem, qualifier (degree of certainty about concluding claim(s), and rebuttals (conditions and circumstances under which final claim(s) does not apply). De Bono's lateral thinking[61] expands and completes this argumentation process, providing a link between additional arguments and claims with a main line of thought.

In health sciences, scientific communication can take the form of discussion sections in medical articles, or everyday practice-based activities like differential diagnosis, or decision. These forms of communication depend on a well-defined approach to problem solving. In medical literature, critical thinking relies, and is sometimes hidden, scattered and diffused under the term of "*judgment.*" This is a polysemous term for Bunge[62] which means: either "*the mental process of making an assertion or thinking of a proposition,*" or "*the ability to make realistic appraisals of matters of fact.*" In our case, this is represented by the phrase, 'He is medically knowledgeable and smart, but has no clinical judgment.' Or, similar to intuition, it may be defined as the ability to recognize at a glance that something is correct or incorrect, right or wrong, promising or futile, and so on.

In current medical literature and practice, "***clinical judgment***" is subject to these multiple understandings.[28–33] Our clinical treatment orders and working diagnoses ('impressions'), or in other domains, the evaluation of evidence and critical appraisal of literature, are exercises in judgment that bring together the clinician's learned volume of knowledge, experience, and all underlying cognitive, interpretive, evaluative, and decision-making processes. Judgment is not always innate; like anything else in health sciences and professions, it is a learned and acquired skill. But let us define it better first.

1.7 More Recent Development of the Health Sciences–Humanities Interface in the Theory, Philosophy, Logic, Decision-Making, and Communication in, and of, Medicine

Like epidemiology, biostatistics, and evidence-based medicine, developments of several major subjects in the humanities, arts, and sciences have expanded into the health sciences and professions. Some of these are retaining their general content, while others are being adapted and expanded into the health domain. Consider these examples:

■ Under the label of **philosophy in medicine and philosophy of medicine**,[63,64] connections between basic paradigms of medicine, empiricism and scientific method, hermeneutics, ethics, and other philosophical entities[65] are expanding. They are now presented in parallel with epidemiological and biostatistical paradigms, such as probability, uncertainty, or causality.[66–68]

Both philosophy of medicine and philosophy in medicine, are currently enriched by 'pure' philosophers who bring to the field additional experience and expertise beyond health sciences.[14]

- The term and domain of **theoretical surgery and theoretical medicine** remains an open field, and still separated from their practice.[69–71]
- **Logic and critical thinking in medicine**[72] appeared first in association with the spirit, content, and objectives of modern epidemiology and biostatistics, albeit tentatively.[60,73–75] From brief allusions in epidemiology and clinical sciences,[60,56] these elements are now becoming a more distinct entity in medicine[60,56,76] as *"systems of thought underlying understanding and decisions in health sciences and processes conceptualizing, evaluating, synthesizing, and evaluating health information as guides to belief and action."* Beyond and besides medicine, critical thinking has also been adapted and applied to the health and social services domain and among its students and those who hold managerial positions in this area.[77]
- As a context-dependent way of thinking and decision-making,[78] **clinical reasoning** now increasingly includes not only diagnostic processes, but also therapeutic decision-making, cognitive errors, and clinical problem solving.[79]
- *Cognition and cognitive science*[80] studies cognition as mental functions and processes from the perspective of the development of new knowledge and concepts leading to thought (understanding) and action. It relies on an increasingly structured cognitive path from an initial thought to a new one. Deviation from such paths underlies a part of medical error and harm; they are not all due to failures in sensory-motor activity alone.[76]
- *Clinical judgment, reasoning, and decision-making*, as critical thinking in the practice of medicine, are based on the "patient/evidence/setting fit." Clinical reasoning is based on a context-dependent way of thinking. Traditionally, decision-making in medical practice depends largely on probabilistic reasoning and value assessment.[81] In addition, the development of structured operational tools is based on decision-making which itself is informed and influenced by general philosophy and clinical judgment. These satisfy both philosophy and its uses,[82] together with clinical epidemiology and general decision-making processes.

  Decision-making is discussed even more broadly in clinical practice, research, public health and management.[83–85] In these disciplines and contexts, it covers not only clinical questions, but also systematic reviews, decision analysis itself, and clinical practice guidelines.[85] In a broader range of practical applications,[86,41] decision-making is included even in the critical reading of medical journals.[87] Besides and beyond medicine, clinical reasoning methodology and applications are also presented in communications geared to nursing professionals.[88]

Do we define such entities and domains equally well in operational and usable terms?

1.8 In a Given Situation, Do We Need Another Discipline for Medicine and Other Health Sciences?

We believe so. Ways of reasoning, decision-making, and communication based on rich past and present experiences are all spread across these more traditional domains. These experiences have been enriched by fundamental and crucial contributions by a host of medical and health science practitioners including biostatisticians, epidemiologists, clinical epidemiologists, philosophers in and beyond health sciences, evidence-based medicine practitioners, and "fundamentalists" in clinical specialties and community medicine. Together they represent a well-fitting mosaic that offers a picture of what we might call the more-encompassing or comprehensive approach to "medical thinking." More narrowly, we may consider this today as "critical thinking in health sciences" or "evidence-based reasoning, decision-making, and communication in health professions."

The main elements of critical thinking in health sciences that have benefited from this crossover from humanities, arts, and sciences are ethics, communication in medicine, logic, evidence, and lathology.

Ethics is less isolated in health sciences than other branches from a broader spectrum of branches of philosophy. Connections and interfaces are being established with other branches of philosophy—**logic**, **critical thinking**, and **argumentation**.[50,52,77,78,86,87]

Through these connections and interfaces between philosophy and the health sciences, experts in medical humanities and medicine are introducing concepts of 'how doctors think' to a wider readership. How doctors think was recently introduced to a wider readership by experts in medical humanities[31] and medicine as well.[32]

Communication in medicine means *imparting, or interchanging thoughts, opinions, or information about health problems through speech, writing, or signs*. It relies on the critical study of discourse and uses the logic-based research exploring such problems in a particular setting and context.

In today's medicine, **logic** is mostly used informally in practice. It is a *system of thought and reasoning that governs understanding and decisions in clinical and community care, research, and communication*. As a normative science, it investigates the principles of valid reasoning and inference, that is, *drawing conclusions from one or more premises*.

Evidence, within in its broadest sense and focused on research and practice, is *any data or information, whether solid or weak, obtained through experience, observational research, observational, or analytical experimental work (trials) which are relevant either to the understanding of a health problem or to decision-making about it*. The best quality evidence is always sought.[60]

Medicine is a domain which is geared to action. We often feel that '*we must do something, even anything*' with a patient or a community and its environment. Action is expected from us, and a justified evidence-based action is rightly sought. Being more experienced now, we must apply similar rules, ways, and methods of reasoning and decision-making to '*do nothing*.' The latter is often more challenging than the former.

In our actions, we tend to look at the positive: good decisions, ensuing actions, and their results. However, we make errors, and we may harm. The study of both **error and harm (lathology)**[76] is subject to the same type of reasoning as is pursued in the case of positive actions and effects. Errors and harms have their own webs of causes and consequences such as ignorance, cognitive errors, poor sensorimotor performance, faulty argumentative reasoning, or communication failures. Fortunately, not every error leads to harm, and harm is not always caused by health professionals' errors. However, through these incidents, our experience and understanding of both error and harm increases.

So far, our use of humanities, philosophy, and common experiences beyond health sciences is the richest in the domain of medical ethics; **metaphysics** and **ontology** aside, **epistemology** and **logic**-originating experience in medicine are of increasing interest. The same may be said of philosophy's current trends, such as **semiotics** (signs), **hermeneutics** (interpretation), and **phronesis** (practical reasoning). Are the coverage and experience in these domains and trends balanced enough in our teaching, research, and practice?

There are critical issues related to this expansion in medical thinking and communicating. These are outlined here for your consideration.

What Could We Call This New Scientific Method?

Evidence-based argumentative medicine, evidence-supported medical thinking, reasoning, and decision-making medicine, or simply medical thinking? Or some other title? Do we currently teach, master, and use organized medical thinking enough?

More about the scientific method follows in Chapter 4 of this book.

What Should Its Objectives Be?

What knowledge, attitudes, and skills should be acquired at both the undergraduate and graduate levels, in relation to practice and/or research? We propose that they should include and cover three major themes: reasoning, decision-making, and communication with patients and other health professionals.

What Topics and Domains Should Be Covered?

Should this new scientific method include cognition, informal logic, probability, uncertainty, critical thinking, argumentation (many articles, or even titles of clinical rounds are claims in formal argumentation), or heuristics, definitions (operational ones and those in specific contexts as part of orismology), research questions, and research design? Many of these subjects are already scattered across current well-established disciplines such as epidemiology and biostatistics. Some are more or less formally tackled in classrooms, rounds, or bedside teaching by experienced clinicians and other health professionals. However, some are not always understood, shared, or used enough.

Besides **'hard' data** and topics, **which 'soft' topics** (those that are harder to define measure and categorize) **should be covered and further developed**?

Which Specialties Should Be Involved and Interested in This 'New' Method?

To begin, both medical and surgical specialties should be engaged. In psychiatry, geriatrics, and clinical psychology, analyses of patient argumentation, claims, values, and communication, as well as their abnormalities, are often used as additional diagnostic tools.

To support and help answer such questions, two recent 'trilogies' have attempted to pave the way for further developments:

- ■ The first one mainly covers the methodology of critical thinking and decision-making in their broadest sense in medicine:
  - basic methodology (evidence-based practice, logic and critical thinking in medicine[60]);

- a self-learning guide for readers and users (a physician's self-paced guide to critical thinking[89]); and
- a review of major pitfalls to be aware of, detect, and correct (fallacy-free reasoning in medicine; improving communication and decision-making in research and practice[56]).

■ The second focuses on:
- applications in medical research (writing, reading, and understanding in modern health sciences; medical articles and other ways of communication[90]);
- the practice of medicine (a primer on clinical experience in medicine in terms of reasoning, decision-making, and communication in health sciences[54]); and
- specific challenges (medical error and harm; their understanding, prevention and control[76])

More questions, challenges, and future applications will certainly emerge.

Let Us Conclude by Raising Some Questions and Proposals

All of the above-mentioned topics remain open areas for discussion. They are subjects of analysis, evaluation, and consensus among interested readers of this text, as well as practitioners, researchers, and parties beyond pure health professions.

Quality and completeness of health information will always vary in some degree from one place and time to another. Health information may be excellent and complete. In other cases, health information as provided by patients, health professionals, and/or community may be even false, for whatever reasons and motives, including politics, policies, and politicking in health matters.

Everything we do in medicine and other health sciences is the subject of critical thinking, reasoning, decision-making, and communication. Training in epidemiology, biostatistics, and clinical teaching make vital contributions to these elements. However this frequently occurs in a haphazard way, which does not necessarily examine all important *gnostic* processes. To do so, do we need to integrate all of this in a kind of basic science of "**medical thinking**," "*iatrognostics*," "*iatrognosis*," "*iatrology*," "*cognitive medicine*," "*interpretive medicine*,"[90] "*iatrophilosophy*,"[62] or "*iatrosophy*" (without any of its historical connotations) and make it as practical as possible?

Methods, techniques, and other tools of understanding, decision-making, and communication in health are still scattered across current medical experience. What is common, and what is specific and particularly useful, from one clinical and paraclinical specialty and health profession to another? Should such a distinct discipline and science of medical reasoning, decision-making, and communication (under this or any other title) be presented to students and future health professionals from the undergraduate level up?

Let us believe (and be convinced) that the time has come to give such a distinct face and purpose (integrated objectives, content, structure, impact) as well as operational qualities to medical thinking across the current overall experience in research and practice.[91,92] Or, let us at least try to do so. Our general and specialty clinical and community medicine expertise, epidemiology, biostatistics, management and administration rely all on rational and practical philosophy, one of their integrative tools.

References

1. Morris JN. *Uses of Epidemiology*. Edinburgh/London/New York: Churchill Livingstone, 1957. (3rd Edition 1975).
2. MacMahon B, Pugh TF. *Epidemiology. Principles and Methods*. Boston: Little Brown, 1970.
3. Barker DJP. *Practical Epidemiology*. Edinburgh and London: Churchill Livingstone, 1973.
4. Jenicek M. *Introduction à l'épidémiologie*. (Introduction to Epidemiology). St. Hyacinthe and Paris: EDISEM and Maloine, 1976.
5. Jenicek M, Cléroux R. *Épidémiologie. Principes, techniques, applications* (Epidemiology. Principles, Techniques, Applications). St. Hyacinthe and Paris: EDISEM and Maloine, 1982. (Edition in Spanish 1987).
6. Gordis L. *Epidemiology*. Philadelphia, PA: W.B. Saunders, 1996. (2nd edition 2000).
7. *Times, Places, and Persons. Aspects of the History of Epidemiology*. Edited by AM Lilienfeld. Baltimore and London: The Johns Hopkins University Press, 1980.
8. *The Challenge of Epidemiology. Issues and Selected Readings*. Discussed and compiled by C Buck, A Llopis, E Najera, M Terris. Washington, DC: Pan American Health Organization, Publication No 505, 1988.
9. Feinstein AR. *Clinical Biostatistics*. St. Louis, MO: CV Mosby, 1977.
10. Kleinbaum DG, Kupper LL, Morgenstern H. *Epidemiologic Research. Principles and Quantitative Methods*. London: Lifetime Learning Publications/Wadsworth CA, 1982.
11. Ingelfinger JA, Mosteller F, Thibodeau LA, Ware JH. *Biostatistics in Clinical Medicine*. New York: Macmillan Publ. Comp., 1983.
12. *Evolution of Epidemiologic Ideas. Annotated Readings on Concepts and Methods*. Edited by S Greenland. Chestnut Hill, MA: Epidemiology Resources Inc., 1987.
13. *Causal Inference*. Edited by KJ Rothman. Chestnut Hill, MA: Epidemiology Resources, 1988.
14. *Philosophy of Medicine. Handbook of the Philosophy of Science, Volume 16*. Dov M. Gabbay, P Thaggard, and J Woods, General Editors for the *Handbook of the Philosophy of Science*, F Gifford for *Philosophy of Medicine*. Amsterdam/Oxford/New York/Sydney/Singapore/Tokyo: New Holland, imprint of Elsevier, 2011.
15. *Biostatistics*. 4 p. in Wikipedia, the free encyclopedia at https://en.wikipedia.org/wiki/Biostatistics, retrieved Aug 26, 2017.
16. *Medical Statistics*. 3 p. in Wikipedia, the free encyclopedia at https://en.wikipedia.org/wiki/Medical _statistics, retrieved Aug 26, 2017.
17. Hill AB and Hill AD. *Bradford Hill's Principles of Medical Statistics. Twelfth Edition*. (First published in Great Britain 1937 as *Principles of Medical Statistics*). London/Melbourne/Auckland: Edward Arnold/Hodder & Stoughton, 1991.
18. Rosner B. *Fundamentals of Biostatistics*. 8th Edition. Boston, MA: Cengage Learning, 2016.
19. Bowers D. *Medical Statistics from Scratch. An Introduction for Health Professionals*. 3rd Edition. Oxford/Chichester/Hoboken, NJ: Willey/Blackwell (John Wiley & Sons), 2014.
20. Bland M. *An Introduction to Medical Statistics*. 4th Revised Edition. Oxford: Oxford University Press, 2015.
21. Paul JR. *Clinical Epidemiology*. Revised Edition. Chicago and London: The University of Chicago Press, 1966.
22. Fletcher RH, Fletcher SW, Wagner EH. *Clinical Epidemiology—The Essentials*. Baltimore, MD: Williams & Wilkins, 1982.
23. Sackett DL, Haynes RB, Tugwell PX. *Clinical Epidemiology: A Basic Science for Clinical Practice*. Boston: Little Brown, 1984.
24. Jenicek M. *Épidémiologie clinique. Clinimétrie*. (Clinical Epidemiology. Clinimetrics.) St. Hyacinthe and Paris: EDISEM and Maloine, 1985.
25. Feinstein AR. *Clinical Epidemiology. The Architecture of Clinical Research*. Philadelphia, PA/London/Toronto: WB Saunders, 1985.
26. Weiss NS. *Clinical Epidemiology. The Study of the Outcome of Illness*. New York and Oxford: Oxford University Press, 1986.

27. Kramer MS. *Clinical Epidemiology and Biostatistics. A Primer for Clinical Investigators and Decision-Makers*. Berlin and Heidelberg: Springer-Verlag, 1988.
28. Thorne FC. *Clinical Judgment. A Study of Clinical Errors*. Brandson, VT: Journal of Clinical Psychology, 1961.
29. Feinstein AR. *Clinical Judgment*. Baltimore: Williams and Wilkins, 1967.
30. White S and Stancombe J. *Clinical Judgment in the Health and Welfare Professions. Extending the Evidence Base*. Maidenhead and Philadelphia, PA: Open University Press/McGraw-Hill Education, 2003.
31. Montgomery K. *How Doctors Think. Clinical Judgment and the Practice of Medicine*. Oxford and New York: Oxford University Press, 2006.
32. Groopman J. *How Doctors Think*. New York: Houghton Mifflin Company, 2007.
33. Facione NC and Facione PA. 'Critical Thinking and Clinical Judgment'. pp. 1–13 in: *Critical Thinking and Clinical Reasoning in the Health Sciences. A Teaching Anthology*. Edited by NC Facione and PA Facione. Milbrae, CA: California Academic Press, 2008.
34. Feinstein AR. *Clinimetrics*. New Haven, CT and London: Yale University Press, 1987.
35. Jenicek M. *Méta-analyse en médecine. Évaluation de l'information clinique et épidémiologique*. (Meta-Analysis in Medicine. Evaluation and Synthesis of Clinical and Epidemiological Information.) St. Hyacinthe and Paris: EDISEM and Maloine, 1987.
36. Petitti DB. *Meta-Analysis, Decision Analysis, and Cost-Effectiveness Analysis. Methods of Quantitative Synthesis in Medicine*. New York and Oxford: Oxford University Press, 1994.
37. Patrick EA. *Decision Analysis in Medicine. Methods and Applications*. Boca Raton, FL: CRC Press, 1979.
38. Weinstein MC, Fineberg HV, Elstein AS et al. *Clinical Decision Analysis*. Philadelphia, PA: WB Saunders, 1980.
39. *Teaching Clinical Decision-Making*. Edited by ED Cebul and LH Beck. New York: Praeger, 1985.
40. Sox JC Jr, Blatt MA, Higgins MC, Morton KI. *Medical Decision-Making*. Boston: Butterworths, 1988.
41. Eddy DM. *Clinical Decision-Making. From Theory to Practice. A Collection of Essays from the Journal of the American Medical Association*. Boston/London/Singapore: Jones & Bartlett, 1996.
42. Gross R. *Decisions and Evidence in Medical Practice. Applying Evidence-Based Medicine to Clinical Decision-Making*. St. Louis, MO/London/Philadelphia, PA: Mosby, 2001.
43. Muir Gray JA. *Evidence-Based Healthcare. How to Make Health Policy and Management Decisions*. New York/Edinburgh/London: Churchill Livingstone, 1997.
44. Sackett DL, Scott Richardson W, Rosenberg W, Haynes RB. *Evidence-Based Medicine. How to Practice & Teach EBM*. New York and London: Churchill Livingstone, 1997. (3rd Edition, Elsevier, 2006).
45. *Users' Guides to the Medical Literature. A Manual for Evidence-Based Clinical Practice*. The Evidence-Based Medicine Working Group, edited by G Guyatt and D Rennie. Chicago: American Medical Association/JAMA & Archives Journals/AMA Press, 2002. (2nd Edition 2008).
46. Brownson RC, Baker EA, Lee TL, Gillespie KN. *Evidence-Based Public Health*. Oxford and New York: Oxford University Press, 2003.
47. *The SAGE Handbook of Qualitative Research*. Edited by NK Denzin and YS Lincoln. Thousand Oaks, CA/London/New Delhi: 2007.
48. Corbin J and Strauss A. *Basics of Qualitative Research*. 3rd Edition. Thousand Oaks, CA and London: SAGE Publications, 2008.
49. Jenicek M. *Clinical Case Reporting in Evidence-Based Medicine*. 2nd Edition. London: Arnold/Hodder Headline Group/Oxford University Press, 2001. (Editions in French, 1997; Italian, 2001; Japanese, 2001; and Korean, 2002).
50. Dewey J. *How We Think*. Boston: D.C. Heath, 1910. (Reprinted by Dover Publications, Inc., Minneola, NY, 1997).
51. Ennis RH. *Critical Thinking*. Upper Saddle River, NJ: Prentice Hall, 1996.
52. Hughes W and Lavery J. *Critical Thinking. An Introduction to the Basic Skills*. 5th Edition. Peterborough, ON/Plymouth, UK/Buffalo, NY/Sydney, NSW: Broadview Press, 2008.

53. Bowell T and Kemp G. *Critical Thinking. A Concise Guide.* London and New York: Routledge/Taylor & Francis, 2002.

54. Jenicek M. *A Primer on Clinical Experience in Medicine. Reasoning, Decision-Making, and Communication in Health Sciences.* Boca Raton, FL/London/New York: CRC Press/Taylor & Francis/ Productivity Press, 2013.

55. Damer TE. *Attacking Faulty Reasoning. A Practical Guide to Fallacy-Free Arguments.* 5th Edition. Belmont, CA: Thomson Wadsworth, 2005.

56. Jenicek M. *Fallacy-Free Reasoning in Medicine. Improving Communication and Decision-Making in Research and Practice.* Chicago, IL: American Medical Association (AMA Press), 2009.

57. Browne MN and Keeley SM. *Asking the Right Questions. A Guide to Critical Thinking.* 7th Edition. Upper Saddle River, NJ: Pearson/Prentice Hall, 2004.

58. Toulmin SE. *The Uses of Argument.* Cambridge: Cambridge University Press, 1958. (Updated Edition 2003).

59. Toulmin S, Rieke R, Janik A. *An Introduction to Reasoning.* New York: Macmillan Publishing Co. Inc., 1979.

60. Jenicek M and Hitchcock DL. *Evidence-Based Practice. Logic and Critical Thinking in Medicine.* Chicago, IL: American Medical Association (AMA Press), 2005.

61. de Bono E. *Lateral Thinking. A Textbook of Creativity.* London: Penguin Books, 1990. (First published by Ward Lock Education, 1970).

62. Bunge M. *Philosophical Dictionary. Enlarged Edition.* Amherst, NY: Prometheus Books, 2003. (1st Edition 1999).

63. Lederman EK. *Philosophy and Medicine.* Hants/Aldershot and Brookfield, VT: Gower Publishing Company, 1970. (Revised Edition 1986).

64. Wulff HR, Pedersen SA, Rosenberg R, Introduction by A Storr. *Philosophy of Medicine. An Introduction.* 2nd Edition. Oxford and Boston, MA: Blackwell Scientific Publications, 1986. (2nd Edition 1990).

65. Wulff HR and Götzche PC. *Rational Diagnosis and Treatment. Evidence-Based Clinical Decision-making.* Oxford and Malden, MA: Blackwell Science, 1976. (3rd Edition 2000).

66. Pellegrino ED and Thomasma DC. *A Philosophical Basis of Medical Practice. Toward a Philosophy and Ethic of the Healing Professions.* New York and Oxford: Oxford University Press, 1981.

67. *The Philosophy of Medicine. Framing the Field.* Edited by HT Engelhardt Jr. Dordrecht/Boston, MA/ London: Kluwer Academic, 2000.

68. *The Philosophy of Medicine Reborn: A Pellegrino Reader.* Edited by HT Engelhardt Jr and F Jotterand. Notre Dame, IN: University of Notre Dame Press, 2008.

69. Lolas F. Theoretical medicine: A proposal for reconceptualising medicine as a science of actions. *J Med Phil,* 1996;21(6):659–70. doi:10.1093/jmp/21.6.659.

70. Lorenz W and Rothmund M. Theoretical surgery: A new specialty in operative medicine. *World J Surg,* 1989;13:292–9.

71. Koller M, Barth H, Celik I, Rothmund M. A short history of theoretical surgery. *Inflamm Res,* 2004;53(Suppl 2):S99–S104.

72. Murphy EA. *The Logic of Medicine.* Baltimore, MD: The John Hopkins University Press, 1976. (2nd Edition 1997).

73. *Logic in Medicine.* Edited by CI Phillips. London: BMJ Publishing Group, 1988. (2nd Edition 1995).

74. Jenicek M. *Epidemiology. The Logic of Modern Medicine.* Montréal: EPIMED International, 1995. (Editions in Spanish, 1996, and Japanese, 1998).

75. Jenicek M. *Foundations of Evidence-Based Medicine.* Boca Raton, FL/London/New York/Washington, DC: Parthenon Publishing/CRC Press, 2003.

76. Jenicek M. *Medical Error and Harm. Understanding, Prevention, and Control.* Boca Raton, FL/ London/New York: CRC Press/Taylor & Francis/Productivity Press, 2011.

77. Jones-Devitt S and Smith L. *Critical Thinking in Health and Social Care.* Los Angeles/London/New Delhi/Singapore: SAGE Publications, 2007.

78. Thompson A. *Critical Reasoning. A Practical Introduction.* 2nd Edition. London and New York: Routledge/Taylor & Francis, 2002.

79. Kassirer JP and Kopelman RI. *Learning Clinical Reasoning.* Baltimore/Hong Kong/London: Williams & Wilkins, 1991.
80. Stanford Encyclopedia of Philosophy. *Cognitive Science.* 16 p. at http://plato.stanford.edu/entries /cognitive-science/, retrieved Nov 19, 2013.
81. Feinstein AR. *Clinical Judgment.* Baltimore: Williams & Wilkins, 1967.
82. Engelhardt HT Jr, Spicker SF, Towers B. *Clinical Judgment: A Critical Appraisal. Proceedings of the Fifth Trans-Disciplinary Symposium on Philosophy and Medicine, Held at Los Angeles, California, April 14–16, 1977.* Dordrecht/Boston/London: Kluwer, 1979.
83. Downie RS, MacNaughton JU, Randall F. *Clinical Judgment. Evidence in Practice.* Oxford: Oxford University Press, 2000.
84. Rao G. *Rational Medical Decision-Making. A Case-Based Approach.* New York/London/Toronto: McGraw-Hill, 2007.
85. Weinstein MC, Fineberg HV, Elstein AS et al. *Clinical Decision Analysis.* Philadelphia, PA: WB Saunders, 1980.
86. Götzsche PC. *Rational Diagnosis and Treatment. Evidence-Based Clinical Decision-Making.* 4th Edition. Chichester: John Wiley & Sons, 2007. (1st Edition Wulff H, 1976).
87. Pesut DJ, Herman JA. *Clinical Reasoning. The Art and Science of Critical and Creative Thinking.* Albany, NY/Scarborough, ON/London: Delmar Publishers/International Thomson Publishing Company (ITP), 1999.
88. Jenicek M. *A Physician's Self-Paced Guide to Critical Thinking.* Chicago: American Medical Association (AMA Press), 2006.
89. Jenicek M. *Writing, Reading, and Understanding in Modern Health Sciences. Medical Articles and Other Forms of Communication.* Boca Raton, FL/London/New York: CRC Press/Taylor & Francis/ Productivity Press, 2014.
90. Horton R. The grammar of interpretive medicine. *Can Med Ass J (CMAJ),* 1998;159:245–9.
91. Jenicek M. Towards evidence-based critical thinking medicine? Uses of the best evidence in flawless argumentations. *Med Sci Monit,* 2006;12(8):RA149–RA153.
92. Jenicek M, Croskerry P, Hitchcock DL. Evidence and its uses in health care and research: The role of critical thinking. *Med Sci Monit,* 2011;17(1):RA12–RA17.

Chapter 2

Philosophy for Medicine: Key Contributions of Philosophy to Medical Thinking Today—A Short Reminder and Refresher*

Executive Summary

As practitioners in health professions, we sometimes see philosophy as a highly intellectual and refined activity, whose end is not always to do something practical. As healthcare professionals, in nearly all cases, we are compelled and expected to do something rather than nothing. However, our decision "to do nothing" in some cases is still subject to the same thinking as to "do something."

Philosophy is a discipline of "thinking about thinking." All of its main branches are essential for good practice of medicine. Within these branches of philosophy, axiology, semantics, ontology, probabilistic philosophy, and "philosophy of something" are equally important in medicine today. Other subsets of those branches must not be forgotten.

Plato, Aristotle, St. Thomas Aquinas, René Descartes, David Hume, Immanuel Kant, Friedrich Nietzsche, John Stuart Mill, Charles Sanders Peirce, and Bertrand Russell are among many who have historically paved the way for contemporary, pragmatic philosophers (some of them also being health professionals) like Stephen E. Toulmin, Thomas S. Kuhn, Edward De Bono, Henrik R. Wulff, or Raymond Pellegrino among others.

---

* This chapter does not replace a more intensive and extensive reading of monographs quoted in the bibliography to this chapter. It only guides the reader to them.

Having defined philosophy in both its historical context and present state, let us translate it for use in our daily practice, research, and teachings. What would we do without "philosophy *of* medicine," "philosophy *in* medicine" and "philosophy *and* medicine?" We can do this by examining steps in clinical work throughout history, through the eyes of their protagonists—the authors who have written about philosophical challenges such as knowledge or uncertainty and others, and by applying and using such challenges in the context of epidemiology and evidence-based medicine, as well as in the context of medical specialties such as psychiatry, internal medicine, surgery, or others. The profile given to exploring these challenges in major medical journals is encouraging, relevant, and promising.

If we are able to understand and use philosophy more broadly, as we already understand and use epidemiology or biostatistics, it will be beneficial for the patient and our community. Even we, as health professionals, will benefit from being reassured that we are doing what is right, and we are doing it well.

In This Chapter

Executive Summary 21
Thoughts, Thinkers, and Things to Think About 23
2.1 So, What Exactly Is Philosophy? 25
2.2 What Are the Basic Branches of Philosophy and Which Ones Are the Most
      Important for Medicine? 26
      2.2.1 What Is, Then, Metaphysics? 27
      2.2.2 What Is, Then, Epistemology? 27
      2.2.3 What Is, Then, Logic? 28
      2.2.4 What Is, Then, Ethics? 28
      2.2.5 What Is, Then, Esthetics? 29
2.3 Who, Then, Is a Philosopher? 30
2.4 And What about Philosophy and Medicine? 31
      2.4.1 Philosophy in Medicine 31
      2.4.2 Philosophy of Medicine 32
      2.4.3 Philosophy and Medicine 32
      2.4.4 Medical Philosophy 32
2.5 So, Where Are We Today? 33
Let Us Conclude 33
References 34

Thoughts, Thinkers, and Things to Think About

*Most philosophers, most great men, most
anatomists, and most other men of eminence
lie like the devil.*
William Hunter
(1718–1783)
Not all, Bill!

Medicine is a sister of philosophy.
Tertulian (Quintus Septimius
Tertullianus)
circa 160 AD
H.G. Reichert, *Latin Proverbs.*
**How much philosophical (medicine)
and how much practical (philosophy)
are health sciences? Let's see in this and
other chapters.**

*Science is what you know, philosophy is
what you don't know.*
3rd Earl Bertrand Arthur William Russell
(1872–1970)
**From philosophy to science then,
Sir Bertrand?**

*What we should do, I suggest, is to give up
the idea of ultimate sources of knowledge
and admit that all knowledge is human;
that it is mixed with errors, our prejudices,
our dreams, and our hopes; that all we can
do is hope for the truth even though it is
beyond our reach.*
Sir Karl Raimund Popper
(1902–1994)
Anglo-Austrian Philosopher and Professor
Conjectures and Refutations
(Introduction), 1960
**However, Sir Karl, hope, as one of
three major Christian virtues, should
never be lost!**

The essential characteristic of philosophy, which makes it a study distinct from science, is criticism. It examines critically principles employed in science and daily life; it searches out any inconsistencies there may be in these principles, and it only accepts them when, as the result of critical inquiry, there is no reason to reject them.
3rd Earl Bertrand Arthur William Russell
(1872–1970), 1912
Aren't we doing it also in today's medicine, Sir Bertrand?

Science … is the natural and integral part of man's whole life, activity which, at base, is a blend of logic, intuition, art and belief …
Warren Weaver
(1894–1978)
So is medicine As blend of philosophy and science.

Philosophy is like trying to open a safe with a combination lock; each little adjustment of the dial seems to achieve nothing, only when everything is in place, does the door open.
Ludwig Wittgenstein
(1889–1951)
Conversation in 1930
Let us try to open as many doors in medicine as we can.

The philosophy of one century is the common sense of the next.
Henry Ward Beecher
(1813–1887)
Not a small challenge, Henry!

A word from the author of this book already reminded us to look beyond reasoning about health problems and our will to act in the best way for our patients and community. Our best understanding and decision-making about health problems relies on principles, modern methods, and techniques of modern philosophy applied throughout the medical experience.

Such understanding should improve our actions to ensure the best possible well-being of our patients and of entire communities.

Is a chapter about the essentials of philosophy in relation to the health sciences necessary? We believe so. Sometimes we forget what are the applications and uses of classical and modern philosophy. Sometimes, definitions in our domains can vary and differ in time, location, domain, setting, and context. For those reasons, let us examine them in this chapter and in all others as well. Chapter 7 is devoted specifically to the challenge of definitions today.

Knowledge, reasoning, and values are among the research and practice necessities that philosophy offers us to inform the most reasonable and rational ways of how to exercise our duties in the best way. Experience, data, information, and evidence are essential for such approaches.

Let us see in this chapter what philosophy today has to offer to all of us as health sciences thinkers and doers.

2.1 So, What Exactly Is Philosophy?

The definition of the word philosophy itself is "love of wisdom," from the Greek *philos* (love) and *sophia* (wisdom).[1] Today it is defined as '*the discipline that studies the most general concepts such as being, mind, knowledge, norm and other and general hypotheses like existence or knowability*'.

After centuries of definition, formulation, and redefinition of philosophy, the contemporary philosophy is perhaps best defined in a simplest way as:

- "***thinking about thinking***";[2] or
- *rationally critical thinking about the general nature of the world* (metaphysics or theory of existence), *the justification of belief* (epistemology or theory of knowledge), *and the conduct of life* (ethics or theory of value);[2]
- *a systematic analysis and critical examination of fundamental problems such as the nature of reality, mind, perception, self, free will, causation, time and space, and moral judgments;*[3]
- *the study of general and fundamental problems, such as those connected with reality, existence, knowledge, values, reason, mind, and language;*[4]
- *a systematic analysis and critical examination of fundamental problems and nature of being, reality, thinking, perception, values, causes, and choices underlying principles of physical and ethical phenomena.* Traditionally, its fundamental branches are metaphysics, epistemology and logic, and ethics;[5,6] and
- *as an activity—the attempt to understand the general principles and ideas that lie behind various concepts of life.*[3]

For a health professional, accustomed to more precise decisions like those for medicine, surgery, pediatrics, psychiatry, or nursing, the ones for philosophy, its branches and sub-domains are more than diverse.

Rational reasoning, critical thinking, and argumentation are the most important tools in philosophy in our domain of interest as seen across the chapters which follow. They are essential for making practical decisions and implementing them in daily life, and especially in all cases in which science and scientific method produce elements of philosophy.

2.2 What Are the Basic Branches of Philosophy and Which Ones Are the Most Important for Medicine?

Basic branches and areas of inquiry in philosophy are[7]:

- *metaphysics* (study of existence), which includes various aspects of existence, essence, space, time, self, cause, God;
- *epistemology* (study of knowledge), oriented toward theory itself, theory of knowledge, truth, with method, evidence, analysis;
- *logic* (study of reasoning), which includes the theory of argument, validity, proof, definition, consistency;
- *ethics* (study of value, theory of good, right, duty, responsibility, utility) and political philosophy (study of action and force).

For medicine should we not also add to these branches:

- *aesthetics* (study of action, theory of beauty, art, taste, standard, judgment, criticism[7]); and
- specialized branches as "*philosophy of something*" or 'subjects by areas' such as philosophy of history, of language, of law, of mathematics, of mind, of politics, of religion, of science, of biology, of education, and last but not least, of medicine, nursing and other health sciences and professions?

Axiology, defined by Vuletic[8-expanded] as an umbrella term for the study of values, be it ethical, epistemic, esthetic, or values for research and practice, is also an important element of philosophy for medicine.

From all of these branches, philosophy's basic subjects most relevant for health sciences are

- *logic* (study of reasoning);
- *semantics* (study of meaning);
- *ontology* (study of being);
- *epistemology* (study of knowledge);
- *ethics* (study of values); and
- *probabilistic philosophy* which exactifies different concepts such as causation (in ontology), truth or meaning. It measures and exactifies possibility, chance, and randomness.[9]

In its applications, we recognize philosophy of education, history, language, law, life, mind, religion, science, medicine, and all other health sciences and professions as well.

As with any other subject and domain in life, philosophy is a mastered activity which must be taught, learned, practiced, and evaluated.

2.2.1 What Is, Then, Metaphysics?

Metaphysics is a branch of philosophy representing the study of reality characteristics such as existence, the meaning of time and space, the relationship between the body and the mind, properties of wholes and parts of objects, events, processes, causation, determinism, and free will, arguments for belief in God, and immortality.[partly from 10–12]

As the foundation of philosophy, it studies and provides answers to its main questions: "**What is** .....?"[13], "What is **really** real?" and "What **should** be real?"[14] Landauer and Rowlands[11] and Larchie et al.[12] propose the following as its main branches:

1. *ontology*, the study of being or existence;
2. *natural theology*, the study of God and creation; and
3. *universal science*, i.e., the study of first principles like the law of identity.

Some notable historical figures involved in the development of metaphysics include Plato (427–347 BC), Aristotle (384–322 BC), René Descartes (1596–1650), John Locke (1632–1704), David Hume (1711–1776), Immanuel Kant (1724–1804), and Georg Wilhelm Friedrich Hegel (1770–1831). In medicine, the study of reality is behind diagnostic processes, causation of good and bad health events, and processes of care and research; all of these areas are both practical and metaphysical subjects of interest.

2.2.2 What Is, Then, Epistemology?

Epistemology is the study of ways of acquiring knowledge. *Epistemology is a branch of philosophy which is concerned with the nature, origin, and scope of knowledge.*[4] It answers the question "**How do we know?**"[13]

Epistemology questions possibilities of obtaining knowledge, methods of obtaining knowledge, its meaning, as well as how to be certain about it. Epistemology deals with our concept of knowledge, how we learn and acquire knowledge, and what we can know. It should help us to distinguish truth from error and provide criteria that must be provided for something to be believed in and be convinced about it. It is subdivided into:

1. *alethiology* (the study of nature of truth);
2. *formal epistemology* (uses of logic and probability in the study of epistemological questions and problems);
3. *meta-epistemology* (study of methods and aims of epistemology); and
4. *social epistemology* (study of social dimensions of knowledge).[13]

Some of its important subjects of interest (specifics) are concepts, definitions, words, emotions, integration, values, certainty, deduction, induction, abstraction, focus, and evasion.[12–22] Historical contributors to the study of epistemology include Plato (427–347 BC), Aristotle (384–322 BC), St. Thomas Aquinas (1225–1274), René Descartes (1596–1650), David Hume (1711–1776), Immanuel Kant (1724–1804), John Stuart Mill (1806–1873), Charles Sanders Peirce (1839–1914), and Bertrand Russell (1872–1970). In medicine, examples of epistemological studies may be

- ways to elucidate causes of both good and bad health phenomena;
- how we come to know about the effects of medical interventions;
- internal and external validity and accuracy of diagnostic tests; or
- predictive value of prognostic factors and markers.

These ways may be individual or generalized and objectified by epidemiology and biostatistics in clinical and community health research and practice. In epistemology, **rationalism** focuses on the mind as source and provider of knowledge. **Empiricism** focuses on our senses which produce experiences leading to knowledge.

In epistemology, **propositional knowledge,** that is, "knowledge *that*" is a subject of interest. In the world of numbers, we "know *that*" 2 + 3 = 5. "Knowledge *how*" refers to our ability to add numbers. "Knowledge *itself*" is most often defined as "a justified true belief, based on propositions stemming from both truths and beliefs." "*A priori* knowledge" is independent from, or precedes, the one which is based on experience, inquiry, research—an "*a posteriori* knowledge."

More introduction about historical evolution of how to see and understand knowledge as well as contemporary epistemology may be found by the uninitiated in general encyclopedias, monographs, or articles (some referring to epidemiology as part of epistemology[20]).

In monographs, epistemology is presented either as close to the gnostic process (discussed later on in this book), which goes from perception to memory, consciousness, reason, and testimony[19], or as a review of its major problems, topics, and challenges such as rational inquiry, cognitive progress, and cognitive limitations of the quest for truth.[20]

2.2.3 What Is, Then, Logic?

Logic in general is *the normative study that investigates the principles of valid reasoning and correct inference, as well as their consequences.*[5,6] Inference is meant here as the drawing of conclusions from one or more premises. In epidemiology, it is the process of passing from observations and axioms to generalizations, causal inference being its main task. In biostatistics, it means rather the development of ways of generalizations from sample data, usually with calculated degrees of uncertainty. The meaning of inference depends on the context.

Logic in medicine is *a system of thought and reasoning which governs understanding and decisions in clinical and community care, research, and communication.* It defines valid reasoning, which helps us to understand the meaning of health phenomena and leads us to the justification of the choice of clinical and paraclinical decisions and how to act on such phenomena.[6]

Logic may be **formal** by using symbols and mathematical ways of expression of reasoning, or **informal** by analyzing arguments as they occur in everyday language. Aristotle (384–322 BC), Francis Bacon (1561–1626), David Hume (1711–1776), and Bertrand Russell (1872–1970) are among its historical contributors and representatives.

2.2.4 What Is, Then, Ethics?

Ethics is moral philosophy, a study of how we live and what the best way to live might be. It answers the questions, "What **do I do**?" and "What **I should do**?"

Ethics has three main branches:[4,13]

1. *meta-ethics*, i.e., the study of the nature and truth of ethical thought;
2. *normative ethics*, i.e., how one should act and what is the right course of action; and
3. *applied ethics*, dealing with concrete problems, such as abortion, euthanasia, and other curative and preventive strategies, decisions, actions, and their consequences.

Aristotelian ethics, Confucian ethics, and the works of Plato (427–347 BC), Immanuel Kant (1724–1804), and Friedrich Nietzsche (1844–1900) are among the foundations of modern ethics.

Medical ethics may be seen as *the study of values of health, disease, and care and the morality of health professionals' actions, behavior, and conduct.* Today it goes well beyond Hippocratic ethics in the patient–doctor relationship. Medical ethics includes:

- *patient–health professional* relationship, information, and shared decisions;
- *relationships*, shared decisions, and communication *between health professionals* (between doctors themselves, between doctors and nurses, dentists, physiotherapists, clinical psychologists, medical archivists, health administrators, etc.);
- development, implementation, uses, and evaluation of *new medical technologies*;
- *organ* and other biological tissues collection and *transplantation*;
- *health information* storage, dissemination, and exchange; and
- *any kind of shared and not shared decisions about actions and inactions about health, disease, and death (assisted or not).*

Principles of medical ethics apply to all health professions. **Are health politics and policies a branch and subject of ethics**? Yes, they are. It is a subset of ethics by virtue of the studying and proposing rules for permissible actions in the community in general, or within the health community and professions.

2.2.5 What Is, Then, Esthetics?

Esthetics *means the study of beauty, art, enjoyment, their perception and values, as well as matters of taste and sentiment.* It also may be considered as **philosophy of art**. In our context, it is a species of value theory or axiology, which is the study of sensory and sensory-emotional values, also called judgment sentiment and taste.[23–26]

For Bunge,[9] the status of this branch of philosophy remains uncertain because there are no known objective standards for evaluating its subjects. Despite a number of opinions, definitions, and classifications, there seem to be neither testable hypotheses for esthetics, nor hypothetico-deductive systems and theories of evaluation. Plato (427–347 BC), Immanuel Kant (1724–1804), Friedrich Nietzsche (1844–1900), Paul Tillich (1886–1965), and Susanne K. Langer (1895–1985) are among the major historical contributors to esthetics.

Esthetics in medicine[27,28] is important both for the provider and the recipient of care. These include a surgeon practising reconstructive and esthetic (plastic) surgery, an ophthalmologist, or dermatologist, and also any practitioner required to have proper bedside or medical office manners, and even public health strategists in their management of community health problems and environment.

The general concepts, values, historical aspects, and relevant readings of esthetics in medicine are reviewed in several encyclopedic readings.[28–31]

2.3 Who, Then, Is a Philosopher?

Bunge's definitions are worthy of quoting: Teasingly and most broadly, a philosopher is *"any normal human being past age two."* More seriously and more narrowly, *"any person who asks philosophical problems, holds philosophical views, or teaches them, or does original research on philosophical problems."*[9]

Like other scientists, philosophers discover or invent problems, conduct research, produce new ideas, and discover relations among them. However, their scope of interest is much broader than solving research questions. As honest and competent scholars, they look at concepts of things, changes, novelty, time, life, mind, society, justice, knowledge, meaning, truth, norm, and right.[9]

In medical practice and research, we are all philosophers and philosophize to some degree. We think not only as good observers and as experienced qualified practitioners in our specialties, but also as epidemiologists, biostatisticians, decision-makers, and communicators. Pragmatic philosophy should bring all this together. How to do it depends on our paradigm of biological phenomena such as health, disease, care, and all major concerned individuals, health professionals, and patients as well.

The paradigm of human biology and medicine is more complex by its nature than paradigms in exact sciences, such as physics or chemistry. This is because:

■ Human biology and medicine is a more complex paradigm than other exact sciences, such as physics and chemistry. The inputs to human biology and medicine, health information, are most often incomplete and evolving. They are revealed in real time, not in a laboratory. They are most often probabilistic, not always deterministic.

■ The nature of biological phenomena is heterogeneous by variations in time (trends), and place (epidemicity, pandemicity, endemicity, clustering in people, time, and place).

■ Biological responses may be of different nature too: reactions (preformed and often repetitive health and pathological responses), adaptations (in time acquired adjusted best responses of the organism to various stimuli), or dysadaptations (failed or limited adaptations, pathologies and disease).

■ Let us add to all the above that our incomplete knowledge may be also caused by missing information ("it's never enough!"), wrong information ("I didn't know!"), and the misuse of what is left ("it cannot be otherwise!").

As a result, health information, whether written, oral, or electronic, is of heterogeneous nature, amplified by objectives, strategies, expectations, and preferences of research, practice, management, economics and other policies, politics, and politicking in the health and disease domain.

We must think clearly across this kind of paradigm to improve our understanding of health phenomena. Should philosophy help us to put all this together? We believe so.

2.4 And What about Philosophy and Medicine?

> In the above line of thought, '**philosophy for medicine means**'
>
> '*thinking* about *medical thinking.*'
>
> This way of thinking is common to all health sciences.

We may see and understand medical philosophy or philosophy for medicine from two main angles: as "philosophy *in* medicine" and "philosophy *of* medicine."[32,33] Pellegrino et al.[33] differentiate also between "philosophy and medicine" as well as "medical philosophy."

Hence, four modes of philosophy for medicine (in sequence of Reference 33):

- philosophy *and* medicine;
- philosophy *in* medicine;
- medical philosophy; and
- philosophy *of* medicine.

As in any other domain of human endeavor, philosophy means "*systematic analysis and critical examination of fundamental problems and the nature of being, reality and thinking, perception, values, causes and choices underlying principles of physical and ethical phenomena. Its fundamental branches are metaphysics, epistemology, logic and ethics.*"[24]

Until today, most attention was paid to medical ethics, and rightly so. However, other branches of philosophy have their equal place in medicine like logic, epistemology, ontology, or metaphysics.[26]

Philosophy in the domain of healthcare, instead, is concerned with ethical and political issues arising from healthcare research and practice.[27] In this case, the institutional and societal aspects of healthcare are in focus. Its focus may be best illustrated by some questions related to healthcare field, such as:

- Who requires, needs and deserves healthcare?
- What constitutes elements to calculate costs of care represented by institutional costs and treatments themselves?
- What are the necessary parameters for clinical trials and quality assurance?
- Who, if anybody, can decide when a patient needs 'comfort measures' including euthanasia?

Let us specify more two such complementary facets of philosophy for medicine: Philosophy *in* medicine and philosophy *of* medicine.

2.4.1 Philosophy in Medicine

Philosophy is still considered by some as a domain of a speculative nature and removed from reality. Today, modern philosophy is closely related to the practice of, and of primary importance for, medical reasoning and decision-making. From its four main branches, that is, metaphysics and ontology (being and reality), epistemology (knowledge), logic (inference), and ethics (values), ethics is perhaps most widely established, valued, and practiced.

However, other branches are also important. Metaphysics examines problems such as what is disease and health and what are their causes. Epistemology looks at what do we know about health phenomena, how do we know it, and how certain we are about such knowledge; how health professionals think, explain phenomena of interest; and how they make decisions in diagnosis and treatment.[27] Logic, as a branch of philosophy, is now interspersed between clinical and fundamental epidemiology, biostatistics, health economics and administration, and etiological research and more rooted there than in clinical disciplines.

In our context, philosophy *in* medicine means "*the uses and application of philosophy to health, disease and medical care.*"[5] It examines the methods used by medicine to formulate hypotheses (like questions about diagnosis and treatment) and directions on the basis of evidence (what to do), as well as the grounds on which claims (diagnoses, treatment decisions and effects, prognoses made) about patients and health problems may be justified.

Hence, philosophy *in* medicine is about the uses and applications of philosophy regarding various problems in medicine. It means the application of specific, recognized branches of philosophy, such as logic, metaphysics, axiology, ethics, or esthetics to medical matters.[33]

2.4.2 Philosophy of Medicine

Philosophy *of* medicine encompasses rather *philosophical considerations of the nature of medicine's own additional contributions to philosophy in general* such as the experience from clinical trials or other studies of cause-effect relationships; *the focus in on the advancement of the theory of medicine*[5] For Pellegrino et al.[33], *the philosophy of medicine consists in a critical reflection on the matter of medicine— on the content, method, concepts, and presuppositions peculiar to medicine **as medicine**.* Philosophy of medicine has the same relationship with philosophy as philosophies of history, law, art, and others.

Philosophy *of* medicine is currently well reviewed in its recent historical context as an introductory entry by JA Marcum.[30] Both "*in*" and "*of*" directions, as well as other branches of philosophy, often including ethics, are explored in a more or less balanced way in several key monographs.[31–33] Across current literature, distinctions between philosophy *of* medicine and philosophy *in* medicine are either blurred or not made, for whatever reason. Several periodicals are now devoted to both philosophy in medicine and of medicine, such as the *Journal of Medicine and Philosophy* (mostly ethics) or *Theoretical Medicine*.

2.4.3 Philosophy and Medicine

For Pellegrino et al.,[33,35] philosophy and medicine are distinct and a discussion of these is a dialogue between two independent entities. In Pellegrino's work, philosophy and medicine are only a loose pairing, not as an integrated entity which includes both.

2.4.4 Medical Philosophy

Medical philosophy is the loosest term of the four explored here. It is considered as *any informal reflection on the practice of medicine—usually by physicians on clinical medicine based in their reflections on their own clinical experiences.*[33] It is a kind of wisdom shared by reflective physicians such as William Osler (1849–1919) or Lewis Thomas (1913–1993). Distinctions as above in Sections 2.4.1–2.4.3 followed only later.

2.5 So, Where Are We Today?

Over the last two generations, philosophy *in* medicine has been advanced both in the context of clinical practice and research mainly by physicians like Wulff and Gotzche in Denmark[34] or Pellegrino's group in North America,[33,35] or hand in hand by a philosopher and physician[5] and others.[36,37] Philosophy *of* medicine leaned more toward philosophy.

Philosophical matters related to medicine and other health sciences are currently illustrated:

- by steps in clinical work;[38]
- by historical context from antiquity until today;[39]
- through the eyes of their protagonists from one era to the other;[40]
- by covering selected philosophical challenges, such as knowledge, uncertainty, or esthetics and others;[41]
- in the contemporary context of epidemiology[42,43] or evidence-based medicine[44]; or
- in the context of medical specialties such as psychiatry[45].

Philosophy of medicine is also explored in an increasing number of major medical journals, such as the *Journal of Evaluation in Clinical Practice*,[46–49] *Medical Humanities*,[50] *Preventive Medicine*,[43] *Journal of the Royal Society of Medicine*,[51] and elsewhere.

In addition to these early initiatives, a much broader framework, view, and scope of "general" philosophy used by philosophers from around the world presented an important review and analysis of both philosophy *of* medicine and philosophy *in* medicine. In *Philosophy of Medicine*,[52] edited by F. Gifford, its numerous contributors from philosophy consider many important topics such as concepts of health and disease, diagnosis, causal inference and cause-effect relationships as seen from observational etiological research and clinical trials (experimental approach), their translation into research and practice of evidence-based medicine, nursing, and public health, and other more fundamental challenges of "general" (unrelated to profession or specific domain) philosophy, like theories, models, or ontology and other topics.

Philosophy of healthcare[53] is here to stay. As well as medicine itself, it reflects several elements discussed in this chapter.

Let Us Conclude

Consider this understanding of how to address fundamental questions in philosophy:

> *Philosophy is not so much about coming up with the answers to fundamental questions as it is about the process of trying to find these answers, using reasoning rather than accepting without question conventional views or traditional authority. [...] New ideas emerge through discussion and the examination, analysis, and criticism of other people's ideas. [...] Many later philosophers also adopted the device of dialogues to present their ideas, giving arguments and counterarguments rather than simple statement of their reasoning and conclusions.*[54]

This book is about the ways and processes that clinicians and others may use to try and find answers to important issues in medical and clinical thinking, rather than simply providing the answers that clinicians might need. Let us always not only search for the best evidence in medicine, but also to understand the acceptability of such evidence and how to use it in making decisions and sharing our experience with others, whether in oral or written communications.

From all branches of philosophy, we will be most concerned both in our research and practice about logic and its ways of critical thinking, argumentation, and decision-making, both in patient-centered and community-centered care and research. All these branches are behind all our understanding of the nature and origins (causes) of patient's problems, the clinical care of them, daily decisions about them, and forecasting their outcomes and future care. The safety and survival of the patient as well as the quality of care, rely on it.

Ethics in health sciences and professions are now well established, structured, formalized, and legalized by health associations, systems, and industry.

Epidemiologists, biostatisticians, clinicians, health administrators, and economists have been leading efforts to integrate philosophy, often in their own way, in the health domain. Other branches of philosophy deserve the same attention. The further development and uses of ethics look increasingly usable and promising.

Philosophy in medicine is evident in phrases like, "… *It has been epidemiologically proven, that …*" or "… *Our biostatistical analysis provides a good picture and inference about health problem causes and their management …*" is well supported by or even "… *It makes a good sense that …*" These phrases illustrate a philosophical standpoint in terms of logic, argumentation, decisions, or ethics. Additional standpoints are the subject of chapters which follow. The current extent of medical philosophy is a subject of ongoing open question and questioning, initiatives worthy of encouragement.

As health professionals, we cannot identify ourselves solely as ethicists, logicians, or epistemologists, we are, and must be, all of them. We use philosophy in our daily trials to understand and decide, be it in the diagnosis, search for causes, prevention and treatment, or prognosis. We also use philosophy while evaluating benefits (and harms) for, and to, the patient, hospital, and other health communities. And we also use philosophy to assess the performance of caring health professionals.

Do we have a choice to proceed otherwise? We do not believe so.

References

1. Reese WL. *Dictionary of Philosophy and Religion. Eastern and Western Thought.* Expanded Edition. Amherst, NY: Humanity Books/Prometheus Books, 1999.
2. The Oxford Companion to Philosophy. Edited by T Honderich. Oxford and New York: Oxford University Press, 1995.
3. Thompson M. *Philosophy.* New Edition. *Ty-"Teach Yourself" Books.* Lincolnwood (Chicago), IL: NTC/Contemporary Publishing and London: Hodder Headline Plc, 2000.
4. Wikipedia, the free encyclopedia. *Philosophy.* 18 p. at http://en.wikipedia.org/w/index.php?title=Philosophy&oldid=64427867, retrieved March 6, 2015.
5. *The Cambridge Dictionary of Philosophy. Second Edition.* General Editor Robert Audi. Cambridge and New York: Cambridge University Press, 1999.
6. Jenicek M and Hitchcock DL. *Evidence-Based Practice. Logic and Critical Thinking in Medicine.* Chicago, IL: American Medical Association (AMA Press), 2006.
7. Kipfer BA. *The Order of Things. Hierarchies, Structures, and Pecking Orders.* New York: Workman Publishing, 2008.
8. Vuletic MI. *The Nature of Philosophy.* 5 p. at http://www.vuletic.com/hume/ph/philosophy.html, retrieved Jan 30, 2015.

9. Bunge M. *Philosophical Dictionary.* Enlarged Edition. Amherst, NY: Prometheus Books, 2003.
10. Helicon Publishing Ltd. *Instant Reference Philosophy. Ty-"Teach Yourself" Books.* London, UK and Lincolnwood, IL: Hodder Headline Plc and NTC/Contemporary Publishing, 2000.
11. Landauer J and Rowlands J. *Importance of Philosophy.* 14 p. at http://www.importanceofphilosophy .com|, retrieved Jan 30, 2015.
12. Larchie and Lander at Lander Edu. *The Divisions and Definition of Philosophy.* 7 p. at http://philosophy .lander.edu/intro/what.stml, retrieved Jan 30, 2015.
13. Wikipedia, the free encyclopedia. *Epistemology.* 17 p. at http://en.wikipedia.org/w/index.php?title=Ep istemology"oldid=649959229, retrieved March 16, 2015.
14. Truncellito DA. *Epistemology.* The Internet Encyclopedia of Philosophy. 12 p. at http://www.iep.utm .edu/epistemo/, retrieved March 16, 2015.
15. Klein PD. *Epistemology.* In Editor E Craig Routledge Encyclopedia of Philosophy Online. London: Routledge, 1998, 2005. 6 p. at http://www.rep.routledge.com/article/P059, retrieved January 31, 2015.
16. Martinich AP and Stroll A. *Epistemology. Encyclopaedia Britannica Article.* 42 p. at ebcid:com.britannica .oec2.identifier.ArticleIdentifier?tocId=91060..., retrieved Jan 31, 2015.
17. Steup M. *Epistemology.* Stanford Encyclopedia of Philosophy (online). 34 p. at http://plato.stanford /edu/entries/epistemology/, retrieved March 16, 2015.
18. Battersby M. Applied epistemology and argumentation in epidemiology. *Informal Logic,* 2006; 26(1): 41–62.
19. Audi R. *Epistemology. A Contemporary Introduction to the Theory of Knowledge.* 2nd Edition. New York and London: Routledge, Routledge Contemporary Introductions to Philosophy, 2003.
20. Rescher N. *Epistemology. An Introduction to the Theory of Knowledge.* Albany, NY: State University of New York Press, 2003.
21. *A Dictionary of Epidemiology.* 5th Edition. Edited by Miquel Porta. A Handbook Sponsored by The I.E.A. Oxford and New York: Oxford University Press, 2008.
22. Scruton R. *Aesthetics. Encyclopedia Britannica Article.* 33 p. at ebcid.com.britannica.oec2.identifier .ArticleIdentifier?tocId=91060..., and http:33www.britannica.com/print/topic/7484, retrieved Jan 31, 2015.
23. Slater BH. *Aesthetics. Internet Encyclopedia of Philosophy. A Peer-Reviewed Academic Resource.* 13 p. at http://www.iep.utm.edu/aestheti/print, retrieved Jan 31, 2015.
24. Wikipedia, the free encyclopedia. *Aesthetics.* 26 p. at http://en.wikipedia.org/wiki/Aesthetics, retrieved March 13, 2015.
25. Philosophy Archive. *Philosophy of Aesthetics. From Philosophy Archive.* 8 p. at http://www.philosophyarvhive .com/index.php?title=Philosophy_of_Aesthetics, retrieved March 16, 2015.
26. *Aesthetics.* 11 p. from the *New Word Encyclopedia,* at http://www.newworldencyclopedia.org/entry /Aesthetics, page last modified Feb 15, 2016, last retrieved Dec 2, 2017.
27. Wikipedia, the free encyclopedia. *Aesthetic Medicine.* 5 p. at http://en.wkipedia.org/wiki/Aesthetic _medicine, retrieved March 16, 2015.
28. Wikipedia, the free encyclopedia. *Philosophy of Medicine.* 7 p. at http://en.wikipedia.org/wiki/Philosopy _of_medicine, retrieved Jan 30, 2015.
29. Wikipedia, the free encyclopedia. *Philosophy of Healthcare.* 5 p. at http://en.wikipedia.org/wiki/Philosophy _of_healthcare, retrieved Jan 30, 2015.
30. Marcum JA. *Philosophy of Medicine.* 25 p. from Internet Encyclopedia of Philosophy pages at http:// iep.utm.edu/medicine/, retrieved Jan 30, 2015.
31. Lederman EK. *Philosophy and Medicine.* Revised Edition. Hants/Aldershot and Brookfield, VT: Gower Publishing Company, 1970. (Revised Edition 1986).
32. Jenicek M. *A Primer on Clinical Experience in Medicine. Reasoning, Decision-Making, and Communication in Health Sciences.* Boca Raton, FL/London/New York: CRC Press/Taylor & Francis/Productivity Press, 2013.
33. *The Philosophy of Medicine Reborn: A Pellegrino Reader.* Edited by HT Engelhardt Jr and F Jotterand. Notre Dame, IN: University of Notre Dame Press, 2008.

34. Wulff HR and Gotzche PC. *Rational Diagnosis and Treatment. Evidence-Based Clinical Decision-making.* 3rd Edition. Oxford and Malden, MA: Blackwell Science, 1976. (3rd Edition 2000, 4th Edition at John Wiley by PC Gotzche 2007).

35. Pellegrino ED and Thomasma DC. *A Philosophical Basis of Medical Practice. Toward a Philosophy and Ethic of the Healing Professions.* New York and Oxford: Oxford University Press, 1981.

36. Wulff HR, Pedersen SA, Rosenberg R, Introduction by A Storr. *Philosophy of Medicine. An Introduction.* 2nd Edition. Oxford and Boston, MA: Blackwell Scientific Publications, 1986. (2nd Edition 1990).

37. *The Philosophy of Medicine. Framing the Field.* Edited by HT Engelhardt Jr. Dordrecht/Boston/London: Kluwer Academic, 2000.

38. Bunge M. *Medical Philosophy. Conceptual Issues in Medicine.* Singapore/Hackensack, NJ/London (UK): World Scientific Publishing Co. Pte. Ltd, 2013.

39. Van Der Eijk PJ. *Medicine and Philosophy in Classical Antiquity: Doctors and Philosophers on Nature, Soul, Health and Disease.* Cambridge, UK: The Press Syndicate of the University of Cambridge/Cambridge University Press, 2005.

40. *Philosophy and Medicine.* Volume I and II. Edited by KJ Boudouris. Studies in Greek Philosophy Series. International Association for Greek Philosophy and International Center for Greek Philosophy and Culture. Alimos, GR: 1998.

41. *Philosophy for Medicine. Applications in a Clinical Context.* Edited by M. Evans, P Louhiala, and R Puustinen. Oxford and San Francisco, CA: Radcliffe Medical Press, 2004.

42. Broadbent A. *Philosophy of Epidemiology.* Basingstoke: Palgrave Macmillan, 2013.

43. Morabia A and Costanza MC. Editorial. Philosophy and epidemiology. *Preventive Medicine,* 2011, 53: 213–214.

44. Howick J. *The Philosophy of Evidence-Based Medicine.* Oxford, UK/Chichester (West Sussex)/Hoboken, NJ: Wiley-Blackwell/BMJ Books, 2011.

45. Culver CM and Gert B. *Philosophy in Medicine: Conceptual and Ethical Issues in Medicine and Psychiatry.* New York: Oxford University Press, 1982.

46. Loughlin M, Bluhm R, Fuller J, Buetow S, Upshur REG, Borgerson K, Goldenberg MJ, Kingma E. Philosophy, medicine and health care—Where we have come from and where we are going. *J Eval Clin Pract,* 2014, 20:902–907.

47. Mitchell D. Philosophy at the bedside—Phenomenology, complexity and virtue in the care of patients. *J Eval Clin Pract,* 2014, 20:970–974.

48. Bullock E and Kingma E. Interdisciplinary workshop in the philosophy of medicine: Medical knowledge, medical duties. *J Eval Clin Pract,* 2014, 20:994–1001.

49. Lemoine M, Darrason M, Richard H. Where is philosophy of medicine headed? A report of the International Advanced Seminar in the Philosophy of Medicine (IASPM). *J Eval Clin Pract,* 2014, 20:991–993.

50. Rudnick A. An introductory course in philosophy of medicine. *Medical Humanities,* 2003, 30:54–56.

51. Weatherall DJ. Philosophy for medicine. *J Roy Soc Med,* 2004, 97(8):403–405.

52. *Philosophy of Medicine.* Edited by F Gifford (General Editors: DM Gabbay, P Thagard, and J Woods.). A *Handbook of the Philosophy of Science.* Amsterdam/New York/Singapore/Sydney/Tokyo: Elsevier and North Holland, 2011.

53. Wikipedia, the free encyclopedia. *Philosophy of Healthcare.* Last edited on Oct. 11, 2017. https://en.vikipedia.org/w#windex.php?title=Philosophy_of_healthcare&oldid=80488157. Last retrieved Dec 2, 2017.

54. Buckingham W, Burnham D, Hill C, King PJ, Marenbon J, Weeks M et al. *The Philosophy Book. Big Ideas Simply Explained.* London/New York/Melbourne/Munich/New Delhi: DK Publishing, 2011.

Chapter 3

Medicine's Own Contribution to Today's Thinking in Health Sciences and Professions: Not Only Philosophy, But Also Art, Craft, Scientific Method, and Evidence*

Executive Summary

Today the field of medicine includes health protection (actions to eliminate possible risks to health), disease prevention (policies to eliminate a disease and minimize its effects), and health promotion as approaches that can improve and strengthen the health of individuals and communities. To reach such goals, medicine is practiced as an art, as a science which relies heavily on the scientific method, and as a craft—actions based on sensory-motor skills and dexterities which rely on both art and science.

The results and impacts of disease, health, and medicine are less often deterministic and more often subject to probabilities, uncertainty, fuzziness, and chaos. The science of medicine refers to a structured and organized way of using probability, uncertainty, and facts for the benefit of the patient.

* This chapter is based, with permission of the publisher, on Chapter 1 in: Jenicek M. *A Primer on Clinical Experience in Medicine. Reasoning, Decision-Making, and Communication in Health Sciences.* Boca Raton, FL/London/New York: CRC Press/Taylor & Francis/Productivity Press, 2013. Revised, edited, updated.

Medicine consists of both theory and practice. The theory of medicine includes conceptions, views, and propositions that explain phenomena of interest. Philosophy and its branches (logic, ethics, and epistemology) are the foundation of medical theory. The practice of medicine refers to actions and processes as exercises of a physician's knowledge of both facts and theory, including their reasoning, actions, and evaluation.

The practice of clinical and community medicine therefore is not only based in evidence, but also values patients and the practitioner's own narratives. All of these approaches are grounded in critical thinking, informal logic argumentation, and increasingly structured decision-making.

Besides evidence-based medicine (EBM), other approaches to medicine have increased, including: integrative medicine, individualized medicine, patient-centered medicine, patient-centered care, integrated behavioral healthcare, patient-centered primary care, patient-centered integrated care, personalized medicine, person-centered health policy, and evidence-informed person-centered healthcare, among others. Are they contradictory or complementary to EBM? We suggest that these approaches are complementary to EBM.

In This Chapter

Executive Summary 37
Thoughts, Thinkers, and Things to Think About 39
Introductory Comments 43
3.1   Art, Craft, and Science of Medicine 45
    3.1.1   Medicine as Art 45
    3.1.2   Medicine as Craft 48
    3.1.3   Medicine as Science 49
        Scientific Theory 49
        Scientific Method 49
3.2   Paradigms behind the Science of Medicine 52
    3.2.1   Probability and Clinical Uncertainty 52
    3.2.2   Fuzzy Theory in Medicine 53
    3.2.3   Chaos Theory in Medicine 54
3.3   Theory and Practice of Medicine: Which One Will You Learn, Use, and Practice? 54
    3.3.1   Theory of Medicine 55
    3.3.2   Practice of Medicine 55
3.4   Newer Trends and Paradigms in the Theory and Practice of Medicine:
    Evidence-Based Medicine and Other Evidence-Based Health Sciences 56
    3.4.1   But What Exactly Is Evidence-Based Medicine? 56
    3.4.2   What Are the Steps in the Practice of Evidence-Based Medicine? 56
    3.4.3   Evidence-Based Clinical Medicine (EBM) 58
    3.4.4   Evidence-Based Community Medicine and Public Health (EBPH) 58

3.4.5 Evidence-Based HealthCare...59
3.4.6 Grading Evidence and Evaluating the Whole EBM Process.............................. 60
3.5 Beyond the Evidence-Based Medicine Original Concept: Evidence-Based Critical
Thinking Medicine, Reflective Uses of Evidence, Patient-Centered Medicine Trends 62
3.5.1 Critical Thinking... 62
3.5.2 Reflective Uses of Evidence... 63
3.5.3 Patient-Centered (Person-Centered), Personalized, Integrative Medicines 63
Let Us Conclude: What Exactly Should We Teach, Learn, and Practice Then?.........................65
An Evidence and Critical Thinking-Based Medicine Then?...65
References 67
Suggested Additional Readings 70

Thoughts, Thinkers, and Things to Think About

*Art is the imposing of a pattern of
experience and our esthetic enjoyment is
recognition of the pattern.*
Alfred North Whitehead (1861–1947), 1943
in Dialogues of Alfred North Whitehead (1954)
**And a catchy way to present our
thoughts and decisions!**

Art is the sex of imagination.
George Jean Nathan
(1882–1958)
American Mercury (July 1926)
**How should we then make medicine
more imaginative than it is today?**

*Facts are not science—as
the dictionary is not literature.*
Martin H. Fisher
(1879–1962)
Fischerisms (Howard Fabing and Ray Mart)
The Glossary and References in this book are!

*Science is what you know, philosophy is
what you don't know.*
3rd Earl Bertrand Arthur William Russell
(1872–1970)
British philosopher
And yes, medicine is both!

The aim of pure basic science, unlike those of applied science, are neither fast-flowing nor pragmatic. The quick harvest of applied science is the usable process, the medicine, the machine. The shy fruit of pure science is understanding.
Lincoln Barnett
(1809–1979)
Isn't then medicine also pure basic science?

Science is the knowledge of consequences, and dependence of one fact upon another.
Thomas Hobbes
(1588–1679)
So is medicine!

Science .... Is the natural and integral part of man's whole life, an activity which, at base, is a blend of logic, intuition, art and belief. ...
Warren Weaver
(1894–1978)
So is the blend of medicine!

The ability to reason is the fundamental characteristic of human beings.... Virtually every conscious human activity involves reasoning: we reason whenever we solve problems, make decisions, assess character, explain events, write poems, balance chequebooks, predict elections, make discoveries, interpret works of art, or repair carburetors. We reason about everything from the meaning of life to what to have for dinner.
William Hughes and Jonathan Lavery (2008)
We also reason at every step of clinical care, making diagnoses, prescribing drugs, performing surgery, or caring for bedridden patients and their friends and family.

*Science is the attempt to make the chaotic
diversity of our sense-experience correspond
to a logically uniform system of thought.*
Albert Einstein
(1879–1955)
Out of My Later Years (1950, 14)
**Aren't health sciences today less chaotic
due to their system of thought?**

*Science is nothing but trained and organized
common sense ...*
Thomas Henry Huxley
(1825–1895)
Collected Essays (1893–1894)
"Agnosticism"
**Providing that we can well define
"common sense" in operational terms!**

*Science may be described as the art of the
systematic oversimplification.*
Sir Karl Raimund Popper (1902–1994)
Quoted in the *Observer* (August 1, 1982)
**Isn't is rather systematic clarification,
Sir Karl?**

*The great tragedy of Science – that the slaying
of a beautiful hypothesis by an ugly fact.*
Thomas Henry Huxley
(1825–1895)
"Biogenesis and Abiogenesis,"
in the *British Association Annual Report, 1870*
What would we do without ugly facts?

*Starting third year is like going to a foreign
country. You don't speak the language,
you don't understand the customs, and the
natives are not necessarily friendly.*
Anne Eva Ricks (1982)
Even earlier, Anne!

*The person who knows "how" will always
have a job. The person who knows "why"
will always be his boss.*
Diane Ravitch (1985)
**Some knowing "whys" follow in
this book.**

*Be assured that no man can know his own
profession perfectly, who knows nothing
else; and he who aspires to eminence in any
particular science, must first acquire the habit
of philosophizing on matters in general.*
Abraham Colles (1773–1875)
**Isn't this what we are doing on these
pages?**

*Knowledge makes the physician, not the
name or the school.*
Paracelsus (1493(?)–1541)
**But the school is a provider of
knowledge!**

*Learning without thinking is useless.
Thinking without learning is dangerous.*
Confucius (551–478 BC)
So, dear reader, learn and think!

*Facts are not science—as
the dictionary is not literature.*
Martin H. Fischer (1879–1962)
**The rest is in our Glossary
at the end of this book.**

*So many views, approaches and paradigms
of medicine, so challenging to make them
operational, to learn medicine in those lights and
putting them into practice? Just imagine how even
more challenging it is for your clinical teachers,
elders and role models!*

Introductory Comments

How should we see and understand medicine before starting to learn it? Let us define it first. So many ways to see medicine! In this introductory chapter, let us try to understand them beyond pure theory and realize their relevance for our understanding and practice.

Let us start by medicine itself. Do we really need to define it? We believe so. Its definition specifies not only its content but also its extent and then, also the expectations from our work.

Definitions of medicine abound. Medicine is currently defined by *Mosby's Medical Dictionary* as *"the art and science of diagnosis, treatment, and prevention of disease, and the maintenance of good health."*[1] In 2006, largely in the conformity with prevailing trends, we have stressed that *"This definition applies both to the care of individual patients and to the care of the community."*[2] Another more recent (and much broader) definition identifies medicine as *"the profession and calling concerned with the care of the sick, including care by skilled professional staff, lay healers, and family members. 'Medicine' is a wide-ranging field of human activity, not confined to the profession that requires a university education."*[3] The latter definition implies a much broader focus, content and methods and techniques, more actors, less reliance on the scientific method, and often different target populations.

This book focuses on the former—the care of the individual and the community. In this spirit, medicine includes health protection, disease prevention, and health promotion. Each of these is described further below.

Health protection: The activity which focuses mainly on the actions *"that can be taken to eliminate as far as possible the risk of adverse consequences for health attributable (most often) to environmental hazards."*[3]

Disease prevention: *"Policies and actions to eliminate a disease or minimize its effect."*[3] Preventing disease includes five different approaches, including:

Primordial prevention *"consists of conditions, actions, and measures to minimize hazards to health and that hence inhibit the emergence and establishment of processes and factors (environmental, economic, social, behavioural, cultural) known to increase the risk of disease."*[4] Defined as such, it largely overlaps the definition of health protection.

Primary prevention *"aims to reduce the incidence of disease by personal and communal factors."*[4,5]

Secondary prevention *"aims to reduce the prevalence of disease by shortening its duration."*[4,5] If this is so, then most of clinical medicine falls in this domain. Are all physicians then practitioners of some kind of prevention? To a large extent, they are. (N.B. Screening for disease and early treatment is a good example of this level of prevention.)

Tertiary prevention *"consists of measures aimed at softening the impact of long term disease and disability, and handicap; minimizing suffering, and maximizing potential years of useful life."*[4] Hence, even the duration of disease is not in focus but rather the severity, spectrum, and gradient of the disease.[5]

Quaternary prevention *"consists of actions that identify patients at risk of overdiagnosis or overmedication and that protect them from excessive medical intervention."*[4,6]

Health promotion as *"the policies and processes that enable people to increase control over and improve their health."*[3] In health promotion, communities, their behavior and their environment are largely in focus.

Medicine, as a multifaceted domain, may be seen from several different angles. It incorporates:

- art and science;
- theory and practice;
- knowledge, attitudes, and skills;
- finding and using the most rational way the best evidence;
- critical thinking, argumentation, and decision-making in our practice of medicine;
- execution of sensory and motor skills; and
- evaluation of how well have we done.

Understanding and addressing these different aspects of medicine means that we approach medicine as both a rational and purposeful professional exercise, and as an act of belief, goodwill, and best intentions. While these approaches are disparate, both are needed. Without a rational and purposeful professional exercise, the second risks becoming nothing but an act of faith, however sincere and well intentioned it might be. A patient's physical, mental, social, and spiritual health maintenance or improvement, as well as a health professionals' job satisfaction, all depend on them.

The complexity of the range of approaches to, and aspects of, medicine creates formidable expectations on what knowledge and skills physicians must master, including:

- assimilating a considerable volume of facts such as elements of anatomy, hundreds of syndromes for further pattern recognition, drug dosages, and pieces of legislation or administrative rules governing medical practice;
- acquiring automatisms necessary for the execution of many clinical maneuvers such as those required to perform a physical examination or to practice emergency medicine;
- communicating effectively (listening and talking) with the patient, the patient's family, as well as members of the health team;
- assessing patient risks;
- making diagnoses and prognoses;
- listing problems and creating a hierarchical classification system;
- making decisions;
- mastering exploratory medical and surgical procedures (performance);
- managing patients after intervention (follow-up and care, control of disease course);
- evaluating the effectiveness and efficiency of cure and care;
- respecting medical, cultural, and social ethics as well as of patient values, preferences, and expectations; and
- expressing empathy.

Practicing medicine means not only applying our humanism, compassion, knowledge, and skills, but also basing our actions on the fundamentals of philosophy, science, facts and evidence, as well as on art and logic in their universal sense. Medicine is an integral part of such a universe and often, we do not realize the extent to which we follow its general rules. This book is not only about reasoning and making decisions when dealing with patients in a clinical setting, but also when working with groups of individuals in communities under our care. It also covers what we should know and the application of this knowledge.

3.1 Art, Craft, and Science of Medicine

Viewing medicine in this comprehensive way requires an exploration of what the art, craft, and science of medicine are, how they differ, and how they complement each other. These remain subjects of an open and ongoing discussion. In the sections below, each of these terms are defined within the medicine paradigm.

3.1.1 Medicine as Art

The **art of medicine** may be defined as *a mastery of dealing with human interactions, feelings and sensations, ideas, making meaningful lateral and holistic connections, and contributing thusly to the body of medical knowledge, attitudes, and skills.*[7]

Is there a better way to define art of medicine? Quantitative research (based on counting and measurement) and qualitative research methodology (based on understanding and interpretation) are both necessary to understand the workings of medicine today. In fact, there is no other way to evaluate and understand the expectations of both Canadian and American physicians and health professionals.[8,9] These expectations include:

- placing patients' needs ahead of self-interest;
- commitment to scholarship;
- responsiveness to societal needs;
- working optimally with other health professionals;
- practicing with integrity, respect, compassion, responsibility, courtesy, sensitivity to patient needs, and to colleagues and other healthcare personnel;
- having high standards of moral and ethical behavior;
- recognizing and managing physician impairment in peers and self;
- being concerned for psychosocial aspects of care;
- recognizing the importance of self-assessment, and willingness to teach;
- understanding requirements for involvement of patients in research;
- being aware of the effects of differences in gender, age, cultural, and social background; and
- acting with honesty and dependability.

Many of these virtues reflect expectations for physicians that were already proposed at the time of Paracelsus (1493–1541), with some notable exceptions such as: " ... *not to be married to the bigot, ... not to be a runaway monk, ... not practice a self-abuse, ... and ... not to have a red beard.*"[10] More seriously, it is clear that health professionals require more than a discrete body of knowledge and skills. Moreover, they are expected to value performance above reward, and are held to higher standards of behavior than non-professionals.[11]

Let us define first the **context of medicine**. It will allow us to better understand even better the justification, uses, and purposes of various methods and techniques of study, understanding, decision-making, and evaluation in the health domain. Everything we do is based on the way we see things around us and on the values given to our actions and endeavors. The same is true in medicine. For instance, the consideration and practice of euthanasia is heavily influenced by our understanding and interpretation of the Judeo-Christian commandment "Thou shall not kill" in a given setting of faith, culture, and societal values. The order *primum non nocere* ("first, do not harm") in the Hippocratic oath can be challenged in situations when some harm is necessary to heal and prevent a worse outcome. Health promotion, screening for disease, or treatment of complex health problems, will depend not only on medical considerations of relevance or effectiveness, but also on economics, politics, administration, and management in health sciences and society as a whole.

Similarly, the value and justification of our reasoning, decisions, methods, and techniques in medicine depend on the context of our practice. For example, a lecturer who enters a classroom and tells his or her unprepared students that today they will learn about case control studies in etiological research should expect to be asked why. Therefore, let us first define major paradigms in medicine, that is, the ways we perceive major issues and characteristics of health, disease, and care.

To be a good physician, it is necessary to develop the art of medicine and to master medicine as a science in two areas:

1. In **clinical medicine**, the art and science relate to a clinic or the bedside, where observation and treatment of patients occurs.
2. **Community medicine, preventive medicine, and public health** occur where a body of individuals live in a defined area and have a common interest, organization,[6] characteristics, or all three.

The art of medicine must be applied in all of these.

Historically, medicine was learned first and mostly as an art. In general, **medical art** has several pragmatic definitions and components. Some of them, like skills, might fall today to the category of *medical crafts*.

Medical crafts can be described as:

■ the employment of means to accomplish some desired end;
■ a system of rules serving to facilitate the performance of certain actions;
■ a system of principles and rules for attaining a desired end;
■ a method of doing well some special work;
■ the systematic application of knowledge or skill in effecting a desired result;
■ manual expertise;[12]
■ acquired skill as the result of knowledge and practice;
■ a practical application of any science;
■ a pursuit of occupation in which skill is directed toward the work of imagination, imitation, or design, or toward the gratification of the aesthetic senses[13] (N.B. "Élégance" or gratification of senses are subjective and hard to define in pleasing practices of medical interviewing and communication, aesthetic or reconstructive surgery or physical examination);
■ the skill required for expressing language, speech, and reasoning;[14]
■ a system of principles and methods employed in the performance of a set of activities;
■ a trade or craft that applies such a system of principles and methods (Example: The art of plastic surgery);

- a skill that is attained by study, practice, or observation: the art of the physician;
- a skill arising from the exercise of intuitive faculties (N.B. This being important in differential diagnosis or emergency medicine);[15] and
- both a skill and requiring the use of creative imagination.[16]

These definitions all focus on art as a ***way of doing things***. Other definitions, however, highlight the ***product of such endeavours***, that is, not only oil paintings, but also a successful rhinoplasty or facelift. Such an extensive list of even the most general definitions of art illustrates not only how differently we can approach things around us, but also that art, evidence, science, philosophy, or logic are not purely abstract terms. In fact, they have important practical meanings and implications, as we will illustrate.

The **art of medicine** requires:

- a clinician with an open mind and flexibility of reasoning;
- the ability to establish a good relationship with the patient, and communicate with them (or, bedside manners);
- tutoring or guidance from peers in reasoning, decision-making, and acting;
- compassion;
- empathy;
- a clinician's attitude toward nature and patient;
- an aptitude to individualize interpretations, decisions, and care each patient;
- manual and sensory skills;
- clinical flair and intuition, i.e., an aptitude to infer from previous experience, without active and concrete recall, in order to make appropriate decisions;
- clinical imagination;
- the capacity to persuade the patient to take responsibility for his or her own health and to convince the patient that the clinician will also share that responsibility;
- the aptitude to convert serendipity into insight of patient problems;
- the preservation and maintenance of human dignity (this is one difference between medicine and the advanced technical manipulation of human beings); and
- the aestheticism, elegance, and style in the conceptualization, execution, evaluation, and communication of a clinical experience lived.

All these components of the art of medicine are of a highly subjective nature. Thus they are hard to define and measure, and often even harder to teach. However correctly defined terms that are operational, mutually understood, non-overlapping, and reproducible permits us to understand everything we observe, do, and study (including the subjects and individuals involved as well medical and non-medical circumstances important to the problem). Otherwise, speaking beautifully and 'scientifically' does not warrant meaningful, purposeful work.

Hence, the art of medicine are the emotions, sensations, feelings, and mental operations upon which the physician's behavior is based.[17]

The study, development, use and evaluation of all definitions in this book and elsewhere, which we might call ***orismology*** (from the Greek *orismos*, meaning 'definition' and *logos*, meaning 'study') is explained in more detail in Section 2.1.3.3 of Chapter 2 of this book and in subsequent chapters.

> The art of medicine may also be defined as *the systematic application of sensory and motor skills, creative imagination, faithful imitation, innovation, intuition, and knowledge in speech, reasoning, or motion in the care of the health of patients and communities*.[2]

3.1.2 Medicine as Craft

As in other fields, both art and science in medicine require technical skills. Both of these focus on creating order from seemingly random and diverse experiences, building on an understanding of the world and sharing their experience with others. However, there are important differences between art and craft:

The artist creates some kind of more permanent and/or valid statement.

The scientist, however, tends to use observations to discover laws or concepts that may be invalidated later.

The clinical craftsman combines both of these. The clinical craftsman makes realities through actions which are based both on art and science, unique in their quality, adequacy, impact, and value for the patient, and the craftsman's human, social and physical environment.

Craft is defined as a practical art, trade, or occupation requiring especially manual skill and dexterity. It is a skill, especially involving practical arts. Crafts are defined either by their relationship to functional or utilitarian products or by the use of particular media such as wood, clay, glass, textiles, and metal.[18,19]

Studio crafts are those which are practiced by independent artists working alone in small groups. (N.B. Isn't this what most surgery-based specialties are doing? One may suggest that most surgical-based specialties are similarly practiced by independent artists, working alone in small groups, which requires manual skill and dexterity.)

Engineering provides another example of a field that crosses the boundaries of art, craft, and science. It is generally recognized as a "craft" that is more scientific and systematic than an "art," but not quite a "science." It applies science in ways that leave a lot of room for individual expression and produces tangible items, which appears to be a requirement for 'craftsmanship'.[20]

In this way, crafts can be considered as a "grey" zone after the arts and science of medicine. Practically all surgery-based specialties (all surgical subspecialties, gynecology and obstetrics, ORL, ophthalmology, etc.) depend on a high degree of craftsmanship and art as defined above. Moreover, sensorimotor skills are a dominant feature of medical crafts. In this way, do not skills in history taking, physical examination, case presentations, communication, learning skills, non-verbal communication, or specialty evaluations (mental status, bodily systems, etc.) also contain a high dose of craftsmanship?

As the debate if medicine is art or science continues,[7,17,21–27] we may agree that it is an interface of both. A medical student or clerk must consider elements of both and master them as much as possible. Therefore, medicine refers to the application of the fundamentals of art, science, and crafts as defined above to the treatment and prevention of disease, health protection, and health promotion.

3.1.3 Medicine as Science

But we also call medicine a science. Is it?

Science, in general, is *the study of the material universe or physical reality in order to understand it.*[12]

Science *in* medicine means "*discovery, implementation, uses and evaluation of evidence in understanding human health, disease, and care decisions, implementation and evaluation which are based on the scientific method.*"[2]

The **science *of* medicine** does not conform to this definition. In our view, the science of medicine is organized reasoning and is complementary to the art of medicine. When both are combined, we gain a better understanding of what good medicine, in the fullest sense of the term, should be.

Scientific Theory

Scientific theory is a *plausible and consistent explanation for observable phenomena.*[28] In the sciences, it comprises a *collection of concepts, including abstractions of observable phenomena expressed as quantifiable properties, together with rules, called scientific laws, that express relationships between observations of such concepts.*[29]

Theories are mostly constructed to explain, predict, and to master phenomena such as health and disease in the world of medicine.

Theories are generated when an original idea is subjected to experimentation. If the evidence from the experiment supports the idea, a theory is formulated. When a theory is used to better understand a concept or experience, and new evidence is discovered in the process, the theory is modified in a circular way from the original idea that was reviewed.[29]

In medicine, the path from the first diagnostic impression to the final diagnosis follows very similar steps and logic.

In modern science, a scientific theory is a tested and expanded hypothesis that explains many experiments and fits ideas together in a framework. Specifically, to reach the level of a scientific theory, a theory must be tested numerous times, by many different scientists in many different places and must be proven every time.[30] This is similar to the process of generating the best evidence in the world of diagnosis, or treatment effectiveness, in medicine.

Scientific Method

What, then, is "scientific" in medicine? All that is obtained, analyzed, and used according to a general scientific method makes up the scientific components of medicine.

Schafersman points out rightly that science in general is not merely a collection of facts, concepts, and ideas as part of a definition of science: "*science is a method of investigating nature—way of knowing about nature—that discovers reliable knowledge about it.*" In this definition, "*reliable knowledge is knowledge that has a high probability of being true because its veracity has been justified by a reliable method.*"[31] Reliable knowledge is called sometimes a "*justified true belief.*"[31]

Scientific thinking is a thought process and mental tool that uses the scientific method to study or investigate the nature or the universe. Scientific thinking in everyday life is an expanded fundamental form of critical thinking: "**Critical thinking** *is thinking correctly for oneself that successfully leads to the most reliable answers to questions and solutions to problems.*"[31]

The central components of scientific and critical thinking are:

- **empiricism**, using evidence which can be identified by sensory way;
- **rationalism** as practice of logical reasoning; and
- **skepticism** as a constant questioning of our beliefs and conclusions.

As good scientists and critical thinkers, we constantly examine the evidence, arguments, and reasons for our views, perceptions, and beliefs. Using scientific research and thinking, we can produce **scientific theories**, that is, "*unifying and self-consistent explanations of fundamental natural processes or phenomena that are totally constructed of corroborated hypotheses.*"[31]

The **scientific method** is used to describe a body of techniques for investigating phenomena, acquiring new knowledge, or correcting and integrating previous knowledge. It is based on empirical or measurable evidence, subject to specific principles of reasoning. Experiments are an important tool of scientific method needed to be designed to test hypotheses.[32]

Four essential elements lie behind the scientific method:

- *iteration(s)* are acts repeating the inquiry process, either to generate and unbounded sequence of outcomes, or with the aim of approaching a desired goal, target, or result;
- *recursion(s)* as the act of defining phenomena (things, functions) in terms of themselves or of their types. In computer science, it is a method where a solution of a problem depends on solutions of smaller instances of the same problem (as opposed to iteration);
- *interleaving(s)* as a method to make systems more efficient, fast, and reliable by arranging data in non-contiguous manners; in computer science, dividing memory into small chunks to solve memory issues for motherboards and chips; and
- *ordering*, in logic, any of the numbers or categories of relations that permit at least some numbers (or all) of their domain to be placed in order.

Characterizations of observations, definitions, and measurements as subjects of inquiry, hypotheses, predictions, and experiments are behind the practice of the scientific method and research.

The scientific method has its own objectives as follows.

Objectives of the Scientific Method

The scientific method is used to achieve one of five objectives:

1. **Creating research on the basis of currently available experience and evidence.** Creating research is based on various observations, formulations of the problem, defining the problem of interest, and obtaining relevant background evidence providing elements to solve the problem.
2. **Formulating hypotheses and research questions to explain a problem (most often a cause-effect relationship).** The formulation and development of hypotheses and research questions is followed by their conceptual evaluation, establishing testable consequences that allow for the acceptance or rejection of hypotheses and questions. In addition, hypotheses

and questions-based experiences are used to make quantitative and qualitative predictions that are testable based on new observations and experience.

3. **Defining** what we will do.

4. **Conducting either observational and/or experimental studies to test hypotheses and predictions**. In this case, empirical tests are built and performed. It includes a search for both favorable and unfavorable evidences which include examples and counterexamples.

5. **Analyzing results, driving conclusions, reporting the experience**. These steps include the critical examination and biostatistical processing of data in search of error and anomalous events (outliers), making inferences, and the evaluation of hypothesis(es) in the light of the background knowledge and evidence and experience acquired through the study. Formulations of meaningful conclusions in light of the new experience and proposals for future directions for research and/or practice on the basis of the newly acquired experience follow.

Steps of the Scientific Method

Science then is anything based on the scientific method which requires several steps:[31]

- defining and characterizing the **domain** of interest;
- formulating the research **question(s)** once the problem is defined;
- specifying **objectives and reasons of research**;
- formulating a **hypothesis** as a testable proposition to be accepted or rejected, which is built on operational definitions of phenomena as dependent and independent variables to observe;
- formulating **definitions** of all health and other phenomena of interest (domains of interest, problem itself, dependent and independent variables subject of etiological studies, setting of events including setting of healthcare, society, and physical environment to make further steps practicable, analyzable and results interpretable);
- making **predictions** as a formal way to test a hypothesis (hypotheses);
- specifying the **type of study**: observational study of occurrence, cause-effect analysis by observational or experimental design;
- analysing quantitative and qualitative **observations and sets of observations**;
- detection and control of **errors, biases, and fallacies** to improve study claims (conclusions);
- identifying conditions and circumstances in which findings and conclusions stemming from them do not apply (also called **falsifiability** of results);
- replicating the study to confirm the **consistency** of findings;
- making **decisions, recommendations, and directions** for future research on the basis of the study and the previously acquired experience and knowledge;
- taking **action** to rectify or further improve the situation; and
- **evaluating** the effectiveness of corrective measures, rectifications, improvements, and failures.

Behind the scientific method lies several different ways of thinking, such as probabilistic thinking, induction, deduction, the hypothetico-deductive method, and others detailed more exhaustively elsewhere.[34-36] The reader may also find other aspects of ways of thinking (induction, deduction, abduction), in Chapter 2, Section 4.2.2, of this book.

3.2 Paradigms behind the Science of Medicine

Historically, the science of medicine has focused on rigorous observation, measurement, and interpretation. With the development of microbiology, biochemistry, histology, pathology, genetics, and other basic sciences, the goal of medicine became a search for the **true** picture of a disease, the identification of **real** causes, and a search for the **best** treatment. Such an approach is clearly deterministic: the absolute truth (as much as possible) was sought rigorously.

Today, experimental medicine is often based on such an approach. Models are built, undesirable factors are controlled or excluded, and rigorous experimental conditions are established in the search for an unequivocal result. Exact information, reality without error, is the ideal and the basis for the **deterministic paradigm of medicine**. However, the **deterministic paradigm of science and life is now progressively being replaced by a probabilistic approach**.

3.2.1 Probability and Clinical Uncertainty

In the probabilistic approach to medicine, the deterministic paradigm is eschewed to reflect uncertainties. As an example, survival after surgery is *probable* but not certain as unanticipated complications may arise. It is *probable* that susceptible individuals in the midst of an epidemic of a new strain of influenza will become infected but it is not certain. Such probabilities and chances can be quantified in terms of rates or decimal fractions. Rates may be compared in terms of ratios and some causal relationships can be derived to some degree from such comparisons.

Clinical uncertainty recognizes that any endeavor in the health sciences is subject to **random and systematic error**, even in the most controlled conditions. Moreover, **information** for decision-making is **almost never complete** and decision makers always work with a considerable measure of **uncertainty**.

Let us define **uncertainty in medicine** as "*any situation where probabilities of different possible phenomena or outcomes are not known due to our poor knowledge of them whatever reason of such imperfect knowledge might be.*" Uncertainty may be caused by purely psychological reasons, the quality and quantity of data (probabilistic assessment and quantification of events and information), relevance of information for a specific purpose, as well as how we handle them in our reasoning and decision-making.

Let us now turn our attention to **probability** as the *quantification of the uncertainty*. As in economics and finance, research and practice in medicine becomes probabilistic when faced with the ubiquitous reality of uncertainty and missing information. As an example, all subjects who smoke will not develop lung cancer and all subjects who abstain from drinking will not be absolutely free of the risk of hepatic cirrhosis. Just a few generations ago, a middle-aged man with a productive cough of abundant sputum and a loss of weight was supposed to have tuberculosis, especially if there was confirmation based on Koch's mycobacterium isolation at the laboratory. With our current knowledge of competing problems, such as bronchiectasies, silicosis, silico-tuberculosis, or neoplasms of the lung and bronchial tree, and without the exclusion of other competing health problems, this diagnosis becomes probable, but not entirely certain.

> **Clinical uncertainty** is a reality today. It is a result of:
>
> ■ incomplete knowledge of the clinical problem (entity, etiology, controllability, prognosis, natural and clinical course of the disease);
> ■ incomplete information given by the patient;
> ■ incomplete information obtained by the physician;
> ■ erroneous information given by the patient (shame, lack of memory, lie);
> ■ erroneous recording of information by the physician;
> ■ erroneous interpretation of information by the physician;
> ■ observations that are missing, or not sought;
> ■ information not recorded; and
> ■ erratic reasoning and intellectual handling of information by health professionals.

All clinical decisions are, and will be, made with a variable degree of uncertainty depending on a variable probability of events and outcomes. Neglecting them often leads to medical error and harm.[37,38]

For example, using various rates of morbidity, mortality, or of other health events in the assessment of risk to the patient is a quantification of our certainty (or uncertainty) about problems of health or care. Calculating and presenting their confidence intervals is one of the ways to quantify our uncertainty about disease frequency. However, uses of confidence intervals in today's biostatistics are much broader.[39,40]

For Timmermans and Angell,[41] managing uncertainty is an important element of evidence-based clinical judgment. Managing uncertainty includes some important characteristics: it mixes together evidence and experience, exhibits an awareness of all the factors necessary to reach a satisfactory medical decision, includes both epidemiological and social skills, and is firmly grounded in a Western allopathic and professionalized approach to medicine.[38] Shouldn't all medicines also reflect such characteristics?

3.2.2 Fuzzy Theory in Medicine

Another contributor to our uncertainties is a fuzzy theory. Fuzzy theory,[42–44] discussed in more detail elsewhere,[5,45] is the view that that the physiological, pathological, and other clinical phenomena of interest are not necessarily dichotomous (healthy or sick, handicapped or not, etc.). It proposes that many health phenomena are a matter of degree and should be analyzed and understood as such. Being obese or in pain is a matter of degree and there is no 'excluded middle.' Grading and categorizing clinical phenomena that are defined in operational terms makes them manageable for decision-making and care.

Uncertainties and imprecision are pervasive in medicine. Fuzzy logic in medicine is a developing concept that seeks to make the right decisions in such situations. It is now increasingly used in various specialties, including neurology, psychiatry, anaesthesia, dermatology, epidemiology, and elsewhere. Where it is used, and applications of fuzzy logic, are increasing.[46]

Building on this concept, Burton[47] questions how our brain manages the idea of certainty, proposing that it is neither a conscientious choice nor even a thought process. His central premise is that certainty and similar states of 'knowing what we know' are sensations that feel like thoughts, but arise out of involuntary brain mechanisms that function independently of reason. So far, bio-statistical and epidemiological management of probabilities to quantify uncertainty remains the most meaningful and operational tool available to a health professional, layman, and laywoman.

3.2.3 Chaos Theory in Medicine

Medical phenomena may be not only fuzzy but also "chaotic." Subias[48] suggests that biorhythms, a chaotic/non-chaotic ratio underlying an individual's experience, provides a more exact evaluation of the state of health and illness, and a diagnosis and prognosis which would not be possible by other means of traditional medicine.

In the framework of this theory, human functions are not seen as stable (homeostasis) but they are also subject to '**chaotic**' **behavior** defined as *"an aperiodic, seemingly random behaviour in a deterministic system that exhibits sensitive dependence on initial conditions"*[49,50] or *"apparently random or unpredictable behaviour in systems governed by deterministic laws."*[49] Phenomena that are subject to chaos are unpredictable and their cause-effect relationships are unpredictable. If true, correct diagnosis, treatment decisions, and prognosis in such circumstances may be a challenge.[51]

Chaos theory illustrates the limitations of a linear, reductionist approach to our understanding and management of natural phenomena, including medical phenomena. Chaos theory has evolved from merely descriptions of behavior, to the discovery of laws that describe the behavior of these systems. One of the names of these activities is "**complexity theory**."[52]

All of these various concepts exploring uncertainties in medicine leads to a view that healthcare delivery consists of numerous simple and "complex" systems ranging from those that are deterministic to those with features of randomness. Deterministic systems feature predictable outcomes, other don't. Deterministic and other systems are considered "**complex systems**" and they are subject to "**complexity theory**."[53–55] We are only at the beginning of our understanding of this theory and systems.

In this context, rather than being synonymous to rigorous laboratory work only, the **science *of* medicine** becomes *a structured and organized way of using probability, uncertainty, and facts in preventive medicine and clinical care to best benefit the patient and the community. It is a logical and systematic approach to the exploration, organization, and interpretation of data from initial observations to clinical decisions and final conclusions concerning problems of interest. The latter are defined, measured, categorized, classified, analyzed, and interpreted with a satisfactory degree of reproducibility.*

Such a scientific approach to medicine should be applied to the entire scope of medical activities. The debate about this approach, however, continues.[56]

3.3 Theory and Practice of Medicine: Which One Will You Learn, Use, and Practice?

Medicine must be mastered both from a theoretical and practical standpoint. We must know what is behind our actions and we must practice it in the light of its theoretical foundations.

3.3.1 Theory of Medicine

Murphy's renewed call for theory *of* medicine[57] has reinvigorated the place for both theory and practice of medicine in how we see medicine today. In general, the term "theory" means *"a coherent group of general propositions used as principles of explanation for a class of phenomena ... a particular conception or view of something the be done or of the method of doing it ... a system of rules or principles."*[58]

Theory *of* medicine is *"the body of principles of the science and art of medicine as distinguished from the 'practice of medicine', or the application of those principles in actual practice."*[59] Colloquially speaking, it is anything that happens in the head of the physician, researcher or practitioner of medicine before oral or written orders are given or actions, manual or technological, are taken.

Wikipedia specifies that "scientific" theory refers to *"a proposed explanation of empiric phenomena, made in a way consistent with the scientific method. Such theories are preferably described in such a way that any scientist in the field is in a position to understand, verify, and challenge (or 'falsify') it. In this modern scientific context the distinction between theory and practice corresponds roughly to the distinction between theoretical science and technology or applied science."*[60]

Modern reflections about both theoretical medicine[61] and theoretical surgery[62,63] intimately link reasoning as a part of theory and actions together with non-surgical support systems like basic sciences, clinical epidemiology, social sciences, even patient, and so on.[62,63] Theoretical surgery was hence proposed as *"a nonoperative decision analysis and clinical basic research supporting system for surgery. It consists of an essential, predominant integration concept completed by a supplementary cooperation concept."*[62,63] Several journals were created to cover the domain of the theory of medicine in the English language like the *Journal of Theoretical Medicine, Theoretical Medicine,* and *Theoretical Medicine and Bioethics.*

3.3.2 Practice of Medicine

Practice in general means *"the action or process of performing or doing something."*[58]

Practice of medicine in lexical terms means *"the utilization of knowledge in a particular profession, the practice of medicine being the exercise of one's knowledge in the practical recognition and treatment of disease."*[59] We may also view this type of practice as *"**reasoning** about patient and/or community health and disease followed by and coupled with corrective **action(s)** and **evaluation** what was done."* Hence, the practice of medicine does not mean only action but also what preceded and triggered it (reasoning) and what followed it (evaluation).

Practice of medicine is then *"an action, sensorimotor or other, in the domain of health and disease resulting from critical thinking about the problem and decisions what to do. Physician's mental activity in this role is then an integral part of the practice of medicine as it also underlies the theory of medicine."* 'Just thinking' must evolve into action or "justified doing nothing." Hence, a proper learning of medicine must include how to think before one acts, how to act and understand what has been done, and how. Simply put, *the practice of clinical medicine is about problem solving and solutions.*

"**Rational medicine**" may be seen as precursor of evidence-based medicine, being defined in the Sixties as "*practice of medicine based upon actual knowledge.*"[59] Distinctions between "actual knowledge" and "evidence" (without specifying which evidence is the best) remain blurred.

3.4 Newer Trends and Paradigms in the Theory and Practice of Medicine: Evidence-Based Medicine and Other Evidence-Based Health Sciences

Evidence-based medicine has emerged as a way to build on medical experience and bring even more rigorous evaluation into the realms of health, disease understanding, and caring. Medical experience is captured by research and practice, and incorporate fundamental and clinical epidemiology, biostatistics, health management, economics, and administration. In our view, the paradigm of EBM is common in all health sciences, professions, and their practice and research, including evidence-based dentistry, evidence based nursing, evidence-based dietetics and nutrition, and others. Let us see the EBM concept in this chapter in this light. If we substitute "patient" for "community" this paradigm applies equally for community medicine, preventive medicine, and public health.

3.4.1 But What Exactly Is Evidence-Based Medicine?

Since the appearance of the Evidence-Based Medicine Working Group's position papers[64,65] in 1992, this paradigm of medicine was and continues to be a subject of an ever-increasing number of monographs and papers. Among its definitions are an astonishing number which do not specify what EBM "is" but what EBM "requires," "means," and so on. As an example, "*evidence-based medicine (EBM) requires the integration of the best research evidence with our clinical experience and our patient's unique value and circumstances.*"[66]

> From an epistemological perspective, EBM can be defined as,
>
> "*a set of principles and methods to ensure that population-based policies and individual decisions are consistent with all the most credible evidence while relying on both type 1 and type 2 cognitive processes to weight the trade-offs involved in alternative courses of action.*"[64]

3.4.2 What Are the Steps in the Practice of Evidence-Based Medicine?

For Straus et al.,[65] the five steps of practice of EBM comprise:

1. converting the need for information into an answerable question;
2. tracking down the best evidence with which to answer that question;
3. critically appraising that evidence for its validity, impact, and applicability;

4. integrating the critical appraisal with our clinical expertise, and with our patient's unique biology, values, and circumstances; and

5. evaluating our effectiveness and efficiency in executing steps 1–4 and seeking ways to improve them both for the next time.

Hence, EBM ensures a closer application of the scientific method to what we intend to do, will do, and the result it achieves.

Contemporary medicine rightly relies not only on the best available evidence about the proofs of the origins, nature, and manageability of health and disease, but also on additional considerations such as clinical settings and circumstances, patient values and preferences, and the best available knowledge and experience of its assessors, evaluators, users, and all decision-makers in clinical and community care. This reality is responsible in part for the evidence-based domain of medicine.

In medicine, evidence itself is a broad entity encompassing "*any data or information, whether solid or weak, obtained through experience, observational research or experimental work (trials).This data or information must be relevant and convincing to some (best possible) degree either to the understanding of the problem (case) or the diagnostic, therapeutic, or otherwise care oriented clinical decisions made about the case.*" our definition

In this way, "*Evidence' is not automatically correct, complete, satisfactory and useful. It must be first evaluated, graded and used based on its own merit.*"[5] Which one to choose and for what purpose are the best remain great challenges for its user and decision-maker.

In the light of evidence as defined above, the basic steps of EBM (with minor variations across the literature)[2] can be expanded into nine:

1. formulating the question concerning the problem, patient, or community that has to be answered *(identifying the need for evidence)*;
2. searching for the evidence *(producing the evidence)*;
3. selecting the best evidence available for clinical or community health decision-making *(using the evidence)*;
4. linking the evidence with clinical and community health knowledge, experience, and practice with the patient's and/or community values and preferences *(integrated uses of evidence)*;
5. implementing useful findings in clinical (clinical care) and community (public health policies and programs) medicine's decisions and practice;
6. using the evidence in clinical and/or community care to solve the patient's or community problem *(uses of evidence in specific settings)*;
7. evaluating the effectiveness of the uses of evidence in this case and situation *(weighing the impact)*;
8. evaluating the implementations and the overall performance of evidence-based medicine and/or evidence-based public health practitioner and activity *(evaluating*

structure, process, and impact of evidence-based actions, economical and managerial real and desired characteristics); and

9. teaching and expanding EBM practice and research *(going beyond what was already achieved)*.

Isn't the approach and rigor of EBM becoming more similar to the scientific method in general?

3.4.3 Evidence-Based Clinical Medicine (EBM)

Evidence-based clinical medicine (EBM)[64] may be seen then through its current numerous definitions as:

- *the process of systematically finding, appraising, and using contemporaneous research findings as the basis for clinical decisions;*[65] *(**too little today**)*
- *the conscientious, explicit, and judicious use of current best evidence in making decisions about the care of individual patients;*[66] *(**limited for uses as operational definition**)*
- *a practice of medicine based on the integration of the best research evidence with clinical experience and patient unique values and circumstances;*[65] *(**but how?**)*
- *consistent use of the best available evidence, preferably from current peer-reviewed sources in electronic and print media, to inform decisions about optimum patient management; decisions should consider the needs and preferences of individual patients;*[3] *(**much better**)* and
- *the practice of medicine in which the physician finds, assess and implements methods of diagnosis and treatment on the basis of the best available current research, their expertise, and the needs of the patient.*[ours, based on Reference 64–67] The expertise means here special skills or knowledge acquired by a person through education, training, or experience (***expertise includes also the respect and practice of medical ethics***).

Wherever so many definitions appear, the defined entity still requires further refinements and clarifications. Moreover, connecting these definitions and incorporating ethical considerations are needed.

3.4.4 Evidence-Based Community Medicine and Public Health (EBPH)

Evidence-based community medicine and public health (EBPH)[68–71] can be described as:

- *the application of best available evidence in setting public health policies and priorities. … Evidence-based public health is an approach that makes informed, explicit use of validated studies to arrive to judicious decisions on public health policies and best practices;*[5]
- *the process of systematically finding, appraising, and using contemporaneous clinical and community research findings as the basis for decisions in public health;*[69] and
- *the conscientious, explicit, and judicious use of current best evidence in making decisions about the care of communities and populations in the domain of health protection, disease prevention, and health maintenance and improvement (health promotion).*[67–71 (modified)]

3.4.5 Evidence-Based HealthCare

Evidence-based healthcare,[72] as formulated by Muir Gray, integrates in its concept both clinical and community medicine, care, and public health.

In the sense of the above, the EBM-driven initial steps of both clinical and community medicines are then:

1. Formulation of a clear clinical or community medicine **question** from a patient or community problem which has to be answered;
2. A literature search for relevant sources of information (i.e., **evidence**); and
3. Critical **appraisal** (analysis, evaluation, and grading) of the original and integrated evidence. Its main points include the relevance of the evidence to user's issue and setting, the objectivity of evidence presented, the clarity of a bias-free methodology, the justification of conclusion about evidence presented, confidence about findings (evidence) presented, and the applicability to particular individuals, site, setting, practice, rules, and culture.

For example, critical appraisal of a cause-effect study provides answers to several questions such as:

- Are we dealing with a questionable and uncertain problem?
- How well is the problem defined?
- Was the question properly formulated?
- Was the search for evidence (e.g., other studies) adequate and complete?
- What is the design of an etiological study? How valid is it?
- Are biostatistical considerations such as sampling or analysis and epidemiological considerations, like exposure to possible multiple causes, adequately handled and answered?
- Were clinical aspects of the disease considered (e.g., subjects' characteristics, co-morbidity, outcomes, follow-up, others)?
- How was the effect (impact) of a presumed cause (validity of results) evaluated?
- Which criteria of causality, if any, are fulfilled by the study results?
- Was the broader balance between harm, benefits, costs, and controllability assessed, and is it adequate?
- Is the best evidence available used in the study?
- Are the study results usable in the user's setting (for example, caring for a specific patient, groups of patients, community groups), and in which settings are they not?
- If relevant, how much could, and should, such findings be generalized?
- Were potential competing causes considered and evaluated?
- If this problem was also the subject of other studies, should a systematic review and research synthesis of all these available experiences be attempted, and would such expanded research bring additional relevant information?

Physicians in their clinical practice should answer several questions before choosing and using available evidence from the literature or from their own experience to inform their decisions in clinical and community care. These questions include:

1. What is the problem to be solved?
2. Is there a clearly formulated question to be answered?
3. To what kind of study or demonstration can we refer to obtain such an answer?
4. What are the results?
5. Are those results valid?
6. Are such results relevant for understanding and/or decision-making about the problem at hand?
7. Are the results applicable to the particular group of patients with whom we are concerned?
8. Are the study results applicable to a specific ("my") patient?

The current edition of the *User's Guides to the Medical Literature*[68] lists most of these questions and offers many answers. Evidence, supported by clinical and fundamental epidemiology, biostatistical methods, and grading of evidence (mostly for cause-effect relationships), and applied to clinical activities and problem solving, is at the core of this EBM strategy. In addition to the above questions, more specific problem-solving practical questions will determine the type of research that can be elucidated and its inherent methodology. Figure 3.1 provides examples of such links between research, clinical domain applications, and problems to be solved.

In the domain of cause-effect relationships (noxious agent → disease, treatment → cure, etc.), the hierarchy of evidence goes from the weakest (clinical anecdotes, single or multiple clinical cases descriptions) to observational analytical studies (case control or cohort) and their systematic reviews and research synthesis. Hierarchies of evidence beyond etiology still remain subject to our better understanding. Both EBM and EBPH are not even two decades old. They are still in development and remain widely discussed domains and paradigms in many health sciences and professions.

In our view, the EBM paradigm is common to all health sciences and professions and their practice and research, such as evidence-based dentistry, evidence based nursing, evidence-based dietetics and nutrition, and others.[70] Let us consider the EBM concept explored in this chapter in this light. If we substitute "patient" for "community," this paradigm applies equally well for community medicine, preventive medicine, and public health.

3.4.6 Grading Evidence and Evaluating the Whole EBM Process

Evaluating any action and activity in medicine means looking at its essence and nature, its structure, its process of its uses, and its impact. An important international group of authors formed a GRADE group to evaluate selected EBM activities and concerns. GRADE is an acronym for the "*Grades of Recommendation, Assessment, Development and Evaluation*" group.

In the GRADE group's first article, in a 20-part series[73,74] spanning from 2011 to 2015, the group states its contributions as to "*provide guidance for rating quality of evidence and grading strength of evidence of recommendations in health care. It has important implications for those summarizing evidence, for systematic reviews, health technology assessment and clinical practice guidelines.*"

Questions in medical research, clinical domains of application, and examples of practical problems to be solved

Examples of questions in medical research	Examples of clinical domain and type of research to answer the question	Examples of practical problems to be solved (fields of application)
DIAGNOSIS AND NEW EXPLORATORY TECHNOLOGIES		
What is the subject of diagnosis? How serious is it? How do we arrive at diagnosis?	• Forming clinical entities • Measuring disease severity • Understanding the diagnostic process	• Evaluation of internal and external validity of diagnostic and screening tests • Establishment of diagnostic criteria for daily practice and disease surveillance
HEALTH EVENT OCCURRENCE		
When, where, and in whom problems (health events) appear?	• Descriptive longitudinal or cross-sectional studies at the hospital and in the community • Studies of natural or clinical course of cases	• Epidemiological portrait of disease • Disease spread • Epidemiological surveillance • Disease clustering
CAUSAL RESEARCH		
Why did it happen? What and who is responsible?	• Etiological research by observational studies • Causes identification	• Disease etiology research by comparative studies of exposure to various factors and disease occurrence using cohort and case control studies • Elucidation of causes of disease spread
INTERVENTION (Prevention and/or treatment)		
Can we control case(s) or disease? Did we control case(s) or disease? Will it control (or solve) the problem?	• Efficacy, effectiveness, and efficiency evaluation • Systematic reviews and meta-analyses of interventions and their effect	• Phase 1–4 clinical trials • Field trials • Pharmaco-epidemiological studies • Impact of secondary and tertiary prevention (mainly) • Meta-analyses and systematic reviews of interventions effect • Decision analysis
PROGNOSIS		
What might or will happen later?	• Study of disease outcomes • Survival studies • Descriptive and analytical studies of probabilities of events derived from case studies (disease course)	• Epidemiological and clinical forecasting of exposures to beneficial or noxious factors, disease occurrence and spread based on clinical follow-up and epidemiological surveillance

Figure 3.1 Questions in medical research, clinical domains of application, and examples of practical problems to be solved. Look for the definitions of some new terms in Chapters 2 and 3 and in the Glossary.

This group's contributions are richest in the evaluation of the essence and nature, as well as the structure and process, of medical activities and care. However, evaluation of the impact of these initiatives and recommendations will only be possible after more extensive usage in research and practice. Ideally, any process for categorizing and assessing knowledge and activities should reflect further resulting impacts on the health of individuals, communities, and on the health system and activities which adopt them.

3.5 Beyond the Evidence-Based Medicine Original Concept: Evidence-Based Critical Thinking Medicine, Reflective Uses of Evidence, Patient-Centered Medicine Trends

Producing, finding, and evaluating the best evidence are not enough for good clinical and community medicine practice. Using it in the framework of critical thinking is. Let us conclude, then, that medicine is taught and learned through all these multiple approaches described earlier in this chapter. We will see these paradigms reflected in medical reasoning, communication, and decision-making discussed in the chapters which follow.

3.5.1 Critical Thinking

What exactly is critical thinking today? Its concept, content, methodology, and applications are more closely aligned with practical and pragmatic medicine than we might initially think. Thank you, philosophers!

The definitions which follow are complementary, and they reflect well the scientific method in medicine and what we are doing in our daily reasoning about health problems and our patients. A selection of these definitions is:

> – *Reasonable reflective thinking that is focused on deciding what to do or believe.*[75]
> – *Critical thinking is the intellectually disciplined process of actively and skillfully **conceptualizing**, **applying**, **synthetizing**, and/or **evaluating** information gathered from, or generated by, **observation**, **experience**, **reflection**, **reasoning**, or **communication** as a guide to **belief** and **action**.*[76]

*"In its exemplary form, critical thinking is based on universal intellectual values that transcend subject matter divisions: **clarity, accuracy, precision, consistency, relevance, sound evidence, good reasons, depth, breadth, and fairness**.*

*It entails the examination of those structures or elements of though implicit in all reasoning: **purpose, problem, or question-at-issue, assumptions, concepts, empirical grounding; reasoning leading to conclusions, implications and consequences, objections from alternative viewpoints, and frame of reference**. Critical thinking—in being responsive to variable subject matter, issues, and purposes—is incorporated in a family of interwoven modes of thinking, among them: scientific thinking, mathematical thinking, historical thinking, moral thinking, and philosophical thinking."*[76] **Let us add to these modes medicine and all other health sciences!**

> A ***purposeful, self-regulatory judgment*** *which results in interpretation, analysis, evaluation and inference, as well as explanation of the evidential, conceptual, methodological, criteriological, or contextual considerations upon which that judgment is based. ...*[77]

Hall proposes eight tools in effective thinking, each of them with its inherent strengths, weaknesses, and limitations.[78]

Of these, four tools relate to data processing and include:

1. **Memory** as an essential element of thought, however fallible it may be.
2. **Association** between phenomena and ideas on which thinking is based.
3. **Pattern discernment** and **pattern recognition**, be it visual, structural, or cause-effect perceptions. For example, a diagnostic process or adverse effects considerations depend largely on them.
4. **Reason** and **reasoning** as tool of moving from one idea to another.

Another four related to how data are generated that is later subject to the processing detailed above include:

5. **Experience** as a primary source of raw elements for thinking about. Among other domains of medical thinking, it is most often essential for decision-making.
6. **Invention** as an important tool in generating hypotheses, proposing interpretations, and in offering explanations of a subject of interest and thinking.
7. **Experimentation** as a rational direction, redirection, and limitations giving toll to our thinking.
8. **Intuition** as an instant tool at a given moment of the thinking process, not necessarily true as self-evidence, and not always self-supported. Emergency medicine would be considerably more difficult without intuitive thinking, however limited it might be from one case to another.

All our clinical practice, medical research, and public health are a perpetual exercise of critical thinking about health problems, including how we understand them, making and choosing decisions about what to do and evaluating the results of what we have done.

3.5.2 Reflective Uses of Evidence

Producing the best evidence is not enough. The best evidence must also be applied through the critical thinking process as defined and outlined above. This subject requires a chapter apart, and will be addressed in Chapter 4.

3.5.3 Patient-Centered (Person-Centered), Personalized, Integrative Medicines

Modern health sciences and practice require both a solid grounding in the scientific method and attention to the individuals who must benefit from the best possible understanding and decision-making about individuals in clinical and community settings. Until now, evidence-based medicine has contributed mainly to the former, especially with regard to dealing with case study examinations of cause-effect relationships between noxious and beneficial factors affecting health. Defining improved clinical expertise, patient values, and patient circumstances must be approached with equally well-structured elements of methodological rigor and practice, which are both reproducible and evaluable in various care settings. This rapidly developing interest in the attention given to individual patient characteristics, patient environment, and type of care that is created, developed and increasingly practiced by more than one entity is termed, variously, patient-centered care,[77] patient-centered medicine, personalized medicine, and patient-centered healthcare. These fields all focus on individuals and very often with few or unique cases, but are they identical?

Patient-centered care is a *way of doing things that sees the people using health and social services as equal partners in planning, developing, and monitoring care to ensure the services delivered meets their needs. This means putting people and their families at the center of decisions and seeing them as experts, alongside professionals, to get the best outcome.*[80]

Personalized medicine is an approach of medical practice, when the clinical, genetic, genomic, and environmental features of the patient determine the intervention of choice to prevent or treat a disease.[81]

A clinical-epidemiological and biostatistical approach to patient health problem solving is not enough. It must be expanded through qualitative research, case studies, clinical case reporting, broader ways of critical thinking and argumentation as well as through patient care ethics from a modern philosophy perspective in increasingly operational manners, forms, and techniques.

Are these newer patient-focused "medicines" and other entities equally well or better defined in their identity, objectives, practices, and evaluation as pertains to their content, structure, process, and impact?

Patient-centered care and medicine are complementary to evidence-based medicine. They are what trigger's care and the endpoint of evidence-based practice and the final decision step in individual care.[82,83] Their equal importance must be emphasized, understood and further justified. After patient-centered care and medicine, what next then?

Integrative medicine seeks to restore and maintain health and wellness across the person's lifespan by understanding the patient's unique set of circumstances and addressing the full range of physical, emotional, social, spiritual, and environmental influences that affect health.[84] Integrated management of both the identification of treatment of individualized health challenges and the appropriate care of them requires integrated systems—which remain to be developed. The process of webs of causes, and consequences from, and in, the biological, social, cultural, and health sciences and care, and beyond, must be part of this integrated management and integrated in this system.

Patient-centered (person-centered), personalized, integrative medicines are not contradictory to evidence-based medicine. Rather, at the end of the classical process of medicine, as proposed, they fulfill and expand its fourth step, that is, integrating the critical appraisal (of evidence) with our clinical expertise, and with our patient's unique biology, values, and circumstances.[65]

An extensive critique of evidence-based medicine started was at the end of Nineties[83] and continues, mainly in the *Journal of Evaluation in Clinical Practice*. Whatever is the rationale of such thinking trends about all these "new medicines," their scope, and directions are complementary rather than exclusionary.[85] We agree.

Let Us Conclude: What Exactly Should We Teach, Learn, and Practice Then?

In a recent paper[87] the authors summarized the importance of critical thinking in this way:

> Obtaining and critically appraising evidence is clearly not enough to make better decisions in clinical care. The evidence should be linked to the clinician's expertise, the patient's individual circumstances (including values and preferences), and clinical context and settings. We propose critical thinking and decision-making as the tools for making that link.
>
> Critical thinking is also called for in medical research and medical writing, especially where pre-canned methodologies are not enough. It is also involved in our exchanges of ideas at floor rounds, grand rounds and case discussions; our communications with patients and lay stakeholders in healthcare; and our writing of research papers, grant applications and grant reviews.
>
> *Critical thinking is a learned process which benefits from teaching and guided practice like any discipline in health sciences. Training in critical thinking should be a part or a pre-requisite of the medical curriculum.*[87]

An Evidence and Critical Thinking-Based Medicine Then?

Teaching an evidence- and critical thinking–based medicine should provide students with the essential knowledge, attitudes, and skills that are needed to put in practice this kind of medicine for the full benefit of all parties involved in care and research. Medicine today embraces experiences from natural sciences that are strong in scientific method and quantitative methodologies. It embraces and integrates together with the above experiences from humanities:[88–92] academic disciplines that study the human condition primarily by methods of analytical, critical, or speculative nature, including informal logic, argumentation, and/or critical thinking from philosophy.

Learning and practicing medicine today is based on a blend of two ways of health problem solving. On one side is scientific, quantitative, probabilistic, and managed uncertainty inquiry. This is the practice of the **science of medicine**. On the other lies an interconnected web of **medical humanities**. These blend uses of the arts, literature, ethics, religion, history, sociology, and law together with cognitive sciences and philosophy. Within the science of medicine, logic, structured reasoning, and argumentation are taking an increasingly prominent place.

Medical humanities are defined as *"an interdisciplinary field which includes humanities (literature, philosophy, ethics, history and religion), social science (anthropology, cultural studies, psychology, sociology) and the arts (literature, theatre, film and visual arts) and their application to medical education and practice."*[89] Their purpose is to improve the delivery of effective healthcare through a better understanding of disease in the society and in the individual. Rather than occupational and professional skills based on scientific principles and their applications, medical humanities contribute to providing more general knowledge and intellectual skills behind the former. At least two titles[90,91] and the *Medical Humanities* journal currently cover currently this domain. The debate about medical humanities continues.[92]

Quo vadis medicina ex testimoniis? What further directions will evidence-based medicine, and other health sciences and professions, take?[93–95] We will certainly see in the near future. Several titles provide an introduction for not only **how to see and understand EBM**,[5,64,65,68,96,97] and how to read EBM articles[66] and other means of communication,[97] but also **how to do it**.[5,65–68]

Today medicine should be viewed through all these multiple approaches as summarized above. It is less relevant to identify exactly where this element of teaching belongs: theory or practice of medicine, evidence- or something else-based medicine (narrative-based, patient-centered), scientific method and theory-based (allopathic) medicine, or alternative medicine that is philosophy and beliefs-based? Newcomers to the medical field, regardless of whether they will practice in a clinical or non-clinical environment, will all face the challenges of how to integrate multiple views into some meaningful reasoning and decision-making behind any element of our practice or research.

Medicine and other health sciences and professions are domains dealing with biological phenomena which are harder to define than phenomena in basic sciences like chemistry or physics. This is due to our limited ability and capacity for observation and measurement, limited understanding of health phenomena, their nature (etiology and underlying biological mechanisms), different understandings and values shared by physicians and their patients. To augment this biological basis, we must add technological, social, economical, and cultural considerations to be integrated wherever it is necessary to solve a health problem. Multiple challenges for medical thinking, philosophical, epidemiological, biostatistical, or managerial ensue from this thinking. These include:

- **definability**, i.e., our capacity and ability to express, ideally in operational terms, about what are we dealing with as health and care of it;
- **comparability**, i.e., our capacity to judge health values relatively to time, place, person's possibilities or alternatives;
- **representativity**, i.e., our ability to see our problems as a part of some other one, its part, or entirety;
- **reproducibility**, i.e., those of study results or any other original findings and observations;
- **repeatability**, i.e., of whatever was seen or experienced (tests, acts, results);
- **generalizability**, i.e., how far can we go in our understandings and actions beyond what we have witnessed as a sample or part of a bigger entity;
- **applicability**, i.e., a realistic estimation of uses of our experience beyond the original time-place-persons setting;
- **causality**, i.e., what (as cause) leads to what (as effect), be it a noxious health factor leading to a health problem, or beneficial action such as treatment or prevention leading to the improvement or elimination of disease or sickness, or improvement in health; and
- **validity for practice** in terms of uses for decision-making about the solution of a health problem.

All these challenges are important subjects of medical thinking worthy of further attention across the chapters which follow. They will be explored in Chapter 4 as subjects of methodology for modern thinking. Readers interested in more about the content and topics of Chapter 3 may find some useful additional references[98–113] at the end of the References section.

References

1. *Mosby's Medical Dictionary.* Revised 2nd Edition. St. Louis, MO: The C.V. Mosby Co., 1987.
2. Jenicek M and Hitchcock DL. *Evidence-Based Practice. Logic and Critical Thinking in Medicine.* Chicago: American Medical Association (AMA Press), 2006.
3. Last JM. *A Dictionary of Public Health.* Oxford and New York: Oxford University Press, 2007.
4. *A Dictionary of Epidemiology.* 5th Edition. Edited by M Porta, S Greenland, JM Last, Associate Editors. A Handbook Sponsored by the I.E.A. Oxford and New York: Oxford University Press, 2008.
5. Jenicek M. *Foundations of Evidence-Based Medicine.* Boca Raton, FL/London/New York/Washington, DC: The Parthenon Publishing Group/CRC Press, 2003.
6. *WONCA Dictionary of General/Family Practice.* Copenhagen: Laegeforeningens Forlag, 2003.
7. Morrell P. *Medicine: Art or Science?* 7 p. at http://www.homeoint.org/morrell/otherarticles/artsci.htm, retrieved June 28, 2010.
8. *Project Professionalism.* Philadelphia, PA: American Board of Medicine, 1998.
9. Sugar LM, Catton PA, Tallet SE, Rothman AI. Assessment of residents' professional attitudes and behaviours. *Annals RCPSC,* 2000;33:305–9.
10. *Paracelsus. Selected Writings.* Edited by J Jacobi and translated by N Guterman. Princeton, NJ: Princeton University Press, Bollingen Series XXVIII, 1979.
11. Cruess SR, Cruess RL. Professionalism must be taught. *BMJ,* 1997;315:1674–7.
12. Bunge M. *Medical Philosophy. Conceptual Issues in Medicine.* Singapore/New Jersey/London: World Scientific Publishing Co., 2013.
13. *The New Shorter Oxford English Dictionary on Historical Principles.* Edited by I. Brown. Volume 1, 4th Edition. Oxford: Clarendon Press, 1993.
14. *The New Encyclopaedia Britannica.* Volume 1. Micropedia. Chicago: Encyclopaedia Britannica, 1992.
15. *The American Heritage Dictionary of English Language.* 4th Edition. 2000. Electronic Edition at http://www.bartleby.com.
16. Entries 'Art' and 'Philosophy, Western'. *Encarta® Encyclopedia.* ©1993–1997, Microsoft Corporation, Electronic Edition. See also: http://www.encarta.msn.com.
17. Gregg D. The art and the science of medicine. *Boston Med Surg J,* 1923(Sep 27);189:438–40.
18. 'Craft'. *Random House Webster's Unabridged Dictionary.* Antwerpen: Random House Inc, 1998 and 2003.
19. Wikipedia, the free encyclopedia. *Outline of Crafts.* 2 p. at http://en.wikipedia.org/wiki/Outline_of _crafts, retrieved October 6, 2010.
20. Harriet H. The "art" of clinical decision-making. *Science-Based Med,* 2008(May 13). 12 p. (with responses) at http://www.sciencebasedmedicine.org/?p=106, retrieved June 28, 2010. Comment 1 ("Science or art?"), by *#oveshooton*, from engineering (p. 2).
21. Guttentag OE. The phrase, "art and science of medicine". *Calif Western Med,* 1939(Feb);50:86–7.
22. Fillers. Endpiece medicine: Art or science? *BMJ,* 2000;320:1322 doi 10 1136/bmj 320 7245 1322/a (Published 13 May 2000).
23. Herman J. Medicine: the science and the art. *Med Humanities,* 2001;27:42–6.
24. Harrington JA. Art or science? Understanding medicine and the common law. *Health Law J,* 2001;9:129–48.
25. Panda SC. Medicine: Science or art? *Mens Sana Monogr,* 2006;4:127–38.
26. Kirkpatrick JN and Groninger H. Putting it all together: The art and science of medicine. *Virtual Mentor,* 2006(July);8:452–8.

27. Tucker NH. President's message—Medicine: Art versus science. *Jacksonville Med* (Dec 1999). 2 p. at http://www.dcmsonline.org/jax-medicine/1999journals/december99/presmess.htm, retrieved June 28, 2010.
28. Conservapedia. *Scientific Theory.* 4 pages at http://ww.coservapedia.com/Scientific_theory, retrieved June 27, 2010.
29. Wikipedia, the free encyclopedia. *Scientific Theory.* 8 pages at http://en.wikipedia.org/wiki/Scientific_theory, retrieved June 27, 2010.
30. Simple Wikipedia, the free encyclopedia. *Scientific Theory* [Another entry with an identical title]. 2 p. at http://simple.wikipedia.org/wiki/Scientific_theory, retrieved June 27, 2010.
31. Schafersman SD. An introduction to science. Scientific thinking and the scientific method. 8 p. at http://www.geo.sunysb.edu/esp/files/scientific-method.html, retrieved Sep. 3, 2017.
32. Wikipedia, the free encyclopedia. *Scientific Method.* 31 p. at https://en.wikipedia.org/wiki/Scientific_method, retrieved Sep 3, 2017.
33. Jenicek M. *Fallacy-Free Reasoning in Medicine. Improving Communication and Decision-making in Research and Practice.* Chicago: American Medical Association (AMA Press), 2009.
34. Gorham G. *Philosophy of Science. A Beginner's Guide.* Oxford: Oneworld Publications, 2009.
35. *Exploring the Scientific Method. Cases and Questions.* Edited by S Gimbel. Chicago and London: The University of Chicago Press, 2011.
36. Nola R and Sankey H. *Theories of Scientific Method. An Introduction.* Montreal/Kingston/Ithaca: McGill-Queen's University Press, 2007.
37. White S and Stancombe J. *Clinical Judgment in the Health and Welfare Professions. Extending the Evidence Base.* Maidenhead and Philadelphia, PA: Open University Press/McGraw-Hill, 2003.
38. Jenicek M. *Medical Error and Harm. Understanding, Prevention, and Control.* Boca Raton, FL/London/New York: CRC Press/Taylor & Francis/Productivity Press, 2011.
39. Gardner MJ and Altman DG. *Statistics with Confidence—Confidence Intervals and Statistical Guidelines.* London: British Medical Journal, 1989.
40. 'Classical' theory of probability. Section 3.3.1.1, pp. 53–55 in Ref. 5.
41. Timmermans S and Angell A. Evidence-based medicine, clinical uncertainty, and learning to doctor. *J Health Soc Beh*, 2001;42(4):342–59.
42. Fuzzy logic and fuzzy sets theory. Section 3.3.1.3, pp. 58–62 in Ref 5.
43. Gleick J. *Chaos. Making a New Science.* New York and London: Penguin Books, 1987.
44. Zadeh LA. Knowledge representation in fuzzy logic. Pp. 1–26 in: *An Introduction to Fuzzy Logic. Application in Intelligent Systems.* Dordrecht, NL: Kluwer Academic, 1992.
45. Fuzzy sets and fuzzy logic. Section 3.7, pp. 83–89 in: Jenicek M and Hitchcock DL. *Evidence-Based Practice. Logic and Critical Thinking in Medicine.* Chicago: American Medical Association (AMA Press), 2005.
46. Torres A and Nieto JJ. Fuzzy logic in medicine and bioinformatics. *J Biomed Biotech*, 2006; Article ID 9108:1–7.
47. Burton RA. *On Being Certain. Believing You Are Right Even When You're Not.* New York: St. Martin's Press, 2008.
48. Subias JL. *Applications of chaos theory in medicine.* 6 p. at http://www.didyf.unizar.es/info/jlsubias/Cor_tv04.eng.htm, retrieved April 1, 2010.
49. Denton TA, Diamond GA, Gelfand RH, Khan S, Karaguezian H. Fascinating rhythm: A primer on chaos theory and its application to cardiology. *Am Heart J*, 1990;120:1419–40.
50. *The New Encyclopaedia Britannica. Micropaedia.* Vol 7. Chicago, IL: Encyclopaedia Britannica Inc., 1992.
51. Chaos theory vs. probability theory. Beyond classical logic and probability. Section 3.3.1.2, pp. 55–58 in Jenicek M. *Foundations of Evidence-Based Medicine.* Boca Raton, FL/London/New York/Washington, DC: Parthenon Publishing Group/CRC Press, 2003.
52. Goodwin JS. Chaos and the limits of modern medicine. *JAMA*, 1997;278(17):1399–40.
53. Litaker D, Tomolo A, Liberatore V, Stange KC, Aron D. Using complexity theory to build interventions that improve health care delivery in primary care. *J Gen Intern Med*, 2006;21:S30–S34.
54. Sturmberg JP and Martin CM. Complexity and health—Yesterday's traditions, tomorrow's future. *J Eval Clin Pract*, 2009;15:543–8.

55. Martin C and Sturmberg JP. Perturbing ongoing conversations about systems and complexity of health services and systems. *J Eval Clin Pract,* 2009;15:549–52.

56. Waymack MH. Yearning for certainty and the critique of medicine as "science." *Theor Med Bioeth,* 2009;30:215–29.

57. Murphy EA. *The Logic of Medicine.* 2nd edition. Baltimore, MD and London: The Johns Hopkins University Press, 1997.

58. *Random House Webster's Unabridged Dictionary.* Antwerpen: Random House Inc, 1998 and 2003.

59. *Dorland's Illustrated Medical Dictionary.* 24th Edition. Philadelphia, PA and London: W.B. Saunders Company, 1965.

60. Wikipedia, the free encyclopedia. *Theory.* 8 p. at http://en.wikipedia.org/wiki/Theory, retrieved June 27, 2010.

61. Lolas F. Theoretical medicine: A proposal for reconceptualising medicine as a science of actions. *J Med Phil,* 1996;21(6):659–70; doi:10.1093/jmp/21.6.659.

62. Lorenz W and Rothmund M. Theoretical surgery: A new specialty in operative medicine. *World J Surg,* 1989;13:292–9.

63. Koller M, Barth H, Celik I, Rothmund M. A short history of theoretical surgery. *Inflamm Res,* 2004; 53(Suppl 2):S99–S104.

64. Sackett DL, Rosenberg WM, Muir Gray JA, Haynes RB, Scott Richardson W. Evidence-based medicine: What it is and what it isn't. *BMJ,* 1996;312(13 Jan):71–2.

65. Straus SE, Scott Richardson W, Glasziou P, Haynes RB. *Evidence-Based Medicine. How to Practice and Teach EBM.* 3rd Edition. Edinburgh/London/New York: Elsevier/Churchill Livingstone, 2005.

66. Dixon RA, Munro JF, Silcox PB. *The Evidence-Based Medicine Workbook. Critical Appraisal for Clinical Problem Solving.* Oxford: Butterworth-Heinemann, 1997.

67. Evidence-Based Medicine Working Group (G Guyatt et al.). A new approach to teaching the practice of medicine. *JAMA,* 1992;268:2420–25.

68. Evidence-Based Medicine Working Group. *Users' Guides to the Medical Literature. A Manual for Evidence-Based Clinical Practice.* Chicago: American Medical Association (AMA Press)/JAMA & Archives Journals, 2002. 2nd Edition edited by G Guyatt, D Rennie, MO Meade, and DJ Cook. New York and Chicago: McGraw-Hill Medical and JAMA & Archives Journals (AMA), 2008.

69. Jenicek M. Epidemiology, evidence-based medicine, and evidence-based public health. *J Epidemiol* (Japan Epidemiological Association), 1997;7(4):187–97.

70. Jenicek M and Stachenko S. Evidence-based public health, community medicine, preventive care. *Med Sci Monit,* 2003;9(2):SR1–SR7.

71. Brownson RC, Baker EA, Leet TL, Gillespie KN. *Evidence-Based Public Health.* Oxford and New York: Oxford University Press, 2003.

72. Muir Gray JA. *Evidence-based Healthcare. How to Make Health Policy and Management Decisions.* New York and Edinburgh: Churchill Livingstone, 1997.

73. Guyatt GH, Oxman AD, Schünemann HJ, Tugwell P, Knottnerus A. GRADE guidelines: A new series of articles in the *Journal of Clinical Epidemiology. J Clin Epidemiol,* 2011;64:380–382. The first article of this GRADE series.

74. Guyatt GH, Schünemann HJ, Djulbegovic B, Akl EA. Guidelines panels should not GRADE good practice statements. *J Clin Epidemiol,* 2015;68:597–600. The last article of this GRADE series.

75. Ennis RH. *Critical Thinking.* Upper Saddle River, NJ: Prentice Hall, 1996.

76. Scriven M and Paul R. Critical Thinking Community. *A Working Definition of Critical Thinking.* At http://lonestar.texas.net/~mseifert/crit2.html, retrieved June 2005.

77. Facione PA. *Critical Thinking: A Statement of Expert Consensus for Purposes of Educational Assessment and Instruction.* Research findings and recommendations prepared for the Committee on Pre-College Philosophy of the American Philosophical Association. Newark, DE: American Philosophical Association, ERIC Document #ED 315–423, 1990.

78. Hall J. *Tools of Thinking: Understanding the World through Experience and Reason.* Chantilly, VA: The Great Courses (The Teaching Company), A Transcript Book of the Course, 2005.

79. Health Innovation Network, South London. What is person-centred care and why is it important. 7 p. at http://www.hin.southlondon.org, retrieved January 14, 2017.

80. The College of Family Physicians of Canada. *Patient-Centred Primary Care in Canada. Bring It on Home.* Discussion Paper, October 2009. 27 p. at https://www.cfpc.ca/uploadedFiles/.../**BRING**20it2 0on20Home20FINAL20ENGLISH.p..., retrieved Jan 14, 2017.

81. Chan IS and Ginsburg GS. Personalized medicine: progress and promise. *Annu. Rev. Genomics, Hum. Genet.*, 2011(12):217–44.

82. Sheshia SS, Makhinson M, Phillips DF, Young BG. Evidence-informed person-centered health care (Part I): Do 'cognitive biases plus' at organizational levels influence quality of evidence? *J Eval Clin Pract*, 2014(20):734–47.

83. Seshia SS, Makhinson M, Young BG. Evidence-informed person-centred health care (part II): Are 'cognitive biases plus' underlying the EBM paradigm responsible for undermining the quality of evidence? *J Eval Clin Pract*, 2014(20):748–58.

84. What is Integrative Medicine? 1 p. at https://www.dikeintegrativemedicine.org/about/what-is-integrative -medicine/, retrieved April 4, 2016.

85. Miles A, Polychronis A, Grey J. Evidence-based medicine: why all the fuss? This is why. *J Eval Clin Pract*, 1997;3(2):83–6.

86. Bereczski D. Personalized medicine: A competitor or an upgrade of evidence-based medicine? *Personalized Medicine*, 2012;9(2):211–21.

87. Jenicek M, Croskerry P, Hitchcock DL. Evidence and its uses in health care and research: The role of critical thinking. *Med Sci Monit*, 2011;17(1):RA12–RA17.

88. Wikipedia, the free encyclopedia. *Humanities*. 13 p. at http://en.wikipedia.org/wiki/humanities, retrieved February 16, 2011.

89. Aull F. *Mission Statement.* Medical Humanities, New York University School of Medicine. 1 p. at http://medhum.med.nyu.edu/, retrieved March 18, 2011.

90. *Medical Humanities.* Edited by M. Evans and l. Finlay. London: BMJ Books, 2001.

91. *Medical Humanities: A Practical Introduction.* Edited by D. Kirklin and R. Richardson. London: Royal College of Physicians, 2001.

92. Shapiro J, Coulehan J, Wear D. Medical humanities and their discontents: Definitions, critiques and implications. *Acad Med*, 2009;84(2):192–8.

93. Jenicek M. Towards evidence-based critical thinking medicine? Uses of best evidence in flawless argumentations. *Med Sci Monit*, 2006;12(1):RA149–RA153.

94. Jenicek M. Evidence-based medicine: Fifteen years later. Golem the good, the bad, and the ugly in need of a review? *Med Sci Monit*, 2006;12(11):RA241–RA251.

95. Jenicek M. The hard art of soft science: Evidence-Based Medicine, Reasoned Medicine or both? *J Eval Clin Pract*, 2006;12(4):410–19.

96. Geyman JP, Deyo RA, Ramsey SD. *Evidence-Based Clinical Practice. Concepts and Approaches.* Boston, MA/Oxford/Auckland/Johannesburg/Melbourne/New Delhi: 2000.

97. Wulff HR and Gotzche PC. *Rational Diagnosis and Treatment. Evidence-Based Clinical Decision-making.* 3rd Edition. Oxford and Malden, MA: Blackwell Science, 1976. (3rd Edition 2000).

Suggested Additional Readings

98. Pellegrino ED and Thomasma DC. *A Philosophical Basis of Medical Practice. Toward a Philosophy and Ethic of the Healing Professions.* New York and Oxford: Oxford University Press, 1981.

99. Wulff HR, Pedersen SA, Rosenberg R, Introduction by A Storr. *Philosophy of Medicine. An Introduction.* 2nd Edition. Oxford and Boston, MA: Blackwell Scientific Publications, 1986. (2nd Edition 1990).

100. *The Philosophy of Medicine. Framing the Field.* Edited by HT Engelhardt Jr. Dordrecht/Boston, MA/London: Kluwer Academic, 2000.

101. *The Philosophy of Medicine Reborn: A Pellegrino Reader.* Edited by HT Engelhardt Jr and F Jotterand. Notre Dame, IN: University of Notre Dame Press, 2008.

102. Risdale L. *Evidence-Based General Practice. A Critical Reader.* London/Philadelphia, PA/Toronto/Sydney/Tokyo: W.B. Saunders Company Ltd, 1995.

103. *Users' Guides to the Medical Literature. A Manual for Evidence-Based Clinical Practice.* Edited by G Guyatt, D Rennie, MO Meade and DJ Cook. 3rd Edition. New York and Chicago: McGraw-Hill Education/JN-The JAMA Network/JAMAevidence®, 2015.
104. Brown B, Crawford P, Carter R. *Evidence-Based Health Communication.* Maidenhead(Berkshire/England) and New York: Open University Press/McGraw-Hill Education/McGraw-Hill House, 2006.
105. Yamada S, Slingsby BT, Inada MK, Derauf D. Evidence-based public health: A critical perspective. *J. Public Health,* 2008;16:169–72.106. *Mosby's Dictionary of Medicine, Nursing & Health Professions.* 8th Edition. St. Louis, MO: Mosby/Elsevier, 2009.
106. *Definitions of Evidence-Based Medicine on the Web.* 1 p. at http://www.google.ca/search?hl=en&biw=13 39&bih=562&defl=en&q=define:Evidence-..., retrieved October 12, 2010.
107. Jenicek M. *Writing, Reading, and Understanding in Modern Health Sciences. Medical Articles and Other Forms of Communication.* Boca Raton, FL/London/New York: CRC Press/Taylor & Francis, 2014.
108. *Users' Guides to the Medical Literature. A Manual for Evidence-Based Clinical Practice.* 3rd Edition. Edited by G Guyatt, D Rennie, MO Meade, DJ Cook. New York/London/Sydney/Toronto: McGraw-Hill Education, 2014. (Ref. 103 presented by another publisher.)
109. Guyatt G, Jaeschke R, Wilson MG, Montori VM, Scott Richardson W. *What Is Evidence-Based Medicine?* Ch. 2, pp. 7–14 in Ref. 106.
110. Djulbegovic B, Guyatt G. *Evidence-Based Medicine and the Theory of Knowledge.* Ch. 3, pp. 15–8 in Ref. 106.
111. Neumann E, Aki E A, Vandvik PO, Coello PA, Santesso N, Murad MH, Spencer F, Schunemann HJ, Guyatt G. *Assessing the Strength of Recommendations: The GRADE Approach.* pp. 561–73 (Section 28.1, Advanced Topics in Moving From Evidence to Action) in Ref. 106.
112. Evidence-Based Medicine Working Group. Evidence-based medicine. A new approach to teaching the practice of medicine. *JAMA,* 1992;268:2420–5.
113. Lederman EK. *Philosophy and Medicine.* Revised Edition. Hants/Aldershot and Brookfield, VT: Gower Publishing Company, 1970. (Revised Edition 1986).

ESSENTIALS OF REASONING AND CRITICAL THINKING IN HEALTH SCIENCES

Then, How Do Physicians and Other Health Professionals Really (or Should) Think*

Executive Summary

Critical thinking and decision-making (CTDM) in the health sciences and professions, including medicine, has evolved into a well-organized and structured process to be mastered, used, and evaluated in both practice and research. Its methodology is steadily developing, as are the methodologies for epidemiology, biostatistics and other domains applied to risk, diagnosis, treatment, and prognosis.

The objective of CTDM must be better understanding, rational decision-making, or both. It relies on argumentation as a dialogue to improve views and conclusions stemming from the exchanges between interested individuals or bodies. The simplest two-element arguments (reason → conclusion), categorical syllogisms as classical forms of reasoning, or Toulmin's modern argumentation model, might, are, and should be used in Socratic dialogue and problem solving, development, and discussion of research findings or various clinical rounds discussions. All these methods of clinical problem solving, its components, and building blocks must be supported by the best available evidence.

A demonstration of a cause → effect link is the most frequent and important, but not exclusive, form of CTDM. It is widely used and applied to illustrate the cause → effect link between noxious factors and disease occurrence and beneficial factors and health improvement. Etiological considerations are

---

* This chapter is based, with the permission by the publisher, on Chapter 2 in: Jenicek M. *A Primer on Clinical Experience in Medicine. Reasoning, Decision-Making, and Communication in Health Sciences.* Boca Raton, FL /London/New York: CRC Press/Taylor & Francis/Productivity Press, 2013. Revised, edited, updated.

based on both quantitative (frequencies of disease and exposure) and qualitative methodologies, as well as on criteria of causation.

The current state and uses of CTDM benefit and rely not only on experiences in health research, practice development, and evaluation methodologies, but also on wider experiences from the business world, military arts, law, health, and economics. They are all supported by informal logic, argumentation, and critical thinking as developed by modern philosophers.

Medicine remains a domain of probabilities and uncertainties. Its successes and failures depend widely on all the above CTDM components and on their contributors and considerations as summarized here.

In This Chapter

Executive Summary.. 75
Thoughts, Thinkers, and Things to Think About 77
Introductory Comments 78
4.1   General Medical Thinking and Reasoning.. 79
    4.1.1   Basic Considerations Related to Clinical Care and Caregiver Reasoning.............. 80
    4.1.2   Our Thinking and Reasoning: Essential Definitions and Meanings 81
    4.1.3   Tools for Argumentation.. 89
        4.1.3.1   "Naked" Argument (Enthymeme) or Argument at Its Simplest:
            A "Two-Element" Reasoning 89
        4.1.3.2   "Classical" Form of Reasoning: Categorical
            Syllogism or a "Three-Element" Reasoning...............................91
        4.1.3.3   "Modern" Form of Toulmin's Model of Argument: A "Multi-Element"
            Way of Reasoning to Reach Valid Conclusions..................... 95
    4.1.4   Reminder Regarding Some Additional and Fundamental Considerations 109
4.2   Directionality of Reasoning: Inductive, Deductive, and Abductive Ways 111
Let Us Conclude 115
References 119

Thoughts, Thinkers, and Things to Think About

The essential characteristic of philosophy, which makes it a study distinct from science, is criticism. *It examines critically principles employed in science and in daily life; it searches out any inconsistencies there may be in these principles, and it only accepts them when, as the result of critical inquiry, there is no reason for rejecting them.*
3rd Earl Bertrand Arthur William Russell (1872–1970), 1912
Isn't medicine today both science and philosophy (among others)?

The ability to reason is the fundamental characteristic of human beings. … Virtually every conscious human activity involves reasoning: we reason whenever we solve problems, make decisions, assess character, explain events, write poems, balance chequebooks, predict elections, make discoveries, interpret works of art, or repair carburetors. We reason about everything from the meaning of life to what to have for dinner.[1]
William Hughes and Jonathan Lavery (2008)
We also reason at every step of clinical care, making diagnoses, prescribing drugs, performing surgery, or caring for bedridden patients and their friends and family.

With understanding, there is no such thing as inevitability.
Marshall (Herbert) McLuhan (1911–1980)
Without understanding, is there viable decision-making?

Toulmin's method of practical reasoning permits the clinician to test a claim about the management of patients and the meaning of findings reported in a research paper. … The process of questioning our claims and assumptions in clinical decision-making is part of a recent interpretive turn in medicine. …The argument is the fundamental unit of medical thought. …[2]
Richard Horton
Editor of *The Lancet* (1998)
Should we not learn this like anything else?

Scientific papers are not just baskets carrying unconnected facts like a telephone directory: They are instruments of persuasion. Scientific papers must argue you into believing what they conclude; they must be built on the principles of critical arguments. …[3]
Edward J. Huth
former Editor-in-Chief,
Annals of Internal Medicine (1999)
This must also be true of exchanges of thoughts, opinions, and ideas between clinicians in their daily practice, teaching, and learning.

Finding and grading the best evidence in today's world of evidence-based medicine is just fine. The rest depends on how we will use it in your reasoning and decision-making. But what does all this mean?

Introductory Comments

The following situation is an example of how critical thinking and decision-making applies in the context of the health sciences and professions: As a medical student on my first hospital residency, I am listening to a teacher whose knowledge, experience, clinical skills, bedside manners, and approach to patients I admire. If I understand how my teacher reasons and why they are doing what they are doing, I can benefit best from my medical training. How should I understand what the teacher is saying and why the teacher is saying it? Should I reason and learn in an identical or similar manner in order to make the most of my first hospital experience? This chapter will attempt to find the answers to such questions.

4.1 General Medical Thinking and Reasoning

Thinking and reasoning in medicine, regardless of the form they take, are materialized in a series of statements about:

- original ideas triggering the reasoning process;
- leading to the premises that cover triggering ideas; and
- conclusion(s) that follow from premises analysis and integration.

Thinking and reasoning in medicine is organized around three sequential concepts: postulating an original idea that triggers a reasoning process, producing a series of premises, and analyzing and integrating these premises to produce a conclusion. In the analysis of our reasoning processes, all types of statements may be identified by idea indicators, premise indicators, and conclusion indicators words and wordings. Figure 4.1 illustrates such a structure in different types of argumentation as summarized in this section.

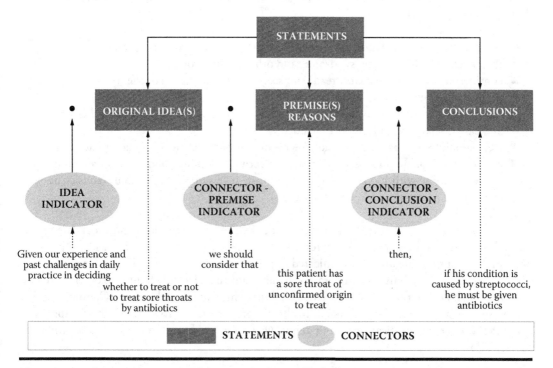

Figure 4.1   Three major types of statements in medical communication: Ideas, premises, and conclusions. (Reproduced with permission from Jenicek M. *A Primer on Clinical Experience in Medicine*. Boca Raton, FL: CRC Press, 2013.)

4.1.1 Basic Considerations Related to Clinical Care and Caregiver Reasoning

Physicians follow several steps and considerations when taking care of their patients:

- learning about the patient's past and present through medical history that includes gathering written and oral information about the past and present (chief complaint and other complaints);
- physical examination and/or mental status assessment, paraclinical exploration (laboratory and other technology-dependent procedures) leading to, and making diagnosis;
- taking into account risks (future health problems) and health problems already present (diagnosis);
- treatment choices, decisions, plan, and orders;
- assessment of prognosis;
- evaluation of the effectiveness, efficiency and efficacy of the collection of above mentioned steps in healthcare; and
- future steps in care to consider.

At each step in this clinical work, clinicians make conclusions as a sort of a claim or endpoint in argumentation. These are based on each action, or inaction, in clinical treatment, and all the positive or negative aspects which result from it. Some of the information used to inform making these conclusions include:

- those data and information are relevant for further assessment of the patient;
- the patient has this disease, syndrome, and other health problem;
- considering what I have heard, read, and seen in this patient, he or she may develop health problems that he or she does not have yet;
- the patient should receive the following medical, surgical, psychiatric, or other treatment and care (social care and support included);
- the outlook for the patient (prognosis) with or without treatment is good or bad; and
- our treatment plan and its execution were effective (did some good in habitual conditions), efficient (in line with money, resources, and time invested) and efficacious (consistent, specious, and beneficial under ideal conditions).

At any step of clinical care, decisions are made, and recommendations and orders are given, through various channels (admission notes, consults, discharge summaries, etc.). Ideas, propositions, and conclusions are also communicated to peers, other health professionals, managers, and administrators, and last but not least, to the patient and their friends, family, and other society members. Such **communication** is a bilateral activity which must 'make sense'. Communication is addressed in later chapters of this book. In this chapter, let us see first how we should approach (and practice) general medical reasoning about what we should understand and then, what we decide to do.

4.1.2 Our Thinking and Reasoning: Essential Definitions and Meanings

Should we learn how to reason? By all means, yes! Correct reasoning is necessary to achieve the objectives of any teaching and learning process such as acquiring desirable, necessary, and useful knowledge, attitudes, and skills.

Our thinking and reasoning serves three distinct and different purposes.

1. The first is **understanding**. Undergoing a mental process to understand the nature of the problem at hand. Problems may be what causes cancer or what is effective to treat a cancer.
2. The second purpose is **decision-making**. We reason about the best ways to solve a health problem, such as deciding if surgery or conservative treatments are the best ways to treat an advanced cancer, what to do in a particular clinical case, or which available surgical procedures and techniques are the best for this patient.
3. Finally, thinking and reasoning is not enough. A clinician needs to move ideas, thoughts, proposals, recommendations directions, rules or orders between individuals (health professionals and their patients and community) and organizations (hospitals, other health services, community groups). **Communication** is thus a vital tool in the thinking and reasoning process.

This chapter is about understanding, Chapter 10 will focus on decision-making, and Chapters 11 and 12 are devoted to the challenge of, and rules for, communication. Let us look at understanding first.

In the spirit of Bloom's taxonomy of learning and teaching processes in general,[4] we must master several abilities:

1. **Knowledge** (observation and recall of information);
2. **Comprehension** (understanding information, translation into the specific context, interpretation, prediction of consequences);
3. **Application** (uses of information or evidence, solving the problem);
4. **Analysis** (identification of patterns, meaning of the whole and its components);
5. **Synthesis** (generalizations, new ideas generation, merging knowledge from several areas, making conclusions and predictions); and
6. **Evaluation of our mental processes** (comparisons of and making discriminations between ideas, assessing the value of claims, making choices based on reasoned argument, verifying the value of evidence, making distinctions between subjectivity and objectivity).

To these we propose adding:

7. **Decision-making** (what to do given the above, communicating with all involved parties like patients, other health and social professionals, and management as partners in the execution of decided actions);
8. **Execution** of decided actions; and
9. **Evaluation of the impact of actions performed** (results as they appear to both providers and recipients of clinical and other healthcare).

All of these depend on reasoning to be effective, and avoid medical errors at any point in the clinical process while also contributing to patient safety and quality of care. How we think and make decisions is increasingly pragmatic, structured, and practice oriented, often as much a part of our thinking as epidemiologists, biostatisticians, surgeons, or psychiatrists.

And so, what lies behind the most important terms we encounter and use in the world of medical reasoning today? The following definitions of some basic concepts in thinking apply well to medicine:

Thinking is a *mental action that, if verbalized, is a matter of combining words in propositions.*[5,6] Needless to say, this general definition applies to, and includes, the mental processes dealing with health and disease. The elements of thinking in general[7] as well as in clinical settings[8] are:

■ *purposes* (goals, objectives, functions);
■ relevant *questions* (problems to deal with and solve);
■ *information* (data, facts, evidence, observations, experiences, reasons);
■ *interpretation* and *inference* (conclusions, solutions);
■ *concepts* (theories, definitions, laws, principles, models);
■ *assumptions* (presuppositions, axioms, taking for granted);
■ *implications* and *consequences* (effects, that which follows logically); and
■ *points of view* (frames of reference, perspectives, orientations, world views).

Reasoning

Reasoning is *thinking leading to a conclusion*. We think about signs what a patient reports experiencing, signs, and symptoms and come to a conclusion about the diagnosis of his or her health problem. We review information and knowledge about a drug and conclude whether it should be prescribed to a patient or not. Our patient asks us what will happen given his or her health problem and what this implies for his or her care and outcomes. We review the evidence and conclude that his or her prognosis is good or bad. Without good reasoning, there is no good medicine.

Formally and more generally, reasoning is the *process of forming conclusions, judgments, or inferences from facts, observations, and/or hypotheses*. Its elements are, like those for thinking generally: purpose, question, information, inferences, assumptions, concepts, implications, and points of view.[6,7]

Types of reasoning. There are numerous methods to reasoning, none of which are mutually exclusive.[8,9] These types of reasoning are: abduction, analogic reasoning, cause-effect reasoning, comparative reasoning, conditional reasoning, criteria reasoning, decompositional reasoning, deductive reasoning, inductive reasoning, modal logic, traditional logic, pros vs. cons reasoning, set-based reasoning, systemic reasoning, and syllogistic reasoning.

When reasoning, we examine various **propositions**, **statements** or **proposals** regarding the problem in question. This creates a new way to look at, or view of, the problem under scrutiny. Ideally, all propositions and statements about risks, diagnosis, treatment or prognosis should be based on the best evidence through which we identify, know, and understand a problem.

Argument and Argumentation

An **argument** is a *vehicle for reasoning*. It consists of *various statements or propositions (logicians call them premises or reasons) from which we infer to make another statement or conclusion*.

The argument is supported and/or justified by propositions that lead us to something new, another statement or conclusion stemming from our argumentation process. In other words, an **argument** is a connected series of statements or reasons intended to establish a position leading to another statement as a conclusion. An argument is a *vehicle of our medical logic*.

Argumentation itself is a *discussion between two or more people in which at least one advances an argument,*[4] *a manner and vehicle for the presentation of arguments*. It means putting forward and integrating propositions by one or more proponents to reach a mutually acceptable solution. In this light, a physician's discussion with his or her patient(s), exchanging ideas between physicians, researching and publishing results, and proposing decisions in medical care and prevention, are part of the wider field of medical argumentation. To obtain the best outcomes and for the patients' utmost benefit, we want our argumentation to be as flawless as possible, an impeccable "**argument-based medicine**."

Argumentation falls into the domain of **reasoning**, a tool used to form conclusions, judgments, or inferences from facts or premises. It is a method used to present of arguments. Correct argumentation with ourselves and with other interested parties is one of the important ways to deal with a given health problem, disease, medical care, and medical error as well. Figure 4.2 illustrates medical considerations in critical thinking, in other terms, 'how doctors think, reason, decide, and do.' We will follow this path throughout this book.

Argumentation may also be seen as *the study of the principles by which beliefs and actions are evaluated and related to one another*. It enables us to discover what beliefs and actions are reasonable in any social (professional practice and research in a community functioning related framework) context and that is concerned with the selection and organization of ideas to justify particular positions.

In medicine, we argue all the time: about patient history, their risks, their diagnosis, how to treat the conditions that were found, what will happen after the prognosis is determined, and what should be done next, and in the long term.

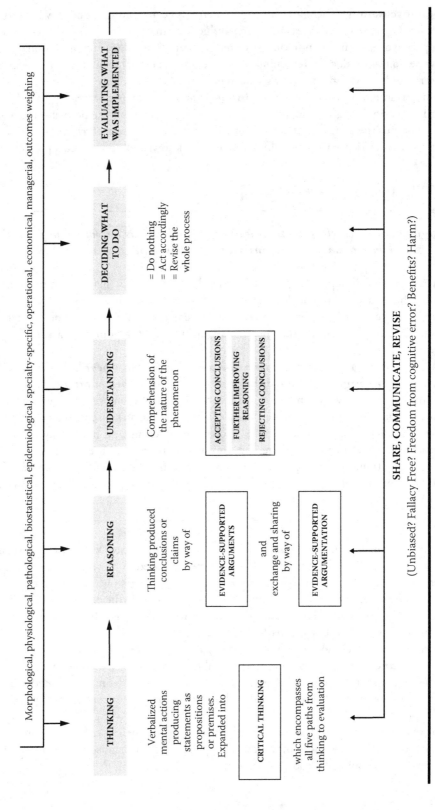

Figure 4.2 **Components and sequence of mental processes and operations in medicine. (Redrawn with modifications from Jenicek M.** *A Primer on Clinical Experience in Medicine.* **Boca Raton: CRC Press, 2013. Reproduced with permission by the publisher.)**

Argumentation is a two-dimension process:

1. As *inquiry*, it leads to the finding of appropriate beliefs and actions.
2. As *advocacy*,[10] it is a tool for using language strategies to justify our beliefs and actions to others.

Premises or statements that are phrased as part of arguments are either *perceptual*, reflecting the nature of things, or *value judgments*, reflecting the worthiness of something, such as goodness, rightfulness, importance, or ethical acceptability. Various premises that are conclusions of arguments are either descriptive, predictive, or evaluative statements. They may be *propositions of facts or values* that assert the existence or worth of something: "*This patient has a fever.*" Or they may be *propositions of policy*, that is, statements of actions to be taken and a desired change: "*We must find out why and treat him accordingly.*" In this case, those advocating change must provide sufficient evidence and arguments to overcome the presumption, the inherent advantage to oppose change, of existing beliefs and policies.

Again, **conclusions** must provide meaningful and usable information to improve our **understanding** of the health problem, **actions** to be taken, or **both**.

How, therefore, should we understand arguments and argumentation processes in the context of critical thinking and decision-making?

Argumentation is "*the communicative process of advancing, supporting, criticising, and modifying claims so that appropriate decision makers, defined by relevant spheres, may grant or deny adherence.*"[11] In this framework, **adherence** refers to informed support by individuals involved in argumentation. They represent **spheres**, that is, collections of people in the process of interacting about, and making, critical decisions. Medical or surgical multidisciplinary teams, medical graduate and undergraduate students can be considered as "spheres" in this context. Spheres may be personal or interpersonal, technical (specialty or profession related) or public, involving individuals and groups under the care and attention of decision-makers. This process is only complete when claims are advanced, supported, criticized, and modified is a way that appropriate decision makers grant, or deny, the conclusion. This is called 'adherence'.

In summary, who appropriate decision makers are is defined by relevant spheres—the collections of people involved in the process of interacting about, and making, critical decisions. The sphere may be a multidisciplinary medical or surgical team, or, in the case of medical research, graduate or medical students. Ultimately, the final step in an argumentation process is when spheres may adhere to (agree with) or deny claims.

Argumentation may be also seen as a manner and vehicle for the presentation of arguments. An **argument**, then, is a unit encompassing various supports for some claim and must offer justifications to relevant decision makers allowing them to adhere to the claim. Generalizations, analogies, authority, causes, signs may underlie all its ways.[11]

Premises that lead to a conclusion or idea of what might be the conclusion of an argument *before* necessary information is gathered are called *presumptions*, that is, positions or argumentative grounds that are available until some sufficient reason is adduced against them. Hypotheses at the beginning of medical research, or working diagnoses before a more complete assessment of a patient can be completed, are presumptions in a critical thinking and decision-making sense. Our argumentation and its results are often subject to error and/or harm due in part to reasoning biases and cognitive errors. Some definitions might help to understand such challenges.

Logic in General and Medical Logic

Medical logic (logic in medicine) is *"a system of thought and reasoning that governs understanding and decisions in clinical and community care, research, and communication."*[5]

Informal logic helps us deal with health problems by looking at arguments as they occur in the context of natural language used in everyday life.

Error and Harm

Error in general is *"an act of commission (doing something wrong) or omission (failing to do the right thing) that leads to an undesirable outcome or significant potential for such an outcome."*[12,13] Reasoning, deciding, or acting poorly can lead to medical errors and harm.

Medical error may then be defined as *"an individual and/or system failure resulting from human behaviour made by a health professional who, in a health establishment or community setting provides direct clinical or community care, acts, or services (e.g., operating surgeon, prescribing internist, consulting psychiatrist, nurse at floors or in a surgical or office setting). It may be knowledge-based, rule-based, or skill (execution)-based and often (but not always) produces* **medical harm**.*"*[5]

These two entities, error and harm, however, must not be confounded.[14] In the first case, medical error is defined as a preventable adverse effect of care, whether or not it is evident or harmful to the patient. This might include an inaccurate or incomplete diagnosis or treatment of disease, injury, syndrome, behavior, infection, or other ailment.[15]

Medical harm is a *temporary or permanent physical impairment in bodily functions (including sensory functions, mental functioning, social and occupational functioning, pain, disease, injury, disability, death) and structures as well as suffering that disrupts a patient's physical, mental, and/or social well-being.* Some errors result in medical harm, but many errors do not. Conversely, many incidents of medical harm are not the results of any errors.[14]

Medical error is therefore an inaccurate or incomplete assessment and management of patient risks and diagnosis. Medical errors can include executing radical or conservative treatment, making an inaccurate prognosis, and improperly extending care. Such faults fall into the category of fallacies, biases, and cognitive errors.[16]

Absence of errors and harm in medical practice is an important warrant of patient safety and quality of clinical and community healthcare. The absence of errors and harm in medical practice is an important outcome of patient safety and quality in clinical and community healthcare.

Fallacies in Thinking and Reasoning

In more general terms, a **fallacy** is some mistake or flaw in reasoning or in an argument. It is a violation of the norms of good reasoning, rules of critical discussion, dispute resolution, and adequate communication.[16,17] **Fallacy in medicine** refers to any error in reasoning pertaining to a health problem, its supporting evidence(s), the handling of evidence in our reasoning, and throughout the process of argumentation, interfering with the best possible understanding and decision-making in the task of health problem solving.[17,18] It may be a product of the physician's reasoning, communication, and decision-making as well. For example, a *cum hoc ergo propter hoc* fallacy refers to the act of drawing conclusions about cause-effect relationships on the basis of loosely defined "associations" or "correlations" instead of on the basis of a more formal cause-effect proof. Anything that precedes medical error and its potential consequences (harm) should not automatically be considered a "cause" of harm until it conforms to criteria of causality.

Fallacious reasoning often occurs when a problem as a whole is reduced to one of its parts, and generalizations from its solution are applied to the whole problem. For example, we may emphasize that an association between a toxic agent and cancer is strong given a high relative risk or odds ratio of exposure. However, the strength of the cause-effect association is just one criterion among many to confirm or reject a cause-effect relationship. Elsewhere, as shown above in the case of a *cum hoc ergo propter hoc* fallacy, a correct temporal sequence is not sufficient. Other criteria must be fulfilled too. Regardless, authors of medical articles about causality involving beneficial (trials) or noxious (etiological observations of uncontrolled individuals and events) factors frequently present high odds ratios or relative risks as a demonstration of causality. This is just part of the picture.

Fallacies in reasoning and decision-making beyond health sciences and professions are now reviewed in an increasing number of websites. Wikipedia's *List of Fallacies*[19] is perhaps the most extensive with over 130 fallacies reviewed and defined, with reference to separate websites for each fallacy and article references supporting each of these topics. Other reference sources for fallacies include *Fallacy Files Weblog*,[20] *Nizkor*,[21] and other initiatives.[22-24] In 2009, we categorized selected fallacies in medicine and the health sciences as: fallacies related to general medical reasoning, medical research and articles, communication between health professionals, and communication between health professionals, their patients, and the laic community.[18] This represents a different classification and taxonomy than the ones used in classical philosophy and logic.

Bias, Cognitive Error, Cognitive Bias

The meaning of the word **bias** in medicine is most strongly influenced by its meaning in biostatistics: a deviation from some real or reference value. In a more general context, bias may be considered a ***non-random, systematic deviation from truth, or a well-defined "reality."*** Often, bias is a term used in an undistinguished way from cognitive error or cognitive bias.

Krishna et al.[25] define bias as "a systematic deviation from what would have been the most effective route to one goal because of commitment to another particular tendency or inclination, especially the one that prevents unprejudiced consideration of a question." In this sense, some biases may also be viewed as fallacies. Bias, then, may occur both in research and in practice with patients and communities.[26] It may be perceived *within a study*, observation and interpretation from one case individual to another, or *between studies* of the same phenomenon or different phenomena.

Classification of biases may be mostly methodological or mixed. Wikipedia's *List of Cognitive Biases* include cognitive biases, conflicts of interest, statistical biases, contextual biases, and prejudices.[27] This web listing of over 100 biases provides definitions, reference articles, and directions to separate websites for each bias listed.[28]

A **cognitive error** or **cognitive bias** (terms often used interchangeably across the literature) identifies a pattern of deviation in judgment that occurs in medical and clinical situations or in medical research reasoning and conclusions.[13,25,26] One example of cognitive error is *"hindsight* *bias*," which refers to the tendency for people with knowledge of an outcome to exaggerate the extent to which they would have predicted that outcome beforehand. In modern medical literature, 'bias' has multiple meanings, including almost any flaw in reasoning and decision-making, especially in medical research (research design, execution, and evaluation). It is increasingly discussed because even 'biased' research results and their uses may be detrimental to patient safety and health. In this context, bias is, in great part, synonymous with fallacy.

General cognitive biases are listed in the List of Cognitive Biases in the appendices of this book.

Cognitive biases[29] of particular interest *for medicine and health sciences* are

- affective error (chagrin factor);
- aggregate bias (ecological fallacy);
- ambiguity effect;
- ascertainment bias;
- availability bias;
- base rate neglect;
- belief bias;
- blind spot bias;
- commission and omission biases;
- confirmation bias;
- diagnosis momentum;
- feedback sanction;
- framing effect;
- fundamental attribution error (negative stereotyping);
- gambler's fallacy;
- hindsight bias;
- information bias;
- order effects (primacy, recency);
- paying the odds;
- posterior probability error;
- premature closure;
- representativeness restraint (prototypical error);
- search satisfaction;
- sunk cost fallacy;
- triage cueing ('geography is destiny');
- yin yang bias; and
- zebra retreat.

Since terms like bias, fallacy, or cognitive error are still used interchangeably across much of the literature, the list of cognitive biases grows.[28,29]

In this section, we have defined some of the basic terms and meanings in thinking. In light of current evidence in the medical paradigm, error and bias-free **argument-based medicine**[16,17] refers to the research and practice of medicine in which understanding and decisions in patient and population care are supported by, and based on, flawless arguments using the best the best available evidence and experience as argument and argumentation building blocks in a structured, fallacy-free manner. We use this understanding to explore the tools that clinicians and others involved in medicine can use as formal structures, to develop argumentation processes for medicine.

4.1.3 Tools for Argumentation

There are several ways to explain and defend our views and positions. It starts with establishing a simple link between two statements, then moving on to more complex and complete forms that better reflect the reality of the problem to be solved. In essence, any kind of argumentation relies on varying numbers of statements, connected and identified by linking words called 'connectors'. Figure 4.1 illustrates this concept and the basic organization of statements, and connections between such statements, in argumentation.

4.1.3.1 "Naked" Argument (Enthymeme) or Argument at Its Simplest: A "Two-Element" Reasoning

In daily reasoning and communication, we usually move from **one reason** (statement, proposition, premise) to some **conclusion** (claim, recommendation, orders) through the use of an **indicator** which links the reason to the conclusion. This simple argument looks like this:

Statement	Element of the Argument
"Our child has a high fever and nothing at home helps,	Reason
↓	
therefore	Inference indicator/ connector
↓	
let us take him to the pediatric emergency."	Conclusion, claim

As another example, we may state that:

Statement	Element of the Argument
"The patient has a fever of unknown origin,	Reason
↓	
meaning that	Inference indicator/ connector
↓	
we must do a diagnostic workup to better understand what is behind this case of fever."	Recommendation, orders, conclusion claim

In this case, the recommendation would lead medical practitioners to investigate the cause of the fever and identify the specific treatment (antipyretics, antibiotics, antiviral agents, surgery, etc.).

In another common situation of daily practice, we proceed from some reason to some conclusion:

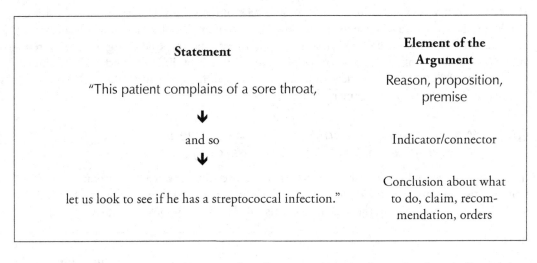

In some situations, we may also proceed in the reverse direction by stating (concluding, claiming) what we intend or want to do:

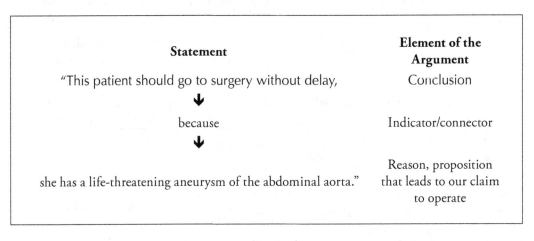

Figure 4.3 is another illustration of an enthymeme used in clinical practice communication.

For Hitchcock, this "one-element" form of reasoning, called **enthymeme**, is a kind of reasoning or argument that is not deductively valid, but which can be made deductively valid by adding one or more premises.[5] Enthymematic ways of reasoning and argumentation are fairly ubiquitous in charged clinical practice. As a vehicle of reasoning, enthymeme may often underlie **abductive reasoning**, one of three basic forms of inference besides induction and deduction. Its form is illustrated in this phrase: "*The surprising fact is observed. If a hypothesis were true, the fact would be commonplace. Therefore, hypothesis is possibly true.*" In abductive reasoning, we reason from observed phenomena to a hypothesis. It only shows, however, that the hypothesis is a possible explanation; more (further

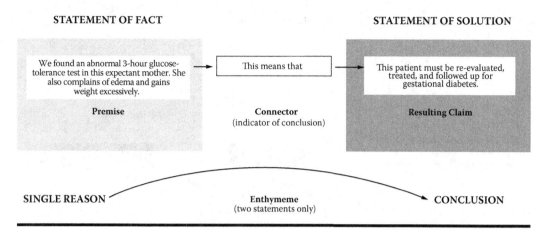

STATEMENT OF FACT   STATEMENT OF SOLUTION

We found an abnormal 3-hour glucose-tolerance test in this expectant mother. She also complains of edema and gains weight excessively.

This means that

This patient must be re-evaluated, treated, and followed up for gestational diabetes.

Premise   **Connector**   **Resulting Claim**
                                 (indicator of conclusion)

SINGLE REASON   **Enthymeme**   **CONCLUSION**
                                   (two statements only)

Figure 4.3   A *"single reason → conclusion"* argument: Enthymeme. (Reproduced with permission from Jenicek M. *A Primer on Clinical Experience in Medicine.* Boca Raton: CRC Press, 2013.)

observation, experiment, reasoning) is needed to fully justify the hypothesis. In Section 4.1.3.2, we will explore syllogistic reasoning which illustrates that the uncertainty in inference may be due to a weak connection between major and middle terms, or the middle terms and major terms in a categorical syllogism. But let us first examine what is exactly a categorical syllogism.

4.1.3.2 *"Classical" Form of Reasoning: Categorical Syllogism or a "Three-Element" Reasoning*

In the most ancient and traditional form of reasoning, we base our understanding and decisions on Classical Greek philosophy dating back more than two millennia. Aristotle's proposal of a **categorical syllogism** remains a model to move from various propositions (premises) to some conclusion.[30,31] Figure 4.4 illustrates a medical example of a categorical syllogism.

The three constituting elements of a categorical syllogism are:

1. A **general statement (*major premise*)** is made: All subjects with blond or red hair are more sensitive to sunlight (ultraviolet light) as a cause of skin cancer.
2. A **specific statement (*minor premise*)** is made about a specific case: This patient has blond or red hair and often vacations in tropical and subtropical countries or goes to sun tanning salons to look "healthy."
3. A **conclusion** resulting from the link between the general and specific statement (i.e., a statement about the specific case in light of the general statement) is made: This patient is at high risk of skin cancer, so this patient should (1) limit his or her exposure to ultraviolet light (conclusion, recommendation); (2) be followed more closely by others for early signs of potentially malignant skin lesions (additional recommendation if supported by other arguments specific to them); and (3) be treated for them if required (additional recommendation if supported by other arguments specific to them).

From one element of a syllogism to another, we insert, most often in natural language, **connectors** between statements or **indicators** of a statement that follows from the preceding in a meaningful way. For example, a **premise indicator** may use words like *"since," "because," "assuming*

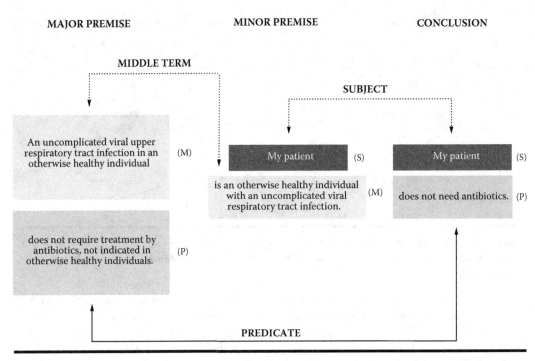

Figure 4.4 Categorical syllogism: A medical example. (Reproduced with permission from Jenicek M. *A Primer on Clinical Experience in Medicine*. Boca Raton: CRC Press, 2013.)

that," "*in view of*," "*given that*," "*in view*," "*due to the fact that*," "*as indicated by*," and so on. A **conclusion indicator** like "*therefore*," "*thusly*," "*hence*," "*for this reason*," "*which means that*," "*which proves that*," "*which lead us to*," "*indicating us what to (do)*," "*showing a mandatory action as follows*," "*allowing us to conclude that*," and "*given that*" are phrases that justify and prepare us for the rightness of the final conclusion of the argument. A more complete list may be found elsewhere (Table 2-1 in Reference 5).

All supporting statements must be based on the best available evidence for the purpose of leading to the evidence-based conclusion. Let us consider another example: "*All sore throats require attention even if they are not caused by a streptococcal infection. Given that my patient has a sore throat, so, I must be sure that he does not have this kind of bacterial infection before reassuring him that he does not need antibiotics.*" Hence:

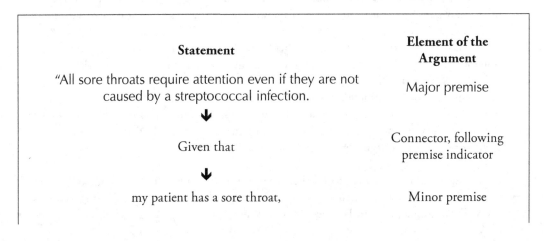

Statement	Element of the Argument
"All sore throats require attention even if they are not caused by a streptococcal infection.	Major premise
↓	
Given that	Connector, following premise indicator
↓	
my patient has a sore throat,	Minor premise

↓

so,   Conclusion indicator

↓

I must be sure that he does not have this kind of bacte-
rial infection before reassuring him that he does not need   Conclusion
antibiotics."

Good evidence must underlie the general considerations regarding how to treat bacterial or non-bacterial throat infections (major premise), the state of our particular patient (minor premise), and their connection leading to the conclusion. Figure 4.5 illustrates this reasoning. Its upper portion represents the original Toulmin's argument and its lower portion represents a translation of this argument into the medical problem and context.

Let us discuss this model more in the sections of this chapter which follow.

In the context of argumentation and medicine, **evidence in medicine** means *any piece of information and data needed and used either for **understanding** a health problem or **making decisions** about it.* In its broadest sense, **evidence in argumentation** means answering questions like *"How do you know?"* or *"What do you have to go on?"* by applying the following strategies:

1. Providing **examples** as materials from which a generalization will be built, something that is true about a problem as a whole.
2. **Statistics**: Quantitative (numerical) information in the form of frequencies, rates, ratios, odds, quantification of associations, and so on.
3. A **rate of change** based on repeated experience in terms of outcomes of experiments or observational analytical studies.
4. **Tangible objects** as actual things or pictures of actual things, like those often used as evidence in criminal law, in medical textbooks, articles, pathology, or bedside teaching and experience.
5. A **testimony of fact or of opinion** as a judgment of people who are in a position of knowing directly as a credible source.
6. A **social consensus** so widely believed that the individuals concerned consider it to be a fact.
7. '**Common knowledge**' is a type of social consensus.^{partly from Reference 31}

Evidence in argumentation does **not** mean solely a cause-effect relationship in observational or experimental analytical (trials) domains. It may concern risk, diagnosis, prognosis, or any other domain of health sciences and it may range from the worthless to the best available evidence. For practical decisions, it is graded according to the nature and purpose of the problem to be solved. Hence, the notion and meaning of the 'best' evidence may vary from one case and problem to another.

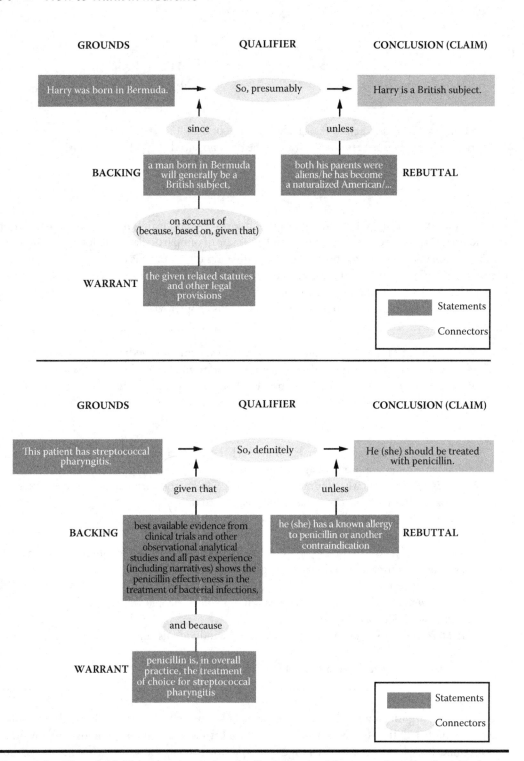

Figure 4.5 Way of thinking, argumentation the Toulmin way. Theory and application. (Redrawn with modifications from Toulmin SE. *The Uses of Argument.* **Cambridge University Press, 1958 and Jenicek M.** *A Primer on Clinical Experience in Medicine.* **Boca Raton: CRC Press, 2013. Reproduced with permission.)**

4.1.3.3 *"Modern" Form of Toulmin's Model of Argument: A "Multi-Element" Way of Reasoning to Reach Valid Conclusions*

In the 1950s, the British-American philosopher Stephen Toulmin proposed a new model of argument[32,33] in the hope that it would better fit our ways of reasoning in today's world, and the questions and problems of modern life. Many modern thinkers agree that it does just that, and it has therefore been applied and used in an expanding number of domains in arts and sciences, medicine included. Compared to previous models, it often reflects reasoning backwards from the conclusion (claim) to all elements (argument building blocks) that contributed to its support and value. However, we anticipate this kind of argumentation can be used when developing and executing a research project, when we admit or see a patient for the first time and develop "the case" from the initial "impression," and in the planning and execution of clinical or community care.

Let us look at modern argumentation from a philosophical and more formal standpoint first, and then in terms of its applications to medicine. Toulmin offered an original example of an argument[20] redrawn here in the form of the upper portion of Figure 4.5. Its lower portion is its medical example, discussed later in this chapter.

Philosophically speaking, Toulmin's model contains six elements, or building blocks, with connectors between them. These six elements are outlined below and in Figure 4.5:

1. The **claim** is a ***conclusion*** to which we arrive through our reasoning supported by the present argument. As an example, we may reason that *"a high incidence of cancers in this rapidly developing industrial area is due to the high level of air pollution."* Our clinical statements such as *"This patient should be admitted," "This patient should be discharged," "This patient must get anti-rejection drugs,"* or *"This patient has pneumonia"* are all conclusions from various argumentative processes leading to such claims. The claim in this example is: *"Harry is a British subject."*

2. The **grounds** are the basis from which we reason. They are the ***fundamental data and information*** of our own findings. For example, *we observed a high incidence of cancers and high levels of industrial air pollution in the area of interest.* In EBM, we may see this as "firsthand evidence;" *"Harry was born in Bermuda"* in this example.

3. The **backing** is the ***body of experience and evidence*** that supports the warrant, or, our past studies and experience or literature review of similar and dissimilar findings. In EBM, we may see this as "secondhand evidence," critically appraised or not (*the following other studies offer similar findings and conclusions*). In this example, *"the following statutes and other legal provisions"* are the backing.

4. The **warrant** is a ***general rule or experience, understanding of the nature of the problem under study.*** This allows us to infer to the claim: similar findings in the literature, methodological experience, and explanation of pathological and physiological mechanisms underlying the health problem, such as our general understanding of the carcinogenicity of specific air pollutants. In EBM, it's our understanding of the nature of first- and secondhand evidence. In this example, *"A man born in Bermuda will generally be a British subject"* is the warrant.

5. The **qualifier** is an expression, often a single word or number, somehow quantifying the certainty with which we make our claim in light of the preceding argument blocks

and connections between them. We may state that the high incidence of cancers is "definitely", "probably", "more certainly than uncertainly" due to the air pollution, or, "80%" of cancer cases are due to the carcinogens in the air, "We are 90% sure that this health problem is an environmental problem,' and so on. In this example, *"presumably"* is a qualifier.

6. **Rebuttals** are conditions or circumstances under which our claim does not apply. They undermine the force of supporting grounds and other building blocks of the argument. In the cancer-related example, rebuttals would be other undetected carcinogens of non-industrial origin (naturally occurring in soil, waters, etc.); difficult differential diagnosis criteria with other competing health problems; individual endogenous factors in the population leading to the high probability of cancer incidence ('cancer families'); and others. In a broader framework, rebuttals may contain ethical considerations, contra-indications, differential diagnoses, or patient preferences and values which may differ from the health professional and/or scientific point of view. As exclusion criteria in a clinical sense, they must be based on the best evidence available and otherwise justified. In this example, *"Both his parents were aliens/he has become a naturalized American"* is a rebuttal.

Connectors between various statements, or building blocks, of the argument, are also elements of Toulmin's model. Connectors include phrases like "since," "on account of (because, based on, given that)," "so," and "unless."

Toulmin's model is typically used in other domains. The example below is from the perspective of a demographer.[32 modified]

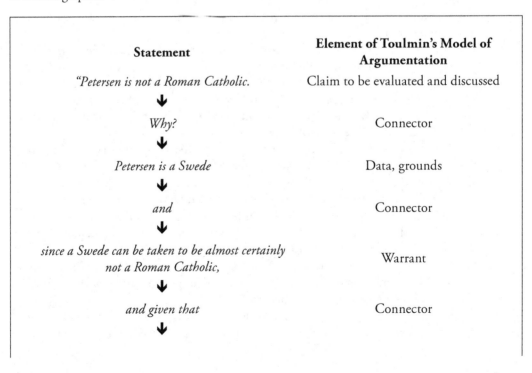

Statement	Element of Toulmin's Model of Argumentation
"Petersen is not a Roman Catholic.	Claim to be evaluated and discussed
↓	
Why?	Connector
↓	
Petersen is a Swede	Data, grounds
↓	
and	Connector
↓	
since a Swede can be taken to be almost certainly not a Roman Catholic,	Warrant
↓	
and given that	Connector
↓	

the proportion of Roman Catholic Swedes is less than 2%,	Backing
↓	
he almost certainly	Qualifier
↓	
is not a Roman Catholic."	Back to the claim as conclusion of an argument

Does all this have anything to do with medicine? It certainly does.

Similarly, in medicine, we may use Toulmin's model to consider the question of a young immunized patient with a rash.

Statement	**Element of Toulmin's Model of Argumentation**
"My young patient, immunized against measles has a rash which looks like measles.	Data and impression
↓	
Why?	Connector
↓	
Besides the clinical manifestations of his or her rash,	Data, grounds
↓	
and since	Connector
↓	
there is a very low probability that a well immunized child would get measles	Warrant
↓	
and because	Connector
↓	
he comes from a community in which almost all children are immunized against measles and the herd immunity there is then high enough to prevent measles spread and high occurrence of cases,	Backing
↓	
so,	Connector (as conclusion indicator)
↓	

> *my young patient almost certainly*
>
> *does not have measles and we must also look at another more probable diagnosis of his or her problem."*
>
> Qualifier
>
> Conclusion, claim stemming from this diagnostic argumentation and argument

N.B. This approach to reasoning recognizes that the protective efficacy of the vaccine is not absolute, and that pattern recognition plays an important role in this approach to reasoning.

More generally speaking in medicine, and in simpler terms, what do we need?

- We need some **grounds** for argumentation, be it spoken or written. Clinical and paraclinical data and information particular to the case serve this purpose.
- We look at grounds in light of a **warrant**, which is some kind of general rule, accepted understanding, and evidence. It is focused on plausibility.
- Whatever we conclude on the basis of grounds and warrant is evaluated in a confirmation, line, or distinct pattern as seen through **backing**. These are the research findings, graded evidence, past practical clinical experience, "external evidence," or "what literature tells us."
- Putting all this together, we try to somehow quantify the certainty or probability that our ensuing claims or conclusions of the argument are correct in terms of a **qualifier**. Understanding the limits or level of certainty or probability is often the hardest challenge of an argument.
- Our **conclusions** or argument **claim** are then the result of synthesis of the above argument building blocks.
- Argument conclusions are valid provided only that there are existing exclusionary circumstances or criteria that Toulmin termed **rebuttals**. Besides qualifiers, rebuttals are often sorely missing (and they should not be) in our conclusions or claim statements.

Based on this approach to argumentation, errors may occur and mistakes can happen if:

- grounds are of poor quality, incomplete or unrelated to the problem under study;
- our understanding of the essence of the problem is not clear;
- the backing is of poor quality, incomplete, or unrelated again;
- there is no certainty regarding our conclusions and claims;
- we do not perceive that exceptions apply to what we conclude about the problem; and
- there is no meaningful link between each of the argument building blocks.

Let us return to our example of the patient presenting with a sore throat and requiring antibiotics example to illustrate Toulmin's way of argumentation.

Statement	Element of Toulmin's Model of Argumentation
"I will prescribe you antibiotics for your bacterial throat infection,	Claim, conclusion of an argument
⬇	
because	Connector
⬇	
looking at your red throat, patched tonsils, tender cervical nodes and fever, and positive results of our rapid laboratory test,	Grounds
⬇	
and since	Connector
⬇	
a treatment with penicillin may be the best choice in your case	Warrant
⬇	
and because	Connector
⬇	
all our past experience and clinical studies show that we must do this to spare you from serious complications of such an infection	Backing
⬇	
so,	Connector
⬇	
let us definitely proceed this way,	Qualifier
⬇	
unless, if you agree,	Connector
⬇	
you are allergic to penicillin,	Rebuttals
⬇	
in which case we should choose another kind of treatment."	New claim, supported by alternative premises or statements applying to a different condition

The lower part of Figure 4.5 represents a graphical structure of this kind of modern argument.

The flowchart in Figure 4.6 illustrates this type of argument as it might be (and is) used in medicine and other health sciences. The flowchart was originally proposed for the writing and understanding of medical articles, with particular attention given to the discussion section of an article and other forms of communication.[34–36] Its principles apply to any other argument and argumentation in health sciences research and practice, as well as communication of both pinpoint and broader experience.

Let us briefly define components of this flowchart, in this exercise on argumentation, what they mean and what they do:

Definition	'What It Does': Role/Purpose/Function	Comments
1. Argument as a whole		
Structured path from an initial idea, across a series of considerations (building blocks), leading to a conclusion (claim) confirming, rejecting, or modifying the triggering thought about the problem.	Defines the problem in context (structured question, hypothesis, setting), gathers and critically appraises each argument building block with attention to a proper connection between them up to the final claim.	A journal article as a whole.
2. Problem in context or thesis		
An ensemble of statements which includes, to varying degrees, hypothesis, research question(s), setting, study objectives, and initial impression of the problem under study. A statement that addresses *'what exactly is the question'* of the argument.	Proposes an original operational and structured idea to be evaluated through an argument process.	To be meaningful and useful for interpretation, the original idea must be supported by a clear hypothesis, research question, objective(s) of the argumentation process, analysis, and evaluation. This is usually in the "Introduction" section.
3. Claim		
Conclusion drawn by the end of reasoning path (argument); the thesis drawn from or evaluated by the study. A *'what do we think about it'* statement.	Confirms or modifies the thesis initiating the argument; generates a new thesis from findings.	***Factual***: Does it exist, what is, was, or will be? ***Definitional***: What is it, how can it be classified? ***Causal***: What caused it, what will it produce? ***Value asserting***: Is it harmful or beneficial? Good or bad? ***Policy/direction giving***: What should we do? The claim is in the "Title" and at the core of the "Conclusions" of the article.

4. Grounds: (syn. **data, support**)

Data and/or information that support the claim. A *'facts and evidence'* statement.	Provides essential and direct basis for the claim.	Grounds are outlined in the "Material and Methods" and "Results" sections.

5. Backing

Information which justifies and makes explicit the warrant. Experimental and theoretical foundations from other sources. A *'given that'* statement.	Provides additional information and clarification(s) for the warrant. Justifies the move from grounds (data) to the claim. Offers cultural assumptions, support, and the theoretical basis for the warrant.	Typically in the "Literature Review" section.

6. Warrant

Explanation of how grounds support the claim; general (other) statements, assumptions, propositions bridging claim and data. Information about the arguer's reasoning. A *'general wisdom about'* statement.	Shows how grounds support the claim. Justifies the move from data and/or backing to the claim.	It may be found in several different sections of an article including "Introduction" and "Discussion" sections.

7. Rebuttals (syn. reservations)

Circumstances invalidating the claim. An *"unless"* statement.	Defines limits of the claim. Offers counter-arguments. Specifies conditions under which the claim does not apply.	Rebuttals are typically found in the "Discussion" section.

8. Qualifier (syn. modality)

The arguer's degree of belief of certainty about the claim. A *"conviction"* statement.	Quantifies strengths and limitations given by the reasoning process and its building blocks to the claim.	Uses terms and phrases like some, many, often, probably, quite, presumably, surely, definitely, almost certainly, may, with a 75% probability, etc. It is usually found in the "Conclusions" section of the article.

The **claim**, which appears in the third building block, represents the result of the argument.

Figure 4.6 represents Toulmin's model of argument with the addition of thesis and adducts entities.[36,37] It is redrawn from left → right orientation to the top ↓ bottom orientation, as flowcharts usually appear in health sciences.

Toulmin's six classical building blocks, *"organs within a living system of argument,"* as he calls them, may be completed conveniently by setting the **problem statement or thesis** within an argumentation paradigm. Pros (warrants stemming from grounds and backing speaking for conclusion) and cons (rebuttals) represent an ensemble of **adducts** within which we search for a balance of elements justifying, or not, our claim(s) or conclusion.

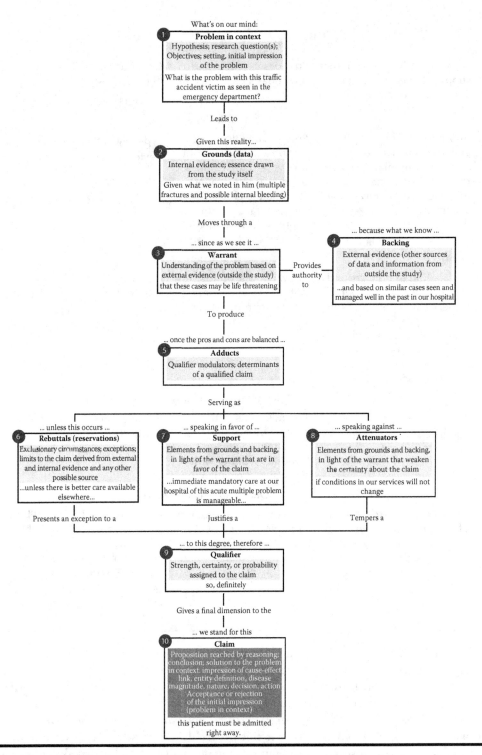

Figure 4.6 A flowchart of a medical argument. Expanded model of Toulmin's modern argument: A medical example. (Based on Figure 2.7 in Jenicek M. *A Primer on Clinical Experience in Medicine*. Boca Raton FL: CRC Press, 2013 and elements from References 36 and 37.)

As we understand from the concepts of argumentation described here, in practice, an argument is either built from some original idea (thesis) through to its conclusion (claim), or it is reconstructed retrospectively and evaluated for its validity and absence of fallacies. Reasoning this way may be either valid or invalid. Deductively valid arguments are those whose conclusions follow necessarily from their premises. Given true premises and a valid argument, the conclusion is necessarily true. Given false premises and a valid argument, the conclusion may or may not be true. The quality of the premises is derived from the argumentation that led to them through new statements and by the quality of evidence (data or information necessary for the understanding of and/or decision-making about a health problem).

Argumentations which are based on any of the above-mentioned three models work if, and only if, they are based on solid evidence underlying each premise, and if this evidence is correctly linked (inferring) to conclusions on which they are based. Any error in evidence and how it is handled through reasoning (argumentation) is a fallacy that may be prevented or corrected. An argument makes sense only if it is exercised within the framework of a well-defined problem in context or thesis.

Thesis

A **thesis** is *"a proposition stated and put forward for consideration, especially one to be discussed and proved or to be maintained against objections."*[38] Ideally, the thesis includes five components: the definition of the **problem in focus** (research or practice situation or event) itself, **objectives** to tackle the problem, **hypothesis(es)**, a research or practice **question**, as well as all necessary operational **definitions** of entities and variables of interest. In most cases, there is no meaningful discussion and argumentation without first detailing the thesis and its components.

In particular, definitions and meanings are vital to the argumentation process.[39] We devote Chapter 7 of this book to this important topic. **Context, setting, and framing** (*vide infra*) are also indispensable for any meaningful discussion.

Problem in Focus

The **problem (topic) in focus** is the health problem that you are working to solve in practice or research.

Definitions

The domain of orismology (i.e., study of definitions), provides a definition for **definitions themselves**: **Definitions** are the formal statements of the meaning and significance of entities of interest (variables, tools, conditions, settings, etc.). To be practical in medicine, definitions should be as *operational* (usable as decision-making tools), precise, and usable in practice and research as possible. Other elements of the term "definitions" include *stipulative* (coining new phenomena), lexical or *reportive* (how the word is actually used), *precising* (eliminating vagueness), *theoretical* (formulating an adequate characterization), *motivational* and *persuasive* (influencing attitudes in a rather metaphysical manner), or *essentialist* (specifying the nature of the phenomenon to which the term refers).[39]

For a health professional, entities are defined in the context of, and in comparison with, other entities in a way that makes them usable and useful. This occurs when entities

■ are clearly separated from other possibly competing entities related to the problem;
■ represent a distinct substrate, different from others;
■ are, if possible and desired, measurable and otherwise subject to quantification (counting);
■ are subject to grading (degree, direction attributing);
■ are categorizable within a classification in a specific context;
■ reflect and relate to a specific decision about an action to be taken;
■ have operational inclusion and exclusion criteria which distinguish such an entity from others; and
■ are mutually understood, hence warranting reproduction, repetition, and re-use.

Regardless of how we deal with the problem of interest, definitions establish whether our understanding and approach of the issue is good, bad, usable, or meaningless. They deserve, and are considered, in a special chapter in this book (Chapter 7).

As an example, where a definition of evidence-based medicine (EBM) as *"the conscientious, explicit and judicious use of current best evidence in making decisions about the care of individual patients"*[40] may be an excellent motivational definition, but if we do not define "evidence" in context, as well as conscientious, explicit, judicious use and **best** evidence, can the reader say, in operational terms, who is a practitioner of EBM and who is not? Can they determine what EBM ultimately is and what it is not? We doubt it.[41]

Elsewhere, for example, saying that "our medicine *is about*" rather than "our medicine *is*" may be read by some as avoiding its definition of itself. In the new domain of knowledge translation, there are so many definitions of definitions that they merit a regroupment, realignment, and update.[42] Definitions are a strategic resource for the arguer. They are ideally clear enough to avoid common fallacies of meaning[19] like vagueness, equivocation (the same word having different meanings in the same argument), and others.[17]

Persuasive definitions are a way to slant, or skew, arguments to gain a particular advantage. Persuasive definitions often alter the meaning of a term by associating it with a term of clear positive or negative connotation. They may or may not be based on evidence. ("That's what they call it and how they do it at 'the other' hospital!") Stipulative and operational definitions are better.

Framing

In the **social sciences and psychology, framing** is the construction of a social phenomenon by mass media or specific political or by social movements and organizations.[30] It is considered an inevitable process of selective influence over an individual's perception of the meanings attributed to words and phrases. Health activities, care, and programs and medical information are and may be subject to framing. Rhetoric is used to encourage certain interpretations and discourage others in journals, books, or even the spoken word. Defining, structuring, and interpreting medical research is a necessary subject of framing which allows, preferably in an unbiased way the "frame" within which a research finding applies (setting, human context, applicability, etc.). It may then be good or bad.

In medicine, defining health problems in the context of the target population (patients, community, etc.), prevailing or specific practices of clinical and community care, or social, political, economical, spiritual (faith) environments means building and specifying a 'frame' within which our views of health problems and events are valid.

In epidemiology, expressing specificity of a causal association in terms of risk differences (absolute risk difference, attributable risk), etiological fractions (attributable risk percent, relative risk reduction), and ensuing interpretation of the importance of findings may depend on how the meaning of each measure is "framed." An absolute measure may be interpreted and considered more important for ensuing practical and research interpretations and decisions than its relative equivalent, and vice versa.

Hypotheses

Our **hypotheses** are propositions to be evaluated, accepted or refuted in light of clinical experience with the case or problem or by a research study.

A hypothesis is a testable proposition to be accepted or rejected, which is built on operational definitions of phenomena as dependent and independent variables to observe and explain.

In epidemiology, a hypothesis is a proposed explanation of epidemiological phenomena, provisionally accepted, until submitted for re-evaluation by an appropriate analytical study; such a proposition is then accepted or rejected by the study in question.

Research and Practice Questions

Questions for clinical or research problem solving[31–34] offer, in various combinations and completeness from case to case, specifications about the:

- *Population* under consideration (in the study and/or beyond the study);
- *Intervention* (treatment, care);
- *Condition* of interest (disease stage, spectrum, gradient, etc.);
- *Controls* when comparisons are made for the sake of interpretations;
- *Outcomes* (possible results);
- **Setting** (specifics about the clinical care human and physical environment); and
- *Time frame* (interval within the course of disease, period over which patients will be followed and studied, etc.).[31]

Initially proposed for use when conducting systematic reviews of evidence, this acronym, **PICCOST** or **PoCICOST** (population, condition of interest, intervention, controls, outcomes, setting, timeframe) and its abbreviated version of **PICO** (population, intervention, conditions, outcomes) identifies meaningful practical and research questions that should be raised in original research studies and practice questions. Initially proposed for systematic reviews of evidence, these models apply equally to questions raised in original research studies and to questions in practice.

All research and practice questions are not created equal. Here are some questions that may be asked, and our assessment of their utility.

1. *"Is this antithrombotic treatment good for you? Ask your Doctor!"* This is a kind of question used in television advertising to reach the largest audience. Let us leave it there and not use it.
2. *"Does antithrombotic treatment do well for patients?"* The least specific and most general question. This is an example of a PC question that reflects the population and condition, but not detailed enough to render a truly useful answer.
3. *"In patients surviving myocardial infarction, does antithrombotic therapy decrease the risk of myocardial re-infarction and death?"* This is an example of a PICO question. It contains the population (patients), the intervention (antithrombotic therapy), condition (myocardial infarction), and outcome (risk of myocardial re-infarction and death).
4. *"In patients discharged from our hospital (Po) after myocardial infarction (C), does antithrombotic therapy (I) in comparison to similar patients who do not receive it (C) improve survival and prevent re-infarction and stroke (O) when such a program is implemented in our hospital and regional clinics (S) over a period of one, five and ten years (T)?"* This is an example, with all its rich detail and precision, of a PoCICOST question.

The components of research questions vary with the nature of the problem and clinical considerations and circumstances. The fourth question is the most "scientific," specifying as much as possible to what and to whom it applies. Let us also note that this more concrete kind of question is most often used for the study of cause-effect relationships. Questions about the validity of diagnostic tests, about disease occurrence (descriptive) studies and elsewhere should contain all relevant components (PICO or more) in various combinations of the above.

Objectives

Objectives are points to be reached in practical clinical problem solving or in research, either **specific** to the problem or **general**, encompassing a broader context into which the problem belongs. For example, we wish to evaluate the effectiveness of vein stenting (or "liberation") to alleviate symptoms of patients suffering from multiple sclerosis (a specific objective of a defined activity) and contribute to the control of the severity of cases of multiple sclerosis (a general objective for the problem of multiple sclerosis as a whole). A thesis or theses are essential in order to evaluate the extent to which an argument is grounded in evidence. An argument may be formally valid *per se*, but not necessarily solid, meaningful, or based on evidence.

Essential building blocks for argumentation already exist, but are disguised in various medical articles and in clinical reasoning in medical practice. Considering a journal article, the thesis may be found in the "Introduction," grounds in "Material," "Methods," and "Results sections," backing and warrant in the "Review of the Literature and Discussion," and rebuttals in the "Discussion." The claim often appears in the *Title* itself and in the *Conclusions* of the article.[22–24]

Currently, there is no formal rule regarding where Toulmin's original argument building blocks should be found. They are typically scattered in bits and pieces across the introduction, material and methods, results, and discussion (IMRAD) and phrased in natural language.

In the following table (Table 4.1), the phrases in the first column, are and should be supported by argument building blocks. In any dialogue or written communication, consider stating, explaining, and supporting them.

Table 4.1 Natural Language Argument Building Blocks/Indicators and Corresponding Argument Building Blocks

Phrase as Argument Building Block/Indicators	*Argument Building Block*
What is on your mind…	Refers briefly to your **problem in context.**
…given the reality of…	Presents your **grounds** as found in the internal evidence, data, or essence drawn from the study itself.
…since as we see it…	The **warrant** reflects your overall view of the problem under study, your understanding of the problem based on external evidence (outside the study).
…because what we know…	The **backing** describes what you have done to tackle the issue already, found partly in the literature review.
…once pros and cons are balanced…	**Adducts, qualifiers,** and **modulators** are determinants of your qualified claim found in the findings of the study. These are your expressions of the degree of certainty (and uncertainty) in your claim.
…unless this occurs…	The **rebuttals** are your reservations and the exclusionary conditions under which the conclusions of your study do not apply. For example, therapeutic contraindications may be set in this category.
…speaking in favor of…	Selected elements from grounds, etc., that briefly restate **support** for your findings.
…speaking against…	**Attenuators** are how pros and cons are balanced. These include elements from the grounds and backing, in light of the warrant, that weaken the certainty about the claim.
…to this degree, therefore…	In terms of your **qualifier**, your certainty about your claim, your conclusion.
…we stand for this.	These are the conclusions of your study and article, your **claim.** They include the proposition reached, impression of cause-effect link, effectiveness of intervention, entity definition, disease magnitude, nature of the problem, decision, and recommended action.

In informal discussions and conversations throughout our practice—at floor rounds, chatting more informally with colleagues, at the round tables, at lectures, and elsewhere—we use a similar language. Table 4.2 shows how argumentation is "hidden" in the natural language of communication between clinicians in daily life on hospital floors.

Toulmin's argumentation is so attractive and appropriate in medicine because it follows a line of thought that is similar both to the scientific method and reasoning in medical practice and research. In forthcoming chapters, Toulmin's model of argumentation backed by the best specific and general evidence available is discussed as it applies not only to clinical and community medicine research, but also to various ways of reasoning and its communication whether that is through dialogues

Table 4.2 Daily Communication of an Argumentative Nature between Clinicians in Natural Language in a Hospital Setting

Question	Statement	Component of the Argument
Attending: *"I was told that you had a busy morning here. Any new admissions at our floor?"*	**Resident:** *"Yes, we admitted an elderly lady with chest pain."*	***Original idea, problem in context:*** Setting of the problem to be solved.
Attending: *"What led you to admit her?"*	**Resident:** *"Well, the senior resident told me to do so! But more seriously, this patient was transferred to us from the emergency room with a working diagnosis of myocardial infarction."*	***Claim:*** Proposition resulting from our reasoning.
Attending: *"What brought you to this diagnosis and treatment and care orders?"*	**Resident:** *"In the past, this patient had some unchecked chest pains, but this time, her pain radiated to both arms, she had low systolic blood pressure, and we heard a third heart sound on auscultation. On the ECG, we saw a new ST segment elevation, a new Q wave and a new conduction defect."*	***Grounds:*** Basis from which we reason and argue. Facts supporting the claim.
Resident: *"I would like to know if they are any steps that I must follow in future similar cases."*	**Attending:** *"In this and similar cases of myocardial infarction, especially if confirmed by ECG, MRI, serum cardiac enzymes, we give aspirin and clopidogrel, start thrombolytic treatment, and consider coronary angiography and stenting."*	***Warrant:*** General rule that permits us to infer a claim from grounds.
Resident: *"How sure are we that this kind of treatment and care will work?"*	**Attending:** *"All our past experience in this hospital, and several critically reviewed studies and their systematic reviews of outcomes in patients treated this way, give us a high level of confidence, if not almost a certainty, that this kind of care works and it should in this patient."*	***Backing:*** Body of experience and evidence which supports the warrant. AND ***Qualifier:*** A word or phrase that indicates the strength conferred by the warrant and thus the strength of support for our conclusion.

Resident: *"Are there any additional or alternative problems and treatments which we should keep in mind?"*	**Attending**: *"Chest pain as originally seen in this patient may occur and be confounded with manifestations of pericarditis, pulmonary embolism, esophageal perforation, aortic dissection among several other problems to exclude. These other problems should be ruled out."*	***Rebuttals***: Differential diagnosis to consider as a possible exclusionary condition and criterion for other management of this kind of patients.
Resident: *"So, if we successfully rule out all those other problems, does it look like we did the right thing?"*	**Attending**: *"You definitely did! Yes, this is a case of myocardial infarction which required the clinical management you proposed and ordered."*	**Conclusion of the argument.** ***Claim***: Proposition at which we arrive as a result of our reasoning and which we defend in the argument by citing all supporting elements and argument building blocks.

Source: Revised from Reference 43.

between colleagues, progress notes in patients' charts, discussing cases on morning reports, morbidity and mortality review meetings, consults, or discharge notes. Let us keep it in mind.

Modern reasoning, critical thinking and argumentation are becoming relevant well beyond health sciences and professions. For this broad framework, Hitchcock proposes critical thinking as an educational ideal for all.[44]

4.1.4 Reminder Regarding Some Additional and Fundamental Considerations

Is our correct reasoning and argumentation important to maintain and improve the quality of care, patient safety and understanding, and prevention and control of medical error and harm? Yes, it is.

A well thought out and reasoned argumentation process is important to maintain and improve the quality of patient care, patient safety and understanding, and prevention and control of medical error and harm. However, we also need to use the critical foundations of our medical training and the diagnostic, therapeutic, or prognostic processes in tandem with the argumentation process. Indeed, these two should be the foundation of our cognitive and decision-making processes.

To understand this even better, let us start with the practical example of an internist who examines a patient suffering from coronary heart disease. The internist is faced with the dilemma of pursuing the conservative (medical) treatment of coronary pathology and dysfunction, to refer the patient to invasive cardiologists for angioplasty, or to surgeons for coronary bypass surgery. Where errors might occur and how should they be prevented?

The two processes—an argument and argumentation process based on evidences and that of a step-by-step review of our diagnostic, therapeutic, or prognostic processes both for short- and long-term care—must work in concert. Here's how:

1. A decision such as "This patient must be transferred to surgery" can be considered a conclusion or claim (as philosophers say) of the **argumentation process** using evidence of all kinds. Errors may occur not only due to the use of poor evidence or failures to use good evidence from one step of argumentation to another, but also due to how various components are linked together on the way to conclusions and recommendations. The argumentation process and model apply to practically all steps and stages of clinical practice and health and community care.

2. The additional, more specific, **cognition pathways in various clinical practices and components of care** must be recognized in the development of any necessary steps in risk assessment, from their original triggers to their final understanding and ensuing decisions to be considered. The diagnostic process, treatment plan workup, or prognosis with its ensuing short- and long-term actions in care, will be explored in greater detail in Chapter 5. Errors in any of these steps may cause numerous incidents and their consequences.

A step-by-step evaluation of both argumentation and cognition processes must contribute to improvements in the medical error domain. These processes are used at each of the following steps in medical care and may be summarized as follows:

Accumulation of evidence
Acquired knowledge and basic understanding, structured or unstructured, derived from history, literature, physical and paraclinical examination, and past experience.

Reasoning about the case, problem or situation
Structured acquisition of **new knowledge** achieved through differential diagnosis, final diagnosis, and co-morbidity assessment.

Decision-making
Medical, surgical, psychiatric, and other orders and plans for care.

Sensorimotor execution of medical acts
These may include operations, invasive diagnostic procedures, physiotherapy, parenteral applications of drugs, new technologies, implantation of devices, etc.

Getting results
Results may be positive or adverse, or both.

Evaluation
Of all the preceding steps, one-by-one and the entire process;
successes, errors, failures.

Prognosis and further risk assessment
Includes morbidity, co-morbidity, and further outcomes.

Follow-up, surveillance
Forecasting risk factors and markers, prognostic factors and markers, possible outcomes, errors and failures.

Modern argumentation and argument are the foundations of evidence, reasoning and decision-making that is grounded in clinical epidemiology and critical thinking, through this is not always understood. Flawed argumentation and reasoning tends to generate errors and harm, whereas correct argumentation tends to contribute to the quality of medical care and patient safety. In **lathology** (the study and management of error and harm in medicine and other health sciences),[13] knowing, understanding and avoiding fallacies, biases, and cognitive errors eliminate some potential sources of harm that may occur as a result of our reasoning and decision-making. An exhaustive list of biases as flaws in research is beyond the scope of this text but can be found in the literature cited here and paired with more general lists of cognitive biases found elsewhere.[13]

4.2 Directionality of Reasoning: Inductive, Deductive, and Abductive Ways

In epidemiology, the search for causes of disease and illness may be carried out in several ways.[17,41,42] Inductive,[45] deductive,[46–53] and abductive[54–61] reasoning are used both in health research and practice. Understanding the different reasoning processes is necessary to select the best and most appropriate process for different practice and research scenarios.

Inductive Reasoning

In the world of reasoning, **induction** refers to the act of reasoning from the particular to the general. Providing that we define 'massive stroke' well, we may reason: *"Patient A died from a massive stroke. Patient B also died from a massive stroke. More massive stroke victims so far died from massive strokes. Therefore, massive stroke is most probably lethal for all people."*

Induction is also referred to as **enumerative induction**, which may have the following form:[62]

X percent of <u>observed</u> members of group A have property P.
Therefore, X percent of <u>all</u> the members of group A have property P.

Inductive research means using existing information and data, collected for whatever purpose, to generate and/or confirm a hypothesis. In another words, a hypothesis is generated through pre-established facts, data, and information. Sometimes, the derogatory expression *"milking and dredging"* of data is used to describe inductive research. However, despite its limitations, it is often the only available approach. Inductive research can often lead to what philosophers call **inductive reasoning**, in which premises bring only a *limited degree of support* to a study's conclusions.

Deductive Reasoning

Deduction refers to the act of reasoning from the general to the particular. For example, we may reason that *"If all elderly patients who suffer from a massive stroke die, then this elderly patient, who is a victim of a massive stroke, will die."* This kind of argument follows the form of a classical categorical syllogism:

If phenomenon P then phenomenon Q.
Phenomenon P.
Therefore, phenomenon Q.

As an example:

All men are mortal.
Socrates is a man.
Therefore, Socrates is mortal.

(N.B. Given what was said, it cannot be otherwise.)

Deductive research works in an opposite direction to inductive research: a general principle or hypothesis is used as a starting point for data collection, analysis and interpretation in order to confirm or refute this principle. The hypothesis is formulated first on the basis of past experience, independent of the planned research. The study (data collection, analysis, and interpretation) is planned to confirm or refute the hypothesis.

Deductive research should lead more often (at least theoretically) to **deductive reasoning** in which a conclusion (finding) is *definitely true if the premises are true*. A study as a deductive argument provides (at least theoretically) the *absolute support* for study findings (conclusions). The study as a logical argument is deductively valid.

Abductive Reasoning and Inference

Some aspects of argumentation, reasoning, or scientific method in general are also **induction and deduction**, and are not the only pathways to the best explanations. Abduction is another one, considered by many as **inference in general.** For epidemiologists, inference means *the process of logical reasoning that combines observed phenomena with accepted truths or axioms in order to formulate generalizable statements.*[63]

We owe the concept and development of the abduction domain to the founder of American pragmatism, Charles Sanders Peirce (1839–1914). He considered deduction, induction, and abduction as phases or stages of a scientific method of inquiry.

Abduction,[54–61] also called **hypothetical induction,**[62] means *"inference to the best* *explanation*." In abductive reasoning, a number of facts from a multitude of sources, such as general observations, original studies, systematic and unsystematic reviews literature reviews, and syntheses are gathered together as a starting point for research to examine what might be the most likely hypothesis to explain an event, situation, or occurrence. Hence, in abduction, a hypothesis is searched for that would best explain the available evidence. Proposed for public health, abduction is *a method of reasoning that arrives at the most logical inference after considering all the available evidence, and then decides which solution is the best fit.* Abduction is used in artificial intelligence and is (among others) the basis for evidence-based diagnosis.

For Schick,[62] a general form of abductive reasoning is:

Phenomena $\underline{P}$.
Hypothesis $\underline{H}$ explains $\underline{P}$.
No other hypothesis explains $\underline{P}$ as well as $\underline{H}$.
Therefore, it's **probable** that $\underline{H}$ is true.

In Walton's[61] wording:

Generally, if event A occurs, then event B will (might) occur.
In this case, event A occurs (might occur).
Therefore, in this case, event B will (might) occur.

For example, we may reason that "*This child lives in a poor community and environment and our pediatric patient comes from such an environment. Most of such children living in such conditions and environment are prone to malnutrition. Hence our patient may be malnourished.*" The conclusion is logically compatible, but not certain. Table 4.3 summarizes some conceptual characteristics of deductive, inductive, and abductive approaches to reasoning.

Abductive reasoning is a subject of current refinements and developments in research, medical research included. Wells, in exploring clinical thinking in psychiatry, explores how important and appropriate these three types of reasoning (deduction, induction, and abduction) are in medicine and in psychiatry in particular.[62]

Statistical and Causal Inference

Like reasoning, **statistical inference** applies a process to a series of observations and, instead of merely identifying a claim or conclusion as a result of the observations, calculates degrees of uncertainty in comparisons of various data sets. In contrast, **causal inference** is the thought process and methods that assess or test whether a relation of cause to effect does or does not exist.

In medicine, we infer in one of two directions. Either from observing individuals and applying experience from these experiences to the whole problem represented from those individuals, or by seeing how individual patient's problems fit with what we already know about groups of similar patient, the medical care, and the disease they represent. In the former, classical or field epidemiologists often infer from the perspective of observing the characteristics of patients one by one to establish the picture of disease they represent, or by studying disease outbreaks or occurrence in the community.

Figure 4.7 illustrates these two strategies and directions of reasoning. Both are necessary for good understanding and decision-making.

Table 4.3 Conceptual Differences between Deductive, Inductive, and Abductive Approaches to Reasoning

Deductive Reasoning 'Top-Down Logic'	Inductive Reasoning 'Bottom-Up Logic'	Abductive Reasoning 'Inference to the Best Explanation'
Process of reasoning starting from one or more statements (premises) to reach a logically certain conclusion.[49,50] The conclusion is necessarily true provided the premises are true.	The conclusion of the reasoning process is reached by generalizing and extrapolating starting from specific cases and proceeding to general rules.[49,50] The conclusion is only probable.	Logical inference starts with an observation and proceeds to a theory that offers the simplest and most likely explanation for the observation. Unlike in deductive reasoning, the premises do not guarantee the conclusion; it is an inference to the best explanation.
Starting from the general and proceeding to the specific. Proposing a theory or hypothesis(es) and then conducting research in order to test whether the hypothesis(es) can be proven true with specific cases.	Starting from specific (premises, observations) and proceeding to general or broader generalizations (conclusions).	Reasoning that starts from a set of accepted facts and inferring to explanations that are considered most likely or best.
A conclusion is reached reductively by applying general rules that remain consistent over the entirety of a closed domain of discourse.	Data is collected and through observation, patterns of meaning can be extracted.	Further testable *a priori* adoption of a hypothesis as explanation for observed facts results according to known laws. A hypothesis is adopted, and tested, as explanation of observed facts that follow from known laws.
Developing a theory or conclusion first, then working to find evidence that supports or dismisses that theory or conclusion. A general principle or hypothesis is used as a starting point for data collection, analysis, and interpretation in order to confirm or refute a pre-established hypothesis. Deduction proceeds from general to the particular.	A reasoning that derives general principles from specific observations.	A reasoning based on the overall acquired experience in view of the best direction of further research and inquiry.

Deduction means determining the *conclusion*	*Induction* means determining the *rule*.[59]	*Abduction* means determining the *precondition*.
Example of a deductive argument: *Every person who is not immunized against this disease will acquire it. This patient is not immunized, so he/she will get this disease.*	**Example of an inductive argument:** *Based on past experience, every non-immunized person who was also exposed to the agent of infection has got this disease. Therefore, each such person today is at risk for getting this disease.*	**Example of an abductive argument:** *This patient comes from a community that is unprotected by immunization. Most patients living in such a community risk acquiring this disease. Hence, our patient may be unprotected by immunization and risks acquiring this disease.*
Deductive argument: If P then Q. P. Therefore, Q.	**Inductive argument:** If Q then P. P. Therefore, P.	**Hypothetical induction (abduction):** Phenomena P. Hypothesis H explains P. No other hypothesis explains P as well as H. Therefore, it's probable that H is true.[65]
Rule: All men are mortal (P), *Case:* Socrates is a man (Q), *Conclusion:* Therefore, Socrates is a mortal.	*Case:* Socrates is a man (P). *Case:* Socrates is mortal (P). *Conclusion:* Therefore, all men are mortal (P).	*Rule:* All men are mortal (P). *Case:* Socrates is mortal (H). *Conclusion:* Therefore, Socrates is a man (Q).[70]

Source: Selected and compiled from References 45–63.

Let Us Conclude

Whether in clinical practice or research, thinking processes in medicine have two purposes: understanding the nature of the health problem and deciding what to do to solve it. Philosophers' principles, methods, and ways of critical thinking in general are extremely well adapted to thinking and reasoning in the health sciences. Epidemiologists, biostatisticians, health economists, and clinical specialists have developed many original contributions which are crucial for all pragmatic purposes. Our reasoning is geared toward concrete decision-making and actions whose course and results we are responsible for as health professionals.

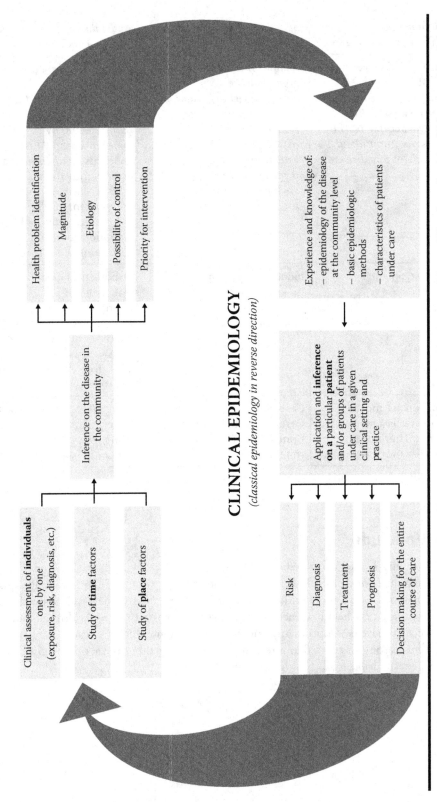

Figure 4.7 Directions of reasoning in fundamental and clinical epidemiology. (Redrawn with modifications from Jenicek M. *Epidemiology. The Logic of Modern Medicine*. Montreal: EPIMED International, 1995. Reproduced with permission.)

> Logicians are often interested primarily in the purity of argumentation and thinking processes themselves. In medicine, even the best argumentative process must be first be based on what is best for the stated purpose. Evidence-based medicine joins critical thinking and evolves into a kind of **evidence-based critical thinking (argumentation) grounded medicine.**

The experience and practice of others, including the military arts and business, is enriching critical thinking and reasoning in the health sciences. We must be open to developments from other fields, and to adapt them in a well-structured way to better manage and understand health problems. In fact, medicine is also a health business battlefield where beyond health economics, our care and its outcomes must take into account the money that passes between the health producer, supplier, and provider (health professionals, hospitals, medical offices or community medicine, and public health units, etc.) and the consumer, patients, and our community.

For lawyers, judges, and expert witnesses in courts of law, pleading for a health cause is (and should be) an exercise in argumentation and critical thinking as it has been outlined here for health sciences. In this diversity of experience, we cannot insist enough on clear, usable and operational definitions of what we see and do. Again, orismology helps. For example:

- An **evidence-based medicine practitioner** may define **evidence as** *"Any data or information, whether solid or weak, obtained through experience, observational research or experimental work (clinical or field trials), relevant to some degree (more is better) either to the **understanding** of the problem (case) or to the clinical and community medicine **decisions** made about the case (meaning clinical case or the community health problem to solve)."*[17]
- A **public health practitioner** considers evidence as *"The assembled information and facts on which rational, logical decisions are based in diverse forums of human discourse, including courts of law, ands in the practice of evidence-based medicine among many others."*[64]
- A **philosopher/critical thinker**, sees evidence as *"The data on which a judgment or conclusion might be based or by which proof or probability might be established ... something to prove."*[6]
- **lawyers**, as might be expected, understand evidence as *"Information and things pertaining to the events that are the subject of an investigation or a case: especially, the testimony or objects (but not the questions or comments of the lawyers) offered at a trial or hearing for the judge or the jury to consider in deciding the issue in a case."*[65]

Today developments of **grading evidence in evidence-based** medicine[66] are based most often on the validity of different types of studies as cause-effect proofs, from the least convincing to the most convincing: from narratives, single case observations, case series (no denominators, no control groups), to observational analytical studies (cohort studies, case control studies), and experimental studies (clinical trials, etc.), and finally, the most convincing, systematic reviews, meta-analyses, and otherwise synthesized experimental and clinical experience and research of observational analytical or experimental experience from multiple studies.

Grading the level of evidence remains for the moment an unfinished topic, and the subject of further development, refinement, and expansion. In various versions, the following 'pyramid of evidence' can be found across the current literature:

Synopses
Meta-analyses
and systematic reviews
Experimental studies (clinical trials)
Observational analytical cohort studies
Observational analytical case control studies
Observational descriptive studies of occurrence
Single clinical case reports and case series reports
Hearsays, anecdotes, narratives, plain ideas, opinions, quotes

This hierarchy of evidence may be valid for cause-effect relationships and their approaches to establishing proof, but other domains requiring evidence may call for another kind of "pyramid" or "hierarchy" of proof. For example, what might a hierarchy of evidence be for physical examination whenever the presence and absence of disease causing a test result is not of primary interest?

Grading the evidence for types of research other than causal relationships between noxious or beneficial factors in relation to health or disease requires a different approach. Besides etiological considerations, any grading must have some sense and practical purpose for decision-making. Ideally, any stage in a grading system must differ from the other by expanding the understanding, changing the understanding (different meanings like different prognosis or differential diagnosis), or modifying clinical decisions (treatment indications). Staging cancer in these terms is well established; staging evidence is still more challenging in these practical terms.

We must always find some mutually acceptable language to assess levels of evidence, or to specify differences between the participating professions and domains, from one situation to another. The same holds true for example for a "case" and, in clinical medicine, for any noxious or beneficial factor and their outcomes, disease signs or symptoms, or the disease itself, its diagnosis or remedial clinical actions (treatments), and their outcomes.

Besides the evidence used in argumentation, the value and relevance of the entire argumentative process depends on its **conceptual framework** or "**framing.**"[67] Within such a framework, we are always defining the problem and its biological and physical setting, raising hypotheses about what's going on, specifying objectives regarding what we intend to do or how we intend to intervene, and at what outcome we wish to arrive in general and specific terms and dimensions. *Our reasoning, understanding, decisions, and actions only have meaning and value if such a framework is determined and known, preferably beforehand*. Last but not least, our reasoning and decision-making must remain free of fallacies which is also a learned experience.

In the chapters that follow, we will see how our ways of reasoning and decision-making apply to various steps and stages of clinical practice and care. These include assessing risk in patients (communities), making diagnosis, choosing and administering treatment, assessing patient outcomes (prognosis), and establishing follow-up and long-term care for individuals under our responsibility. Some other topics that will be reviewed and are relevant to medicine as art and science biological and social phenomena. In biology, these phenomena are most often subject of variability, uncertainty, and probability than in more exact sciences like physics or chemistry, particularly:

■ selected cornerstones which define research and practice as well;
■ definitions for uses in research and practice;
■ causality or determination of cause-effect relationships; and
■ medical error and harm.

The health of our patients and of our community, as well as all the best future developments in healthcare and research, should benefit from initiatives in the above domains. Our best possible ways of thinking are essential for these purposes. Some philosophical and other aspects of today's thinking in medicine, bridging philosophical and clinical experience will definitely prove useful. For example, Wells[63] proposed his approach for psychiatry recently, but his reflections are also valid for many other domains and specialties of medicine.

The rest depends on us.

References

1. Hughes W and Lavery J. *Critical Thinking. An Introduction to the Basic Skills.* 5th Edition. Peterborough, ON and Buffalo, NY: Broadview Press, 2008.
2. Horton R. The grammar of interpretive medicine. *CMAJ (Can Med Ass J)*, 1998;159:245–9.
3. Huth EJ. *Writing and Publishing in Medicine.* 3rd Edition. Baltimore: Williams & Wilkins, 1999.
4. Bloom BS. *Taxonomy of Educational Objectives.* Boston: Allyn and Bacon, 1956.
5. Jenicek M and Hitchcock DL. *Evidence-Based Practice. Logic and Critical Thinking in Medicine.* Chicago: American Medical Association (AMA Press), 2005.
6. Elder L and Paul R. *A Glossary of Critical Thinking Terms and Concepts. The Critical Analytic Vocabulary of the English Language.* Dillon Beach, CA: The Foundation for Critical Thinking, 2009.
7. Paul R and Elder L. *The Miniature Guide to Critical Thinking. Concepts and Tools.* Dillon Beach, CA: Foundation for Critical Thinking Press, 2009.
8. Hawkins D, Elder L, Paul R. *The Thinkers Guide to Clinical Reasoning.* Based on *Critical Thinking Concepts and Tools.* Dillon Beach, CA: The Foundation for Critical Thinking Press, 2010.
9. ChangingMinds.org. *Types of Reasoning.* Variable p. at http://changingminds.org/disciplines/argument/types_reasoning/types_reasoning.htm, retrieved Nov 4, 2009.
10. Ziegelmueller G, Kay J, Dause C. *Argumentation: Inquiry and Advocacy.* 2nd Edition. Englewood Cliffs, NJ: Prentice Hall, 1990.
11. Rieke RD, Sillars MO, Peterson TR. *Argumentation and Critical Decision-Making.* 6th Edition. Boston, MA/New York/San Francisco, CA: Pearson Education Inc., 2005.
12. Agency for Healthcare Research and Quality (AHRQ), U.S. Department of Health & Human Services. *Glossary.* 31 p. at http://www.wbmm.ahrq.gov/popup_gov/glossary.aspx, retrieved Jan 3, 2009, and 30 p. at http://www.wbmm.ahrq.gov/glossary.aspx, retrieved July 7, 2009.
13. Jenicek M. *Medical Error and Harm. Understanding, Prevention, and Control.* Boca Raton, FL/London/New York: CRC Press/Taylor & Francis/Productivity Press, 2011.
14. Institute of Medicine, Committee on Quality of Health Care in America. *To Err is Human. Building a Safer Health System.* Edited by LT Kohn, JM Corrigan, and MS Donaldson. Washington, DC: National Academy Press, 2000.
15. Wikipedia, the free encyclopedia. *Medical Error.* 15 p. at https://en.wikipedia.org/wiki/Medical_eror, retrieved Dec 30, 2016.

16. Dowden B. *The Internet Encyclopedia of Philosophy. Fallacies.* 44 p. at http://www.iep.utm.edu/f /fallacy.htm, retrieved Oct 31, 2006.
17. Jenicek M. *Foundations of Evidence-Based Medicine.* Boca Raton, FL/London/New York/Washington, DC: The Parthenon Publishing Group/CRC Press, 2003.
18. Jenicek M. *Fallacy-Free Reasoning in Medicine. Improving Communication and Decision-Making in Research and Practice.* Chicago: American Medical Association (AMA Press), 2009.
19. Wikipedia, the free encyclopedia. *List of Fallacies.* 12 p. at https://en.wikipedia.org/wiki/List_of _fallacies, retrieved Jan 10, 2017.
20. Weblog: *Fallacy Files.* (Condon J, Karger G et al.). 15 p. at http://www.org/glossary.html, retrieved Jan 3, 2017.
21. *The Nizkor Project. Fallacies,* 2 p. of the content of site (see the index), at http://www.nizkor.org /features/fallacies, retrieved Jan 4, 2017.
22. *Stephen's Guide to the Logical Fallacies.* Brandon, Manitoba, Canada, 1995–2001. 2 p. at http://www .onegoodmove.org/fallacy/copyrite.htm, retrieved Jan 4, 2017.
23. THESECULARWEB. *Logic & Fallacies. Constructing a Logical Argument (1997).* Mathew. 21 p. at https://infidelsa.org/library/modern/mathew/logic.html, retrieved Jan 15, 2017.
24. Zarefsky D. *Argumentation: The Study of Effective Reasoning.* The Transcript Book, 2nd Edition. Chantilly, VA: The Great Courses/The Teaching Company, 2005.
25. Krishna R, Maithereyi R, Surapaneni KM. Research bias: A review for medical students. *J Clin Diag Res,* 2010(4, April):2320–4.
26. CMPA—Overcoming bias in medical practice. Duties and responsibilities, expectations of physicians in practice. (Originally published Dec 2012,P1205-3-E). 3p. at https://www.cmpa-acpm.ca/-/overcoming-bias -in-medical-practice, retrieved Jan 15, 2017.
27. Wikipedia, the free encyclopedia. *Bias.* 14 p. at https://en.wikipedia/org/wiki/Bias, retrieved Jan 14, 2017.
28. Wikipedia, the free encyclopedia. *List of Cognitive Biases.* 19 p. at https://en.wikipedia.org/wiki/List _of_cognitive biases, retrieved Dec 30, 2017.
29. First10EM. Cognitive errors in medicine: The common errors. A four part series. 34 p. at https://first 10em.com/2015/09/15/cognitive-errors/, retrieved Dec 30, 2016.
30. Smith R. *Aristotle's Logic.* In: *Stanford Encyclopedia of Philosophy, Fall 2004 Edition.* Edited by EN Zalta. At http://plato.stanford.edu/entries/Aristotle-logic, retrieved Dec 2004.
31. Zarefsky D. *Argumentation: The Study of Effective Reasoning.* The Transcript Book, 2nd Edition. Chantilly, VA: The Great Courses/The Teaching Company, 2005.
32. Toulmin SE. *The Uses of Argument.* Cambridge: Cambridge University Press, 1958. (Updated Edition 2003).
33. Toulmin S, Rieke R, Janik A. *An Introduction to Reasoning.* 2nd Edition. New York: Collier Macmillan, 1984.
34. Jenicek M. How to read, understand, and write 'Discussion' sections in medical articles. An exercise in critical thinking. *Med Sci Monit,* 2006;12(6):SR28–SR36.
35. Jenicek M. Writing a 'Discussion' section in a medical article: An exercise in critical thinking and argumentation. Chapter 27, pp. 457–65 in: *Biomedical Research. From Ideation to Publication.* Edited by G Jagadeesh, S Murthy, YK Gupta, and A Prakash. New Delhi/Philadelphia, PA/London: Wolters Kluwer Health 0(India)/Lippincott/Williams & Wilkins, 2010.
36. Jenicek M. *A Physician's Self-Paced Guide to Critical Thinking.* Chicago: American Medical Association (AMA Press), 2006.
37. Jenicek M. *Fallacy-Free Reasoning in Medicine. Improving Communication and Decision-Making in Research and Practice.* Chicago: American Medical Association (AMA Press), 2009.
38. *Random House Webster's Unabridged Dictionary 3.0.* Electronic edition on CD. Antwerpen: Random House Inc., 1998 and 2003.
39. Hughes W and Lavery J. Meaning and definition. Pp. 33–60 in: *Critical Thinking: An Introduction to Basic Skills.* 4th Edition. Peterborough, ON and Orchard Park, NY: Broadview Press, 2004.

40. Sackett DL, Rosenberg WMC, Muir Gray JA, Haynes RB, Richardson WS. Evidence based medicine: What it is and what it isn't. *BMJ*, 1996;312(Jan 13):71–2. Doi:10.1136bmj.312.7023.71. (Published 13 January 1996.)

41. Jenicek M. Evidence-Based medicine: Fifteen years later. Golem the good, the bad and the ugly in the need of a review? *Med Sci Monit*, 2006;12(11):RA241–RA251.

42. Jenicek M. *Epidemiology. The Logic of Modern Medicine*. Montréal: EPIMED International, 1995.

43. Jenicek M. *A Primer on Clinical Experience in Medicine. Reasoning, Decision-Making, and Communication in health Sciences*. Boca Raton, FL/London/New York: CRC Press/Productivity Press (Taylor & Francis Group), 2013.

44. Critical thinking as an educational ideal. Pp. 529–31 in: Hitchcock DL. *On Reasoning and Argument: Essays in Informal Logic and on Critical Thinking*. Dordrecht, NL: Springer, 2017.

45. Wikipedia, the free encyclopedia. *Inductive Reasoning*. 8 p. at https://en.wikipedia.org/wiki/Inductive_reasoning, retrieved May 9, 2016.

46. Wikipedia, the free encyclopedia. *Deductive Reasoning*. 5 p. at https://en.wikipedia.org/wiki/Deductive_reasoning, retrieved May 9, 2016.

47. Wikipedia, the free encyclopedia. *Deductive Thinking*. 1 p. at http://wiki.deductivethinking.com/wiki/Deductive_Thinking, retrieved May 9, 2016.

48. *A Dictionary of Public Health*. Edited by JM Last. Oxford and New York: Oxford University Press, 2007.

49. Crossman A. What's the difference between deductive and inductive reasoning? 3 p. at http://sociology.about.com/od/Research/a/Deductive-Reasoning-Versus-Inductive Reaso…, retrieved Aug 1, 2016.

50. Bradford A. *Deductive Reasoning vs. Inductive Reasoning*. 5 p. at http://www.livescience.com/21569-deduction-vs-induction.html, retrieved Aug 1, 2016.

51. *The Philosophy Book. Big Ideas Simply Explained*. Buckingham W, Burnham D, Hill C, Kingt PJ, Marenbon J, Weeks M, Osborne R, Chilman S Contributors. New York: DK Publishing, 2011.

52. Bluedorn H. *Two Methods of Reasoning*. 5 p. at https://www.triviumpursuit.com/articles/two_methods_of_reasoning.php, retrieved May 9, 2016.

53. Internet Encyclopedia of Philosophy, IEP Staff. *Deductive and Inductive Arguments*. 5 p. at http://iep.utm.edu/ded-ind/, retrieved May 9, 2016.

54. Douven I. Abduction. *Stanford Encyclopedia of Philosophy*. 17 p. at http://33plato.stanford.edu/entries/abduction/, retrieved Sep 9, 2016.

55. New World Encyclopedia. *Abductive Reasoning*. 6 p. at http://www.newworldencyclopedia.org/entry/Abductive_reasoning, retrieved Sep 9, 2016.

56. New World Encyclopedia. *Abductive Reasoning*. 6 p. at http://newworldencyclopedia.org/entry/Abductive_reasoning, retrieved May 9, 2016.

57. Psychology Wiki—Wikia. *Abductive Reasoning*. 3 p. at http://psychology.wikia.com/wiki/Abductive_reasoning, retrieved Aug 1, 2016.

58. Haig BD. Scientific method, abduction, and clinical reasoning. *J Clin Psychol*, 2008;64(9):1013–8.

59. Haig BD. Précis of 'An abductive theory of scientific method'. *J Clin Psychol*, 2008;64(9):1020–2.

60. Thagard P and Shelley C. Abductive reasoning: Logic, visual thinking, and coherence. 14 p. at http://cogsci.uwaterloo.ca/Articles/Pages/%7FAbductive.html, retrieved May 9, 2016.

61. Walton D. *Abductive Reasoning*. Tuscaloosa: The University of Alabama Press, 2004.

62. Schick T Jr and Vaughn L. *How to Think about Weird Things*. 6th Edition. New York: McGraw-Hill, 2011.

63. Wells DA. Clinical thinking in psychiatry. *J Eval Clin Pract*, 2015;21:514–7.

64. *A Dictionary of Public Health*. Edited by JM Last. Oxford and New York: Oxford University Press, 2007.

65. Clapp JE. *Random House Webster's Dictionary of the Law*. New York: Random House, 2000.

66. GRADE Series—Guest Editors S Straus and S Shepperd. GRADE guidelines. First article: *J Clin Epidemiol*, 2011;64:380–2. Last article of this series: *J Clin Epidemiol*, 2013;66:124–31. (Reference abridged.)

67. Wikipedia, the free encyclopedia. *Framing (Social Sciences)*. 10 p. at http://en.wikipedia.org.wiki/Framing_(social_sciences), retrieved Sep 19, 2011.

Chapter 5

About What to Think in Step-by-Step Clinical Work and Care: Risk, Diagnosis, Treatment, Prognosis*

Executive Summary

In clinical practice, community medicine, and public health, we reason and make decisions in four particular domains:

1. Assessing risk (probability of new phenomena) in the individual patient and in the community.
2. Detection and diagnosis of disease and other phenomena in individuals and their groups (sporadicity, epidemicity, endemicity, pandemicity).
3. Choosing, implementing, and evaluating success and failures of clinical treatment, prevention, and other active interventions.
4. Forecasting and evaluating potential and real outcomes of health phenomena of interest.

In **risk assessment**, risk factors (events which may be modified) are often of greater interest for pragmatic reasons than risk markers, as uncontrollable predictors of disease and its cure. Results may be seen as significant not only from a biostatistical or epidemiological point of view, but also from values attributed to them by patients and their communities. *Post hoc ergo propter*

---

* This chapter is based, with permission of the publisher, on Chapter 3 in: Jenicek M. *A Primer on Clinical Experience in Medicine. Reasoning, Decision-Making, and Communication in Health Sciences.* Boca Raton, FL/London/New York: CRC Press/Taylor & Francis/Productivity Press, 2013. Revised, edited, updated.

hoc or *cum hoc ergo propter hoc* and other fallacies in causal reasoning should be avoided.

Diagnosis is made by various reasoning methods such as pattern recognition, hypothetico-deductive, probability-based, and deterministic approaches. The evaluation of diagnostic methods examines internal validity (how do diagnostic methods detect disease) and external validity (how do diagnostic methods work in understanding disease from one individual to another). These approaches to diagnostic methods must be considered both for screening and reference diagnostic tests. Anchoring (premature closure of the diagnostic workup), ordering, and triage-related fallacies, ignoring Bayesian diagnostic prior/posterior/revised probabilities or rhetorical manipulations, are some examples of diagnostic reasoning to avoid and correct.

Treatment must be seen as a matter of intervention at various levels of prevention, health protection, and health promotion. Controlled clinical trials and their alternatives focus on the demonstration of a causal relationship between some beneficial factor and improvement in health and disease based on the rules outlined in Chapter 2. The best evidence according to evidence-based medicine rules is sought here. Ignoring webs of causes and consequences, appeals to authorities, tradition or actions at any price, are just some of the fallacies to know, prevent, and rectify.

Prognosis refers to a longitudinal (over time) study of multiple beneficial or noxious factors having both good or bad multiple consequences on what has happened, or will happen, once the disease is acquired. Prognostic factors and markers often differ from risk factors and markers. They are the subjects of 'survival'-type studies, proportional hazard (impact of multiple prognostic factors) evaluations, and other methods. Case fatality, response to treatment rates, remissions, relapses, and disease gradient and spectrum may be in focus. Types of reasoning and argumentation are common to some of the other aforementioned domains of clinical activity. Oversimplifications, divisions (whole entities and their parts) or misleading uses of statistics are additional fallacies to avoid. General rules of reasoning, critical thinking, and decision-making apply to all steps and stages of clinical work and care with individual patients as well as to the management, prevention, and control of disease and health at the community level.

In This Chapter:

Executive Summary 123

Thoughts, Thinkers, and Things to Think About 125

Introductory Comments 128

Health Events 128

Clinical Reasoning about Health Events 128

5.1 *"You Are at Risk."* What Does This Mean and How Can It Be Mutually Understood by Us, Our Patients, and the Community? 129

    5.1.1 What Is 'Risk' in Health Sciences? 130

    5.1.2 Are Risk Characteristics All the Same? Risk Factors and Risk Markers 130

5.1.3 Why Are Some Risk Factors 'Significant' and Others Are Not?........................ 130
5.1.4 Where Does Our Knowledge of Risk Factors and Markers Come From? 132
5.1.5 Risk as a Subject of Argumentation 132
5.1.6 Illustrative Fallacies...132
5.1.7 How Do We Think about Risk? Our Ways of Reasoning about Risk 133
5.2 *"We Have a Problem Here."* Properties of Meaningful Diagnosis 134
5.2.1 Quality and Completeness of the Diagnostic Material...............................134
5.2.2 How Is a Diagnosis Made?...135
5.2.3 How Good Are Our Diagnostic Methods and Techniques?.............................136
5.2.4 Diagnosis as a Subject of Argumentation 139
5.2.5 Illustrative Fallacies...139
5.2.6 How Do We Think and Reason in the Diagnosis Domain?..............................142
5.3 *"That's What We'll Do about It."* Reasoning and Deciding How to Treat
      and If the Treatment Works 142
5.3.1 Types and Levels of Medical Therapeutic and Preventive Interventions 143
5.3.2 Which Treatment Works Best? How Is It Measured?..................................147
5.3.3 Which Treatment Modality Applies to a Particular Patient? 151
5.3.4 Treatment as a Subject of Argumentation 152
Evidence-Based Approach 152
Critical Thinking Approach..152
5.3.5 Illustrative Fallacies...153
5.3.6 How Do We Reason in the Domain of Treatment and Preventive Interventions?...154
5.4 Reasoning about Prognosis: *"You'll Be Doing Well…"* Making Prognosis Meaningful.....155
5.4.1 Differences between the Prognosis Domain and the Risk Domain......................156
5.4.2 What Do We Need to Know about Prognostic Events and Outcomes?................158
5.4.3 What Do We Expect from Prognostic Studies in Order to Reason More
      Effectively about the Future of Our Patients? What Treatment Modality Best
      Applies to a Particular Patient?..160
How Should We Apply What We Know to an Individual Patient?...................................162
5.4.4 Prognosis as a Subject of Argumentation 162
5.4.5 Illustrative Fallacies...163
5.4.6 How Do We Think in the Domain of Prognosis? Considerations for Further
      Work and Understanding in the Area of Prognosis.....................................164
Let Us Conclude 165
References 166

Thoughts, Thinkers, and Things to Think About

*There are four questions which in some
form or other every patient asks of his
doctor: (a) What is the matter with me?
This is **diagnosis**. Can you put me right?
(b) What will be my **treatment** and
prognosis? (c) How did I get it? This is
causation. (d) How can I avoid it in the
future? This is **prevention**. He may not be
called upon to attempt a full answer to his*

*patient, but he must give a fair working
answer to himself.*
George Newman
(1870–1948)
in *The Lancet* (1931)
**What can we say 80 years later?
The same perhaps, but with some
new perspectives, approaches, and
answers.**

*He is the best prophet who guesses well, and
he is not the wisest man whose guess turns
out well in the event, but he who, whatever
the event be, takes reason and probability
for his guide.*
Euripides
(489–406 BC)
**Isn't it what we are doing in today's
epidemiology?**

*Forecasting is very difficult, especially if it is
about future.*
Edgar B. Fiedler
(1929–2003), 1977
So is prognosis in the health domain!

Hindsight is always twenty-twenty.
Billy Wilder
(1906–2002), 1979
'Always' or 'mostly,' Billy?

*When you have mastered the numbers, you
will in fact no longer be reading numbers,
any more that you read words when reading
a book. You will be reading meanings.*
Harold Geneen
(1910–1997), 1984

**Isn't this similar to what we do
when counting and measuring what
we see at the bedside and when
looking at lab results?**

*The end cannot justify the means, for the simple and
obvious reason that the means employed determine
the nature of the end produced.*
Aldous Leonard Huxley
(1894–1963), 1937
Some men of faith should also know.

*What we should do, I suggest, is to give up
the idea of ultimate sources of knowledge,
and admit that all knowledge is human;
that it is mixed with our errors, our prejudices, our dreams, and our hopes; that all
we can do is to grope for truth even though
it be beyond our reach.*
Sir Karl Raimund Popper
(1902–1994), 1960
**Yes, it makes us definitely
humble, Sir Karl!**

*The conclusion of your syllogism, I said
lightly, is fallacious, being based upon
licensed premises.*
Flynn O'Brien (Myles Gopaleen)
(1911–1966)
(Chapter 1 in *Swim-Two-Birds*)
Our clinical conclusions are as well!

*For philosophers, reasoning means "thinking leading
to the conclusion." Isn't this what physicians do all
the time? About what and how, let us see here.*

Introductory Comments

Once we know the patient's chief and other complaints or reasons bringing him or her under our care, we usually try to solve several problems. To do this, we take the patient's medical, occupational, and social and other history, perform a physical examination and evaluate his or her mental state. When we do this, we are

- assessing the patient's **risks**. Given the above information, what might be the patient's future health problems? We may think, "*This is a health problem to deal with …*"
- making **diagnoses**, often for the main problem of interest and other associated problems (co-morbidity). We may think, "*This is my diagnosis: …*"
- choosing and administering medical, surgical and/or psychiatric **treatment** for the main problem of interest as well as for associated health problems (co-treatment for co-morbidity). We may think, "*His or her treatment should be then …*"
- making a **prognosis** of outcomes and other future issues that result once the treatment and care of the entire patient's health problems are implemented, during the care, and once it is completed. We may think, "*This is what we can expect and should expect: …*" and
- establishing **plans** of possible long term medical, social and other care beyond current health problem resolution. We may think, "*This is how we should care for this patient beyond the current problem and care: ….*"

In all such cases, in addition to reasoning well, we must arrive at meaningful conclusions, understand a clinical case or cases better, and derive the best possible decisions about what to do. Let us see in this chapter how we think and reason in the most frequently encountered activities at the beginning of the learning process of clinical medicine: patient risk assessment, diagnosis, treatment, and prognosis.

Health Events

All steps in clinical care both rely on, and are subjects of, argumentation and communication. Cause-effect considerations are limited not only to disease, suffering, and their causes (etiological factors of disease), but also the medical (clinical pharmacology, psychotherapy, behavior modification, etc.), surgical (including invasive exploratory methods and techniques), psychiatric, and social support interventions for their patient. These cause-effect considerations extend to whether the interventions benefited the patient, were successful or failed, had adverse effects of treatment and care, caused medical error and harm, and the subsequent impact of all this on health professionals and services, economic and administrative functioning on health community and society beyond. In this book let us give them the common name of **event(s)** or **health event(s)** since any of them (not only disease and its causes) may be and actually are subjects of argumentation, decision-making, and communication.

Clinical Reasoning about Health Events

In the broadest of terms, **clinical reasoning** is *"a context-dependent way of thinking and decision-making in professional practice to guide practice actions. It involves the construction of narratives to make sense of multiple factors and interests pertaining to the current reasoning task.*

It occurs within a set of problem spaces informed by the practitioner's unique frames of reference, work-place context and practice models, as well as by the patient or client contexts. It utilizes core dimensions of practice knowledge, reasoning and metacognition and draws on these capacities of others.[1]

As already mentioned in our introduction, **clinical judgment** is *"the capacity to make and choose data and information to produce useful (true or false) claims in clinical practice and research, to make decisions on the basis of such claims and to act accordingly."* It also means *critical thinking in the practice of medicine based on the "patient/evidence/setting" fit.* Together with elements of knowledge and experience, it relies on the process of integrating meanings and values of clinical and paraclinical observation and data into the making of conclusions and decisions derived from such an integration.

The clinical steps of practice, evaluation, and understanding depend heavily on crucial contributions from fundamental and clinical epidemiology and biostatistics. Let us now highlight some particular perspectives regarding our reasoning about these steps from a wider scope, encompassing clinical epidemiological methods, biostatistical techniques, and other considerations. This is crucial to the understanding shared by learners and their teachers. However, the points that follow do not replace the more formal training from which they are drawn.

5.1 *"You Are at Risk."* What Does This Mean and How Can It Be Mutually Understood by Us, Our Patients, and the Community?

When we speak of risk, we refer to "bad" factors, the causes of health problems, complications, and undesirable outcomes of medical care. "Beneficial" factors, that is, those that improve health and cure disease, relate to treatment. Being "at risk" is perhaps one of the terms and notions most used and misused in daily practice and communication and can signify many things. For laypersons in particular, it sounds "scientific," technical, and knowledgeable. Such "risk of the risk" should be minimized through some basic clarifications. Otherwise, even flawless argumentation is useless in the context.

In the domain of risk, as elsewhere in medicine, we often think in terms of probabilities, answers to "what are my, our, or their chances." A **probability** is *"A measure that ranges from zero to 1 of the likelihood that a random event will occur or the degree to which a statement or assumption is true."*[2] In other words, closer to the epidemiological notion of rate or risk, a probability (*P*) is *the quantitative expression of the chance that an event (A) will occur.* In other words:

$$P(A) = \text{number of times } A \text{ occurs/number of times } A \text{ could occur}^3.$$

(N.B. Probabilities were already discussed to some extent in Chapters 3 and 4.)

Quantifications of realities or predictions of disease presence, occurrence, frequency, or prognosis are made in terms of probabilities. Their comparisons are used in statistical inference, comparing theory and practice or to better understand cause-effect relationships. For example, **rates** of disease, such as 20/1,000 or 0.020 (20/1,000 in decimal form) are probabilistic expressions. Holland provides further explanations of probabilities (without equations) to clinicians.[4]

5.1.1 What Is 'Risk' in Health Sciences?

Risk is the probability that a *new* event will happen. It is essential that both the patient and his or her physician should speak about and understand the same event. Risk should be specified often on a case-by-case basis, especially if laypersons are involved.

Risk of disease and other events is a probability derived from observations and comparisons of two or more sets of **incidence rates**, that is, frequencies of new events over a defined period of time often related to some denominators of various size (%, per 1,000, 100,000, etc.). Such denominators include both events and non-events, sick and healthy individuals, and so, in some target population of interest (to which observations apply). Incidence rates are particularly useful to follow the spread of the disease over time.

N.B. Prevalence rates as frequencies of events at a given moment or over a defined period of time, independently of when they occurred, are useful as a diagnostic *a priori* predictor of a possible health problem. They are particularly useful in understanding the overall burden of the disease at a given moment (point prevalence) or over a certain period of time (period prevalence). Prevalence rates may sometimes be used as estimators of risk from the relationship between prevalence, incidence, and duration of the disease, provided that the duration of cases is comparable and stable over time. This is rather exceptional, however. Consider with caution!

5.1.2 Are Risk Characteristics All the Same? Risk Factors and Risk Markers

For practical and research purposes, risk factors and risk markers are not interchangeable. Any patient may experience exposure to risk factors and risk markers. However, **risk factors** can be modified, either raising or lowering the risks of diseases related to these factors. Some examples of risk factors include smoking and health, physical activity, drug abuse, dietary patterns, occupational and environmental physical and chemical agents, or exposure to infectious agents, resistance, and others.

Risk markers, on the other hand, are those characteristics which may also be useful predictors of desirable or undesirable events, but which cannot be modified. Examples include age, gender, some immutable cultural, societal, or faith values, and more. Risk factors are of primary importance in advising the patient of the chances of successful treatment or prevention.

5.1.3 Why Are Some Risk Factors 'Significant' and Others Are Not?

We always strive to establish some hierarchy of importance of risk factors in deciding what we should control first, and what might be done later. The notion of importance is most often derived from comparisons of two or more groups exposed to the factor of interest and its consequence(s) in cohort studies, or from comparisons of past or present exposure in already diseased and non-diseased individuals in case control studies. Both observational only or experimental studies may yield various estimations of various cause-effect relationships as in Chapters 4 and 8 of this book. More follows in this chapter too. Having said this, which factors (causes or consequences) are more important than others? Which are most useful for decisions in practice and research?

The theoretical concept of cause-effect relationships presented in the previous chapter also applies to any kind of intervention in medicine at any level of prevention: control of exposure to noxious factors, immunization in primary prevention, treatment in secondary prevention, avoiding metastases, or ensuring the comfort of a terminal patient in tertiary prevention. The same criteria of cause-effect relationships apply to various risk measurements (absolute, relative, attributable, fraction of the web of causes). Any evaluation of the role of noxious causal factors or treatment impact, such as effectiveness or adverse effects and their evaluation by additional methods, are derived from this basic consideration and approach.

Once comparisons of outcomes in groups are made, interpreters bring their experiences to the attention of readers and listeners. Results are interpreted as being 'significant,' 'highly significant,' or 'statistically significant.' *p* values from the statistical analysis of data are used to show the strength of evidence in analytical studies, be they observational or experimental. *p* values are also used to evaluate the degree of dissimilarity between two or more series of observations. Once again, let us remember that as a measure of the impact of treatment in clinical or epidemiological terms, *p* values can only 'clear the way' (if they are small) for the epidemiological and clinical assessment of results of clinical trials.[5] **The *p* value is** *"usually the probability of obtaining a result as extreme as, or more extreme than, the one observed if the dissimilarity is entirely due to variation in measurement or in subject response—that is, if it is the result of chance alone."*[6]

In research, some funding agencies or institutions may still be happy with 'small *p*'s,' indicating that a drug leading to different outcomes shows a very low probability of not working (null hypothesis would be true). This, however, does not indicate the magnitude of the effect. Hence, *p* values and significance of findings in terms of inferential statistics should be carefully interpreted and given their proper meaning. If authors are satisfied stating that differences in disease outcomes between groups are statistically significant, they must keep the following in mind:

1. **What is statistically significant is not necessarily significant from an epidemiological point of view.** Statistically significant studies may still show low relative risks (a poor strength of association) or etiological fractions (specificity of improvements due to the treatment under study).
2. **All epidemiologically important results are not necessarily of equal clinical importance: What is epidemiologically important is not always equally clinically important.** For rare phenomena and outcomes that are not severe or life-threatening, strong associations may exist, but they are of lesser clinical importance in comparison to more frequent and serious health problems where even less epidemiologically important findings might be of more clinical interest.

In other words, if one needs to know some *p* value beyond its customary clearing power in the chain of quantitative analysis of clinical trial results, findings are probably not significant from the point of view of clinical reasoning and decision-making. For example, smoking is epidemiologically more important in relation to lung cancer than in relation to cardiovascular problems. However, given the frequency of cardiovascular problems, control of smoking may be in some instances more clinically important for this area than for lung cancer.

Always specify exactly what you mean when saying that something is 'highly significant,' 'significant,' or 'not significant.' Funnily enough, authors of some medical articles find that the results of their own studies are often 'highly significant' whereas results of competing studies are not. Moreover, what is significant for clinicians may not always corroborate with the views of field epidemiologists. Significance, then, does not travel well from one specialty to another.

In the domain of treatment evaluation (*vide infra*), the fundamental epidemiological measures of treatment (or prevention modality) efficacy and effectiveness are the relative risk (strength of association) and the etiological fraction (specificity of association). These risks are calculated traditionally based on the occurrence of undesirable events (complications of disease, disease cases, and deaths), using tradition and experience from field studies in community medicine. The same can be done for expected improvements, provided they are well defined in clinimetrically acceptable terms.

5.1.4 Where Does Our Knowledge of Risk Factors and Markers Come From?

Most such knowledge comes from observational analytical studies of disease etiology. These studies are either of a cohort (sometimes called prospective) or case control (sometimes understood as retrospective) nature. Practically all textbooks on epidemiology, including our current one,[7] cover these challenges in more detail. Experimental studies are rather exceptional given the ethical unacceptability of controlled trials of a noxious factor and its consequences. What is left are observations and analyses of "natural experiments," that is, situations which allow comparisons of sets of observations reflecting the nature of a trial as they occur without being determined by the observer and analyst.

5.1.5 Risk as a Subject of Argumentation

The quality of our knowledge, understanding, and use of risk is, like any other step of clinical work, a subject of argumentation in which:

- the best evidence is used in grounds, backing, warrants, rebuttals, and qualifiers leading to our conclusion about the causality problem and its value and relevance for practice and research;
- meaningful links are established between component building blocks of our argument;
- the cause-effect criteria are fulfilled; and
- everything falls into a clear and well defined conceptual frame.

5.1.6 Illustrative Fallacies

Fallacies as errors in reasoning are too numerous to list here, and have been better summarized elsewhere.[8] However, many fallacies are also related to the formulations of questions about risk factors and other causes, study design, interpretation, or applications. In considerations of possible risk factors or markers in the etiology of disease, let us mention:

1. The ***post hoc ergo propter hoc* fallacy** assumes that because a health problem (or its improvement) occurs after exposure to a suspected noxious or beneficial factor, a change in health status occurred as a result.
2. The ***cum hoc ergo propter hoc* fallacy has several self-explanatory synonyms:** association/causation fallacy, correlation not cause fallacy, correlation for cause fallacy, *non causa pro causa* and others. The culprit here is the ambiguous term 'association' meaning either causality or something else when there is none. In an example from the non-medical world, when two show business stars are said to be 'romantically linked' this means that the two stars have fallen in love, or are engaged, married, involved with someone else, associated for pragmatic business and/or publicity reasons, whether

romance is involved or not. The same should not happen in matters of health and disease and their causes and consequences. Also, as already mentioned in Chapter 2, a temporary sequence of events is not sufficient proof of a cause-effect relationship.

3. *'It speaks for itself'* fallacies, *'appeal for common practice'* fallacies, *'appeal to antiquity/tradition'* (***ad antiquitam, ad antiquitatem***), *'false conservatism'* fallacies or *'newness' (originality)* fallacies still occur as substitutes for the real causality in the risk and treatment domains.[8]

4. Other fallacies appear under the name of **'bias'** in the clinical epidemiological literature. They are related to design flaws in etiological studies, the definition of variables, organization and recording in studies, misrepresentation and misinterpretation of clinical course of the disease, selected individuals ending and not ending as participants in research studies, and their compliance with research protocols and early losses from the study.

5. Some common biases include:

   a. *'Berkson bias'* is a type of selection bias where the population for a study is selected from a sub-population (like hospitalized patients only in case control studies), rather than a general population which will affect the representativeness of the study.

   b. *'Neyman bias'* is related to the attrition of cases in etiological studies due to the fact that most serious, deceased 'too early' as well as not serious cases escape attention in analytical studies covering longer periods of time.

   c. ***Hindsight bias*** refers to a tendency to judge events, their causes or consequences (outcomes) as well as our interpretations and decisions about them on the basis of what we know after such events occur, rather than on the basis of what we knew before we faced those events and made our decisions. We may say, in retrospect, we did not have the same (and often richer) information that we have now. Everyone is wiser after an experience than before it; *"After the war, everyone is a general"* or *"I knew it all along"* as popular sayings go. Our judgment of patient risks, rightness of diagnosis, therapeutic decisions, and making prognosis may all be affected by this kind of directional reasoning.

Such biases (fallacies) are more extensively covered in the epidemiological literature.[8–11]

N.B. The lists of fallacies and biases in this chapter are not exhaustive and they are presented in this book only for illustrative purposes.

5.1.7 How Do We Think about Risk? Our Ways of Reasoning about Risk

There are several paradigms, mental processes, types of reasoning and pathways of thinking underlying risk assessment in the patient, including:

- occurrence considerations;
- cause-effect considerations;
- inductive and deductive paths of reasoning;
- considerations and analysis of webs of causes, temporal sequence, and interaction between multiple risk factors;

- consideration and analysis of webs of consequences, temporal sequence, and interaction between multiple consequences;
- validity assessment for understanding: the "scientific value" of information about risk;
- uses of both vertical thinking (within a specific argument) and lateral thinking (several topics, options, arguments, and choices about them); and
- validity assessment for practical decision-making in general and in a particular individual: "this patient" (patient's fit into grounds and backing).

These are all necessary for our reasoning, understanding, and decision-making about a patient's risks.

5.2 "We Have a Problem Here." Properties of Meaningful Diagnosis

Diagnosis relies on two elements:

1. **Quality and completeness of data and findings** from patient history, physical and paraclinical examinations; and
2. **What we do with all this information** on our reasoning path to diagnose patient problem(s) or, in other words, **how** the **diagnosis is made**.

Clinicians arrive at their opinions based on **soft data**, which is harder to define, measure, quantify, and classify. These data include pain, nausea, injected eyes, feeling sad, and many other observations, particularly in psychiatry. **Hard data** is the opposite: blood cell count, body temperature, skinfold thickness, cholesterol levels, and radiological findings of bone fractures, for example. The '**hardening**' of soft data is a process used to make soft data more meaningful for understanding and decision-making. For example, pain is quantified on a scale from 0 to 10 or as a pictogram, and overnight sputum is estimated as a spoonful, half-cup, or small cup. Both entities are useful, although hard data are easier to work with in **clinimetrics** or the quantification, qualification, categorization, and other identifications of what we saw, heard, and felt (and sometimes smelled and tasted) as clinicians working with the patient.

5.2.1 Quality and Completeness of the Diagnostic Material

Once the patient specifies his or her complaint or reason for consultation, his or her physician completes the idea about the complaint through a series of **open** ("*How do you feel today?*" "*What else worries you?*") and **closed** ("*Is your chest pain still there?*" "*Can you move your right knee better today than yesterday?*") questions. Most often, interviews begin with open questions, and closed questions usually follow in order to specify the problem. Patient history and physical findings are enriched by paraclinical explorations and findings: diagnostic imagery, biochemistry of body liquids and tissues, clinical microbiology, biopsy, and other diagnostic methods in pathology. All of this information enters our reasoning process, leading to diagnosis.

5.2.2 How Is a Diagnosis Made?

Several steps are involved in making a diagnosis ranging from simple recognitions to organized and structured pathways from initial observations to conclusions about them.[12] First the patient is **observed globally**, then manifestations of interest are **isolated** from the global observation. Next, the manifestations of interest are properly **described** in reproducible terms:

■ a **dimension** (making sense of what was seen and described) is given to them;
■ allowing their **interpretation** by an associative process, linking previously observed elements with additional perceptions and clinical observations; and then
■ a final inference on the patient's state by classifying it in a diagnostic category as the end of this clinimetric process, that is, path from observations to the final **diagnosis itself**.

There are several thinking ways to make a diagnosis:

1. Diagnosis by **pattern recognition** is based on fitting what we saw into previously learned patterns. If we see a patient in shock, with a sharp retrosternal pain irradiating into the left arm, we may think about a myocardial infarction and order further testing and work up to accept, or reject, our working diagnosis and initial impression.

2. Diagnosis by **arborization or multiple branching** is a procedure followed by going from one point of observation to another, each step depending on what was found beforehand. Clinical **algorithms and guidelines** may be based on this method. For example, we may consider a stab wound in the abdomen of a patient in the emergency room. If the anterior fascia is penetrated, we proceed to a peritoneal lavage. If the red blood cell count exceeds a certain amount, we might consider exploratory laparotomy. If not, 24 hours' hospital observation might be a preferred alternative. The movement from one step to another on the procedure path depends unequivocally on the result of the previous step. More about algorithms and guidelines will follow in Chapter 10.

3. Diagnosis by **exclusive exploration of data** is an inductive procedure. Multiple data are gathered first and then dredged to obtain hypotheses which can be formulated on the basis of the sequence and combination of clinical data available. This leads to a variable degree of certainty.

4. A **hypothetico-deductive diagnosis** path proceeds from one or several working ideas or hypotheses to an ad hoc evaluation allowing the acceptance or rejection of original ideas (differential diagnosis). For example, a young person complaining of nausea, vomiting, and abdominal pain will elicit differential diagnoses of appendicitis, mesenterial lymphadenitis, nephrolithiasis, gastro-enteritis, or extra-uterine pregnancy. A judicious set of hypotheses will be linked to patient characteristics, information obtained and clinical setting of the case. Proceeding from one highest probability to another, a Murphy's **steepest ascent method** is considered characteristic of an experienced physician.[13] Therapeutic and other decisions using **decision trees** (also *vide infra*) are based on an approach similar to Murphy's steepest ascent method.[14]

5. A **probability-based diagnosis** is based on linking the meaning of clinical information in terms of its sensitivity, specificity, and predictive value of the diagnostic

method. From the prevalence of the disease in the patient community combined with such 'conditional probabilities' as the occurrence of positive or negative results and the sensitivity and specificity of the diagnostic procedure, a 'revised' or 'posterior' probability is obtained through this kind of Bayesian procedure (*vide infra*).

6. In a **deterministic diagnostic pathway**, unambiguous rules are followed on the basis of compiled knowledge: "***If*** *a throat culture is positive for a bacterial infection,* ***then*** *treatment by antibiotics is mandatory*." This kind of diagnostic reasoning is an extension or sequence of deterministic and/or categorical diagnostic reasoning.

7. **Computer-assisted** diagnosis is based on "if … then" categorical and deterministic reasoning.

5.2.3 How Good Are Our Diagnostic Methods and Techniques?

Most often, we are interested in the internal and external validity of the diagnostic procedures we perform. We want to know how good they are on their own and how good they are when used repeatedly and among different patients, communities, and settings. By diagnostic method, we do not only mean laboratory tests in clinical biochemistry, hematology, or microbiology. The same logic and criteria apply to manual and sensory diagnostic maneuvers in physical examination, mental state evaluation, and even screening tests. **Screening tests** are presumptive diagnostic techniques whose purpose is not to establish a definitive diagnosis and prescribe treatment, but to lead patients with positive results to a more complete diagnostic evaluation and treatment, if needed.

In essence, each diagnostic method is another kind of proof of a cause-effect relationship: a given morphological or physiological state leads to a positive test result. In practice, we already take such relationships for granted and look at how positive or negative test results corroborate with having an anomalous pathological state, or not. Most often, two tests are performed on each patient: the reference test (biopsy, imagery, surgery), and a test to be evaluated if it confirms or correctly rejects the results of the reference test.

For example, we may reason that a family physician's diagnosis of a possible colorectal cancer is a screening procedure (rectal bleeding and other considerations) leading the patient to histopathologic confirmation and surgery as required. Table 5.1 shows the four most important criteria of a good test[4] and an example.[15]

Sensitivity tells us how many cases may be detected from all cases in a group of patients of interest. In our example, every one in every four cases would be missed. If the disease is treatable and fatal if not treated, we want to have a test as sensitive as possible. By using sensitive tests, ***we want to detect as many cases as possible and treat them accordingly***.

Specificity, on the other hand, tells us how many healthy individuals are confirmed as such by a negative result of the test. This information is useful in cases which lend themselves to requiring an in-depth diagnostic workup and treatment. In our example, about one-third of patients fall into this undesirable category. By using highly specific tests, we aim to exclude individuals who do not have the disease from further care.

When a test is highly **sp**ecific, its **p**ositive result rules **in** the diagnosis. The mnemonic, **SpPin**, reflects this property of a diagnostic test.[16] A highly specific test will rule out patients who do not require further care through its negative results. Positive test results, whatever their sensitivity might be, make us more certain that the patient has the disease. If the patient did not have the disorder, a negative test result would confirm it.

Table 5.1 Basic Contingency Table to Evaluate the Internal Validity of a Diagnostic Test

		Result of a Reference Diagnostic Method or a True State of Health		
		Diseased persons (patient **has** cancer)	Persons without disease (patient **does not have** cancer)	
Result of a diagnostic clinical procedure or of a laboratory test: Family physician's working diagnosis	Positive: Patient **may have** cancer	True positive results or TP (disease confirmed): 12	False positive or FP (health not confirmed) absence of disease: 46	Total of positive results for a test (TP+FP): 58
	Negative: Patient **may not have** cancer	False negative or FN (cases of disease missed): 4	True negative or TN (absence of disease confirmed): 83	Total of negative results for a test (TN+FN): 87
		Total of diseased persons targeted by the test (TP+FN): 16	Total of healthy subjects who are candidates for a diagnostic procedure (TN+FP): 129	

Sensitivity: TP/TP + FN = 12/12 + 4 × 100 = 75%
Specificity: TN/TN + FP = 83/83 + 46 × 100 = 64.3%
Predictive value of a positive test result (syn. Positive predictive value): TP/TP + FN = 12/12 + 46 × 100 = 20.7%
Predictive value of a negative test result (syn. Negative predictive value): TN/TN + FN = 83/83 + 4 × 100 = 95.4%
Other clinical reasoning underlying computations using rates, ratios, likelihoods and odds for a future more in depth (beyond this text) uses:
Likelihood ratio (LR): Ratio of the probability of the test result among individuals with the target disorder (diseased) to the probability of that same test result among individuals who are free of that target disorder (non-diseased, healthy).
Likelihood ratio for a positive test result: LR = sensitivity (1-specificity)
Likelihood ratio for a negative test result: LR = (1-sensitivity)/specificity
Odds: The ratio of the probability of the occurrence of an event to that of non-occurrence. The probability that something is one way to the probability that it is another way.
Pre-test odds: prevalence/(1-prevalence)
Post-test odds: pre-test odds × likelihood ratio
Post-test probability: post-test odds/post-test odds + 1
Source: Reworked and redrawn from data in Reference 15.

A highly sensitive test would find most of those individuals who do have the disease of interest through a positive result. This is a highly desirable property in screening programs for disease; community medicine and public health specialists aim for the maximum number of cases to be detected to control the problem. On the other hand, a clinician facing an individual patient may be sure that when using a highly sensitive test yielding a negative result, the patient in question does not have the disease. In other terms, when using a highly **s**ensitive test, its **n**egative result rules **out** the diagnosis. The mnemonic, **SnNout**, reflects this property of a highly sensitive test.[16]

The **predictive value of a positive test result** tells the clinician what the probability is that the patient really has the disease. We want to be certain of the result *before* doing something (treatment) which would follow diagnosis. *We want to be sure that the patient really has the disease if tested positive for it.* We are concerned by possible adverse effects and cost, time, and other requirements of needless procedures in patients who do not need these procedures or for whom they are eventually contra-indicated. In our example, more than one half of positively tested patients would fall into this situation.

The **predictive value of a negative test result** indicates the probability that the patient really does not have the disease if the patient is tested negative. The clinician wants to have certainty before deciding **not** to take action (to treat). In our example, the physician may be almost certain that *doing nothing was a good decision* (95.4%, in our case).

Bayesian reassessment of predictive values of tests shows how, depending on the prevalence of the health problem of interest (*a priori* probability of disease), related to prevalence, sensitivity, and specificity information which yields a revised probability of test predictive values. In the eighteenth century, Reverend Thomas Bayes studied betting, probabilities, and chances, and eventually proposed a theorem connecting the conditional and marginal probabilities of events. Bayes theorem reflected that the so-called *a priori* probability (before the test is performed) related to post-test probabilities (given the test performed) including sensitivity and specificity, yielded a revised probability for a predictive value of the text taking into account both of the above.[17] (N.B. We have indicated appropriate formulas and equations elsewhere.[18]) It is a way of understanding, in our case, how probability (like the predictive value of a diagnostic or screening test) is updated or revised in light of a new piece of evidence, or prevalence (disease frequency or occurrence in the community).[19]

The Bayesian approach to biostatistics in the health sciences domain is one of the paradigms that uses observed data to draw inferences. Gustafson specifies correctly that the Bayesian approach distinguishes itself from other approaches and paradigms, *"At the heart of Bayesian analysis is Bayes theorem, which describes how knowledge is updated on observing data."*[20] Bayes theorem differs then from probabilistic statements about mechanistically random processes using probabilistic statements about fixed, but unknown quantities of interest. Bayesian analysis has been used in a variety of contexts ranging from marine biology to medicine (diagnostic and screening testing), philosophy of science (relationships between evidence and theory), and even in the development of "Bayesian" spam blockers for email systems.[20]

As an example, Bayesian reasoning is worthy of consideration in situations when prevalence of disease in the target or patient's community is too high or low. Even without using appropriate tests to assess the extent to which the result on a diagnostic test changes the probability that a patient has a disease (like Fagan's[21] nomograms or formulas[22]) we can predict what would happen if we tested extensively, or otherwise systematically, for AIDS in a community in which the prevalence of AIDS is extremely high. We might, and would likely, obtain more false negative results than in a very low prevalence community. The predictive value of a negative test result in a high risk community would be lower, and we might miss a good number of patients who require prevention and care. These patients would likely be left unattended in the community, with all negative consequences for them and their contacts. Clinical epidemiology offers us more information about the Bayesian management of diagnosis and subsequent clinical remedial decisions.

Diagnostic tests are not only used individually, but also in series and in parallel known as **serial testing**, or otherwise referred to as **sequential** or **parallel testing**. In the case of **sequential testing**, we perform one test (preferably the most sensitive one) first and if positive, add another test and so on. Each test added to the diagnostic process depends on the result of the test that preceded it. This way, the entire sequential testing procedure is more specific at its end than a single test. In the case of **parallel testing**, we perform several tests at once and independently of the result of another test. What one test does not detect, the other will. The sensitivity of this type of testing is better than the sensitivity of using a single test.

5.2.4 Diagnosis as a Subject of Argumentation

Making a diagnosis is a process of reasoning aimed at finding the **cause(s)** of a **particular** configuration of signs, symptoms, and test results in a particular patient. In other words, in making a diagnosis, we seek to establish a causal link between some unusual morphology, function, or biological, physical, chemical, or social agent and some particular manifestations of disease, illness, or sickness. As such, the process of making a diagnosis shares many features with the **general** causal reasoning that is required to establish the cause(s) of diseases and the effectiveness of treatments.

5.2.5 Illustrative Fallacies

Fallacious reasoning and decision-making may occur anywhere.[8] Some of them are related to the structure of our diagnostic argumentation or to its building blocks and components. They are more extensively reviewed by us in another title.[8] Only a few of them will be quoted here:

1. In *anchoring or premature closure*, we tend to overly relate to early observed features of disease presentation in the diagnostic process and to jump prematurely to conclusions. This happens when everything stops at the 'working diagnosis' or 'impression' at patient admission without proceeding to a more definitive diagnosis.
2. When making an *ascertainment bias (fallacy)*, our thinking is pre-shaped by our expectations or by what we specifically hope to find. We do not detach ourselves enough from preformed notions, expectations, or beliefs that may impact the subsequent interpretation of data.
3. *Diagnostic creep (diagnosis momentum) fallacy* is committed if the lack of more relevant evidence and information is replaced by an accumulation of opinions creeping in from the patient via paramedics, nurses, and others before they reach, 'pre-diagnosed,' the physician-diagnostician. An *order effect fallacy* may be considered a subcategory of the diagnostic momentum: The first information obtained is better remembered and treated than subsequent information. *Triage cueing* in emergency medicine may also serve as another example of where this fallacy can occur.
4. We commit a *representativeness restraint* fallacy if we ignore a possible diagnosis because patient features and manifestations of the health problem are atypical. Pattern

recognition is one of the cornerstones of heuristic practice, but should not exclude alternative options.

5. *'Calling off'* or *'search satisficing' fallacy* means calling off procedures from pre-established diagnostic or therapeutic planning and work up once some important problem is found. The identification of one serious injury does not exclude a still undetected multiple trauma, other co-morbidity and co-treatments. **Sutton's slip**, or robbing a bank because that's where the money is, that is, *going for the obvious* or the *hindsight bias* are other reductionist practices that may also be placed in this category of right or wrong reasoning errors.

6. *Vertical line failure fallacy* is due to exclusively following only the vertical line of thinking and ignoring De Bono's lateral thinking. We reason about one problem when there are in fact many, and often interconnected, problems. Delayed or missed diagnoses may be minimized by coupling both vertical and lateral thinking.

7. *Ignoring Bayes fallacy* is committed by ignoring and/or misrepresenting any element of Bayesian diagnostic making, such as prior or posterior probabilities, internal validity of diagnostic methods, and their improper linking. *Base rate neglect fallacy* and *availability/non-availability fallacy* both belong to this category of erroneous reasoning.

8. *Availability and non-availability fallacy* takes place when we judge a disease from events or experiences that readily come to the physician's mind. As epidemiologists used to say, "*Looking for horses rather than zebras on hearing the sound of hoofs*" should be avoided. Faulty Bayesian reasoning may result from 'diagnostic impressionism' based on disproportionate estimates of the frequency of a particular diagnosis or condition. 'Zebras' should not be excluded from differential diagnosis. On the other hand, ignoring 'zebras' is an omission of lateral thinking in favor of vertical thinking only. This fallacy should be carefully pondered as an error or omission.

9. *Base rate neglect fallacy* happens when we fail to take into account the prevalence of the health condition in a Bayesian approach to diagnosis and replace it with the typical presentation of the health condition in a 'natural' setting at the clinical practice site (emergency room). This failure may result in the overestimation of the disease. Elsewhere, a heuristic approach may be the only possible (and maybe successful) approach.

10. *Diagnostic oversimplification fallacy (false dilemma)* occurs in reasoning and arguments which are based on exclusive and exhaustive 'yes or no' considerations when other alternatives and options exist. This fallacy may take place in differential diagnosis. For example, after receiving a kidney transplant, a patient develops a fever. Is the fever due to an infection related to the surgery itself, or is it a sign of organ rejection? Are these two options the only possible ones, or are there others? What about a new, concurrent infectious disease? A drug reaction? Some other co-morbidity? Infection or rejection may be the most prevalent considerations, but are not the only ones. Needless to say, a differential diagnostic process should be based on all clinically important possibilities and options.

11. The ***argumentum ad verecundiam*** ('**argument from bashfulness**') *fallacy* is almost as ubiquitous in daily hospital practice in advancing and/or accepting of claims based solely on the prestige, status, or respect of its protagonists and proponents. For example: Two clinical clerks discuss the relevance of a lumbar puncture in a multiple trauma sufferer. "*Why should we perform this procedure on this patient? …. Because the staff physician said so.*" This is an unquestioning appeal to the prestige of someone whose dictum is not always supported by evidence, reasoning, or argument. Such appeals should be distinguished from appeals to the legitimate authority of peer-reviewed scientific publications, where data are reported and arguments are given. Of course, a clinical clerk or intern must do what the attending physician orders. But the order is not in itself a justification for doing the procedure. If one wants to know why it is the right thing to do in the circumstances, substantive reasons should be given. The *ad verecundiam* fallacy occurs not only in the diagnostic domain, but also in treatment decisions and prognosis.

12. Applied to diagnosis, ***ignoring Ockham's razor fallacy*** means the following: If you can explain all the observations, reported symptoms, and test results by a condition which you know the patient has, do not bother ruling out another condition which might explain some or all of the same data. The razor is a useful rule of thumb, but not an infallible guideline. Sometimes a patient who has suffered a fall has two broken bones, not just the one visible on the X-ray. Sometimes a patient has two infections, not just the one identified by laboratory testing. It is a fallacy to think that knowing that a patient has a condition which explains all the data **proves conclusively** that the patient does not have some other condition as well which would explain some or all of the data. To think this way is to take something which follows inductively (probabilistically) from the data as following deductively (necessarily). Ockham's razor is a warrant that can be defeated by further information. It is therefore a defeasible, and not a necessary, warrant.

13. The '***is–ought*** *fallacy* is based on an assumption that if something is now in practice, it **ought** to be so. This assumption, or warrant, is not justified. You need some reason to think that what you are now doing has a good basis other than the fact that you are doing it. "*In our practice, the periodical examination for male patients over 50 includes doing a chest x-ray. A chest x-ray ought to be an integral part of the periodical examination of healthy senior adults.*" (This, of course, is not the case.)

14. The '***criterion/criteria*** *fallacy* also exists. As in etiological research, substituting one criterion of validity for the validity of a diagnostic tool as a whole (provided that other criteria are fulfilled too) may not be satisfactory. For example, we may conclude that a diagnostic test's low sensitivity shows that the test is not good. However, although the test is not good for screening, if the same test is highly specific (as it occurs), it may be valuable in clinical practice to confirm the diagnosis and that the patient should be evaluated further and treated for his or her problem.

5.2.6 How Do We Think and Reason in the Diagnosis Domain?

There is no unique and uniform way to make and use diagnosis in clinical care. Mental processes, types of reasoning and pathways of thinking underlying diagnosis-making include:

- common sense;
- intuition;
- pattern recognition;
- dealing with diagnosis as a logical argument and its outcome (result, claim) in terms of vertical thinking;
- probabilistic considerations;
- deterministic building of diagnosis;
- inductive path, exhaustive approach;
- hypothetico-deductive path;
- direction-driven algorithmic path;
- decision analysis if diagnosis is a part of a multiple-component decision considerations;
- differential approach between multiple options, differential diagnosis, uses of lateral thinking;
- building-up and assessing diagnosis through critical thinking imbedded in a modern argument;
- causal assessment (this anomaly leads to this test result);
- validity assessment for practical uses, in general and in a particular individual (compatibility with subjects in grounds and backing); and
- fallacy watch and corrections.

Any of these ways, alone or in combination, will vary from one diagnostic problem solving approach to another.

The challenge of making diagnoses is further amplified by the reality of medical practice, especially in emergency medicine. It is additionally difficult anywhere where information is missing or vague, where there are not enough health professionals to deal with serious patient problems, and where there are constraints of time, facilities, space, and equipment. Discursive, mostly deductive, and analytical thinking as described briefly above must, and often is, replaced by non-discursive, mostly inductive, and intuitive thinking proposed as a dual process model of reasoning in medicine.[22]

Stolper et al.[23] also recognizes that complex tasks often require both analytical and non-analytical processes in situations marked by uncertainty, and acknowledges that *'gut feelings'* are another element to consider. Because these concepts relate to situations of uncertainty, incomplete knowledge, and other constraints, they apply not only to diagnosis, but also to other steps of clinical work and related decision-making. We will discuss these more in the next chapter which explores decision-making.

5.3 *"That's What We'll Do about It."* Reasoning and Deciding How to Treat and If the Treatment Works

Once the diagnosis is made, treating the patient in the best way possible, and using the best treatment possible, is our focus. The methods we use to decide on the appropriate treatment are the same be it a conservative treatment by drugs, a radical and reconstituting treatment by surgery, or psychotherapy in psychiatry, nursing care, or social support. In addition, there is nothing that would exclude using the general rules of reasoning and decision-making in alternative medicines such as homeopathy, osteopathy, chiropractic, herbalism, aromatherapy, or therapeutic touch in nursing, or any restoring procedures like physiotherapy or beauty enhancers like sun tanning. Mainstream medicine (also called 'allopathic' medicine by naturopaths) and its alternatives are all subject to the same logic, reasoning, and decision-making. Once again, cause-effect relationships are at the core of our concerns and considerations.

As Figure 5.1 shows, understanding and evaluation of the treatment and its results requires multiple comparisons of events and phenomena happening at three steps in sequence:

1. **initial states** (before subjects are exposed or not to treatment and other factor of interest);
2. clinical **maneuvers**, and what happens after such exposure (maneuvers subject of comparison); and
3. resulting outcomes (**subsequent states**).

In each of these steps, the principal subject of interest (chief complaint and health problems, morbidity), associate health problems (co-morbidity), treatment for the chief problem, co-treatment for co-morbid states, and the expected and/or unexpected outcomes of each of them, as well as success or harm resulting from each intervention (maneuver) are studied and determined.

To understand if and how treatment works, a step-by-step comparison of treated and untreated groups is necessary. This is illustrated by Figure 8.1 in Chapter 8, and is also presented here with minor modifications to emphasize treatment aspects, for the convenience of the reader, as Figure 5.2 in this chapter.

In the risk domain, we deal with noxious factors and undesirable events such as the case occurrence of a particular disease. In the treatment domain, we most often pay attention to positive phenomena such as beneficial factors (treatment and care) and improvements in health: cure, lessening the severity of disease, and prevention. Adverse effects of care may be an exception. Both categories of phenomena are an ensemble of **health events that are subject to conceptually similar reasoning**, dealing with probabilities, uncertainties, their quantification, comparisons, interpretation, and use in our decision-making. Methodologically, they are subject to similar logic and reasoning. Let us keep this in mind throughout the present chapter.

5.3.1 Types and Levels of Medical Therapeutic and Preventive Interventions

Five types of preventive or therapeutic interventions can be considered as medical therapeutic and preventive interventions:[24]

1. **modification of the factor** or cause of disease. For example, sodium chloride intake in relation to hypertension may be partly replaced by the consumption of other salts;
2. **modification of exposure**, in terms of avoidance, lesser doses, or its spread in time: abstention from some foods or alcohol, a gluten-free diet in phenylketonuria, etc.;
3. **modification of the response**, such as augmenting subject resistance through vaccines, better nutrition, drugs, operations, etc.;

4. **avoidance of response**, such as in personal hygiene; or
5. **suppression of the target organ (modification of the morphology)**, such as performing an appendectomy or hernia repair. A woman whose mother and sister died of breast cancer may ask her surgeon to perform a bilateral mastectomy, eliminating the biological terrain for a high-probability cancer, given that various endogenous and exogenous factors or causes remain unknown.

We want to know if treatment works at any level of prevention. There are five levels of prevention:[25]

- **Primordial prevention**, a more recent entity, refers to the control of conditions, actions, and measures that minimize hazards to health and hence inhibit the emergence and establishment of processes and factors (e.g., environmental, economic, social, behavioral, cultural) known to increase the risk of disease. Primordial prevention is accomplished through many public and private health policies and intersectorial action. Focusing on the exposure to potential causes, it may be considered part of primary prevention because no disease is involved yet.
- **Primary prevention of medical error and medical error produced harm** means controlling the incidence (occurrence of new cases over a certain period of time). It is generally a task for primary care, family medicine, and public health.
- **Secondary prevention of medical error and medical error-produced harm** means controlling the prevalence (occurrence of all cases at one moment or over a certain period of time) of an error event. Given that prevalence is a function of its average duration and incidence, secondary prevention includes both the control of incidence and disease duration.[7] The control of disease duration is more closely connected to clinical medicine; in preventive medicine, sector 'screening for disease' (or for medical error and harm) remains an important tool.
- **Tertiary prevention of medical error and error-produced harm** means controlling the gradient and severity of disease cases, and its long-term impact with regard to disability, impairment, and handicap. Minimizing suffering and maximizing potential years of useful life[partly from Reference 25] is also its objective. Tertiary prevention focuses exclusively on consequences of a health problem, not its causes.
- **Quaternary prevention** consists of actions that identify patients at risk of overdiagnosis or overmedication, and that protect them from excessive medical intervention, actions that prevent iatrogenesis.[25] Quaternary prevention may prove to be of interest for operational research, especially if supported by further evidence.

Given this multiple sense of prevention, isn't then clinical and community medicine as a whole 'preventive'? Specific epidemiological methods and techniques used in disease prevention in general are described in the epidemiological, public health, and evidence-based medicine literature.[7,26–28] The concept of cause-effect relationships as discussed above (and in Chapter 8) also applies to any kind of intervention in medicine at any level of prevention: control of exposure to noxious factors, immunization in primary prevention, treatment in secondary prevention, avoiding metastases, or

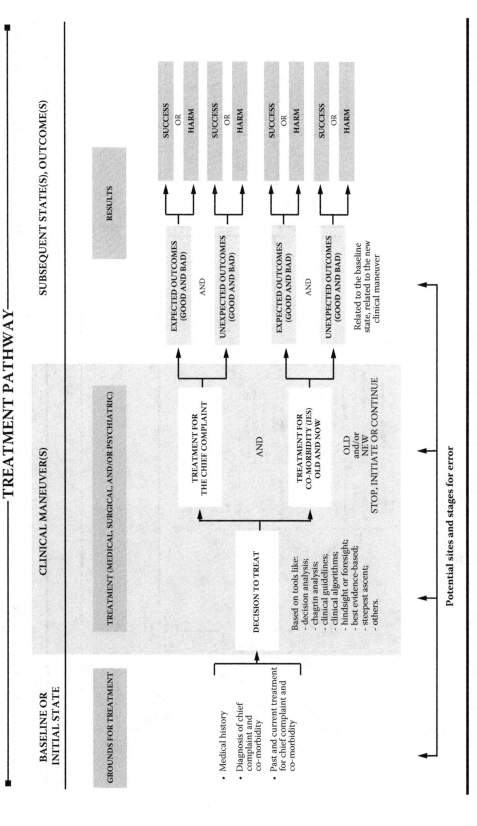

Figure 5.1 **Pathway of treatment to be understood. (Redrawn with modifications from Jenicek M.** *Medical Error and Harm. Understanding, Prevention, and Control.* **Boca Raton, FL: CRC Press/Taylor & Francis/Productivity Press, 2011. Reproduced with permission.)**

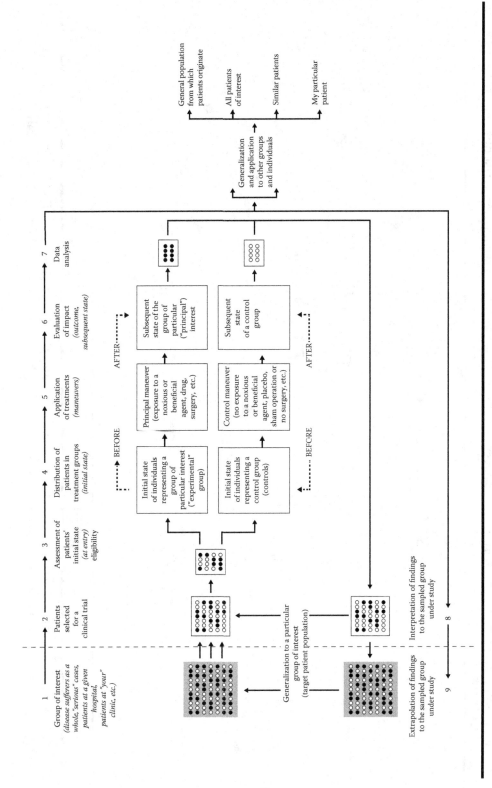

Figure 5.2 Steps of analytical study of treatment and its effects and generalizability of results. (Redrawn with modifications from Jenicek M. *Epidemiology. The Logic of Modern Medicine.* **Montreal: EPIMED International, 1995 and Jenicek M.** *A Primer on Clinical Experience in Medicine.* **Boca Raton, FL: CRC Press, 2013. Reproduced with permission.)**

ensuring the comfort of a terminal patient in tertiary prevention. The same criteria of cause-effect relationships apply as well as various risk measurements (absolute, relative, and attributable). Any evaluation of treatment impact, such as effectiveness or adverse effects, and their evaluation by additional methods, are derived from this basic consideration and approach.

Paradigms, mental processes and types of reasoning underlying treatment evaluation and decisions regarding a patient represent the same considerations as those of reasoning regarding the risk, plus:

- equal chances for patients, treatments under comparison, evaluators of effect (randomization and blinding);
- equipoise when faced with the research question and the search for the answer;
- considering the clinical trial as an argument leading to the acceptance or rejection of the treatment under evaluation (vertical thinking);
- weighing other options in terms of lateral thinking;
- weighing benefits and risks (adverse effects);
- making distinctions in outcomes evaluation: efficacy, effectiveness, efficiency of treatment, consistency of its effect, and outcome;
- considering clinical trials as an evaluation of another cause-effect relationship;
- choosing the treatment for a particular patient with his or her eligibility to trials serving as grounds and backing for treatment recommendation (claim).

5.3.2 Which Treatment Works Best? How Is It Measured?

Treatment evaluation consists of various procedures, methods, and techniques needed to determine as objectively as possible the relevance, effect, and impact of various therapeutic activities relative to their pre-established objectives. Does a new analgesic control arthritis pain? Does a coronary bypass improve cardiac function? Does psychotherapy relieve anxiety in a patient under stress? All these interactions as cause-effect relationships must be examined with the same logic as that used for the assessment of criteria of causality, as explained in Table 5.2 (p. 148).

In interventional or experimental studies, however, it is not the subject who chooses to be exposed (or not) to the factor under study, but rather the health professional. A researcher or practising clinician decides who will be exposed to the active treatment or its inactive alternative (placebo) using statistically valid random assignments or otherwise. Since the factor under study (treatment, nursing care, rehabilitation, etc.) is expected to bring about a cure, healing, functional improvement, alleviation of pain, or comfort to the patient, there are fewer ethical obstacles to "voluntarily and deliberately" exposing the patient to such factors.

The major tools of evaluation of medical interventions are clinical and field trials. New interventions, that is, all those which have not yet been more objectively evaluated go through five distinct phases:[7]

Phase I: a clinical trial that is performed on healthy subjects in a descriptive manner. The purpose is to see how healthy individuals will respond to a drug physiologically, morphologically, and otherwise.

Phase II: A clinical trial that aims to determine how patients (disease sufferers) will respond to the treatment (drug, etc.). There may be a small control group for basic comparison.

Table 5.2 Basic Characteristics of Prognosis as Opposed to Risk

Topic of Interest	Risk	Prognosis
Individual	What will happen to healthy subjects	What will happen to subjects who already have disease under study
Occurrence of expected effects	Less frequent or rare	Frequent
Controllability of independent variable	Risk characteristics: • uncontrollable: risk markers • controllable: risk factors	Prognostic characteristics: • uncontrollable: prognostic markers • controllable: prognostic factors
Aim of study	• primary prevention • better assessment of individuals	• secondary and tertiary prevention • better clinical decisions
Population size	Many subjects are often studied (large size of studies)	Few patients are often available for the study (small size of studies)
Major focus of interest	Often: • causes • non-medical factors • risk factors	Often: • consequences • medical factors • prognostic markers
Time factor	Occurrence of events toward a given moment (incidence, mortality, etc.)	Occurrence of events evolving in time ("survival" curves)
Target population	Mainly community at large	Hospital-bound individuals (bedridden patients, clinics, etc.)
Accessibility and compliance of participants	Poor or variable	Usually good
Interest and motivation of investigators	Variable	Usually high
Cost of study	Usually higher	Usually lower
Competence of investigators to do study	Usually better	Variable

Source: Partially from Reference 37.

Phase III: A clinical trial that shows if the treatment can, and does, really work. The classical randomized double-blind controlled clinical trial belongs in this category. Limited spectrum and gradient of disease is studied first and further expanded later on.

Phase IV: A clinical trial that is expected to show how the treatment will work once it is put to general use. A non-selective group of 'clean' cases (no co-morbidity and no treatment for co-morbidity) of 'whoever comes through the door' is studied.

Phase V: A clinical trial that may be considered as a late Phase IV, post-marketing study in which 'dirty' cases are involved. This includes individuals with co-morbidities (multiple additional health problems besides the problem of main interest) and co-treatment for such additional health problems in all their interaction of indication and response.

While these phases may seem arbitrary on the surface, they are in fact rigorously scientific. They only increase in their power of causal proof of treatment and cure and in their reproduction of the reality of targeted populations, patients, and setting of care. Three areas and levels of intervention have their own specificities, requirements, and resulting methodologies for determining the best treatment options and require a specialized focus: disease treatment and cure, disease prevention, and health maintenance or health promotion.

Any treatment is an intervention, and it represents a cause in relation to its expected impact (result and effect such as cure or improvement in health and disease). Four questions arising from the concept of treatment are usually explored:

- Is the proposed action **sound** (does it make sense)?
- Is the **structure** of the intervention adequate (how is it organized)?
- Is its **process** acceptable (does it happen as desired)?
- What is the **result** or impact of the treatment (what does it do)?

Any result stemming from these interventions may be evaluated on four different levels:

Level 1: Does the treatment work in ideal conditions (uniform, laboratory or hospital)? This represents the **efficacy** of the treatment (can the treatment work?). In other words, *"Are treatments or prevention specious and consistent?"*

Level 2: Does the treatment work in habitual conditions (everyday life)? The **effectiveness** of the treatment is then understood.

Level 3: Does the treatment work adequately in relation to the amount of money, time, and resources spent? In other words, what is the price of the gains wrought by the treatment? The **efficiency** of the treatment is examined this way. Health economics reasoning is of particular interest, even if a monetary value or utility is replaced by another one.

Level 4: Does the treatment continue to work once put into action? The **constancy** of the performance is highly desirable.

Health economics, operational research, and healthcare organizations focus on the efficiency of interventions. In clinical practice, we particularly want to know the treatment efficacy and effectiveness. Evaluating effectiveness or efficacy is just a matter of comparison either with the **current** situation (rates without intervention of interest) yielding **effectiveness** or to some reference point, likely the **best** situation. The latter offers an idea regarding the **efficacy** of the proposed intervention.

Any evaluation of treatment impact is an analytical study, either by observation or experimentation. Clinical trials are the embodiment of the experimental method across sciences reflected in

Figure 5.1. Subjects are partitioned based on the will of the experimenter, preferably at random into two or more groups, that is, a treated group and another group that is untreated or treated by some alternative procedure or drug. Data are then collected in a 'controlled' manner: Experimenters are 'blinded' in their readings by ignoring the group to which the subjects (patients in the trial) belong and patients ignore to which group they belong. A 'randomized double blind controlled clinical trial' is born. It allows more objective conclusions to be drawn about the cause (treatment of interest or something else) of the outcomes in the trial.

Not only can patients be randomized, so can treatment modalities in the case of an episodic disease with multiple spells, such as migraine and asthma. An N-of-1 trial (random assignment of treatments for disease spells in a single patient suffering from an episodic health problem) is believed to improve patient management.[29] Wherever trials are not feasible or available, the impact of treatment may be, and is, evaluated as a cause-effect relationship through observational studies (case control studies, studies with historical controls, analysis of time trends, etc.).

Given the heterogeneity of trial designs, comparisons, target groups and selected patients, findings from multiple trials are brought together by way of **research integration**, which is essentially an epidemiological study of a set of studies[30–32] of the homogeneity and heterogeneity of their design and results. The goal of research integration is to obtain a more comprehensive idea about a health problem, such as the beneficial impact of treatment or an adverse effect of a noxious factor. Some methodologists emphasize that there are two approaches to research integration:

- The more quantitative approach, **meta-analysis**, is a mostly statistical integration of various fractions, odds, or ratios found in original studies, subject to integration. Point and interval estimates of 'typical odds ratios' are an example of this type of research integration.
- **Systematic reviews** represent a more qualitative approach, in which the person/place/time characteristics of the trial (or other study) are systematically identified and retrieved one by one from one study to another. The picture of homogeneity and heterogeneity across studies is thus obtained, analyzed, and interpreted. A kind of *'epidemiology of original studies'* is done this way.

Both approaches are necessary. Without both, the meaning of quantitative integration would be more than limited. For other methodologists, meta-analysis covers both quantitative and qualitative studies (trials) which can be compared in terms of their subject, nature, and design. Systematic reviews analyze heterogeneous and less comparable studies. The most often used indexes (mathematical relationships) both in original and integrated studies are absolute risk differences or attributable risks in the case of noxious factors or absolute benefit differences or relative benefit (attributable benefit) fraction increases. N.B. Methodologically speaking, a relative benefit notion here is the equivalent of the etiological fraction notion in fundamental epidemiology.

An example of the case of a beneficial factor (treatment) and cases cured or prevented is demonstrated below:

Rate of recovery in the case of treatment: 80%
Rate of recovery in the case of not being subjected to this treatment: 20%
Absolute rate due to the treatment: 80% − 20% = 60%
Relative benefit fraction: 80% − 20%/80% = 75%, meaning that 75% of recoveries are due to the therapeutic intervention of interest.

In the case of the study of a preventive factor such an immunization (vaccination) where newly occurring disease cases (over a defined period of time) rather than recoveries are counted, it would mean a vaccine effectiveness (vaccine protective rate) of 75%, that is, 75% of all expected cases would be avoided (prevented) by (or are due to) immunization. Some may say simply that "*This vaccine is 75% effective.*"

An example of the case of exposure to a noxious agent and new cases of disease is illustrated below. For the sake of simplicity and explicitness, 'round' rates are used in the following example, like 80%, 20%, and so on. In reality, rates may be less 'talking' like 35/100,000, 4/1,000,000, and so on, in cancer or adverse effects epidemiology and studies.

N.B. A small reminder about vocabulary. The term 'exposure' is used across the literature both to exposure to noxious agents and development of disease cases as well as the 'exposure' to beneficial treatment and non-appearance, disappearance, or improvement of disease cases.

Let us consider then:

Incidence rate in the exposed group: 80%

Incidence rate in the non-exposed group: 20%

Relative risk: incidence rate in the exposed group (80%) / incidence rate in the unexposed group (20%) = 4.0

Attributable risk, i.e., absolute rate attributable to the factors of interest (from a web of causes shared by both groups under comparison): 80% − 20% = 60%

Attributable risk percent (syn. attributable fraction, attributable proportion, etiological fraction) is in our example: 80% − 20%/80% = 75% of the total of cases (rate) due to the exposure to the web of its causes is due to the noxious factor of interest. Almost two thirds of all cases observed are due to the factor of interest among others.

Some may say simply that "*This factor represents here three quarters of the entire web of causes.*" If a preventive program to avoid exposure and its consequences were to be implemented, such as smoking cessation to avoid lung cancer, 75% of all cancers occurring in a smoking and non-smoking community under study (smokers and non-smokers all together) would be prevented (would not occur) if smokers stopped smoking. The closer the role of the etiological factor of interest is to 100% of all cases due to all factors forming the web of causes, the more prevalent, dominant, exclusive, or specific is the role of the etiological factor under study.

5.3.3 *Which Treatment Modality Applies to a Particular Patient?*

Ideally, at least for a clinical epidemiologist, your patient's characteristics should be similar to the characteristics of patients selected and participating in clinical trials assessing the treatment of interest and confirming the effectiveness of treatment. In other words, you should be asking yourself: "*Would my patient be eligible to participate in a clinical trial from which information about treatment effectiveness is coming?*" It is even more ideal if your patient's characteristics were compatible with the characteristics of patients participating in the trial and ultimately, who have responded favorably to treatment. They may differ in all those aspects. However, randomization aside, clinical trial reports do not routinely provide detailed information about the characteristics of patients who responded well.

5.3.4 Treatment as a Subject of Argumentation

We may look at the choice, use, and evaluation of treatment as a kind of pleading for it: an argument leading to some claim or conclusion. We can do this using two approaches: an evidence-based medicine (critical appraisal) approach or an argumentation (critical thinking) approach. These approaches are outlined here.[32]

Evidence-Based Approach

Appraising the choice, execution, and effect of treatment is a more traditional approach to critical appraisal in evidence-based medicine. The following questions can be used to assess the treatment:

- Are we dealing with a questionable and uncertain problem?
- How well is the problem defined?
- Was the question to be answered properly formulated?
- Was the search for evidence (other studies) adequate and complete?
- What is the design of an etiological study? How valid is it?
- Are biostatistical considerations like sampling or analysis, and epidemiological considerations like exposure to possible multiple causes, adequately handled and answered?
- Were clinical aspects of the disease considered (subjects' characteristics, co-morbidity, outcomes, follow-up, and others)?
- How was the effect (impact) of a presumed cause (validity of results) evaluated?
- Which criteria of causality are fulfilled by the study results?
- Was the broader balance between harm, benefits, costs, and controllability assessed, and is it adequate?
- Is it the best evidence available?

Critical Thinking Approach

Critical thinking can also be used to assess treatment. Consider using the following questions:

- What is the proponents' claim?
- What was the original question?
- How solid and complete are grounds needed for the solution of the problem?
- Is there any good backing for the claim?
- Does the overall existing information provide some usable understanding of the nature of the problem (warrant)?
- Are there any conditions (considerations) that might invalidate (rebuttals) or weaken ('negative' adducts) the ensuing final claim?
- How well are such building blocks of an argument interconnected to support or limit the claim?
- In the case of a cause-effect problem: Does the overall evidence fulfill the criteria of causality? Which ones?

- How certain are we about our claim (qualifier specified)?
- Were possible competing claims considered and evaluated?
- Are the results usable in the user's setting (caring of a specific patient, groups of patients, community groups) and in which settings are they not?
- If relevant, how much could, and should, such findings be generalized?
- Were possible competing causes considered and evaluated?

Both approaches and related paradigms are complementary, not exclusive; both are necessary.

5.3.5 Illustrative Fallacies

Our reasoning and judgment in the domain of treatment, as everything else in our medical reflections, may be prone to errors. Some of these fallacies[8] are worth mentioning. These fallacies are related to data and information, to the design of the studies (trials) that produced them, to their interpretation, or to all three aspects. The same faulty mental processes and types of reasoning underlying risk or diagnosis apply with additional considerations to treatment evaluation and decisions regarding a patient as discussed in this chapter as follows:

1. **Boeotian's fallacy (ignoring webs of causes and webs of consequences fallacy)** refers to simplistic reasoning due to the ignorance of such as various treatments offered for a particular disease and webs of treatment consequences such as more than one desirable and/or undesirable outcome(s). Formulation of questions about the treatment, its trials, and interpretations, may be affected by pretending that this is the only treatment of interest, alternatives to the clinical trial design do not exist, or that the only chosen outcome is worthy of analysis and interpretation.
2. From a biostatistical point of view, omitting **multivariate** (more than one independent variable) analysis and/or **multivarible** (more than one dependent variable) analysis is also fallacious approach to treatment understanding.
3. **Confirmation fallacy**, or **confirmation bias**, stems from looking only for evidence that confirms the hypothesis (such as effectiveness of a particular drug) and omitting the evidence that does not confirm the hypothesis. Evidence for the hypothesis may be weaker than broader evidence gathered later on.
4. **Fallacy of commission** or **action fallacy** is due to the tendency to change the course of events (patient's outcomes) by choosing the treatment because this creates some action as opposed to doing something. This is embodied in the phrases: "*It's better to do something than nothing!*" and "*I would look incompetent and indecisive if I said let's leave it as it is.*"
5. **Omission fallacy (omission bias)** is the opposite of the above. It can be described by the phrase "*I prefer to do nothing, I will avoid errors this way and possible adverse and undesirable outcomes of whatever I choose and will occur.*"
6. **Overconfidence fallacy** is the omission of critically appraised evidence that the treatment works or not, replacing it with hunches, absent, or incomplete evidence, and exaggerated faith in our own opinion. This is summed up by the phrases "*It has always worked for me!*" and "*It has always worked in this hospital!*"

7. **Appeal to authority fallacy** is a result of misjudging the problem and reasons for decisions because of the position of the decision maker or someone who is an authority in a different domain. For example: "*As chairman of this Committee, I must tell you that these clinical treatment guidelines are correct,*" or "*As manager of this hospital, I must say that this protocol of care is not the best from among all available alternatives,*" or "*I am a resident; I run this floor! Since you are a clinical clerk, do what I tell you.*" Anonymous authorities and associations with past or present disreputable persons, bodies, or literature, are used as references to solve problems and challenges in the domain of treatment.

Let us avoid the above-mentioned fallacies, as well as many others.[8]

5.3.6 How Do We Reason in the Domain of Treatment and Preventive Interventions?

In the domain of treatment and preventive intervention, as in any other domain of clinical reasoning and decision-making, we argue *for* something. For example: "*This drug treatment is best for you,*" or "*Surgery is not an option for you,*" or "*This vaccine is 80% effective.*" Even in such informal language, our recommendations are 'claims' or conclusions of an argument in favor or disfavor of such treatment.

We take a number of steps to see if preventive interventions are good and complete enough for our recommendation. We look at data, studies and other references as 'grounds.' We check other available information from our experience, from colleagues, literature or electronic sources to see if such 'backing' may be linked and useful with 'grounds.' We examine the explanatory value of such links as a 'warrant' of our conclusions. Can we say (and why?) how sure we are about our claim? Such a 'qualifier' expresses our certainty that our recommendation is good. A patient may effectively ask, "*Doctor, are you sure that your recommendation of surgery is correct?*" If the patient asks, "*Isn't my problem exceptional and not applicable to your generally recommended strategy?*" we must weigh our answer in terms of all positive elements and exclusionary elements. "Rebuttals" can be both positive and negative adducts, which lead us to our conclusions and recommendations.

All elements of our reasoning are based on what we have seen in the patient and on the epidemiological and biostatistical information we have. Our assessments of the certainty and uncertainty, probabilities of events such as disease prevalence, incidence, case fatality, duration, causal association quantifications and criteria (rates, ratios odds), our knowledge of chances of cure (effectiveness of treatment), and longer term outcomes as part of prognosis all are based on these sources of information. Our best treatment recommendation will depend then on the quality and completeness of clinical and epidemiological evidence underlying the information which is at our disposal and on our correct ways of using such evidence in a fallacy free argumentation path.

The professional and scientific information and argumentation we use, fallacious or not, will often be hidden in the natural language of all parties involved. We should be able to retrieve it anytime.

5.4 Reasoning about Prognosis: *"You'll Be Doing Well…"* Making Prognosis Meaningful

From the beginning of a clinical experience, patients will ask the health professionals involved in their care, *"What will happen to me?"* Patients expect not only a favorable prognosis but also that such a prognosis will be as realistic as possible. As an example, a clinician discovers that a middle-aged, multiparous mother has endometrial cancer and her attending physicians suggests a hysterectomy and other treatments as needed. She may ask a series of questions: *"Is what you propose necessary?"* *"What will happen if I choose not to have this operation?"* *"What other possible problems should I expect and when?"* or *"What is my remaining life expectancy with, or without, my problem and its treatment?"*

What will you tell her? In other words, what is your prognosis in this case? Again, our answers are not only a product of our knowledge of prognostic facts and experience. It is also a result of our reasoning about that information and experience translated into the argumentation and exchange of ideas with the patient and with other colleagues who are caring for her.

Prognosis is more than the art of foretelling the course of disease or *"the prospect of survival and recovery from a disease as anticipated from the usual course of that disease or indicated by special features of the case in question."*[34] Contemporary prognosis is not a guess or a product of clinical flair. It is an estimation of probabilities, as is the evaluation of risk. The basic clinical epidemiological approach is governed by a similar spirit. In risk assessment, probabilities of developing disease are estimated according to the characteristics of the individual and his general environment. In prognostic assessment, probabilities of various good and bad events, as well as outcomes, are assessed in the already diseased individual. While risk is usually related to one event (falling ill), prognostic studies are multidimensional in that they deal with several outcomes, not just death. Whereas risk depends mostly on non-medical factors, prognosis is largely determined by clinical factors, human biology and pathology.

With these considerations in mind, let us understand prognosis then as:

> *"**An assessment** of **the patient's future** (based on probabilistic considerations of various beneficial and detrimental clinical outcomes as causally or otherwise determined by various clinical factors, biological and social characteristics of the patient), and of the **pathology under study (disease course)** itself. Its main purpose is to **prevent undesirable events** and to **intervene precociously to modify disease course** and drive it to its **best possible outcome(s)**. Hence, prognosis is an important element of medical decision-making that goes well beyond reassurance of the patient as part of good bedside manners. It is a **professional act** like any other, be it diagnosis, surgery or medication."*[7,35]

Fries and Ehrlich[36] emphasize several characteristics of prognosis. These considerations, outlined below, apply to a variable degree and in combination based on the health problem. The discussion of each prognosis should then be modified accordingly. Prognosis:

- is a prediction, a probabilistic consideration under uncertainty;
- may be dealt with in both qualitative and quantitative terms;
- is multidimensional, reflected by webs of causes and webs of consequences (outcomes);
- covers in meaningful terms a specific time period;

- varies often from one subgroup of the health problem to another and must be dealt with as such and as a composite phenomenon; and
- does not rely exclusively on treatment; other prognostic factors may be involved including patient characteristics, co-morbidity, type and setting of general care, etc.

A contemporary clinician must proceed with the same rigor to examine their prognosis, evaluating what will happen to an individual patient, as others do when dealing with disease at the community level. The clinician must know, and use, all relevant information from community and clinical epidemiology findings to assess the probability of the worst possible events in order to prevent or alleviate them. As patients or health professionals, we need to know and share prognosis for three major reasons:

1. For the patient, the *best possible estimation of the disease's future course and outcome* gives him or her either reassurance and improvement of mental well-being, or (if the prognosis is poor) allows for timely considerations for the best possible quality of life remaining.
2. For physicians and nurses, good prognostic information allows for the *best therapies and care* to be planned for the patient.
3. For social services, good prognostic information allows for a *timely and optimal reintegration of the patient* into the family, occupation, and environment to an extent and degree corresponding to the foreseeable health status.

Given the considerable human and material resources involved, prognostic studies must arrive at conclusions that are as close to the future reality as possible.

5.4.1 Differences between the Prognosis Domain and the Risk Domain

Making a prognosis is more complicated than assessing risk. As in the risk domain where various risk markers and factors must be evaluated separately, **prognostic characteristics** fall into two categories: **prognostic markers,** which cannot be modified and upon which disease course is dependent, and **prognostic factors,** which can be modified; consequently disease course can also be modified. Knowledge of both is necessary to make a good prognosis. In addition, methodological aspects of prognosis differ from risk assessment. In prognosis, methodological aspects depend on different individuals under study, the duration of events, different causal factors, and the main topics under study. Figure 5.3 summarizes these differences.

Traditionally, knowledge of risk factors in medicine was automatically extrapolated to the field of prognostic factors. Doing so, however, can be quite misleading. For example, smoking is a powerful risk factor for lung cancer, but is it justified for a clinician to suggest that a lung cancer patient stop smoking at an advanced stage of disease? Is it wise to suggest that an octogenarian with a small facial basocellular lesion minimize exposure to the sun in order to avoid skin cancer, even if the patient is carefully followed, screened, and surgically treated in time?

Some risk factors lose their power as prognostic factors, and some are important at both levels. For example, alcohol abuse is a powerful risk factor for chronic hepatitis and liver cirrhosis. Patients with chronic hepatitis and liver cirrhosis will further deteriorate if they continue to drink. Thus, alcohol is a powerful prognostic factor as well. An alcoholic, cirrhotic patient should stop drinking, but a lung cancer patient whose life expectancy is two years at best might possibly continue smoking without greatly altering the disease's course, even though smoking caused the fatal

Topic of interest	Risk	Prognosis
Basic characteristics of prognosis as opposed to risk		
Individual	What will happen to healthy subjects	What will happen to subjects who already have disease under study
Occurrence of expected effects	Less frequent or rare	Frequent
Controllability of independent variable	Risk characteristics: • uncontrollable: risk markers • controllable: risk factors	Prognostic characteristics: • uncontrollable: prognostic markers • controllable: prognostic factors
Aim of study	• primary prevention • better assessment of individuals	• secondary and tertiary prevention • better clinical decisions
Population size	Many subjects are often studied (large size of studies)	Few patients are often available for the study (small size of studies)
Major focus of interest	Often: • causes • non-medical factors • risk factors	Often: • consequences • medical factors • prognostic markers
Time factor	Occurrence of events toward a given moment (incidence, mortality, etc.)	Occurrence of events evolving in time ("survival" curves)
Target population	Mainly community at large	Hospital-bound individuals (bedridden patients, clinics, etc.)
Accessibility and compliance of participants	Poor or variable	Usually good
Interest and motivation of investigators	Variable	Usually high
Cost of study	Usually higher	Usually lower
Competence of investigators to do study	Usually better	Variable

Figure 5.3   Basic characteristics of prognosis as opposed to risk. (Modified from Reference 37.)

neoplasia in the first place. In this context, the ethicist should be asked: Is a recommendation to quit smoking in this particular case justifiable and acceptable from an ethical point of view?

Operationally, risk remains the focus of primary prevention, whereas prognosis and ensuing clinical decisions fall into the field of secondary and tertiary prevention. Consequently, effective secondary and tertiary prevention will depend on knowledge of prognostic markers and factors in their best qualitative and quantitative terms. Certain states, already being consequences of other prognostic factors, lead to the diversification and aggravation of the disease spectrum and ultimately of its gradient.

By **disease spectrum** we mean the range of different systemic manifestations of the disease like the glandular, oculoglandular, oropahryngeal, pleuropulmonary or typhoid forms of tularemia.

Disease gradient is, on the other hand, an expression of different grades of disease according to the severity of cases.[4] Subclinical, flu-like, benign, chronic, and fatally necrotic cases encompass the gradient of viral hepatitis.

Finally, prognostic factors arise not only from the web of causes of principal disease outcomes, but also from concurrent diseases or newly appearing co-morbid states (such as cross infections, metabolic imbalances, etc.). Indeed, all may act upon the outcome of the disease of main interest and/or on any other co-morbidity or additional new disease or health problem. Nonetheless, probabilistic estimations and analyses of exposure to risk or to prognostic factors and their outcomes are still often merged and confounded in current literature.[36,38] Let us always read with care.

5.4.2 What Do We Need to Know about Prognostic Events and Outcomes?

A good or bad (qualitative) prognosis also requires quantification in terms of probabilities. A probabilistic prognosis can be expressed in many different ways. They can be expressed:

- ■ by establishing a **survival rate** after five years of observation, as is usually done in studies of cancer patients;
- ■ by determining a **case fatality rate** at any moment (N.B. Mortality may also be a measure of risk and prognosis since it is the product of incidence density and case fatality rate);[7]
- ■ by detecting a **response rate to treatment** at any moment of a follow-up period (such as an improvement rate after treatment of leukaemia patients). Response rates can include a **remission rate** following a defined treatment (provided that a remission period and its criteria are well-defined) and a **relapse rate** (with the same conditions as above); and
- ■ by establishing a longitudinal picture of events during the natural or clinical course of disease, known as a **survival curve**.

Of particular interest is a survival curve. A **survival curve** is essentially a sequence of rates (proportions) of events of interest in time. Originally, a proportion of patients (usually cancer sufferers) surviving or dying at a given moment were the subject of study. Today, the terms 'survival' or 'survival studies' are rather awkward or misleading, because in addition to deaths, any event appearing during the natural or clinical course of disease may be the subject of a "survival" analysis. These can include disease spells, recurrence, co-morbid events, adverse reactions, and so on.

Figure 5.4 is an example of survival curves of an event with or without treatment. Such curves, as indicated by arrows in the figure, show that survival curves may be used to study trends.

From such descriptions, hypotheses about the evolution of prognosis can be made. As the shadowed sections illustrate, comparisons of survival curves are used in etiological research to analyze and demonstrate the role of prognostic factors, noxious or beneficial, in good or bad prognosis.

> The methodology of studying survival also applies to outcomes of disease other than death. These include the development of complications, another spell of disease such as a migraine attack or an epilepsy "mal," surgical complications after an operation, adverse effects of treatment, and others. During the past two decades, a new term, '**time-to-event analysis**,' has been applied to these studies of morbid events. In studies of treatment effectiveness, time-to-event analysis may be even more specific. For example, in such studies of migraine treatment, time-to-event analysis becomes '**time-to-relief analysis**'; or, elsewhere, it may become '**time-to-effect analysis**.'

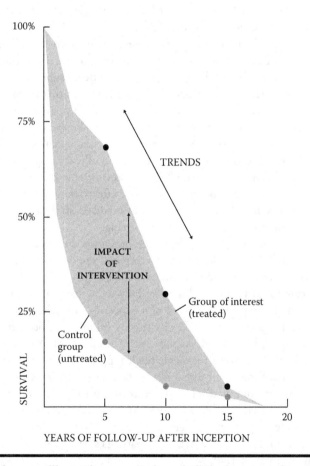

Figure 5.4 **Survival curves illustrating prognosis and clinical course of treated by venesection and untreated patients in sufferers from idiopathic hemochromatosis. (Expanded and modified from Reference 39 as Fig. 3.1 in Jenicek M.** *A Primer on Clinical Experience in Medicine.* **Boca Raton, FL: CRC Press, 2013. Reproduced with permission.)**

5.4.3 What Do We Expect from Prognostic Studies in Order to Reason More Effectively about the Future of Our Patients? What Treatment Modality Best Applies to a Particular Patient?

Like studies of risk, prognosis studies may use either descriptive, observational analytical, or experimental methodologies, but most are longitudinal cohort studies. As in descriptive studies of risk, descriptive studies of prognosis serve several purposes to:

- generate hypotheses on probable causes of a good or bad prognosis in patients;
- identify patients at high probability of a bad prognosis; and
- give argument components and support necessary for clinical decision analysis and clinical decisions themselves in view of the above.

Analytical observational (cohort and case control studies) research prognosis methodologies can use comparative studies of 'survival' in time. These can be either inductive or deductive. Many of these use an inductive approach to data where the information already exists in clinical charts. In cohort studies of prognosis, where hypotheses are constructed deductively and study designs built *ad hoc*, conclusions can be more solid than those in retrospective studies.

Finally, intervention studies, such as clinical trials, may be based on the comparison of survival curves (or prognostic curves) in different groups of patients subjected to different treatment modalities. A simple comparison of the frequency of outcomes in treatment groups usually represents an assessment of treatment impact in the short term. A comparison of prognostic (survival) curves is an important method of evaluation of a treatment's long-term impact. In these studies, the natural (placebo) and clinical course are compared, or various clinical courses (under various treatment modalities) are assessed with regard to their best efficacy and effectiveness.

Another type of study addressing cause-effect relationships are comparative studies.

These studies of a course of disease examine cause-effect relationships between various non-clinical and clinical events and disease outcomes. Specialized statistical techniques are used to understand relative risk of a particular outcome occurring.

Regardless of the type of analytical study in the prognosis domain, the principles remain the same. Whether the study is observational or experimental the same clinimetric rigor and causal reasoning are used as in any other study in clinical epidemiology.

Making a prognosis based simply on knowing how many patients will survive a certain time period (e.g., five years following the detection of a cancer or any other disease) might yield very poor information. This is because thee the exact timing (moment of occurrence) of the events in **this five-year period** would be ignored. As shown by Fletcher et al.,[40] several diseases may show a comparable survival rate at a given moment. Such a prognosis can be made with fairly good accuracy for a rapidly dissecting aortic aneurysm; subjects mainly die within the first one or two years following its discovery, and its discovery is known immediately. However, for a disease like chronic granulocytic leukemia, the exact timing when the disease occurred is not known with certainty. It may have developed over a period of years. While a five-year survival rate can be observed in chronic granulocytic leukaemia, more patients survive beyond the first year and years after within the same five-year period.

A better approach to describe and properly analyze prognostic events is to develop a life table, and then estimate a survival curve based on the table.

A **life table** is a summarizing technique used to describe the pattern of mortality (or of any other event of clinical interest) and survival (i.e., non-event) in populations.

A **clinical life table** *"describes the outcome experience of a group or cohort of individuals classified according to their exposure or treatment history."*[24,40] It is *"a summarizing technique used to describe the pattern of morbidity and survival in populations."*[25]

Once a life table is developed, then a survival curve can be estimated from it. Once survival curves are established through an appropriate survivorship study, a survival analysis, that is, comparison of curves, can be carried out. A **survival curve** is "a curve that starts with 100% of the study population and shows the percentage of the population surviving at successive times for as long a period as information is available."[24,41] There are three major reasons to establish, analyze, and use survival curves:

1. Survival curves depict trends and the evolution of prognostic events in time.
2. Analyses of time trends represented by survival curves allow hypotheses generations about possible causal factors behind differing trends depicting prognosis.
3. The comparison of survival curves contributes to the establishment of causal relationships between disease course and prognostic and other factors.

> We must reiterate that '**survival**' is not merely 'avoiding death,' when death represents the disease outcome of interest. Survival is a state enjoyed until the occurrence of some event or outcome of interest relevant to the disease. It can be any discrete event such as a relapse, recovery, disease spell (well-defined), or any other change of disease course. The term 'survival' is chosen here because of its persistent use, although it represents 'time-to-event,' 'survival time,' or any 'prognostic' function of interest.

If the endpoint in "true" survival studies is too difficult or expensive to detect, some other "surrogate" point which is more readily measurable, well-correlated with the disease, and biologically well-justified for substitution, may be selected and analyzed.[42] In survival studies of cancer, surrogates for tumour response may be its progression, reappearance of the disease, or the predefined particular value change of carcinoembryonic antigen.[43]

In the statistical literature, establishing a survival curve is called a **survivorship study.** This is defined as the:

> *...use of a cohort life table to provide the probability that an event, such as death, will occur in successive intervals of time after diagnosis (or other time point defined a priori), and conversely, the probability of surviving each interval. The multiplication of these probabilities of survival for each time interval for those alive at the beginning of that interval yields a cumulative probability of surviving for the total period under study.*[41]

In these studies, estimation of "survival" is based on information available about all patients including cases of incomplete follow-up for reasons unrelated to the outcome of interest such as patients dropping out, moving away, dying from other causes, and so on.

Survival analysis is then a *"class of statistical procedures for estimating the survival function and for making inferences about the effects of treatments, prognostic factors, exposures, and other covariates."*[41] Only principles of survival analysis are outlined in this section. Numerical examples abound in the medical literature, and quantitative methodology of survival analysis is described in the statistical literature. However, since clinicians are the use prognostic findings, make decisions, and communicate these prognoses to patients, all clinicians should know what information they need to provide for such an analysis and how to understand its findings.

How Should We Apply What We Know to an Individual Patient?

As in the domain of individual application of treatment evidence, general applicability of research evidence to individual patients and its integration with care is equally valid in the domain of prognosis. The applicability of a prognostic study to an individual patient under a physician's care may be summarized here in just a few questions:

> ■ Would my patient be eligible for a study of prognosis whose results should apply to him or her?
> ■ Would my patient finish such a study?
> ■ Would my patient finish in the 'winning group,' that is, those ending with a good prognosis?
> ■ Are his or her clinical and demographic characteristics similar to those of the patients involved in the research on prognosis on the basis of which we reason?

Needless to say, the third question is more difficult to answer than the three others.

Neither socio-demographic comparability nor clinical and paraclinical characteristics of the disease in the patient are sufficient to determine applicability in the domain of prognosis. The clinician must also ensure that the clinical setting and care, its accessibility and coverage, as well as the human and material resources needed for such care, are compatible. In other terms, does the patient evolve in a similar environment of care (primary care, hospital, long-term care, social services, and living conditions)?

Often, our prognostication is not flawless and it may be subject to multiple fallacies to know, avoid, and correct.

5.4.4 Prognosis as a Subject of Argumentation

Prognosis is another process of reasoning leading to a conclusion. As such, it too is a subject for the argumentative approach. We are best served when we use the best evidence embedded in all building blocks of an argument in developing our reasoning process for making a prognosis.

The paradigms, mental processes, and types of reasoning which are the foundations of making prognoses in a patient are subject to all other considerations and reasoning similar to those in the study and interpretation of risk, diagnosis, and treatment. In the matter of considerations for prognosis as a subject of argumentation, we add:

■ possible disease outcomes, a problem of both description and cause-effect link evaluation;
■ distinctions made between prognostic markers (uncontrollable) and prognostic factors (controllable);

- temporal sequence and of interactions between prognostic factors and markers;
- consequences of the course of disease and its treatment, also called the web of outcomes;
- understanding prognosis in terms of vertical thinking (within the study) and lateral thinking (multiple studies, experiences and pathways to solve the problem); and
- assessing the compatibility between the specific patient under our care and other patients that served as study subjects.

In addition to these considerations, premises need to be understood in the argumentation process. Premises may include patient characteristics, past therapeutic experience, exposure to various risk and prognostic factors as well as experience with the effects of preventive and therapeutic interventions. Ultimately the conclusion of a prognosis argumentation process is that the patient will fare well, or poorly, within a defined time span.

As is the case for any other argument in the risk, diagnosis or treatment domains, concluding (or claiming, as philosophers/logicians/critical thinkers say) is an endpoint of the reasoning process for making a prognosis. This process is based on direct information (grounds, data), available past experience (backing), and an explanatory link between them (warrant) which provides some probability of the righteousness of the claim (qualifier). Some exclusionary information (rebuttals) must also be considered that may invalidate our claims, such as that our prognosis is good or bad. There is no learning and understanding of prognosis without discussing building blocks of modern argument and argumentation such as these.

5.4.5 *Illustrative Fallacies*

The prognosis domain of clinical considerations also has its own flaws and fallacies like risk assessment, diagnosis, or treatment.[8] A few examples outlined in this section introduce us to this area of errors in reasoning and decision-making.

1. **Division and composition** refers to taking the truth about some whole as applying to each one of its parts or *vice versa*. This is a fallacy that occurs in research, practice, and the outside world. For example, the statement: *"The prognosis of cancer is bad!"* Often yes, but is it true for all of its stages, all sites, and given all types of medical facilities and care available? Not necessarily. Prostate cancer has a better prognosis than pancreatic cancer. Similarly, angioplasty can do marvels for single artery coronary disease, but not necessarily in advanced atherosclerosis involving several coronary arteries.

2. **Fallacy of division** means concluding that the properties of an entity as a whole apply to each of its parts. A systematic review of the effectiveness of an anticancer drug improving prognosis across the entire cancer domain does not mean that it applies to each type of cancer under consideration, all of its (their) stages, and coincidence with other treatments.

3. **Fallacy of composition** is the opposite of the above. It means that since some part (and other parts) of a whole has a given property, the entire entity which these parts constitute should also have that property. Finding adverse effects of a new antibiotic in treating bacterial skin infections does not mean that this drug will necessarily produce the same adverse effects in other systemic infections.

4. **Oversimplification** occurs if we look at prognosis too globally, without '*atomization*,' a term used by logicians for breaking down a huge problem into manageable pieces. For example, a good or bad prognosis may simply mean a principal outcome of the disease of interest like death and some of its determining clinical and other factors. Another prognosis may concern the prediction of the occurrence of additional other diseases, treatment for such co-morbidity, or outcomes of the latter. To say that a prognosis is 'good' or 'bad' does not necessarily refer only to survival or indicate that the patient will walk out alive from the hospital. Saying that the prognosis in this patient is good or bad does not always mean a good or poor survival or life expectancy. For example, exposure to some prognostic beneficial factor like treatment may lead to a better prognosis in terms of a better course of the major health problem under treatment, it may improve the course of other co-morbid states (other diseases of interest), or it may be a good prognostic factor in relation to other health problems occurring with the index health problem, like cross-infection, new degenerative processes, or injuries without necessarily affecting overall survival.

   An exposure to some prognostic beneficial factor like treatment may lead to a better prognosis in terms of a better course of the major health problem under treatment, it may improve the course of other co-morbid states (other diseases of interest), or it may be a good prognostic factor in relation to other health problems occurring with the index health problem, like cross-infection, new degenerative processes, or injuries without necessarily affecting overall survival.

5. **Misleading use of statistics** can be a particularly challenging in making prognoses as they are used so frequently. Prognoses are often stated in terms of probabilities, or in terms of measures of a central tendency. For example, "*Abdominal mesothelioma is incurable, with a median mortality of only eight months after discovery.*" Does this mean that a patient diagnosed with abdominal mesothelioma will be dead within eight months? Among other considerations, cases are **not always uniformly** distributed around a median (middle-ranking) value. In this instance, the 50% of recorded patients with abdominal mesothelioma who died in eight months or less were clustered in this short period, but the 50% who lived for eight months or more were spread out over a period which ranged up to several years. Statistical distributions **apply only to a prescribed set of circumstances**. In this instance the reported median applied to patients given conventional treatment; it would be different in the case of some alternative, better treatment protocol.

5.4.6 *How Do We Think in the Domain of Prognosis? Considerations for Further Work and Understanding in the Area of Prognosis*

Intuition is even less important in prognostication than in treatment decisions. It is more an attitude of faith than logic fueled by evidence. The best available evidence should be used to support building blocks of our argumentation. Fallacy-free connections between argument blocks (grounds, backing, warrant, adducts for the conclusion and rebuttals, ensuing conclusion, and claim) is what makes medicine based on critical thinking and grounded in evidence.

Prognostic studies are derived from a time-extended follow-up of outcomes in clinical trials or observational analytical studies. More than one group of patients are then involved and compared.

Absolute and relative probabilities of outcomes are formulated as a **hazard**, absolute for a given group or relative to some other control group. Observational longitudinal studies are a more traditional approach for understanding prognosis. These studies examine outcomes of disease to establish a particular probability of outcome (event) in time, like other disease spells, occurrence of new complications, new co-morbidity, cure, or death.

Risk, as the probability of new cases of disease in the community in previously healthy subjects, has already been discussed. Let us emphasize again that risk as an assessment of disease occurrence is essentially **an evaluation of the cause-effect relationship between some factors and disease** before it occurs in individuals who do not have it, and who might get it. **Prognosis**, instead, **is the probability** of some events (outcomes) **occurring in individuals who already have the disease**. For some, prognosis also includes other predictions of outcomes in individuals who still either do not have the disease, or have not been treated for it or anything else. This distinction between risk and prognostic characteristics (factors and markers) is often confounded in the current literature.

Despite the considerable development of a conceptual and methodological basis of prognosis, this field remains 'young'. Thousands of survival and other prognostic studies have taken place, but once published, their results are still used less often in practice than information obtained from the areas of diagnosis and treatment. However, prognostic information that goes beyond educated guesswork is necessary for patient counseling, and it is crucial when deciding what problem is worthy of prevention (secondary and tertiary prevention in particular).

As the field develops, prognostic scoring systems are now increasingly the subject of pragmatic evaluations. As already mentioned above, Hussain et al.'s study[43] of such systems in the field of gastrointestinal bleeding is an excellent example of such initiatives. It is still necessary to know if the structured approach to prognosis (called '**actuarial judgment**')[44] or the clinical approach supports the preference of actuarial judgment based on experience in psychiatry and medicine.

The prognostic performance of physicians may vary considerably from one physician to another and adversely affect care in emergency situations and in critical care. In cardiology, inter-physician variability may be substantial. In coronary artery disease, statistical predictions can provide better predictions than the "expert" clinical judgment of individual cardiologists.[45] Any prognostician should expect that his or her patient may not be happy with a sole quantitative prognosis, but the patient may also ask *"Why?"*

Returning to this section's introductory example, the attending physician advising a patient to have a hysterectomy should, on the basis of the above-mentioned considerations, give the patient the second half of the answer, *"You will be fine, because..."* In other words, the physician tells the patient that specific prognostic data from description, research of causes, and clinical trials or other types of outcome research, speak in her favor given that her situation is similar to other patients in these studies. The physician can conclude by telling her: *"But given your past and present specific characteristics, here is how sure you can be about the following..."*.

Let Us Conclude

Understanding and communicating risk, diagnosis, treatment, and prognosis at any stage of the clinical process requires an often monumental volume of information from reading, teaching, listening, and watching from our experiences. We must know understand these processes, and how they differ with respect to specific to patients. What should we keep in mind?

In summary, our views of risk assessment in the patient, diagnosis, treatment, and prognosis have been and are shaped by various traditional and less traditional disciplines. These include fundamental epidemiology, clinical epidemiology, biostatistics, emerging cognitive science, decision-making, and philosophy (informal logic, critical thinking, argumentation). Where our ways of reasoning come from among all the above-mentioned fields is less important than integrating them into some common view and uses from which all, patients and medical professionals as well, would benefit for the sake of the best possible quality of care.

At any level and step of clinical work, we must consider underlying cause-effect relationships, judge them, and use them in our interpretations and decisions. Our broader views go well beyond causality. For example, in the diagnostic domain, evaluating the internal validity (how the test detects disease itself) and the external validity (how the test performs in practice once its internal quality is determined) further rationalize our diagnostic processes.

Epidemiological, biostatistical and other methodologies will proportionally vary from one clinical activity to another. However, logic and critical thinking are, and increasingly will be essential at any level of what we are doing in daily practice and medical research. All our statements, such as *"You must stop smoking [...] alcohol ruined your liver [...] take this pill, it will ease your pain [...] if you don't do this, you will shorten the years you have left"* are claims or conclusions of our argumentation held either between us, or with our patients, about such problems. Let us understand what is required and apply it more successfully in practice.

Wishing to read more before and beyond references in this chapter, especially related to clinical research? Babu's *Clinical Research Methodology and Evidence-Based Medicine,*[46] Glasser's *Essentials of Clinical Research,*[47] and Portney and Watkins' *Clinical Research: Applications to Practice*[48] may prove useful and valuable for those readers who wish to know the broader context in which clinical thinking and reasoning is used and applied.

References

1. Higgs J, Jones MA, Loftus S, Christensen. *Clinical Reasoning in the Health Professions.* 3rd Edition. Amsterdam/Boston/Heidelberg/London: Elsevier/Butterworth Heinemann, 2008.
2. *A Dictionary of Public Health.* Edited by JM Last. Oxford and New York: Oxford University Press, 2007.
3. Everitt BS. *The Cambridge Dictionary of Statistics in the Medical Sciences.* Cambridge/New York/Melbourne: Cambridge University Press, 1995.
4. Holland BK. *Probability Without Equations. Concepts for Clinicians.* Baltimore, MD and London: The Johns Hopkins University Press, 1998.
5. Goodman SN. Toward evidence-based medical statistics. 1: The *P* value fallacy. 2: The Bayes factor. *Ann Intern Med,* 1996;130:995–1004(Part 1) and 1005–13(Part 2).
6. Ware JC, Mosteller F, Ingelfinger JA. P values. pp. 49–69 in: *Medical Uses of Statistics.* Edited by JC Bailar III and F Mosteller. Waltham, MA: NEHM Books, 1986.
7. Jenicek M. *Foundations of Evidence-Based Medicine.* Boca Raton, FL/London/New York/Washington: The Parthenon Publishing Group/CRC Press, 2003.
8. Jenicek M. *Fallacy-Free Reasoning in Medicine. Improving Communication and Decision-Making in Research and Practice.* Chicago: American Medical Association (AMA Press), 2009.
9. Feinstein AR. *Clinical Epidemiology. The Architecture of Clinical Research.* Philadelphia, PA and London: W.B. Saunders Company, 1985.
10. Fletcher RH, Fletcher SW, Wagner EH. *Clinical Epidemiology. The Essentials.* 3rd Edition. Baltimore/Philadelphia, PA/London: Williams & Wilkins, 1996.
11. Gordis L. *Epidemiology.* 2nd Edition. Philadelphia, PA/London/New York: W.B. Saunders Company, 2000.
12. Identifying cases of disease. Clinimetrics and diagnosis. Chapter 6, pp. 107–46 in Ref. 7.

13. Murphy EA. *The Logic of Medicine.* Baltimore and London: The Johns Hopkins University Press, 1976.
14. Decision analysis and decision-making in medicine. Beyond intuition, guts, and flair. Chapter 13, pp. 341–78 in Ref. 7.
15. Goulston KJ, Cook I, Dent OF. How important is rectal bleeding in the diagnosis of bowel cancer and polyps? *Lancet,* 1986;2:261–5.
16. Straus SE, Scott Richardson W, Glasziou P, Haynes RB. *Evidence-Based Medicine. How to Practice and Teach EBM.* 3rd Edition. Edinburgh, London, New York: Elsevier/Churchill Livingstone, 2005.
17. Bayes T. An essay towards solving a problem in the doctrine of chances (Read 23 December 1763). *Biometrika,* 1958;45:296–315.
18. Variability of predictive values of diagnostic and screening tests. Section 6.4.1.7, pp. 122–124 in Ref. 7.
19. Fu R. Bayes's Theorem. pp. 73–5 in: *Encyclopedia of Epidemiology.* Edited by S Boslaugh and L-A McNutt. Los Angeles/London/New Delhi/Singapore: SAGE Publications, 2008.
20. Gustafson P. Bayesian approach to statistics. pp. 72–3 in: *Encyclopedia of Epidemiology.* Edited by S Boslaugh and L-A McNutt. Los Angeles/London/New Delhi/Singapore: SAGE Publications, 2008.
21. Fagan TJ. Nomogram for Bayes' formula. *N Engl J Med,* 1975;293:257.
22. Croskerry P. Clinical cognition and diagnostic error: Applications of a dual process model of reasoning. *Adv in Health Sci Educ,* doi:10.1007/s10459-009-9182-2, published online 11 August 2009.
23. Stolper E, Van de Wiel M, Van Royen P, Van Bokhoven, Van der Weijden T, Dinant GJ. Gut feelings as a third track in general practioners' diagnostic reasoning. *J Gen Intern Med,* 2010;26(2):197–203. doi:10.1007/s11606-010-15240-5.
24. The impact of treatment and other clinical and community health interventions. A "Does it work?" evaluation. Chapter 9, pp. 229–268 in Ref. 7.
25. *A Dictionary of Epidemiology.* 5th Edition. Edited by M.Porta, S Greenland, and JM Last, Associate Editors. An IEA Sponsored Handbook. Oxford and New York: Oxford University Press, 2008.
26. An overview of program evaluation. pp. 1–30 in: Rossi PH, Lipsey MW, Freeman HE. *Evaluation. A Systematic Approach.* 7th Edition. Thousand Oaks, CA: SAGE Publications, 2004.
27. *Wallace/Maxcy-Rosenau-Last Public Health and Preventive Medicine.* Edited by RB Wallace, N Kohatsu, and JM Last. New York: McGraw-Hill Medical, 2008.
28. *Oxford Textbook of Public Health.* 3rd Edition. Edited by R Detels, WW Holland, J McEwen, and GS Omenn. New York and Oxford: Oxford University Press, 1997.
29. Scuffham PA, Nikles J, Mitchell GK, Yealland MJ, Vine N, Poulos CJ, Pillans PI, Bashford G, del Mar C, Schluter PJ, Glasziou P. Using N-of-1 trials to improve patient management and save costs. *J Gen Intern Med,* 2010;25(9):906–13. doi:10-1007/s11606-010-1352-7.
30. Jenicek M. *Méta-analyse en medicine. Évaluation et synthèse de l'information clinique et épidémiologique. (Meta-Analysis in Medicine. Evaluation and Synthesis of Clinical and Epidemiological Information.)* St. Hyacinthe, QC and Maloine, Paris, 1987. (The first textbook on meta-analysis in medicine.)
31. Petiti DB. *Meta-Analysis, Decision-Analysis and Cost-Effectiveness Analysis. Methods for Quantitative Synthesis in Medicine.* New York and Oxford: Oxford University Press, 1994.
32. Analyzing and integrating a body of knowledge. Systematic reviews and meta-analysis of evidence. Chapter 11, pp. 297–326 in Ref. 7.
33. Jenicek M. *A Physician's Self-Paced Guide to Critical Thinking.* Chicago, IL: American Medical Association (AMA Press), 2006.
34. *Dorland's Illustrated Medical Dictionary.* 27th Edition. Philadelphia, PA: WB Saunders, 1988.
35. Prognosis. Studies of disease course and outcomes. Chapter 10, pp. 269–94 in Ref. 7.
36. *Prognosis. Contemporary Outcomes of Disease.* Edited by JF Fries and GE Ehrlich. Bowie, MD: The Charles Press, 1981.
37. Jenicek M and Cléroux R. *Épidémiologie Clinique. Clinimétrie (Clinical Epidemiology. Clinimetrics.)* St. Hyacinthe, QC and Paris: EDISEM and Maloine, 1985.
38. Eiseman B. *What Are My Chances?* Philadelphia, PA/London/Toronto: The Saunders Press, a W.B. Saunders Company, 1980.
39. Bomford A and Williams R. Long term results of venesection therapy in idiopathic heamochromatosis. *Quart J Med, New Series XLV,* 1976;180:611–23.

40. Prognosis. Chapter 6, pp. 111–35 in: Fletcher RH, Fletcher SW, Wagner EH. *Clinical Epidemiology. The Essentials.* 3rd Edition. Baltimore/Philadelphia, PA/London: Williams & Wilkins, 1996.
41. *A Dictionary of Epidemiology.* 2nd Edition. Edited by JM Last for the International Epidemiological Association. New York and Oxford: Oxford University Press, 1988. (See also Ref. 17.)
42. Ellenberg SS and Hamilton JM. Surrogate endpoints in clinical trials: Cancer. *Stat Med,* 1989;8:403–13.
43. Hussain H, Lapin S, Cappell MS. Clinical scoring systems for determining the prognosis of gastrointestinal bleeding. *Gastroenterol Clin North Amer,* 2000;29(June, No 2):445–64.
44. Dawes RM, Faust D, Meehl PE. Clinical versus actuarial judgment. *Science,* 1989;243:1668–74.
45. Lee KL, Prior DB, Harrell FE Jr. et al. Predicting outcome in coronary disease. Statistical models versus expert clinicians. *Am J Med,* 1986;80:553–60.
46. Babu AN (with contributors). *Clinical Research Methodology and Evidence-Based Medicine: The Basics.* Tunbride Wells, Kent: Anshan Limited, UK, 2008.
47. *Essentials of Clinical Research.* 2nd Edition. Edited by Stephen P. Glasser. Heidelberg/New York/Dordrecht/London: Springer International Publishing, 2014.
48. Portney LG and Watkins MP. *Foundations of Clinical Research. Applications to Practice.* 3rd Edition. Philadelphia, PA: F.A. Davis Company, 2015.

MAJOR SUBJECTS AND CHALLENGES IN MEDICAL THINKING NOT TO BE MISSED: CHOOSING WHAT WE WANT TO DO, DEFINING WHAT WE ARE DOING, CAUSE-EFFECT RELATIONSHIPS, MEDICAL ERROR AND HARM

III

Chapter 6

Thinking about What We Intend to Do: Thesis and Its Seven Cornerstones— "What Is on Our Mind before Talking about Anything Else? About What Exactly Are We Talking?"*

Executive Summary

In medical thinking, and indeed in all scientific thinking, it is vital to first establish what we plan to do, then execute the plan, to understand all that follows: the results of the reported experience, its relevance, impact, and guiding value. The meaning and importance of ideas in each of these steps depends *directly* on the research proposal outlined in the introduction which precedes both the research itself and its subsequent reporting. Recent emphasis on the development of a well-formulated research question is an important step forward. However, more must be said. In exercises of critical thinking, argumentation, and communication, success depends on how everything that we intend to do it is formulated from the beginning.

---

* This chapter is based, with permission by the publisher, on Chapter 3 in: Jenicek M. *Writing, Reading, and Understanding in Modern Health Sciences. Medical Articles and Other Forms of Communication*. Boca Raton, FL/ London/New York: CRC Press/Taylor & Francis/Productivity Press, 2014. Revised, edited, updated.

A more complete research thesis may contain up to seven components, depending on the subject and circumstances. These include the description of the research topic, the critically appraised best evidence available, the research objectives, the research hypothesis, the research question itself, definitions of all of the above entities and their components, and the context and setting in which research is done.

Do readers always find these components in research grants applications, design of research studies, and intended medical articles and other communication? They are equally important in other studies as well as in the description of medical practice and care experience.

Depending on the nature of the problem, our knowledge of it, and the policies of journals and other media, the specific components of a research paper thesis may be explicit or implicit. The author must be ready to defend their thesis and provide necessary additional information on request. The thesis—and its seven components—must be clear to both highly expert and novice readers.

In This Chapter

Executive Summary 171
Thoughts, Thinkers, and Things to Think About 173
Introductory Comments 174
6.1 Our Thesis of This Chapter 175
6.2 Article in Health Sciences as an Argumentative Path 175
6.3 Research Thesis and Its Seven Cornerstones, Which Define Both Research
    and the Presentation of Its Results as a Written or Oral Communication 176
    6.3.1 Research Problem or Topic of Interest: "About What Do We Wish to Talk?" 178
    6.3.2 Critically Appraised Best Evidence Available: "Where Are We Now?" 179
    6.3.3 Objectives of a Research Study: "Why Do We Do All This and What Do
          We Want to Achieve?" 179
    6.3.4 Research Hypothesis: "What Is Our Idea
          about the Nature of the Problem to Be Elucidated?" 181
    6.3.5 Research Question as a Formulation of the Research Problem: "What Is,
          Then, an Answerable Question about Our Hypothesized Problem?" 181
    6.3.6 A Word About Research Questions in Qualitative Research 183
    6.3.7 Definitions Used; the Essence of Understanding: "How Do We Delineate
          the Meaning of Everything We Are Using and Working With?" 185
    6.3.8 Context and Setting of the Study: "What Is the Reality of All Happenings
          in Which the Study Is Valid?" 185
Let Us Conclude 186
References 187

Thoughts, Thinkers, and Things to Think About

A good problem statement often includes (a) what is known, (b) what is unknown, and (c) what is sought.
Edward Hodnett
(1901–1984)
Isn't our thesis here to begin with?

If you do not ask the right questions, you do not get the right answers. A question asked in the right way often points to its own answer. Asking questions is the A-B-C of diagnosis. Only the inquiring mind solves problems.
Edward Hodnett
(1901–1984)
What would we do without a thesis?

This chapter is dedicated also to two notable medical journal editors for their thoughts about medical articles: (1) Edward J. Huth from the Annals of Internal Medicine,[1] for his view of scientific papers as an ***"instrument of persuasion"*** *and (2) Richard Horton from* The Lancet,[2] for his view of medical papers as ***"interpretive medicine,"*** **in other words, an exercise in argumentation. The "cornerstones" of medical articles as thesis, introductions to them, are the opening gateway to the best possible persuasions, argumentations, and interpretations. A good research question is only one of them.**

Anything is possible if you don't know what are you talking about.
Chris A. Mack's (1960–)
Law of Logical Argument
Shouldn't we know?

*Computers are useless: They can only
give you answers.*
Pablo Picasso
(1881–1973)
**Isn't it only up to us to ask right
questions? This chapter should help.**

*Finding and grading the best evidence in today's
world of evidence-based medicine is just fine.
The rest depends, however, on how you will use
it in your reasoning and decision-making. But
all this starts by formulating well what are we
intending to do.*

Introductory Comments

Medical research projects and the articles based upon them may be a simple expository essay or a research report based on the scientific method. Do we have rules for writing essays that are the same as those for scientific papers? Are there common traits, components, and attributes for most of the medical papers which we should understand, respect and apply, no matter the type of medical article being written?

Of course they are. The reader must know what the author (and the researcher whose work is behind the article) is talking about and why. In the case of a research article, the reader must know why the research itself was done, or why, in the case of an essay, the article itself was written. Everyone, and in particular those who provided the financial and other resources for the research, must be convinced about the reason and relevance of the study or issue in question, and how it will contribute to the health sciences.

There is a saying that *"You will only sleep as well as you make your bed beforehand."* Can such a saying also apply to writing medical papers that report health science research findings, ideas, views, and proposals? Absolutely. The research cornerstones which follow apply equally well to writing research projects, applications for research funding, and other discussions and procedures aimed at starting research.

In this chapter, we use medical articles as an example of an activity which requires a set of pre-specifying information which clarifies what we have done, what we are doing, and what we intend to do. For our purposes, medical articles may include:

■ a plan of a particular **daily clinical activity** such a diagnostic workup or choice of treatment or other care;

■ a formulation of a **research project or proposal**;

■ an information about **ongoing research and practice activity** as direction for its ongoing evaluation;

■ a **review** of such activity in view of its conclusions; and

■ a **presentation** of this activity as professional or research communication such as oral communication, periodical or final research report, activity report, or medical scientific and other article and other communication medium.

Our discussion of medical article writing must be seen in this broader light and framework. Even informal discussions among health and management professionals may raise questions about these topics. Without such specifications, our listeners and readers may misunderstand what we are thinking about, what we are doing, and how are doing it, and what we find through our work. We will continue to examine the medical article in this context.

6.1 Our Thesis of This Chapter

In this chapter, let us argue that preparing research, executing research, and writing a scientific paper about it today is not only a question of the form and quality of content, nor the data or information observed and presented based on a universally accepted **structure and organization**. It is more than that. As Fried and Wechsler wrote in their 2001 paper, *How to Get Your Paper Published,* "*Publication of the results of an original scientific study entails producing a manuscript with content that reflects a well-designed, well-executed research question. It is a well-written description of the process, the results, and the wide implications.*"[3] In fact, the way that the scientific paper is written and constructed must reflect and convey the reasoning and critical thinking underlying the message of the paper.

> Even the best research results may not reach their recipients if the communication is poor, the critical thinking and argumentation is illogical, and there is a lack of shared understanding between authors and their readers. **Any medical article is, at its heart, an exercise in critical thinking, argumentation, and communication. Its success depends on how this is designed and conveyed right from its very beginning. Let us propose this as the thesis of this chapter.**

6.2 Article in Health Sciences as an Argumentative Path

Let us consider that you are the researcher and you want to convince everyone that your years of highly competent work and research results are correct, relevant, and useful. How will you do so? In the spirit of the above, and after reading recent books[4–8] and articles[9–12] about medical article writing, you will establish that the crux of a modern, meaningful research article is a continuous argumentative path, that flows from the foundation of your research, through to the resulting medical paper.

The modern health sciences article starts at the very moment when the thesis of the paper is developed, the research is conceived, the motive of the paper is formulated, and the research plan is developed. As a prerequisite, the best available evidence must support all steps and research components in this path. The path is only as good as:

1. How the problem of interest, with all its conceptual and execution components, is **defined** at the beginning of the research, whether it is based on individuals or on other available information.
2. How the research is structured and undertaken from the way it is **organized**, to how the data is **gathered** and subsequently analyzed.
3. How findings are **interpreted** and presented as reports, medical papers, or shared oral communications.

Considering these three parts, the strongest element is usually the second, how the research is structured. There are a variety of research structures: randomized multiple-blind controlled clinical trials, case control studies based on webs of causes and consequences followed by the multivariate and multivariable analysis of its findings, or epidemiological surveillance of adverse effects of healthcare errors and their consequences (harm). However, an article as an exercise in argumentation is initiated at its very beginning by some initial claim which is clarified and proven throughout the whole argumentative process.

This three-step sequence corroborates with the view of a two-step "research → publication" procedure and its connection to scientific writing in general. Writing in the field of architecture Walliman[13] writes:

> *Good communication is required at every stage of the project, but the main writing tasks are located at the beginning and end of the research project—at the beginning to explain what you will do in the research, and at the end, to explain what you have done and what you have found out.*

The quality of a medical paper's original research depends on how well the research underlying it is defined at its beginning, as well as the rigorous methodology followed through to its interpretation and communication as a research report, medical article, or any other way to share the experience with others.

Communicating research or any other professional experience is an exercise in argumentation, intended to convince the reader or the recipient of the message, of the righteousness of findings, their relevance for research and practice, and directions for further attention and inquiry. Throughout the process, the strengths and weaknesses of the experience are shared with interested parties. That, in essence, is the focus of this book. It is not a prescriptive list of rules to follow. Such rules belong to health sciences editors and editorial boards. The ideas presented here are subject to a wider discussion. Some of the ideas are implicit, and therefore do not require discussion, and some are explicit—which means they are clearly understood and thus also do not need further discussion such as some checklists or clinical guidelines. Researchers, medical article writers, readers, and editors all have a voice in these matters.

Is scientific thinking and the method underlying its reporting as outlined in the Introductory Comments and Chapter 3 in this book enough to make scientific reporting meaningful? Something more is needed: Building a medical paper as a way of, and a tool for, reasoning, decision-making, and communication of a health problem and question.

6.3 Research Thesis and Its Seven Cornerstones, Which Define Both Research and the Presentation of Its Results as a Written or Oral Communication

Any medical article's analysis, discussion, and interpretation of research findings are meaningful only in so far as they are grounded and expressed within an argument that is threaded throughout all elements of the article. A well-formulated research question is simply not enough. While a research question is essential for a meaningful research paper, more is needed to understand the article message. McGaghie, Bordage, and Shea[14] stress five requirements and qualities as starting points of a scholarly manuscript:

1. The introduction builds a logical case and context for the problem statement. That is, coverage of the argumentation is expected.
2. The problem statement is clear and well-articulated. More than a research question is needed.
3. The conceptual (theoretical) framework is explicit and justified. The thought process behind the research, or how is framed or proposed, should provide a clear understanding of the research question.
4. The research question, as well as the research hypothesis, is clear, concise, and complete.
5. The variables being investigated are clearly identified and presented.

Thus, in addition to any "research question," any health research paper based on the scientific method requires clear, operational, analyzable, and evaluable *a priori* formulations of at least seven clearly stated cornerstones of research formulation and development listed in Figure 6.1. Definitions and the research setting may also be added.[15 expanded]

These seven elements are all part of a research thesis which comprises more than simply a hypothesis or a research question only. Without these elements, any research study, its findings, and resulting medical articles risk being meaningless. Funders and agencies will require and expect such specifications in the form of a **research thesis**, based on a meaning that is fundamentally different from an academic dissertation as part of the academic studies. In our context, it is a series of statements to be confirmed, rejected, or replaced through argumentation by a new claim and/ or thesis. How should we understand the "thesis" in the context of medical articles? Is it the same notion as in philosophy and its applications in general?

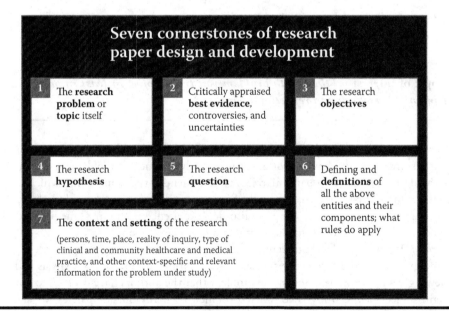

Figure 6.1 Seven cornerstones of research paper design and development. (Redrawn with modifications from Jenicek M. *A Primer on Clinical Experience in Medicine*. Boca Raton: CRC Press, 2013.)

Northey and McKibbin[16] define a thesis as a **central and controlling idea behind the message.** It may be presented as a **working thesis**, which is a sort of planning *thesis*, a focal point around which the presented material and message are organized. A *restricted thesis* is one that narrows the material to examine it thoroughly within a described set of restrictions or limits. A *unified thesis* blends together "double-headed" or sometimes contradictory theses of the same topic. A *precise thesis* avoids vague terms like, "uncomfortable patient" and instead uses more specific terminology such as, "patient in pain."

A **thesis statement** for biomedical research, or for its reporting, is perhaps more than the few sentences suggested across general research methodology. In this context it defines the meaning, relevance, and usability of health research findings, and the articles in which they are presented to second and third interested parties. Ideally—and where space in the journal and topic of research permits—it should be presented in an explicit rather than implicit form. That is, it should be thoroughly expressed in the background, introduction, and other opening opportunities of a medical paper. Implicitness and its justification are imputable to the author, who should be always ready to defend it.

As a roadmap for what to expect from the paper, a thesis introduces the author's first specification of the significance of the presented topic; it is an interpretation of a question or subject, not the subject itself. Eventually it makes a claim that others might dispute.[17] The thesis statement delineates the argument that is presented in the work and it says what the author (authors) is (are) trying to prove in the document.[18] Depending on the nature of the problem and our knowledge of it, thesis components may be explicit or implicit (if clear without exception) in research papers.

In medical articles about causality, all thesis components may be of interest. In review articles, position papers, or essays, one or more components may be of interest only. These are outlined in Section 6.3.1.

6.3.1 Research Problem or Topic of Interest: "About What Do We Wish to Talk?"

> The **topic of interest** is "*the health problem you try to solve, at least in part, through your intended research and reflection about it.*"

The research problem must be defined, and that definition and classification must be clear, stating where our research belongs, how important it is to study this health problem, and what the reasons are that lead us to do it. In particular, it is vital to identify the domain into which our article falls, and to which our research contributes. Some examples of domains include hypertension, ischemic heart disease, psychosis, affective disorder, experience with a new medical technology, understanding and prevention of medical error and harm, and so on.

An *a priori* knowledge of the problem based on personal and collective experience, a literature search, and evaluation and research synthesis in terms of meaningful meta-analysis and systematic reviews, gives appropriate value to the problem that the authors have decided to study. Even if the main subject of the study is considered implicit by many outside parties, we should first make it clear for ourselves while not lengthening our research proposal with an abundance of such details.

6.3.2 Critically Appraised Best Evidence Available: "Where Are We Now?"

The evidence that you have developed is presented before anything else is done. The critically appraised evidence available will determine the quality of the research paper design and development providing that it

- is based not only on a more or less exhaustive literature review, but also on all other relevant sources of information, yielding critically appraised, problem solution-related **best evidence**;
- includes also all known major **contradictions** in the matter under study;
- reviews all relevant **controversies** known;
- identifies relevant **uncertainties** about the problem; and
- covers **competing views** about the problem under scrutiny worthy of comparisons and analyses, all in relation to the problem under study and subject of a medical article.

Hence, a meaningful "literature review" is more than "who said what so far" about the matter of interest.

6.3.3 Objectives of a Research Study: "Why Do We Do All This and What Do We Want to Achieve?"

Research objectives in medicine and other health sciences may be broadly defined as *'Points we want to reach in a study, such as clinical trial, diagnostic test evaluation, or cost-effectiveness assessment of medical care and intervention, community health program or some kind of research synthesis and interpretation of the above'*.

For Kalmund,[19] research objectives should be "SMART":

- **s**pecific,
- **m**easurable,
- **a**chievable,
- **r**ealistic,
- **t**imeframed,

but also:

- **a**ccountable and
- **c**ompatible.

Objectives fall into two categories, either:

> ■ **general** objectives which are often expressed in qualitative terms and specify desired achievements beyond the study, typically within a larger framework of initiatives; and
> ■ **specific** objectives which are often expressed in both qualitative and quantitative terms and which pertain to the study itself.

For example: The University of Oxford Department of Primary Health Care developed a study in the domain of diabetes and vascular disease which addressed the role of diabetes, dyslipidemias, and nutrition in the primary and secondary prevention of cardiovascular disease in primary care based populations. In this study, **general research objectives** could include the development of trials using complex interventions, evaluation of monitoring techniques for disease management, and promoting patient self-management of chronic diseases.[20] A **specific objective** might be the various outcomes in diabetic patients in relation to their compliance with specific drug, nutrition, activity, and care regimens within a multi-center trial of primary care patients in family medicine.

Others differentiate between *task* **objectives** that set the stage for the research (focus on research mechanics) and *research* **objectives** (focus on the results themselves).[21] Research objectives detail the objectives to be achieved by the health professional him/herself, that is, what the research adds to Bloom's three types of learning, educational activities, and acquired skills[22,23] such as **knowledge**, **attitudes**, or **skills** that will be gained by individuals, professionals, or the larger health community as a result of this research. The Association of American Medical Colleges objectives to improve medical communication are a good example of these three foci of evaluation.[22] Other research objectives define what aspect or characteristic of an intervention is evaluated. For example, the evaluation of drug treatment in a trial would include objectives around the intervention **structure** (how it is organized), its **process** (how it works in terms of function description, understanding, control, and/or modeling), or its **impact** (explanation, immediate effect and its forecasting). They also identify what contributions the study will bring to patients as individuals or community and at which **level of prevention** they address—primary, secondary, tertiary, quaternary, and the type of impact that is of interest in the study—efficacy, effectiveness, or efficiency.

Sometimes, objectives include not only the assessment of specific treatment effectiveness, but also the gathering of data itself to address gaps in the current research base. The focus here may be to systematically assess the effectiveness of combinations of treatment for specific patient groups (including those who are commonly excluded from clinical trials), examine the outcomes of care for specific disorders, or to conduct health policy and health economic studies of the impact of the changes in the organization, delivery and financing of care on access quality, and outcomes of treatment.[21–23 generalized]

Research objectives in pharmacology and drug research most often focus on cause-effect relationships, for example, whether a drug works or not. In other types of research studies, such as occurrence studies, outcome studies, and surveillance for unexpected and expected adverse or undesirable effects, research objectives are modest (like determining a simple occurrence of frequency of events) and their results are powerful generators of hypotheses. Their purpose should be to provide the information necessary for conceiving subsequent causal research or health intervention testing.

Case studies and other qualitative research and mixed-method inquiries have their own research objectives. These are typically focused on understanding and problem and hypothesis generation for further quantitative, qualitative, and mixed-methods research.

Once research objectives of a study—regardless of the type—are defined, a research hypothesis will need to be generated.

6.3.4 Research Hypothesis: "What Is Our Idea about the Nature of the Problem to Be Elucidated?"

> Let us define a **research hypothesis** as '*a proposition to be evaluated, accepted or rejected by the research study and its results*'. Hence, a research hypothesis is much more than a statement, in the language of statistics, about some relationship between dependent and independent variable(s) of interest.

Another definition of a research hypothesis is that it is a proposition or set of propositions, set forth as an explanation for the occurrence of some specified group of phenomena, either asserted merely as a provisional conjecture to guide investigation (a working hypothesis) or accepted as highly probable in light of established facts.[24,25] It can also be defined as a preliminary or tentative explanation or theory by the researcher of what the researcher considers the outcome of the investigation will be.[26]

A research hypothesis as a testable statement is a starting point for any research. The hypothesis must be phrased so that it is clear and testable.[26] A good hypothesis must have an elucidating power, furnish an acceptable explanation of the phenomenon, be formulated in simple and understandable terms, be verifiable, and fit the existing knowledge (conditional).[22,23 modified]

6.3.5 Research Question as a Formulation of the Research Problem: "What Is, Then, an Answerable Question about Our Hypothesized Problem?"

> In a broader research context, the **research question in general** is a *matter of some difficulty and uncertainty, and subject of dispute or controversy, that must be answered by the study*. A health research question is '*an expression of doubt and uncertainty about the nature and solution of a health problem in their specific context, to be discussed, solved and answered by an intended inquiry*'. We may see it also as a '**hypothesis followed by a question mark**'.

Let us reword one component of this: In a historical context of research question development, as reviewed by Heddle,[27] Thabane et al.,[28] and Lytwyn[29] remind us that the key purpose of a research question is not only in determining research structure orientation and other methodological aspects of the research itself. It also plays an important role in reporting results in medical articles and communications by improving the clarity of the problem and the thought process in developing the research plan. This increases the chances of finding the solution of the problem of interest, guiding analysis decisions, and anticipating issues and resource needs.

Asking the question in the right way also improves efficiency by reducing the need to revisit the question. It leads to effective review of the literature and retrieval of best evidence at the beginning of the research. At its end, it allows the reader and the researcher as well to understand what was accomplished, if the research was relevant, and useful to the reader's needs. A well-formulated research question increases chances that the research will be published. **Open, exploratory questions** are "*What is ...*" kinds of questions, such as: "*What are the outcomes of myocardial infarction?*" **Directive questions** specify the problem, its determinants, and related circumstances, such as: "*What is the five-year survival of patients with this type of cancer if treated or not by this best available treatment?*"

A series of mnemonics and acronyms have been developed as a way to capture a directive form of creating the research hypothesis. The **PICO**[30] format (**p**atient/problem, **i**ntervention or other kind of exposure, **c**omparison intervention or exposure, **o**utcomes) was originally proposed by Mulrow, Oxman,[31] and Counsell.[32] This format has evolved to **PICOT**[24] or (clumsily acronymized) **PoCICOST format**[24] and structure, as summarized in the following synopsis as Figure 6.2.

These constituting elements of the research question must be used selectively (i.e., not all of them every time) according the nature of the health problem to be solved. They must be relevant in the context of any particular challenge.

> ## PoCICOST Question
>
> **Po** **Population**, or selected patients who represent or not a larger demographic, social and health status entity. A 'target' population or population to which research study results should and will apply.
>
> **C** **Condition of interest**, such as disease stage, spectrum and gradient.
>
> **I** **Intervention**, such as medication, surgery, health education, health promotion, economic or social reorganization and so forth to modify the current health situation.
>
> **C** **Control(s)**, i.e., groups for comparison allowing the establishment of contrasts as a measure of the success of treatment or any other intervention, noxious or beneficial for individuals under care and attention.
>
> **O** **Outcome(s)**, as all possible results (changes of health status) stemming from exposure to some beneficial (treatment, prevention) or noxious (disease causes) factors occurring during the handling and study of the health problem of interest.
>
> **S** **Setting**, i.e., the organization and functioning of life, social and other related conditions, activity, and care (including the current research study of interest) and specific healthcare environment and services within which the study of the health problem is carried out. Study results may also differ from such environment to another. Outcomes research among others depends on it.
>
> **T** **Time frame**, or periods and durations of exposure to beneficial or noxious factors and/or the duration of the study of the development of their consequences. Meta-analyses, time trends studies, outcomes research or survival studies need all a well defined time frame for which the study is valid.

Figure 6.2 PoCICOST Question.

An example of a **PoCICOST** directive question might be: "*In patients from our city, discharged from our hospital care (**Po**) after surviving a myocardial infarction (**C**), do platelet therapies (**I**), improve the prognosis of (or the probability of) such undesirable outcomes such as cardiovascular death, myocardial re-infarction, and stroke, and such patients' survival with or without the risk of increased comorbidity (**O**), as compared to other patients to whom this therapy was not given (**C**), when under the care of our university affiliated outpatient clinic (**S**) over a longer term period of five years (**T**)?*"[24 modified]

Another example is: "*Does the new emergency medical services system (**I**) improve survival and other outcomes, and prevent complications (**O**) in traffic accident, stroke, and cardiac arrest victims (**P**), in this emergency medical services underserviced rural area with a new standard high quality hospital care (**S**) as compared to the old system and similar system changes in the neighbouring urban environment (**C**) over the period of five years (**T**) since its implementation?*"

Such questions are only meaningful if all their components are well-defined both in gnostic and operational terms. This includes defining the patients themselves, hospital and extra-hospital services, events (such as stroke, cardiac arrest, traffic accident, complications), type of services, quality of care, target population and area of the study, and any other health-related phenomena beyond the basic, possibly related independent, and dependent variables. Such definitions as detailed in Chapter 7 are crucial for our understanding of any medical article and the research which underlies it. The results of the study should be presented and discussed (and may be only discussed) in light of the above mentioned **PoCICOST** specifications and limitations. Omitting or ignoring them would mean making more or less supported educated guesses, and/or offering more or less substantiated proposals, for a more advanced study.

The **PICO format** of research questions is appropriate for those searching for cause-effect relationships between noxious or beneficial effects and health deterioration or improvement. However crucial a cause-effect study may be, what about research questions regarding problems other than etiology? Some elements of these **structured research questions** have also begun to appear in part or *in toto* as elements of structured summaries required by, and presented by, an increasing number of leading medical journals (*The Lancet, Annals of Internal Medicine*, and others). As already mentioned in the previous chapter, these may include *background* (some or all elements of the thesis as outlined above), *objective, design, setting, participants* (patients and others), *intervention* (exposure to noxious or beneficial factors), *measurements* (of results, outcomes in health and/or care), other *results* or *findings*, their *interpretation, limitations* (in understanding and knowledge, decision purposes, scope of use, impact), and *conclusions*. To all the above, "*funding*" is added to further clarify the objectivity of the (ideally) bias-free study.

6.3.6 *A Word About Research Questions in Qualitative Research*

In qualitative research[33] as briefly outlined in Section 2.5 in Chapter 2, research questions are *broader* than in quantitative research given the characteristics, focus, and objectives of this type of research. These questions differ from the questions at the beginning of a scientific method-based quantitative research project (see Chapter 2) on the basis of:

- the will to explore the nature of the problem with an open and clear mind, unobstructed by other experience, or potentially biased by previous experience;
- the use of open questions which lead to other questions (both open and closed) which first identify valuable information and refine it in the further process of qualitative inquiry;

- the will to bring together researchers, research subjects, and other involved parties and stakeholders to address a given health problem solution with information and ideas in a mutually unaffected way; and
- conceiving subsequent research of mostly inductive nature in which observations precede hypotheses generation and their further proofs within, and beyond the original study, and those generated by other studies, some of them being of deductive nature.

The **PICO**, **PICOT** or the expanded **PoCICOST** formats, were conceived for a quantitative research of deductive nature and do not always apply here. Questions in qualitative research and case studies have a simpler **substance** and **form**, which may be worded by "who," "what," "where," "why" (with all limits of causal proof in qualitative research), or "how," intentionally 'pretending' that the researcher does not know and wishes to know more. In this way the qualitative researcher wants to know and better understand "webs of causes" and "webs of consequences" that are so characteristic in etiology of health problems, their control, cure, and prevention. Some examples include:

What does an adequate healthcare means for a laic population in the health system of this province or state?

How do older and chronically ill people perceive their chances to be admitted in a long term institutional care facility?

Why do physicians prefer to work in an urban environment rather in underserviced rural regions?

Who are, and what is, the profile of practical nurses successful in subarctic regions of the country?

What are the services offered to the elderly citizens in all senior residential facilities in our area?

From the perspective of health professionals who run health systems, *where* should e-health systems and facilities be implemented first in the health system?

How might existing facilities be used better to satisfy requirements for new technologies in orthopedic surgery?

It is almost superfluous to remind even a novice, that our *who, what, where when, why* and *how,* and *in whom* words and questions also indicate the type and nature of the study in the following ways:

- a "*what*" question falls into the domain of diagnosis or cause of a health problem.
- "*where*," "when," or "in whom" questions cover the health problem occurrence and description of a health event.
- "*why*" questions search for causes of either noxious or beneficial health events; and
- "*how much*" and "*how many*" questions provide answers that reflect the magnitude and dimension of the phenomenon of interest.

The mixed-methods research questions methodology in health sciences are still developing. How similar the methodology is to the quantitative research based question (of the **PICO**, **PICOT**, or **PoCICOST** type) will depend on the predominant component of a given mixed method question. In other cases, qualitative aspects may prevail. All reasons for such questions and their components must be well-defined. Some rules for such definitions follow in the Section 6.3.7 which follows and also in Chapter 7 of this book.

6.3.7 Definitions Used; the Essence of Understanding: "How Do We Delineate the Meaning of Everything We Are Using and Working With?"

All elements of the research question require strong, clear definitions. This includes the topic, domain, and components of a research question, target populations, dependent and independent variables under study, study subjects, methods of counting, measurement, classification, analysis, and interpretation of findings. Definitions must be usable (operational), reproducible, and mutually understood by producers and consumers of medical research. Poorly defining what we are studying, and how we are doing it, risks making our research meaningless. Many types of definitions are currently in use. Not all of them are usable and operational. This situation sets the stage for **medical orismology**,[24] the study, use, and evaluation of definitions pertaining to medical practice and research. Chapter 7 is devoted to this important topic.

6.3.8 Context and Setting of the Study: "What Is the Reality of All Happenings in Which the Study Is Valid?"

All the cornerstones of a research study and its reporting (the problem, objectives, hypothesis, research question, and related definitions) are valid *only* in the specific scientific and professional **context** and **setting** (or environment) of medical practice and research, its professionals, and their patients. Both of the latter elements must also be well-defined by researchers and authors. Without such specifications, even the most well-conceived and executed research, and its presentation in the form of a medical article, could become meaningless.

All these cornerstones must appear directly, or be identifiable indirectly, in a medical article to be shared between its authors and readers. They are relevant not only at the beginning of any research and article reporting it, but also throughout the research design and its culmination. They are equally important in the "*Conclusion*" and "*Recommendation*" sections of medical articles. Concluding sections should specify if such cornerstones were covered, and questions raised at the beginning were answered. Questions include not only the research question, but also other research and article cornerstones like objectives, hypotheses, and fit in the current volume of related information and experience available to date.

Let Us Conclude

Editorial boards of respected medical journals and other periodicals have a challenging task today in selecting, prioritizing, and providing feedback to the health information offered to them. Burdened by inherent necessary and ever-increasing expertise, they do so remarkably well. The scientific committees of medical and other health professionals' conventions have a similar, often difficult, but always rewarding, mission.

To write and present a medical paper, authors must make many specialists happy: the experts and novices in the authors' own clinical and public health specialty, biostatisticians, epidemiologists, health economists, administrators, and managers of healthcare. Authors must balance the art of the research analysis from a variety of perspectives with the scientific and clinical inquiry that is the heart of their work, with the ultimate imperative to improve outcomes. Moreover, all this must be integrated into one coherent article. Considerations of biostatistical aspects (errors, samples, contrasts between observations, linkage of dependent and independent variables in etiology search), epidemiological considerations (who, where, when, why and controllability in time/place/persons/disease interactions), and health economics and administration concerns about the problem (at what human and material price) are connected to the goals and considerations (views, desired objectives, understanding, and interventions) of a "scientist" or clinician as practitioner and user of information in his or her understanding and decision-making (nature of findings, explanation of the underlying mechanisms, biological plausibility, relevant findings identification, search for missing links, implications, and strategies for what to do next).

What we plan to do, what we are currently doing, why we are doing it, and for whom, are considerations that should be developed for more purposes than a medical article.

All these considerations are also important when we formulate:

■ a research project;
■ an application for a research grant;
■ oral and written communications to share projects with peers, listeners, and readers, through scientific and administrative meetings; or
■ communications to inform interested parties from a field beyond health sciences and professions.

In these and other similar situations, the following relevant elements research and practice activities, and their management and administration, need to be specified:

■ the subject, or topic, of our activity(ies);
■ objectives of these activities, research questions, and/or hypotheses to be tested and clarified;
■ definitions of components, entities, and variables relevant to the subject;
■ intended target population for the activity (patients, community, and its subgroups of interest);

- proposed activity that will be implemented;
- research or professional methodology used;
- expected or obtained results, and an analysis of their meaning for research and/or practice;
- assessment of the methodology and proposed or obtained results in terms of structure, process, and impact;
- references from literature and other sources of past and present experience; and
- suggestions for further research and/or practice activity.

This information is important to share both before the research or initiative is implemented, and after reporting results, proposing activities to improve the well-being of individuals and communities, as well as the work and functioning of researchers and health professionals. A medical article is just one of the tools to reach such objectives.

What originates, precedes, and ultimately defines the value of a medical paper at the end of the research process, is a correct and explicit specification of the problem under study, the purpose of the research, how to perform it, its results, their evaluation, what was done, and in which specific context. Excellent structure, sections, language, or style follow. They are well-covered by the authors of *Biomedical Research: From Ideation to Publication*[34] together with valuable complementary information to this article(s).

Let us also pay attention to the domain of definitions (orismology), as we will do in the forthcoming Chapter 7. Definitions are one of the seven cornerstones of research thesis, and largely define the medical article itself. In addition, we should consider the design and execution of a study and examine the "product," the medical article, as an exercise in argumentation, informal logic, and critical thinking supporting the research cornerstones. Hence, what was done with the best evidence produced? What does it mean?

Let us reiterate: To be understood by the audience, the seven cornerstones of research (problem, objectives, hypothesis, questions to answer, definitions used, context, and setting) must be established at the beginning of the research itself and implicitly or explicitly presented throughout the paper or other communication. Further understandings, applications, decisions, and their impact that result from the findings of the research paper or communication largely depend on them.

References

1. Huth EJ. *Writing and Publishing in Medicine*. 3rd Edition. Previously titled *How to Write and Publish Papers in Medical Sciences* (1982, 1990). Fried PW, Wechsler AS. How to get your paper published. *J Thorac Cardiovasc Surg*, 2001;121:S3–S7.
2. Horton R. The grammar of interpretive medicine. *Can Med Ass J (CMAJ)*, 1998;159:245–9.
3. Fried PW and Wechsler AS. How to get your paper published. *J Thorac Cardiovasc Surg*, 2001;121:S3–S7.
4. Taylor RB. *Medical Writing. A Guide for Clinicians, Educators, and Researchers*. New York/Dordrecht/Heidelberg/London: Springer, 2011.
5. Huth EJ. *Writing and Publishing in Medicine*. 3rd Edition. Previously titled *How to Write and Publish Papers in Medical Sciences* (1982, 1990). Baltimore, MD/Philadelphia, PA/London: Williams & Wilkins, 1999.
6. *How to Write a Paper*. 4th Edition. Edited by GM Hall. Malden, MA and Oxford, UK: BMJ Publishing Group and Blackwell Publishing, 2008.

7. Hackshaw A. *How to Write a Great Publication*. Malden, MA/Oxford/London: BMJ Publishing Group and Blackwell Publishing, 2011.
8. Fraser J. *How to Publish in Biomedicine. 500 tips for Success*. 2nd Edition. Oxford and New York: Radcliffe Publishing, 2008.
9. Lundberg GD. How to write a medical paper to get it published in a good journal. *MedGenMed (Medscape General Medicine)*, 2005;7(4):36.
10. Leung AKC. Writing a medical article: Guidelines for prospective authors. *Can Fam Physician*, 1987;33(Oct):2249–52.
11. Kotur PF. How to write a scientific article for a medical journal? *Indian J Anaesth*, 2002;46(1):21–5.
12. Siwek J, Gourlay ML, Slawson DC, Shaughnessy AF. How to write an evidence-based clinical review article. *Am Fam Physician*, 2002;65(2):251–8.
13. Walliman N. *Research Methods. The Basics*. London and New York: Routledge/Taylor & Francis, 2011.
14. McGaghie WC, Bordage G, Shea JA. Manuscript introduction. Problem statement, conceptual framework, and research question. *Acad Med*, 2001;76(9):923–4.
15. Jenicek M. The four cornerstones of a research project: Health problem in focus, objectives, hypothesis, research question. Chapter 3, pp. 27–34 in: *Biomedical Research. From Ideation to Publication*. Edited by G Jagadeesh, S Murthy, YK Gupta, A Prakash. New Delhi/Philadelphia, PA/London: Wolters Kluwer Health/Lippincott/Williams & Wilkins, 2010.
16. Northey M, McKibbin: *Making Sense. A Student's Guide to Research and Writing*. 7th Edition. Oxford/New York/Don Mills, ON: Oxford University Press, 2012.
17. The Writing Center at UNCC - Chapel Hill. *Thesis Statements*. 5 p. at http://writingcenter.unc.edu/resources/handouts-demos/writing-the-paper/thesis-statements, retrieved Jan 19, 2012.
18. Wikipedia, the free encyclopedia. *Thesis Statement*. 1 p. at http://en.wikipedia.org/wiki/Thesis_statement, retrieved January 19, 2012.
19. Kalmund P. *Setting Thesis Research Objectives. Masters Programme*. 1 p. at http://www.staff.vu.edu.au/Peterkalmund/html/objectives.htm, retrieved on May 17, 2008.
20. University of Oxford: Department of Primary Health Care. *Diabetes and Vascular Disease Research Objectives*. 1 p. at http://www.primarycare.ox.ac.uk/research/vascular/objective, retrieved on May 17, 2008.
21. ResearchCompanion.com. *Sample Objectives*. 3 p. at http://www.researchcompanion.com/objectives.html, retrieved on May 17, 2008.
22. Association of American Medical Colleges. *Report III. Contemporary Issues in Medicine: Communication in Medicine. Medical School Objectives Project, October 1999*. Washington, DC: Association of American Medical Colleges, 1999.
23. American Psychiatric Association, Psychiatric Research Network (PRN). *Research Objectives*. 1 p. at http://www.psych.org/mainMenu/Research/PracticeResearchNetworkandHealthServices..., retrieved on May 17, 2008.
24. Jenicek M. *A Primer on Clinical Experience in Medicine. Reasoning, Decision-Making, and Communication in Health Sciences*. Boca Raton, FL/London/New York: CRC Press/Taylor & Francis/Productivity Press, 2013. (Released 2012).
25. *Random House Webster's Unabridged Dictionary 3.0*. Electronic (CD) Edition. Antwerpen: Random House, 1998.
26. Stockton Riverside College. *Research Design and Implementation: Formulating a Hypothesis*. 10 Power Point® slides at http://www.learningtechnologies.ac.uk/downloads/100/Research%20Design%20and%20Implementation.ppt, retrieved on May 21, 2008.
27. Heddle NM. The research question. *Transfusion*, 2007;47:15–7.
28. Thabane L, Thomas T, Ye CY, Paul J. Posing the question: Not so simple. *Can J Anesth*, 2009;56:71–9.
29. Lytwyn A. *Formulating Researchable Questions in Health Care*. Health Research Methodology graduate program (HRM 721) Unit 2 presentation, Hamilton, McMaster University, July 2, 2013. Quoted with presenter's permission.
30. Straus SE, Scott Richardson W, Glasziou P, Haynes RB. *Evidence-Based Medicine. How to Practice and Teach EBM*. 3rd Edition. Edinburgh and New York: Elsevier/Churchill Livingstone, 2005.

31. Mulrow CM, Oxman A (Editors). *How to Conduct a Cochrane Systematic Review.* 3rd Edition. San Antonio, TX: San Antonio Cochrane Center, 1996.

32. Counsell C. Formulating questions and locating primary studies for inclusion in systematic reviews. *Ann Intern Med,* 1997;127:380–7.

33. Mantzoukas S. Facilitating research students in formulating qualitative research questions. *Nurse Educ Today,* 2008;28:371–7.

34. Section F: *Scientific Communication.* pp. 411–87 in: *Biomedical Research. From Ideation to Publication.* Edited by G Jagadeesh, S Murthy, YK Gupta, A Prakash. New Delhi/Philadelphia, PA/London: Wolters Kluwer Health/Lippincott Williams & Wilkins, 2010.

Chapter 7

Definitions: Thinking about What We Are Thinking, Specifying More What We Intend to Do—*"What Do You Mean by That?"**

Executive Summary

Any message in health sciences and professions depends on how everything within the message is defined. This is more than simply including definitions of interacting variables in the study of causal and other relationships in observational and experimental causal research. Definitions are required to clearly and fully articulate the domains of our activities, subjects of research and professional activity, individuals and communities, and interacting variables in the study. There must be definitions for what is being done, what has to be done, the target populations of the above, and who are the recipients of our information and, ultimately, care.

The importance of good definitions goes beyond a single research study or article. If such health information is examined across studies as meta-analysis and all other systematic reviews of evidence, comparable definitions between studies are necessary. In addition, the heterogeneity of definitions across studies should be scrutinized for a meaningful synthesis.

We define the domain of study, development, analysis, evaluation, and uses of definitions as "orismology." In health sciences, a heterogeneous

---

* This chapter is based, with permission by the publisher, on Chapter 4 in: Jenicek M. *Writing, Reading, and Understanding in Modern Health Sciences. Medical Articles and Other Forms of Communication.* Boca Raton, FL/ London/New York: CRC Press/Taylor & Francis/Productivity Press, 2014. Revised, edited, updated.

ensemble of at least 13 different kinds of definitions exists. Inspirational and motivational definitions are perhaps the most attractive for many but they are useless beyond this purpose and create a false feeling that the reader understands what is being discussed. There are at least eight desirable qualities and attributes of definitions in health sciences. Particular challenges are composite definitions with multiple inclusion and exclusion criteria for what is in, or out.

Definitions must precisely describe research questions and the research itself as a whole. Mutual understanding is necessary to solve problems. It is still an emerging domain requiring better structure, focus, uses, and evaluation.

In This Chapter

Executive Summary 191
Thoughts, Thinkers, and Things to Think About 192
Introductory Comments 194
7.1   What Might, Then, Be a Thesis for This Chapter as an Essay? 195
7.2   What Are Definitions and Their Type in General? The Sort of Definitions We Use 195
7.3   Definitions in Medicine and Health Sciences and Their Subject 196
7.4   Why Are Definitions So Important? 199
7.5   Types of Definitions in Current Medical Research and Practice Uses 199
7.6   Desirable Qualities and Attributes of Definitions in General 202
7.7   Desirable Qualities and Attributes of Definitions in Medicine and Other Health
        Sciences 203
7.8   The Challenge of Composite Definitions 203
        Inclusion and Exclusion Criteria for Definitions 204
7.9   Adjectives and Other Challenges of Definitions 205
        A Word about Critical Appraisal: A Critical Appraisal <u>of What</u>? 207
Let Us Conclude 208
References 209

Thoughts, Thinkers, and Things to Think About

How many a dispute could have been deflated into a single paragraph if the disputants had dared to define their terms?

Aristotle

(384–322 BC)

How many of the exchanges of our ideas in medicine today could be deflated if we would dare to define our terms?

I hate definitions.
Benjamin Disraeli
1st Earl of Beaconsfield
(1804–1881)
**But what can you do without them
when called to write medical articles,
the Right Honorable Sir Benjamin?**

*Why did you start, what did you do, what
answer did you get, and what does it mean
anyway? This (seems to me to be) a logical
order for a scientific paper.*
Sir Austin Bradford Hill
(1897–1991)
in the *British Medical Journal* (1965)
**Without definitions about what are we
talking? Isn't it also true to most of the
other communications in medicine, be
it between doctors, and sharing with
patients, and the community at large?**

A problem well stated is a problem half solved.
Charles F. Kettering
(1876–1958)
Inventor and Medical Philanthropist
**Providing that everything in it is well
defined!**

*The beginning of wisdom is the definition
of terms.*
Socrates
(c. 470–399 BC)
**How could we disagree, especially in
this book!**

*Honey, I love you! … How apicultural of
you, my bumble bee!*
**But to understand each other better in
those affection matters, what do you
mean by love, apiculture, and bee?**

*Can we argue about anything which is not
well-defined at its very beginning?*

Introductory Comments

Authors of medical research want their audience to understand the relevance of their findings and to use these findings, whether in systematic reviews or meta-analyses of a body of evidence, about a particular topic. Can this occur without valid and uniform definitions of each element used in such an endeavor? We do not think so. Both in this instance and in situations of clinical decision-making and sharing experiences with others, we believe good definitions are essential for both research and communication.

Why do we pay so much attention to definitions in this book? The answer is simple: Definitions are vital to how we understand for ourselves, and how we communicate information to others. At the beginning of a research project, we define its domain, topic, elements of observation and analysis, and what we will do and why. At the end of a research project, by virtue of publishing its results, we define the elements of our message in order for them to be understood and to make our results usable for further research and practice. Our ways of defining what we experience is another essential part of communication in medicine and all health sciences.[1] Further uses of definitions determine the success, applicability, and relevance of what we do, and what we share.

The importance of good definitions goes beyond a single research study or article. If such health information is studied across studies as meta-analysis and all other systematic review of evidence, comparable definitions are necessary from one study to another. Only in this way can we scrutinize heterogeneous studies for a meaningful synthesis.

Our decisions depend on definitions. Clear and usable definitions are particularly vital to understanding systematic or non-systematic comparisons and reviews of observations and findings from various sources, meta-analyses, and syntheses of research and evidence. In these cases, authors are considering and assessing research being conducted at a variety of centers, from different researchers, often across the world. Ensuring that what is being examined and reported on is accurate and consistent between and among research projects, and accurately accounting for differences, requires precision and specificity. Definitions here are not merely a useful add-on, they a necessity.

Definitions are necessary at the beginning of any thinking process. The importance of the best possible definitions is even more obvious when research findings, evidence, and experience are evaluated, combined, and integrated in meta-analyses and systematic reviews. How much are such initiatives worth if the initial definitions across the field of interest are incorrect themselves, hazy, overlapping, heterogeneous, different, and of unequal value? In those cases, should we not synthesize, stratify by definition types, analyze, and integrate the body of evidence accordingly?

Non-ambiguous definitions are essential elements of characterization, the first step in the scientific method. Unclear operational purposes of characteristics produce numerous fallacies of definition. By nature, definitions at the beginning of any scientific endeavor are heterogeneous; in the broadest context, they should be neither ambiguous nor vague. Also, definitions should do more than expand vocabulary and provide meaning. If needed, they should offer theoretical and/or practical explanations, influence understanding and decisions, and reflect some kind of value (importance). In addition to these general expectations, definitions of any variable or observation in medicine should allow proper measurement, classification, decision-making, action, and evaluation. Without proper and usable definitions, any research and subsequent medical article which is produced is meaningless.

7.1 What Might, Then, Be a Thesis for This Chapter as an Essay?

In the spirit of the ongoing debate about medical articles and their writing and reading,[2] the thesis of this chapter might be that:

1. Usable operational definitions are necessary for any analysis of a clinical practice problem, the actions needed to solve it successfully, and the thought processes that are necessary to make appropriate decisions.
2. Any research question leading to an evidence-based inquiry, as well as its solution and implementation, is only as good as the definition of its components in operational terms. These terms should be used across the volume of research to answer just such a question. It is, in essence, its prerequisite.
3. The domain of definitions, on which the success of our communication and the impact of our ensuing activities depend, is still a heterogeneous and disparate ensemble of entities. Review, better understanding, and subsequent uses of definitions are needed in health sciences to ensure meaningful research and effective practice.

Let us see how we can explain and justify such a proposal. Although we have covered definitions partially in the past[1,3] with particular attention to research and practice, more should be said, at the cost of some repetition, about definitions and their role in medical article writing and reading.

7.2 What Are Definitions and Their Type in General? The Sort of Definitions We Use

A **definition** is an *"explanation of the meaning of a word or expression, either as established ('dictionary definition') or as it is to be used ('stipulative definition')."*[4] For Yagisawa,[5] it is a *"specification of the meaning or, alternatively, conceptual content, of an expression,"* Once the meaning of a definition is clarified, its usability is of primary importance and concern for health sciences.

Philosophers recognize several kinds of definitions: analytical, contextual, coordinative, by genus and species (in use, *per genus and differentiam*), explicit, implicit, lexical, nominal, ostensive, persuasive, précising, prescriptive, real, recursive, stipulative, and synonymous.[5] From a general critical thinking perspective, consider that definitions may be:[5–7 modified]

- *stipulative* (delineating new phenomena);
- *lexical* or *reportive* (how the word is actually used);
- *theoretical* (formulating an adequate characterization);
- *ostensive* (by giving an example);
- *motivational* or *persuasive* (influencing attitudes by their metaphysical or ecclesiastical nature);
- *operational* (decision-making tools);[1]

- *by synonym* (for example, pneumoconiosis is a lung disorder due to dust inhalation); or
- *essentialist* (presenting a theory about the fundamental nature of the phenomenon to which the term refers).

Further, some essentialist definitions may be *cause-based* (streptococcal pharyngitis is a throat infection caused by a Streptococcus), *circular* and *by synonym*, too.

But how do we view definitions in medicine, especially in relation to medical written and oral communication?

7.3 Definitions in Medicine and Health Sciences and Their Subject

Ours, and others', definitions may be quite different in daily life, in professional communication and research as well. Definitions we use differ based on the health problem and domain, by purposes of intended activities, by available information, or by information needed for an activity of interest. Currently, definitions in the health sciences represent a heterogeneous ensemble, which is in need of semantic clarification, structure, and categorization. The domain of study, development, analysis, evaluation and uses of definitions, which we may call *orismology* (from the Greek *"orismos"* = definition and *"logos"* = study),[1] is now among the first determinants of research success and its adoption. How can we understand it today?

What must be defined? To be successful, convincing, and correct in our endeavors both in practice and research, we must first define many distinct entities, well beyond some causes and their consequences. We must define:

- *domains of our activities* whether in health sciences, sociology, management, care, or other;
- the *subject(s) of our research and professional activity* (medicine, clinical practice, community medicine, public health);
- *individuals and communities* involved in the research, which may include patients, community, healthcare institutions, social, cultural, geographical, physical environment;
- *interacting variables in the study of causal and other relationships.* These include dependent variables such as health and disease in individuals and communities, and independent variables such as physical, chemical, biological, social, cultural, faith, economical and other environmental factors, hereditary burden, genetic factors, or human and physical components involved in health and community care including new and old technologies;
- *what is, or has to be done,* in research, practice, education, and information including maintenance of the status quo and its changes;
- *target populations* of the above and *recipients of our information and care;* and
- *setting of research and practice experience,* that is, other personal and environmental factors related to individuals and communities.

Figure 7.1 illustrates two major types of definitions:

■ those that cover mental frameworks and the settings for our thinking processes and activities, such as concepts, theories, domains, and contexts; and
■ those specifying observations within processes, activities, and their results based on interacting phenomena and entities which include independent and dependent variables and phenomena in our research of associations, causes, and their effects.

The definitions may be worded using a single term or entity, or as composites, compounded terms consisting of two and more parts. For example, "fever" or "anemia" in their simplest sense may be defined by a single term. "Knowledge translation" (KT) is a composite term within which a definition of "knowledge" and "translation" leads to the definition of "knowledge translation" and its understanding as a compounded definition.

Definitions as formal statements may be seen in several overlapping ways as *constructs* (complex images formed from a number of simpler elements), *contexts* (parts of written or spoken statements that precede a specific message and influence its meaning and/or effect), *theories* in the sense of particular conceptions or views of something to be understood or done, or as a *system of rules and principles*. Definitions convey *concepts* as mental combinations of objects of thought. In our context, they are words or groups of words designating some *entity of medical and other health interest*.

Definitions in medicine are not limited solely, as it sometimes happens, to independent and dependent variables in some cause-effect relationship under study. They are derived both from basic sciences and clinical experience. Definitions are used in the clinical medical environment to reflect:

■ *a structural pathology and/or function* (ulcerative colitis, asthma);
■ *symptom and/or sign presentation* (migraine, allergy, panic reaction, pain);
■ *deviation from physiological and/or morphological norms* (anemia, hypertension);
■ *etiology* (pneumococcal pneumonia, histoplasmosis);
■ *negative effect of noxious factors*;
■ *both positive and negative effects of clinical and other actions, interventions, and care, and their outcomes*;
■ *characteristics of care providers and their recipients*; and
■ *other views* like in psychiatry where they are based on distress, dysfunction, disadvantage, disability or irrationality or other phenomena.

Understandably, some definitions include and are valid only in a particular *setting* that also must often be defined beforehand. These settings include the surrounding physical, social-economic, cultural, technological, and/or healthcare environments. They must be specified whenever their validity and uses depend on them.

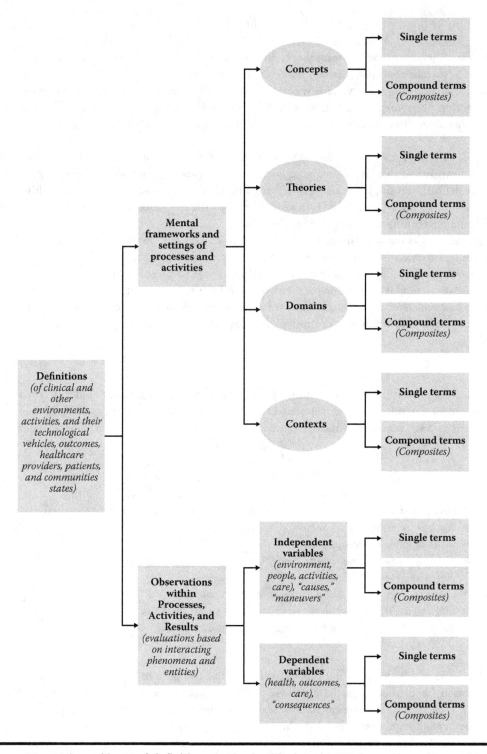

Figure 7.1 Major subjects of definitions in the health domain. (Redrawn from Figure 4.1 in: Jenicek M. *Writing, Reading, and Understanding in Modern Health Sciences*. Boca Raton: CRC Press, 2014. Reproduced with permission.)

7.4 Why Are Definitions So Important?

When definitions are not clearly stated, diagnostic errors, decision-making errors, and patient outcomes are all at stake. Moreover, the ways in which we define what we will do, what we are doing, and what this process yields are crucial both for health research itself and its reporting in the form of a medical paper. Any kind of meaningful scientific argumentation depends first on how entities of interest are defined: the health problem, dependent and independent variables, the sample, target population, techniques and methods of study and inquiry, laboratory and other analytical procedures, and so on.

In research, *defining the problem to be solved* typically means *defining variables in a study*, but we should also *define their framework*: concepts, domains, disciplines, contexts, researchers, the health professionals involved and their working environment, and their patients. Both variables and their framework require our equal attention, the latter often being more challenging than the former. Even the best research and its results may be invalidated by a sheer absence of definitions or by poor, non-operational and irreproducible definitions. In the evidence-based management of a health problem, we add a third step in the sequence of defining the problem—"*What do we mean by this?*" or "*Defining all this.*"

Thus, the total sequence of defining the problem in patients and elsewhere consists of:

---

1. Assessing the patient
↓
2. Formulating (in usable terms) a clinical problem to be solved
↓
3. Defining all components of the question and work thesis
↓
4. Acquiring the best evidence for understanding, decision-making, and health problem solving
↓
5. Assessing and choosing the best evidence for the intended purpose
↓
6. Applying (using) the evidence
↓
7. Evaluating if the effect and impact of such an application, **as defined by the outcomes,** produced the expected results

---

7.5 Types of Definitions in Current Medical Research and Practice Uses

Definitions represent an amazingly heterogeneous ensemble and many different kinds of definitions exist. These include:

1. **No definition at all (missing, absent definitions):** "*We all know what it is, no definition is needed, it is so obvious dear ignorant reader.*" In this case, the authors simply do not bother to define what is of interest. This could happen, for example, if we define evidence-based medicine (EBM) only as '*what it requires*' (integration of the best research evidence with our clinical expertise and our patient's unique values and

circumstances) without saying directly '*what it is*.' However, EBM and its composites are now better defined.[8,9]

Within EBM, the definition of 'evidence' itself may be (and is) currently understood and defined in various ways. It can be:

- not defined at all;
- implicitly and narrowly understood as some kind of demonstration of a cause-effect relationship only;
- meant as the best evidence only, a challenge in any domain other than clinical trials and systematic reviews of causal proofs;
- defined in broader and mostly operational terms: "*Any data or information, whether solid or weak, necessary either for the understanding of a problem and/or decision-making about the problem.*"[10] (What is the 'best' evidence is another additional question, challenge, and definition, at present and in the future);
- even more broadly, in the domain of evidence-based decision-making as "*information based on historical or scientific evaluation of a practice that was accessible to decision makers in the Canadian healthcare system.*"[11] It can be experimental, non-experimental (observational), expert opinions (consensus)-based, or of historical or experiential nature.[11]

2. **Inspirational and motivational definitions**: Let us consider an example. In 1996, five authors agreed upon the following often-quoted definition of EBM, i.e., "*Evidence-Based medicine is the conscientious, explicit, and judicious use of current best evidence in making decisions about the care of individual patients.*"[12] If we want to use this definition to distinguish between who is a practitioner of EBM and who is not, we need to clarify in operational terms, perhaps with inclusion and exclusion criteria, what is a conscientious use, an explicit use, and a judicious use of the term, and in extremis, what is evidence and which evidence is the best. Without such distinctions between adjectives in this case, the definition may be excellent from a motivational and ideological perspective, but its operational uses are limited.[13] A nebulous definition, intentionally or not, may make many potential users comfortable and expand its marketing value of the subject. We assume, "*We all know about what we are talking about, don't we?*" But do we really talk about the same thing?

3. **Strategy-motivated definitions**: Some definitions are tailored to reflect an implicitly or explicitly desired strategy to deal with a defined problem and entity.

4. **Value (judgment)-based definitions**: These definitions include judgments or values, for example, "*Osteoarthritis is a debilitating, professionally and socially incapacitating degenerative chronic disease of joints which requires onerous management of its consequences and long term medical care.*" (N.B. The preceding is exaggerated for the sake of explicitness.)

5. **Cause-based and cause-containing definitions**: For example, "*Radiation pneumonitis is a radiation-caused lung injury,*" or "*Thiamine deficiency in alcoholics is an alcohol abuse-related disorder due to a poor dietary intake of vitamin B_1.*" Is 'streptococcal pharyngitis' suitable for an etiological study of Streptococcus as a cause of pharyngitis? Such definitions are often circular like this one.

6. **Content-listing definitions**: For example, "*Thiamine deficiency includes anorexia, muscle cramps, paresthesias, irritability, wet beri-beri (peripheral vasodilatation, heart*

failure, pulmonary and peripheral edema) or dry beri-beri (peripheral sensory neuropathy, Wernicke encephalopathy, Korsakoff syndrome)." Diagnostic entities are often defined but what are the contents, or what comprises, the condition or disease diagnosis.

7. **Context-specifying definitions**: For example, "*In an office practice where full laboratory support is not available, myocardial infarction must be considered in any case of a sudden, shoulder-radiating retrosternal pain at rest, associated with cold sweat, orthopnea, nausea or vomiting as additional manifestations.*"

8. **Uncertain, or evolving definitions**: Definitions of new, emerging and evolving entities and domains lack consensus and suffer from a persistent variable degree of uncertainty. Again, evidence-based medicine, knowledge translation, chronic fatigue, and even chest pain or health (physical, mental, social, spiritual), for example, may be subject to ***multiple definitions***, until their etiology, classification, management, and uses are better known and solved. For example, both *knowledge translation* and *knowledge transfer* are currently the subjects of 22 definitions apiece and *translational research 24.*[14]

9. *A posteriori*–**developed definitions**: These definitions are hard to detect. Did the authors develop definitions *during* the development of the research protocol or were definitions established only *after* the research was completed? This may occur and contribute to inductive or deductive research problem solving, for example, when health phenomena unexpectedly develops, as it frequently does, only during ongoing research: bleeding, hepatomegaly, new adverse reactions, new technology failures, errors, harm, etc.

10. **Specialty-bound** and **type of care-dependent definitions**: Are diabetes, chest pain, or arthritis always the same entity for an internist, cardiologist, endocrinologist, pathologist, physiologist, clinical biochemist, surgeon, or geriatrist?

11. **Subject-missing definitions**: Like the definition of *critical appraisal,* critical appraisal *of what?*

12. **Purpose-missing definitions**: Like *grades or grading of evidence:* The purpose of grading of evidence is not always known in advance and uses of grades in terms of ensuing decision-making, from one grade to another are often untested.

13. **Patient/physician-centered definitions**: This is when the same condition can be viewed either as a sign (physician), symptom (patient), or both.

14. **Definitions of other scientific endeavors or entities**: These are heterogeneous for other reasons: purpose, vocabulary, ambiguity, vagueness, explanatory power, and focus on attitudes and values.

> In medicine, in our opinion, definitions of any variable, entity, or observation should allow their proper measurement, classification, decision-making, action, evaluation and reflect change (by changing themselves).

15. **Operational definitions**: In health research, **operational definitions** are the most desirable if they:

– define an entity of observation and analysis (health problem to be dealt with, drug, surgery, pain, bleeding, etc.), with inclusion and exclusion criteria as clearly as possible whenever it is needed and appropriate
– allow the detection of change and its magnitude if criteria, events, and their consequences change;
– clearly separate one entity from others; and
– lead to making different distinct diagnostic, therapeutic, prognostic, or risk control decisions in comparison with other definitions and entities, or whether a defined subject belongs to a defined entity or not.

In medical article writing and reading, flawed reasoning in building and creating definitions leads to fallacious reasoning, interpretation, and decision-making. If deficient definitions are used, their subsequent claims will not match the formulation of theses and research questions. Their ambiguity may invalidate even the best research protocol, its execution, and the interpretation of findings in any article or other research report.

7.6 Desirable Qualities and Attributes of Definitions in General

Clear, specific, and unequivocal definitions are essential elements of characterization, which is the first step of the scientific method. Unclear operational definitions, purposes, and characteristics may produce many fallacies of definition.[15,16] Definitions are a strategic resource for the arguer, ideally clear enough to avoid common fallacies of meaning[16] like vagueness, equivocation (same word having different meanings in the same argument), and others.

A good definition must have several desirable characteristics. Good definitions must:[5–7 modified]

■ state the essential attributes;
■ elucidate;
■ be non-circular, it is not self-contradictory (conflicting conditions are absent);
■ neither too broad nor too narrow;
■ <u>not</u> verbalized in ambiguous, obscure, or figurative language;
■ <u>not</u> negative when it can be affirmative;
■ <u>not</u> self-contradictory (conflicting conditions are absent); and
■ is **operational**, that is, usable in practice by possessing clear inclusion and exclusion criteria and specifications together with the attributes already mentioned above. It must be suitable in all situations where used **repetitively** and by **more than one health professional, user, or reader.**

In a practical sense, virtues of definitions should therefore be:

■ their reproducibility (usability in different studies, practices, settings, clinical and other environments);
■ representative (of what they are supposed to define);

- comparability (from one use to another);
- applicability (usability for various purposes and in various settings); and
- evaluable (able to be evaluated; do the definitions really work, and are they usable in the above-mentioned situations and circumstances?).

Can we write and understand medical research, practice medicine, and communicate about it without good definitions as specified above?

7.7 Desirable Qualities and Attributes of Definitions in Medicine and Other Health Sciences

For health professionals, definitions are usable and useful if they:

- discriminate and are clearly separated from other possibly competing entities related to the problem;
- represent a distinct substrate which is different from others;
- are, if possible and desired, measurable and otherwise subject to quantification (counting);
- are subject to grading (degree, direction attributing);
- are categorizable within a classification in a specific context;
- reflect and relate to a specific decision about an action to be taken;
- have operational inclusion and exclusion criteria which distinguish such an entity from others; and
- are mutually understood, hence warranting reproduction, repetition, and re-use.

Failure to ensure that definitions in medical and health communications have these requirements is then considered a **fallacy of definition**[15] with potential negative, if not ruinous, effects if used in further argumentations.

7.8 The Challenge of Composite Definitions

Some definitions stem from more than one entity. If those entities mean different things from one understanding to another, definitions may have a different meaning from one case and use to another. Philosophers call these definitions *biconditional* or *multiconditional (pluriconditional) analytical definitions*. For our purpose, we may call them **composite definitions** in the health sciences. The composite definition concept applies both at classical clinical entities and new domains, concepts or techniques as well. Both are equally challenging, often in different ways.

In the classical clinical problem domain, a case of an acute coronary heart disease is comprised of cardiac biomarkers (paraclinical and laboratory findings in blood indicating myocardial necrosis), cardiac symptoms (phenomena perceived by the patient), cardiac signs (manifestations perceived by the clinician), and ECG findings.[17] A special challenge remains the definition of many new composite terms like *evidence-based medicine*. What is evidence within this term, and is it necessary? It took approximately six to 12 years to attempt to define 'evidence' within the term EBM.[10,11] Other challenges may be terms such as knowledge translation[14,18–20] (what are "knowledge" and "translation" themselves in a given context?) and critical appraisal[19] (a term not containing a subject appraisal of "what" and what does "critical" mean in this composite term?). The definitions of the elements constituting the term may largely define the meaning and definition of the composite term as an entity, but the latter may differ depending on the former.

The authors of *Evidence-Based Medicine: How to Practice and Teach It*[9] were well aware of the composite nature of some definitions. To address this, they proposed not only *what* EBM requires (the integration of the best research evidence with our clinical expertise and our patient's unique values and circumstances), and what it is about, but they also defined related terms—what is *best research evidence, clinical expertise, patient values*, and *patient circumstances* within the concept.

Inclusion and Exclusion Criteria for Definitions

Good composite definitions are necessary for practical reasons. By necessity, they may sometimes be lengthy. They must include not only the nature of the problem, but also selected elements from the natural history of disease, past and present clinical activities, and context of practice. Moreover, in defining clinical phenomena, both **inclusion** and **exclusion criteria** are subjects of orismology.

For example, in a clinical trial, a group of ThermoCool AF Trial Investigators[20] compared antiarrhythmic drug therapy and radiofrequency catheter ablation in patients suffering from paroxysmal atrial fibrillation. In this situation and using **inclusion criteria**, a case (patient eligible for enrollment in the trial) was defined as an individual:

- with an experience of atrial fibrillation as an electrophysiologically confirmed event for its *nature*;
- suffering from at least three symptomatic atrial fibrillation episodes within the six months before randomization as part of the *patient clinical history*; and
- not responding to at least one anti-arrhythmic drug (*past and present clinical care*).

Exclusion criteria for the same case were defined in domains related to patient characteristics, patient history regarding the problem including past and present competing events and states, and past and present care. These are outlined below.

Patient characteristics:

- patients younger than 18 years;
- life expectancy of less than 12 months; and
- contraindication to antiarrhythmic or anticoagulation medications.

Patient history of this problem, past and present competing events and states:

■ documented left atrial thrombus;
■ myocardial infarction within the previous 2 months;
■ patients with atrial fibrillation of more than 30 days in duration;
■ an ejection fraction of less than 40%;
■ marked or severe limitations in activity due to symptoms; and
■ left atrial size of at least 50 mm in the parasternal long axis view.

Past and present care:

■ previous ablation for an atrial fibrillation;
■ amiodarone therapy in the previous 6 months;
■ coronary artery bypass graft procedure in the previous 6 months;
■ thromboembolic event in the previous 12 months;
■ severe pulmonary disease;
■ prior valvular cardiac surgical procedure; and
■ presence of an implanted cardioverter-defibrillator.

In definitions of a case or another clinical phenomenon, the composite nature of the definition is a necessity. Their elements are necessary for inquiry and decision-making.

In the earlier clinical example of paroxysmal atrial fibrillation, we might equally detail the definition of this phenomenon by specifying the "paroxyscity" (duration and nature of the episode) or fibrillation. We may consider:

■ Is this anything other than a deviation from a sinus rhythm?
■ What is its duration and what is the nature and picture of dysrhythmia?
■ How frequent are they and over what period of time?
■ Are such differences important in the follow-up and interpretation of a clinical trial focusing on such pathological physiological phenomenon?
■ Or, is it just "detailing" without a clear purpose?

This level of specificity or detailing is absolutely necessary if differences could have an impact on the interpretation of the study results and its adoption in practice. Are such "sub-definitions" necessary and useful? They are, if ignoring them is detrimental to clinical decisions or to the interpretation of research findings. Decisions about them depend on the investigators; simply selecting the most often referred to definition from the literature and using it may not be enough for a given purpose and context.

7.9 Adjectives and Other Challenges of Definitions

The original definition of knowledge translation in the health sciences[18] mentioned earlier, or a definition of critical appraisal (*vide infra*) are examples of a particular challenge of the use of adjectives in definitions. One of the updated definitions of **knowledge translation** states that it is "*A dynamic and iterative process that includes the synthesis, dissemination, exchange and ethically sound* *application of knowledge to improve health, provide more effective health services and products, and strengthen the healthcare system.*"[19] What is "dynamic," and what is "ethically sound," or "iterative?" These terms should be specified and explained in such a way that all interested and involved operationally minded parties can understand them and use them in a specific context, case, setting, and situation. As with any composite definition, its other elements often merit a "definition within a definition." Even defining what is "new" needs a specification if it applies to different types of patients, a new procedure, a new drug, new outcomes, a new way of observing or analyzing findings, or other differences.

Critical appraisal (in medicine and other health sciences) is another example of a challenging definition. In health sciences, it may be defined more broadly as an *"application of rules of evidence to a study to assess the validity of data, completeness of reporting, methods and procedures, conclusions, compliance with ethical standards, etc.,"*[18] either applied to the entire research[19–22] or limited to a particular medical article and literature only.[23] This is a composite definition. The better we define "critical appraisal (of what?)" first, then "rules of evidence," "validity of data," "completeness of reporting," or "compliance with ethical standards" (which ones?), the better our critical appraisal will be.

Definitions themselves, regardless of how we deal with the problem of interest, establish whether our understanding and approach are good, bad, usable or meaningless. They should be neither **ambiguous** (terms that have more than one meaning) nor **vague** (single meanings that have borderline cases). The initial definitions of a new entity are often **definist,** transforming the assumption that one's own position is true, into a definition. Or more pointedly stated, defining a term so that one's controversial position is made easier to defend.

Persuasive definitions are a form of *slanting* in which a definition is used to gain an argumentative advantage. They often alter the meaning of a term by associating it with a term of clear positive or negative connotation. They may, or may not, be based on evidence. ("*That's what they call it and how they do it at 'the other' hospital!*") Stipulative and operational definitions are preferable.

Other fundamental entities in medical sciences are challenging and subject to multiple definitions of various quality and completeness in health sciences. These include oft-used terms like "guidelines" or already mentioned "evidence-based medicine."

Guidelines may be defined as a formal statement about a defined policy, function, or activity. Examples include guidelines for screening procedures, the "clinical preventive services guidelines," "clinical practice guidelines," guidelines for the ethical conduct of practice and research in occupational health, epidemiology, and so on. There may be sanctions against those who violate the guidelines, but generally guidelines are more loosely structured than codes of conduct and seldom strictly enforced.[24] It can also be a formal statement about a defined task or function. Examples include clinical practice guidelines, guidelines for application of preventive screening procedures, and guidelines of the ethical conduct, in which the rules are intended to be strictly adhered to and may include penalties for violation. In Europe, "*directives*" are stronger than "*recommendations,*" which are stronger than "*guidelines.*" In North America, "*guidelines*" is effectively synonymous with "*recommendations.*"[25]

Clinical practice guidelines may be defined as one of the following:

■ patient care protocols, preferably evidence based, that have been established by experts and may be required for accreditation, reimbursement of expenses, etc., by administrators, such as those who operate a "health maintenance organization;"[24]

■ systematically developed statements (based on the best available evidence) to assist practitioner and patient decisions about appropriate healthcare for specific clinical (practice) circumstances;[26] or

■ our definition which is, *"any data or information, solid or weak, obtained through experience, observational research, or experimental work. This data must be relevant and convincing to some degree either to the understanding of the problem (case) or to the clinical decisions (diagnostic, therapeutic, or care oriented) made about the case. 'Evidence' is not automatically correct, complete, satisfactory and useful. It must be first evaluated, graded and used based on its own merit."*[1]

A similar diversity may be observed in defining **evidence-based medicine**. Some definitions are:

■ the conscientious, explicit, and judicious use of current best evidence in making decisions about the care of individual patients;[12]
■ our definition, which is *"the practice of medicine in which physicians find, assess, and implement methods of risk assessment, diagnosis, treatment, and prognosis on the basis of the best available current research, their expertise, and the needs, values and preferences of the patient, and medical ethics considerations in a specific setting of practice and society."* It may be considered also as *"the systematic application of the best available evidence to the evaluation of options and to decision-making in clinical management and policy settings."*

Within the **composite EBM definition**, the definition for evidence itself includes:

■ any ground or reason for knowledge or certitude in knowledge. In other words, proof, whether immediate or derived by inference; a fact or body of facts on which a belief or judgment is based; or
■ an observation, fact, or organized body of information offered to support or justify inference or beliefs in the demonstration of some proposition or matter at issue.[see also 27]

A Word about Critical Appraisal: A Critical Appraisal <u>of What</u>?

In simplest terms, critical appraisal means thinking about what we are doing, ***"How well are we doing it?"*** This type of thinking has evolved through the past two decades. The term was originally used as a part of evidence-based medicine to assess written communication like articles and other communication vehicles. Understanding of the term has expanded into a vast array of subjects and fields of application. It was originally used without being more specifically defined, what it is and how to evaluate and use it.

The focus of critical appraisal in medical literature is expanding well beyond the cause-effect-relationships in etiology and control of health phenomena and problems.

Today, critical appraisal encompasses three slightly different definitions that vary slightly in their vocabulary and scope. These include:

1. **A definition for public health professionals** where critical appraisal is a *"systematic evaluation of a process, service, research design, etc., consisting of a detailed scrutiny and logical analysis of all phases of the process with the aim of ensuring that it conforms to acceptable standards, or if it does not, identifying the shortcomings of the service, process, research design, and procedures."*[24]
2. **A definition for epidemiologists.** In this definition, critical appraisal means the *"application of rules of evidence to a study to assess the validity of the data, completeness*

of reporting, methods and procedures, conclusions, compliance with ethical standards, etc. The rules of evidence vary with circumstances."[16]

3. **A definition for clinicians**, proposed originally only as a term (Sackett et al.) was reworded later as "*the application of rules of evidence to clinical (signs and symptoms), paraclinical (laboratory and diagnostic tests) and published data (advocating specific treatment manoeuvres or purporting to establish the etiology or prognosis of disease in order to determine their validity (closeness to truth) and applicability (usefulness in one's clinical practice. Critical appraisal then is focused primarily on 'evidence' derived from empirical research studies published in the scientific literature. …Critical appraisal is indispensable as a technique for evaluating the strength of factual claims in healthcare. However, it is addressed only to the facts and not to the arguments.*"[28]

4. "Critical appraisal" may be **reduced to research only**:[29,30] "*Critical appraisal is the process of carefully and systematically examining research to judge its trustworthiness, and its value and relevance in a particular context.*"

    And ensuing research articles: "*Critical appraisal is a systematic process used to identify the strengths and weaknesses of a research article in order to assess the usefulness and validity of research findings.*"[31]

    Critical appraisal ways of thinking now expand into other domains such as qualitative research. This method of evaluation applies to both qualitative and quantitative approaches to clinical practice and is commonly used by both for physicians and nurses.[32–35]

5. The **current focus of critical appraisal** is either on the critical appraisal of medical literature only or on a wider range of initiatives, including applications and new methodology in numerous health professions like nursing, dentistry, pharmacology, general practice, and family medicine, and other branches and domains of practice and research. Case reporting and clinical case reporting are one of them.[36]

Its definition remains broad so far. Other definitions abound and increase in numbers over the years. Critical appraisal definition and understanding is an example of how broad definitions may be for a certain time.

Let Us Conclude

What do these thoughts about definitions suggest?

1. Definitions "define" research questions and subsequent basic, clinical and epidemiological research as a whole and their results.
2. Definitions "define" clinical practice problem solving.
3. Definitions are essential for any meaningful communication between health professionals, mutual understanding, and problem solving.
4. Orismology in health sciences is an emerging domain requiring better structure, focus, uses, and evaluation. It merits our attention and improvement.

Most available definitions in medicine today, such as those for hypertension, diabetes, cancer and its stages, are well-made and suitable for use by both practitioners and researchers. Definitions of psychiatric disorders in the current edition of the DSM (*Diagnostic and Statistical Manual of the American Psychiatric Association*)[37] are as complete as they can be, without being final. This is a remarkable achievement indeed, given the inherent omnipresence of 'soft' data in psychiatry. Fortunately, medical definitions in both practice and research are not always composite terms.

> Flawed reasoning in building and creating definitions leads to fallacious reasoning, interpretation, and decision-making that, in turn, produce poor results. If deficient definitions are used, anyone subsequently using the results based on those definitions risk the reality that their claims will not match the formulation of their theses and research questions, and the purpose of the medical article will be lost. As already emphasized, good and ideally uniform definitions increase in importance where systematic reviews and meta-analysis (i.e., of analysis and synthesis of information on the same subject from various sources across the available information) are concerned.

Indeed, we require further research and developments in medical orismology,[1] the study, use, and evaluation of definitions in medical practice and research. It is one of the cornerstones that define the value, replicability, and usability of findings in research and practice as presented in medical papers. This chapter illustrates only where we are today with all current definitions and their understanding, nosology, management qualities, and uses.

> Let us reiterate: All the cornerstones of a research study and its reporting (the problem, objectives, hypothesis, research question, and related definitions) are valid only in a specific **context** of scientific and professional nature and **setting** or environment of medical practice and research, its professionals and patients. Both the former and the latter must be well defined by researchers and authors. Without such specifications, even the best conceived and executed research and its presentation (medical article) risk being meaningless.

Let us continue to further expand the domain of orismology, and to structure and orient it more effectively. Let us also develop systematic reviews and meta-analyses of evidence based on diverse and anarchical and heterogeneous definitions in original studies. With the cornerstones of research and other subjects of medical communication defined, the path from original ideas to publication is now well covered by several references,[38,39] and some other scattered elsewhere. Publication itself, in the form of a medical article as an exercise in argumentation, informal logic, and critical thinking is the subject of our next essay chapter.

References

1. Jenicek M. *A Primer on Clinical Experience in Medicine. Reasoning, Decision-Making, and Communication in Health Sciences.* Boca Raton, FL/London/New York: CRC Press/Taylor & Francis/Productivity Press, 2013.

2. Jenicek M. The four cornerstones of a research project: Health problem in focus, objectives, hypothesis, research question. Chapter 3, pp. 27–34 in: *Biomedical Research. From Ideation to Publication.* Edited by G Jagadeesh, S Murthy, YK Gupta, A Prakash. New Delhi/Philadelphia, PA/London: Wolters Kluwer Health/Lippincott/Williams & Wilkins, 2010.

3. Jenicek M. *Fallacy-Free Reasoning in Medicine. Improving Communication and Decision-Making in Research and Practice.* Chicago: American Medical Association (AMA Press), 2009.

4. Gupta A (in the *Stanford Encyclopedia of Philosophy). Definitions.* 27 p. at http://plato.stanford .edu/entries/definitions, retrieved Aug 1, 2013.

5. Yagisawa T. Definition. pp. 213–5 in: *The Cambridge Dictionary of Philosophy.* 2nd Edition. General editor R Gaudi. Cambridge and New York: Cambridge University Press, 1999.

6. Meaning and Definition. Chapter 2, pp. 33–60 in: Hughes W, Lavery J. *Critical Thinking. An Introduction to the Basic Skills.* 5th Edition. Peterborough/Buffalo, NY/Plymouth/Sydney: Broadview Press, 2008.

7. Wikipedia, the free encyclopedia. *Definition.* 9 p. at http://en.wikipedia.org/wiki/Definition, retrieved July 28, 2013.

8. Straus SE, Glasziou P, Richardson WS, Haynes RB. *Evidence-Based Medicine. How to Practice and Teach It.* 3rd Edition. Edinburgh and New York Elsevier/Churchill Livingstone, 2005.

9. Straus SE, Glasziou P, Richardson WS, Haynes RB. *Evidence-Based Medicine. How to Practice and Teach It.* 4th Edition. Edinburgh/London/New York/Toronto: Churchill Livingstone/Elsevier, 2011.

10. Jenicek M. *Foundations of Evidence-Based Medicine.* Boca Raton, FL/London/New York/Washington, DC: The Parthenon Publishing Group/CRC Press, 2003.

11. *Canada Health Action. Building the Legacy.* Papers Commissioned by the National Forum on Health. Volume 5. *Making Decisions. Evidence and Information.* Sainte Foy: Éditions MultiMondes, 1998.

12. Sackett DL, Rosenberg WMC, Muir Gray JA, Haynes RB, Richardson WS. Evidence based medicine: What it is and what it isn't. It's about integrating individual clinical expertise and the best external evidence. *BMJ,* 1996;312:71–2.

13. Jenicek M. Evidence-Based medicine: Fifteen years later. Golem the good, the bad, and the ugly in need of a review? *Med Sci Monit,* 2006;12(11):RA241–251.

14. WhatisKT. *KT Terms.* Evolving number of p. at http://whatiskt.wikispaces.com/KT+terms, retrieved Jan 22, 2012.

15. Downes S. *Stephen's Guide to the Logical Fallacies.* Brandon, Manitoba, Canada, 1995–1998. Evolving number of p. (including subsites) at http://www.intrepidsoftware.com/fallacy/welcome.php and related sites, retrieved Dec 06, 2004. See also http://assiniboinec.mb.ca/user/downes/fallacy.

16. *A Dictionary of Epidemiology.* 5th Edition. Edited for the International Epidemiological Association by M. Porta. Oxford and New York: Oxford University Press, 2008.

17. Luepker RV, Apple FS, Christenson RH, Crow RS, Fortman SP et al. Case definitions for acute coronary heart disease in epidemiology and clinical research studies. A Statement from the AHA council on Epidemiology and Prevention; AHA Statistics Committee; World Heart Federation Council on Epidemiology and Prevention; the European Society Working Group on Epidemiology and Prevention; Centers for Disease Control and Prevention; and the National Heart, Lung, and Blood Institute. *Circulation,* 2003;108:2543–9.

18. Canadian Institutes of Health Research. *About Knowledge Translation.* 1 p. at http://www.cihr-irse .gc.ca/e/29418.ktml, retrieved Feb 14, 2012.

19. Straus SE, Tetroe J, Graham I. Defining knowledge translation. *CMAJ,* 2009;181(3–4):165–8.

20. Willer DJ, Pappone C, Neuzil P et al. for the ThermoCool AF Trial Investigators. Comparison of antiarrhythmic drug therapy and radiofrequency catheter ablation in patients with paroxysmal atrial fibrillation. A randomized controlled trial. *JAMA,* 2010;303(4):333–340.

21. Burls A. *What is Critical Appraisal?* 8 p. at http://www.medicine.ox.ac.uk/.../What_is_critical_appr ..., retrieved Feb 14, 2012.

22. Ontario Public Health Libraries Association (OPHLA). *Clinical Appraisal of Research Evidence 101.* 16 pdf p. at http://www.health.gov.on.ca/english/.../caore.pdf, retrieved Feb 14, 2012.

23. Young JM and Solomon MJ. How to critically appraise an article. *Nat Clin Pract Gastroenterol Hepatol,* 2009(2);6:82–91.

24. *A Dictionary of Public Health.* Edited by JM Last. Oxford and New York: Oxford University Press, 2007.

25. *A Dictionary of Epidemiology. Fifth Edition. A Handbook Sponsored by the I.E.A.* Edited by M. Porta. Oxford and New York: Oxford University Press, 2008.

26. Field MJ and Lohr KN (Editors). *Guidelines for Clinical Practice, Directions for a New Program.* Washington, DC: Institute of Medicine, National Academy Press, 1990. See also: Davis D, Goldman J, Palda VA. *Handbook on Clinical Practice Guidelines.* Ottawa: Canadian Medical Association, 2007.

27. Madjar I and Walton JA. What is problematic about evidence? pp. 28–45 in: Morse JM, Swanson JM, Kuzel AJ. *The Nature of Qualitative Evidence.* Thousand Oaks, CA: SAGE Publications, 2001.

28. Colak E. *Critical Appraisal & Critical Thinking.* 2 p. at http://www.individual.utoronto.ca/ecolak /EBM/evidence_and_eikos/critical_ppraisal_and_critical thinking.htm, retrieved July 30, 2017.

29. Burls A. What is critical appraisal. 8 pages at www.whatisseries.co.uk/what-is-critical-appraisal/, 2009. Retrieved August 7 2017.

30. Johansen M and Thomsen SF. Guidelines for reporting medical research: A critical appraisal. *International Scholarly Research Notices,* 2016, Article ID 1346026, 7 p. at http://dx/doi/org /10.1155/2016/1346026, retrieved August 7, 2017.

31. Young JM and Solomon MJ. How to critically appraise and article. *Nat Clin Pract Gastroenterol Hepatol,* 2009;6(2):82–91.

32. *Critical appraisal of qualitative research.* Chapter 4 by Hannes K in: Noyes J, Booth A, Hannes K, Harden A, Harris J, Levin S, Lockwood C (Editors). *Supplementary Guidance for Inclusion of Qualitative Research in Cochrane Systematic Reviews of Interventions.* Version 1 (updated August 2011). Cochrane Collaboration Qualitative Methods Group, 2011. At http://cqrmg.cochrane.org /supplemental-handbook-guidance, retrieved July 28, 2017.

33. CBMa Center for Evidence-Based Management. *Critical Appraisal of a Case Study.* Adapted from Crombie, *The Pocket Guide to Critical Appraisal;* the critical appraisal approach used by the Oxford Centre for Evidence medicine, checklists of the Dutch Cochrane Centre, BMJ editors checklists of the EPPI Centre. Center for Evidence Based Management (July 2014), Critical Appraisal Checklist for a Case Study. 1 p. at https://www.cebma.org/wp-content/.../Critical-Appraisal-Questions-for-a -Case Study, retrieved Aug 7, 2017.

34. Bootland D, Coughlan E, Galloway R, Goubet S, Mcwhirter E. *Critical Appraisal from Papers to Patient.* Boca Raton, FL/London/New York: CRC Press (Taylor & Francis Group), 2017.

35. Mhaskar R, Emmanuel P, Mishra S, Patel S, Naik E, Kumar A. Critical appraisal skills are essential to informed decision-making. *Indian J Sex Transm Dis,* 30(2):112–9.

36. Roever L and Reis O. Critical appraisal of a case report. *Evidence-Based Medicine and Practice,* 2015,(1):1.

37. American Psychiatric Association. *Diagnostic and Statistical Manual of Mental Disorders. Fifth Edition. DSM-5™.* Washington, DC and London: American Psychiatric Publishing, a Division of American Psychiatric Association, 2013.

38. Hulley SB, Cummings SR, Browner WS, Grady DG, Newman TB. *Designing Clinical Research.* 3rd Edition. Philadelphia, PA: Wolters Kluwer Health/Lippincott Williams & Wilkins, 2007.

39. *Biomedical Research. From Ideation to Publication.* Edited by G Jagadeesh, S Murthy, YK Gupta, A Prakash. New Delhi/Philadelphia, PA/London: Wolters Kluwer Health/Lippincott, Williams & Wilkins, 2010.

Chapter 8

How to Think about Cause-Effect Relationships: Multiple and Single Observations*

Executive Summary

How should we think about and evaluate cause-effect relationships? Cause-effect relationships exist both between "bad" and "good" causes. "Bad" cause-effect relationships are those between noxious agents that cause disease, and the subsequent illness and harm that is the effect. "Good" cause-effect relationships are treatments for disease and illness and the subsequent consequences of their use, like cases of disease prevented, improved, or healed. Both kinds of factors (causes) are the subjects of the same rules of causality to conclude about their effects (consequence).

We may assess the causality while comparing series of cases of exposure and their consequences by quantitative observations or studies of multiple groups. Conclusions are based both on judgment and quantifications of exposures and their consequences. We may also try to assess the causality in single case or few situations on the basis of judgment only with all the inherent limitation of such purely qualitative approach. This approach may lead to hypothesizing as a lead to more convincing quantitative studies.

To say that being exposed to an industrial solvent 'is associated' with occupational disease occurrence or that taking a certain drug 'is associated' with its presumed adverse effects or improvement in a patient's health, is

---

* This chapter is based, with permission by the publisher, on Chapter 6 in: Jenicek M. *Writing, Reading, and Understanding in Modern Health Sciences. Medical Articles and Other Forms of Communication.* Boca Raton, FL/ London/New York: CRC Press/Taylor & Francis/Productivity Press, 2014. Revised, edited, updated.

like the tabloid media saying that "Star X" "is romantically linked" to "Star Y." That is to say, it can mean anything. Any report on causality, such as those found in medical articles, must offer far more evidence to support a claim of causality. Indeed, a medical article or research report must offer as much evidence for causality to readers as possible, either directly by the authors or by offering enough elementary information that allows them to determine causal demonstration, and thus allowing them the opportunity to evaluate for themselves the cause-effect relationship of the issue under study. Descriptive, purely observational studies without any control groups or comparable observations do not bring a causal proof; however, they offer extremely valuable information for hypothesizing about causality and generation of a further, proper, ad hoc causal study.

Both observational and experimental studies of causes, by their content and organization, must confirm or reject as many criteria of causality as possible: reporting straightforward *p*-values, relative risks, or odds ratios is not enough. In this chapter, we identify six assumptions or prerequisites, six major criteria, conditional criteria, reference proofs and confirmations that are necessary for research studies. Additional criteria are brought to bear where the causality of a given problem goes beyond the reported study itself.

A critical appraisal of etiological studies is based on the step-by-step evaluation of such studies. This requires careful review and assessment of each element in the study—from the research thesis to the selections of subjects and groups for the study through to the analysis and extrapolation of findings—to the original population and setting and beyond, individual patients, other groups or health problems. These considerations of causality, as reported in medical articles, apply equally to both the original research and to systematic reviews.

In This Chapter

Executive Summary 213
Thoughts, Thinkers, and Things to Think About 215
8.1   Uncertainty, Probabilities, Disease Frequency behind Our Disease Occurrence
     and Its Causes 219
     8.1.1   Disease or Other Event Frequencies and Fractions in Causal Reasoning 219
            Point Estimates and Confidence Intervals 226
     8.1.2   Beyond Causality: Combining Frequencies, Fractions, Risks, and Proportions 226
     8.1.3   Quantifying Our Uncertainties 226
8.2   Thinking about Causes 228
     8.2.1   How We Look at Causes: Single or Multiple Observations as Sets, Chains,
            Webs, and Concept Maps of Causes 228
     8.2.2   Ways of Searching for Causes: Single or Multiple Observations and Findings 233
     8.2.3   Criteria of Causality 235
     8.2.4   Criteria for Accepting Etiology or Other Cause-Effect Relationships 235

8.3 Fallacies in Medical Reasoning and Scientific Thinking in General 239
8.4 Role of Causal Reasoning in Medical Thinking 241
8.5 Considerations of Causality in "Cognition-Based" Medicine; Non-Epidemiological
Reasoning Focused on Specific Cases; Single-Event Observations.................................241
8.6 Single-Subject Research Design 241
8.7 Other Ways of Considering Causality 243
8.8 Critical Thinking, Communication, and Decision-Making and Their Connection
to Medical Ethics 243
Let Us Conclude 244
References 247

Thoughts, Thinkers, and Things to Think About

*We are too much accustomed to attribute
to a single cause that which is the product
of several, and the majority of our
controversies come from that.*
Attributed to Baron Justus von Liebig
(1803–1873)
German Chemist
**Yes, sets, webs, and chains of causes are
here to stay with us!**

*It is too bad that we cannot cut the
patient in half in order to compare two
regimens of treatment.*
Bela Schick
(1877–1967)
Austrian Pediatrician
*Aphorisms and Facetiae of
Bela Schick, "Early Years"*
by I.J. Wolfe
Why not a good clinical trial?

Statistics are not substitute for judgment.
Robert P. Lamont
(1867–1948)
U.S. Secretary of Commerce
Right, even more in medicine!

The great tragedy of Science—that the slaying of a beautiful hypothesis by an ugly fact.
The Right Honorable
Thomas Henry Huxley
(1825–1895)
"Biogensis and Abiogenesis"
in the *British Annual Report, 1870*
Aren't we doing this all the time in etiological research?

Accident is the name one gives to the coincidence of events, of which one does not know the causation. … Accidents only exist in our heads, in our limited perception.
Franz Kafka
(1883–1925)
in Gustav Janouch's
Conversations with Kafka (p. 55)
tr. H. Goronovy Rees (1953)
Aren't we avoiding these kinds of accidents by doing causal inquiries?

Every action must be due to one or other or seven causes: Chance, nature, compulsion, habit, reasoning, anger, or appetite.
Aristotle
(284–322 BC)
Rhetoric (1.10)
tr. W. Rhys Roberts (1954)
And more, the venerable one!

When you have mastered the numbers, you will in fact no longer be reading numbers, any more than you read words when reading a book. You will be reading meanings.
Harold Geneen
(1910–1997)
Businessman
with Alwin Moscow
in *Managing* (1984, p. 9)
So, in this book too!

*Science is the knowledge of consequences,
and dependence of one fact upon another.*
Thomas Hobbes
(1588–1679)
Leviathan (1651, p. 5)
**Hence casual reasoning or something
more?**

*The most savage controversies are those
about matters to which there is no good
evidence either way.*
3rd Earl Bertrand William Russell
(1872–1970)
Etiological research should help!

*Some circumstantial evidence is very
strong, as when you find a trout in the
milk.*
Henry David Thoreau
(1817–1862)
**Does not evidence from etiological
research locate a trout in its waters?**

*Human actions are not mechanical effects
of causes; they are purposive executions
of decisions between alternative possible
choices.*
Arnold J. Toynbee
(1889–1975)
A Study of History (1961, 2.259)
A human cause to add?

*Medicine is the science of uncertainty and
the art of probability.*
Emily Mumford
From Students to Physicians (1970)
**That's the reason behind the
etiological research, Liz!**

Science and clinical practice move in opposite directions. Science moves from individual observations to a generalizable theories and laws. Clinical practice brings this generalizable body of knowledge to bear to benefit an individual. Science has a unique and essential role in clinical practice. Clinical practice is not a science but an endeavour that uses science. Good science is necessary but insufficient for good practice.
Nuala B. Kenny
in the *Canadian Medical Association Journal* (1997)
But what we would do without it, Nuala?

It all depends on how we see a cause-effect relationship.

How should we translate basic philosophical tenets and a broad general experience into health sciences thinking? How frequent are health phenomena like disease, health, prevention, and treatment? What causes them? And what do we do with them? This kind of basic philosophical thinking is enriched by specific reasoning about health entities and phenomena, and by more quantitative methodology that is now omnipresent in medicine. Can we imagine health sciences without epidemiology and biostatistics today?

To begin, let us specify what a cause is in the domain of cause-effect relationships within the health sciences. The *Encyclopedia Britannica* defines a cause as *"That factor which is possible or convenient for us to alter in order to produce or prevent an effect. … This concept contains two components, production of an effect and an understanding of its mechanisms."* A cause may be then defined in our (more specific) context as *a (health) event without some subsequent (health) event would not have occurred or because of which it occurred.*[1] Causal factors may include:

■ all endogenous and exogenous factors of individuals and the environment which modify health status and health occurrence in individuals and communities;
■ all decisions (medical or otherwise), and other factors modifying disease occurrence and influencing disease course; and
■ all phenomena determining clinical decisions and public health interventions.[2]

A "cause" must then be modifiable, and its modification must lead to a change of its effect (patient state, disease spread). The relationship between this "cause" and "effect" is what interests us here. Cause-effect relationships between the "bad" (causes) and their "bad" consequences such as disease occurrence and worsening are of as much interest as those between "good" causes like treatment or preventive measures and their "good" consequences. "Good" consequences may include no new cases of disease (no disease) incidence or improvement of existing cases like in patient care, clinical trials, and other health programs.

In this chapter, let us summarize some basic methodology. Causal thinking in medicine and the philosophy of medicine has been developed through the domains of epidemiology and biostatistics over the past century and has become ubiquitous across the medical experience. Through this work, studies of health phenomena like disease, health, actions of various beneficial or noxious factors, and any other physiological or morphological entities of interest may be seen as falling in two principal categories of inquiry:

1. **Descriptive studies**, which report health phenomena beyond a single observation. The principal objective of such studies is to offer a portrait of what happened and what was observed during a specific period of time or within a specific situation. It is somewhat exceptional for such studies to be used as cause-effect proofs. However, they often offer important propositions about possible cause-effect relationships which should be confirmed or rejected by further analysis and research, addressed in the next category. Medical articles must report not only exactly *what* happened, but also what should be done next and what directions for further research and immediate practice might be.

2. **Analytical studies** offer the best possible opportunities to demonstrate causality. These studies are based on *observations of uncontrolled events* in the healthcare environment and community-at-large, *or experimental research* such as clinical trials, field trials, laboratory studies, and environmental research. As an example, toxicology offers an excellent opportunity to demonstrate causality. Each type of research, such as case control studies, (concurrent) cohort studies, or cohort studies of past experiences (historical cohort studies, retrospective cohort studies) offer some examination of a cause-effect relationship. Medical articles that report these studies must allow the reader to judge for themselves the degree to which the underlying studies fulfill the criteria of causality. The knowledge gained through this exploration should aid further research and provide insight into immediate decisions in healthcare and community health practice.

3. **Descriptive studies of single phenomena and disease occurrence** like clinical case reports are not definitive proof of cause-effect relationships, but they are the first and essential portal to such proofs. Both the generation of hypotheses and reporting is part of such portals.

8.1 Uncertainty, Probabilities, Disease Frequency behind Our Disease Occurrence and Its Causes

Ideally, as caring clinicians and practitioners, we want to be certain about what we understand and what we should do with our patients and communities. However, our knowledge and experience are almost always limited in some way. We are required, then, to attribute degrees of probability to health phenomena and actions.

8.1.1 Disease or Other Event Frequencies and Fractions in Causal Reasoning

To understand disease frequency and its causes, we need numbers of events (disease, exposure to causal factors, their results), either as **absolute numbers (frequencies)** or **fractions (relative frequencies** such as **rates, ratios, or odds)**. The concept of causality fundamentally requires the comparison of events in various groups of individuals. Events may include cases of disease, exposure to noxious factors, drug therapies, having surgery, having complications, suffering from adverse effects of treatment and care, and so on. Events are presented and studied in two forms: frequencies or fractions.

Frequencies are simply the number of events that are occurring or have occurred. For example: 250 cases of chronic obstructive pulmonary disease (COPD) exist in our community. The number (n) is a total of events that were observed, a frequency of COPD.

Frequencies (such as 1,000 cases of cancer) and their **rates** (1,000 cases per 100,000 subjects in the community, that is, a rate of 1/100 or 10/1,000, etc.) represent **absolute values** of what we observed, usually presented as a total of events observed in a given category, set, or group.

Fractions are two related frequencies as expressions of the relationship between them. Frequencies of events are numerators presented as parts of some whole, and the whole is presented as the denominator. For example, 25 cases of chronic obstructive pulmonary disease occur in a community of 35,000 inhabitants. This means that there are 25 diseased and 34,775 non-diseased inhabitants. In epidemiology, fractions are typically presented as **rates** (proportions) or **ratios**.

Rates are a result of pairing a set of observations in the numerator, such as disease cases (*a*), with a set in the denominator including those same observations (*a*) and some additional ones such as non-cases (*b*). These two like sets create a community: *a/a + b*. A rate in our example is then 25/(25 + 34,775). It can be presented as such or multiplied by some coefficient like 100,000 for comparability: 25/35,000 × 100,000, that is, 7,142.85/100,000.

For less frequent phenomena like cancer, rates per 100,000 may be presented. For frequent phenomena like diarrhea cases during a foodborne disease outbreak per 100, adverse drug effects may be reported per 1,000,000, and so on. As in our COPD case, rates may also be presented as a percentage (07.14%) or as decimal fractions (0.00714) for various computational purposes.

Ratios are *relationships* between different entities in the numerator (*a*) and the denominator (*b*): *a/b*. In our COPD case, the ratio is 25/34,775. The entity in the numerator is not included in the denominator. For example, comparing rates of events (incidence of events in one community) to other rates of events (incidence of events in another community) yields **ratios** such as cancer incidence rate in smokers over the cancer incidence rate in non-smokers (risk ratio in this case).

Odds (cross-product ratio, relative odds) are ratios of the probability of occurrence of an event to that of non-occurrence of that same event in another set of observations.[3,4] In other words, it is the *ratio of the probability* that something is one way compared to the *probability that it is other way*.[3,4] **Odds**, in fact, are fractions which have *events* in the nominator, and *non-events* in the denominator. For example, where there is a community of 1,000 people, and 100 have been diagnosed with cancer and the remaining 900 do not have a cancer diagnosis, the odds of having cancer are 100/900. That is, odds in one group of subjects is presented *over* the odds in another group yield an **odds ratio**. Ratios and odds give us an idea about **relative values** of what we see and compare.

Likelihood refers to the general state of being likely or probable that an event has already occurred and would yield a specific outcome. Formally, it differs from *probability* as probability refers to the occurrence of future events, and likelihood refers to events that have already occurred. Statistically speaking, a **likelihood ratio** is the ratio of the values of the likelihood function at two different parameter values or under two different data models.[3,4] In other words, a likelihood ratio is the likelihood that some observed outcome will occur if a set of parameters exist, compared to the likelihood that a second observed outcome will occur if the same set of parameters does not exist. Considered as a diagnostic methods and test, a likelihood ratio test is the probability that a given test result would occur in a person with the target disorder divided by the probability that the same result would occur in a person without that disorder.[3]

In the simplest terms, rates consist of numerators (frequency of a health phenomenon, cases of disease, etc.) and denominators (frequency of all individuals in the group, diseased or not).

Put another way, the denominator represents the whole community from which numerators originate and to which they belong. It is not always easy in practice and research to define and identify denominators of rates. This has led to a humorous definition of epidemiologists as "*human beings in eternal search of good denominators.*"

In a rate, the numerator is included in the denominator, plus additional groups. For example, a rate may have a diseased population in the numerator, and both diseased and non-diseased populations in the denominator. In a ratio, the numerator and denominator are exclusive groups. That is, if something is in the numerator (like diseased individuals), then only something else is in the denominator (other than diseased individuals), it is a ratio. A ratio may be also a relationship of two rates, like a ratio of disease rate in subjects exposed to a factor of interest as a ratio to a rate of subjects who are not exposed to it.

In causal relationship studies, rates are a measure of the magnitude of a phenomenon and relative risks are measures of the strength of a causal association. The difference between risks (attributable risks) or their proportional magnitude from a larger body of risk (etiological or attributable fractions) measure the specificity of a causal association. In words, risk provides an understanding of the preponderance of one factor among others, which constitute sets or webs of causes of disease or other phenomenon under study. More about this follows.

Figure 8.1 represents a basic model of comparison of two groups of events from which an event frequency is derived. It serves with other considerations to assess causality, what it represents, and to what it applies (target population or patients as individuals). A subset (sample) of individuals representing a larger (target) population to which the results of the study should apply, and be representative of, is selected. Groups that are exposed and not exposed to the event (noxious factor, treatment, or other beneficial intervention) are formed. They are compared at their "initial state" or state *before* the event of interest, and after the "intervention," "event," "maneuver," or "exposures" occurs or is executed. Additional events (like co-morbidity or co-treatments) may also be considered. "Subsequent states" or event outcomes subsequent to the initial outcome, in groups are then compared for their differences and distinctions. Causality and the role of the actions under study are clarified. Findings are then evaluated based on what they actually apply to: the original target population, individuals beyond the original target population (further generalizations), particular and specific patients, or individuals in the community, and so on.

Examples of tools for statistical reporting a magnitude of a health problem are then:

■ Rates
■ Incidence rates
■ Prevalence rates

Examples of tools for statistical reporting for establishing a relationship, or causality are then:

■ Ratios
■ Odds ratios

Examples of tools for statistical reporting for strength of causality then:

■ Relative risk
■ Odds ratios
■ Attributable risk
■ Etiological fraction

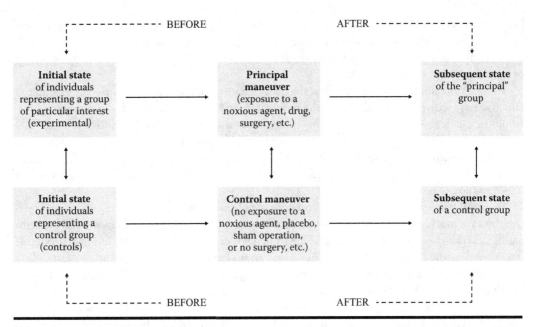

Figure 8.1 A basic model of a cause-effect analytical study in medicine. (Redrawn from Jenicek M. *Epidemiology. The Logic of Modern Medicine.* Montreal: EPIMED International, 1995, and with modifications from References 6–8. Reproduced with permission.)

Below is an oversimplified example of noxious factors and following cases of disease events studied both by cohort and case control studies. This example should help us understand how disease cases, death, or favorable or unfavorable outcomes and exposures to various beneficial or noxious factors frequencies and their comparisons are applied to various uses and interpretations as further detailed in this section and chapter:

Frequencies of disease, death, or change in health status are numerous. Morbidity (disease prevalence and incidence), mortality, case fatality, and their relationships in the form of rates, ratios, or odds are the most important ones. Figure 8.2 represents another simplified example of some such frequencies. It describes the situation in a group of workers exposed over a period of time to an industrial carcinogenic substance from which some workers develop cancer and some die. Quantification in this example is self-explanatory.

Morbidity rates are rates of disease cases in a community defined in time and space. The two most important are prevalence rates and incidence rates. **Prevalence rates**, which can be described as, disease frequency (cases, spells, manifestations, individuals treated, etc.) at a given point in time (point prevalence) or over a period of time (period prevalence), independent of the moment of its occurrence as it appears in a population of interest (cases and non-cases confounded). Prevalence provides researchers with an idea of the *overall magnitude* of the health problem either at a given moment or over a defined period of time. Chronic disease, handicaps, and other health problems of long duration are often in focus. In **incidence rates**, frequencies of *new* cases of disease or another event in a defined period of time (hours, days, years) are related to a population in which they occur (preferably subjects susceptible to get it). In the case outlined above, $a/a+b$ and $c/c+d$.

Incidence rates allow us to measure the speed of disease spread from one period of time to another. New cases, incidence spells, incidence of various manifestations, or incidence of newly diagnosed cases may be of interest from one problem to another. Infectious disease, injury, cancer, and cardiovascular diseases are often followed this way.

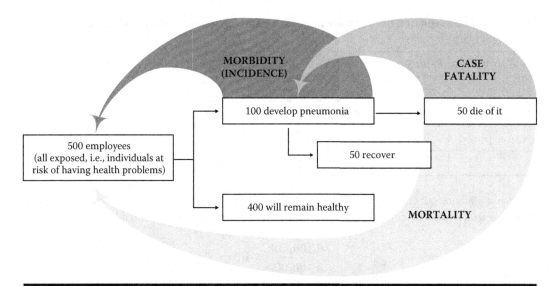

Figure 8.2 Morbidity, mortality, and case fatality in a health event. Periods of exposure and event occurrence are defined. (Redrawn from Jenicek M. *Epidemiology. The Logic of Modern Medicine*. Montreal: EPIMED International, 1995, and References 6–8. Reproduced with permission.)

Deaths in communities or any other group of interest are studied through mortality and case fatality rates. There are two types of fatality rates: mortality rates and case fatality rates. **Mortality rates** are rates of death in such a community for *all individuals*, healthy, diseased, or suffering from other health problems confounded in the denominator of a rate. They may encompass general mortality rates or specific rates, which may be specific to disease, age, sex, and other demographic or social specific elements. **Case fatality rates**, on the other hand, are deaths occurring in a given number of cases of disease toward a given moment (cumulative events) or over a certain period of time. They are therefore an occurrence of deaths by a disease between *cases only* (those who suffer from it already).

Rates reflect the *absolute* magnitude of a given health problem. To get an idea of the *relative* magnitude, we need health event ratios, event odds, and other ways to compare rates, risks, or deaths. The most important ones for medical understanding and decision-making are relative risks, attributable risks, and etiological fractions (attributable risk percent).

In analytical studies, **ratios**, addressed earlier, are fractions relating two entities (two different health events or their related characteristics) in which the entity in the numerator is not reproduced (with something else added) in the denominator. **Odds** (cross-product ratios, relative odds) are ratios of the probability of occurrence of an event to that of non-occurrence, or the ratio of the probability that something is one way to the probability that it is another way. In our case of a case control study in Table 8.1—ad/bc.

Relative risk (relative benefit increase or reduction) is a fraction relating incidence of events in one group of subjects, such as those exposed to some factor, to another group or groups not exposed to it. Relative risks are quantifications of the *strength of the causal relationship*. In the case of a study of noxious factors, the higher the relative risk, the stronger the causal association. If the relative risk of a presumably noxious factor is lower than 1.0, the factor (agent) has a protective

Table 8.1   Data from a Cohort Study and Case Control Study. A Numerical Example (Fictitious Data)

Cohort (Longitudinal) Study				Case Control (Transversal) Study		
	New Cases	Non-Cases	Total	–	Cases	Non-Cases
Exposed	A (80)	B (99,920)	100,000	Exposed	a (80)	b (50)
Non-exposed	C (20)	C (99,980)	100,000	Non-exposed	c (20)	d (50)
				Total	100	100

effect, not a noxious one. Cohort studies (observations of new events over a certain period of time) of groups (cohorts) to be compared serve this purpose. In the example outlined in Table 8.1:

$$\frac{80/100,000}{20/100,000} = 4,0$$

Hence, relative risk may also be called a *ratio of rates* or *rate ratio*.

Odds ratios, described elsewhere, also provide a kind of estimation of the strength of a causal association in case control studies. In this situation, odds ratios can provide an understanding of the relationship between exposures/non-exposure by reporting the frequency of exposure as a ratio to non-exposure. In our example (Table 8.1):

$$\frac{a/d}{b/c} = \frac{80 \times 50}{20 \times 50} = \frac{4,000}{1,000} = 4.0$$

N.B. If case control studies are based on incident cases and if the proportion of subjects exposed is similar as in the cohort study, both cohort and case control studies yield comparable estimations of the strength of causal association.

Attributable risk (risk difference, absolute risk reduction) is the difference between the rate of events in a group of interest (exposed to a noxious or beneficial factor) and the rate of events in a non-exposed group. The rationale behind an attributable risk is that in the case of a multi-factorial cause (web of causes) of the disease or health event shared both by the exposed or non-exposed group, the difference is due to the factor in question, the rest of the web of causes and their consequences being the same for both groups compared. In our cohort study (Table 8.1):

$$80/100,000 - 20/100,000 = 60/100,000$$

In another example, in searching for cause(s) of a foodborne infectious disease, we want to detect the most probable contaminated dish from among many, eaten in various combinations by a group of people. By establishing an attributable risk (risk difference) for each meal as consumed or not (attack rate of disease in this dish's eaters compared to such an attack rate in non-eaters), we may consider as the most probable vehicle of infection the dish showing the greatest attributable risk among them all. Specificity of causal association from one meal to another is shown by the biggest risk difference, relative risks show its strength, and etiological fractions (see below) show the role and predominance of each dish in a given web of causes (all dishes under consideration as potential sources/causes of infection in the entire study).[3,6] Nosocomial (hospital) infections or other outbreaks of events with underlying sets or webs of causes may also be analyzed this way.

An **etiological fraction** (attributable benefit fraction) is a proportion of events in exposed subjects which is due to the factor of interest from the web of causes of the health problem under study. It is estimated either as a proportion of the attributable risk from the total of the risk in the exposed group (in the cohort or longitudinal studies) yielding an ***attributable risk percent*** or as an odds ratio minus one (in case control studies), ***attributable odds***. These calculations provide some insight into the *specificity of one causal factor* and its prevalent role in the web of causes. We presume that other causes from the web of causes are similarly present and manifested in the exposed and unexposed groups of interest. The closer the etiological fraction is to 100%, the more specific (exclusive, prevalent, dominant) the role of this factor is among all other causal factors under consideration. In our cohort study:

$$\frac{80/100,000 - 20/100,000}{80/100,000} \times 100 = 75\%$$

that is, three-quarters of cases in the exposed are due to the exposure under study; this factor is predominant among others being part of the web of causes.

Hence, strength and specificity (exclusivity) criteria of causality may be estimated quantitatively by using ratios and other quantifications.

Dose–effect relationships (biological gradient) and concomitant variations may be studied by biostatistical methods. For example, clinical or field trials of vaccine protective effect (protective efficacy ratios are one of the epidemiological tools used) require both epidemiological and biostatistical methods; the rest relies mostly on qualitative judgment. The magnitude and spread of health problems are quantified by rates.

As the frequency of bad events following exposure to a bad factor may be quantified and compared, so beneficial interventions (medicines, surgeries, care) can be related to their beneficial effects. In both cases, groups with a higher frequency of results are in the numerator, those with a lower frequency represent the denominator of such ratios in such comparative expressions. Only the name changes in some instances in the following comparison:

Bad Events (Factors and Outcomes)	Good Events (Factors and Outcomes)
Individual risk (frequency, rate) **of bad events**	**Individual risk** (frequency, rate) **of good events**
Relative risk of bad events	**Relative risk of good events**
Attributable risk of bad events	**Attributable benefit increase**
Etiological (attributable) fraction of bad events	**Attributable benefit fraction**
Relative risk increase (Difference in rates in exposed and unexposed)	**Relative benefit increase** (Difference in rates of outcomes in treated and untreated groups)
Number needed to harm: Number of individuals exposed to the factor which would lead to one additional person being harmed compared with individuals who are not exposed to this factor), i.e., 1/attributable risk difference, hence the reciprocal of the attributable risk difference.	**Number needed to treat:** Number of patients who must receive the treatment (beneficial factor) to create one additional improved outcome in comparison with the control treatment group, i.e., 1/absolute risk reduction, hence the reciprocal of the attributable risk reduction.

Epidemiological and biostatistical terms continue to be refined. The American College of Medicine's *ACP Journal Club* periodically updates the glossary of these terms.

Point Estimates and Confidence Intervals

Such various risks, rates, proportions and ratios are presented across the medical literature as **point estimates**, as illustrated in our study example. The uncertainty of these measurements is quantified by computing the **confidence intervals** (*CI*), usually reported as ranges within those true values for the whole population (community or patients) most probably are, that is, 95% *CI* or 99% *CI*.

8.1.2 Beyond Causality: Combining Frequencies, Fractions, Risks, and Proportions

Rates and ratios can be treated separately, each reflecting a particular problem. They can also be combined to evaluate diagnostic considerations. In particular, various frequencies, rates, and ratios can help identify priorities and make decisions for health programs and medical care. As an example, at various levels of prevention choices must often be made between various health programs. Table 8.2 shows how incidence or prevalence frequencies and fractions, etiological and prognostic fractions, and other considerations are combined in our choice of possible most successful interventions.

All frequencies and fractions used in these considerations have a specific meaning from the point of view of causality (importance of the event and its controllability and success of intervention). Some, like risks, are important for primary prevention. Others are important for different levels of health intervention, such as prevalence for secondary prevention or prognostic frequencies and fractions beyond primary prevention.

8.1.3 Quantifying Our Uncertainties

An absolute certainty in medicine is rare. Our experience, understanding, and decision-making processes often vary due to our previous experience with different patients and settings. Such uncertainties are worth measuring, interpreting and using for practical decisions.

We are well aware that all our observations, analyses, and studies are subject to various random and systematic errors. Repeating studies of herd immunity (what proportion of the population is immune after an immunization program) or integrating results from clinical trials yield ranges of results. Repeating studies that integrate results from different clinical trials yield ranges of results rather than the same result on every occasion. Errors, samplings, detection, counting, and health professionals' activities and clinical practices may all contribute to the variation of findings from one study and population to another. For example, can we be certain that a finding of 70% herd immunity is appropriate to guide us to implementing an immunization program or not? For all these and other reasons, we make decisions on the basis of point and interval estimates.

Point estimates provide an idea of "exact" frequencies, proportions, rates, incidence, and so on, such as 70% in the case of our herd immunity study (the term "herd immunity" is used in infectious disease epidemiology for the proportion of subjects in a given community who are resistant to the disease of interest). **Interval estimates** offer ranges within which a "true" value lies, such as 65%–75% in the herd immunity example. More precisely, they are intervals within which the true estimates would fall given the variations of such estimates that might be seen in multiple studies of the same problem in the same group of patients or community. Confidence intervals of 95% or 99% specify our certainty regarding where our observations might be found.

Table 8.2 Uses of Frequencies, Rates, Ratios, or Proportions at Various Levels of Prevention and Choices in Health Program Considerations

Priority	=	*Occurrence*	×	*Clinical Importance*	×	*Controllability (in proportional terms)*	×	*Operational Considerations of Health programs (target population)*
Level of Prevention								
PRIMORDIAL AND PRIMARY (control of disease incidence)		Incidence		Disease severity (case fatality rate, severity score, etc.)		Etiological (attributable) fraction of risk		General population proportion reached by the disease prevention program
SECONDARY (control of disease prevalence by controlling the duration of cases)		Prevalence		Disease severity (case fatality rate, severity score, etc.)		Etiological (attributable) fraction of prognosis (survival, or duration of disease)[a]		Group of patients reached by the healthcare program
TERTIARY AND QUARTERNARY (control of disease spectrum and/or gradient without affecting its duration)		Clinical events		Disease severity (case fatality rate, severity score, etc.)		Etiological (attributable) fraction of prognosis (outcomes' occurrence timing and duration in terms of disease spectrum and/or gradient)[b]		Group of patients reached by the healthcare program

Source: Modified, expanded, and redrawn from Reference 8.

Note: All components may be considered in terms of absolute frequencies, rates, or proportional rates, depending on the view of importance. N.B. For detailed definitions of levels of prevention see Section 3.3.1 in Reference 8.

[a] From observational analytical studies, more desirable from clinical and community trials.
[b] Mainly from clinical trials.

The **range of observations** also counts to understand our uncertainties. If multiple studies indicate a herd immunity range of 50%–90% (too wide in this example for the sake of explicitness) a true value within such an interval may have practical implications. For example, assume that we know that in the case of a particular infectious disease, a herd immunity of 80% is enough to make immunization unnecessary. If the true value is 60%, immunization would be necessary, whereas if it were 85%, it would not. Additional information about the diversity of individuals and their states is given then by the analysis of ranges of observations within and between various sets. Novices in this area must be aware that **confidence intervals and ranges of observation are different subjects** and that they have **different meanings.** Both are relevant, useful, and provide complementary information.

Quantifying uncertainties is as important as reporting our results. Physiological and pathological parameters, like averages or quantiles, rates, ratios, proportions, relative, risks etiological fractions, or protective efficacy rates, are expressed by interval estimates to indicate the level of certainty with findings regarding the problem under study. Confidence intervals are another important element of this process. Overlapping confidence intervals of effectiveness of treatment in various clinical trials helps us to understand whether such results are similar or dissimilar. An important resource authored by British biostatisticians has presented an overall fundamental and detailed overview of obtaining, interpreting and using confidence intervals in describing health phenomena and using them.[9]

8.2 Thinking about Causes

Absolute and relative frequencies and rates of ratios of health events assists in understanding causes and consequences of disease or health. But more is required. It is also important to understand relationships and expanded meaning of causes and consequences based on models of their relationship which can vary from one health problem and situation to another. Some frequent relationships are explored in this section.

8.2.1 How We Look at Causes: Single or Multiple Observations as Sets, Chains, Webs, and Concept Maps of Causes

Since any given health phenomenon may have more than one cause and consequence, multiple approaches toward analyzing causes are necessary. There are at least six main approaches to examining causes in medicine. These are outlined below.

1. Looking at health problems and their causes often starts with the idea of a **single cause–single consequence relationship**. This is illustrated here:

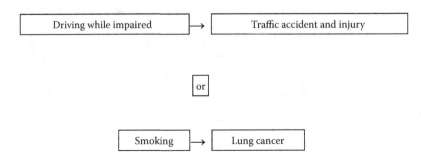

However, a traffic injury may be caused not only by drinking, but also by fatigue, stress, drug abuse, the driver's poorly controlled chronic or acute morbidity, experience, road and vehicle condition, and other factors. We are also aware that smoking is not the only cause of bronchogenic carcinoma. Other causes include passive smoking, miners' exposure to radon gas, asbestos, metals like arsenic, chromium, nickel or iron oxide, other industrial and environmental carcinogens, familial predisposition, predisposing diseases like pulmonary fibrosis, chronic obstructive lung disease, and sarcoidosis. All of these factors must also be taken into consideration as potentially causal or contributing agents.

2. In medicine, multiple causes as "**sets of causes**" are often at the origin of a health problem. Multiple consequences as "**sets of consequences**" may follow the action of the same beneficial factor. We choose here to call these "sets" rather than webs as other authors have termed them.[5] We believe that webs are better described as a separate approach, outlined in the fourth approach here. This is because sets and webs require different biostatistical and other methods and techniques of analysis like path analysis[10] and various multivariate independent variables and multivariable dependent variables techniques and analyses.[11] Friedman offers a good introduction to them in the context of epidemiology.[12] Figure 8.3 illustrates this concept and paradigm applied to a set of causes of medical error and harm and a set of consequences of alcohol abuse.

   There are numerous possible sets of causes of medical error and harm, including combinations and even interactions. These causes vary from case to case as a result of:
   - professional competencies of the healthcare providers (knowledge, attitudes, skills);
   - dispositional states of all health professionals involved (outlook, mood, inclinations, ethics);
   - the psychological and physiological condition (stress, fatigue) of all health professionals involved;
   - patient specifics;
   - dispositional and interactive states (clinical, participation, communication);
   - logistic failures (communication, information, management);
   - professional setting (physical environment, tools, agents and technologies used);
   - rules (protocols, guidelines to follow);
   - critical thinking failures (argumentation, conditionals, rebuttals, lateral thinking, conditions *sine qua non*); and
   - good or bad logistic failures (ensuing decisions made and not made, their execution and evaluation).

   An example of a set of consequences are those related to the abuse of alcohol. These include several medical, surgical, neurological and psychiatric problems, violent behavior, breakdown of family and professional relationships, road and work injuries, suicide, and homicide. A set of causes for heart disease includes hereditary predisposition, physical inactivity, diabetes, high blood pressure, diet, stress, and other factors. Aspirin produces a set of beneficial consequences leading to the control of fever, having an analgesic effect, being a mild anticoagulant preventing coronary heart disease and perhaps still other unknown effects representing a set of consequences.

3. **Chains of causes** (like "*one thing leads to another*") or **chains of consequences** (like "*from one bad thing to a worse one*" or "*from a good thing to an even better one*") may apply to still other cases. Figure 8.4 presents an example of a chain of causes.

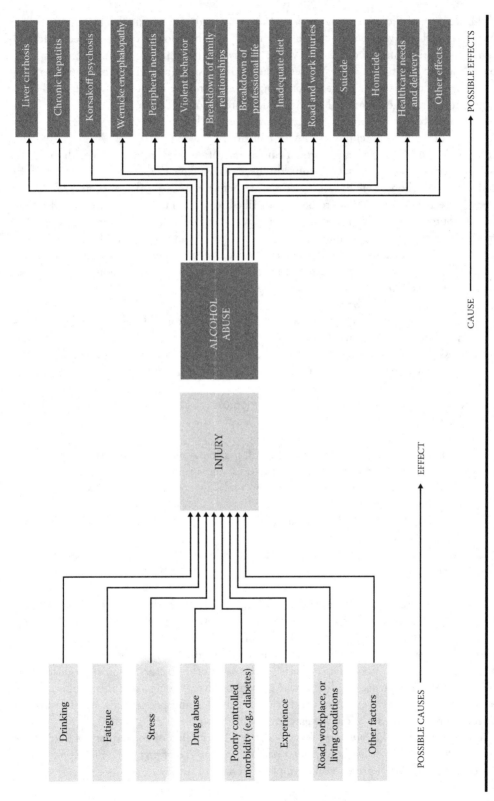

Figure 8.3 Sets of causes and consequences in epidemiology. (Redrawn with modifications from Jenicek M. *Epidemiology. The Logic of Modern Medicine*. Montreal: EPIMED International, 1995 and Reference 6. Reproduced with permission.)

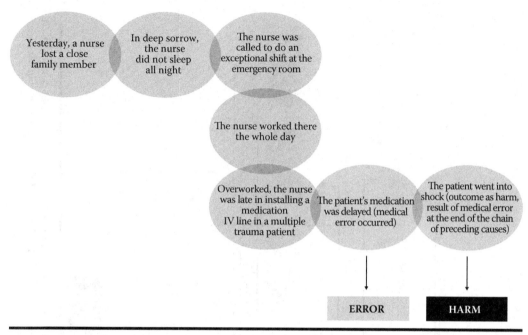

Figure 8.4   Chain of causes: A hospital setting example. (Redrawn, with modifications, from Fig. 2.9 in: Jenicek M. *A Primer on Clinical Experience in Medicine.* Boca Raton: CRC Press, 2013. Reproduced with permission.)

4. Causes and consequences may be also seen, studied, and understood as **webs**. Webs of causes and consequences acknowledge the multidirectional, causal, and other relationships between multiple causes and consequences, what we have termed **webs of causes** and **webs of consequences**. These are studied not only to better understand cause-effect relationships, but also to determine the best ways to intervene and address these causes and consequences. Figure 8.5 represents the modified Friedman's web of causes of myocardial infarction:[6]

5. For a better understanding of problems, **concept maps** are developed and used for learning, teaching, and research. Originally, they were developed mostly for the non-medical world.[13–16] In concept maps, causal factors are considered a part of an even broader concept that visualizes overall thinking about a health problem, its components, and the interactions between them. Concept maps may include webs of causes and consequences, views about the mechanisms underlying health problems, clinical considerations, decisions, and actions. Figure 8.6 is a good example of a concept map; causal factors are highlighted as parts of this wider health problem context.

    N.B. Usually, concept maps are developed and presented in sequence, ramification, and direction from top to bottom. Arrows indicate such a sequence and direction. How can this figure be read and understood? In this presentation, we propose a sequence, ramification and direction from left to right. Arrows indicating cause-effect relationships show the direction from cause to effect rather than the direction of the development and reading of the concept map. The sequence and direction are preserved in the spatial distribution of the concept map elements from left to right. In this example, we can identify several areas and paths indicated by their *connectors*.

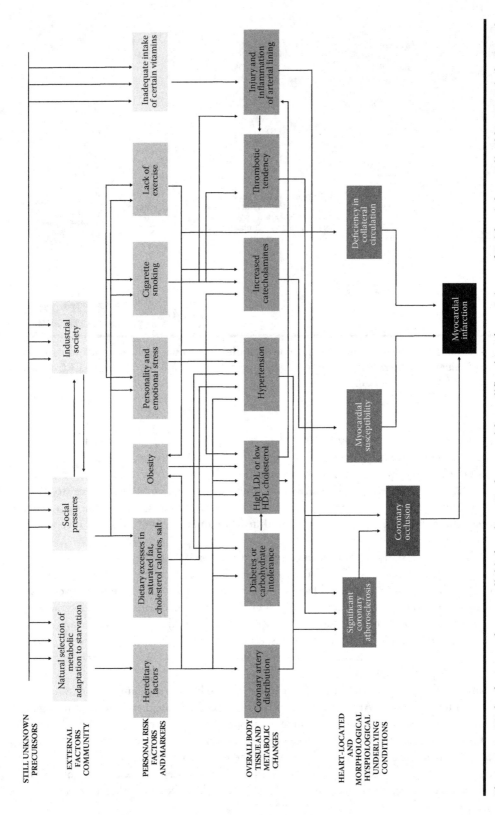

Figure 8.5 Web of causes of myocardial infarction. (Redrawn, with modifications from *Primer of Epidemiology*. Edited by GD Friedman. 5th Edition. New York and London: McGraw-Hill, Medical Publishing Division, 2004 and Jenicek M. *A Primer on Clinical Experience in Medicine*. Boca Raton: CRC Press, 2013.)

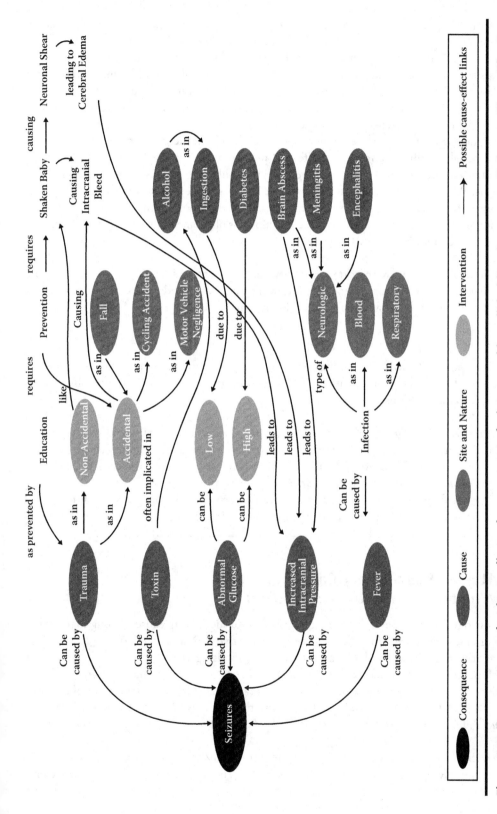

Figure 8.6 A concept map of understanding and management of seizures used in a clinical learning process. (Redrawn with modifications from West DC, Pomeroy JR, Park JK, Gerstenberger EA, Sandoval J. Critical thinking in graduate medical education. A role model concept mapping assessment? *JAMA*, 2000;284(9):1105–10.)

In this light, the upper and central portion of the concept map covers a good part of cause-effect relationships. Peripheral areas reflect more sites, mechanisms, interventions, and outcomes. Visually, concept maps might be confused with webs of causes or consequences maps by uninitiated persons. However, concept maps go well beyond a simple cause-effect path or web. Concept maps are now being developed and used in teaching clinical medicine,[14,15] in various clinical specialties, in community medicine (disease prevention),[16,17] and elsewhere in health sciences and other domains.[18–20]

6. A particular challenge in the study of multiple etiological factors in their webs or sets is their possible **additive effect** or an **effect of potentiation** in a synergy of their action. An additive effect occurs when the combined effect of multiple factors is a sum of their isolated effects. Potentiation of effect occurs when the combined effect of multiple causal factors is more than the sum of the effects of each. Clinical pharmacologists know perhaps more than other specialists about the study and the effect of this phenomenon in the domain of disease treatment by multiple drugs and their effects.

Our views of causality are important well beyond the scientific search for causality. In daily practice, they affect our anamnestic inquiry, review of systems, methods, and extent of treatment, outcomes assessment and follow up, and extension of care.

From an epidemiological perspective connectors can draw conclusions between various thinking and concluding considerations. The following phrases can be used to link observed phenomena and situations:

■ *"can be," "caused by," "causes,"* and *"due to"* may follow a chain or web of causes and their consequences developing into a cause of the next or another consequence;
■ *"as in"* or *"type of"* refer to the location, body systemic site, and some aspects of diagnosis;
■ *"can result in"* indicates outcomes or consequences; and
■ *"requires," "prevention of," "treated with,"* and *"prevented by"* suggest interventions at various levels of prevention (primary or secondary in this case).

8.2.2 Ways of Searching for Causes: Single or Multiple Observations and Findings

In epidemiology, there are several different approaches for identifying causes among many other subjects of interest.[5,6] These include inductive,[21] deductive,[22–25] and abductive[26–35] reasoning. Abductive reasoning, in particular, is an increasingly promising way of reasoning is currently a subject of intense refinements and developments in research, including medical research.[33–35]

There are two types of inference of interest to us. **Statistical inference** uses a series of observations to calculate degrees of uncertainty in comparisons of various data sets. **Causal inference** is *"the thought process and methods that assess or test whether a relation of cause to effect does or does not exist."*[4]

In medicine, we infer in two directions. In the first, we infer *from* observing individuals individually and applying the experience *to* the whole problem which those individuals represent. 'Classical' or field epidemiologists often do this by looking at the characteristics of patients one by one to establish the clinical picture of disease they represent, or studying disease outbreaks or cancer occurrence in the community). The "clinical epidemiology" approach is used in clinical medicine. In this approach, we observe *from* what we already know about groups of similar patients, medical care and their diseases and infer (see how they fit) *to* solve individual patients' problems. Figure 4.7 (in Chapter 4) illustrates these two strategies and ways of reasoning. Both are necessary for good understanding and decision-making.

8.2.3 *Criteria of Causality*

The still-evolving concepts and rules of causality in health sciences and its criteria are largely based on those of the British philosopher John Stuart Mill, expanded and adapted for health sciences much later by Sir Austin Bradford Hill.[36,37] Later, these concepts were applied to smoking and health by the U.S. Surgeon General's Advisory Committee on Smoking and Health.[38] The chronological journey of the concept and rules for causality was reviewed by Evans.[39] Over the past two generations, epidemiologists and biostatisticians have made several key contributions to the evolving understanding and structuring of causality,[40–42] as documented by Feinstein.[43]

There are multiple causation criteria of causation that need to be discussed and confirmed from one case to another in any discussion of causality. Most of these criteria are subjects of reflection; others are subjects of calculation, quantification, and interpretation. These criteria and considerations for their use are outlined in Table 8.3 in the following Section 8.2.4. Case by case, and in a selective manner, all such considerations and criteria may be used in various building blocks of an argument.

8.2.4 *Criteria for Accepting Etiology or Other Cause-Effect Relationships*

How causality is demonstrated is essential for our understanding of the etiology of health phenomena and for our decisions about what to do if such a relationship is found. These demonstrations are based both on judgment and the computation of multiple potential causal factors as related to the consequences of such factors (webs, sequences, and sets of interacting factors) which are responsible for similarly interrelated resulting phenomena of disease(s) occurrence or course. In the health sciences, we often consider more than one cause behind a health problem. Figure 8.5 (in Section 8.2.1) illustrates that there may be a considerable number of *types* of causes behind a single health problem like myocardial infarction. For example, in considering the issue of myocardial infarction and elsewhere, the causes could be classified as illustrated in Figure 8.7 and outlined here:

- a *set* **of causes**, an ensemble of space-time independent factors (some cases in cancer etiology as another example);
- a *sequence* **of causes** like causes of medical error (fatigue → missing orders → wrong care chosen → its poor sensor-motor execution); or
- a *web* **of causes** (space-time dependent etiological interactions) like nutrition, smoking, physical activity, social pressures, heredity, and other causal factors.

We owe our understanding of such challenges to many outstanding past and present biostatisticians and epidemiologists throughout the recent history of modern medicine and other health

Table 8.3 Criteria of Causation and Their Use: An Example

Criteria of Causality	Surgeon General's Report on Smoking and Health (Especially Lung Cancer)[38]
Temporality	Yes
Strength	Yes
Specificity:	
Manifestational	Poorly known
Casual	Yes
Biological gradient	Yes
Consistency	Yes
Biological plausibility	Yes
Coherence with relevant knowledge	To be followed
Analogy	Hard to assess
Experimental proof	Yes

sciences. Figure 8.8. summarizes assumptive and proper criteria of cause-effect relationship both for a single study (A) and for the problem across studies as a whole (B). Definitions of terms which may escape some readers may be found in References 5, 6, and 8.

This figure illustrates five major points:

1. A conclusion that confirms or rejects causality is a question of both computations and judgment. Observational cohort, case control studies, and experimental studies like clinical or field trials in hospital or community settings use these types of essential information. Some of these include:
   a. *P*-values to assess the randomness of the criteria;
   b. relative risks or odds ratios help us understand the strength of causal relationships and attributable risks; and
   c. etiological fractions to quantify the specificity of a cause-effect relationship.
2. Multivariate analyses or path analyses expand our understanding of "webs of causes" and "webs of consequences" as space-time interrelationships and connections of all kinds within the domain of causality.
3. Most other considerations are results of judgment.
4. Various considerations based on judgment and other criteria are used in argumentations and critical thinking assessments leading to conclusions about what is the cause or consequence and what is not.
5. Conclusions and recommendations are made on the basis of valid and meaningful modern argumentation and critical thinking.[15]

Some authors have created a checklist of criteria that, when identified, establish a causal relationship. Examples of these include the Surgeon General's public health conclusions about

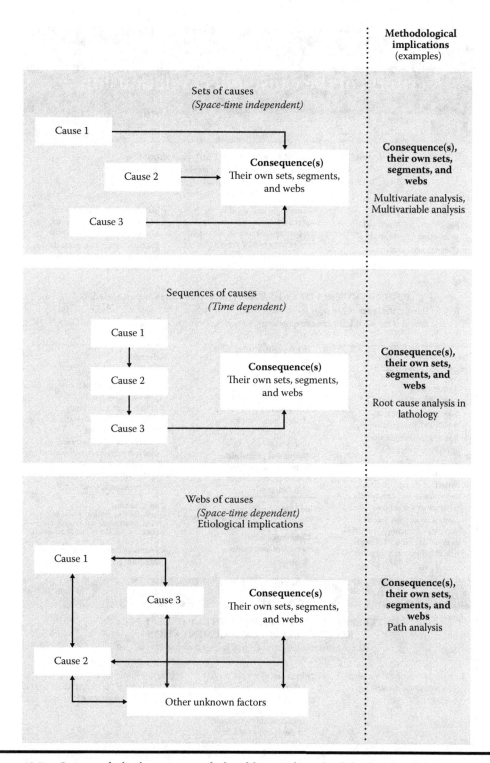

Figure 8.7 Causes, their time-space relationships, and methodological implications in etio-logical research and presentation of its results. (Redrawn from Jenicek M. *A Primer on Clinical Experience in Medicine.* Boca Raton: CRC Press, 2013.)

Fundamental prerequisites and assessment criteria of the cause-effect relationship

A Individual (for a specific case and study) cause-effect criteria under scrutiny:

ASSUMPTIONS OR PREREQUISITES (what should be confirmed before any causal criteria apply)
Possible roles in argumentation: grounds, rebuttals.

- Excludes **randomness**
- Results are consistent with **prediction** (conditional)
- Observational studies use, to the extent possible, the

- **same logic and similar precautions** as those used in experimental research, although the objectives may differ
- Based on **clinimetrically valid data**

- Data are subject to **unbiased observations, comparisons and unexaggerated analysis**
- **Factors** that are **uncontrollable and uninterpretable** are ideally absent

PROPER CRITERIA OF CAUSATION (for a study already performed)
These criteria apply not only for studies based on new health phenomena (studies of risk) but also for what happens once these phenomena occur (prognostic or hazard studies)

Major
(to be evaluated individually)

- **Temporality** ("cart behind the horse")
- **Strength** (relative risk, odds ratio, hazard ratio)
- **Specificity** (exclusivity or predominance of an observation and its effect)
- **Manifestational** ("unique" pattern of clinical spectrum and gradient as a presumed consequence of exposure)
- **Causal** (etiological fraction, preventable fraction, protective or curative effect, attributable risk, risk difference, attributable

risk percent, attributable hazard, proportional hazard)

- **Biological gradient** (more exposure → stronger association)
- **Consistency** (assessment of homogeneity of findings across studies, settings, time, place, and people)
- **Biological plausibility** (explanation of underlying mechanisms or nature of association)

Conditional
(not always necessary for new discoveries)

- **Coherence with prevalent knowledge**
- **Analogy**

Reference
(within the framework of the scientific method)

- **Experimental proof** (preventability, curability): Clinical trials, other kinds of controlled experiments, or "cessation studies"
- A **cessation** or **withdrawal study**, controlled or not, with all its limitations, sometimes may be the only available equivalent to experimental proof

Confirmation
(providing a clear problem definition, research question, relevant dependent and independent variables and target population)

- **Systematic review** and **meta-analysis** of evidence

B Criteria for the causal reasoning process and demonstration of causality as a whole:

INTERPRETATION OF THE BROUGHT UP CAUSAL PROOF RELYING ON PROPER ARGUMENTATION
(Argumentation is outlined in Chapter 5 of this book)

1. A single criterion is not used as a sole proof of causality

2. Each and every causality criterion was evaluated and interpreted by a fallacy-free argumentation leading to confirmation or refutation of cause and its effect

3. Completeness and validity of the identified criteria was assessed

Figure 8.8 Fundamental prerequisites and assessment criteria of the cause-effect relationship. (Modified and expanded from References 5, 6, and 8.)

smoking and health,[38] Guyatt et al.'s clinical epidemiology evidence about corticosteroids and osteoporosis,[41] and Broadhead et al.'s assessment of social support and mental health in allied health sciences.[42] A medical article must offer as many "pro and con" elements for a judgment on causality as possible. These elements may either be based on what is directly known through conclusions made in the article, or indirectly building on readers' and other authors' own expanded systematic reviews of evidence, meta-analyses for interpretations, and recommendations that are beyond the original message. The fundamental strength of how well a causal relationship is demonstrated is based on an expanded model of Feinstein's proposal[43] in a broader context,[5,6] as illustrated in Figure 8.9.

This figure follows a similar path of thought as Figure 5.3, only extrapolations and extensions of results may be different within a study and beyond a study. The figure also shows that analytical observational studies of etiology or experimental inquiries like clinical trials:

- use a well-formulated and defined question about causality for a desired target population and application of study conclusions;
- provide an essential comparison of two or more groups study individuals *before* action is taken ('initial state'), and after action is taken by a toxic agent, drug, etc.;
- compare exposure to various factors ('maneuvers') and assess results and outcomes of exposures ('subsequent' states comparisons); and
- use comparisons made in a structured discussion the argumentative way and their results to determine if they apply to the identified target population, or other communities beyond the originally intended target population.

These four observational elements must be based on good definitions, measurement, and both quantitative and qualitative analysis made by the authors of a medical article and presented to the reader. The analysis may be presented directly or referred more indirectly. Either way, the reader should be able to evaluate and understand the article using the reasoning and research outlined above and in our Chapter 4 on argumentation and critical thinking in medical articles.

An example of how criteria can be evaluated for causality was outlined by the Surgeon General's evaluation of smoking and health.[38] In this ground-breaking 1973 report, the Surgeon General evaluated causation criteria by listing their applicability to the issue individually. This list is presented in Table 8.3.

Subsequent to the Surgeon General's report, similar evaluations were undertaken in an increasing number of domains, including social support and various aspects of health,[40] and medicine as well.[39] From all these causal criteria and considerations, especially strength, specificity of a cause-effect relationship and biological gradient are subject to quantification. For this purpose, disease frequency is used in absolute and relative terms.

8.3 Fallacies in Medical Reasoning and Scientific Thinking in General

Perhaps the most important source of fallacies in medical and scientific thinking in general is to derive conclusions and make proposals about causal relationships based on only one fulfilled criterion of a cause-effect link. For example, if some relative risks or odds ratio are found to be unusually high, we can conclude that the causal link may be strong but we know nothing else.

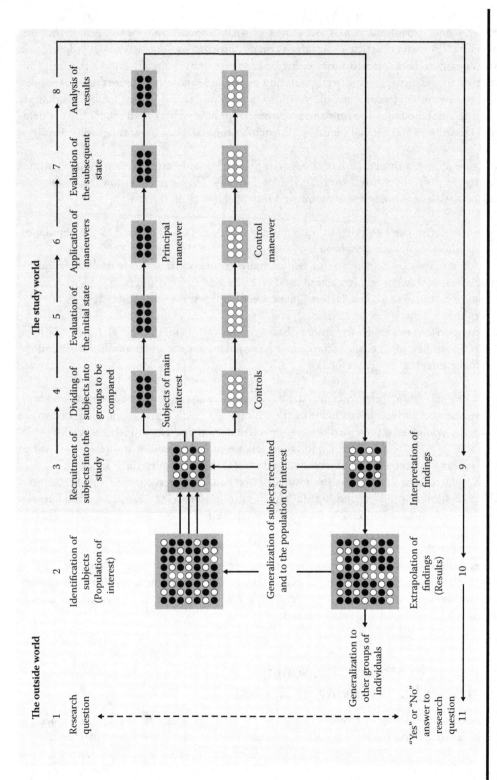

Figure 8.9 Structure and organization of analytical studies in health sciences as a guide to their conception and presentation. (Redrawn from References 5, 6, and Jenicek M. *Writing, Reading, and Understanding in Modern Health Sciences*. Boca Raton: CRC Press, 2014.)

A different situation may occur in a field trial of a new vaccine's effectiveness. In this situation, if the field trial indicates a high protective efficacy ratio (proportion of the whole of cases prevented by intervention), let us say 80%, this is a good indicator of causality provided that other causal criteria are fulfilled. A controlled clinical trial is closer to this ideal than other observational analytical or other type of research.

Covering the entire main body of fallacies in medicine might be overwhelming for uninitiated readers and it goes well beyond the scope of this introductory reading. We have devoted a book to the topic entitled *Fallacy Free Reasoning in Medicine*[44] that may be welcomed by some readers as an extension of this chapter and section. Some fallacies of common importance in the risk and cause assessment domains as covered in this chapter. Other are quoted in next chapters only for illustrative purposes; as already mentioned above, they are overviewed in a more structured way elsewhere.[44]

8.4 Role of Causal Reasoning in Medical Thinking

Causal reasoning is not the only reasoning in medicine, however important and primordial it is. We also reason about other problems to solve, such as ethical considerations in medical care, assessing patient attitudes and values, and others. In the framework of a broader concept of argumentation and critical thinking, causal reasoning proves useful at most of the steps and in assessing the building blocks of the argument, grounds, backing, and perhaps is most prominent in the warrant. If we wish to reach a conclusion about the cause of some consequence, there is no other way than to do so by a cause-effect review as outlined in this chapter.

8.5 Considerations of Causality in "Cognition-Based" Medicine; Non-Epidemiological Reasoning Focused on Specific Cases; Single-Event Observations

Alternative approaches to causality are also one of the foundations of **cognition-based medicine**[45] and **anthroposophic(al) medicine**[46–49] as defined by their authors in the literature. In these domains, reasoning and decision-making is based on individual clinical cases. Their primary element is the criteria-based assessment of therapeutic causality at the level of the individual patient. In this approach, the main points of interest are a singular (individual) therapeutic cognition, the valid causality in single cases of interest, the cause-effect relationship, treatment, and its outcomes. This initiative was developed to attempt to answer the EBM question "What applies to this particular patient?" and contribute to the evaluation of treatment effectiveness where clinical trials and other experimental and observational analytical cause-effect proofs are still infrequent or impossible.

8.6 Single-Subject Research Design

A single-subject research design is devised to draw cause-effect phenomena from observations in a single individual, whatever its limitations might be. In observational research, at least one situation before, and one after some intervention, is compared. In experimental research of repetitive episodic clinical events, interventions instead of individuals may be randomized yielding an "N-of-1" clinical trial as proposed by Guyatt et al.[50,51]

We agree with Law et al.'s[52] prerequisites for such inquiries: Target outcomes must be observable and quantifiable for accurate measurements, well-defined in operational terms allowing for their presence or absence, exerting their supposed effect in a relatively short time, and the effect itself being temporary and reversible once the treatment is discontinued. A withdrawal design and multiple baseline design is also valuable in the study of single subjects. Strengths and weaknesses rely essentially on the single patient nature of inquiry.

All these "non-epidemiological" approaches to causality may be good generators of hypotheses, but they also have numerous limitations. They focus mainly on the immediate effect of

Causal relationships may be considered whenever the Gestalt (i.e., feature, pattern, structure, or shape) reflects some possible cause given individual patients' responses. A "shape" or "form" of correspondence (shape-experimental method) is proposed as an alternative to the statistical-experimental method of possible causal associations. Most often, however, the cause-effect relationship must be known to some degree beforehand to be considered a "figural" proof. Across the literature, terms like "fit," "pattern," or "correspondence" are used alternatively to express situations where patterns related to time, place, treatment modalities, disease gradient and spectrum and other factors are observed and linked together in both directions of causation or association. Let us add then following proposals for hypothesizing across the cognition-based and anthroposophical medicines mostly on the basis of single or few cases:

1. **Observing the obvious**. Where figural or pictorial "correspondence" or "fit" and figural or pictorial experiment means finding certainty by looking at an 'obvious' link, such as surgical repair as the solution for stopping an artery from bleeding.

2. **Complex uniform pattern of response**. This criterion demonstrates that causal proof is another way which differs from epidemiological and biostatistical considerations in etiological research. A unique and complex pattern of response is proposed as a demonstration of possible causality. This consideration requires, however, some pre-existing knowledge of possible webs of causes and webs of consequences as established by clinical epidemiological and biostatistical research.

3. **"Time-manifestations" pattern for relationship or association**. The relationship **or** association between the time pattern of the treatment and the time pattern of symptom relief (or other outcome). The "N-of-1" clinical trials[50,51] fall into this category of causal proofs. A repeated effect (outcomes) after repeated treatments is also of interest here.

4. **"Space-manifestations" pattern for relationship or association**. Different patterns (sites, applications, etc.) of the same treatment as exposure lead to different patterns of response specific to the manner in which treatment is applied.

5. **"Morphologic-pictorial" relationship or association**. Different sites of treatment applications (spinal anesthesia, other anesthetic nerve blocks, and acupuncture sites) lead to specific responses related to a particular site.

6. **"Intensity-manifestations" relationship or association**. This is an alternative dose-effect consideration as an already used criterion in mainstream causal research. This criterion is applied again to individual patients.

7. **"Drug-outcomes" relationship or association**. This criterion reflects a possible causal link between treatment intervention and as of yet unobserved and undocumented improvement of additional unknown and causally yet unrelated outcomes.

8. **"Therapeutic idea-disparate manifestations" relationship or association**. An idea (complex intention) about what should happen is confirmed exactly by the outcome of the intended complex. For example, heterogeneous and initially presumably unrelated health problems are considered as having some potential common basis. A circular thinking fallacy cannot be excluded in this type of correspondence.

9. **"Interventions" and "manifestations" bidirectional (ping-pong) relationship**. This is a type of reflective-experimental correspondence: One act leads to another act that mirrors the primary act and its outcomes. As an example, consider that there is the treatment of autistic children through music. Exposing these children to increasingly melodious music first leads to verbal communication and then to increasingly melodious speech.

clinical maneuvers and they often presume that some knowledge about the causality under study is already available. Fallacies related to before-after evaluations such as *post hoc ergo propter hoc* consideration, circular thinking, and others may be an additional inherent risk to this way of reasoning in the clinical case reporting domain.

8.7 Other Ways of Considering Causality

For Agbabiaka et al.,[53] **other approaches to causality** fall into three broad categories of:

▪ **expert judgments**, both epidemiological and non-epidemiological;
▪ **algorithmic questions-answers** that use yielding some kind of likelihood of cause-effect relationship; and
▪ **Bayesian ways** using specific findings to estimate probabilities of drug causation from prior and posterior probabilities.

8.8 Critical Thinking, Communication, and Decision-Making and Their Connection to Medical Ethics

Is there a connection between medical ethics and reasoning, communication, and decision-making in health sciences? We would argue that there is. They are not only vehicles governed by the rules of ethics, but also part of medical ethics themselves. Correct rules and ways of reasoning, communication, and decision-making lie behind good ethics in the health domain. In the opposite direction, good ethics are needed as a framework for reasoning, communication, and decision-making in all health professions.

> We may **define medical ethics** as *"rules of conduct for a health professional to distinguish between right and wrong. They serve as a moral basis in medical, nursing and other care, research and administration."* Medical ethics falls into the broader framework of bioethics and ethics in its largest sense.[54]

Medical ethics may be virtue-based, principle-based, or duty-based. Six values apply to medical ethics, including:

■ *autonomy* (the patient has the last word);
■ *beneficence* (acting in the best interest of the patient);
■ *non-maleficence* (*primum non nocere*);
■ *justice* (fairness and equality in the distribution of resources and care);
■ *dignity*; and
■ *truthfulness and honesty* (informed consent).

Many professional institutions like have their own codes of ethics. These include the American Medical Association (*AMA Code of Ethics*), British Medical Association (*BMA Code of Ethics*), Canadian Medical Association (*CMA Code of Ethics*), and others. Medical ethics are also covered in general bioethics and in all major religions such as Christianity, Judaism, Islam, Buddhism, and Hinduism.

Mutual understanding, participatory decision-making, and meaningful multilateral and multidirectional communication all depend on structured and problem solving, directed argumentation, and shared critical thinking and its content. We may then consider argumentation, critical thinking, decision-making, and communication not only as having to be ethical themselves, but also as an integral part of medical ethics itself.

There are numerous modern medical ethics challenges. These include encounters and between patients and their clinicians—physicians, nurses, and other allied professionals, as well as decisions made by those clinicians. Ethics challenges also concern the adoption and uses of new medical technologies, surgical interventions, medical genetics, gene therapy, assisted suicide, euthanasia, stem cell research and its applications, procreative techniques, organ and tissue transplantations, or uses and abuses of psychiatry beyond its own domain. Argumentation, communication, and the uses of their results largely define our success.

Let Us Conclude

All in all, our thinking processes in medicine, be it in clinical practice or research, have two purposes: understanding the nature of the health problem and/or deciding what to do to solve it. Philosophers' principles, methods, and ways of critical thinking in general are extremely well adapted to what we are doing in health sciences. Epidemiologists, biostatisticians, health economists, and clinical specialists have developed many original contributions which are crucial for all pragmatic purposes. Our reasoning is geared to concrete decision-making and actions whose course and results we are responsible for as health professionals.

Beyond health sciences, we are enriching our experience and practice through the experience and practice of others. Military arts or business experience as mentioned in our 'Word from the Author' and 'Introduction' are just two of many helpful areas. We must be open to them and adapt

Logicians may be interested primarily in the purity of argumentation and thinking processes themselves. In medicine, even the best argumentative process must be based on the best evidence for the stated purpose first. That is where evidence-based medicine joins critical thinking about the uses of the best evidence and evolves into a kind of **evidence-based critical thinking (argumentation) grounded medicine**.

them in a well-structured way to manage health problems. In fact, medicine is also a health business battlefield where our care and its outcomes must take into account the money that passes between the health producer, supplier and provider (health professionals, hospitals, medical offices or community medicine and public health units, etc.) and the consumer, patients, and our community. For lawyers, judges, and expert witnesses in courts of law, pleading for a health cause is (and should be) an exercise in argumentation and critical thinking as it has been outlined it here for health sciences.

In this diversity of experience, we cannot insist enough on clear, usable, and operational definitions of what we see and do. Again, orismology helps. For example:

- an **evidence-based medicine practitioner** may define evidence as "*any data or information, whether solid or weak, obtained through experience, observational research or experimental work (clinical or field trials), relevant to some degree (more is better) either to the **understanding** of the problem (case) or to the clinical and community medicine **decisions** made about the case (meaning clinical case or the community health problem to solve).*"[4,6]
- a **philosopher/critical thinker**, evidence is "*the data on which a judgment or conclusion might be based or by which proof or probability might be established … something to prove.*" [55]; and
- **lawyers**, as might be expected, evidence is "*information and things pertaining to the events that are the subject of an investigation or a case: especially, the testimony or objects (but not the questions or comments of the lawyers) offered at a trial or hearing for the judge or the jury to consider in deciding the issue in a case.*"[56]

Grading evidence in evidence-based medicine[57] is based most often on the validity of different types of studies as cause-effect proofs, from the least convincing to the most convincing. While this area remains an unfinished topic, and the subject of further development, refinement and expansion, the following grading the validity of evidence of causality by types of its study, from the weakest to the strongest outlines the different levels of evidence, graded from least valid to most:

Narratives, single case observations, case series (no denominators, no control groups)
↓
Observational analytical studies (cohort studies, case control studies)
↓
Experimental studies (clinical trials, etc.)
↓
Systematic reviews, meta-analyses and otherwise synthesized experimental and clinical experience and research of observational analytical or experimental experience from multiple studies.

In various versions, the following "*pyramid of evidence*," from the strongest to the weakest can be found across the current literature:

> Synopses
> Meta-analyses and systematic
> reviews
> Experimental studies (clinical trials)
> Observational analytical cohort studies
> Observational analytical case control studies
> Observational descriptive studies of occurrence
> Single clinical case reports and case series reports
> Hearsays, anecdotes, narratives, plain ideas, opinions

Such hierarchy of evidence may be valid for cause-effect relationships and their ways of proof, but other domains requiring evidence may call for another kind of "pyramid" or 'hierarchy' of proof. For example, what might a hierarchy of evidence be for physical examination or diagnosis whenever the presence and absence of disease causing a positive or negative test result is not of primary interest?

Grading evidence for types of research other than causal relationships between noxious or beneficial factors in relation to health or disease like in the domain of validation of diagnostic tests, requires a different approach. Besides etiological considerations, any grading must have some sense and practical purpose for decision-making. Ideally, any stage or grade in a grading system must differ from the other by expanding the understanding, changing the understanding (different meanings like different prognosis or differential diagnosis), or modifying clinical decisions (treatment indications). Staging cancer in these terms is well done; staging evidence is still more challenging in these practical terms.

From one situation to another, we must always find some mutually acceptable language or specify differences between the participating professions and domains. The same holds true for example for a "case" and, in clinical medicine, for any noxious or beneficial factor and their outcomes, disease signs or symptoms, or the disease itself, its diagnosis or remedial clinical actions (treatments), and their outcomes.

> Besides the evidence used in argumentation, the value and relevance of the entire argumentative process depends on its **conceptual framework** or "framing." Within such a framework, we are always defining the problem and its biological and physical setting, raising hypotheses about what's going on, specifying objectives regarding what we intend to do or how we intend to intervene, and at what we wish to arrive in general and specific terms and dimensions. *Our reasoning, understanding, decisions, and actions only have meaning and value if such a framework is determined and known, preferably beforehand.*

Last but not least, our reasoning and decision-making must remain fallacy-free which is also a learned experience. Let's now see, in the chapter that follows, how our ways of reasoning and decision-making apply to various steps and stages of clinical practice and care such as assessing risk in patients (communities), making diagnosis, choosing and administering treatment, assessing patient outcomes (prognosis), and establishing follow-up and long-term care for individuals under our responsibility.

References

1. Jenicek M and Hitchcock DL. *Evidence-Based Practice. Logic and Critical Thinking in Medicine.* Chicago: American Medical Association (AMA Press), 2005.
2. Jenicek M. *Foundations of Evidence-Based Medicine.* Boca Raton, FL/London/New York/Washington, DC: The Parthenon Publishing Group, a CRC Press Company, 2003.
3. *A Dictionary of Public Health.* Edited by JM Last. Oxford and New York: Oxford University Press, 2007.
4. *A Dictionary of Epidemiology.* 5th Edition. Edited by M Porta, S Greenland, and JM Last, Associate Editors. A Handbook Sponsored by the I.E.A. Oxford and New York: Oxford University Press, 2008.
5. Jenicek M. *Epidemiology. The Logic of Modern Medicine.* Montréal: EPIMED International. 1995.
6. Jenicek M. *Foundations of Evidence-Based Medicine.* Boca Raton, FL/London/New York/Washington, DC: The Parthenon Publishing Group/CRC Press, 2003.
7. Jenicek M. *Medical Error and Harm. Understanding, Prevention, and Control.* Boca Raton, FL/London/New York: CRC Press/Taylor & Francis/Productivity Press, 2011.
8. Jenicek M. *A Primer on Clinical Experience in Medicine. Reasoning, Decision-Making, and Communication in Health Sciences.* Boca Raton, FL/London/New York: CRC Press/Taylor & Francis, 2011.
9. *Statistics with Confidence. Confidence Intervals and Statistical Guidelines.* Edited by MJ Gardner and DG Altman. London: British Medical Journal, 1989.
10. Li CC. *Path Analysis—A primer.* Pacific Grove, CA: The Boxwood Press, 1975.
11. Introduction to Multivariate Analysis. Chapter 12, pp. 225–245 in: Friedman GD. *Primer of Epidemiology.* 5th Edition. New York and London: McGraw-Hill, Medical Publishing Division, 2004.
12. Friedman GD. *Primer of Epidemiology.* 5th Edition. New York and London: McGraw-Hill, Medical Publishing Division, 2004.
13. West DC, Pomeroy JR, Park JK, Gerstenberger EA, Sandoval J. Critical thinking in graduate medical education. A role model concept mapping assessment? *JAMA,* 2000;284(9):1105–10.
14. Pinto AJ, Zeitz HJ. Concept mapping: A strategy for promoting meaningful learning in medical education. Pelley JW. *Concept Mapping—a Tool for Teaching Integrative Thinking.* A 30 p. PowerPoint presentation at http://www.iamse.org/development/2005/webcast_050305.pdf, retrieved Feb 3, 2011.
15. Pelley JW. *Effective Learning through Concept Mapping.* 4 p. at http://www.ttuhsc.edu/.../Concept%20Mapping%20in%20Med%20School.pdf - Similar, retrieved Feb 3, 2011.
16. Anderson LA, Gwaltney MK, Sundra DL, Brownson RC, Kane M, Cross AW, Mack Jr. R, Schwartz R, Sims T, White R. Using concept mapping to develop a logic model for the prevention research centers program. *Prev Chron Dis Pub Health Res Pract Pol,* 2006;3(1):1–8. At http://www.cdc.gov/pcd/issues/2006/jan/05_0153.htm.
17. Cinnamon J, Rinner C, Cusimano MD, Marshall S, Bekele T, Hernandez T, Glazier RH, Chipman ML. Evaluating web-based static, animated and integrative maps for injury prevention. *Geospatial Health,* 2009;4(1):3–16.
18. Baldwin CM, Kroesen K, Trochim WM, Bell IR. Complementary and conventional medicine: A concept map. *BMC Compl Alt Med,* 2004;4(Feb 3):online. doi: 10.1186/1472-6882-4-2, PMCID: PMC356920.
19. Concepts Systems Inc. *Concept Mapping Methodology. Bibliography and Recent Publications.* 4 p. at http://www.conceptssystems.com/.../bibliography_examples_of_cm_projects_4.pdf, retrieved Feb 3, 2011.
20. BMC Complementary and Alternative Medicine. *Concept Mapping. Published Literature.* 7 p. at http://www.socialresearch methods.net/research/cm.htm, retrieved Feb 3, 2011.

21. Wikipedia, the free encyclopedia. *Inductive Reasoning.* 8 p. at https://en.wikipedia.org/wiki/Inductive_reasoning, retrieved May 9, 2016.

22. Wikipedia, the free encyclopedia. *Deductive Reasoning.* 5 p. at https://en.wikipedia.org/wiki/Deductive_reasoning., retrieved May 9, 2016.

23. Wikipedia, the free encyclopedia. *Deductive Thinking.* 1 p. at http://wiki.deductivethinking.com/wiki/Deductive_Thinking, retrieved May 9, 2016.

24. Crossman A. What's the difference between deductive and inductive reasoning? 3 p. at http://sociology.about.com/od/Research/a/Deductive-Reasoning-Versus-Inductive Reaso..., retrieved Aug 1, 2016.

25. Bradford A. *Deductive Reasoning vs. Inductive Reasoning.* 5 p. at http://www.livescience.com/21569-deduction-vs-induction.html, retrieved Aug 1, 2016.

26. *The Philosophy Book. Big Ideas Simply Explained.* Buckingham W, Burnham D, Hill C, Kingt PJ, Marenbon J, Weeks M, Osborne R, Chilman S, Contributors. New York: DK Publishing, 2011.

27. Bluedorn H. Two methods of reasoning. 5 p. at https://www.trivioumpursuit.com/articles/two_methods_of_reasoning.php, retrieved May 9, 2016.

28. Internet Encyclopedia of Philosophy, IEP Staff. Deductive and Inductive Arguments. 5 p. at http://iep.utm.edu/ded-ind/, retrieved May 9, 2016.

29. Douven I. Abduction. *Stanford Encyclopedia of Philosophy.* 17 p. at http://33plato.stanford.edu/entries/abduction/, retrieved Sep 9, 2016.

30. New World Encyclopedia. *Abductive Reasoning.* 6 p. at http://www.newworldencyclopedia.org/entry/Abductive_reasoning, retrieved Sep 9, 2016.

31. New World Encyclopedia. *Abductive Reasoning.* 6 p. at http://newworldencyclopedia.org/entry/Abductive_reasoning, retrieved May 9, 2016.

32. Psychology Wiki—Wikia. *Abductive Reasoning.* 3 p. at http://psychology.wikia.com/wiki/Abductive_reasoning, retrieved Aug 1, 2016.

33. Haig BD. Scientific method, abduction, and clinical reasoning. *J Clin Psychol,* 2008;64(9):1013–8.

34. Haig BD. Précis of 'An abductive theory of scientific method'. *J Clin Psychol,* 2008;64(9):1020–2.

35. Thagard P and Shelley C. Abductive reasoning: Logic, visual thinking, and coherence. 14 p. at http://cogsci.uwaterloo.ca/Articles/Pages/%7FAbductive.html, retrieved May 9, 2016.

36. Hill AB. The environment and disease: Association or causation? *Proceedings of the Royal Society of Medicine,* 1965;58(5):295–300.

37. Hill AB. Observation and experiment. *N Engl J Med,* 1965;248:905–1001.

38. Surgeon General's Advisory Committee on Smoking and Health. *Smoking and Health.* Washington, DC: Public Health Service Publ. No 1103, 1973.

39. Evans AS. Causation and disease. A chronological journey. *Am J Epidemiol,* 1978;108:249–57.

40. *Causal Inference.* Edited by KJ Rothman. Chestnut Hill, MA: Epidemiology Resources Inc., 1988.

41. Guyatt GH, Weber CE, Mewa AA, Sackett DL. Determining causation—A case study: Adrenocorticosteroids and osteoporosis. Should the fear of inducing clinically important osteoporosis influence the decision to prescribe adrenocorticosteroids? *J Chron Dis,* 1984;37:343–52.

42. Broadhead WE, Kaplan BH James SA et al. The epidemiologic evidence for a relationship between social support and health. *Am J Epidemiol,* 1983;117:521–37.

43. Feinstein AR. *Clinical Epidemiology. The Architecture of Clinical Research.* Philadelphia, PA: WB Saunders, 1985.

44. Jenicek M. *Fallacy-Free Reasoning in Medicine. Improving Communication and Decision-Making in Research and Practice.* Chicago: American Medical Association (AMA Press), 2009.

45. Kiene H. What is cognition-based medicine? *Z Ärtzl Fortbild Qual Gesundh Wes,* 2005;99:301–6.

46. Kiene H, von Schön-Angerer T. Single-case causality assessment as a basis for clinical judgment. *Alternative Therapies in Health and Medicine,* 1998;4(1):41–7.

47. Kiene H. *Komplementäre Methodenlehre der Klinische Forschung.* Berlin/Heidelberg/New York: Springer-Verlag, 2001.

48. Kiene H. Causality, anthroposophic medicine and statistics. *J Anthroposoph Med,* 1996;13(1):42–8.

49. Wikipedia, the free encyclopedia. *Anthroposophical Medicine.* At http://en.wikipedia.org/wiki/Anthroposophical_medicine, retrieved Mar 1, 2008.

50. Guyatt G, Sackett DL, Taylor DW, Chong J, Roberts R, Pugsley S. Determining optimal therapy—Randomized trials in individual patients. *N Engl J Med,* 1986;314:889–92.
51. Guyatt G. N of 1 randomized trials: A commentary. *J Clin Epidemiol,* 2016;76:4–5.
52. Law M, King G, Pollock N. *Single Subject Design.* Research Report No 94-2. McMaster University, Faculty of Health Sciences, Neurodevelopmental Clinical Research Unit, June 1994.
53. Akbabiaka TF, Savovic J, Ernst E. Methods for causality assessment of adverse drug reactions. *Drug Safety,* 2008;31:21–37.
54. Wikipedia, the free encyclopedia. *Bioethics.* 8 p. at http://en.wikipedia.org/wiki/Bioethics, retrieved Oct 25, 2011.
55. Elder L and Paul R. *A Glossary of Critical Thinking Terms and Concepts. The Critical Analytic Vocabulary of the English Language.* Dillon Beach, CA: The Foundation for Critical Thinking, 2009.
56. Clapp JE. *Random House Webster's Dictionary of the Law.* New York: Random House, 2000.
57. GRADE Series—Guest Editors, S Straus and S Shepperd. *GRADE Guidelines.* First article: *J Clin Epidemiol,* 2011;64:380–2. Last article of this series: *J Clin Epidemiol,* 2013;66:124–31. (Reference abridged.)

Chapter 9

Thinking about Medical Error and Harm: Flaws in an Operator's Reasoning and Decision-Making among Others*

Executive Summary

Two major trends appear in the modern approach to the problem of medical error. Either healthcare is seen as a system which produces medical error, or it is the final operator and decision-maker that make a faulty decision leading to harm for the patient. Both views are the intertwined; the individual or operator error cannot be left as a black box in the context of the system error. This chapter is about how medical error, especially in regard to thinking and decision-making, should be understood on the individual (operator) basis before it is integrated into the analysis and interpretation process. As an introspection or review with peers, it should precede any further scrutiny or assessment of any kind.

The process of medical care includes the entry of the patient into medical care, the physician's evaluation and diagnosis, the decision to treat, the act of medical care itself, and the evaluation of its effect. Errors may occur as a result of failure in sensory perception, communication, medical thinking, and flawed processes in reasoning and decision-making which include wrong or

---

* This chapter is based, with the permission of the publisher, on multiple elements (as referenced), mainly in Chapter 6 in our own title: Jenicek M. *Medical Error and Harm. Understanding, Prevention, and Control.* Boca Raton, FL/London/New York: CRC Press/Taylor & Francis/Productivity Press, 2011.

right actions executed, evaluated, and followed by foreseeable predictions in terms of prognosis and outcome follow-up.

Each of the steps in medical care, from gathering evidence, reasoning about the case and diagnosis, executing sensory-motor medical acts, to evaluating results, establishing prognosis, and surveillance and forecasting, all rely on the validity of the practitioner's clinical-epidemiological reasoning and the quality of their argumentation. Evaluation of errors and the quality of clinical and community care depends on both the evaluation of evidence, its uses, and the argumentation which supports decisions, and all the steps that comprise making those decisions, in the clinical and community care process. Paths in the structure of medical care, analysis, and their endpoints differ from paths in research, however complementary they might be.

This chapter provides an understanding of what errors might be generated through the reasoning, understanding, and decision-making process, what to do with them, and how to integrate them in the evaluation of the system.

In This Chapter

Executive Summary...251

Thoughts, Thinkers, and Things to Think About 253

Introductory Comments 256

9.1   Defining Medical Error and Medical Harm..257

9.2   System Error vs. Individual Human Error...257

9.3   A Reminder of Some Fundamental Considerations...................................259

9.4   Flawed Argumentation and Reasoning as Sites and Generators of Error:
       Argumentation and Human Error Analysis for Logic 260

       9.4.1   Mistakes and Errors in Medical Lathology 264

       9.4.2   Fallacies, Biases, and Cognitive Errors in Medical Lathology 265

9.5   Where and When Errors Can Happen: Cognitive Pathways as Sites of Error...........267

       9.5.1   Reviewing Diagnosis: Searching for Errors in the Clinimetric Process 269

       9.5.2   Reviewing the Path from Diagnosis to Treatment Decisions and Orders..........272

       9.5.3   Reviewing Decisions as Sources of Harm 274

       9.5.4   Reviewing Actions as Sources of Error......................................274

       9.5.5   Getting Results and Their Impact Evaluation 275

       9.5.6   Errors in Making Prognosis 276

       9.5.7   Follow-Up, Surveillance, Forecasting-Related Errors 278

Let Us Conclude 279

References 282

Thoughts, Thinkers, and Things to Think About

*Only those who do nothing at all make no
mistakes ... but that would be a mistake.*
Anonymous (undated)
**Aren't we all working hard not to
make them?**

*If you don't make mistakes, you're not
working on hard enough problems. And
that's a big mistake.*
Author unknown
We make them even on the small ones!

*Things could be worse. Suppose your errors
were counted and published every day, like
those of a baseball player.*
E.C. McKenzie (1980)
They often are!

*An error doesn't become a mistake unless
you refuse to correct it.*
E.C. McKenzie (1980)
**Providing that we are able to make a
distinction between a mistake and an
error. If you are not able to, why not
reading this chapter to begin with?**

*A man of genius makes no mistakes. His
errors are volitional and are the portals of
discovery.*
James Joyce
(1882–1941)
Irish Novelist
in *Ulysses* (1922)
**Only, there are not many geniuses
between us!**

Strong people make as many mistakes as weak people. Difference is that strong people admit their mistakes, laugh at them, learn from them. That's how they become strong.
Richard Needham
(1912–1996)
Canadian Cartoonist
Not at the patient's expense, please!

Don't argue for other people weaknesses. Don't argue for your own. When you make a mistake, admit it, correct it and learn from it immediately.
Stephen Richards Covey
(1932–2012)
American Educator
Argumentation is a way to improve them, Stephen!

Don't ever make the same mistake twice, unless it pays.
Mae West
(1892–1980)
Unfortunately, we often do, Mae, even if it does not pay!

Never say, "oops."
Always say, "Ah, interesting."
Author unknown
So, shouldn't we explain it?

Recently, I was asked if I was going to fire an employee who made a mistake that cost $600,000. No, I replied, I just spent $600,000 training him.
Thomas J. Watson, Jr.
(1914–1993)
Would you do the same thing with a surgeon, or emergency physician, or intensive care nurse who lost a patient due to error?

*After a long, arduous and expensive
education, doctors are expected to get it
right. But they are fallible human beings
like the rest of us. Mistakes are stigma-
tized rather than being seen as chances for
learning. … yet doctors are given very little
training in understanding, anticipating,
detecting and recovering errors.*
James Reason
British Psychologist
2009
Let's try!

*Wishing to learn from our errors, aren't we
often hesitant, whatever the reason might be,
to have assessed them by retrospection for our
good or poor reasoning and decision-making
and for their possible deficiencies to minimize
harm and maximize patient safety? Before
sharing our error analysis with others, what
prevents us to do it for ourselves in the privacy
of our own introspection at the first place?
Nothing. Let us just begin with analyzing and
understanding the path of our own actions.*

The focus of this chapter is medical error and harm, a particular challenge in thinking and reasoning. Medical error and harm are two distinct interfacing problems which require their own
proper understanding and management. It is vital to understand that medical error and harm are
not synonymous. Their webs of causes and webs of consequences may be different, and not every
medical error leads to harm, and vice versa.

Medical error is subject to a process of thinking which is common to all health professionals:
physicians, nurses, clinical psychologists, chiropractors, and all others, including alternative and
complementary medicines. In this chapter we will examine the term "medical error" within the
context of the health sciences and the professionals who practice them. Within this context, medical error can be attributed to multiple failures of the system or human failure at the end of some
causal chain. Medical error is not only a problem faulty logic and/or cognition in health professional's thinking, but also of medicine itself, ergonomics, system components, and functioning
failures and flaws.

Is it enough to prove that an error occurred? We believe that it isn't. A proof of who or what
was responsible of error or not is equally important to be corrected.

Introductory Comments

This chapter offers the reader guidelines for where to detect faults in a health professional's reasoning and decision-making, and where corrections should be made. Although the web of latent (remote) or active (proximate, immediately preceding) errors leading to incidents may be complex, there is always an operator at the end who introduces or fails to introduce necessary elements into his or her reasoning, understanding, and decision-making to avoid such failures. In our culture, which is reluctant to assign individual blame, much attention has been paid so far to system components such as technologies, communication, and environment, as well as psychological and physiological factors in care providers. Much less has been said about where the sites of error in chains of our reasoning and decision-making might be when applied to various components of patient care such as risk assessment, diagnosis, treatment, prognosis, and prevention.

A recent study of errors in surgery by Fabri and Zayas-Castro[1] analyzes surgical complications in 332 patients over a 12-month period of time. The results attribute 63.5% of complications to surgical technique, 29.6% to errors in judgment, 29.3% to inattention to detail, and 22.7% to incomplete understanding. More than half (58%) of errors were slips and 20% were mistakes. Human causes of error prevailed, organizational/system errors or breaks in communication were less frequent, and system errors (2%) and communication errors (2%) were noted. More of such studies are needed in other medical specialties.

In the *Quality in Australian Health Care Study*, iatrogenic (surgery and beyond) patient injuries considered as adverse events were found to be associated with 16.6% of hospital admissions. The major causes found were complications of, or failure in, the technical performance of an indicated procedure or operation (34.6%) and failure to synthesize, decide and/or action available information (15.8%). Some other causes of interest related to this chapter were acting on insufficient information (1.8%), slips and lapses, errors due to "absentmindedness" in activities in which the operator is skilled (1.6%), and lack of knowledge (1.1%). Multiple procedural failures were also noted.[2] In another Australian pilot study of medical errors, a 21% occurrence of knowledge and skills errors was noted.[3] Let us try to say more about human flaws in reasoning and decision-making behind medical error in this chapter.

Medical or nursing students are more accustomed to the scrutiny of their thinking process and accept this scrutiny as a part of the learning process and the evaluation of their knowledge, attitudes or skills. Accomplished health professionals are often hesitant to share any kind for such analysis with a third person for psychological, legal, monetary, or otherwise punitive reasons. They are sometimes also hesitant as a result of encouragement from hospital administrators, insurers, and attorneys to avoid words that might trigger litigation like "error, harm, negligence, fault or mistake."[4] The meaning of these terms may vary in the understanding of administrators, insurers, attorneys, patients, and other laics. In all cases, any reader who wishes to correct and improve his or her actions should do such evaluations for himself or herself first, and examine how his or her reasoning, decision-making, and behavior fit as part of the "operator (clinician)-health technology-patient system". Clinicians should then be encouraged to share the knowledge they gained with others.

Errors of action are of double nature. They are a result of an effort in sensory-motor skill—for example, a clinician may set a bone improperly, or fail to see a lesion on an x-ray. Or, the error may be in how the clinician reasoned, or thought, through a series of information inputs, to identify a diagnosis. It is this type of error that is of interest to us in this chapter. Thanks to critical thinkers in philosophy, psychologists, epidemiologists and others, the accumulation of valuable, usable and operational methodology acquired in this domain throughout last generations allows us to treat this question more than a black box.

Semantics in the error and harm domain are detailed elsewhere, such as in our *Medical Error and Harm* book.[5]

9.1 Defining Medical Error and Medical Harm

As we have already mentioned, medical error and medical harm are sometimes homozygous, sometimes heterozygous, and sometimes "heredity (hereditary)-unrelated" twins. Less symbolically speaking, the links between them produces and invokes the attention and involvement of multiple specialties while dealing with their challenges.

Besides medicine itself, the study and the management of the medical error requires a significant involvement with disciplines like philosophy (logic, critical thinking), psychology, operational research, and computer sciences. The management of medical harm will rely on the essential mastery of clinical specialties in which harm occurs—clinical epidemiology, biostatistics, and evidence-based medicine. In lathology, both are brought together in different proportions and balance, from and between the domains of error and harm.

> In the context of medical thinking, **human error in medicine** is a flaw in reasoning, understanding, and decision-making made by an operator (typically, a clinician or researcher) regarding the solution of a health problem or in the ensuing sensory and physical execution of a task in clinical or community care. It leads to an inaccurate or incomplete assessment of a patient's (or community's) risks and diagnosis, conservative or radical treatment, prognosis, follow-up, and care. It may or may not lead to medical harm.
>
> **Medical harm**, on the other hand, refers to a temporary or permanent physical, mental, or social impairment in body functions, such as pain, disease, injury, disability, death, suffering, and other deleterious effects due to a disruption of the patient's physical, mental, and/or social well-being. It may be intended or unintended, preventable or not.

9.2 System Error vs. Individual Human Error

The ongoing debate about whether medical error is a system error or a human error at its effective or "sharp end" is still open. In the discussion about how should we deal with medical error, either as a system/multi-party/multi-factorial or an individual/active/human/operator one, we must not ignore simply the latter. The ultimate decisions in clinical and community care always belong to the physician and any other health professional responsible for practice, care, and research.

> Moreover, no one has yet precisely defined the borders between latent and active errors. Is **active error** only one committed by an operator at the *end* of the medical care process, or is it anything which happened *since* the admission of the patient or another precise moment and time in patient and community care? For the moment, let us define it from one type of error to another.
>
> **Latent error** is a term used for errors that result from *underlying* health system and structure, organization, preceding recent or remote events, and failures. Latent error or failure may then be human, technical, external, and/or design-construction-material related.

Operators, those at the "sharp end" of the error, may be of one, or several, types. Errors committed by operators are outlined here, beginning at the outset of a patient-clinician interaction, and moving to the outcomes of such an interaction. Error may occur due to the failure of any of the stages of the medical care process outlined below. To be remedied, all stages should be scrutinized and corrected.

Errors and their consequences are then **failures**.

In our context, a **failure** is defined as "non-performance or inability of the system or its component (humans included) to perform an intended function in a specific person/time/place context and specific conditions to reach an intended objective." Therefore, not all faults are failures.[5 modified] An intended objective in this context may be the best possible understanding of a health problem, its management, improvement in individual or community health and maintenance of any of the above.

To what kind of failures in physician's work should we pay attention?

■ **Sensory-perception-communication failures** are failures of observation of the problem (literature, past experience, observation of the patient or the community, etc.). Misreading labels in clinical pharmacology or patient charts before surgery, omission of medical orders, fatigue or stress are just some examples. This is a *noticing* challenge.

⬇

■ **Medical thinking-reasoning-decision-making** is a **flawed process**. Physician's activities "are just not logical." Reasoning and critical thinking supporting conclusions about a patient's diagnosis, treatment plan, or prognosis are frequently based on poor evidence, poorly linked and irrelevant for the conclusion. This is an *interpretation* challenge.

⬇

■ A **decision challenge** is one that is not based on a structured and explicit decision-making process, be it a decision analysis, heuristics, algorithms, consensus, hindsight thinking, or something else.

⬇

■ The **action undertaken** to treat the patient **is wrong or the action is not properly executed**: The operator's sensory and motor skills fail in the execution of preceding decision and orders for action. These may include actions like administering a prescribed medication from orders, failing a surgical intervention, or making an unrealistic prognosis (not yet litigated at courts of law). As an execution break-up whatever sensor motor "*fausse route*" is behind the error and its consequences of interest. This is a challenge of 'how and what to do' based on what was decided.

⬇

■ The **intervention is inadequately evaluated** for its structure, process (execution), and impact. This is a challenge of "knowing what was achieved by all this."

⬇

■ The **prognosis is made without often necessary distinctions** from patient history, between risk factors and prognostic factors, and co-morbidity.

The purpose of this chapter is to highlight considerations in the medical thinking/reasoning/decision-making processes, their points of potential, and the real error to which we must address.

This is the only possible approach if we wish to fully understand causes of medical error and to do something about it.

Across the current literature the individual reasoning and decision-making process are typically treated as some kind of black box, although it should not be. There is always an individual—or individuals—behind interpretations and actions that are to be decided and executed. The increasingly robust evidence about the critical thinking and decision-making experience and its increasingly structured methodology, as well as the progressing clinical experience and applications in this domain, reflect this. It is never enough to blame error solely on the system. However psychologically, professionally, or socially it might be resented, system and individual/human/active errors must be examined, understood, corrected, and prevented in the future.

9.3 A Reminder of Some Fundamental Considerations

Let us begin with a practical example: an internist has a patient suffering from coronary heart disease. He or she faces the dilemma to pursue the conservative (medical) treatment of coronary pathology and dysfunction, or to refer the patient to invasive cardiologists for angioplasty, or to surgeons for a coronary bypass surgery. Where might errors occur in this reasoning process, and where should they be prevented?

A catheter for angioplasty malfunctions, the patient does not need angioplasty after all, and patient prognosis worsens: Where is the reason, where is the culprit? Whatever path the internist recommends to their patient, there are potential errors. If they recommend angioplasty, a catheter used in the procedure may malfunction. Or, once referred and the angioplasty is performed, the patient may not have needed the procedure at all. Identifying where the error lies in this process requires a considered examination of the thinking process by all.

There are two visions of the cognitive and decision-making processes that need to be examined: an **argument and argumentation process** based on evidence, and the step-by-step **diagnostic, therapeutic, or prognostic process**, both in the short- and long-term care. From an argumentation process, a decision, such as "This patient must be transferred to surgery," may be seen, in philosophers' terminology, as a conclusion or claim of an **argumentation process** using evidence of all kinds.[6,7] Errors may occur not only due to uses of poor evidence or omission from one step of argumentation to another, but also how various components are linked together on the way to conclusions and recommendations. The argumentation process and model apply to practically all steps and stages of clinical practice and health and community care.

The second decision-making process that requires examination is the diagnostic, therapeutic, or prognostic process. All the steps in the various clinical practices and components of care processes, from the original presenting problem, through to the final understanding and decisions for consideration, must be recognized in the development of necessary steps in the risk assessment (as seen partly in the preceding chapter) related to the diagnostic process, treatment plan workup, or prognosis with its ensuing short- and long-term actions in care. Faults in any of those steps may be causes of numerous incidents and their consequences.

A step by step evaluation of both argumentation and cognition processes must contribute to improvements in the medical error domain. All those processes are used at each of the following steps in medical care: Correct or incorrect argumentation, reasoning, critical thinking, and decision-making underlay this whole process.

■ **Evidence buildup**, acquired knowledge, and basic understanding structured or unstructured (history, literature, physical and paraclinical examination, past experience)

⬇

■ **Reasoning** about the case, problem or situation, structured acquisition of **new knowledge** (differential diagnosis, final diagnosis, co-morbidity assessment)

⬇

■ **Decision-making** (medical, surgical, psychiatric, and other orders and plans for care)

⬇

■ **Sensory-motor execution of medical acts** (operation, invasive diagnostic procedures, physiotherapy, parenteral applications of drugs, new technologies devises implantation, etc.)

⬇

■ **Getting results** (positive and adverse)

⬇

■ **Evaluation** (of all preceding steps, one by one and of the whole process; successes, errors, failures)

⬇

■ **Prognosis and further risk assessment** (morbidity, co-morbidity, further outcomes)

⬇

■ **Follow-up, surveillance, forecasting** (risk factors and markers, prognostic factors and markers, possible outcomes, errors and failures)

9.4 Flawed Argumentation and Reasoning as Sites and Generators of Error: Argumentation and Human Error Analysis for Logic

We do not always recognize that modern argumentation underlies most of our reasoning and decision-making, as we have discussed in detail elsewhere.[6–8] Let us again review some basic terms, principles, rules, and guides, scattered in previous chapters. To begin, diagnosis and differential diagnosis, treatment choices, or predictions in prognosis may all be seen as fruits of arguments. Why? There are several ways to understand this reasoning path, listed here.

1. In simplest situations in daily practice, we proceed simply from some reason to some conclusion: "*This patient complains of sore throat* (reason, proposition, premise), *then* (indicator, connector), *let us have a look if he has a streptococcal infection.*"

2. We may also recall from our high school years the Aristotelian thinking through a categorical syllogism: *"All sore throats require an attention if they are not caused by a streptococcal infection* (major premise) ... *my patient has a sore throat* (minor premise) ... so, ... *I must be sure that he has not this kind of bacterial infection before reassuring him that he does not need antibiotics"* (conclusion).

3. Another way of reasoning and decision-making is putting in practice the modern way of argumentation proposed by Toulmin,[9,10] detailed more later. In this spirit:[6] *"I will prescribe you antibiotics for a bacterial infection of your throat* (claim, conclusion of an argument), *because looking at your red throat, patched tonsils, tender cervical nodes and fever, and positive results of our rapid laboratory test* (grounds). ... *A ten-day treatment by penicillin may be the best choice in your case* (warrant) ... *All our past experience and clinical studies show that we must do this to spare you from serious complications of such an infection* (backing) ... so, *let us definitely proceed this way, if you agree* (qualifier) ... *unless you are allergic to penicillin* (rebuttal), *in which case we should choose another kind of treatment."*

The above methods of reasoning are highly applicable to how we deal with medical error. The theoretical foundations of argumentation may be found in more detail in our[6–8] and other[9,10] writings from which we may remind some following basic concepts before applying them to medical error.

Let us just review here very briefly some essential terms, concepts, and ways of thinking and reasoning relevant to the context and content of this chapter:

Argumentation falls into the domain of **reasoning**, i.e., as a tool to form conclusions, judgments, or inferences from facts or premises.

An **argument** is a connected series of statements or reasons intended to establish a position—that is, leading to another statement as a conclusion.

An argument is a vehicle of our **medical logic** as a system of thought and reasoning that governs our understandings and decisions in clinical and community care, research, and communication.

Informal logic helps us to deal with health problems by looking at arguments as they happen in the context of natural language used in everyday life.

Argumentation is a methodological employment or presentation of arguments. Correct argumentation with ourselves and with other interested parties is one of important ways to deal with a given health problem, disease, medical care and medical error as well.

In the light of the current evidence in medicine paradigm, **argument-based medicine**[8,11] means research and practice of medicine in which understanding and decisions in patient and population care are supported by and based on flawless arguments using the best research and practice evidence and experience as argument and argumentation building blocks in a structured, fallacy-free manner.

As already suggested above, medical reasoning fits extremely well into the framework of **modern argument** as developed by Stephen Toulmin.[9,10] Chapter 4 is devoted more to this modern argumentation method and its six components:

- ■ **claim** (in initial propositions and conclusion);
- ■ **grounds** (fundamental data and information);

- **backing** (body of experience and evidence);
- **warrant** (rules related to experience and understanding of the nature of the phenomenon of interest);
- **qualifier** (expression of our certainty about the problem); and
- **rebuttals** (exclusionary conditions in which our conclusions in the argumentative process do not apply).

Figure 9.1 offers a visualization of the application of the Toulmin model to the error and harm domain.

The argumentation process is outlined below in the simplest terms.

- We need some **grounds** for argumentation. Clinical and paraclinical data and information particular to the case in question serve this purpose.
- We submit grounds under the light of a **warrant**, i.e., some kind of general rule, accepted understanding and evidence. Plausibility is the focus.
- Whatever we conclude on the basis of grounds and warrant is evaluated in confirmation, line, or distinct pattern as seen through **backing**, that is, research findings, graded evidence, past practical clinical experience, "external evidence," and "what literature tells us."
- Putting all this together, we try to quantify somehow our certainty or probability that our ensuing claims or conclusions of the argument are right in terms of a **qualifier**, often the hardest challenge of an argument.
- Our **conclusions** or argument **claim** are then the result of synthesis of the above argument building blocks.
- Argument conclusions are valid providing only that there are not any existing exclusionary circumstances or criteria, called rebuttals by Toulmin. Besides qualifiers, rebuttals are often sorely missing (and they should not) in our conclusions or claim statements.

Based on this, an error occurs and mistakes happen if:

- grounds are of poor quality, incomplete, or unrelated to the problem under study;
- our understanding of the essence of the problem is not clear;
- the backing is of poor quality, incomplete, or unrelated again;
- we are not sure how much are we sure about our conclusions and claims;
- we act as if exceptions would not apply to what we conclude about the problem; and
- there is no meaningful link between each of the argument building blocks.

Ensuing incidents and accidents and their consequences (harm) may be seen then on the basis of:

- the formal quality of the argument;
- the quality and complexity of evidence which is fed into the argument; and
- the inclusion or exclusion of other system errors, be it latent or active which may prove necessary as parts of argument building blocks.

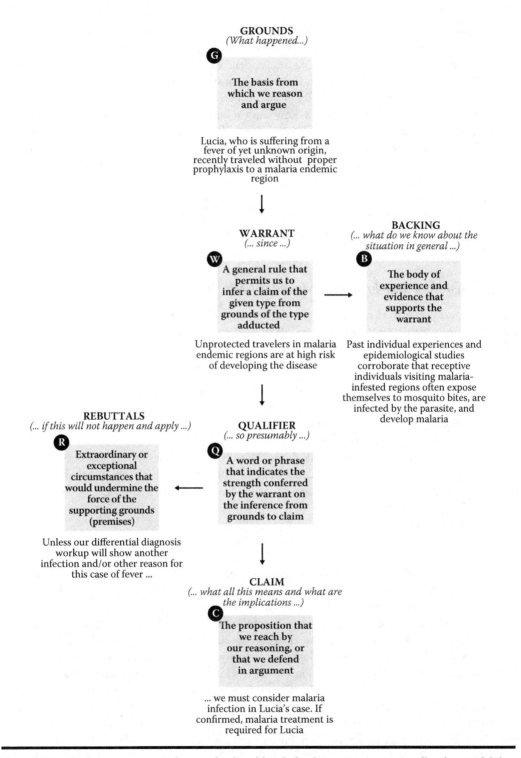

Figure 9.1 **Modern argumentation method and its six basic components. Application to driving accidents and their consequences. (Reproduced with permission from Jenicek M.** *Medical Error and Harm. Understanding, Prevention, and Control.* **Boca Raton, FL: CRC Press, 2011.)**

An **operator**, such as an internist, clinical pharmacologist, or psychiatrist making a treatment plan, a surgeon choosing whether to use an invasive exploratory or operating instrument, or an emergency medicine physician intubating an accident victim all make right or wrong decisions and actions which have potential harms. Other practice and activity components might be worthy of inclusion in our reflection about causes of medical error.

If we do not evaluate operator errors, how can we understand the differences between person and system errors? Furthermore, how can we correct and improve the operator's work? This is what lies behind such questions like "How did you arrive to your decisions and actions in the care of this patient?" It is also important to absolve an individual of responsibility of an error and harm before attributing a medical error to some system.

Thus far the problem of faulty logic and critical thinking is only summarily acknowledged in taxonomy of error proposals. For example, currently available taxonomies[5] summarily include knowledge, failure and retrieval, and usage of stored instructions but not more specific failures in reasoning and related decision-making.

9.4.1 Mistakes and Errors in Medical Lathology

Lexically speaking, **mistakes** and **errors** are synonyms. More refined distinctions have been proposed for the human error domain.[12] The following definitions are offered in this spirit. They are worthy to be quoted here again:

> A **mistake** is an error in action, calculation, opinion, or judgment caused by poor reasoning, carelessness, insufficient knowledge,[13] a wrong judgment, wrong statement proceeding from faulty judgment, inadequate knowledge, or inattention,[14] a misconception or misunderstanding.[13]
>
> An **error** as a synonym of "mistake" may be seen in our context as an act that through ignorance, deficiency, or accidents departs from or fails to achieve what should be done; mistake implies misconception or inadvertence and usually expresses less criticism than error.[15]
>
> **Lapses** are failures of memory.

In this framework, Reason[12] makes distinctions between slips and mistakes, as already outlined in Chapter 3. **Slips** are rather attentional and perceptual failures,[12] whereas **mistakes** are due to failures of mental processes. Hence, errors as failures in reasoning, logic, or argumentation fall under the current category of mistakes. Erroneous diagnosis with its consequences is then a mistake. An overworked doctor who forgets to execute clinical orders written in the patient's chart is considered to have "committed" a lapse accordingly to current terminology and semantics. Misreading a decimal point in medication dosage label is a slip under the current general human error considerations and terminology. Forgetting to administer the prescribed medication, however, is a lapse. Understanding medical error as the result of faulty judgment, reasoning, or argumentation whose conclusions lead to patient's harm, is at the core of our preoccupation of human medical error attributable to the individual health professional himself or herself.

9.4.2 Fallacies, Biases, and Cognitive Errors in Medical Lathology

Medical error as mistake may be due to faulty reasoning and decision-making. These types of faults fall into the world of fallacies, biases, and cognitive errors. They may be defined and illustrated for the domain of error and harm by way of an example, illustrated here.

Fallacy

In most general terms, a **fallacy** refers to some mistake or flaw in reasoning or argument. A fallacy is a violation of the norms of good reasoning, rules of critical discussion, dispute resolution, and adequate communication.[16] For example, a ***cum hoc ergo propter hoc* fallacy** refers to the act of drawing conclusions about cause-effect relationships on the basis of loosely defined "associations" or "correlations" instead of a more formal cause-effect proof. Anything which precedes medical error and its potential consequences (harm) should not be considered automatically as "cause" of harm until it conforms to criteria of causality.

Bias

The word of **bias** in the medical world is most strongly influenced by its meaning in biostatistics, as deviation from some real or reference value. More generally bias may be understood as a non-random, systematic deviation from truth, state, or a well-defined "reality."

Often, bias is a term used in an undistinguished way from cognitive error or cognitive bias. For example, drawing conclusions about a population on the basis of a sample that is biased or prejudiced in some manner, sometimes called the fallacy of **biased sample** or fallacy of **underreporting of facts and variables** which are relevant information for problem solving. The ensuing arcane explanations are biases in the aforementioned sense.

Cognitive Error (Cognitive Bias)

A **cognitive error** or **cognitive bias**, terms often used synonymously across the literature, denotes patterns of systematic deviation in judgment that occurs in a particular and consistent way, in our case, in medical and clinical situations or in medical research reasoning and conclusions.

Outcome bias refers to the influence of knowledge gained at the outcome of a process, typically upon evaluations of decision quality. The result of this is that sometimes it enables mediocre processes to be judged as good and good processes as mediocre.[16]

Hindsight bias (loosely synonymous with outcome bias) is also a cognitive error. It is a tendency for people with outcome knowledge to exaggerate the extent to which they would have predicted the event beforehand; it can have an adverse impact on retrospective investigations of events that cause harm.[17]

Cognitive distortion(s) in psychiatry and cognitive therapy has a slightly different meaning with overlapping characteristic with fallacies and cognitive errors as listed in Appendices of this book. For mental health professionals they are exaggerated or traditional thought patterns that are believed to perpetuate the effects of psychopathological states such as depression or anxiety.[18] They are thoughts which cause individuals to perceive reality inaccurately. They often reinforce negative thoughts or emotions related to subjects of interest.[8-20] Examples: Always being right, blaming, disqualifying the positive, fallacy of change, fallacy of fairness, jumping to conclusions, magnification or minimization, all-or-nothing splitted thinking or dichotomous reasoning among others.[18]

The term **bias**, as currently used across the medical literature, has multiple meanings, including almost any flaw in reasoning and decision-making, especially in the medical research domain: research design, execution, and evaluation. Bias has been increasingly covered and discussed[16-26] because even "biased" research results and their uses may be detrimental to patient safety and health. A few examples of biases which may compromise internal and/ or external validity and can potentially harm medical research results include susceptibility biases, protopathic bias, design, trial execution, overcharging biases, information, transfer, and performance. Information about the extensive list of biases as flaws in research is beyond the scope of this text. It can be explored further in the quoted literature and paired with the more general list and reviews of cognitive biases and fallacies.

Lists and reviews of cognitive biases and errors, as well as of fallacies, grow and expand. Beyond the scope of this and other chapters in this book, these lists cover considerable numbers of

- cognitive biases and cognitive errors in general[27]
- cognitive biases and cognitive errors in medicine (in diagnosis in particular)[28]
- fallacies in general[29]
- fallacies in medicine and other health sciences and professions[8]

Many readers might like to consult directly these easily accessible sources, too voluminous in the context of this and other chapters.

In addition to the bias challenge itself, extensive arrays and definitions of known fallacies, biases, and cognitive errors often overlap. This lack of semantic and terminological requires further clarification. In our preceding monograph,[8] we provide a more detailed discussion of the fallacy/ bias/cognitive error domain and provide more valuable collections of fallacies, biases and cognitive errors with their definitions, examples, and ways to correct them increase in numbers and quality. We should be aware of as many as possible most important errors in reasoning in particular clinical and research situations to correct or avoid them properly. Current lists[8,30-42] are still not exhaustive and they evolve in time. Any particular clinical or research situation may create some new ones to discover, define, understand, and avoid. The medical error is one of such situations.

The relevance of fallacies, biases, and cognitive errors may vary from one medical specialty to another. For example, Gunderman[43] points out that in radiology attribution, availability, commission/omission, confirmation, framing, hindsight, regret, and satisfaction of search biases behind potential and real errors are particularly relevant. Fabri and Zayas-Castro[1] identify the most frequent errors in surgery as errors in technique, carelessness/inattention to detail, judgment error, and incomplete understanding of the problem. To this list, Paradis[26] adds susceptibility, design, information, transfer, performance, citation, optimism, and conflict of interest biases. But what about other medical specialties? Should we not seek to identify and understand of fallacies, biases, and cognitive errors in other medical specialties as well? Our understanding of medical error should be as free from fallacies, biases, and cognitive errors as possible. This is an ideal which will not be ever reached but it should always be attempted. "It can't be done" is not an answer.

9.5 Where and When Errors Can Happen: Cognitive Pathways as Sites of Error

While improving clinical practice by finding that our patient risk assessment, diagnosis, treatment plan, prognosis, or prevention decisions are wrong can identify a problem, it cannot identify where in the process of practice the error happened. Nor does it identify what was responsible for the error, and where there are opportunities for improvements. These steps can be seen as a cognitive process path from initial stimuli and ideas to observations, making sense from them and reaching some new knowledge as a basis for understanding or decisions what to do. These steps can answer at what moment the error occurred, or at what part, stage, or step in clinical activities could be a weak point to watch (Table 9.1, p. 268).

In this chapter, we examine the diagnosis, treatment, prognosis, and risk assessment steps that are relevant and interesting to understanding medical error better at the human level. In the next chapter, we will examine what are the strategies to prevent and control medical error.

A physician follows several steps and makes a range of assessments while taking care of his or her patient:

- learning about the patient past and present through medical history which includes gathering written and oral information about the past and present (chief complaint and other complaints);
- physical examination and/or mental status assessment, leading to and making diagnosis;
- reviewing the risks (future health problems) and health problems already present (diagnosis);
- selecting treatment choices, making decisions and plans and issuing orders;
- assessing the prognosis;
- evaluating the effectiveness, efficiency, and efficacy of all the aforementioned steps in healthcare; and
- future steps in care to consider.

At each of these steps in clinical work, conclusions are a sort of a claim (the endpoint in argumentation), or conclusion, of both the positive or negative aspects and impact of our care. These claims may include statements like:

- "Those data and information are relevant for further assessment of the patient."
- "This patient has this disease, syndrome, and other health problem."

Table 9.1   Tracing Errors, Sites, and Sources across Clinical Steps

Steps in Clinical Work	Possible Site and Type of Error
Patient entry under healthcare ↓	• Recruitment, eligibility
Problem identification ↓	• Patient complaint(s)
Impression (diagnostic) ↓	• Hypothesis, working idea
Clinical workup plan ↓	• Plan for investigation and examinations to order

Data collection (interview, clinical and paraclinical examination) ↓	• Qualitative and quantitative
	  • measurements,
	  • counting,
	  • categorization, and
	  • classification

Analysis ↓	• Differential diagnosis (options) • Horizontal assessment of evidence • Soundness, structure, process, and impact of possible ways of care
Working (final) diagnosis ↓	• Diagnostic technique used (pattern recognition, exhaustive exploration, steepest ascent method, and algorithmic way)
Decision making ↓	• Vertical assessment of evidence (including that of treatment) • Decision analysis (including treatment options, probabilities, values, utilities chaining, and path tracing) • Chagrin analysis • Patient care algorithm workup • Patient's preferences and values integration with his/her physician's preferences, values, and options
Decision ↓	• Conclusions about evidence (best available and other) • Final diagnosis • Treatment plan and orders (harmonizing physicians and patient's preferences, values, and options) • Various other claims and critical thinking conclusions about diagnosis, treatment plan, outcomes, and prognosis • Given prognosis, ensuing additional care
Action ↓	• Implementing procedures which include ongoing corrective actions based on progressing, unexpected, and expected results

Evaluation ↓	• Effectiveness, efficacy, and efficiency of care • Expected and unexpected adverse effects • Patient tolerance of procedures, satisfaction, and possible future preferences
Outcomes assessment and prognosis	• Assessment of the soundness, structure, process, and impact of the whole clinical care experience, both in this patient and in other patients within an overall practice

- "Looking at what I have heard, read, and seen in this patient, he or she may develop health problems which he or she still does not have."
- "This patient should receive the following medical, surgical, psychiatric, or other treatment and care."
- "The outlook for this patient (prognosis) with or without treatment is good or bad."
- "Our treatment plan and its execution were effective (did it some good in habitual conditions), efficient (in line with money, resources and time invested) and efficacious (consistent, specious and beneficial result under ideal conditions)."

Figure 9.2 summarizes possible sites and types of errors from one step of clinical work to another.

Errors may occur at any step in these work, research, and practice steps. If we do not analyze, interpret, and know more intimately lathologic aspects of those steps, can we attribute our errors to the system etiology of error only? We believe that we cannot.

9.5.1 Reviewing Diagnosis: Searching for Errors in the Clinimetric Process

It is not enough to simply say that a diagnosis is wrong. Once finding that our diagnosis was wrong, we must endeavor to know where exactly our error occurred. Clinimetrics are useful in this endeavor.

At the beginning of the 1980s, Alvan Feinstein[44–47] originally proposed the term ***clinimetrics*** for the measurement of clinical phenomena, or, "*the domain concerned with indices, rating scales and other expressions that are used to describe or measure symptoms, physical signs, and other distinctly clinical phenomena in clinical medicine.*"

Clinimetrics relies on two important processes, ***mensuration*** and ***measurement***:

- ***Mensuration*** refers to the production of raw individual data from medical history, physical examination, paraclinical explorations, and other primary sources.
- ***Measurement*** refers to the processing of raw data, not only to give this data (signs, symptoms, etc.) some dimension, such as severity, but also labeling them qualitatively through classification, group formation, and validation as syndromes and other diagnostic entities indicative of further specific attention and care.

Steps in clinical work and possible sites and types of errors

Steps in clinical work	Possible site and type of error
Patient entry under healthcare	Recruitment, eligibility
Problem identification	Patient complaint(s)
Impression (diagnostic)	• Hypothesis • Working idea
Clinical workup plan	Plan of investigation and examinations to order
Data collection (interview, clinical and paraclinical examination)	Qualitative and quantitative • measurements • counting • categorization • classification
Analysis	• Differential diagnosis (options) • Horizontal assessment of evidence • Soundness, structure, process, and impact of possible ways of care
Working (final) diagnosis	Diagnostic technique used (pattern recognition, exhaustive exploration, steepest ascent method, algorithmic way)
Decision-making	• Vertical assessment of evidence (that of treatment included) • Decision analysis (inc. treatment options, probabilities values, utilities chaining, and path tracing) • Chagrin analysis • Patient care algorithm workup • Patient's preferences and values integration with his/her physician's preferences, values, and options
Decision	• Conclusions about the best and other evidences • Final diagnosis • Treatment plan and orders (harmonizing physicians and patient's preferences, values, and options) • Various other claims and critical thinking conclusions about diagnosis, treatment plan, outcomes, and prognosis • Ensuing additional care given prognosis
Action	Procedures implementation which include corrections accordingly to occurring and progressing, unexpected and expected results
Evaluation	• Effectiveness, efficacy, efficiency of care • Expected and unexpected adverse effects • Patient tolerance of procedures, satisfaction, possible future preferences
Outcomes assessment and prognosis	Assessment of the soundness, structure, process, and impact of the whole clinical care (in this patient and in other patients—overall practice)

Figure 9.2   Steps in clinical work and possible sites and types of errors.

In this context, medical error does not only mean that some diagnostic instrument such as a biochemical test or fiberoptic imaging sonde has broken or did not work properly; the culprit may be a faulty activity at any point in the clinimetric process. Identifying that such moments and activities may be due to human error, and not only to machine error, is necessary. It is not enough to relate a diagnostic error to poor internal validity of a diagnostic test relying on a specific substance or instrument in terms of sensitivity, specificity, its predictive values, or reproducibility. Our sensory perceptions and their intellectual management equally count. All (or none) may be faulty.

Figure 9.3 illustrates seven steps in the clinimetric process, from initial observations to diagnosis.

Steps 1–3 are steps in **observation** or **mensuration** (Feinstein's term making distinction from measurement). Steps 4–6 are those of **explanation**. Step 7 is the final diagnosis, the culmination of all the steps from the first perception of the patient based on his or her complaint or motive for consultation, to the final **conclusion** (claim) about the patient's state. As noted, a faulty diagnosis leading to a wrong treatment and ensuing harm may be caused by errors at any of these steps in the diagnostician's work, raising several questions worthy of introspection for the purposes of training.

Clinicians may ask themselves:

- Did I understand well the patient's chief complaint and motive (reason) for consultation?
- Did I get the necessary information from patient's medical and other history?
- Did I properly observe the patient? If not, what error did I commit and what might be its consequences?
- Did I isolate all relevant manifestations and information as perceived by myself and by the patient? If not, what error did I commit and what might be its consequences?
- Did I describe them in a measurable and reproducible way? If not, what error did I commit and what might be its consequences?
- Did I perform the diagnostic test, maneuver, or procedure properly? If not, was the reason? Was my error of sensory or motor nature, or both? At what level did eventual lapses and mistakes occur?
- Did I use an *a priori* knowledge of internal and external validity of a diagnostic test, maneuver, procedure, or verbal exploration (like in psychiatry)?
- Was I, or am I, using tests of poor sensitivity, specificity, positive or negative predictive value, or reproducibility?
- Did I choose well, and perform properly, other clinical and paraclinical diagnostic tests, maneuvers, or procedures? If the answer is yes, did I perform an appropriate parallel, serial, or otherwise repeated testing where required and mandatory?
- Did I omit the Bayesian reasoning in diagnosis making?
- Did I properly identify and give dimension to my observations? If not, what error did I commit and what might be its consequences?
- Did I properly interpret the patient's state? If not, what error did I commit and what might be its consequences?
- Did I properly made my diagnosis making correct extrapolations and categorization, and giving clinical meaning to my conclusion, or claim? If not, what error did I commit at this stage of the diagnostic process and what might be its consequences?

- Did I review possible cognitive errors throughout the whole path to the diagnosis process?
- Is my diagnosis explicit enough and my directions detailed enough about what to do with this patient in treatment and further follow-up? If not, what error did I commit and what might be its consequences?
- What might and should be corrected and avoided, why, and how?
- What should I do better next time at any step and moment of this diagnostic pathway?
- How could, and should, I evaluate if my approach to making a diagnosis? Is it less prone to error? Do patients benefit from these changes?
- Ultimately, was my decision to diagnose justified?

This kind of "**clinical reasoning root cause analysis**" should be considered, tried, and evaluated despite all its possible limitations.

There are multiple phenomena as factors in the health processes and environment which may be reasons for lack of focus on diagnostic failure and ensuing possible harm. Croskerry[48] recognizes several of them: amorphous nature of many illnesses, invisibility, accountability, attitude of silence and culture of silence, denial discounting and distancing, non-disclosure, investigation, natural cause of illness, lack of awareness, lack of understanding of the decision-making process, unavailability of tangible solutions, tolerance, and poor business case.[48]

9.5.2 Reviewing the Path from Diagnosis to Treatment Decisions and Orders

The clinimetric or gnostic path is one diagnostic process, but we may also consider another path, this one from the diagnosis to treatment decision, orders, and their success or failures. For this purpose, let us examine the treatment selection, choice of treatment, and its outcomes as successes and failures, as a path in Figure 5.1 (in Chapter 5). This path encompasses not only the principal or key health problem and its treatment, but also parallel and lateral mode paths of the treatment of co-morbidities. de Bono[49,50] coined these ways of thinking as cutting through traditional step-by-step thinking patterns to generate new or additional concepts and ideas, known as the lateral way. This approach allows for the consideration of multiple problems and treatments at a time, in concert with the vertical (like the main health problem and its treatment) problem solving.[7,8,43,44]

In the lateral approach, the treatment choice, decision, execution, and its results (and other outcomes) may be seen and analyzed as a three step procedure starting from the treatment 'baseline' or initial state followed by treatment maneuver(s), medical surgical or others, resulting in a 'subsequent state' or various outcomes.[46,47] Because patients may have other health problems or diseases (co-morbidity) besides the key health problem (disease) and as such are subject to co-treatments for co-morbidities, both parallel and lateral ways of reasoning and decision-making must be used. The challenge of co-morbidity was recently reviewed again by de Groot et al.[51] Co-morbidity and treatment for co-morbidity with their ensuing outcomes are relevant at all levels of clinical exploration and care decisions.

Medical errors may occur if the clinical baseline information is wrong or incomplete, if the decisions to treat key morbidity and co-morbidities are wrong, and if expected and unexpected outcomes of both are missed, poorly detected and evaluated as well as both their successes and harms. Good or flawed fulfillment of good or wrong medical orders is how a reasoning and decision-making error is executed or implemented.

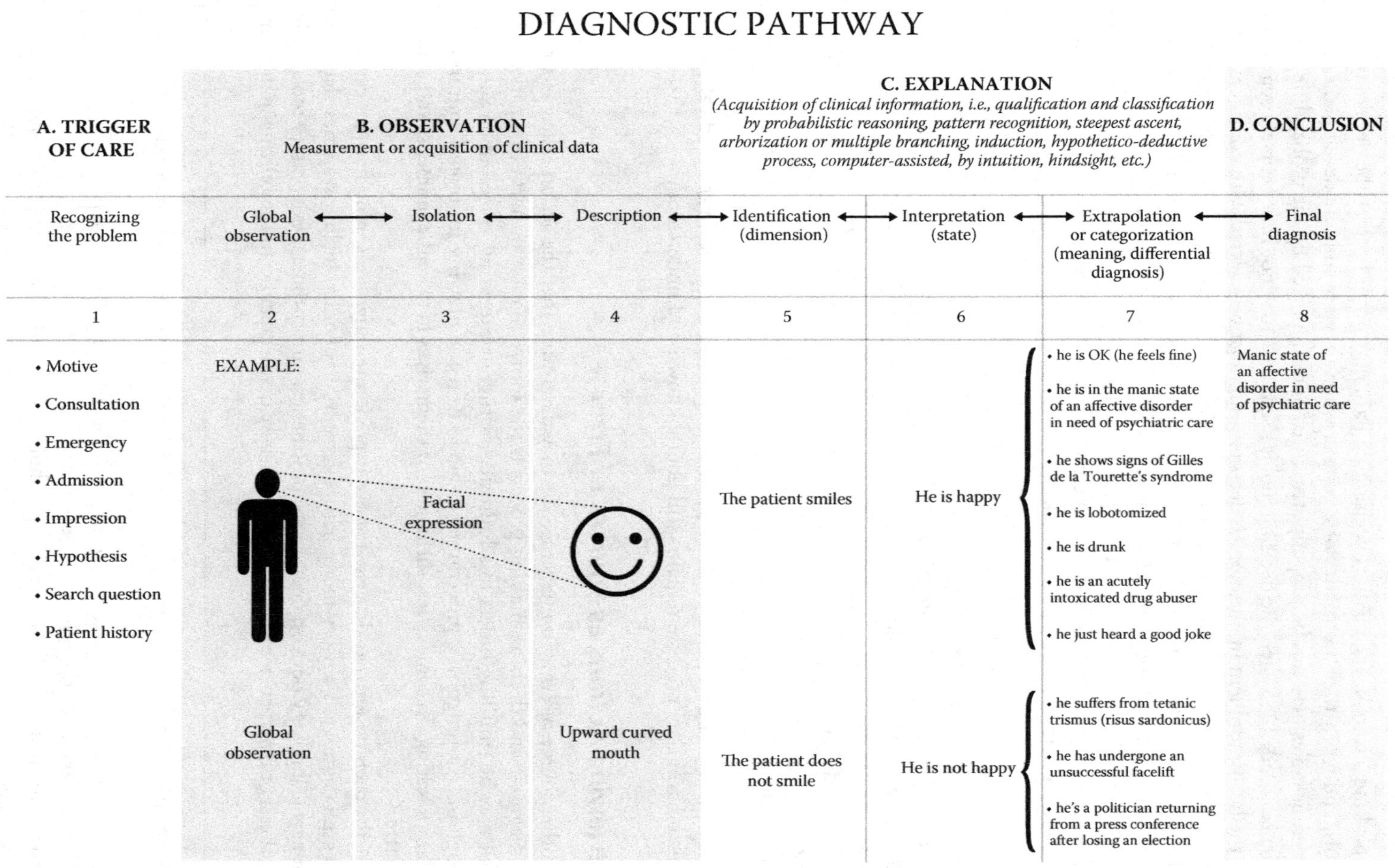

DIAGNOSTIC PATHWAY

A. TRIGGER OF CARE	B. OBSERVATION Measurement or acquisition of clinical data			C. EXPLANATION (Acquisition of clinical information, i.e., qualification and classification by probabilistic reasoning, pattern recognition, steepest ascent, arborization or multiple branching, induction, hypothetico-deductive process, computer-assisted, by intuition, hindsight, etc.)			D. CONCLUSION
Recognizing the problem	Global observation	Isolation	Description	Identification (dimension)	Interpretation (state)	Extrapolation or categorization (meaning, differential diagnosis)	Final diagnosis
1	2	3	4	5	6	7	8

EXAMPLE:

- Motive
- Consultation
- Emergency
- Admission
- Impression
- Hypothesis
- Search question
- Patient history

Global observation

Facial expression

Upward curved mouth

The patient smiles

The patient does not smile

He is happy

He is not happy

- he is OK (he feels fine)
- he is in the manic state of an affective disorder in need of psychiatric care
- he shows signs of Gilles de la Tourette's syndrome
- he is lobotomized
- he is drunk
- he is an acutely intoxicated drug abuser
- he just heard a good joke

- he suffers from tetanic trismus (risus sardonicus)
- he has undergone an unsuccessful facelift
- he's a politician returning from a press conference after losing an election

Manic state of an affective disorder in need of psychiatric care

Figure 9.3 Steps in the clinimetric process through the diagnostic pathway. (Redrawn from Jenicek M. *Epidemiology. The Logic of Modern Medicine.* Montreal: EPIMED International, 1995, and Reference 5. Reproduced with permission.)

9.5.3 Reviewing Decisions as Sources of Harm

Generally speaking, errors in the medical decision domain may occur both at the development of decision tools, and when they are used. For example, when they are initially developed decision analyses, trees, or tables may not be properly structured and supported by the probabilities, utilities, or utilities, or evidences needed.[52] When the decision tool is used, they may not have been chosen appropriately for the health problem in question. A decision tool must be selected with consideration of the health problem, but also the background information and evidence available, specific to the topic (health problem), and how the decision tool will be used in a particular setting of clinical care, by a particular team, using particular equipment to accomplish the task.

Since the 1970s, Detmer et al.[53] have reminded us that heuristic situations do not facilitate decisions either. From the domain of management and administration, Caruth and Hadlogten[54] stress several mistakes to avoid in decision-making:

- failure to recognize the problem;
- incorrect problem identification;
- insufficient consideration of alternatives;
- inadequate evaluation of risk;
- repetitive decisions;
- unnecessary decisions;
- delayed decisions; and
- lack of follow-up.

How frequent are such mistakes in decision-making process itself within the medical domain and how much harm they produce remains still poorly known and understood.

9.5.4 Reviewing Actions as Sources of Error

There is another source of error in medicine. We may determine that the action taken as a result of a sound diagnosis and decision-making process is the source of error or harm in a patient. An action taken may be fulfilling orders to administer a drug, or executing agreed upon surgery or invasive diagnostic or prognostic procedures, or blood or tissue drawing for biopsy, cultures and other laboratory testing. In some cases, these actions themselves may be the moments and sites for error and harm.

Whereas the decision error as discussed above is predominantly a reasoning flaw, an execution error is, to a great degree, of a sensory-motor nature. Executions of orders include surgeries, deliveries, implants of new technology devices, dental care, prosthetics, intracorporeal exploratory tools, delivery of anaesthesia or emergency medicine, and intensive care therapeutic and stabilizing maneuvers.

All activities and actions in the medical specialties dependent on sensory-motor skills require:

- the best possible motor, tactile, visual, or auditory skills for the task;
- their mastery at a proper learning level;
- proper disposition of caregivers (psychological, equipoise, freedom from stress, fatigue, etc.);

> - harmonized ergonomics in the man-machine advanced world; and
> - unhindered communication and other interaction facilitating conditions within and between teams with complementary training, professions, cultures, philosophy, preferences, and values.

Errors may occur, then, due to execution flaws for any of five above reasons: Did the error occur because the physicians did not have required skills? Did he or she learn them satisfactorily? Was he or she in a proper disposition to execute properly required actions and maneuvers? Did the ergonomics of a given action facilitate or complicate interventions? Did the required interaction between health professionals involved contribute to, or was the main cause of error?

The ergonomic assessment of care and contribution to the patient safety includes:[55]

- involvement in the evaluation and implementation of organizational strategies which encourage the patient safety incidents and near misses;
- measurement and recording of those incidents themselves including the variables having possibly impact on patient safety; and
- giving directions to interventions aimed at improving patient safety.

Gawron et al.[56] explored the concept of human factors engineering. These authors describe human factors engineering as systems designed in a way systems and human/machine interfaces that are robust enough to reduce error rates and the effect of error within the system. The goal of human factors engineering is the optimal relationship between humans and systems. Root cause analysis, fault tree analysis, Petri nets, Reason's generic-error modeling system, failure mode, and effect analysis were already used and attempted in various medical and surgical domains of human factors engineering.

Ergonomic analyses focus on systems with both human and machine elements and interrelationships as part of an integrated whole of sets of interacting and interdependent entities. Ergonomic analyses are being used in the quality movement in business and other settings. Drury[57] believes that ergonomics will prove useful in open systems and strategic issues, organization design and leadership, measurement-based operation, appropriate uses of technologies as well as in individuals, teams, and the change process.

Does this "error-free manufacturing" share some common traits with "producing improvements in patient health?" Increasingly over the past decade ergonomics has been considered in the health domain and in patient safety. However, its use as a tool in health evaluation is limited. It is used largely by health professionals for quality improvement processes in non-clinical settings.

9.5.5 Getting Results and Their Impact Evaluation

Errors may also occur at the evaluation level. In this case, the evaluation itself may erroneously conclude that a specific treatment of other health intervention was flawed. This too may harm the patient.

Several different, but complementary, aspects and angles of evaluation are currently used in health quality assurance in healthcare,[58] health administration, care and planning, and surgery.[56–58] To work in these applications, we expand some of Donabedian's three original concepts of evaluation (structure/process/impact or outcomes). These modifications to evaluation are outlined as follows:

A. Multi-angular evaluation

- Soundness   ***"Does it make <u>sense</u>?"***
  Surgeon's knowledge and experience; evidence in its broadest sense; its plausibility and its reasons.

- Structure   ***"How is it organized?"***
  Are all elements of a given activity present in a clear direction and within an acceptable logical structure?

- Process   ***"How does it work? Does it work as desired and expected?"***
  Operational research or operations research is devoted in part to this type of evaluation.

- Impact or outcome(s)   ***"What does it do? Does it produce some effect?"***
  (Clinical trials and their alternatives, observational analytical studies)
  "Does it work in *ideal* conditions?"
  This is called **efficacy**.
  "Does it work in *habitual* conditions?"
  This is called **effectiveness**.
  "Does it work *proportionately* in relation to money, time, and human and material resources spent?"
  This is called **efficiency**.

B. Evolving changes in the above evaluation

- Constancy   ***"Does the above <u>information change</u> or not, over time, in different places, patients, care providers, and settings?"***
  (Fluctuations of soundness, structure, process, and/or impact.)

- Consistency   ***"Does it make the same sense?"***
  (Do the results follow the line of previous experience? Do they have a meaning similar to what we already know in terms of biological, contextual, and practice plausibility based on previous studies and their findings?)

Some treatment or other component of medical care may be considered as sound, but this does not mean that its uses are well organized in a proper process. Its impact may be good in ideal conditions, not necessarily in different settings, and its uses may be deemed irrational given what we have invested in their practice. Even if such desired conditions are reached, quality of care may change over time and it may acquire during such process different meaning, better or worse. Using a simple *"It works"* as an assessment of treatment without more precision and qualification may cause harm.

9.5.6 Errors in Making Prognosis

Prognosis means not only a prediction of being well or not over a certain period of time. As part of a diagnosis, a prognosis leads to considerations of further treatment and care if the prognosis is not good. To make accurate decisions and predictions, more than one piece of information is usually needed.

A prognosis should include considerations of:

■ both positive and negative outcomes in their sequence over time;
■ treatments and care moments as detected over time;
■ alternative portraits of disease course with or without treatment and care plans considered wherever and whenever possible;
■ components of disease spectrum and gradient leading to, or being sites responsible for, a good or bad prognosis;
■ effectiveness of interventions that alter the prognosis, known in advance as much as possible. The intervention that alters the prognosis may not be the same as the one altering the risk of developing the disease;
■ distinctions between risk factors and prognostic factors (called sometimes hazard factors); and
■ distinctions between risk characteristics and hazard (prognostic) characteristics, which are sometimes blurred.

Similar to the risk domain, where we make distinctions between risk markers which cannot be modified, and risk factors which can be modified to lower the probability of developing disease, knowledge about prognostic markers and prognostic factors will lead us to better understand what is effective or not to improve patient prognosis, that is, the disease course once it is established.[59,60] An additional point is the fact that some prognostic factors may be more or less important than similar risk factors. For example, smoking is a more important risk factor than a prognostic one. Alcohol abuse may have an equal role in the development of liver disease and in its further course (prognosis) once the diagnosis of alcoholic hepatitis or cirrhosis are established. In this sense, for example, five-year survival rates as measure of prognosis may not prove always satisfactory for all right care decisions. They remain, however, as one of the valuable leads for a better management of patient prognosis.

Using prognostic trees to detect sites of possible error is limited given the fact that in contrast to decision trees, currently available prognostic trees do not include interventions and their outcomes and utilities. In looking at prognosis this way, errors in prognosis and subsequent decisions in caring for the patient who has already developed a disease may be due and/or explained by mistakes (not making necessary distinctions and related over-encompassing care decisions) related to any point mentioned above. Errors in prognosis may occur if prognosis for the patient, prognosis for the key problem, and prognosis for, and in view of, co-morbidities are confounded. If we conclude that "Prognosis is good," is it for, and of what, of the above?

Evidence-based medicine reminds us that the best evidence should be used in harmony with, among others, patient preferences and values and the setting of care. Using even the best evidence on prognosis requires also some kind of **fit within the setting of care**.

Fit within the setting of care includes:

■ **fit of patient characteristics** with those who served as basis for prognostic information;
■ **fit within available research**, that is the purpose of reference prognostic studies should be in line with the patient problem such as methods of follow-up, medication, and surgery used;

- **fit within medical care** so that the setting, rules, and everyday run of care should be close to those of our patient;
- **fit with caregivers** which means that physicians, nurses, and other healthcare professionals should have complementary competencies, ways of practice, and the general "hospital culture;" and
- **fit with prognosis**, as already discussed in the above paragraphs of this section.

Errors in prognosis and possible harm from it may also result from discrepancies between reference values and information and their application in a specific clinical environment. Prognosis, as in any step in clinical care which precedes it, may be erroneous and may generate other errors if it is it is poorly defined, poorly described, poorly analyzed, or generated poor conclusions, recommendations and further medical care orders.

9.5.7 Follow-Up, Surveillance, Forecasting-Related Errors

Follow-up reviews of error events and harm should extend beyond the original statement and interpretation of the medical error event. In the medical error domain, surveillance is currently limited to serious cases in a high risk environment. Should the **surveillance and forecasting of medical error** follow the general rules of epidemiological surveillance[61] and be reported to those who have the right to know so that action can be taken?

> **Epidemiological surveillance** in this case, should ideally be a systematic and continuous collection, analysis, and interpretation of data, closely integrated with the timely and coherent dissemination of results and assessment. Surveillance should be performed irrespective of the gravity of the problem at a given moment. The gravity of the problem fluctuates in time.

Without surveillance of medical error, including its frequency and high occurrence of causes permitting and justifying the endeavor, better causal research, evaluation of the consistency and constancy of error events and their prevention are limited.

> **Epidemiological forecasting** is a method of estimating what may happen in the future given a particular health phenomenon that relies on the extrapolation of existing trends.[61] Its subjects of interest may be of clinical, demographic, community, epidemiological, and other nature. Even in the forecasting domain, initiatives should take into account sufficient numbers of events which make forecasting possible beyond the hypothetical level.

To make surveillance and forecasting more meaningful in the medical error domain, simple registries of cases without possible causal factors relevant for prevention and control may prove of limited value. The identification of medical error related variables, data, and information understood through deductive reasoning may prove more feasible and rational than **inductive exploration**, where multiple data collection processes are used based on the fear that "nothing must be forgotten." Only more recently, **probabilistic risk analysis** was proposed as a tool to make additional predictions based on few or rare cases in the framework of medical error, harm, and sentinel events.[62,63]

Follow-up, surveillance, and forecasting in the medical error domain merit further development and wider application and uses. In the epidemiological sense, is not medical error another 'disease' which should be properly detected, treated effectively, and prevented? Preventing disease would be much harder without proper surveillance and forecasting which has been found so useful in other domains of clinical and field (community) epidemiology.

Let Us Conclude

The model needed for the evaluation of sources of error is very close to components and sources of teaching and learning skills in surgery:[64,65] Errors and harm in surgery, like in an evaluation of errors and harm more generally, may originate from faulty fundamental assets to acquire (knowledge, attitudes, skills), misuses of passive and active teaching tools, as well as from methods of communication.

The current discussion and experience of error and harm focus mostly on a single or a particular type of error. In addition to this fundamental approach, should we consider in the future a kind of **meta-evaluation of human error** across its spectrum and gradient which includes various medical errors of interest? In both approaches, medical error falls by its nature into three interlinked categories, outlined here.

1. Medical errors may be a product of faulty knowledge, attitudes, and skills of the health professional. Unsound evidence is used, or the best sound evidence is not used.
2. Evidence used in medical understandings and decisions may be unsound, poorly structured, executed in an inappropriate process, and with an unclear impact in terms of effectiveness, efficacy and efficiency, not constant and inconsistent in time and space. All the above may happen at any step of medical care as described in Section 9.3 of this chapter. In this examination of errors, the entry of patients into healthcare may be questioned, or patient interviews, both medical and psychiatric may be flawed, or the physical and para-clinical examination yields wrong data and information. Other errors might include that risks of health problems which might be expected in the patient are not appropriately estimated, or diagnosis and differential diagnosis may be wrong and the diagnosis of other problems (co-morbidity) may be wrong and/or incomplete. Still other errors may be that the plan of care may be too narrow or too broad, well, or poorly defined; or treatment modalities may be misdirected, incomplete, or omit co-morbidities; prognosis may be wrong and omit co-morbid states and the occurrence of additional new health problems, their treatment, and interactions with the main problem. Finally, an error may occur it the follow-up to treatment is not long or complete enough to control the long-term effects and needs.
3. The sources of error at the individual level may include inadequate knowledge, attitudes, and skills as well as poor critical thinking and argumentation. Technology problems may include both their design and uses in a good or bad physical environment of technology at work. In addition to that, systems may be in fault: the human may interact inappropriately with the machine, members of the healthcare team may poorly interact between themselves, and the communication at any level of any system may be compromised.

Figure 9.4 illustrates this concept in simplified matrix form.

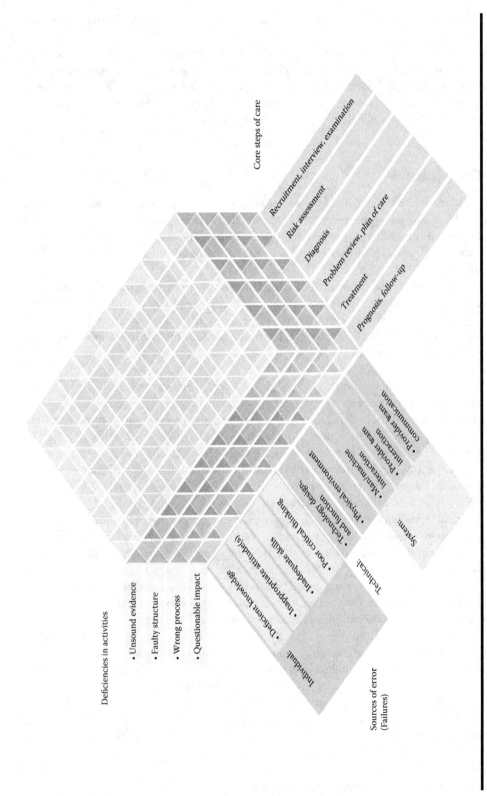

Figure 9.4 Distribution of medical errors accordingly to the level of acquired professional competency, steps in clinical care, and the desirable quality attributes of medical interventions. (Redrawn from Jenicek M. *Medical Error and Harm. Understanding, Prevention, and Control.* Boca Raton: CRC Press, 2011.)

This kind of '**mapping of the spectrum of medical error and the gradient of the harm it produces**' should prove an additional asset in planning prevention and control of the medical error problem across clinical and community care.

Moreover, in light of this chapter, what should we do to analyze the human individual component in a structured way? The way of argumentation and critical thinking: Claims of any kind, at any level of the analysis and evaluation of the process and results of care, should be based on a structured argumentation in which conclusions are based on clinically and logically meaningful grounds, backing, warrant(s), qualifiers, and rebuttals supporting the overall understanding of the problem under study.

Building on this understanding, the loci of potential error and harm and attention required across the stages of clinical care are as follows.

1. Define the kind of error possibly associated with the harm observed.
2. Consider the human (operator) error first before you expand your inquiry at the system level.
3. Check step-by-step clinical care process for possible location of mistakes leading to the error event.
4. Consider flaws in reasoning, decision-making, and sensory-motor actions.
5. Begin the process by examining if the error event is a result of how the patient entered care, that is, whether the chief complaint and reason for consultation or hospitalization was right, missed, or misdirected. If so, a wrong treatment may follow.
6. Identify, if possible, the precise stage in the clinimetric process which is the wrong step responsible for further wrong decision in patient care: observation, qualification, categorization, or others?
7. Were the rules of hypothetic-deductive thinking, proper pattern recognition, algorithms, or other diagnostic guidelines well chosen given the case and circumstances?
8. Verify possible faults in the making of a differential diagnosis and final diagnosis, and their completeness, in view of multiple morbidities (co-morbidity).
9. Clarify how treatment decisions and orders were justified and made: check errors in treatment guidelines or algorithm choices, decisions based on heuristics, decision analysis, or others.
10. Analyze and explain actions in care as potential loci for mistakes (flaws in reasoning and decision-making) and slips and lapses (mostly of sensory-motor nature).
11. Try to understand how prognosis was made. Did it take into account relevant prognostic markers and factors, co-morbidity and co-treatments for co-morbidity, patient characteristics, and the clinical and community care setting? What are the decisions in the light of the wrong prognosis which my lead to future potential errors in care and harm?
12. Is the proposed patient follow-up and surveillance justifiable by all preceding steps, and how does it fit beyond a single case forecasting for this type of health problem and the healthcare related to it?
13. Analyze the system if operator's errors do not explain satisfactorily the error event of interest. If not, consider a system analysis.

Should we see this approach to the clinical error understanding as a kind of root cause analysis at the human operator level? Each and every human participant in the "system" which produces error and harm may contribute to them at any stage and point in medical care. These may include flaws in:

- initial hypothesizing, question(s) to answer, and objectives for further action;
- perception of bodily, mental, and behavioral manifestations;
- interpretation of what was seen and its coupling with good or bad supporting background evidence;
- making conclusions like diagnosis or treatment orders;
- execution or actions, mostly of sensory-motor nature;
- the evaluation of actions;
- patient or community follow-up; and
- the lack of feedback evaluation of flaws and their correction.

Hence, human medical errors may be caused by flaws in argumentation and critical thinking while producing, interpreting, using, and evaluating evidence and how the evidence is used. Before any analysis of system error is attempted, human error should either precede, or be part of any mutifactorial analysis within the system. This should involve all individuals who are part of such systems and interact with all additional operational, technological, environmental, and other physical, biological, and social components of systems which ultimately produce error and ensuing harm. However imperfect our understanding of the human contribution to error by perception, reasoning, decision-making, and action might be, we cannot leave it as a black box within the system concept and its analysis in lathology.

Whatever is offered as an evaluation of error will depend in the first place on the how cases, reports, and any other information will end up in our hands. The presentation of findings and their interpretation will be, after all biostatistical and epidemiological considerations, an exercise in critical thinking and decision-making.

References

1. Fabri PJ and Zayas-Castro JL. Human error, not communication and systems, underlies surgical complications. *Surgery*, 2008;144:557–65.
2. Wilson R McL, Harrison BT, Gibbert RW, Hamilton JD. An analysis of the causes of adverse events from the *Quality in Australian Health Care Study. MJA*, 1999;170:411–5.
3. Makeham MAB, Dovey SM, County M, Kidd MR. An international taxonomy for errors in general practice: A pilot study. *MJA*, 2002;177:68–72.
4. Delbanco T, Bell SK. Guilty, afraid and alone—Struggling with medical error. *N Engl J Med*, 2007;357(17):1682–3.
5. Jenicek M. *Medical Error and Harm. Understanding, Prevention, and Control.* Boca Raton, FL/London/New York: CRC Press/Taylor & Francis/Productivity Press, 2011.
6. Jenicek M and Hitchcock DL. *Evidence-Based Practice. Logic and Critical Thinking in Medicine.* Chicago: American Medical Association (AMA Press), 2005.
7. Jenicek M. *A Physician's Self-Paced Guide to Critical Thinking.* Chicago: American Medical Association (AMA Press), 2006.

8. Jenicek M. *Fallacy-Free Reasoning in Medicine. Improving Communication and Decision-Making in Research and Practice.* Chicago: American Medical Association (AMA Press), 2009.

9. Toulmin SA. *The Uses of Argument.* Updated Edition. Cambridge and New York: Cambridge University Press, 2003. (1st Edition: Idem, 1958).

10. Toulmin S, Rieke R, Janik A. *An Introduction to Reasoning.* 2nd Edition. New York: Collier Macmillan, 1984.

11. Jenicek M. Towards evidence-based critical thinking medicine? Uses of best evidence in flawless argumentations. *Med Sci Monit,* 2006;12(8):RA149–RA153.

12. Reason JA. *Human Error.* Cambridge and New York: Cambridge University Press, 1990.

13. Dictionary.com. *Mistake—10 Dictionary Results.* 4 p. at http://dictionary.reference.com/browse/mistake, retrieved Feb 10, 2009.

14. Merriam-Webster OnLine. *Mistake.* 1 p. at http://www.merriam-webster.com/dictionary/mistake[2], retrieved Feb 10, 2009.

15. Merriam-Webster OnLine. *Error.* 8 entries (2 p.) at http://www.merriam-webster.com/dictionary/error, retrieved Feb 10, 2009.

16. Dowden B. *The Internet Encyclopedia of Philosophy. Fallacies.* 44 p. at http://www.iep.utm.edu/f/fallacy.htm, retrieved Oct 31, 2006.

17. Henriksen K and Kaplan H. Hindsight bias, outcome knowledge and adaptive learning. *Qual Saf Health Care,* 2003;12(Suppl II):ii46–ii50.

18. Wikipedia, the free encyclopedia. *Cognitive Distortion.* 6 p. at https://en.wikipedia.org/wiki/Cognitive_distortion, retrieved July 12,2017.

19. Beck AT. *Depression. Causes and Treatment.* Philadelphia, PA: University of Philadelphia Press, 1972.

20. Burns DD. *The Feeling Good Handbook: Using the New Mood Therapy in Everyday Life.* New York: W. Morrow, 1989.

21. Chapter 21. Scientific decisions in choosing groups. (pp. 458–99) and Chapter 22. Scientific decisions for data and hypotheses (pp. 500–32) and elsewhere in: Feinstein AR. *Clinical Epidemiology. The Architecture of Clinical Research.* Philadelphia, PA and London: W.B. Saunders Company, 1985.

22. Absence of bias. Section 8.8.6 (pp. 206–9) in: Jenicek M. *Foundations of Evidence-Based Medicine.* Boca Raton, FL/London/New York/Washington, DC: The Parthenon Publishing Group, a CRC Press Company, 2003.

23. Lilford RJ, Mohammed MA, Branholts D, Hofer TP. The measurement of active errors: Methodological issues. *Qual Saf Health Care,* 2003;12(Suppl II):ii8–ii12.

24. Absence of bias. Section 6.8.6 (pp. 180–3) in: Jenicek M. *Epidemiology. The Logic of Modern Medicine.* Montreal: EPIMED International, 1995.

25. Redelmeier DA. The cognitive psychology of missed diagnoses. *Ann Intern Med,* 2005;142(2):115–20.

26. Paradis C. Bias in surgical research. *Ann Surg,* 2008;248(2):180–8.

27. Wikipedia, the free encyclopedia (John Manoogian III). *List of Cognitive Biases.* 19 p. at https://en.wikipedia.org/wiki/File:The_Cognitive_Bias_Codex_-_180%2B_biases_designed by_John_Manoogian_III_(jm3).png, retrieved Sep 15, 2017.

28. Croskerry P. The importance of cognitive errors in diagnosis and strategies to minimize them. *Acad Med,* 2003;78(8):775–80.

29. Wikipedia, the free encyclopedia. *List of Fallacies.* 13 p. at https://en.wikipedia.org/wiki/List_of_fallacies, last retrieved Dec 4, 2017.

30. Croskerry P. Cognitive and affective dispositions to respond. Chapter 32, pp. 219–27 (Table 32-2) in: Croskerry P, Cosby KS, Schenkel SM, Wears RL. *Patient Safety in Emergency Medicine.* Philadelphia, PA/Baltimore, MD/New York/London: Wolters Kluwer | Lippincott Williams & Wilkins (Health), 2009.

31. The Nizkor Project. *Fallacies.* Evolving number of p. (including subsites) at http://www.nizkor.org/features/fallacies/, retrieved Oct 10, 2006.

32. Thompson B. *Bruce Thompson's Fallacy Page.* Evolving number of p. (including subsites) at http://www.cuyamaca.net/bruce.thompson/Fallacies/intro_fallacies.asp, retrieved Nov 1, 2006.

33. Curtis GN. *Fallacy Files.* Evolving number of p. (including subsites) at http://www.fallacyfiles.org/taxonomy.html, retrieved Oct 30, 2006.

34. *EvoWiki Encyclopedia of Fallacies*. Evolving number of p. at http://wiki.cotch.net/index.php/List_of _fallacy_pages, retrieved Mar 12, 2007 and Oct 29, 2006.
35. Downes S. *Stephen's Guide to the Logical Fallacies*. Brandon, Manitoba, Canada, 1995–1998. Evolving number of p. (including subsites) at http://www.intrepidsoftware.com/fallacy/welcome.php, retrieved Dec 06, 2004. See also http://www.assiniboinec.mb.ca/user/downes/fallacy.
36. Damer TE. *Attacking Faulty Reasoning. A Practical Guide to Fallacy-Free Arguments*. 5th edition. Belmont, CA: Thomson Wadsworth, 2005. (2nd Edition: Belmont, CA: Wadsworth Publishing Company, A Division of Wadsworth, Inc., 1987.)
37. Holt T. *Logical Fallacies. An Encyclopedia of Errors of Reasoning*. An evolving number of p. at http://www.logicalfallacies.info/, retrieved Oct 10, 2006.
38. Anon. *Logical Fallacies and the Art of Debate*. 10 p. at http://www.csun.edu/~dgw61315/fallacies.html, retrieved Feb 17, 2007.
39. Lindsay D. *A List of Fallacious Arguments*. 23 and other evolving p. at http://www.don-lindsay-archive .org/skeptic/arguments.html, retrieved Feb 15, 2007.
40. Lindsay D. *A List of Fallacious Arguments*. 20 pages at http://www.don-lindsay-archive.org/sceptic /arguments.html, retrieved March 25, 2009.
41. Changing Minds.org. *Fallacies: Alphabetic List (Full List)*. 3 p. and subsites at http://changingminds .org/disciplines/argument/falalcies/falalcies_alpha_htm, retrieved March 25, 2009.
42. BambooWeb Dictionary. *List of Cognitive Biases*. Variable number of pages bias by bias at http://www .bambooweb.com/articles/L/i/List_of_cognitive_biases.html, retrieved Mar 4, 2009.
43. Gunderman RB. Biases in radiologic reasoning. *AJR*, 2009;192(March):561–4.
44. Feinstein AR. Clinical biostatistics LVII. A glossary of neologisms in quantitative clinical science. *Clin Pharm Ther*, 1981;(Oct);30(4):564–77.
45. Feinstein AR. *Clinimetrics*. New Haven, CT and London: Yale University Press, 1987.
46. Feinstein AR. *Clinical Biostatistics*. St. Louis, MO: C.V. Mosby, 1970.
47. Feinstein AR. *Clinical Epidemiology. The Architecture of Clinical Research*. Philadelphia, PA and London: W.B. Saunders Company, 1985.
48. Croskerry P. Perspectives in diagnostic failure and patient safety. *Healthcare Quarterly,*2012;15(Special Issue):50–6.
49. de Bono E. *Edward de Bono's Thinking Course*. Harlow, Essex: BBC Active, 2006. (Lateral and parallel thinking)
50. de Bono E. *Lateral Thinking. A Textbook of Creativity*. London: Penguin Books, 1990. (Reprint from Ward Lock Education, 1970).
51. de Groot V, Beckerman H, Lankhorst GJ, Bouter LM. How to measure comorbidity: A critical review of available methods. *J Clin Epidemiol*, 2003;56:221–9.
52. Decision analysis and decision-making in medicine. Beyond intuition, guts and flair. Chapter 13, pp. 341–78 in Ref. 40.
53. Detmer DE, Fruback DG, Gassner K. Heuristics and biases in medical decision-making. *J Med Educ*, 1978;53(Aug):682–3.
54. Caruth DL, Hadlogten GD. Mistakes to avoid in decision-making. *Innovative Leader,*2000;9(7), 2 p. at http://www.winstobrill.com/bril001/html/article_index/articles/451-500/article477_body..., retrieved Feb 2, 2009.
55. Edworthy J, Hignett S, Hellier E, Stubbs D. Patient safety. *Ergonomics*, 2006;49(5–6):439–43. See also other related articles in this issue.
56. Gawron VJ, Drury CG, Fairbanks RJ, Berger RC. Medical error and human factors engineering. *Am J Med Qual*, 2006;21(1):57–67.
57. Drury CG. Ergonomics and the quality movement. *Ergonomics*, 1997;40(3):249–64.
58. Basic approaches to assessment: Structure, process, and outcome. Chapter 3, pp. 77–128 in: Donabedian A. *Explorations in Quality Assessment and Monitoring. Volume I. The Definition of Quality and Approaches to Its Assessment*. Ann Arbor, MI: Health Administration Press, 1980.
59. Jenicek M. *Epidemiology. The Logic of Modern Medicine*. Montreal: EPIMED International, 1995.
60. Jenicek M. *Foundations of Evidence-Based Medicine*. Boca Raton, FL/London, New York/Washington, DC: The Parthenon Publishing Group, a CRC Press Company, 2003.

61. *A Dictionary of Epidemiology.* 5th Edition. Edited by M. Porta. Oxford and New York: Oxford University Press, 2008.
62. Alemi F. Probabilistic risk analysis is practical. *Q Manage Health Care,* 2007;16(4):300–10.
63. Alemi F. Tutorial on discrete hazard functions. *Q Manage Health Care,* 2007;16(4):311–20.
64. Jenicek M. Clinical case reports and case series research in evaluating surgery. Part I. The context: General aspects of evaluation applied to surgery. *Med Sci Monit,* 2008;14(9):RA133–143.
65. Jenicek M. Clinical case reports and case series research in evaluating surgery. Part II. The content and form: Uses of single case reports and case series research in surgical specialties. *Med Sci Monit,* 2008;14(10):RA149–RA162.
66. The justification of surgery. Chapter 4, pp. 95–162 in: Donabedian A. *Explorations in Quality Assessment and Monitoring. Volume III. The Methods and Finding of Quality Assessment and Monitoring: An Illustrated Analysis.* Ann Arbor, MI: Health Administration Press, 1985.

Chapter 10

Thinking to Decide in Clinical and Community Medicine: Subjects, Thinking Tools, and Vehicles for the Best Possible Decisions in Practice and Research*

Executive Summary

Reasoning for the purpose of understanding and reasoning for the purpose of making decisions are two distinct but complementary approaches to managing problems of health and disease. All decision-making processes require reasoning and judgment, as well as choices within these stages: recognition → formulation → generation of alternatives → information and evidence search → selection from among options of what to do → action.

Decisions in patient and community care (health programs) can be made using either structured or unstructured approaches. Structured approaches include consensus, various mathematical models, and clinical decision analysis techniques. Unstructured approaches rely on the clinician's information inserted within the decision process. In this way, decision-making activities in medicine involve approaches, techniques, and tools that both seek

---

* This chapter is based, with the permission of the publisher, on multiple elements, presented in Chapter 4 in: Jenicek M. *A Primer on Clinical Experience in Medicine. Reasoning, Decision-Making, and Communication in Health Sciences.* Boca Raton, FL/London/New York: CRC Press/Taylor & Francis/Productivity Press, 2013. Revised, updated, edited, expanded.

direction and provide direction. Cost-benefit analysis may be used as part of a decision-making process. They assess efficacy, effectiveness, efficiency, or equity of decisions, actions, and their consequences. All these processes are useful to answer the various complementary questions they reflect.

The decision-making process is also a kind of argumentative process. Modern argumentation uses in the decision-making domain prove useful and necessary. Tools which provide directions include both tactical tools such as clinical algorithm development, uses, and evaluation, and strategic tools such as clinical practice guidelines. Evidence-based clinical decision-making focuses on generally available evidence for care, its importance, and its applicability to individual patients and their groups of special interest. Assessment of the workplace setting in which decisions are made is integrated within the evidence-based decision-making process.

Strategic tools as a structured process are expected to limit variations, reduce costs, make decisions more "scientific," and have an educational value. They are not prescriptive, but are clinical protocols; distinctions have to be made and respected.

Decision-making-related fallacies are often of a heuristic nature given the reality of clinical practice, especially in emergency and surgery settings. All newcomers to the environment and reality of clinical and community care must understand how decisions are made and their strengths and weaknesses in order to adopt the best medical care options.

In This Chapter

Executive Summary.. 287

Thoughts, Thinkers, and Things to Think About 289

Introductory Comments 291

10.1 Decision Theory, Decision Analysis, and Decision-Making in General and in Medicine ... 293

10.2 How Decisions Are Made in Daily Life.. 294

    10.2.1 Direction Searching Tools through Unstructured Ways of Decision-Making..... 295

    10.2.2 Direction Searching Tools through Structured Ways of Decision-Making 297

        10.2.2.1 Decision Analysis... 297

        10.2.2.2 Cost-Benefit/Effectiveness/Utility Analysis in Clinical
                  Decision-Making...301

        10.2.2.3 Decisions as Conclusions of an Argumentative Process........................ 302

    10.2.3 Direction-Giving Tools in Decision-Making 305

        10.2.3.1 Tactical Tools: Clinical Algorithms 305

        10.2.3.2 Evidence-Based Clinical Decision-Making Path 310

        10.2.3.3 Strategic Tools for Making the Right Decisions: Clinical Practice
                  Guidelines and Clinical Protocols 310

10.3 Illustrative Fallacies in the Decision-Making Domain 314

    10.3.1 Fallacies from an Individual Perspective: Individual-Related Fallacies................. 314

10.3.1.1 Reasoning-Based Fallacies: Fallacies Related to the Thinking Process
behind Decision-Making 314
10.3.1.2 Fallacies Related to Decisions Themselves 316
10.3.2 Collective-Related Fallacies: Groupthink 317
Let Us Conclude... 318
References.. 319

Thoughts, Thinkers, and Things to Think About

*Nothing is more difficult, and therefore
more precious, than to be able to decide.*
Napoléon Bonaparte (1724–1821)
Not only in military arts!

Thought is behaviour in rehearsal.
Sigmund Freud (1856–1939)
in the early 1930s
And it is expected from us!

*A physician who is 90 per cent "certain"
about any decision will always seek additional information in the hope that it will
increase the "confidence" with which he
makes such a decision. The decision …
will be either correct or incorrect, and the
outcome is independent of the confidence
with which the decision is reached. When
additional information cannot possibly alter
the decision, but only gives rise to a greater
sense of comfort on the part of the physician,
such additional information is of no benefit
to the patient. Its only benefit is in reducing
the discomfort of the physician.*
Harold M. Schoolman (1924–2009), 1977
**Even this is sometimes enough for an
overworked health professional, even if
he or she knows this kind of limit!**

*Efficiency is concerned with doing
things right.
Effectiveness is doing the right things.*
Peter F. Drucker (1909–2005)
Man who invented management (1977)
Let us add this to our Glossary!

*A problem is defined and isolated; informa-
tion is gathered; alternatives are set forth;
an end is established; means are created to
achieve the end; a choice is made.*
James McGregor Burns (1918–2014)
Founder of Leadership Studies (1978)
Way to go, Jim!

*1. The information you have is not what
you want.
2. The information you want is not what
you need.
3. The information you need is not
available.
4. The information you can obtain costs
more than you want to pay.*
Finagle's Laws of Information
(John W. Campbell Jr.)
in the 1940s
**In many instances, one must decide
anyway!**

*People whose lives are affected by a decision
must be part of the process of arriving at
that decision.*
John Nesbitt (1910–1960)
Narrator, Announcer, Producer,
Screenwriter (1984)
How true about our patients!

Doctor, you are asking me what I think
about what should be done in my case? But,
I am paying you as an educated person in
medicine, which I am not, to decide for me.
So, decide!
As told by a patient to the author in his
young years in a dynamic and changing
country whose values he was learning and
understanding.
It does not always work that way!

Good evidence is not necessarily a high priority
for intervention. In fact, a high priority for
intervention may often lack good evidence.
Evidence of priority is not a priority of evidence.
It is just additional evidence. Clinicians must
learn not only how to auscultate the heart, count
blood cells, or remove an appendix, but also how
to arrive at the right decisions.

Introductory Comments

Mastering proper reasoning is a vital step in mastering correct decision-making in medicine. But what are the initiatives and contributions of the domain of decision-making within medicine? The process of finding, producing, and evaluating clinical and other evidence in the health sciences and professions must be extended toward methods for using said evidence. Decision-making as a thinking and reasoning process is one such extension. Its current definitions illustrate that it is not only a thinking process but it also implies methodology from epidemiology, health economics and management, and medicine itself. Health economics, however, are not forgotten in today's evidence-oriented medicine.

In the spirit of the above, the health economics/clinical economics/economic analysis/economic evaluation/cost-effectiveness/cost-benefit analysis complex was reported to the attention of general medicine, gastroenterology, oncology, orthopedics, nephrology, internal medicine, and elsewhere. Hence, how can we define the decision domain in health sciences and clinical professions?

In public health, the term ***decision theory*** means *"a specialized branch of logic that provides a conceptual framework and formal rules for decision-making."*[5]

Decision analysis is: *"a system of logic that uses elements of game theory and operational research to identify all available choices and their outcomes at each stage in designing a plan for preventive or therapeutic interventions. Each of the choices and probabilities of the outcome of each choice can be visually presented in a decision tree. The relative value of each outcome can be expressed as a utility or quality of life measurement."*[1,5]

In psychology, decision-making is regarded as *"the cognitive process resulting in the selection of a belief or a course of action among several alternative possibilities. Decision-making is the process of identifying and choosing alternatives based on the values and preferences of the decision-maker."*[2]

Across the literature, the concepts of decision-making, economic analysis, and contributions to the terms and processes of cost-effectiveness, and cost-benefit analyses may be overlapping and often blurred.

Decision-making in medicine is the process of selecting what to do in preventive and curative care from among a range of already understood options, while also taking into account the health problem as a whole.

Let us consider the following examples:

■ A fetal-pelvic disproportion is found in an expectant mother—what should we do? Given our clinical findings, past experience, and medical literature, should we perform a forceps delivery, normal delivery, or a cesarean section?

■ An ambulatory patient complains of a sore throat. Should we prescribe antibiotics or not with or without further clinical and paraclinicial workup?

■ An elderly retired steelworker, after a recent multiple coronary bypass surgery, is almost unable to walk due to advanced and general osteoarthritis. Should a knee replacement be considered for him?

■ In community medicine, a new vaccine against a viral infection is available for a community with low herd immunity against it. Should we implement an early immunization program to prevent an outbreak and further disease spread? Even if we have enough good evidence about what works in the circumstances, how should we use it? How should we reason to arrive at the best solution for those patients' problems?

This chapter should at least in part introduce us to the reasoning pathways of clinical problem solving.

Making correct decisions may be challenging not only when working with new, advanced, expensive, and sophisticated technologies, but also in daily clinical practice when dealing with everyday problems! The latter, due to their sheer number, also require the best possible decisions to benefit as many patients as possible and to minimize the costs and risks of less appropriate decisions. Understanding decision theory, decision analysis, and decision-making help us find answers to our daily questions. As we will see in this chapter, good clinical decision-making and its success depend, as do many other endeavors in medicine, on the correct knowledge, attitudes, skills, and dispositions in the decision-making domain.

Knowledge as part of the cognitive domain *encompasses both retention of data and information about the subject, and the capacity to apply them to specific tasks.*[3] Errors occur if the operator's knowledge, especially when it is evidence-based, is deficient and insufficient.

Attitudes as part of the affective domain may be considered as *learned tendencies to act and decide in a consistent manner toward a particular object and situation.* In the context of decision-making, it also refers to having *the capacity to sense and recognize the situation, act in a controlled, predictable, and consistent manner relevant to the problem at hand.*[3] The decision maker's attitudes must be appropriate for the task to avoid errors in decision-making.

Skills as part of the psychomotor domain, are defined in general as *expertness, practical ability, facility in doing something, dexterity, and tact.*[1] In the decision-making domain, they are considered to be the abilities to use a structured decision-making methodology to solve problems in practice. Errors may occur if the decision maker's skills are inadequate for the successful execution of the task.

Disposition means the *right state of mind and inclination regarding something, the natural or prevailing aspect of one's mind as manifested in behavior and relationships with patients and peers. A disposition is a habit, a preparation, a state of readiness, or a tendency to act in a specific way.*[4] Acquiring an appropriate disposition is also an objective of this chapter.

At the end of this chapter, the reader should ask himself or herself:

- What do I know about how to make the right decisions? Is my knowledge actively or passively acquired?
- What are my attitudes (values and judgment of them) toward decision-making to solve my clinical problem? Do I consider them worthy of consideration and why? How do I foresee their role, success, or failure?
- Am I equipped, trained, and experienced enough to mentally and physically make the right decisions in clinical and community care?
- Are my evaluation skills pertaining to my decisions good enough to propose, implement, and assess them?

The pages that follow should help provide answers to these questions.

10.1 Decision Theory, Decision Analysis, and Decision-Making in General and in Medicine

Until now, we have dealt with health problems by trying to better understand the meaning of what we perceive: the problem, the patient or patients, and related evidence. What do we know about how to make decisions regarding what to do with them?

Decision theory is the theory of rational decisions, often called **rational choice theory**.[5] Since the seventeenth century, social sciences, political and business sciences have developed decision theory as a set of quantitative methods for reaching optimal decisions. To summarize decision theory in brief, initial solvable decision proposals and conditions are linked to possible consequences, which are not known with certainty, and expressed as sets of probabilistic outcomes. Outcomes are assigned "utility" values based on the assessment and preference of the decision maker. An optimal decision is one that maximizes the expected utility.[6]

Decision theory in medicine has been the subject of developments, reviews, and critiques since the 1970s.[7] An even more recent view outlines that decision theory must:[8]

■ be evidence-based;
■ be explanatory and predictive;
■ be broader than a hypothesis; and
■ ideally, encompass relevant data and prior theory, rather than reinvent the wheel or ignore contrary evidence.

Decision-making requires not only reasoning and judgment, but also choices. Memory, reasoning, and concept formation lay behind the steps and stages of the decision-making process.[9] These steps and stages are

recognition
↓
formulation
↓
generation of alternatives
↓
information (evidence) search
↓
selection
↓
(resulting in) action

The most valuable experience, methodology, and applications for clinical research, practice, and health management produced by experts in medical decision-making domain is now available in an increasing number of ad hoc reader-friendly books[10–16] and articles.[17] This and other experiences are also summarized in a chapter of our *Foundations of Evidence-Based Medicine*[15] and in two other monographs,[18,19] which provide additional background information and an expanded bibliography for this chapter.

10.2 How Decisions Are Made in Daily Life

Any decisions, including whether to treat or not, to further pursue a diagnostic work up, and to follow up and care for a patient over a prolonged period of time, can be made either in an unstructured way or in a structured way as an organized step-by-step process. The unstructured approach is most often emotionally motivated.

Other motivations and reasons are

- Teachers and older colleagues are often **blindly idolized**: They are never wrong; we do what they do.
- We are often **emotionally attached** to what has been laboriously learned. Why adopt and practice laparoscopic surgery if our proven general surgery was always good enough?
- Sometimes, **clinical ritualism** is *de rigueur*: This diagnostic maneuver is a part of the "complete examination" let us do it then.
- Sometimes, decisions are dictated by the **defensive practice of medicine**. Physicians may wish to avoid lawsuits and do not want to risk performing surgery if it is not the preferred treatment method. They may also "over-immunize" children or travelers.
- "**Something must be done**" often rules. There is the "*art of doing nothing*" and the "*art of waiting*." An old surgical saying holds that "*It takes two years to get into the abdomen and twenty years to learn to stay out.*"
- Sometimes decisions are made **without taking into account epidemiological information and methods**.
- **Politically motivated** decisions like screening or immunization campaigns fortunately occur less and less frequently.
- Some decisions are dictated by an **extraneous power** and/or justified socially, historically, culturally, or by faith. The debate about abortions is not over.
- Simple "**blind willingness to please**" decisions are still made. Anything that pleases the patient, the physician and/or onlookers or any parties connected to the patient may take precedence over rational decision-making.

Unstructured decisions in medicine are frequent; sometimes they work well, other times they do not. However, they are most often feasible in busy practices, due to their time, human, and material resource constraints.

10.2.1 Direction Searching Tools through Unstructured Ways of Decision-Making

Unstructured approaches to decision-making are also known as shortcut decision-making. Shortcut decision-making does not necessarily result in longer-term internal change.[20] Some unstructured decision-making methods are listed below.

1. **Gut feeling exploration**,[15–17] focusing on intuitive feelings such as "*sudden awareness of a clinical problem through thoughts that come to one's mind without apparent effort as something potentially serious and worthy of solution.*"[17] It may be based on a considerable wealth of evidence, experience, and knowledge; it is not "blind."
2. **Distilled clinical judgment** includes knowledge of facts, experience, intuition, common sense, and gut feeling.[20] It goes beyond gut feeling; decisions are made on the basis of hypothetico-deductive thinking, from major *a priori* formulated clues to the most probable diagnosis and treatment of possible problems. If a patient develops a fever after a kidney transplant, it may be equally due to an infection or to rejection of the organ. In the case of an erroneous diagnosis, antibiotics would not prevent organ rejection with its possible fatal consequences for the patient, but immuno-suppression would not help in the case of an infection. In such situations, a "steepest ascent type of thinking"[21] is mandatory.

3. The **Gestalt** or **pattern recognition** method is useful in other situations and allows for appropriate "right" decision-making. A patient with nocturnal distress and dyspnea, who sleeps on several pillows and holds the bed frame with both hands 'to breathe better,' exhibits a pattern suggesting cardiac insufficiency.

4. When competing health conditions are at stake, two decisions can be considered. In a "**minimax**" approach, a solution is sought which would give a minimum probability of a maximum loss. In a situation where a patient may have a streptococcal infection of the throat, and laboratory testing is not available, a clinician may decide to prescribe antibiotics to prevent any late systemic complications (maximum loss) of this infection. In a "**maximin**" or 'Las Vegas approach,' decisions are made to reach a maximum probability of a minimal loss. In cancer medicine, a chemotherapeutic or physical agent leading to fewer secondary effects in cases of competent efficacy is often chosen for treatment.

5. Decisions made on the basis of the **magic of numbers**. Is something which is "statistically highly significant" always better? How much and in what practical terms?

6. **Heuristic decision-making** happens in extremis of restraining and constricting conditions of emergency, crisis, or threat, whatever their cause and reason might be. It may often be a kind of "black box" of decision-making for which reasoning mechanisms must still be analyzed and better understood. This kind of *"rule of thumb"* decision-making is well known to all clinicians. It may lead both to right or wrong decisions.

7. **Other shortcut decisions**, most often without detectable heuristics, occur as a result of:
   a. **reaction** as an immediate response bypassing the cortical decision centers.
   b. **conditioning** as a pre-programmed reaction based on past experience and training.
   c. **habit** as simple repetitions of what worked last time.
   d. **intuition** as "**choices without thinking**" is the product of a subconscious mind searching through our experiences and finding a good match for what we are facing.
   e. **using scripts** as prepared short or protracted steps for what to say or do that we keep for various situations: *"How are we doing today?"* in sales instead of *"Hello"* without expecting an answer. At the bedside, we expect an answer, even to a script.

All in all, decision-making is mental processes which can be implemented using two different systems, each outlined below:

System 1: A heuristic process

A heuristic process is an instant "rules of thumb" reaction without calculations or deliberations. Educated guess, trial and error, anchoring and adjustments (starting the decision process by something already known which is fitted into a specific situation or individual), availability of related information, or representativeness of first impressions are all part of heuristics, both in general and specifically with health sciences. From a general decision-making perspective, heuristics is considered a parallel-processing system good for making rough, best possible estimates in a fast and as realistic a way as possible, in a given setting and availability of information.[24]

> **System 2: A structured assessment process**
>
> A second approach is based on a serial and structured processing of essential, necessary, and available information to make a decision about a given problem. In health sciences, Croskerry[23] considers a good part of clinical practice as being part of System 1. System 2 is an approach that has been developed over recent decades and encompasses decision-making experience and methodology.

In this chapter, let us have a look especially at System 2.

10.2.2 Direction Searching Tools through Structured Ways of Decision-Making

Human nature of patients and physicians means that information in medicine is never complete and never entirely true. Decisions are always probabilistic, no matter how confident the attitude of senior colleagues may be. As a result, decisions are always made with a variable degree of uncertainty. However, this does not mean that decisions are inevitably made in a disorganized and chaotic way—they can be structured. These structured approaches to decisions may be arrived at in different ways. This structured clinical thinking represents the basis of **decision analysis** in medicine. Some of these structured approaches are listed here.

1. It is important that agreements be reached between several specialists and experienced professionals in the field. One approach is to produce a **consensus** of the group, representing either a unanimous or a prevalent agreement by its members. There are several highly organized and structured approaches for making a consensus decision. For example, in the so-called **Delphi method**, the least important (or frequent) opinions are progressively removed from the array of choices. Such a reduced set is re-evaluated, additional deletions are made, and the whole process is repeated until the group reaches the best possible option. Decisions can also be rated.
2. Decision analysis can also be based on several **mathematical models**, such as decision trees, Markov models, Monte Carlo simulation, survival analysis, and the hazard function, fuzzy logic, or sensitivity analysis.[24] Only decision analysis in general will be discussed here.
3. **Computer-assisted decision-making** facilitates the use of structured approaches in medical decision-making, and allows decisions to be made on the basis of a wider body of information, data, and premises, which go well beyond the capacity of a single deciding individual or group.

10.2.2.1 Decision Analysis

A structured approach to making the best possible medical decisions is accomplished through a process called **clinical decision analysis**. This method is already used in finance, business, military affairs, industry, and economics. Why not also use this approach in medicine? This approach must take into account the unique medical environment—considering human nature and the patient's opinion.

The clinical decision analysis approach, as an organized intellectual process, can be used provided that the required data and information can be accumulated, and that there is sufficient time, conditions, and need to use this process. The basic vocabulary and the meaning of the clinical decision analysis approach is outlined here.

Conceptually, a **medical decision** represents the choice of the best option to assess risk (explanatory decisions), to treat patients (managerial decisions), or to make a prognosis (both explanatory and managerial, if treatment decisions are involved). The process of making a medical decision (medical decision-making) is a process by which one arrives at a given medical decision, the latter being the result or endpoint of such a process.

Decision analysis tackles precisely such situations. It is a systematic approach to decision-making under conditions of uncertainty.[25] It has also been defined as *"a derivative of operations research and game theory to identify all available choices, and potential outcomes of each, in a series of decisions that have to be made (e.g., about aspects of patient care as diagnostic procedures, preventive and therapeutic regimens, prognosis). Epidemiological data play a large part in determining the probabilities of outcomes following each potential choice."*[26]

Clinical decision analysis is an application of decision analysis in a clinical setting.

It has three main components: **choices available** either to the patient, his or her physician or both; **chances** as probabilities of outcome for each choice; and **values of treatment** options and their outcomes for interested parties. It systematizes (organizes) decision-making, clarifies decision-making, and leads to the "correctness" of decisions. A **decision tree** is one of the most important graphical, analytical, and probability and quantification-based structure of clinical decision analysis. Its objective is to lead us to the best decisions about diagnosis, treatment, prognosis, and other aspects of quality care which are most beneficial for the patient and other involved parties.

Clinical decisions incorporated into the decision tree are not only decisions to treat or not to treat. They may also be concerned with whether or not to add another (presumably more modern and better) diagnostic method in serial or parallel testing to the clinical process preceding treatment decisions, additional medical or nursing care following an operation, social support, and home care to convalescent patients and so on.

Figure 10.1 is an example of a decision tree used to visualize a situation in emergency medicine. We want to decide the best way to treat a patient presenting an acute abdomen. How can this be done, analyzed, and interpreted? Only a shortened summary and principles of this decision-making tool will be given here for our elementary understanding; more details, especially the computational aspects may be found elsewhere.[27,15,11] Interested readers may also notice that decision trees can cover single stage events like the problem to operate or not with ensuing outcomes and their values. Many clinical problems, especially chronic and episodic issues, in which events may occur repetitively at various moments in time or after multiple interventions, have different values and utilities. Such disease courses are analyzed by Markov models which divide them into multiple "Markov states" with their own events/decisions/outcomes/utilities sets which follow in time.[28] Our example is from the former simpler situation.

The obvious objective of this type of decision analysis using a decision tree approach is to find, among all options in a given clinical situation, the decision or way that would be the most beneficial to the patient. As paradoxical as it may appear, the approach described here, which is

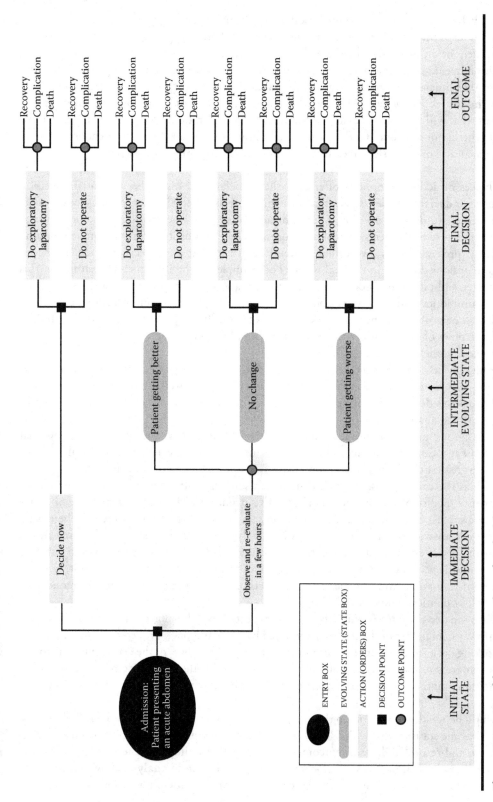

Figure 10.1 Graphic representation of a decision tree. Example of an acute abdomen decision challenge. (Redrawn from Jenicek M. *Epidemiology. The Logic of Modern Medicine.* **Montréal: EPIMED International, 1995 and from Jenicek M.** *A Primer on Clinical Experience in Medicine.* **Boca Raton/London/New York: CRC Press, 2013 [References 18 and 19]. Reproduced with permission.)**

full of probabilities, values, and computations, contributes much to the humanitarian aspect of medicine. It helps find, by objective means, a better clinical procedure or a choice of treatment for a given patient or for particular disease sufferers in general.

Decision trees are temporal and spatial representations, in a proper clinical sequence of options, offered to the clinician at specific points within clinical work. The tree is comprised of a series of **decision nodes** (conventionally identified by squares) and its **outcome nodes** including probabilities of what will happen after each decision under consideration. Decisions included in these tools are whether or not to add a diagnostic method, to treat or not to treat, to choose different treatments, and so on. Decision trees are structures containing three basic elements:

1. Choices of action or options offered to the clinician and his or her patient(s). Decision points or **decision nodes** (squares in our Figure and elsewhere) indicate options for example, immediate or delayed decision, operate or not. More than one choice may be presented at each juncture in the decision-making process. Wherever possible, and without abandoning reality, preferably only two options should be attached to each decision node. However, more options do exist in the real world. For example, in the introductory example in this chapter, a physician must decide whether to treat a sore throat by antibiotics right away, not give antibiotics at all, or give antibiotics later depending on the result of a throat culture.
2. Chance or **probability nodes** (marked as circles in our figure and elsewhere) or probabilities of outcomes of each choice, such as recovery, complications, or death. They may follow each moment (node) of choice.
3. **Values** given to each given outcome or **end utilities**. Case fatality, recovery or complications rates, related monetary, managerial or operational values as well as the patient's own values may be considered and analyzed as endpoints of a decision tree. They represent final points from which analysis starts.

   Assigning utility to an outcome is a question of judgment, and we already know that judgment means attributing a value to something. In fact, the assignment of utility is one of the greatest challenges of decision analysis. Should the outcome be some monetary value (such as the cost of subsequent cure and care), some measure of pain and/or suffering, the patient's quality of life, impact on a patient's surrounding, a physician's measure of therapeutic success or failure, or a score based on some or all of the above elements? There is no clear-cut answer to this problem. Decision analysis and its solution are valid only in the context of pre-established probabilities and utilities. These values are given to each outcome by the patient in the first place, by a physician in terms of a desired realistic result, or by an administrator or community health policy decision-maker in terms of economic (monetary), social, or political gains.
4. Once the decision tree is built, the highest expected overall value ("utility") from available pathways, 'branches of the tree' is determined by a **folding back procedure**. This consists of working back from the final points or the "tips of the branches" of the decision tree, through the progressive multiplication of end utilities and probabilities of outcomes following each decision point, up to the initial question reflected by the first decision point of the tree.

Having a better idea of what to do this way, we may consider a **sensitivity analysis** ('robustness' analysis for some statisticians) which looks at how a decision would change if probabilities, reference values, and/or probabilities of outcomes and their value (utility) were to change. Balancing various likelihoods of clinical risks and benefits through a **threshold analysis** allows determining situations and ('toss up') moments from which benefits for the patient outweigh risks of clinical procedures of interest and preference.[29] As we may see, this method systematically assesses essential treatments available, possible outcomes, and desirability of each outcome of interest.

Decision trees are one example of a type of clinical decision analysis. Considered more broadly, there are both advantages and disadvantages to the wider topic of clinical decision analysis.

Clinical Decision Analysis Advantages	Clinical Decision Analysis Disadvantages
• Much less costly than the search for the best decision through experimental research, which is often sophisticated in design and complex in execution and analysis. • Can be easily translated into clinical decisions and public health policies. • An important tool in medical education. It allows students to better structure their thinking and to navigate the maze of decision-making.	• Less valuable if clinical data and information are of poor quality and/or uncertain. • May take up precious time in emergency situations, especially if left in the hands of a less-experienced decision analyst. • Utilities may have different values and weights in different individuals, be they patients, doctors, or community decision-makers (administrators, politicians, economists, etc.) or those of individual patients versus their community.

10.2.2.2 Cost-Benefit/Effectiveness/Utility Analysis in Clinical Decision-Making

While classical clinical trials answer the main question about treatment effectiveness to solve a patient's problem, economic evaluation like cost-effectiveness evaluation is a valuable "piggyback approach." This yields additional important information[30] for several purposes which may all be used as outcomes and utilities, including hospitalization, physician visits, and tests. Today's economic assessment of medical malpractice also includes decision analyzes using decision trees, Markov models from the prognosis (survival) domain, and receiver operating characteristic curves analysis from the diagnosis domain.

Many physicians still dislike taking costs into consideration when making a clinical decision. However, every clinical decision has its additional price, not only in monetary terms, but also in terms of complications, incapacity, handicaps, and so on. In this context, a **cost-effectiveness analysis** *seeks to determine the costs and effectiveness of an activity, or to compare similar alternative activities to determine the relative degree to which they will obtain the desired objectives and outcomes.*[26] On the other hand, a **cost-utility analysis** is an economic analysis in which outcomes are measured in terms of their social value. A widely used utility-based measure is *quality-adjusted life years.*[26]

The economic evaluation of medical care assesses four aspects of care:[26 modified]

1. **Efficacy**: A beneficial result under ideal conditions. An answer to *"Can it work?"* question.
2. **Effectiveness**: Beneficial and other results under "ordinary," prevailing or customary conditions and patients. An answer to *"Does it work?"* question.

> 3. **Efficiency**: Effects of the end results in proportion to the effort (human and material resources, time) invested in the healthcare activity. An answer to the question "*What is the cost for what result?*"
> 4. **Equity**: Fairness and impartiality of healthcare activities may also have a cause or effect on care. Equitable access to healthcare is an important economic concern. An answer to "*How well are costs and benefits distributed?*" question.

In **clinical decision analysis**, the **cost-benefit approach** is a "scaled down and reoriented analysis" in accordance with the definition above. Monetary values are often replaced by clinically important "costs," such as operative case fatality, case fatality in treated and untreated individuals in the general population, occurrence of side effects of diagnosis and/or treatment, and occurrence of co-morbidity and its impact. Survival or any other measure of "positive" impact is used as an indicator of "benefit." The subject of evaluation is **efficiency** based on the question "What does it cost, and of what value is it?" in clinical terms. Monetary values can be taken into consideration, but they are not the principal focus of analysis. Rather, they are integrated into a larger frame of clinical considerations.

10.2.2.3 Decisions as Conclusions of an Argumentative Process

Just like medical understanding, the medical decision-making process should be considered an exercise in argumentation as already outlined in Chapter 4. Clinical decision analysis, as explained in Section 10.2.2 provides elements specific to decision analysis. In turn, these elements provide the building blocks of an argumentative process leading to clinical care and research decisions. It does not replace evidence-based decision-making as originally suggested by Dickinson.[31] Let us view decision-making in an integrative manner through Toulmin's modern argumentation model, as adapted by Rieke et al.[32] and modified here for the domain of decision-making.

TOULMIN'S MODERN ARGUMENTATION MODEL, ADAPTED FOR DECISION-MAKING

> 1. **Claim and conclusion**: Our decision to treat or not, pursue a diagnostic workup, or provide additional long term care given the prognosis is a **claim** stemming from argumentation and the **conclusion** of its supportive process.
> 2. **Grounds**: What our examination of the patient, records, and knowledge about conditions and care reveal are essentially the **grounds** for argumentation. Grounds must be based on good evidence. Grounds for argumentation in the decision-making context are statements made about persons (patients and/or healthcare professionals), conditions (care), events (clinical interventions, related outcomes), or things (methods and techniques used, etc.) representing the available support to provide a reason for a claim.
> 3. **Warrant**: As a **warrant**, clinical decision analysis should provide specific information based on the decision process about the understandings and rules related to the subject of the decision process which suggests whether or not the clinical decision is plausible.

Warrants, as they are in any other domain of argumentation, are broader, more general statements and understandings or "rules" related to the issue as a basis for the claim. The focus of the warrant is whether or not the decision is plausible.

4. **Backing**: In the decision-making domain, **backing** refers to specific support for the claim including instances, statistics, testimony values, or credibility distinct to the grounds or warrant.[32 modified] Past experience from basic and clinical research and practice from other and similar related situations are used most often as warrants and/or backing. Backing information is very specific to the claim at hand whereas the warrants are past experience or evidence from basic clinical research and practice in general. Backing includes testimonies in medicine as evidence in support of a fact or statement, or statements based on personal experience and/or knowledge. They may be good or bad if the claim is implausible, or if it goes beyond reporting a person's professional and other personal qualifications, experiences, and competencies. In some cases this kind of very specific backing may be invaluable.

5. **Qualifier**: The qualifier is an expressed perception of the degree of certainty about or claims and conclusions. It can only be derived from evidence based on past experience.

6. **Claim(s)**: Claims are statements that we want others to accept and act upon, gaining their *adherence*, i.e., informed support of involved parties. For Rieke et al.,[32] claims may be:

    a. *Factual claims* are confirmed by objective data from reliable sources, for example affirming that certain conditions exist in the material world and could be observed. Research conclusions (smoking causes lung cancer), clinical care progress notes in patient charts as "**SOAPs**" (**s**ubjective observations and perception, **o**bjective clinical and paraclinical findings, **a**ssessment of the patient in the light of the above, and plan for further care of an observed clinical case) or orders (this surgical patient must also be seen by an internist or clinical pharmacologist) are factual claims.

    b. *Value claims* assert the quality of a person, place, thing, or idea. Making a claim about how good, or how bad, a particular clinical facility is, or specialist, or procedure, is ascribing a value to a claim.

    c. *Policy claims* are orders or guidelines that provide information and guidance for clinical or personal behavior or activities. In this sense, clinical orders and guidelines are also policy claims.

7. **Rebuttals**: A **rebuttal** represents the basis on which the claim will be questioned by a decision-maker.[32] Rebuttals should be considered as presenting contrary or alternative information diverting our decisions in the light of the possible alternative clinical settings, practice, patients, and values, past or present. It has a broader sense than Toulmin's modern argument as defined in Chapter 4.

8. **Reservation**: To address rebuttals, Rieke et al.[32] propose a **reservation**, that is, a qualification of the original claim that answers a rebuttal. Reservations are statements of the conditions under which a claim would not apply. In this context, contradictory clinical and paraclinical findings in a clinical workup of a patient's case which broaden and require differential diagnosis and subsequent dependent treatment decisions may be seen as reservations.

The completeness of the use of argument building blocks may vary from one case to another. Let us see how the management decision of an acute abdomen illustrated in the following table maps to these argument building blocks adapted for decision-making.

Claims, Conclusions (both)	Possible decisions first proposed, then confirmed or not are: 1. operate, or not operate 2. operate now or later
Grounds	What we see in the patient: visceral pain, parietal pain, colic, vomiting, constipation, diarrhea, jaundice, hematemesis, hematuria. Other grounds might include gynecologic, family, travel, and surgery histories, peristaltic "rushes" sounds, abdominal wall tenderness, abdominal masses, and guarding on deep palpation, hip flexion or costo-vertebral tenderness, resistance and pain, urine and stool test, plain and contrast x-ray studies, angiography, ultrasonography, computerized tomography and radionuclide scans, endoscopy, and paracenthesis.
Backing	Our past experience with decisions, probabilities, and utilities provides **backing** for our reasoning.
Warrant	We understand it better if we know past decision analyses of this problem, their meaning, and their results (operate or not); they are our **warrant** in the present decision-making process. How certain can we be about our claim?
Qualifier	Our certainty as **qualifier** may be extrapolated from probabilities from the past experience and the present state of our actual patient.
Rebuttals	Rebuttals are circumstances which may invalidate the claim. Differential diagnosis and its results are one of them: Differential diagnosis behind acute abdomen may include volvolus, intussusceptions, mesenteric adenitis, malignant and vascular diseases in the elderly, cholecystitis, appendicitis, bowel obstruction, cancers, salpingitis, dysmenorrhea, ovarian lesions, urinary tract infections, atypical manifestations of any above, unexplained unrelenting diffuse abdominal pain without commensurate peritoneal signs or abnormalities in elderly or cardiac patients, pulmonary conditions such as pneumothorax or lower lobe pneumonia and other thoracic infections, acute rheumatic fever, polyarteritis nodosa, or acute intermittent porphyria, and others. They may all play the role of **adducts**, either in favor or as **rebuttals** of our final claim or solution. Physical findings may also play the role of grounds and rebuttals as well: guarding, tenderness, and rigidity, distension or deterioration after conservative treatment, radiologic findings of pneumoperitoneum, bowel distension, extravasation of contrast material, space-occupying lesions on scans (with fever), endoscopic findings of perforated or uncontrollable bleeding lesions or blood, bile, pus, urine, or bowel contents on paracenthesis. They are indications for urgent operation in patients with an acute abdomen.[33]

As in our example, decision analyses based on decision trees may be a multistage process. The decision analyses and their conclusions may then also be a multistage process. It includes a sequence of argumentation processes and their conclusions, potentially even more than two, within the specific conceptual and methodological frame of decision analysis. At the conclusion of this process, decisions are made.

A structured decision-making process as a result of an argumentative process, ensures that critical decisions are based on clearly articulated arguments that have been tested through refutations and disagreements. In essence, they "have survived'" criticisms and remain open to potential future ones. Openness to uncertainty, internal and external dialogue, dialectic, rhetoric, and willingness to act are their necessary attributes.[28] For example, the acceptance of any new medical technology as a critical decision must carry such attributes.

Critical decisions are based on clearly articulated arguments that have been tested through refutations and disagreements. They "have survived" criticisms and remain open to potential future ones. Openness to uncertainty, internal and external dialogue, dialectic, rhetoric, and willingness to act are their necessary attributes.[28] For example, the acceptance of any new medical technology as a critical decision must carry such attributes.

Argumentation and critical decision-making in the clinical decision-making domain are then the process by which interested parties seek the best choices and decisions under uncertain and ambiguous situations.[32 modified] Physicians, nurses, their patients, and other stakeholders in health should use these approaches in daily activities and practices, not only in research.

10.2.3 Direction-Giving Tools in Decision-Making

Once the best option (evidence) is obtained either through decision analysis, clinical trial, consensus, or other means, directions for decisions may be established. Such directions may have a tactical or strategic character. **Tactical tools** (in military arts, "the tools needed to win the battle") focus on specific objects, solving an important part of the problem, for example, a diagnostic work-up for breast cancer or diabetes. *Clinical algorithms* belong to this category. **Strategic tools** (in military arts, "the tools needed to win the war") try to give the best directions (management skills) in a broader context. What should be done when caring for breast cancer patients from diagnosis and treatment to follow-up? How should patients suspected of having diabetes be cared for? *Clinical practice guidelines* are a good example of strategic tools in medicine.

As seen in the previous section, important progress has been made regarding the best way to navigate the mazes of possible decision options that appear in diagnosing and treating health problems. Once these best ways (and decisions) are found, they should be organized in an ensemble of optimal steps leading to the best result and benefit for the patient, or for the community if disease control is in question. Such a "best kit" must be built on the best available evidence. This evidence may come from decision analysis as described in original clinical and community research studies, meta-analysis of the best clinical and epidemiological experience of the deciding physician, or the physician's careful assessment of the specific situation relative to the patient or community.

10.2.3.1 Tactical Tools: Clinical Algorithms

Clinical **algorithms** and **decision tables** are offered in increasing numbers to the practising community. These tactical tools seek to fill a need for easy-to-use and practical guides to clinical decisions. Experienced clinicians may be tempted to draw up graphical guides in a form of flowchart or decision chain. Others draw colored "quick fixes" for subsidized, mostly advertising-oriented periodicals for practitioners, and call them "continuing education." There is a better way to develop and use clinical algorithms.

Clinical algorithms are *step-by-step written protocols for health management.*[34-36] They consist of *an explicit description of steps to be taken in patient care in specified circumstances.*[26] Clinicians may ask what diagnostic and therapeutic steps should be taken to properly treat a sore throat, or how should a case of multiple trauma in, and en route to, an emergency room be managed.

> Clinical algorithms are a specific category of algorithms. **An algorithm is defined as** *"a set of rules for approaching the solution to a complex problem by setting down individual steps and delineating how each step follows from the preceding one."*[35] Its character as a "uniform procedure"[35] and a "finite number of steps" for a solution to a given specific problem[34,36] is usually emphasized.

Algorithms as Flowcharts

Given its visual impact, the graphical form of algorithms is most widely used in medicine. An algorithm in its most well-known graphical form is a kind of flowchart. By definition, a **flowchart** is a

> *...graphical representation of the progress of a system for the definition, analysis, or solution of a data processing (or manufacturing) problem in which symbols are used to represent operations and data (or material flow and equipment), and lines and arrows represent inter-relationships among the components.*

Other terms for a flowchart are a **control diagram, flow diagram,** or **flow sheet.**[36]

Both decision trees and algorithms are flowcharts, with important differences. The fundamental difference between the two is that a **decision tree** portrays the choices available to those responsible for patient care, as well as the probabilities and values of each possible outcome that will result in a particular strategy in patient or community care. It is an **open system**, like a menu in a restaurant. Algorithms, on the other hand, are a **closed system**; they are orders reflecting what *should* be done, what actions *should* be taken, but without a prescribed list of options.

Clinical algorithms have proven useful in almost all medical specialties and fields of practice. However, like any diagnostic or therapeutic method, technique or instrument, as a medical tool clinical algorithms must have a well-structured and understandable form, a reason for their creation and use, and they must be evaluated for their advantages and weaknesses in their use and impact. Figure 10.2 illustrates an algorithm for the clinical workup and management of a stab wound of the abdomen[37] presented here in a standardized fashion.

N.B. Today and where available, modern imaging techniques might be preferred by some over peritoneal lavage to demonstrate fluid accumulation in the abdominal cavity.

The algorithm guides the practitioner from an initial evaluation of the patient, through successive steps, represented alternatively by clinical findings and actions to be taken. An action may be either a final diagnosis or a surgical or medical procedure to correct the situation. This sequence progresses to the exit point from the algorithm, usually the resolution of the clinical problem, depending on the type of action points. Algorithms may be purely diagnostic (no treatment indicated), purely interventional, or a mixture of both.

Algorithms are graphically represented in a standardized way. Formally, clinical boxes (rounded rectangles), decision boxes (hexagons), action boxes (rectangles), and link boxes (small ovals) are

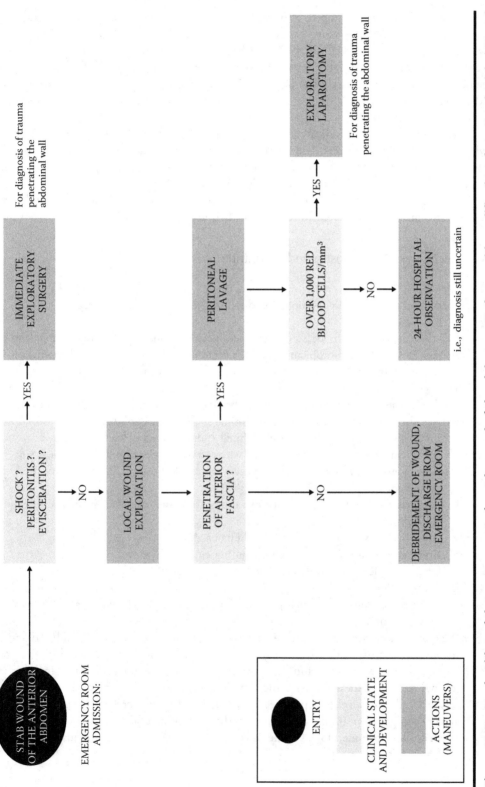

Figure 10.2 An algorithm of the management of a stab wound of the abdomen. (Redrawn with modifications from Oreskovich, MR and Carrico, CJ, *Ann Surg*, 1983;198:411–9. See also References 18 and 19.)

put in a sequence flowing from top to bottom and from left to right. Arrows, never intersecting if possible, are unobstructed by writing except in decision boxes, 'yes' arrows pointing right, 'no' arrows pointing down. Sequential numbering of boxes in the directions as noted is appropriate, with the entire algorithm preferably covering a single page. The presentation of an algorithm in medicine is becoming increasingly standardized,[38,39] illustrating entry points as square rectangles, decision points as hexagonal frames or vertically standing squares and endpoints (also called "terminators") as oval squares.[40]

An algorithm approach is indicated in specific clinical conditions, under specific states of knowledge, or for particular users, and working environments. Where clinical practice guidelines are presented or viewed in an algorithmic form, the same information applies equally to the domain of clinical practice guidelines. (See Section 10.2.3.3 of this chapter.)

In the next section, we address challenges with the algorithm,[41–43] and how we can build and evaluate algorithms to better understand them and their uses.

How to Recognize Well-Constructed Algorithms

The construction of clinical algorithms should follow these clearly defined steps:

1. The clinical **problem** to be solved by the algorithm must be well formulated and defined.[41] The clinical problem may be related to diagnosis, health phenomenon occurrence, target population, users, expected results, or other. Current practice must be also described.

2. Expected **results** of algorithm use must be specified (gains for practice, economy, patient, physician workload, etc.). "Discriminators,"[44] that is, points in clinical workup leading to a suggested action, are well defined and described in explicit terms.

3. Clear **indications** are given as to when, where, and by whom the algorithm is supposed to be used and to what kind of patients it should be applied. These indications should include:

   a. **patients** eligible for the algorithmic approach (target population for use of the algorithm);

   b. **situations** in which algorithms should be used;

   c. **sites** and **settings** are identified, including emergency rooms, operating theatres, family practice offices, and other; and

   d. **users** of algorithms.

   These four specifications help in making pragmatic decisions (where, when, and in whom an algorithm might and should be used).

4. The **clinical situation** statement → diagnostic statement → therapeutic and/or diagnostic options must be clearly defined in a realistic time-and-space relationship.

5. Enough **data** and **information** must be retrieved from the literature. This includes original studies, data analysis, clinical trials, consensus studies, medical audits, or personal and other clinical experience, or simple "gut feelings" or "flair" to justify each step of the algorithm. It must be clear, from the description of the proposed algorithm, which of the above-mentioned elements was used in its construction and justification;

the **best available evidence** for the purpose must support the algorithms' constituting elements.

6. Each node indicating an action to follow must be supported not only by the best **evidence**, but also by its justification through an **argumentative process** and its claims and conclusions in which the best evidence is used. We may reason poorly even when we have the best evidence at hand!

7. **Entry and exit points** of the algorithm need to be defined.

8. **Diagnostic steps** must be organized in order of their decreasing severity.

9. **Therapeutic steps** are organized either in order of their lifesaving importance (the worst first) or in order of their increasing cost and complexity (from the cheapest to the most expensive).

10. All **indications in boxes** (graphical components of the algorithm) are clear, explicit and as complete as necessary.

11. The algorithm should be drawn in a conventional, consistent manner that is **understandable** to the user.

If an algorithm respecting the above-mentioned rules is put into practice, its performance and effect must be evaluated.

How to Evaluate Clinical Algorithms

An algorithm and its use is a type of clinical maneuver like any other (diagnostic or therapeutic); its process (use) and impact must be evaluated, its weaknesses and strengths should be known. Evaluating the **process of algorithm use** means determining its security, appropriateness, economy, user friendliness, recipient (patient) friendliness, accidents, errors, and potential harm.

Several questions are important when **evaluating the impact** of algorithm use:

■ Does the algorithm correctly evaluate the patient's state?
■ Does it produce errors leading to undesirable effects, even if properly used?
■ Does it cover an important proportion and spectrum of daily cases?
■ Does it cover an important gradient of cases?
■ Most importantly, does using the algorithm improve a patient's state more than any alternative approach in diagnosis and therapeutic decision-making?

An algorithmic approach proves useful in the assessment of new technologies. Also, algorithms may be used to tell new technologies how to function. Controlled clinical trials, although the golden standard in treatment impact (effect) assessment, are rarely used in the evaluation of the use of algorithms. They should become standard. Beyond these examples, the evaluation of algorithms across the literature focuses mainly on "process" evaluation. The "effect" evaluation is often more difficult.

What are algorithms worth? Komaroff answers this question:

Algorithms are no substitute for experience, sensitivity, or compassion... algorithms can help us to articulate how we make decisions, to clarify our knowledge and to recognize our ignorance. They can help us to demystify the practice of medicine, and to demonstrate that much of what we call the "art" of medicine is really a scientific process, a science which is waiting to be articulated.[45]

There is a big difference between an "impression-based" and an "evidence-based" algorithm. A medical algorithm today may be seen also as a graphic presentation of a clinical practice or community medicine activity guideline and be the subject of valid guideline rules.

10.2.3.2 Evidence-Based Clinical Decision-Making Path

Entering the best evidence into the decision process creates a decision path in the form of a flowchart as illustrated by Figure 10.3. In this illustration, the decision process starts by the best **evidence** in general for the appropriate problem, its **relevance**, and then **applicability** to a particular patient provided that the clinical **setting** in which the decision is made fits. **Patient** values, preferences, and choices and other **ethical considerations** serve as an ultimate condition and rebuttals before the final decision is made. This acronym—**ERASPEC**—outlines how clinical decisions should be made.

10.2.3.3 Strategic Tools for Making the Right Decisions: Clinical Practice Guidelines and Clinical Protocols

Preoccupation with providing the best possible quality of care while containing costs have been the impetus for the development and implementation of clinical practice guidelines within health administration and professional institutions at local and international levels. **Clinical practice guidelines (CPG)** should respond to questions of how cancer patients should be cared for after surgery, or how diabetics or hypertensive patients should be cared for, and what is the best long-term care for arthritis.

Clinical Practice Guidelines

But what, then, are clinical practice guidelines?

The following characterizes modern medical guidelines in this way:

...they briefly identify, summarize and evaluate the highest quality evidence and most current data about prevention, diagnosis, prognosis, therapy including dosage of medications, risk/benefit and cost-effectiveness. Then they define the most important questions related to clinical practice and identify all possible decision options and their outcomes. Some guidelines contain decision or computation algorithms to be followed.[46]

Clinical practice guidelines have been defined as *"systematically developed statements to assist practitioner and patient decisions about appropriate health care for specific clinical circumstances."*[47] In their mostly methodological review of CPGs applied to chronic spinal pain

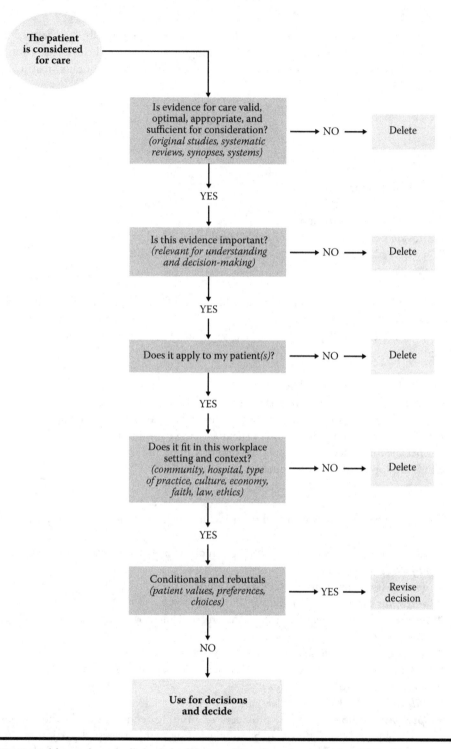

Figure 10.3   Evidence-based clinical decision-making flowchart or algorithm: Necessary general considerations. (Redrawn from Jenicek M. *A Primer on Clinical Experience in Medicine.* Boca Raton: CRC Press, 2013. Reproduced with permission.)

management, Manchikanti et al.[48] state that clinical practice guidelines as defined above should lead to the best practice based on a thorough evaluation of the evidence from published studies on the outcome of treatment. However, CPGs cover not only treatment, but also other steps in clinical care.

More precisely, good CPGs should:[49]

- limit variations in practice;
- reduce necessary costs;
- give a scientific direction to care;
- provide useable summaries of the best evidence-based practices; and
- have an educational value for risks and benefits of medical interventions and care.

CPGs should be valid, reliable, reproducible, clear, flexible, and applicable in various settings of care.[47] CPGs can be developed through expert opinion and consensus or "evidence-based guidelines," as preferred today.[50,51] Several stages and steps describe how evidence-based CPGs are developed:

- a clinical problem is formulated;
- the best evidence is drawn from the literature and past experience;
- a systematic review of evidence is done as a basis for draft practice guidelines;
- a draft practice is put to a test use in the practicing community;
- feedback is integrated into the final version of CPGs; and
- CPGs are approved and disseminated.

CPGs must be reported in a standard form[52] which includes (with some modifications):

- definition of the *problem* and description of the *present practice* and situation;
- *objective* of the proposed CPGs;
- *options* (the maze through CPGs that guides the clinician);
- *outcomes* (health and economic);
- *evidence* about all major aspects of the problem and how it was obtained, synthetized, and graded;
- *benefits*, *harms*, and *costs*;
- *values* of potential outcomes (for clinicians and their patients as well);
- summary of *recommendations*;
- *validation* of CPGs themselves; and
- *sponsors* (authors of CPGs, providers of funding, endorsers and other important stakeholders). N.B. CPGs may be influenced by many interested parties such as the profession, business, the government, or insurance companies. Thus their sponsors must be noted to avoid, or expose, potential bias.[48–50]

Examples of current CPGs abound. They have been developed for all major cancers (breast, colon, rectal, lung, ovarian, prostate, leukemia), ischemic heart disease, back pain, diabetes, pneumonia, schizophrenia, stroke, myocardial infarction, biliary tract disease, depression, pre-term birth, acute pain, and many others. For example, *Canadian Clinical Practice Guidelines*[53] cover 30 key medical and therapeutic areas. Some CPGs may take the form of structured narrative directions to follow or an algorithm.[51-54]

Developing evidence-based guidelines is not a quick and easy task. Diagnostic and treatment options, as well as their validity, effectiveness, and desirable and adverse outcomes, must be ideally supported by the best available evidence. This evidence should be provided to those who use CPGs.

Guidelines focusing on the process of care cannot always be founded on evidence.

Consensus development may also yield excellent results. Guidelines for pre-hospital[55] and in-hospital[56] cardiopulmonary resuscitation, published by several leading medical journals and currently in field use, are such examples.

CPGs have two additional challenges: their implementation and evaluation of how they are used;[57,58] and evaluation of their effectiveness.[58] Good guidelines have to be used, but they must yield better results than unguided heterogeneous practices and care.[59] Several competing guidelines may be developed for the management of the same problem, thus evaluation to determine which is best may be necessary. Systematic reviews of such decision-making tools may become more frequent in the near future if guidelines continue to proliferate.

Fletcher[60] correctly stresses that CPGs are just recommendations for the evidence-based care of **average** patients, not rules for **all** patients. He notes, "*Although guidelines may point out the best research evidence to guide the care of average patients, they are not the substitute for clinical judgment, which should be applied to each individual patient.*"

Hence, **CPGs in the framework of evidence-based medicine** are an important part of a longer process. In the case of a novel treatment, Lilford and Braunholtz,[61 modified] suggest that a CPG proposal should be justified in several ways:

- **clinical trials** show its effectiveness;
- **meta-analyzes** confirm it;
- **decision analysis** weighs costs and benefits in favor of treatment;
- this preferred treatment option is made part of **clinical practice guidelines**;
- the impact of guidelines is evaluated by **clinical audit**;
- implementation is handled by managerial action like **clinical governance**; and
- all of the above represent **evidence-based care.**

Most recently, the National Guideline Center[62] and editors of the *Annals of Internal Medicine*[63] have proposed "guidelines to guidelines" together with examples of applications to delirium prevention[64] and cost-effectiveness assessment in the domain of health economics.[65]

Clinical Practice Guidelines vs. Clinical Protocols

CPGs and clinical protocols offered to clinicians are different entities, especially from the point of view of their purpose and rules. **Clinical practice guidelines** are **not** a **compulsory procedure** to follow; they are discretionary, unless specified otherwise. They are proposals to the clinician and/ or his or her health institution to adopt or reject them, regardless of well they are built, evidence-based and argumentatively justified and otherwise scientifically and clinically sound. Again, they are not intended as a substitute for the judgment of the physician or other health professional, and they are not the only approach to consider for the best practice.

Clinical protocols originate in the domain of clinical trials and pharmacology. Based on clinical trial protocols, clinical protocols are rather **prescriptive**. They are structured and organized step-by-step activities specifically designed to be followed in a given structure and setting. A practitioner working within the structure of a clinical protocol **must** follow the protocol if he or she agrees to participate in a given activity. A merging of both clinical practice guidelines and clinical protocols is currently under consideration in computerized settings.[66]

10.3 Illustrative Fallacies in the Decision-Making Domain

Fallacies as errors in reasoning and decision-making, often referred to as biases, cognitive errors, or decision errors. They may be related either to the motivation to decide, to the decision oriented thinking process, or to act of deciding itself.[67,68] Still, terms like fallacies, biases, cognitive errors, or mistakes may be used interchangeably across the literature beyond fundamental philosophy and cognitive sciences basic domains. Let us quote here just a few examples applicable to the clinical problems. The world of medical fallacies is much wider and covered elsewhere by us.[69]

For Roberto,[70] poor decisions are not always due to incompetence, inexperience, lack of intelligence, or bad intentions. They arise because of other factors such as faulty reasoning leading to erroneous decision-making. Decisions are not just events. They are, in fact, processes to be analyzed and understood and the causes of their failures should be identified and remedies drawn from such experiences.

There are several fallacies related to reasoning, leading to faulty decisions, that are relevant to decision-making in health sciences. These are itemized in the following section.

10.3.1 Fallacies from an Individual Perspective: Individual-Related Fallacies

There are two main groups of fallacies in reasoning that lead to faulty decisions. One group is related to individual reasoning and decision-making, the other to collective team reasoning and interaction producing decisional failures. Sometimes, both groups are interwoven.

Individual-related fallacies may be reasoning-based, from the motivation to decide domain, or related to decisions themselves. Let us have a look first at some examples of individual-related fallacies.

10.3.1.1 Reasoning-Based Fallacies: Fallacies Related to the Thinking Process behind Decision-Making

There are a number of fallacies related to the thinking process behind the decision-making process. These are briefly described here. Each of these types of fallacies can impact on the integrity of the decision-making process.

Satisficing in this the context of decision-making, means choosing an acceptable solution instead of looking for the optimal one. In some cases, good enough may not be the best option. Proven surgeries or medications may be subject to satisficing choices instead of choosing the best proven alternatives available. Optimization of decisions is replaced by searching and opting for alternatives only to the point where an acceptable solution is found.

Overconfidence bias is due to what it says: physicians or nurses who are overconfident in their judgment in general, overly optimistic in diagnosis, and managing patient care.

Availability bias is generated by our tendency to place too much emphasis on the information which is readily available when decisions are to be made. In this type of reasoning bias, both diagnostic and therapeutic decisions may be at stake.

Sunk cost trap. Another type of fallacy is based on a concept called a 'sunk cost trap.' In a sunk cost trap, decision-makers tend to escalate commitment to a course of action in which they have already made substantial investments of time, and material and human resources. Continuing to gamble in a casino after multiple losses or continuing to practice surgical techniques into which we have already invested so much time, energy, or hospital and other technology resources may become sunk cost traps.

A **sunk-cost effect fallacy** occurs when once we have put effort into something, we are reluctant to pull out because of the loss we would incur, even if continued refusal would lead to an even more important loss. Choosing surgery before a conservative treatment may be an example of this fallacy.

Recency effect or **temporizing** is a type of fallacy that places too much emphasis on recent events. For example, the immediate experiences leading up to the impending decision may take on increased importance due to their proximity to the decision-making exercise.

Confirmation bias is reflected in the tendency of individuals to gather and base decisions on data and information that confirm their existing views, and downplay information that is contrary to their pre-existing hypotheses. For example, "*do not resuscitate*" orders may be subject to this kind of biased decision-making.

A confirmation bias means also actively seeking *a posteriori* elements of support which will confirm the decision we already made. For example, "*You see, you did better after taking this medication than others who didn't.*"

Overreliance on pattern recognition and pattern matching is still another type of fallacy. It is a fallacy where individuals recognize patterns based on prior experience, and attempts are made to match the current situation to these past experiences. This type of fallacy may reduce considerations of the whole series of alternatives. Decisions must be made in views of the current range of best options. However, pattern recognition and matching are not the same when experienced by novices and health professionals. In the former, "feeling uncomfortable about," "something goes wrong," or "something is not right" is worth considering in decision-making, but finding reasons or patterns leading to such perceptions should be the next step in a novice's performance.

In structured decision-making, problems are defined, alternatives are generated, options are evaluated, actions are chosen and implemented and their result is evaluated.

Intuition alone may lead to wrong decisions if a more formal analysis of a decisional process is available.

Reasoning by analogy is a double-edged decision-making tool. On one hand, analogical reasoning minimizes repetition of mistakes. On the other, it downplays or ignores differences and new phenomena and considerations which should necessarily refine or reorient decisions. Establishing lists of what is analogous and what is not and beyond helps.

The **ambiguity effect fallacy** means choosing an action or option with which we are familiar in probabilistic terms, and understand is effective, *before* another action whose outcomes are not known, or not well known in probabilistic terms. Once the probabilities of the later actions are known, they may be better than the probabilities of the former. Choosing a treatment known for its effectiveness always follows a *"playing it safe"* route. Medical ethics are in favor of the "playing it safe" option even if some logicians might think the contrary.

Hyperbolic discounting means choosing actions yielding smaller benefits for the short term, rather than a larger long-term benefit of another alternative action. "Making the patient comfortable" may be preferred by some to alternative decisions to treat the patient and significantly improve his or her survival.

A **source credibility fallacy** may occur if we prefer decisions of a person who is credible, an expert, and trustworthy. This fallacy may occur if we blindly follow the conclusions of consults by other experts from other specialties without assessing evidence from requesters as compared to the providers of a consult.

Other fallacies in decision-making may occur and they remain an open list in the medical decision domain.

A **commitment fallacy** occurs when we follow a social and/or professional commitment that we translate into our decisions. The Hippocratic Oath to act and help accordingly may be pursued, despite contrary evidence of the appropriateness of action. Our action derives from the fear of professional and/or social rejection while being blind to the evidence not to act in the circumstances.

10.3.1.2 Fallacies Related to Decisions Themselves

Sometimes fallacies are based on the very act of making decisions themselves. There are three fallacies related to the following concept.

1. **Bounded rationality**: Decisions are rational within the limits of the decision-maker's knowledge, experience, cognitive capability, and the time they have available to make the decision. This kind of **bounded rationality** appears to be suitable for medicine. Best choices are not necessarily made due to the limitations of the human mind, the structure within which the mind operates, the best evidence available and the ways we handle it. Decision-maker's rationality will then always be bound and cannot be completely overcome.
2. **Anchoring and adjustment heuristic**: Another fallacy in decision-making is an **anchoring and adjustment heuristic**, which means basing understanding and the ensuing decisions on known "anchors" or familiar positions. As an example, where a set of possible actions are available to choose from, we tend to adopt one of them based on our familiarity without considering other actions based on a broader view of the

problem. This may happen in the differential diagnosis domain and the selection of actions which follow competing diagnoses.

3. **Availability heuristic**: The term **availability heuristic** refers to the tendency to make judgments based on what we can remember rather than on complete data and information. Necessarily, this judgment is affected by the frequency and likelihood of events that occur within a clinician's practice. Delaying a decision until more information is available may compensate for incompatible information coming from vivid memory. However, delayed decisions are incompatible with the reality of emergency, surgery, or critical care medicines.

Fallacies, biases, and other judgment and decision errors are open ended, expanding and ever-changing domains. They must be followed, understood and corrected continuously. Hence, even our reference devoted specifically to fallacies[69] from which many of the above are drawn, must not be seen as the final word about our understanding and decision-making errors. Many others will decidedly follow.

10.3.2 Collective-Related Fallacies: Groupthink

Thinking in groups and as a group creates another category of reasoning and decision-making traps that leads to potential errors and fallacies. Based on experience from the world of politics in general and foreign policy,[71,72] Janis[71] concludes that erroneous decisions are sometimes made under stress and pressure by groups whose members think "collectively" and value, above all, the sense of belonging by "going along to get along." Mental efficiency, reality testing, and moral judgment may deteriorate as a result of in-group pressure. Pressure generates a strong need for affiliation, stress generates group cohesiveness.

Members of groups are committed to prior group decisions and under pressure to conform. In a group, friendship is valued even with weaker members. This attitude prevails over building rational individual and complementary contributions to decisions chosen by the group. In "groupthink," striving for unanimity overrides group members' motivation to realistically appraise alternative courses of action. Does such an attitude exist in health professions? One only needs to casually observe what happens in hospitals, in clinical services, or in academic departments in medicine and other health professions to be able to answer the question.

Roberto[70] recognizes three types of dysfunctional decision-making cultures: a *culture of no*, a *culture of yes*, and a *culture of maybe*. These situations result from the chronic inability to move from conflict to consensus and from deliberation to action. Even if members of the group disagree, by being silent or otherwise, they opt for one of these three approaches and cultures.

Do healthcare, academic, and research environments not often have similar characteristics? Groupthink may occur and be important in various domains. These include the development of clinical guidelines, health administration functioning and orientation of emergency medicine, strategies in surgical specialties or public health and preventive medicine programs, and policy development, implementation, and evaluation. In the health domain, related administrative and scientific meetings, colloquiums, symposiums, consensus groups, specific topic-oriented working groups and their recommendations, even clinical rounds at various levels, do not escape group-related decision-making errors and fallacies.

Let Us Conclude

Patient- or management-centered decisions making both require a **sound *a priori* decision analysis** as discussed in this chapter. **Decision analyses and their products, like algorithms** (with their other components such as research, experience or meta-analysis), **often do not travel well**. They are badly needed in certain environments where incomplete and imperfect data, information for straightforward matters, and/or the proliferation of new medical technologies, such as diagnostic methods and treatments in medicine and surgery are prevalent. Decision analysis, like meta-analysis, may represent an alternative and/or complement to controlled clinical trials, whenever they are costly and/or ethically unacceptable or when additional information is sought. However, like meta-analysis, decision analysis is only as good as its database.

Diagnostic (base rate) errors present a different challenge for the use of decision-making processes. Variable meaning is attributed to findings based on their representativeness. Variable use of relevant findings exists. Unequal weight given by different clinicians in their work and decisions to different findings (anchoring), and even wording of problems (framing), may affect the decision process and its result.

Making clinical diagnoses presents some particular challenges in using decision-making processes. As we have seen, variable meaning is attributed to data and information based on how representative the information is. Relevant findings are used to variable degrees by different practitioners. Clinicians ascribe different weight to findings (anchoring) and even frame problems differently based on their work experience and perceptions. Both of these may affect the decision process and the result of that process.

Balla et al.[73] argue that not all clinical situations lend themselves to the use of decision-making processes, nor can all practitioners exercise them equally. They note that biases exist between expert and novice users. They suggest that expert decision analysis belongs to expert people, not novices. Diagnostic (base rate) errors abound. Variable meaning is attributed to findings as for their representativeness.

Moreover, reluctance to use decision analysis does not focus on its substance, intellectual quality, or scientific acceptability. Its greatest challenge is that it is somewhat inflexible and not adaptive enough for ever-changing daily life in different clinical environments and community health fields. These authors[73] conclude:

> *We are not suggesting that it is neither feasible nor necessary to apply decision analytic methods to every clinical situation. Yet the insights into decision processes provided by the theory and the discrepancies between clinical intuition and formal theories should become part of the background and understanding of every clinician.*

Decision analysis was also found to be preferable to second opinions for surgical decisions.[74]

We live in an action-oriented era and the domain of health endeavors is itself action oriented— clinicians face intense pressure to *do something* in the face of a medical problem. Interestingly but not surprisingly enough, decision-making and decision analysis rarely include "***doing nothing***" as decision points, choices, and options. Hippocrates might not be pleased.

The quantitative methodology of decision analysis requires further refinements.[75–77] Refinements in the evaluation of its results, considerations of human values, and the assessment of human weaknesses in clinical practice are necessary ingredients for the improvement of decision-making in clinical practice, community health, and medical research. This would probably explain why the results of clinical decision analyses may at times appear more counterintuitive than they really are.

Several additional readings might prove useful for the reader. Given the size and extent of this chapter and its main focus at the thinking process, computational examples were put aside. They may be found among others in our *Foundations of Evidence-Based Medicine* (its Chapter 13).[15] MA Roberto's *The Art of Critical Decision-Making*[70] provides an introduction to the analysis and rules of decision-making through case analyzes of selected good or bad decisions in political and civic life. The philosopher/nurse team of PA Facione and NC Facione brings us closer to health sciences while building on foundations of critical thinking and decision-making in general, in their *Thinking and Reasoning in Human Decision-Making: The Method of Argument and Heuristic Analysis*.[78] Wulff and Göetsche propose and additional approach via evidence-based clinical decision-making.[79] Medical errors are preventable. Understanding and improving medical decision-making is one way to make the "epidemiology of medical errors"[80,81] easier.

As we may see, medical decision-making is a particular thinking and reasoning process, distinct from other processes, focused at understanding and communication. Let us put it at its best use.

Need a broader general view of decision-making? Hamilton's text and course[22] might prove valuable for novices in the decision-making domain in general.

References

1. *A Dictionary of Public Health.* Edited by JM Last. Oxford and New York: Oxford University Press, 2007.
2. Wikipedia, the free encyclopedia. *Decision-making.* 13 p. from https://en.wikipedia.org/wiki/Decision-making, retrieved Feb 12, 2017.
3. Anon. What are knowledge, skills and attitudes? At: http://www.apaseq.com/docs/knowledge.doc, retrieved May 2, 2009.
4. Wikipedia, the free encyclopedia. *Disposition.* 1 p. at 0http://en.wikipedia.org/wiki/Disposition, retrieved Feb 9, 2011.
5. Jeffrey R. Decision theory. Pp. 207–9 in: *The Cambridge Dictionary of Philosophy.* 2nd Edition. R Audi, General Editor. Cambridge and New York: Cambridge University Press, 1999.
6. *Decision Theory.* Encyclopaedia Britannica Article. 1 p. at ebcid:com.britannica.occ2.identifier .Articleidentifier?tockd=90297..., retrieved from electronic edition June 27, 2010.
7. Albert DA. Decision theory in medicine. A review and critique. *Milbank Mem Fund Quart/Health and Society,* 1978;56(3, Summer):362–401.
8. Reyna VF. Theories of medical decision-making and health: An evidence-based approach. *Med Dec Making,* 2008/Nov–Dec 2008:829–33. doi: 10.1177/0272989X08327069, downloaded from *mdm. sagepub.com,* retrieved Oct 16, 2010.
9. TIP:0000 Learning Domains. *Decision–Making.* 1 p. at http://tip.psychology.oreg/decision.html, retrieved January 16, 2010.
10. Patrick EA. *Decision Analysis in Medicine: Methods and Applications.* Boca Raton, FL: CRC Press, Inc., 1979.
11. Weinstein MC, Fineberg HV, Elstein AS, Frazier HS, Neutra RR, McNeil BJ. *Clinical Decision Analysis.* Philadelphia, PA: WB Saunders, 1980.

12. Sox HC, Higgins MC, Owens DK. *Medical Decision-making.* 2nd Edition. Hoboken, NJ/Toronto/Chichester: Wiley-Blackwell, 2013.

13. *Decision-making in Health Care. Theory, Psychology, and Applications.* Edited by GB Chapman & FA Sonnenberg. Cambridge and New York: Cambridge University Press, 2000.

14. Maynard A. Evidence-based medicine: An incomplete method for informing treatment choices. *The Lancet,* 1997;349:126–8.

15. Decision analysis and decision-making in medicine. Beyond intuition, guts, and flair. Chapter 13, pp. 341–78 in: Jenicek M. *Foundations of Evidence-Based Medicine.* Boca Raton, FL/London/New York/Washington: The Parthenon Publishing Group/CRC Press, 2003.

16. Alemi F, Gustafson DH. *Decision Analysis for Healthcare Managers.* Chicago, IL and Washington: Health Administration Press and AUPHA Press, 2007.

17. Stolper E, Van de Wiel M, Van Royen P, Van Bokhoven M, Van der Weiden T, Dinant GJ. Gut feelings as a third track in general practitioners' diagnostic reasoning. *J Gen Intern Med,* 2010;26(2):197–203. doi: 10.1007/s1606-010-1524-5.

18. Clinical and community medicine decision-making. Chapter 4, pp. 163–204 in: Jenicek M. *A Primer on Clinical Experience in Medicine. Reasoning, Decision-making, and Communication in Health Sciences.* Boca Raton, FL/London/New York: CRC Press/Taylor & Francis/Productivity Press, 2013.

19. Decision analysis and decision-making in medicine. Beyond intuition, guts, and flair. Chapter 13, pp. 341–78 in: Jenicek M. *Foundations of Evidence-Based Medicine.* Boca Raton, FL/London/New York/Washington, DC: The Parthenon Publishing Group, a CRC Press Company, 2003.

20. Kramer MS. *Clinical Epidemiology and Biostatistics. A Primer for Clinical Investigators and Decision-Makers.* Berlin/Heidelberg/New York/London: Springer-Verlag, 1988.

21. Murphy EA. *The Logic of Medicine.* Baltimore, MD: The Johns Hopkins University Press, 1976. (2nd edition, 1997).

22. Hamilton R. *How to Decide. The Science of Human Decision-making.* Chantilly, VA: The Great Courses (The Teaching Company), A Transcript Book, 2016.

23. Croskerry P. Clinical cognition and diagnostic error: Applications of a dual process model of reasoning. *Adv in Health Sci Educ,* 2009;14:27–35. doi: 10.1007/s10459-009-9182-2. DOI 10.1007/s11606-010-15240-5.

24. Tom E, Schulman KA. Mathematical models in decision analysis. *Infect Control Hosp Epidemiol,* 1997;18:65–73.

25. Raiffa H. *Decision Analysis: Introductory Lectures on Choices under Uncertainty.* Reading, MA: Addison-Wesley, 1968.

26. *A Dictionary of Epidemiology. 5th Edition.* Edited for the International Epidemiological Association by Miquel Porta. Oxford and New York: Oxford University Press, 2008.

27. Tips for teachers of evidence-based medicine: Making sense of decision analysis using a decision tree. *J Gen Intern Med,* 2009;24(5):642–8. doi: 10.1007/s11606.009-0918-8.

28. Sonnenberg FA, Beck JR. Markov models in medical decision-making: A practical guide. *Med Decis Making,* 1993;13:322–38.

29. Pauker SG & Kassirer JP. The threshold approach to clinical decision-making. *N Engl J Med,* 1980;320:1109–17.

30. Tarride J-E, Blackhouse G, Bischof M, McCarron EC, Lim M, Ferrusi IL, Xie F, Goeree R. Approaches for economic evaluations of health care technologies. *J Am Coll Radiol,* 2009;6:307–16.

31. Dickinson HD. Evidence-based decision-making: An argumentative approach. *Int J Med Inform,* 1998;51:71–81.

32. Rieke RD, Sillars MO, Peterson TR. *Argumentation and Critical Decision-making.* Sixth Edition. Boston, MA/New York/San Francisco: Pearson Education Inc., 2005.

33. Doherty GM. The acute abdomen. Chapter 21, pp. 451–63 in: *Current Diagnosis & Treatment. Surgery.* 13th Edition. Edited by GM Doherty. New York/Chicago, IL/London: McGraw-Hill Medical, 2010.

34. Stedman TL. *Stedman's Medical Dictionary.* 25th Edition. Edited by W Hensyl. Baltimore: Williams & Wilkins, 1990.

35. *Encyclopaedia Britannica.* Chicago: William Benton, 1968.

36. *McGraw-Hill Dictionary of Scientific and Technical Terms.* 4th Edition. SP Parker Editor-in-Chief. New York: McGraw-Hill Book Corp., 1989.
37. Oreskovich MR & Carrico CJ. Stab wounds of the anterior abdomen. Analysis of a management plan using local wound exploration and quantitative peritoneal lavage. *Ann Surg,* 1983;198:411–9.
38. Society for Medical Decision-making Committee on Standardization of Clinical Algorithms. Proposal for clinical algorithm standards. *Med Decis Making,* 1992;12:149–54.
39. Pearson SD, Margolis CZ, Davis S, Schreier LK, Gottlieb LK. The clinical algorithm nosology: A method for comparing algorithmic guidelines. *Med Decis Making,* 1992;12:123–31.
40. Khalil PN, Kleespies A, Angele MK, Thasler WE, Siebeck M, Brunns CJ, Mutschler W, Kanz K-G. The formal requirements of algorithms and their implications in clinical medicine and quality management. *Langenbecks Arch Surg,* 2011;396(1):31–40.
41. Direction giving tools in decision-making. Section 10.4, pp. 313–8 in: Jenicek M. *Epidemiology. The Logic of Modern Medicine.* Montréal: EPIMED International, 1995. (Edition in Spanish 1996, and in Japanese 1997).
42. Tactical tools: Clinical algorithms and decision tables. Section 13.4.1, pp. 360–6 in: Jenicek M. *Foundations of Evidence—Based Medicine.* Boca Raton, FL/London/New York/Washington: The Parthenon Publishing Group/CRC Press, 2003.
43. Hansen DT. Development and use of clinical algorithms in chiropractic. *J Manipul Physiol Ther,* 1991;14:478–82.
44. Green G, Defoe Jr. EC. What is a clinical algorithm? *Clin Pediatr,* 1978;17:457–63.
45. Komaroff AL. Algorithms and the "art" of medicine. *Am J Public Health,* 1982;72:10–11.
46. Wikipedia, the free encyclopedia. *Medical Guideline.* 3 p. at http://en,wikipedia.org/wiki/Medical _guideline, retrieved Jan 28, 2011
47. *Guidelines for Clinical Practice: From Development to Use.* Edited by MJ Filed & KN Lohr. Washington: National Academy Press, 1992.
48. Manchikanti L, Singh V, Helm II S, Schultz DM, Datta S, Hirsch. An introduction to evidence-based approach to intervention techniques in the management of chronic spinal pain. *Pain Physician,* 2009;12:E1–E33.
49. Veale B, Weller D, Silagy C. Clinical practice guidelines and Australian general practice. *Aust Fam Physician,* 1999;28:744–9.
50. Qasem A, Snow V, Owens DK, Shekelle P for the Clinical Guidelines Committee of the American College of Physicians. The development of clinical practice guidelines and guidance statements of the American College of Physicians: Summary of methods. *Ann Intern Med,* 2010;153:194–99.
51. Turner T, Misso M, Harris C, Green S. Development of evidence-based clinical practice guidelines (CPGs): Comparing approaches. *Implementation Science,* 2008;3:45. doi: 10.1186/1748-5908-3-45. 8 p. at http://www.implementationscience.com/content/3/1/45, retrieved Jan 28, 2011.
52. Hayward RSA, Wilson MC, Tunis SR, Bass EB, Rubin HR, Haynes RB. More informative abstracts of articles describing clinical practice guidelines. *Ann Intern Med,* 1993;118:731–7.
53. *Canadian Clinical Practice Guidelines. 2008 Edition.* Edited by DE Greenberg & M Muraca. Toronto: Elsevier Canada, 2008.
54. Pearson SD, Margolis CZ, Davis S, Schreier LK, Sokol HN, Gottlieb LK. Is consensus reproducible? A study of an algorithmic guidelines development process. *Med Care,* 1995;33:643–60.
55. Cummins RO, Chamberlain DA, Abramson NS, Allen M, Baskett P, Becker L, Bossaert L, Delooz H, Dick W, Eisenberg M, Evans T, Holmberg S, Kerber R, Mullie A, Ornato JP, Sandoe E, Skulberg A, Tunstall-Pedoe H, Swanson R, Theis WH. Recommended guidelines for uniform reporting of data from out-of-hospital cardiac arrest: The Utstein Style. *Ann Emerg Med,* 1991;20:861–74.
56. Cummins RO, Chamberlain D D, Hazinski MF, Nadkarni V, Kloeck W, Kramer E, Becker L, Robertson C, Koster R, Zaritski A, Bossaert L, Ornato JP, Callanan V, Allen M, Steen P, Connolly B, Sanders A, Idris A, Cobbe S. Recommended guidelines for reviewing, reporting, and conducting research on in-hospital resuscitation: The in-hospital "Utstein style". A statement for Healthcare Professionals from the American Heart Association, the European Resuscitation Council, the Heart and Stroke Foundation of Canada, the Australian Resuscitation Council, and the Resuscitation Councils of Southern Africa. *Resuscitation,* 1997;34:151–83.

57. Davis DA, Taylor-Vaisey A. Translating guidelines into practice. A systematic review of theoretic concepts, practical experience and research evidence in the adoption of clinical practice guidelines. *Can Med Assoc J,* 1997;157:408–16.

58. Hayward RSA, Guyatt GH, Moore K-A, McKibbon A, Carter AO. Canadian physicians' attitudes about preferences regarding clinical practice guidelines. *Can Med Assoc J,* 1997;156:1715–23.

59. Worrall G, Chaulk P, Freake D. The effects of clinical practice guidelines on patient outcomes in primary care: A systematic review. *Can Med Assoc J,* 1997;156:1705–12.

60. Fletcher RH. Practice guidelines and the practice of medicine: Is it the end of clinical judgment and expertise? *Schweiz Med Wochenschr,* 1998;128:1883–8.

61. Lilford RJ, Braunholtz D. Who's afraid of Thomas Bayes? *J Epidemiol Community Health,* 2000;54:731–9.

62. Hill J & Alderson P. A summary of methods that the *National Guideline Center* uses to produce clinical guidelines for the *National Institute for Health and Clinical Excellence. Ann Intern Med,* 2011;154:752–7.

63. Laine C, Taichman DB, Mulrow C. Trustworthy clinical guidelines. (Editorial.) *Ann Intern Med,* 2011;154:774–5.

64. O'Mahony R, Murthy L, Akunne A, Young J for the Guideline Development Group. Synopsis of the National Institute for Health and Clinical Excellence Guideline for Prevention of Delirium. *Ann Intern Med,* 2011;154:746–51.

65. Wonderling D, Sawyer L, Fenu E, Lovibond K, Laramée P. *National Clinical Guideline Centre* cost-effectiveness assessment for the *National Institute for Health and Clinical Excellence. Ann Intern Med,* 2011;154:758–65.

66. Raza Abidi S, Raza Abidi SS. Towards the merging of multiple clinical protocols and guidelines via ontology-driven modelling. 5 pdf p. at http://www.cs.dal.ca/~sraza/papers/aime09merging.pdf, retrieved Feb 7, 2011.

67. ChangingMinds.org. *Theories about Decision-Making.* Various number of p.at http://changingminds.org/explanations/theories/a_decision.htm, retrieved April 11, 2009.

68. ChangingMinds.org. *Theories about Decision Errors.* Various number of p. at http://changingminds.org/explanations/theories/a_decision_error.htm, retrieved Feb 14, 2009.

69. Jenicek M. *Fallacy-Free Reasoning in Medicine. Improving Communication and Decision-making in Research and Practice.* Chicago, IL: American Medical Association (AMA Press), 2009.

70. Roberto MA. *The Art of Critical Decision-making.* Transcript Book. Chantilly, VA: The Great Courses/The Teaching Company, 2009.

71. Janis IL. *Victims of Groupthink; A Psychological Study of Foreign Policy Decisions and Fiascoes.* Boston, MA: Houghton Mifflin Company, 1972. (2nd Revised Edition 1983).

72. Tetlock PE. Identifying victims of groupthink from public statements of decision makers. *J Pers Soc Psychol,* 1979;37(8):314–24.

73. Balla JI, Elstein AS, Christensen C. Obstacles to acceptance of clinical decision analysis. *Br Med J,* 1989;298:579–82.

74. Clarke JR. A comparison of decision analysis and second opinions for surgical decisions. *Arch Surg,* 1985;120:844–7.

75. Fryback DG. Reflections on the beginnings and future of medical decision-making. *MDM,* 2001;21:71–3.

76. Beck JR. Medical decision-making: 20 years of advancing the field. *MDM,* 2001;21:73–5.

77. Habbema JDF, Bossuyt PMM, Dippel DWJ, Marshall S, Hilden J. Analyzing clinical decision analyses. *Stat Med,* 1990;9:1229–42.

78. Facione PA, Facione NC. *Thinking and Reasoning in Human Decision-making: The Method of Argument and Heuristic Analysis.* Milbrae, CA: The California Academic Press, 2007.

79. Wulff HR, Götzsche PC. *Rational Diagnosis and Treatment. Evidence-Based Clinical Decision-Making.* 3rd Edition. Oxford/London/Malden, MA: Blackwell Science, 2000. 4th Edition under new title: Götzsche PC. *Rational Diagnosis and Treatment: Evidence-Based Clinical Decision-Making.* 4th Edition. Chichester and Hoboken, NJ: J. Wiley, 2007.

80. Meyer G, Lewin DI, Eisenberg J. To err is preventable: Medical errors and academic medicine. *Am J Med,* 2001;110:597–603.

81. Jenicek M. *Medical Error and Harm. Understanding, Prevention, and Control.* Boca Raton, FL/London/New York: CRC Press/Taylor & Francis, 2011.

SHARING OUR THOUGHTS ON ORAL AND WRITTEN COMMUNICATION WITH PEERS, PATIENTS, AND COMMUNITIES

IV

Chapter 11

<hr style="border: 2px solid black" />

Communicating Our Thoughts with Peers and Patients—Mostly Oral Clinical Communication, Its Content, Objectives, and Vehicles*

<hr style="border: 2px solid black" />

Executive Summary

Communication in medicine, a part of the emerging domain of communicology, represents a transactional process in which messages (evidence-based or not) are filtered through the perceptions, emotions, and experience of those involved. Interpersonal communication is not only the linchpin of medical practice, but also an important element of health information usage and of the evaluation of its contribution to the improvement of medical practice.

In this chapter, we will consider two types of vehicles for communication: intellectual vehicles and instrumental vehicles. Intellectual tools include: unfocused quizzing ("pimping"); argumentation/critical thinking-based and evidence-grounded exchanges of data; and information and decision options. Clinicians also use more traditional scholarly methods of communication, by reading, writing, understanding, and use of medical articles; other types of clinical case(s) reporting; and through ongoing teaching and training methods that are preferably evidence-based and argumentation supported Socratic dissent. Greater benefits are derived from these communication methods

* This chapter is based largely, with permission by the publisher, on Chapter 5 in: Jenicek M. *A Primer on Clinical Experience in Medicine. Reasoning, Decision-making, and Communication in Health Sciences.* Boca Raton, FL/ London/New York: CRC Press/Taylor & Francis/Productivity Press, 2013. Revised, updated, edited.

when their associated rules, strengths, weaknesses, and applications are understood.

Instrumental vehicles have a vehicle by which communication is relayed. In medicine, this includes that is collected by communicating with the patient through vehicles like admissions and patient charts, and charts revised during subsequent visits and through other kinds of narratives and clinical reporting. Morbidity and mortality reports and rounds; less formal "hallway" discussions; communication of an administrative nature; emergencies and error reporting; electronic communication device usage; journal clubs; consults, referrals and discharge notes; scut work; formal lectures; and medical articles and other scientific papers are other instruments used to make and communicate medical decisions. Textual, creative, and affective skills are required to execute these communication elements well.

Two particular areas of focus center on case reporting, and fallacies in communication. Case reporting is ubiquitous across all the medical professions. As effective means of communication in the field, the content of any case reporting must include specific objectives (from a large list of options) and a structure that eases the message transfer. Communication fallacies can be reflected across all instruments of communication. They may be both of a rhetorical and non-rhetorical nature.

Knowledge translation as "an interactive process that includes the synthesis, dissemination, exchange and ethically sound application of knowledge to improve health, provide more effective health services and products and strengthen the healthcare system," relies heavily not only on communication methods, but also on health structures, knowledge, information providers and recipients, and other specific settings. Effective communication is necessary for its success.

In This Chapter

Executive Summary 325
Thoughts, Thinkers, and Things to Think About 327
Introductory Comments 330
11.1 How to View Communication in General and in Its Medical Context 330
11.2 Intellectual Vehicles of Communication: Some Less and More Interrogative Ways
       of Sharing Knowledge and Experience 332
    11.2.1 Commonest One-Way Intellectual Vehicles of Communication:
        Barking Orders, Just Watch Me, Do It after Me 332
    11.2.2 Pimping: A Refined Form of Bullying 332
    11.2.3 Uttering Wisdom 335

11.2.4   Argumentation, Critical Thinking-Based and Evidence-Grounded Exchange of Data and Information: A "What Do You Think?" Type of Medicine I 335

11.2.5   Socratic Method, Dissent, and Dialogue: A Refined Form of Pimping: A "What Do You Think?" Type of Medicine II 339

11.3 Instrumental Vehicles, Opportunities, and Environments for Professional Communication: Oral and Written Exchanges of Experience in Clinical Practice 342

11.3.1   Patient Interviews: Admissions and Opening of Patient Charts........................345

      11.3.1.1 Verbal, Oral, and Written Communication...345

      11.3.1.2 Nonverbal Communication.. 348

11.3.2   Revisiting the Patient: Updating the Opening Interview and Record by Bedside Communication and Progress Notes (SOAPs) 351

11.3.3   Narratives and Clinical Case Reports 352

      11.3.3.1 Clinical Consultations as Narratives..352

      11.3.3.2 Clinical Vignettes and Clinical Case Reports.......................................353

11.3.4   Morning Reports..355

11.3.5   Morbidity and Mortality Reports and Rounds 355

11.3.6   Journal Clubs 356

11.3.7   Other Types of Rounds 357

11.3.8   Mostly One-Way Communication Vehicles: Consults, Referrals, Discharge Notes, and Summaries...357

11.3.9   Scut Work 358

11.3.10 Formal (Magisterial) Lectures 358

11.3.11 Medical Articles and Other Scientific Papers...359

11.3.12 Other Forms of Communication..359

11.4 Illustrative Fallacies in Communication 360

11.5 Emergence of Knowledge Translation as a Way of Thinking and Communicating........ 364

Let Us Conclude: From Patient Problem-Solving Dialogue to a Broader Communication in Medicine 367

References 368

Thoughts, Thinkers, and Things to Think About

To think justly, we must understand what others mean: to know the value of our thoughts, we must try their effect on other minds.
William Hazlitt
(1778–1830)
English Writer (1826)
Shouldn't we equally understand our colleagues and patients by talking to them?

*Precision of communication is more
important than ever, in our area of hair-
trigger balances, when a false, or misunderstood word may create as much disaster as a
sudden thoughtless act.*
James Thurber
(1894–1961), 1961
Just think what is being said on floors!

The Medium is the Message.
Marshall (Herbert) McLuhan
(1911–1980)
Canadian Philosopher (1964)
**Do we know well which one
in medicine?**

*Scientists estimate that medical student
notes account for more than 60% of a
chart's weight.*
Frederick L. Brancati
(1959–2013)
Physician-Diabetologist (1992)
**Which ones should be shared with
others, Fred?**

*There are two rules that all medical students
must learn:
Rule #1: The attending is always Right.
Rule #2: Don't forget Rule #1.*
Howard Bennett
Pediatrician (1994)
**Resemblances with the military service
communication are purely coincidental!**

*At the end of a patient visit, review once
more (1) the working diagnosis and (2) the
proposed plan to deal with it. Then ask: "Is
there anything else?" You will be amazed
(and patients will be gratified) at how often
a less obvious reason for the visit is revealed.*
Christopher D. Stanton
Family Physician (1999)
This kind of open dialogue is invaluable!

Whatever one sees, one must read, and whatever one reads, one must see. This is the only way to learn clinical medicine.
T.C. Goel
Retired Surgeon (1999)
Reading is a one-way communication to continue in the opposite direction!

Any type of communication, oral or written occurs more easily if you have something meaningful to clearly say or put down on paper.
Paraphrasing Sholem Asch
(1880–1957), 1955
And to share it in both directions!

*The culmination of the research process is the communication of results. This final stage may be the most important part of the process (in) that only shared information can clarify, amplify and expand the professional body of knowledge. … The **discussion** section is the heart of a research report.*
Leslie Gross Portney, PT, and
Mary P. Watkins
(Authors, 2009)
Isn't this also the case for all clinical communication with peers and patients?

I told you that I felt funny.
From the tombstone of one of our? patients.

For some, what isn't on Twitter or YouTube, or conveyed by cell phone or email does not count. But does it? Yes, really, it does! In the health domain, the "isn't" counts even more in an irreplaceable direct interaction and communication between warm-blooded human beings.

Introductory Comments

Communication is a vehicle of our reasoning, understanding, decision-making, execution, results, evaluation, and improvements in our endless, often more or less ideal and realistic striving for perfection. Is it enough to reason well, master, and use the best evidence in our decision-making, and execute skillful surgical and medical acts on patients? Obviously not. Quality healthcare is a matter of teamwork bringing together physicians, generalists, and specialists, nurses, dieticians and nutritionists, respirologists, rehabilitation specialists, health administration and administrative staff, social services, and many others.

Communication is essential to succeed in medical care. Deficient communication, poor understandings, and breakdowns are responsible for medical error and harm. How can we communicate effectively in order to provide best care possible? This chapter offers several points to master and ponder starting with understanding the inner workings of the hospital, office, and community, as well as the failures and fallacies that may occur and must be avoided and/or corrected.

Any newcomer in the healthcare environment must thoroughly:

1. Understand what is essential in effective communication: *"What is it all about?"*
2. Know the vehicles and tools of effective communication. These may include encounters with patients, patient charts, reporting clinical cases, floor and other rounds, progress notes, referrals and consults, scientific oral communications, medical review articles, and original studies reports: *"By what means can we get the message across to others?"*
3. Be aware of potential failures in communication, how to avoid and correct them. The most important fallacies in communication illustrate ways to prevent and correct medical error and harm: *"How can we overcome our weaknesses?"*
4. Realize that communication must not only have its own identity, methods, and techniques, but also a purpose. In medicine, communication contributes in an essential way to effective and efficient healthcare, its own and its users' improvement leading to the greatest benefit for and the well-being of the patient.

In this chapter, let us provide an overview of thinking, which is (or should be) mainly behind oral communication. We will examine both professional communication in general and in medicine in particular, since it almost always carries general elements of learning and teaching[1,2] for the parties involved, teachers and trainees, and ultimately the patient. In subsequent chapters we will focus on specific forms of communication vital in medicine. In Chapter 12, we will focus on clinical case reports, case series reports, and clinical vignettes which may be presented either in oral or written form. Written forms of communication, especially a formal "scientific" article is the focus of Chapter 13.

11.1 How to View Communication in General and in Its Medical Context

Making sense and sharing views and experience are based on two types of dialogue, both important for an effective communication and shared decision-making. The first, our own way of critical thinking, is an **internal dialogue**. We think about, and argue, something by, and with, ourselves. We may ask ourselves, did this patient improve enough to discharge him or her, or to stop his or her current treatment? The second is an **external dialogue**. It is a process of *dialectic*, that is, seeking a commonly acceptable solution to a given problem through social and professional dialogue (in our case) with others. Toulmin's modern argumentation, as outlined in Chapter 4, may be used here as it is in an external dialogue. It follows, expands, and brings together internal dialogues. Through external dialogue, we are opening ourselves to the reasoning of others to our internal dialogue and thus own solutions, learning, and change.

In its broadest sense, **communication in general** is a *"process whereby information is enclosed in a package and is channelled and imparted by a sender to a receiver via some medium. The receiver then decodes the message and gives the sender feedback."*[3] All forms of communication therefore require an information and evidence source, a sender (transmitter), a message, a channel of communication, and an intended recipient.

Another understanding is that communication does not simply impart information, it injects a process of influence; *"Communication takes place when one mind acts upon its environment and another mind is influenced, and in that other mind an experience occurs which is like the experience in the first mind, and is caused in part by that experience."*[4] Communication is not only verbal. It is the *"imparting or interchanging of thoughts, opinions or information by speech, writing, or signs"*[5] and *"a process by which information is exchanged between individuals through a common system of symbols, signs, or behavior."*[6]

This last perspective, that communication may take place through verbal, nonverbal, visual, or auditory means, conveyed directly or by various written, spoken or electronic media, is the study of semiotics. It relies on **semantics** (study of meanings), **syntactics** (relationships among signs in formal structures of communication), and **pragmatics** (relationships between signs and their effects on the individuals or groups who use them).[7] Communication is essential in many domains in addition to medicine, such as the military. Several useful general bibliographies covering communication skills across various fields are currently updated and available online.[8]

The new science of **communicology** was defined by Lanigan as *"the study of human discourse in all of its semiotic and phenomenological manifestations"*[9] or simply as *"the science of human communication."*[10] It is introduced to us by at least one monograph[11] and covered also in its own *International Encyclopedia of Communication.*[12] It encompasses communication at the interpersonal, group, and intergroup level. Medical communication happens in all of these.

In 1998, the Association of American Medical Colleges stressed among its objectives that even before graduation, students must acquire the ability to obtain an accurate medical history and to communicate effectively, both orally and in writing, with patients and their families, colleagues, and others with whom physicians must exchange information.[13] It defines **communication in medicine** as a *"transactional process in which messages are filtered through the perceptions, emotions and experiences of those involved. Interpersonal communication remains the linchpin of medical practice."*[13] This linchpin is extremely well introduced and covered in Health Canada's Resource Booklet *Putting Communication Skills to Work.*[14]

As accurately noted by Higgs et al.,[15] effective practice and research in medicine requires equally valid oral, written, and electronic communication between peers and co-workers conveying essential information about how health problems and care are understood and what to do about them. This chapter focuses on the latter.

In the preceding chapters, the authors have demonstrated that the meanings of evidence, argument, and argumentation may vary in their daily use within general and professional settings of communication. Rhetoric, the use of fallacies (sophisms), or fallacious arguments (sophistry) are also subject to these variations when people communicate. Refutations also underlie ways to the right decisions. The process of disproving claims (refutations) is also part of making good decisions. All those terms can be defined the desirable or undesirable way. Table 11.1, as a reminder, illustrates and clarifies this point. The meaning of terms in a medical sense are outlined in right-side column.

Communication as a general activity in medicine has a solid foundation in the literature. This is evidenced by the journal *Communication & Medicine* and in dedicated medicine textbooks listed elsewhere.[16]

11.2 Intellectual Vehicles of Communication: Some Less and More Interrogative Ways of Sharing Knowledge and Experience

Where argumentation is a discussion between two or more people in which at least one advances an argument, it is clear that different types of discussion are more fulsome and satisfactory for different purpose than others. Specifically, some intellectual vehicles of communication are more complete and satisfactory where a discussion includes various statements or propositions allow the inference from them to some conclusion (see Chapter 4). At least five intellectual vehicles of communication are of interest in the context of medicine.

11.2.1 Commonest One-Way Intellectual Vehicles of Communication: Barking Orders, Just Watch Me, Do It after Me

"**Barking orders**" is a common reality in medicine, where situations are intense and demanding, and speed of care is often lifesaving, like emergency medicine and obstetrics. In this case, the "transmitter," attending or any other person who is "running the show" tells the "receiver," the clinical clerk, medical student, or rotating intern what to do and the latter executes the orders. While this form of communication is frequent, it is a one-way street and not representative of a communication for decision-making.

Another one-way vehicle for communication is the form of observation. In this case, a clinician transmits the communication through an approach best articulated as: "**Just watch me!**" It is a passive acquisition of knowledge and fundamental ideas intended to demonstrate a practice that the receiver can, and should, develop further through repeated executions. Like barking orders, there is no exchange of ideas in this form of communication.

A third one-way intellectual communication vehicle is a similar approach where a clinician orders a more junior clinician, resident, or intern to complete a procedure, or execute an already demonstrated skill: a simple "**Do it after me!**" In this case, repeated executions of clinical skills are emphasized. Again, there is not necessarily a meaningful discussion between the senior and junior physician and student; still a learning may be imparted.

11.2.2 Pimping: A Refined Form of Bullying

This method of medical teaching and training[17–19] should not be confused with its more widely known non-medical related meaning, that is, the management of providers of carnal

Table 11.1   Medical and Non-Medical Meanings and Connotations of Some Elements of Reasoning and Communication

Term	General Definition	Medical and Critical Thinking Definition
Argument	An oral disagreement; contention. Emotionally loaded and often tense exchange of words, statements harm and positions not always with that occurred, a mutually acceptable solution in sight.	A vehicle of reasoning; a series of statements intended to establish a position in medical problem solving like diagnosis, treatment or that occurred and curative healthcare.
Argumentation	Confrontational exchange of views or positions between two or more parties. An often emotionally tainted dispute about something.	The methodological use or presentation of medical arguments to solve a problem in medical practice and research through the exchange of ideas and statements between two or more health professionals, patients, and other stakeholders in health.
Refutation	The destructive process of tearing down arguments of others in a game of anything goes; "whip shooting" counter-proposals.	The constructive investigative process of exchange of arguments and counter-arguments based on common understanding and cooperative will to reach a common goal; the best solution for the problem of interest by way of going from disagreement to agreement.
Rhetoric	The undue use of exaggeration or display; bombast; using language to manipulate the listener by mere style or pretention. ("It's only rhetoric!")	The faculty or skill of discovering the available means of persuasion in a given case. A means of instruction involving not only invention, arrangement, style, memory, and what is correct, but also evidence and its delivery. The essence of communication today.
Sophism/ Sophistry	A specious argument to display ingenuity in reasoning by subtle, tricky, superficially plausible, but generally fallacious ways of reasoning, sometimes for the purpose of deceiving someone. Empty appeals that do not really have any significant substance to them. Winning the case, not a search for truth, is the goal.	Argumentative skills to convince others on the basis of the appropriate evidence. Finding truth is the goal of such argumentation.

(Continued)

Table 11.1 (Continued)   Medical and Non-Medical Meanings and Connotations of Some Elements of Reasoning and Communication

Term	General Definition	Medical and Critical Thinking Definition
Evidence	That which tends to prove or disprove something according to its proponents.	Any data or information, whether solid or weak, obtained through experience, observational research or experimental work for understanding of a health problem, decisions about it, and related actions and their effect. (Our definition.)

pleasures. In medicine, pimping is one of the ways of professional communication during various clinical encounters such as morning reports, rounds, and less formal hallway discussions bringing together medical seniors and juniors. In medicine, pimping has three essential meanings:

1. It is a clinical practice where persons in power and entitled to make decisions ("attendings" or senior physicians) ask questions (with blurred expectations) of their junior colleagues (medical students or residents) in order for the latter to correctly execute assigned tasks.
2. The quizzing of juniors with objectives ranging from knowledge acquisition to embarrassment and humiliation; it may be positive or negative.
3. The barraging of juniors with seemingly random and topic/problem unrelated or unanswerable questions to which the juniors most often do not have answers. This frequently leads to humiliation regardless of the intention of the attending or resident asking questions. It creates a feeling of "I do not know" in the face of peers and those who know better.

The "**pimper**" is an attending or resident quizzing subordinates on minutiae and medical trivia during rounds or in class as a questionable test of the junior's knowledge. This might involve a 'pimper' probing subordinates with questions like, "*Speaking of Mrs. Bowie's knee replacement, can you draw the Krebs cycle for me?*"

A "**pimped**" or "**pimpee**" is the unfortunate target and recipient of pimping by pimper(s). At its worst, the pimpee is supposed to acquire a profound and abiding respect for the pimper and quickly learn who is at the top of the local pecking order. At its best, pimping can have a positive impact if it is done through a gentle, constructive, and purposeful approach. In this case, a pimper engages the pimpee in a dialogue to reveal his or her incomplete knowledge as a stimulus to further learning.

Pimping has nothing to do with argumentation. It is a self-purposed endeavor and any meaningful exchange of ideas is not intended by the pimper and not expected by a pimpee.

Student examinations are usually a private matter between the examiner and the examined. Where clinical encounters are flavored by pimping, student knowledge, attitudes, and skills are on public display,[19] regardless of their relationship to the health problem discussed. This does not always help communication between peers.

11.2.3 Uttering Wisdom

The senior physician vocally expresses, "utters wisdom," vocally expressing his often apparently unrelated views regarding the topic of interest or some other topic. Junior physicians or residents do not understand the mental associations underlying the senior's statements, whose relevance and meaning remain unknown. The reason for the message, however valuable it is, remains unknown. The junior is in a "take it or leave it" position. A word of wisdom may also be an attempt to hide the senior's ignorance of the topic.

Consider an exaggerated example. A senior physician, upon examining a patient, comments to a resident, *"This patient may be a good candidate for coronary bypass surgery. As a matter of fact, I just read in the latest issue of* The Lancet *an interesting paper about the cost-effectiveness of immunization in some harder to reach communities in the Canadian North."* The bypass statement may be correct or not. The *Lancet* statement may be correct too, but it is unrelated to the former and irrelevant for a cardiologist's conclusions and proposals.

The utterance of thoughts without explanation and expectation in communication between senior–junior practitioners can often produce a *red herring fallacy*. This fallacy occurs when there is a diversion, usually tangential, from one topic to another. The diversion can be somewhat relevant, or even totally irrelevant, to the issue at hand. The "red herring" notion is derived from fox hunting when smoked red-colored herrings were used by hunters to distract dogs from the scent of the foxes they were hunting.

11.2.4 Argumentation, Critical Thinking-Based, and Evidence-Grounded Exchange of Data and Information: A "What Do You Think?" Type of Medicine I

Successful communication relies on structured critical thinking and argumentation as outlined in Chapter 4. If we define argumentation, in general, as a discussion between two or more people in which at least one person advances an argument, the same holds true in medicine. Physicians discuss among themselves and with other health professionals and patients their cases, the nature of the problem, how to understand it, and what to do about it.

Using the language of argumentation, our recommendations and proposals in communication are in fact the **conclusions** (also called **claim**) of a modern argumentative process. These conclusions are the result of some consensus linking our clinical and paraclinical findings about a particular case (**grounds**) to our past experiences and knowledge (**backing**) and that of others. This in turn, makes sense of such actual and past experiences (**warrant**) to some degree of certainty (**qualifier**) about our argument "claim," that is, what is the diagnosis and how should we treat and care for our patient, provided that some contrary and opposite considerations ("**rebuttals**" in the argumentation sense) do not apply.

Even the best argumentation process makes sense and is useful if several prerequisite considerations are fulfilled, such as the following.

■ questions, objectives, and hypotheses about the case (represented by an individual or a group) are appropriately formulated for analysis and interpretation;
■ all dependent and independent variables that enter our hypotheses are well defined in operational and reproducible terms;
■ the quality of the use of such variables is known;

- the setting of the problem and activities related to it are known, defined, and specified in sufficient details;
- the stakeholders for the health problems are known and their views, understanding and expectations are also known. Doctors, patients, their friends and families, other health and social care professionals, and community actors and decision makers may differ in their views and expectations, but they are all involved to some degree and responsible for what will happen to the patient in the future; and
- both the 'transmitter' in the communication (health professional) and the 'receiver' (patient and others quoted above) know and have some essential common and shared degree of understanding about the subject of current reflections from an argumentative perspective.

Such prerequisites are often crucial for further understanding and solving health problems. Let us say, for example, that several medication errors occurred in a clinical service. As a result, several patients suffered from unexpected sensory problems, unstable blood pressure, nausea, and vomiting caused by overmedication and the suspected administering of medication to the wrong recipients. To solve the problem, the following information must be established:

- the exact nature of the problem and what we want to achieve by tackling it. Do we want to solve the problem of medical errors, of harm to the patient or both? Do we want to solve this problem in patients for whom the drug is indicated, in patients who should not receive this drug or in both?
- the drug (or drugs) involved, its (their) clinical pharmacological characteristics, and both desirable and undesirable (adverse) effects in qualitative and quantitative terms, indications, general patient (demographical), and clinical (principal disease of interest, co-morbidity, treatments and co-treatments for both) characteristics;
- the working environment (wards, intensive care units, operating rooms, elsewhere), the health professionals working there, the type of patients under their care, and the rules and clinical practice guidelines in use in such a setting;
- the person(s) interested in the inquiry and their expectations of the problem-solving process, given his or her specific understanding of the health problem, its management, and control of error and harm. Are the persons interested the patients, their doctors, nurses, pharmacists, pharmaceutical companies, or others? What are their expectations in this problem solving? and
- whether we understand each other. Do the individuals involved have the same understanding of the problem and expectations? This prerequisite answers, *"Are we on the same wavelength?"*

The analyses, interpretations, and corrective measures resulting from this inquiry will depend on how such "rules of the game" are determined beforehand. In particular, cause-effect conclusions apply only if the setting in which they have been defined is known, specified, and shared. The same applies to how such information is used in argumentations about the health problem, whether it be practical or research-oriented.

In communicating about a problem, views, proposals, and premises are communicated and exchanged. This enables us to understand all building blocks of a modern argument in order to solve a clinical problem and the relationships between them. As the example in Table 11.2 shows, even in (and specifically in) daily communication and exchanges about a clinical situation that

Table 11.2 Clinical Rounds as Dialogue with Identification of Argument Components in a Physician's Natural Language

Question	Statement	Component of the Argument
Attending: *"Kim (an intern who was on call tonight), anything new on our floor?"*	**Intern:** *"One of our diabetic and hypertensive patients showed a sudden sensory loss and became hemiplegic. Should he be further evaluated and treated for stroke?"*	***Claim:*** Proposition resulting from our reasoning
Attending: *"Can you tell me what your impression (working assessment) is for this patient?"*	**Intern:** *"This patient most probably had **an ischemic stroke two hours ago**. His **computed tomography** is **normal**. Our consulting neurologist told me to **thrombolyze him right away**. ... By the way, ... →"*	***Grounds:*** Basis from which we reason and argue. Facts supporting the claim.
Intern: *"→ ... do we have some general rules regarding how to handle such cases?"*	**Attending:** *"Yes, as shown by our own review of evidence, **all patients who have an ischemic stroke within three hours should receive IV thrombolysis** to limit the ensuing neurologic deficit. Also, we should consider moving him to a stroke care unit."*	***Warrant:*** General rule that permits us to infer a claim from grounds.
Intern: *"Is this treatment plan mandatory or do we have other choices? Is there anything else we should do?"*	**Attending:** *"It is mandatory. This patient **must** be thrombolyzed and considered for endarterectomy or carotid angioplasty and stenting if carotid stenosis should prove to be an underlying problem."*	***Qualifier:*** A word or phrase that indicates the strength conferred by the warrant and thus the strength of support for our conclusion.
Intern: *"Do we have any competing underlying diagnoses? What should we do to adjust treatment according to the pathology underlying this patient's state?"*	**Attending:** *"**Further diagnostic workup based among other things on CT scan, ultrasonography and magnetic resonance angiography** should help us differentiate this case from intracranial venous thrombosis, aneurysm, arteriovenous aneurysms, or subarachnoidal hemorrhage."*	***Grounds:*** Basis from which we reason and argue. Facts supporting the claim. [Here the question is whether the grounds are in fact correct.]

(Continued)

Table 11.2 (Continued) Clinical Rounds as Dialogue with Identification of Argument Components in a Physician's Natural Language

Question	Statement	Component of the Argument
Intern: *"What kind of evidence do you have available to you for your recommendations and orders?"*	**Attending:** *"Our **systematic review of the evidence** shows that emergency IV thrombolysis of stroke patients improves stroke outcomes like neurologic deficit. ...."*	**Backing:** Body of experience and evidence which supports the warrant.
Attending: *"Well done, Kim!"*	*"**Other treatments must also be considered depending on the underlying lesion:** obstruction by atherosclerosis and other types of stenosis, embolus, lacunar infarction, cerebral infarction, or intracerebral hemorrhage. Also, glucose and blood pressure control are important for all underlying diabetes and hypertension."*	*Confirmation of the claim and additional claims suggested: Proposals for lateral thinking and argumentation for alternatives.*

Source: Adapted from Jenicek M and Hitchcock DL. *Evidence-Based Practice. Logic and Critical Thinking in Medicine.* Chicago, IL: American Medical Association (AMA Press), 2005.

Note: Meanings in clinical jargon: CT = computed tomography. IV = intravenous. To thrombolyze a patient = to give him or her thrombolytic therapy (e.g., by recombinant tissue plasminogen activator).

is to be understood and solved, natural language is most often used to "hide" the more technical vocabulary of argumentation.

As we have argued, professional communication relies (or should rely) on proper argumentation. Earlier, we translated our communication process into Toulmin's way of thinking. Questions and answers in argumentation accurately reflect also the kind of discussion outlined in the Socratic method review of relevant questions. As a review, let us consider these questions as a guide for the communication process viewed as an argumentative-based exchange of data and information.

Questions in this review including the following.

- What is your claim?
- What was the original idea that led to the need for problem-solving?
- What are the data on which you base your claim?
- Do you have some backing for this problem-solving?
- Is there any warrant (supporting understanding) stemming from backing in light of which the data interpretation might be viewed and understood?
- How sure are you about your claim? Using philosophical terms, what is your qualifier philosophically speaking?
- What are the conditions and/or situations in which your conclusions (claim) do not apply? (These are the rebuttals.)

Argumentation in favor of a claim may focus either on building this kind of argument, or on reconstructing the argument. Reconstructing the argument requires extracting available information to understand the argument. Fallacies in this approach are based either on faulty evidence behind the argument building blocks, or on how they are linked together.

Additional challenges are derived when the channel for argumentation is the spoken word. In practice, structured medical student debates must include a range of types of information and argumentative processes to propose a solution to a stated problem. Debates must weigh conflicting information from multiple sources including critically reviewing published research for the quality of evidence (accuracy and validity), relevance, and availability, while remaining skeptical about them. Students must also make evidence-based decisions, explaining risks and benefits of outcome/treatment options and incorporating cost/benefit considerations using multiple sources for problem solving together with impromptu reasoning skills in a team approach to solve the identified problem.[21]

In a debate such as this, it is helpful to consider a series of questions relevant to decision-making[22 modified]

1. Is the clinical situation familiar to the arguer(s)?
2. Is there a single answer, or multiple answers, to the problem under consideration?
3. Are there any important points to be ruled out, or ruled in, without additional explorations, questions, and answers (admission or not, additional clinical and paraclinical workup, etc.)?
4. Can this work within the framework of a complete disease history, pattern, and course?
5. Does the condition require specific care in a hospital or outpatient setting?
6. Does the patient understand and accept the proposed plan for further care as an active participant and co-decision maker in the dialogue?

Communication as a tool for exchanging ideas is usually most meaningful if it helps solve a clinical problem. Even if the best outcome occurs in a single health professional's mind, sharing the argumentative process with others produces even better results.

11.2.5 Socratic Method, Dissent, and Dialogue: A Refined Form of Pimping: A "What Do You Think?" Type of Medicine II

The Socratic method has been qualified as 'polite pimping.' However, it is more than that. In essence, "*it is a* **negative** *method of hypotheses elimination, in that better hypotheses are found by steadily identifying and eliminating those which lead to contradictions.*"[23] In essence, it is a negative method of hypotheses elimination. Better hypotheses are found through a process of identifying, considering, and eliminating those hypotheses which lead to contradictions. Ideally, it is a method that gives everyone the opportunity to contribute to the discussion, to hear what others have to say, to share and improve understanding and experience through multidirectional communication. It is an important communication vehicle in dialogues among health professionals.

The Socratic method uses a distinctive five-part format.

1. The question is stated.
2. An answer is proposed to the question.

3. Objectives and objections to the answer are explored.
4. The answer is revised in light of objections and to determine if it evades those objections.
5. Objections to the revised answer are explored until the answer stands up to all known objections.

The Socratic method of questioning proceeds from one question to another, starting with a first question to clarify the issue. Each subsequent question is built on the information provided by the resolution of the preceding question until the solution to the problem is reached. It is a process in which the original question is responded to as though it were an answer. This in turn forces the thinker to reformulate a new question in light of the progress of the discourse.[23]

This type of dialogue is in some ways the opposite of pimping. For example, rather than asking for a list of reasons or causes of low or high random blood sugar, the Socrates-minded attending may ask others to think about the factors affecting glycemia. The first approach tests students' recollection, the second tests students' capacity to think.[24,25]

Questions, whether open or closed, test subjective preferences based on actual observations and past experiences in search of the best alternative as a solution. Teachers are non-judgmental and make learners feel safe to express their own ideas. Pimpers are often the opposite. They are directional, judgmental, and forceful. Learners must find their own way to the solution as much as possible. Errors in learners' logic are searched for and identified, and common agreement is reached on how incorrect reasoning should be corrected and how such corrections should be reflected in the solution of the problem. In contrast, teachers' questions identify errors in student reasoning and beliefs and subsequent questions are formulated in such a way that they cannot be answered except by a better (correct) argumentative process. Such a Socratic method helps make the best use of what learners already know and leads them not only to solutions of a clinical health problem and question, but also to ways of acquiring additional data and information to solve the particular problem at hand and similar ones in the future.

Hence, successful dialogue ends when the answer resists all known objections. Do we not do this when discussing differential diagnoses or choosing treatment options? The nature of dialogue means that:

■ all dialoguing parties share exploration and examination;
■ student thinking and responses are steered in a direction that is usually known ahead of time by the teacher who works backward to clarify the process of reaching a solution with students;
■ reasoning skills (including handling fallacies) are learned by talking out loud;
■ a variable degree of dependency on authority figures or experts is maintained in problem solving;
■ learners are guided to answering questions, building self-awareness of their deficits, and a recognition and correction of their errors; and
■ learners are engaged through effective questioning in order to hone critical thinking skills, diagnose learning needs, offer immediate 'teaching pearls of wisdom,' seek knowledge, and develop the ability to learn in a self-directed manner.

In medicine, dialogue should lead not only to the sharpening of thought processes[26,27] (Socrates' own main objective), but also to an imparting of knowledge. The focus of questions varies.[26,27 – modified] They may address:

- **clarifications** (Why do you say that? How does it relate to our discussion?);
- **assumptions** (How could you verify or disprove that assumption? What could we assume instead?);
- **reasons and evidence** (What would be an example? What do you think causes that to happen and why?);
- **viewpoints and perspectives** (What is the best diagnostic method, treatment, or care? What would be the alternatives? What are the strengths and weaknesses of your preferences and alternatives?);
- **implications and consequences** (What generalization can be made? What are the consequences? What does it affect? What are the links with what we have learned before?); and
- **questions about questions** (What does it all mean? Why do you think that you asked the question? Was it out of scientific curiosity and/or to improve practice? How does all this apply to our practice?).

Socratic questions used in the evaluation of an argument[27–30 modified] are based on these categories. These evaluation questions help to clarify the decision-making process.

They may include the following:

- What do you mean by … (your observation, diagnosis, treatment decision or prognosis)?
- How did you come to that conclusion?
- Why do you believe that you are right?
- What is the source of your information?
- What assumption has led you to that conclusion?
- What happens if you are wrong?
- Can you give me at least two sources that disagree with you and explain why?
- Why is this significant?
- How do I know you are telling me the truth (based on how your clinical workup of the case or problem)?
- What is the alternate explanation for this phenomenon (case, problem)?

Beyond routine clinical work, a good example of Socratic questioning and dialogue is Grahame-Smith's debate about evidence-based medicine.[31]

All questions, points, and counterpoints in Socratic dialogue are (and must be) supported by the best evidence for the purpose. In Socratic dialogue and dissent, it is up to the person answering a question to provide answers as conclusions of a modern argument and be ready to specify all the necessary building blocks, their connection in his or her proposals and counter-proposals. Answers then must be viewed as claims and conclusions of some argumentative process that preceded each of the questions. Structured argumentation must work in both directions: answers to students' questions based on the argumentative process and student replies to teacher questions as conclusions supported by a modern argument and its building blocks. Hence, the Socratic method integrates multiple reasoning paths as outlined in Chapter 4.

Benefits of the Socratic method in teaching and learning medicine are numerous. They include honing critical thinking skills in the context of patient care and challenging the learner's preconceived notions of medicine by asking questions in a stepwise manner; diagnosing the learner's level and further needs; understanding, engaging and encouraging the learner toward focused self-directed learning; and teaching and learning relevant essentials.[26] The ultimate benefit of Socratic thinking (critical thinking, argumentation, and grounded in best evidence) is our understanding, the decisions that we make in clinical and community care, the benefits for the patient, and the preventing errors and harms in the patient.

11.3 Instrumental Vehicles, Opportunities, and Environments for Professional Communication: Oral and Written Exchanges of Experience in Clinical Practice

Instrumental vehicles of communication are environments, opportunities, and tools for communication between peers. There are numerous examples of these vehicles in medicine. These are summarized in the section below.

- **Taking notes about daily activities.** Notes take the form of everything from **patient charts** and **admission notes**, patient and disease histories and other narratives, to clinical and paraclinical workup, **progress reports** ("*SOAPs*," i.e., *s*ubjective and *o*bjective states and findings, *a*ssessments and *p*lans), **referrals** and **discharge summaries**.
- **Specialty consultations and consult letters.** Sharing on request a clinician's particular expertise for the best benefit of the patient, using the best available, though always incomplete and imperfect decision-making, about care in **specialty consultations** and **consults**.[32–34]
- Informal gathering at **inpatient and outpatient**[35] **morning reports**.[36–39] These gatherings are opportunities to review management of cases and the performance of the attending crew (faculty, house officers, and students) and eventually the care provided by associate health professionals. Topics discussed in these morning reports are legion.[40] Morning reports can be both case-based and skills sessions and include resident/medical student morning report, senior resident morning reports, combined morning reports, and outpatient morning reports.[39] In addition to the physician providing care, physician-scientists[41] and librarians[42] can also be involved, especially if the EBM orientation with[43] or without[44,45] mobile or hand-held electronic devices is considered and given to morning reports.
- **Bedside** and corridor or "**hallway**"[46] more or less formal **teaching** (i.e., teaching once the door to the patient's room is closed) and **floor rounds**.[47]
- **Grand rounds**[48,49] within specialty and inter-specialty groups to clarify selected challenging topics in and beyond everyday practice and care.
- Structured **morbidity** and **mortality reports** in clinical practices, both occasional and regular reports.
- Any **communication of an administrative nature**, business meetings, on-the-spot problem solving exchanges of ideas between interested parties and decision makers (personal and material resources discussions and solutions).

- **Clinical guidelines, clinical protocols**, and other standard procedures of development, implementation, and evaluation.
- **Emergencies, outbreaks** investigations and control, **errors and mistakes** in daily routines requiring surveillance, and corrective measures to prevent **harm**.
- Using **electronic communication devices** (email, messaging, texting, teleconference, etc.) for consultation and other exchanges of ideas, data, or information.
- **Scut work** environment, where clinicians work on menial, tedious tasks in healthcare. Questions exist whether this is a place for communication and learning.

Any of these communication methods reflect argumentative processes, in part or in their entirety. They are further discussed in later sections of this chapter. These fundamental modes of reasoning and decision-making are prone to fallacies in communication which are reviewed in Section 11.4.

Communication methods, with the exception of patient charts and unstructured informal discussions (or chats) may involve other tools. These tools include simple orders, elements of pimping and other humiliating and psychological assaults, teaching by Socratic discourse, and evidence-based modern argumentation. The types of communications which are preferred for argumentation in the medical field are discussed earlier.

Let us consider an example of teaching and learning in surgery. For the sake of explicitness, Figure 11.1 illustrates in a simplified manner the desirable attitudes, knowledge and skills that are acquired in various clinical and paraclinical environments and settings. In each, an array of communication methods is used, namely simple orders, the venerated 'show me, watch me, do it after me' technique and other ways of reasoning and communication as presented earlier in this section. All teaching tools, environments, health professionals, and their patients are potential breeding grounds for fallacies.

Passive teaching tools and environments involve lectures, textbooks, articles, web information, and hearsay.

Active teaching tools consist of a much broader group of events and environments. Many of these take place in-hospital or clinical settings like chart-based analyzes at the bedside; rounds and morning reports at floor events; impromptu intramural chats in elevators, hallways, and cafeterias; hospital operating rooms, emergency departments, imaging (x-ray) and laboratory advice and consulting; specialty consults; and post-discharge support and care (social services, prosthetic care, re-adaptation). Others take place outside of clinical environments—at specialty conventions, workshops, interactive continuing education programs, and technology and management assistance problem-solving which may occur in multiple settings.

Each communication method merits further practice and evaluation, regardless of the way each communication method contributes to the acquisition of desirable knowledge, attitudes, or skills in a variety of settings. To have the full benefits of teaching, training and practice, all methods, types and aspects of communication and their settings must be free of fallacies. As illustrated by Figure 11.1, understanding and evaluating communication is a multi-element and multidimensional problem. It cannot be dealt with all at once, but should instead be fractioned into more manageable pieces, "cube by cube," as in this figure.

Each of the different communication methods and the formats they take imply questions, answers, feedback, and other elements of argumentation that are shared by all parties involved. All participants should discuss questions of common interest in a manner that is free of fallacies, in the same way as is required and expected for related scientific information in medical periodicals and other press. Such discussions cover not only the critical appraisal of bedside evidence and

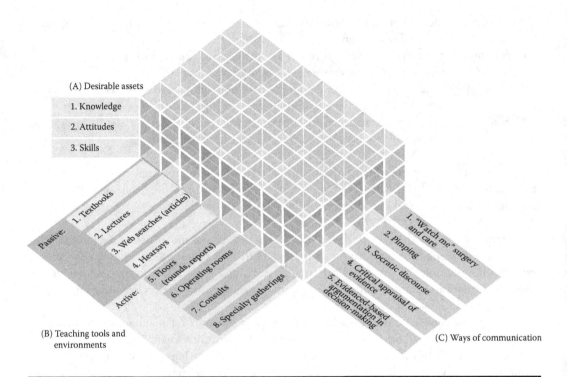

Figure 11.1   Matrix for understanding the evaluation of fallacy-free teaching, learning and practice of surgery.* (Based on Jenicek M. *Evaluating Surgery. Uses of Clinical Case Reports and Case Series in Surgical Specialties*. Draft Document as reported at the Balliol Colloquiums for Evaluating Surgery. Johnathan Meakins, Chair. University of Oxford, UK, September 6–8, 2007.[50] See also Jenicek M. *A Primer on Clinical Experience in Medicine*. Boca Raton, FL: CRC Press, 2013.)

relevant external evidence, but also connections between them and the reasoning towards better decision-making. The teaching aspect of communication thoughts is present in any communication of this kind, but its main purpose is to improve and offer a clearer guideline for understanding and what to do. This must be done between equals and made by equals in their understanding of the problem. As "equals," all participating health professionals must be "on the same wavelength."

One type of communication vehicle that will not be discussed here are medical articles and other scientific papers. They are explored fully in Chapter 12.

Other forms of communication that are specific to certain languages, general and local medical cultures, traditions, experiences and faith may be missed by some readers, but relevant to others. Individual practitioners should determine how to use these other types of communications based on their own judgment.

---

* A clinical teacher who wants to evaluate whether a communication method is free from fallacies by asking himself or herself, "*if bedside and floors teaching based on Socratic discourse improves the knowledge and attitudes of students*" will base his or her evaluation on A1, A2, B4, and C4 teaching and learning elements. Evaluating "*how skills are developing through 'watch me' surgery in operating rooms*" will involve elements A3, C2, and B5. Evaluating "*if surgeons acquire desirable knowledge based on literature from Web searches focused on modern argumentation in decision-making*" will consider elements A1, B2, and C6. "Fractioning" or breaking down the evaluation of teaching and learning in such a manner creates manageable pieces based on clear questions which then lead to a fallacy-free evaluation, understanding, and decision-making process.

11.3.1 Patient Interviews: Admissions and Opening of Patient Charts

Communication between patients and health professionals may be carried out in two ways:

1. Through **oral or written means** we retrieve, convey, and retain information with its proper meaning and understanding to be shared, and reciprocated, between and among, all interested parties, patients, their physicians, and others. This is obviously the vital, ubiquitous, and most established approach.
2. **Nonverbal ways** of communication can be an important addition to verbal communication. They are not only complementary, but must also be considered as more primary methods where linguistic and cultural barriers exist. In some patients whose speech is impaired, sensorium and/or pathology, nonverbal communication may be the only way to establish communication and share the information to ensure proper care.

Let us comment briefly on both of them.

11.3.1.1 Verbal, Oral, and Written Communication

Any patient/doctor encounter is an exercise in communication coupled with physical examination, paraclinical (laboratory biochemistry and hematology) exploration of patient physiology and morphology by imaging techniques, and contextually expanded assessment (social, cultural, faith setting) and needs. The overall approach to such encounters[51–54] is well established, learned, and used throughout the clinical experience. Based on this larger framework, then, what is important for successful communication between the patient and his or her physician in order to provide the patient with the best possible care?

The comprehensive assessment of the adult patient includes:

1. identification of data and source of the history;
2. chief complaint(s);
3. present illness;
4. past history;
5. family history; and
6. personal and social history, and
7. review of systems.[55]

Through this assessment, medical events and relevant client experiences are counted and described wherever necessary and possible. Once a patient–physician relationship is established, a mutual, common, and shared understanding of '*What are we talking about?*' must be built.

As the physician engages in the comprehensive assessment, different questions arise.[51–55]

1. As a prerequisite at any point in the patient encounter, the physician must be ready to **define** what he or she means when asking about pain and being comfortable, or when saying 'this will hurt,' or when sharing with the patient the first impression of the patient's condition, etc. This is easier to express where **hard data** (data that is easier to measure, quantify and categorize in the process of clinimetrics) like bleeding or fever is available. It is more challenging where only **soft data** like pain or mood, values,

and feelings, so important in psychiatry, is available. Let us note that interviews in psychiatry,[53] if performed correctly, are also good examples how soft data might be "hardened" for decision-making purposes.

2. To optimize relationships, objectivity, and value assessments (for the patient, and for physician's diagnostic workup) of any information, encounters frequently begin with **open (open-ended) questions** (e.g., *What brought you here? What happened? How may I help you? How do you feel today?*) Open questions generate hypotheses. They encourage the use of deductive reasoning and can further test preliminary hypotheses.

3. **Closed (closed-ended) questions** follow (e.g., *How does it feel when I touch your tummy this way? In this area? Does it hurt when I press? Does it change when I stop?*). Closed questions test hypotheses. They initiate inductive reasoning and serve to confirm the hypotheses that are dependent on what we asked and saw.

4. **Directive (focused) questions** search for specific information like closed questions, but are more specific and detailed (e.g., *How does the pain in your tummy feel since it first appeared until now?*).

5. **Double questions** simultaneously offer two potential options for responses (e.g., *Do you have any pain in your tummy or do you have also pain in your chest?*). Double questions asked rapidly seek potentially related information, but may be ambiguous and hard to understand by the patient. For that reason, they should be used with caution.

6. **Multiple choice questions** may be asked to define the range of information sought (e.g., *Do you have trouble concentrating, staying concentrated, concentrating on one problem or more, or with some other aspect of your mental functioning?*). These can be confusing for the patient.

7. **"Yes or no"** questions are the most directional and restrictive form of closed questions. They may be needed in some instances for proper decision-making.

8. **Leading questions** are meant to lead the patient to a particular conclusion. They are used sometimes in courts of law, but also in medical and psychiatric interviews (e.g., *You never used medication for your tummy pain, right? ... No? And you changed your dietary habits since having this problem? ... No? Or did you experience any other discomfort during this period? ... So, should we consider this a new problem?*). More precise and more complete information usually cannot be obtained this way despite the somewhat Socratic character of such sequences of questions. They should be avoided.

9. At the end of the encounter, returning **to open question(s)** may solicit additional valuable information for parallel and lateral thinking about other patient problems that should be considered (e.g., *Is there anything else that we have forgotten? Is there anything else that bothers you? Is there some other way I can help you?*).

Through these patient/physician dialogues, three key elements of the patient problem are revealed: information about dependent variables, dimension of the identified phenomena of interest, and to provide meaning to what is discovered. **Information about independent variables** such as the causes of a disease or its cure and **dependent variables** in terms of disease occurrence and recovery, provide the basis for identifying the **phenomena of interest** with respect to the patient. Interviews are critical for any meaningful establishment of these cause-effect relationships and reasoning about them.

The phenomena of interest, such as pain, bleeding, vomiting, or loose stools, must be well defined and usable for categorization and classification if such categories are indicative of specific diagnostic approaches and distinct treatments and follow-up. For this reason, a **dimension** must be given to them whenever it is important for diagnostic and/or therapeutic decision-making and interventions. Dimensions may include frequency, amplitude, duration, localization, projection, episodes, and spells are of interest.[51–53,56]

At the end of the interview, a physician needs to, where possible, give **meaning** to what is discovered during the interview. This signifies making a diagnosis or giving direction regarding the patient's complaints and the reason for the interview.

In this process, the initial "impressions," or first working ideas about further exploration, diagnosis and treatment, that are identified in the meaning of the interview are already a set of claims or conclusions of some type of argumentative process. We can view the initial patient interview through the argumentation process outlined in previous chapters as follows:

1. **Grounds** are provided by the patient interview and completed by further clinical and paraclinical examinations and work-ups.
2. These observations are supported or not by **backing** stemming from general and personal past or present experience.
3. **Warrants** give a meaning based on the connection between the grounds and their backing.
4. From this information, we can assess how certain we can be in our conclusions using **qualifiers**. **Qualifiers** as probabilistic expressions cannot always be satisfactorily quantified given the biological nature of health problems that are addressed in medicine.
5. Ethical considerations, complications, adverse effects, multiple morbidities (co-morbidities), and treatments both for the main problem and co-treatments for co-morbidities may all underlie **rebuttals** of our conclusions and recommendations.
6. As a result then of our patient dialogue or argumentative process, we make diagnostic and therapeutic **conclusions** or **claims** to present either new hypotheses, or their confirmation.

As we can see, argumentation relies heavily on our communication with the patient. Some illustrations in Section 11.4 address how to ensure that this communication is also a fallacy-free process.

In any kind of communication with the patient, interviewing and communication relies on establishing confidence and mutual understanding between the patient and the physician. This is achieved by understanding and solving patient problem(s). Several *ad hoc* titles address very effectively this crucial element of clinical practice.[51–55,57,58]

Bickley and Szilagyi[51] reordered and modified recommend following these steps in the first physician/patient encounter.

- from what you heard during the interview and saw at the physical examination, identify abnormal findings;
- localize these findings anatomically;

- assess the nature and quality of data (findings), their time-space relationship as webs of causes and webs of consequences;
- make hypotheses about the nature of the patient's problems;
- test your hypotheses;
- interpret the findings in terms of the probable process;
- establish a working diagnosis;
- generate the problem list;
- develop a plan (concept maps may help); and
- make this plan agreeable and acceptable to the patient with all respect due to medical ethics.

This proposal of reasoning, assessment, and recording reflects a rather complex reasoning path consisting of a sequence of arguments covering a set of sequential steps in clinical work (risk assessment, diagnosis, treatment, prognosis, further expanded care) as already outlined in Chapter 4.

Each element of a patient–physician interaction is one part of the whole argumentative process. The final outcome of each step represents statements, proposals, and conclusions of the argumentative processes. Ideally, in both oral and written arguments, students and teachers should be able to identify and reconstruct elements of the argumentative process. By the end of any patient interview, it can be useful to conduct a review of mutual physician/patient interaction to ensure that both parties share an understanding of the outcomes of the communication. A shared understanding is not always the case, even where contact with the patient was well established in mostly psychological terms of courtesy, comfort, and connection.[52]

11.3.1.2 Nonverbal Communication

The nonverbal process of communication refers to the sending and receiving of messages by ways other than speech. This includes visual cues, gestures, touch, body language, posture, facial expressions, eye contact, object uses (clothing, hairstyle, personal hygiene, etc.), and "parlanguage" (voice quality, rate, pitch, volume, pitch, volume, rhythm, intonation, stress), among others.[59] Mehrabian[60] and Silverman, Kurtz, and Draper[61] include additional nonverbal communication that they consider as clinically important. These include posture proximity (use of patient–physician space), touch (physical contact during physical examination), body and extremities movements, facial expression, eye behavior, vocal cues, use of time by the patient, physical presence (a heterogeneous ensemble of characteristics such as race, gender, body shape, clothing, grooming), and even environmental cues like location, furniture, placement, lighting, temperature, and color in patient–physician environment.

While face-to-face interactions are the most frequent instances of nonverbal communication in clinical settings, the role and volume of nonverbal communication in general is still a subject of debate both in medical and more general settings. The relative prevalence of nonverbal communication compared to verbal communication is a consideration. Moreover, gestures, mimics, or posture may have different meanings on a case-by-case basis[62] in health sciences, health professions and elsewhere. The additional role of culture and faith is also worthy of attention.

As an example, even clothing may be part of a nonverbal message: white coats, scrubs, and gowns convey and reinforce the professional meaning of what we do. Patient gowns convey the message of dependency, trust, or mistrust. Nonverbal messaging and communication brings additional information to the caring health professional and refines and specifies sometimes more the rest of factual clinical information.

Some other forms of nonverbal communications relevant to the clinical experience are outlined here.

Physical space uses in communication (proxemics) may convey some meaning. Keeping a physical distance between communicating parties may reflect discomfort and may also affect the meaning of oral communication.

Time in communication (chronemics) means the organization and perception of time and reactions to it. The patient's time and that of the patient's caregiver may be precise, scheduled, arranged, and managed, or not. Clinical activities may be done in a fluid or erratic way. Time may not mean only "money," but also "health."

Movement and body position (kinesics) are not only pathognomonic (characteristic or distinctive of disease and other condition) signs, but they also convey a person's attitudes, values, or preferences through their behaviors. Posture and gestures are used, such as "thumbs up" if everything goes well or "thumbs down" if nothing works. A patient's "middle finger" may convey the patient's displeasure, lack of manners, intoxication, or mental state and disease.

Touching in communication (haptics) is more than an examination tool. Holding hands is a tool of sympathy and empathy, back slapping or "high fiving" are signs of comfort, relief, or success of care. Holding a child is an expression of affection and care, not simply a maneuver of care.

Eye gaze (oculesics) is not only of interest for ophthalmologists, neurologists, and psychiatrists as diagnostic tool and reflection of the progress of care. Interest, attention, involvement, mood, and intimacy may be assessed by the length of gaze, glances, patterns of fixation, pupil dilatation, and blinks.

Voice cues (paralanguage, vocalics) such as tone, pitch, accent, and other voice qualities ("voice print") may affect the meaning of the words spoken by the patient and health professional. An "uh-huh" or "hmm" may indicate that a person is listening, thinking about, and paying attention to another. Even health professional comfort, competency, or decision certainty in specific situations may be reflected by voice cues.

Artifacts like choices and preferences of clothing, jewelry, hairstyle, and even art, or the patient's private and hospital space arrangements (furniture and other possessions, placement, visibility, and accessibility of tools and instruments) may say a lot about the patient, the caregiver, and the healthcare environment.

The physical appearance of the patient and his or her caregiver is a nonverbal expression both for the physician (dishevelled patients entering psychiatric care) and the patient (projection of professionalism, involvement, engagement, and devotion in providing healthcare by his or her physician or nurse).

Observation and evaluation of nonverbal communication are particularly important in some clinical specialties. Nonverbal communication is especially relevant psychiatric interview, and in the evaluation of the effectiveness of treatment and care. Many clinical conditions and actions such as endocrinological disorders, obesity, premenstrual syndrome, stress and distress, surgical care, drugs prescribed and used, and others may affect patient nonverbal communication and its interpretation by the patient's physician. A patient may also misread a caregiver's nonverbal messages. Communication between health professionals themselves should also not be forgotten.

In the 1980s, Waitzkin[63] addressed the need for more structured training of health professionals in nonverbal communication with patients. Since this time, applications and methodology developments have evolved further. Not surprisingly, they often cover psychiatry, mental health, and diagnostic activities.[64]

What Role Does Nonverbal Communication Play in Argumentation and Critical Thinking?

Practically speaking, nonverbal communication may play a role as part of an argument building block: A patient's sigh or pointing to where it hurts may be part of grounds in the diagnostic process. Grimacing may signal an adverse reaction to a drug or a rebuttal for further medical decision-making. A "V" sign can be a conclusion or claim that treatment works. Thumbs down means the opposite. However, nonverbal messages must be interpreted and used in a multicultural context and an increasing amount of literature is devoted to this topic. For example, an index–thumb "OK" sign does not always mean success or victory in activities, proposals, and consequently even in patient care. In some countries, it can represent a body orifice where some suggestion of real or proposed activity belongs, if it is not appreciated by the messenger or receiver of this nonverbal expression.

More systematic, methodological development uses and evaluation of nonverbal and especially bilateral communication may be expected in the near future. For example, in the diagnostic domain, it may start by our better understanding of nonverbal messages and communication at any stage of the diagnostic process.

The process for better understanding nonverbal communication in the diagnostic process can be illustrated as follows.

Global observation of a patient's nonverbal message(s)
↓
Isolation of the message of interest
↓
Description of the sign
↓
Its identification and dimension
↓
Its interpretation in terms of patient state
↓
Meaning, extrapolation, and categorization,
hence diagnosis itself of which a nonverbal message is a part,
either together with other messages and signs or sometimes as a single presentation[65]

We still do not know the stages, content, and meaning of nonverbal communication well enough. Let us remember that nonverbal communication may be the only communication in patient–physician interaction where speech, senses, and sensorimotor activities are impaired or impossible, whatever the underlying pathology might be. As such, we should know and use it better in the context of our communication and decision-making in clinical settings.

11.3.2 Revisiting the Patient: Updating the Opening Interview and Record by Bedside Communication and Progress Notes (SOAPs)

Bedside rounds remain an essential opportunity for communication with patients and their other health providers, though more limited than in prior years as a result of other activities and time constraints. Progress notes that result from these encounters should reflect the physician's reasoning and detail his or her assessment and plans for further patient care.[51] Similar strategies apply to repeated encounters with patients in **ambulatory** or **family care**. However, simply reviewing and recording additional information, data, and results from previous encounters is not sufficient.

Progress notes usually follow a format summarized by the acronym **SOAP**. The acronym stands for:

- **s**ubjective observations including all **symptoms** (subjective manifestations of ongoing disease and care) as conveyed to us by the patient. They should be informative enough to provide ideas regarding the location, directionality (radiation and expansion), quality, quantity and severity, timing, setting of the occurrence, remitting and exacerbating factors, alleviating factors and associate manifestations, and their evolving changes of the symptoms;
- **o**bjective observations and findings from the physician's clinical and paraclinical follow-up, new and repeated data, information, and findings. The clinician looks for **signs** of what the patient may be experiencing;
- **a**ssessment of changes in patient clinical course based on the integration of both subjective and objective observations resulting in an updated perspective of the patient's condition; and
- **p**lan which identifies what the clinician has determined should be deleted, modified, or expanded from current care. This may include medication, surgical care, restoration of functions, psychological and/or psychiatric care or social support, and home or ambulatory care. Any plan should include the *patient's perspective*[51]—his or her feelings (fears, concerns), ideas and views of the nature and causes of his or her condition and evolution, impact on his or her life and functioning, and his or her expectations based on past and present experience.

An increasing number of excellent guides, coordinated by Uzelac,[66] are being published for various specialties such as obstetrics and gynecology, pediatrics, emergency medicine, family medicine, urology, dermatology, neurology, and internal medicine.[64] This series offers an overview of many of the most relevant and frequent reasons for patient visits to medical offices, outpatient clinics, emergency services, or admissions for more prolonged hospital care.

From the perspective of "arguers," that is, practitioners of argumentation and critical thinking in medicine, there are six basic and original elements necessary to establish an argumentative process. As we already know, these elements are **conclusions** (plan), necessary **grounds** in subjective and objective information, and **backing**, **warrants** (understanding), **qualifiers** in the assessment of the updated clinical situation, and, whenever **rebuttals** exist, they should be specified along with decisions and recommendations.

Bedside rounds and progress notes represent valuable opportunities not only to teach physical examination skills, but also to model skills in communication and professionalism.[67] These rounds are often expanded to hallway, elevator, or drinking fountains where two or more clinicians continue bedside rounds. The same rules and comments apply, regardless of where they take place.

11.3.3 Narratives and Clinical Case Reports

Narratives and clinical case reports are fundamental part of clinical practice. Whether accepting a new patient in family medicine, or admitting a new patient in hospital care, the process starts by patients telling their stories in context, sharing their concerns and expectations, and importantly, what happened to bring them to the clinician's attention. These form the basis of the patients' own clinical case, charts, and records.

11.3.3.1 Clinical Consultations as Narratives

Telling stories is a part of everyday life. It is also the case in everyday medical practice. Patients tell stories during the first encounters between physicians and their patients, when updating patient charts during subsequent visits and consultations, when a patient moves from one specialist or medical service to another, and so on. Patients tell clinicians about themselves and in turn clinicians share information about themselves, both within or outside the context of the case. This is done to establish mutual confidence and meaningful communication, retention, and use of health information. Such narratives are defined as *an orderly, continuous account of an event or series of events.*[4]

Without narratives in medicine, there would be no meaningful communication between patients and their physicians. Narratives most often precede clinical case reports and may initially be part of them. For some, narratives, even less than case reports, "explain nothing" with regard to cause effect-relationships. However, that is where etiological research, clinical trials, and even simple descriptions of clinical events and those who report them find their ideas and directions for next steps. Narratives must not be forgotten in today's technological world of medicine, but rather further structured, developed, understood, and used as they already have been in general and family medicine,[68–70] applied to surgery[71] connected to ethics,[72,73] clinical case reporting,[74,75] and evidence-based medicine.[76–78]

The narrative serves to build a **relationship**, to **collect data and information**, and to reach a **mutual agreement on a management plan**. They are a type of communication tool.[79]

In terms of general characteristics, narratives:

- cover a well-defined time period as a time frame for the event of interest;
- include both the narrator and listener viewpoints in the story; hence, bilateral communication is essential. Usually, the patient is the story-teller and the physician is the story-interpreter and facilitator of mutual understanding;
- concern not only individuals, but also the settings and circumstances that are relevant for their clinical care;
- help doctors understand what patients really experience for the purpose of clinically caring for them; and
- are the starting point for research, as are clinical case reports. Narratives are where hypotheses are generated and better defined. The design of research studies may be refined by such experience.

These are just some of the reasons why a doctor "who listens" is so appreciated.

Taking a patient's history and giving advice in clinical consultation is an exchange of narratives. Patients tell clinicians what is going on, and in turn clinicians try to explain to them why the course of action is appropriate and why they should comply with treatment recommendations. It is a two-way exchange of different narratives of different genres. In pediatrics, it involves three partners: the child, the parent, and the health services professional.

Running, analyzing, and using narrative requires **narrative competence** which essentially is communication competence. For Charon,[80] it is *"the set of skills required to reorganize, absorb, interpret, and be moved by the stories one hears or reads"*:

- **Textual skills** include identifying, adopting, and recognizing a story's structure, its multiple perspectives, metaphors, and allusions.
- **Creative skills** mean being able to make multiple interpretations, build curiosity, and consider multiple endings.
- **Affective skills** encompass acceptance of uncertainty throughout the story and entering the story's mood. Narratives provide meaning, context, and perspective for information in medicine as well as an understanding of health problems that cannot be obtained by other means. They are an important teaching and learning experience such as through role playing that cannot be reproduced otherwise.[79]

Previously, we defined evidence in evidence-based medicine as any information or data necessary for understanding and making decisions about a health problem.[65] If "evidence" is defined this way, we may consider narratives and narrative-based medicine[81] as one of the tools used to palliate some perceived shortcomings of evidence-based medicine[82] and to complete it in an integrated manner.[74] Montgomery[83] reminds us that when physicians who conduct research perform their clinical duties, they are no longer scientists, but clinicians, that is, physicians who take care of patients.

Narrative sequential presentations unfold the tactful, tactical development of knowledge and experience relevant to determining what is wrong with particular patients and deciding what action to take on their behalf. Case narratives supply a workable medium for representing knowledge that is time- and context-dependent. Once the diagnosis is made, physicians may say, "The patient's story is consistent with a myocardial infarction." Narrative, thus, is essential to thinking and knowing in clinical medicine.[84] We can consider it another example of pattern recognition.

11.3.3.2 Clinical Vignettes and Clinical Case Reports

Clinical vignettes discussed here, and clinical case reports as discussed in Chapter 12, may have different meaning, objectives, and structure in today's literature and communication tools. A clinical vignette is a concise presentation of an interesting or challenging patient encounter.[85] Clinical vignettes are descriptions of a clinical experience, usually with one clinical case, in simple "title and author" information, introduction (preferably with learning objectives), case presentation, literature review (sometimes), discussion, and summary.[86,87]

At its core, a clinical vignette or case report is a presentation of chief complaint, history, physical examination, laboratory and radiographic studies, assessment, and plan. A series of questions asked of trainees and their answers covering the core elements of the vignette are used as a tool to measure and enrich the trainees' knowledge and clinical reasoning. Presentation of the case report and the discussion therein are shaped to highlight either the natural history of a given health problem, the therapeutic relationship between clinician and patient, or patient management to improve knowledge and clinical skills.[85] A virtual cornucopia of clinical vignettes examples was recently assembled by the Society for General Internal Medicine.[86–90]

In a written form, clinical vignettes and case reports are not essays:

> ■ **Essays** are typically literary compositions covering a particular theme or subject from a personal or singular point of view.
> ■ **Clinical vignettes** and **case reports** are more than that:
>   They are purposeful and structured presentations of a health problem with defined purposes and questions asked, answered, resolved, or guided to resolution.

Clinical case reports and **case series reports** are also distinct entities.[88,89]

> ■ A **clinical case report** (CCR) is a structured presentation of a clinical experience with a single patient according to predetermined objectives and has a fact-finding purpose rather than education. It is used to exchange information about observed facts, taking into account the improvement of practice in habitual clinical settings, and to trace potential research directions for the health problem of which the patient is representative. It also can establish directions for further management of the problem and care.
> ■ **Case series reports** (CSRs) are multiple case observations, descriptions, analyzes, and explanation for better understanding and decision-making about the medical and/or surgical management of the health problem that is the subject of the case series. Objectives of CSRs include providing "numerators" of rates for clinical epidemiological research, and identifying prevailing characteristics of patients, sites, management or care, outcomes, and the constancy and consistency of findings. This can provide a basis for a "meta-analysis of cases."

In research, single cases or case series as simple frequencies without denominators and control groups are considered by many as poor, or low, levels of evidence. This may be true in studies of cause-effect relationships and in other types of studies, especially of a descriptive nature. However, they are an important starting point and can provide powerful ideas as part of generating hypotheses. To fulfill this purpose:

■ reasons, objectives, and hypotheses must be stated in advance;
■ all variables of interest must be well defined or provided on request to parties in communication;
■ the structure of the case report must be clear, and at the end; and
■ conclusions must be explicated and discussed.

Clinical case reports are today more objectives, methodology, and uses and applications than their qualification, in daily parlance, "*Ah those, they prove nothing!*" In the past, clinical case reports were not always considered to carry substantive evidentiary value in clinical terms. However, today clinical case reports are more characterized by objectives, methodology, and uses and applications. Clinical case reports will be explored further in Chapter 12 of this book.

11.3.4 Morning Reports

Morning reports[91] are summaries of events that occurred on the hospital floor, service, or department during a specified work period (shift) that the individuals and teams in charge communicate to the individuals and teams who take over at the end of their shift. They may be regular, formal, and institutionalized, or informal as dictated by the reality of the practice. Participants may be members of the house staff, residents, interns, attending physicians, nurses, and others.[91] Newly admitted cases, progress in patients under current care, functioning of services, and unusual events worthy of attention and care may be discussed. Led in informal language, they follow more formal information as illustrated by Table 11.1 in this chapter (Section 11.2.6).

Ideally, cases are discussed in the Socratic manner summarized in Section 11.1.6. Through the morning report, questions focused on problem formulation, diagnosis, and management of patients are addressed to the staff,[91] and their understanding is reached through a mutual exchange of proposals and statements (premises) using a modern argumentation process. In this context, morning reports are an important teaching tool during clinical training.[92,93] Amin et al.[94] offer a valuable review and proposal for how morning reports should be structured.

11.3.5 Morbidity and Mortality Reports and Rounds

Morbidity and mortality conferences and meetings represent a forum for faculty and trainees to explore the management details of particular cases.[95] When they are executed correctly, they contribute to patient care, medical knowledge, practice-based learning and improvement, interpersonal communication skills, professionalism, and problem-based learning and improvement.[92,95] The primary goal is to revisit errors without blame for their better understanding and prevention. Personal failures are not necessarily in focus.

Morbidity and mortality rounds are held less often than other ways of reviewing the current local practice, but still regularly throughout the year and they may be offered to all health professionals. Such meetings address the analysis of a single case or of several cases using the Socratic method and argumentation. Multidirectional communication focused on equality and reciprocity of views exchange remains essential for their success.

Whether **Grand Rounds**, **Noon Rounds**, or **Academic Half Days** are applied to medicine, surgery, and psychiatry, these areas benefit from the morbidity and mortality review experience.[96,97] Even if a live discussion with the patient and discussion with participants is a part of rounds, communication between presenters and listeners is mainly a one-way experience. It is not always easy to fulfill all the requirements of a useful argumentation process, and the needs of participating physicians, a logical order in presentations, and commitment to change through the multifaceted intervention that are morbidity and mortality rounds. Participating physicians needs assessment, multifaceted intervention (rounds' ways of coverage of problems) strategies, logical order in presentations (sequencing), interaction, and commitment to change are not always easily fulfilled.[98]

11.3.6 *Journal Clubs*

Journal clubs are periodic sessions, typically held monthly, that are open to both learners (clinical clerks, interns, residents) and elders (staff). They are typically structured and organized[101] and may be regular, scheduled events with mandatory attendance, defined clear short- and long-term purpose and objectives, and feature leaders trained in selecting the papers for study and in facilitating the discussion.

Topics and problems are presented by more senior learners followed by discussion. The basis for discussion may be:

■ one or more original journal articles covering the topic of interest;
■ an issue of a reputed journal covering one or more important topics of the day;
■ a systematic review of available relevant evidence of the problem of interest; and
■ a non-systematic review of a clinical topic of interest.

A meeting of the journal club is typically led by a senior specialist or some other senior learner in the domain and related fields under discussion. Compared to rounds, a journal club offers more space for the communication and exchange of ideas and a more active role for the learner. Students and juniors have an opportunity here to improve their professional communication. At their core, presentations at a journal club may be:

■ a critical appraisal EBM style of original evidence (journal articles single studies) as partly outlined in Chapter 5;
  – **Critical appraisal** as currently understood is the fundamental way to assess the internal validity, adherence to reporting standards, conclusions and generalizability of a health problem presented in a medical article. Internal validity (how structured and interpreted the document is) is more in focus than contributions to the solution or advancement of the health problem covered. Structured checklists concerning what to answer and not miss are now available for physicians and other health professionals. The University of Oxford Centre for Evidence-Based Medicine offers online various appraisal sheets[99] as does the Ontario Public Health Libraries Association[100];
■ an analysis of the problem in an argumentative manner, that is, how the evaluated evidence is subsequently used in medical decision-making;
■ a systematic review and/or meta-analysis of a chosen topic; and
■ a critical appraisal or a problem analysis using of the above types of evidence, presented in a Socratic manner where all important advanced statements are supported by the best evidence embedded in a modern argument.

These types of presentations support the **interactive character** of journal clubs, which makes them distinct from many rounds and is essential for the argumentative process.

The American College of Physicians publishes a monthly feature the Annals of Internal Medicine's *ACP Journal Club*[102] and *ACP Journal Club Plus*.[103] These monthly journals systematically review selected biomedical original studies and may offer their systematic reviews. These publications can support journal clubs, but cannot replace the benefit of another robust discussion on the topics.

Journal club objectives are not always met. Evaluation of this communication tool shows that participation of learners, and changes in attitude, perception, knowledge, skills, behaviors, and organizational practice do not always follow from journal club presentations. Most importantly, benefits to patients' and other clients' health and well-being are not always evident.[104] A better and more complete evaluation will enhance the role that journal clubs can play in acquiring clinical experience.

11.3.7 Other Types of Rounds

Types of rounds may vary from one medical environment and culture to another. In the North American context, communication opportunities may also include:

- small groups and "academic half days"[105] (may be interdisciplinary);
- grand rounds and clinical conferences[105] (periodic and formal continuing education gatherings to update topics and frequently triggered by recent clinical experience at the institution);
- lectures,[105] more formal presentations involving preclinical students and clinicians of all levels of training and experience;
- workshops, more in-depth, usually methodologically oriented coverage of selected topics implying guided multilateral communication and exchanges;
- "post-take" or admission rounds[106] following on-call periods;
- daily work/working rounds for trainees[105];
- review rounds[106] by trainees and consultants held at the bedside;
- social issues rounds,[106] interdisciplinary, administrative, and social work reviews of patients' status, discharge plans, referrals, and post-hospital follow-up;
- preceptor rounds[106] where teacher and learners develop and improve clinical examination and presentation skills); and
- "down time" or "dead space" uses,[106] as the previously mentioned elevator, drinking fountain, and coffee sipping stand-up "meetings."

Some of these events may be regular, with fixed dates; others are organized and presented to try to answer current events and needs of the moment. All of them, however, are subject to the same general rules of evidence management, argumentation, and communication as outlined above.

11.3.8 Mostly One-Way Communication Vehicles: Consults, Referrals, Discharge Notes, and Summaries

There are numerous communication vehicles that are standard elements of clinical practice. These are one-way communications; they provide information *to* an individual (another clinician or a patient) but do not engage them in a discussion. Examples and descriptions of these vehicles follow.

- A **medical consult** refers to the provision of expert opinion and recommendations by a senior specialist on request. Note that in some jurisdictions like the British Commonwealth and the Republic of Ireland, the title of consultant in medicine mainly recognizes the expertise of its holder. A consultant does not necessarily provide consults.

- A **medical referral** is the transfer of a patient from one physician's care to another.
- A **discharge summary or discharge note** is a summary of a patient's clinical course over the period of time of defined clinical and other institutional care provided by a physician or other health professional. It serves to reiterate the chief patient complaint along with the final diagnosis, both in the past and at discharge, and radical and conservative treatment and care provided. Finally, it includes recommendations for further treatment, care, and follow-up. Many of these elements may not be communicated in current discharge reporting.[107]

Further communication between providers of information and its recipients is not expected in most cases. However, it can be provided on request. As an example, clinicians who provide consults may be asked to exchange explanations and additional ideas with the necessary best evidence at hand. In this case, clinicians must also provide the information in an argumentative manner. As always, all parties involved in the clinical dialogue must ensure that such vehicles fallacy-free.

Another one-way communication vehicle is the act of **following clinical guidelines** is mainly a one-way and passive communication. **Developing clinical** guidelines[108,109] is the product of evidence-based argumentation arrived at by multilateral communication, understanding and the development of guidance acceptable to all interested parties, but the act of following them is not.

11.3.9 Scut Work

Scut work is a necessary everyday activity for all healthcare providers in hospitals. Scut or scut work refers to the repetitive, minimally educational chores that are a major part of most residents' (and other juniors at the hospital) duties. It includes monitoring and maintaining patient vital functions and their related apparatus. This may include intravenous canulation, wound care, and drawing body fluids and tissues for laboratory analyses. Another component of scut work is establishing and maintaining updated written and electronic records about patient care and functioning, communicating with patient relatives, and other non-professional parties.

Frequently disliked by both junior and senior practitioners, scut work is often considered educationally irrelevant, there are opportunities to learn embedded in the process. A faculty mentor who anticipates the trainees' activity, discusses clinical issues with the residents, and creates an educational opportunity building on the required tasks, conditions permitting.[110]

Scut work[110] is also an opportunity to acquire many automated skills even if it does not offer a great deal of two-way communication. While a clinician performs scut work, communication with patients, their friends, and families, and other health professionals in the hospital must be established (even in the most routine daily activities), achieved, and maintained according to the general rules of reasoning and communication outlined in this chapter. It may, but should not be, hampered by a ubiquitous clinical activity overload of all parties involved.

11.3.10 Formal (Magisterial) Lectures

Time-honored formal lectures are a historical and important element of medical education. A selected topic is presented by an experienced lecturer to specific groups of learners. These may be medical students, residents, specialties, and researchers, or interdisciplinary gatherings of health professionals in the hospital, city, or region, or a keynote address at medical, nursing, and other conventions. Lectures are not always appreciated if they are unstructured, not based on more bilateral communication (discussions), and relying solely on literature and other past experience reported secondhand.

How can lectures be made livelier, more motivating, and more grounded in reality for students? An "action movie"-type experience can be adopted and adapted in the following manner:

■ topics can be introduced by a short dialogue with a live invited and consenting patient. Psychiatrists know all too well that such firsthand experience is often invaluable;
■ a "clinical scenario" can be presented as a secondhand experience and actualization that details what happened to and with the patient can be incorporated;
■ a "resolution of the clinical scenario" at the end of the lecture can strengthen the usefulness and relevance of the lecture's fundamental message; and
■ discussion may be relegated to the end of the lecture or an experienced lecturer may insert pinpoint exchanges of views with learners at any moment of a formal presentation of the topic.

How can a lecture (or seminar) be structured to facilitate learner's understanding? The lecture topic and its message structure should be known to learners before the lecture.

Such lecture "programs" should include the following.

■ title (topic) of the lecture;
■ name of the lecturer or all other invited lecturers if more than one;
■ objectives in terms of knowledge, attitudes, and skills to be acquired;
■ contents of the lecture framed as a short list of sub-topics;
■ type of teaching methods to be used in the lecture (oral presentations, discussion, illustrative medical article presentation and analysis, ad hoc exercises and problem solutions, invited debaters, other, selected readings);
■ technical tools like electronic acoustic and visual media, and interactive devices like "smart clicker" and similar interactive apps on smartphones;
■ key references;
■ additional readings; and
■ an optional evaluation. An evaluation is important to determine if learning objectives were attained.

Lectures do not need to be boring. Keeping them as interactive as possible benefit both teachers and learners. In this way even a lecture can enable shared and multilateral communication.

11.3.11 Medical Articles and Other Scientific Papers

As clinical case reports may be presented both in oral and written form, they will be discussed in Chapter 12.

11.3.12 Other Forms of Communication

Other forms of communication which are not reviewed here and which are specific to a certain language, general and local medical culture, tradition, experience, and faith may be missed by some readers. Therefore, readers are encouraged to complete this section based on their expectations, needs and, irreplaceable experience.

11.4 Illustrative Fallacies in Communication

Fallacies in communication can be deliberate manipulations of messages and the way they are conveyed, or the result of erroneous reasoning and decision-making. The number of identified fallacies (as well as of cognitive biases) increases over time, both in medicine[111] and in other domains.[112–117] Building a valuable exchange of ideas with patients and non-health professionals and reaching a clear, mutual understanding of health problems and related care are perhaps the most challenging aspects of communication, and require that we can identify and understand fallacies in communication.

Communication is an individualized experience. Knowledge, attitudes, values, and preferences vary from one patient to another, and from one group of community stakeholders and decision-makers to another. Health professionals communicating among themselves are more or less "on the same wavelength" (or they should be), but this is not the case with patients and the community, especially when dealing with health problems.

> Communication in medicine may be hampered by several elements. We have defined **fallacies in communication** as errors in reasoning and/or decision-making made in the process of understanding and/or solving of a health problem. They can be made by a health professional, produced through a health professional's communication with another health interested party, or in the interaction with another party. Perhaps less often, communication failures result from fallacies as poor reasoning.

In communication, it is also possible for flawless reasoning to be incorrectly used as **rhetorical ploys**. They are non-argumentative deficiencies in reasoning, intentionally misdirecting premises, proposals or claims to reach their proponent's goals. These are often forms of mental trickery and manipulation to varying degrees.

Let us, then, make a distinction between a fallacy as an error in reasoning by ignorance, and those by conscious manipulations of an arguments components and path. An error made in ignorance may be conscious or not, often the result of an unlearned error on the path from premises to conclusions of an argument. Conscious manipulations stem from the use of non-argumentative or extra-logical elements, language, and not-explicated or implicit objectives of lateral thinking in the mind of the proponent of communication. Whether "true" fallacies or rhetorical ploys are behind our interactions, they both fall under the common notion of **communication errors**. In this section, we provide only illustrative examples of such communication errors. A full array can be found in the literature.

Before we begin, let us consider the context of communications in medicine. Clinicians communicate with patients, the community in general, and other clinicians. In medical practices, clinicians encounter two kinds of patients:

1. those who want, and expect, clinicians to solve their problems and will follow the clinician's directives more or less blindly; and
2. those who participate with the clinician to understand and solve their health concerns. This latter group are comprised of laypersons who, because of their intellectual abilities, experience, and judgment broader than the medical field, can assist the physician by asking proper questions and providing other information to direct even better clinical decisions in their case.

In the broader community, almost everyone is concerned about health issues, often because they are not automatically well understood and correct solutions are not always applied to resolve them. These community groups include governments and civic administrations, other planners and providers of material (funding) and human resources (agencies, schools, and higher academic institutions), lawyers and courts of law, security forces (police and army), electronic, print, radio, and television media, and clergy and institutions of faith. The domains of politics, media, and entertainment are also frequently concerned with health issues. They are an even more fertile field for fallacies and remain wide open to rhetorical ploys of all kind. Especially in these areas, reaching the absolute truth about a health problem is not necessarily an ideal and ultimate goal, objective, or claim to be reached by meaningful argumentation. In the struggle for the attention of recipients of messages and claims, their minds must be won for the proponent's causes. Very often, anything goes.

The focus of this discussion is on fallacies in dialogues between physicians and their patient (physician ↔ patient), and between physicians themselves (physician ↔ physician). These fallacies are outlined here.

SLIPPERY SLOPE FALLACY

Slippery slope fallacy (domino theory; argument of the beard; barefoot; beard fallacy; domino fallacy; *reductio ad absurdum*; slippery slope argument)

This fallacy presumes that **if** one event happens, **then** other events must/will also happen (without giving any other supporting reason for each cascading conclusion). For example, a physician may say to his or her patient, "*Your chemotherapy will immunosuppress you, weaken your immunity, you will then develop a cross-infection, we will not be able to control it, and you will die.*" In this example, while the patient will become immunosuppressed as a result of chemotherapy, the subsequent conclusions may, or may not, occur.

In another example, a physician may tell his or her patient:

> If you do not become physically active, modify your eating habits, and stop leading a stressful life, you will become more and more overweight. Once you are overweight, you will develop diabetes, coronary heart disease will follow, and you will have a myocardial infarction. Coronary bypass surgery will have to be performed on you and your life expectancy will be dramatically reduced.

Again, the initial claim may be true but development of all of the subsequent conditions are not guaranteed, regardless of their probability.

A "competent layperson" (patient) may correctly ask the physician for his or her qualifier leading to their claims (conclusions), "*Doctor, how sure are you that all this will happen? What is the probability of such disquieting events? Does all this really apply to me?*" Will the physician always be able to provide a proper answer to such questions?

GAMBLER'S FALLACY

The gambler's fallacy is committed by ignoring that if events are statistically independent, any event in the sequence has an equal chance of occurring. For example, "*Doctor, why not try this drug again? If it did not work for others, it should work for sure for me!*" Gamblers often believe that their luck will change after good or poor bets. This might also be true in medicine if the clinical course and the physician's skills were the same from one situation to another. However, the consecutive decision might be right if the situation, patient chances, and care outcomes are the same. A blind bet on the same chances in different situations leads to the gambler's fallacy and its uncertain outcomes.

APPEAL TO CONSEQUENCES FALLACY (WISHFUL THINKING)

This fallacy occurs when the undesirable consequences of an action are believed to be false based on nothing more than "personal conviction," or wishful thinking. For example: "*To solve your limping and hip pain, I propose surgery X. There are risks to this surgery, but this will never happen to me. If I believed that it might happen, I would never forgive myself for bringing this kind of surgery to your attention.*" The consequences of a belief have no bearing on whether the belief is true or false. While a rational reason to believe is evidence to be taken into account, it is replaced here by motivation.

SELF-EVIDENCE FALLACY (MYSTICAL ASSERTION; BLIND CONVICTION)

Self-evidence fallacy may also be seen as a rhetorical ploy. Statements, propositions or claims that are based on conviction only and unsupported by a valid argument, its premises, and other evidence-based argument building blocks. Qualities attributed to claims are ambiguous, for example, "*It is generally known that electromagnetic fields in some parts of the country cause cancer,*" or "*People using cell-phones while driving cause accidents—it's obvious!*", or "*Everyone knows that drinking coffee helps the brain work better,*" or "*We keep seeing this same type of skin lesion in moisturizer users. Observations speak for themselves!*"

Around 1910, Ambrose Bierce teasingly defined the adjective '*self-evident*' as '*evident to one's self and to nobody else.*' More seriously, as a sole explanation of a given proposition, the French have an expression, "*Ça saute aux yeux!*," or "*It jumps out at you.*" This type of fallacy is ubiquitous in media, advertising, in courts of law, and even in medical writings and practice, and is committed both by professionals and their partners in argumentation, such as by physicians and their patients. The mystical shroud of impressive universality in the above-mentioned statements is not supported by evidence or this evidence is not made explicit enough to support the proposed claims in a valid way. However, claims may be right or wrong depending on the missing premises and their evidence. The remedy to this fallacy is to support claims by strong and valid evidence-based arguments.

APPEALS TO ANYTHING OTHER THAN THE BEST EVIDENCE ('LOW INSTINCTS')

This kind of fallacy is typically a conscious rhetorical ploy. It is based on uses of appeals to any irrational, unrelated, non-evidential states, entities, and issues instead of specific evidence related to various building blocks of argument to justify its conclusions, claims, and ensuing recommendations. In an **appeal to poverty (*argumentum ad lazarum*)** the position is considered to be correct because it is held by individuals who are poor, "*In our community, low income families appreciate our hospital services. Therefore, our hospital services are good.*" In an **appeal to belief**, the belief is considered to be true because many people believe it, "*Most Canadians believe that their healthcare system is the best. Therefore, the Canadian health system is the best.*"

Other appeals are based and count on humor, flattery, emotions, individualism, private motives, guilt, celebrity, or popularity. They are frequently used in cases where there is no valid evidence in grounds, backing, and other building blocks of these arguments that would lead us to an evidence-supported claim. These so-called fallacies are rhetorical ploys because they draw an individual's perspective away from supporting conclusions and recommendation (claim) in a valid argument, and toward desired conclusions that are not necessarily supported by the evidence.

Another type of fallacy within this category is the **fallacy of one-sidedness**. In this type of fallacy, only evidence favoring a specific conclusion (claim) is presented and ignore and/or downplay evidence against that conclusion. For example, "*You should note that 45 studies confirm the effectiveness of rubbing honey into your skin in the treatment of psoriasis.*" Studies to the contrary of this perspective are not shown. Another example is, "*I have seen firsthand that as long as patients see us often and regularly over a one-year period, blood pressure is reduced with none of the traditional side effects of drug therapy.*" Evidence from other patients who experienced a different outcome is not relayed.

Prejudicial language can also create a fallacy that implores the use of non-evidence based arguments. When a proponent of a position uses prejudicial language, like emotive terms, they inject their own perspectives and beliefs rather than evidence into their proposition. An example is, "*No reasonable person in this community would refuse to be immunized against this year's influenza strain,*" or "*Any competent colleague in this Department would refuse to consider a knee replacement in any patient of this age.*" The validity of these statements should be reviewed without prejudicial adjectives like 'reasonable' or 'competent' in the context of these examples.

ALTERNATIVE CHOICE FALLACY

In the alternative choice fallacy, any other option must be better. For example, "*Standard management of multiple sclerosis fails to satisfactorily control this health problem. Neck vein surgery instead is a better and appropriate option.*" The alternative choice may be a worse choice, or may produce the same results, until proven otherwise.

COMPLEMENTARY TREATMENT FALLACY

This fallacy follows attributes the benefit of primary treatments to complementary treatments added to the treatment regimen. This can be characterized by this statement, "*I was told to meditate during the entire treatment program established by oncologists for my cancer. Should I meditate then to improve my chances of non-recurrence and recovery?*" The complementary treatment may not cause harm, or it may. Was a clinical trial conducted of complementary treatment programs? In clinical medicine, combined treatments are tested against single treatments or other treatment combinations. Most often, different outcomes may be in focus (feeling well-cared for versus stopping cancer growth and spread).

PUT THEM ALL TOGETHER FALLACY

This fallacy combines several fallacies together into the same statement (claim) or argument. Take for example the following statement that might be used in a television advertisement,

"90% of physicians in our survey are prescribing Cholysol to their patients to control high choles-terol blood level. Shouldn't you get a prescription for yourself too?"

There is more than one fallacy hidden in this simple advertising statement seen on television. Physicians remain unidentified, a **reference (fallacy) to anonymous (false to some degree) authority** is made. From an unknown set of observations, an inference is made to a specific patient, you; **a fallacy of the general rule** (assuming that something true in a more general context and observation is true in every possible case). Because the drug is prescribed and used by many (**fallacy *ad populum***) does not replace post-marketing studies, trials evaluating not only "clean" cases but also interventions offered ultimately to patients with multiple co-morbidities and co-treatments for co-morbid states. By not mentioning that an exception might exist in this patient, a ***fallacy of accident*** might also be committed.

BLINDING WITH SCIENCE FALLACY

This communication error is based on using scientific jargon as a reflection of the prestige of science to pass one's assertions for something they are not, often instead of legitimate evidence. Consider the following example:

> Our team-based multiangulated analysis of current focused research involving a network of issues in the comparison of our new diet with some of its major alternatives shows as confirming the null hypothesis and the space and imperative for further tackling the problem through promising multivariable and multivariate analyzes in a further experimental and observational analytical research.

It is left up to the recipient of such message to judge the magnitude of the verbal salad articulated by the transmitter. In other words, in plain English, the intervention most likely did not work. Using research jargon may hide poor evidence, unexpected, and undesirable results and outcomes. For consumers of medication and health services, it offers a false reassurance that their problem is handled seriously. Advertising should be free of this kind of "dressing up" of facts.

ARGUMENTUM AD NUMERAM FALLACY

This type of fallacy relies on numbers to support a statement, and thus confounds numbers with the validity of the statement. For example, *"Yes, our diet plan is not cheap. But thousands of current users cannot be wrong!"* This fallacy is often preferred by advertisers, public orators, and other preachers. Numbers of adherents, users, or benefactors supplant evidence of effectiveness and benefits. Moreover, adverse effects and contrary evidence are often ignored.

11.5 Emergence of Knowledge Translation as a Way of Thinking and Communicating

Producing even the best evidence is not enough. Evidence must "travel," through a communication means, effectively from its producers to its users. Users reached by the evidence must use it correctly and patients, other individuals, and communities to which the evidence is applied must benefit from such a knowledge translation process. Knowledge translation relies heavily on effective and fallacy-free communication. Failures in communication may prove to be detrimental to the knowledge translation process and its results.

Most recently, **knowledge translation** has emerged as a new discipline to address how knowledge is communicated and used effectively as a learning process that occurs in learning, and more general, environments.[118–124] The Canadian definition views knowledge translation as "*a dynamic and iterative process that includes synthesis, dissemination, exchange and ethically sound application of knowledge to improve the health of Canadians, provide more effective health services and products and strengthen the healthcare system.*"[118]

Even more simply and pragmatically we may agree that it is "*the science of conversion of current knowledge to patient outcomes.*"[121] An expanded domain of **knowledge translation** continues to develop.[122-124] It is, indeed, a "knowledge—attitudes—skills" translation. The process of conversion, however, is not as straightforward and simple.

First, let us consider the term "**knowledge**" in the context of knowledge translation is defined as:

> a fluid mix of framed experience, values, contextual information, evidence interpretation and expert insight that provides a framework for decision-making, evaluating and incorporating new experiences and information. It may be explicit and tacit, and individual or collective. In organizations, it often becomes embedded not only in documents or repositories, but also in organizational routines, processes, practices and norms.[124]

More generally, it is "*the range of one's information or understanding of facts or ideas acquired by study, investigation, observation or experience.*"[5,6 modified]

However, knowledge is not a static state. As part of the knowledge translation process, it is "translated" into a secondary state. Understanding this translation process is vital to understanding how to best use knowledge translation.

Surprisingly, the word "**translation**" has not yet been defined in the context of knowledge translation. In this context, let us consider translation as:

> multiple ways of moving experience, knowledge, facts and their meaning from their original source and transmitters to their recipients or receivers in the framework of mutual understanding and followed by actions to change receivers' actions and care and health states of their expected beneficiaries.

Taken as a full term, then, knowledge translation implies multidirectional, multilateral, and multiparty continuous communication between numerous stakeholders: researchers, practising physicians, other health professionals, patients, community, policy makers, pharmaceutical and other technology producers and stakeholders in the health of individuals and whole communities.[122,123]

With these terms defined, the process of conversion is now of interest. There are two approaches for understanding knowledge translation as an active process. One of them is to study "knowledge" and "translation" as separate but related entities. This helps us to better understand how different ways of "translation" (moving knowledge from one person, place, or time to another) will change "knowledge" or its surrogate representation.

Epidemiologically speaking, in the "initial state → maneuver → subsequent state" model, "knowledge" is in essence the basic research design equivalent of a "state" (initial or subsequent) or dependent variable. "Translation" is the basic research design equivalent to "exposure" (independent variable or "maneuver," see Figure 5.1 in Chapter 5) in a study of "maneuvers" as actions of noxious or beneficial factors. Subsequent states (after exposure, that is, translation of knowledge) may not only be the knowledge itself, but also the possible consequences of such a knowledge change including its uses and desirable and other effects of a "translation acquired state."

Hence, for example:

Being healthy (initial state)	→	Smoking or not (maneuver)	→	Developing cancer (subsequent state)
Having a certain type and degree of knowledge (initial state)	→	Translating or not translating knowledge (maneuver, results of which are to be tested)	→	Knowledge adopted, used, patient outcomes improve or not (subsequent state)

"Knowledge translation" can also be considered an entity, maneuver itself, or independent variable. This enables us to evaluate if "knowledge translation" changes health practices and care and ultimately the health of patients and community (dependent variables):

Current health practices and/or patients' and/or community health and disease(s)	→	Knowledge translation (its different ways, means, uses, and arrays)	→	Change in health practices and/or patients/and/or community health and disease(s)

Both these approaches may prove useful in the future of this rapidly developing domain. So far, knowledge translation follows this general path:

Evidence-based innovation and production (knowledge)
↓
potential adopters in their practice environment identification
↓
implementation strategies
↓
adoption of strategies to be implemented
↓
outcomes of implemented knowledge in patients, practitioners, system, and/or community
↓
evaluation of what was accomplished.

Failures in communication anywhere in this multistage process may be the cause of numerous cases of medical error and harm.[125] Moreover, a considerable number of patients still do not get treatments of proven effectiveness, or the information they need to make their own decisions. They also get care that is not needed, and their physicians do not get all the evidence they need for their decision-making processes. A better knowledge translation understanding and improvement could remedy this situation.

Let Us Conclude: From Patient Problem-Solving Dialogue to a Broader Communication in Medicine

Teaching and learning in medicine are an exercise in communication of correct knowledge, attitudes, and skills. The transmitting party conveys his or her experience to the receiving party and both adjust their interaction to obtain the best results.

Any meaningful communication in medicine has several pre-requisites. These include:

- an existing meaningful patient/physician or physician/physician relationship as a basis for mutual understanding;
- a clear topic that is understood by both parties;
- semantics, definitions, formulations, and taxonomies, understood and acceptable for both parties;
- definitions and taxonomies that reflect biological distinctions between the entities compared;
- good definitions and taxonomies that continue to inform epidemiological evaluations, and clinical decisions throughout the process;
- methods for reasoning and decision-making are known and understood by both parties communicating;
- modern argumentation and Socratic discourse are mutually perceived, not as detrimental to mutual understanding, but as facilitating the opposite; and
- the movement of ideas and statements is as fallacy-free as possible.

Building on the teaching and learning experience, physicians produce new evidence about treatment effectiveness, development and uses of new technologies, innovative surgery, and disease prevention tools.

Medical communication is now more than a simple physician–patient contact or physician–physician exchange of ideas or facts as covered in this chapter. Both teachers and learners encounter communication as the basis of a larger framework of knowledge translation.

Medical communication may be seen by some as a simple interactive tool, but it is also a topic of study on its own, with its own research questions, methodological challenges, and objectives.[124] Basic clinical communication as outlined in this chapter remains one of the core components of communication in health sciences, medical care, disease prevention, and health promotion. Current trends in "medical communicology" reflect this well.

References

1. *Teaching & Learning in Medical Practice.* Edited by JW Rodney Peyton. Silver Birches, Heronsgate Rickmansworth, Herts.: Manticore Europe Ltd., 1998.
2. Spencer J. ABC of learning and teaching in medicine. Learning and teaching in the clinical environment. *BMJ*, 2003;326:591–4.
3. Wikipedia, the free encyclopedia. *Communication.* 11 p. at http://en.wikipedia.org.wiki/communication, retrieved Oct 25, 2010.
4. Gordon NE. Communication. *Encyclopaedia Britannica.* 13 p. at ebcid:com.britannica.oec2.identifier .ArticleIdentifier?tocId=91096…, retrieved from electronic version on Sept 21, 2010.
5. *Random House Webster's Unabridged Dictionary 3.0.* Electronic edition on CD. Antwerpen: Random House Inc., 1998 and 2003.
6. *Merriam-Webster's Collegiate Dictionary.* 11th Edition. Springfield, MA: Merriam-Webster Incorporated, 2007.
7. Wikipedia, the free encyclopedia. *Semiotics.* 11 p. at http://en.wikipedia.org/wiki/Semiotics, retrieved April 8, 2010.
8. Air War College. Gateway to the Internet. *Communication Skills.* 27 p. at http://www.au.af.mil/au /awc/awcgate/awx-comm.htm, retrieved April 18, 2010.
9. Lanigan RL. Communicology: Towards a new science of semiotic phenomenology. *Cultura. Int J Phil Culture Axiol,* 2007;8:212–6, available also at http://www.international-journal-of-axiology.net /article/nr8/art14.pdf, retrieved Feb 14, 2011.
10. Lanigan RL. Communicology: Approaching the discipline's centennial ('Semiotica y communologia: Historias y propuestas de una mirada cientifica en construccion'). *Razon y Palabra,* 72. 15 p. at www .razonypalabra.org.mx/N/N72/Monotematico/8_Lanigan_72.pdf, retrieved Feb 14, 2011.
11. *Communicology: The New Science of Embodied Discourse.* Edited by D. Eicher-catt and I.E. Catt. Danvers, MA: Rosemont Publishing & Printing, 2010. (See also books.google.ca/books?isbn=0838641474).
12. Blackwell Reference Online. *International Encyclopedia of Communication.* At http://www .communicationencyclopedia.com/public/tocnode?id=g9781405131995_yr20…, retrieved Feb 14, 2011.
13. American Association of Medical Colleges. *Report III. Contemporary issues in Medicine: Communication in Medicine. Medical School Objectives Project October 1999.* Washington, DC: Association of American Medical Colleges, 1999.
14. Professional Education Strategy, Curriculum Working Group, M. Talbot, Chair. *Talking Tools II. Putting Communication Skills to Work.* Ottawa: Health Canada, 2001. (Catalogue No:H39-509/2001-2E.)
15. *Communicating in the Health Sciences.* 2nd Edition. Edited by J Higgs, R Ajjawi, L McAllister, F Trede, and S Loftus. Oxford and New York: Oxford University Press, 2008. (3rd Edition 2012).
16. Textbooks.com. *Communication in Medicine Textbooks.* 4 p. at http://textbooks.com/Catalog/PM6 /Communication-in-Medicine.php?s=1, retrieved June 24, 2010.
17. Brancati FL. The art of pimping. *JAMA,*1989;262(1):89–90.
18. Wear D, Kokinova M, Keck-McNulty C, Aultman J. Pimping: Perspectives of 4th year medical students. *Teach Learn Med,* 2005;17(2):184–91.
19. Detsky AS. The art of pimping. *JAMA,* 2009;301(13):1379–81.
20. Jenicek M and Hitchcock DL. *Evidence-Based Practice. Logic and Critical Thinking in Medicine.* Chicago, IL: American Medical Association (AMA Press), 2005.
21. Lieberman SA, Trumble JM, Smith ER. The impact of structured student debates on critical thinking and informatics skills of second-year medical students. *Acad Med,* 2000;75(No 10/October Supplement):S84–S86.
22. University of California, San Diego, Web site designed by Thompson J. *A Practical Guide to Clinical Medicine. Clinical Decision-Making.* 6 p. at http://medicine.ucsd.edu/clinicalmed/thinking.htm, retrieved March 30, 2005.
23. Wikipedia, the free encyclopedia. *Socratic Method.* 6 p. at http://en.wikipedia.org/wiki/Socratic _method, retrieved March 20, 2010.
24. Hurst JW. *Four Hats. On Teaching Medicine and Other Essays.* Chicago, IL: Year Book Medical, Inc., 1970.

25. Frits HW Jr. Are we Socratic teachers? *Trans Am Clin Climatol Assoc,* 1979;90:109–15.
26. Oh RC. The Socratic method in medicine – the labor of delivering medical truths. *Fam Med,* 2005;37:537–9.
27. The Critical Thinking Community. *Socratic Teaching.* 2 p. at http://www.criticalthinking.org/resources/articles/socratic-teaching.shtml, retrieved Dec 30, 2006.
28. Wikipedia, the free encyclopedia. *Socratic Method.* 5 p. at http://en.wikipedia.org/wiki/Socratic_method, retrieved Sept 22, 2006.
29. Paul R. *A Taxonomy of Socratic Questions.* 2 p. at http://www.wolaver.org/teaching/socratic.htm, retrieved Jan 3, 2007.
30. Paul R. *Critical Thinking: How to Prepare Students for a Rapidly Changing World.* pp. 276–7. Santa Rosa, CA: Foundation for Critical Thinking, 1993.
31. Grahame-Smith D. (Education and debate.) Evidence-based medicine: Socratic dissent. *BMJ,* 1995;310(29 April):1126–7.
32. Carmichael C. (AETC National Resource Center.) *5 Models of Successful Clinical Consultation.* 2 p. at http://www.aidsetc.org/aidsetc?page=et-15-02-05, retrieved Feb 22, 2007.
33. AIDS Education & Training Centers National Resource Center, AETC Training Levels. *Level IV: Clinical Consultation.* 4 p. at http://www.aidsetc.org/aidsetc?page=tr-29-04, retrieved Feb 22, 2007.
34. Lang D. Research and Training Opportunities at the National Institutes of Health, Clinical Electives Program. *Pediatric Consult Service. Four Week Session.* 2 p. at http://www.training.nih.gov/student/cep/p_consult.asp, retrieved Feb 2, 2007.
35. Spickard A, III, Ryan SP, Muldowney A, Farnham L. Outpatient morning report. A new conference for internal medicine residency programs. *J Gen Intern Med,* 2000;15:822–4.
36. Parrino TA and Villanueva AG. The principles and practice of morning report. *JAMA,*1986;256:730–3.
37. Shankel SW and Mazzaferri EL. Teaching the resident in internal medicine. Present practices and suggestions for the future. *JAMA,* 1986;256:725–9.
38. Harris ED Jr. Morning report. *Ann Intern Med,* 1993;119:430–1.
39. Kennedy CC, Cook RJ, Eggert CH, Krajicek BJ, Leenstra JL, West CP. *Developing a Blueprint for Morning Report.* 10 p. at https://www.im.org/AAIM/PUBS/Docs/2006TCMR/MorningReport.pdf, retrieved Feb 10, 2007.
40. Archer TP, Young JJ, Mazzaferri EL. *Morning Report. Internal Medicine.* New York and St. Louis, MO: McGraw-Hill, 2000.
41. Marks AR, Editor in Chief. Physician-scientist, heal thyself … *J Clin Invest,* 2007;117:2.
42. Barbour GL, Young MN. Morning report. Role of the clinical librarian. *JAMA,* 1986;255:1921–2.
43. Sackett DL, Straus SE for Firm A of the Nuffield Department of Medicine. Finding and applying evidence during clinical rounds. *JAMA,* 1998;280:1336–8.
44. Schwartz A, Hupert J, Elstein AS, Noronha P. Evidence-based morning report for inpatient pediatric rotations. *Acad Med,* 2000;75:1229.
45. Houghtalen RP, Olivares T, Greene Y, Booth H, Conwell Y. Resident's morning report in psychiatry training. Description of a model and survey of resident attitudes. *Acad Psychiatry,* 2002;26:9–16.
46. Weinhlotz D, Edwards JC, Mumford LM. *Teaching During Rounds. A Handbook for Attending Physicians and Residents.* Baltimore, MD and London: The Johns Hopkins University Press, 1992.
47. Lye PS, Simpson DE, Wendelberger KJ, Bragg DS. Clinical teaching rounds. A case-oriented faculty development program. *Arch Pediatr Adolesc Med,* 1998;152:293–5.
48. Myint PK, Sabanathan K. Role of grand rounds in the education of hospital doctors. *Hosp Med,* 2005;66:297–9.
49. Mueller PS, Segovis CM, Litin SC, Habermann TM, Parrino TA. Current status of medical grand rounds in departments of medicine at U.S. medical schools. *Mayo Clin Proc,* 2006;81(3):313–21.
50. Jenicek M. *Evaluating Surgery. Uses of Clinical Case Reports and Case Series in Surgical Specialties.* Draft document as reported at the Balliol Colloquiums for Evaluating Surgery, Jonathan Meakins, Chair. University of Oxford, Oxford, UK: September 6–8, 2007.
51. Bickley LS and Szilagy PG. *Bates' Guide to Physical Examination and History Taking.* 10th Edition. Philadelphia, PA/Baltimore, MD/New York/London: Wolters Kluwer Health | Lippincott Williams & Wilkins, 2009.

52. Partnership with patients. Building a history. Chapter 1, pp. 1–31 in: Seidel HM, Ball JW, Dains JE, Flynn JA, Solomon BS, Stewart RW. *Mosby's Guide to Physical Examination*. 7th Edition. St. Louis, MO: Mosby/Elsevier, 2011.

53. Billings JA, Stoeckle JD. *The Clinical Encounter. A Guide to the Medical Interview and Case Presentation*. St. Louis, MO/London/Toronto: Mosby, 1999.

54. Kurtz S, Silverman J, Draper J. *Teaching and Learning Communication Skills in Medicine*. 2nd Edition. Oxford and San Francisco, CA: Radcliffe Publishing, 2005.

55. Robinson DJ. *The Psychiatric Interview Explained*. Port Huron, MI and London, ON: Rapid Psychler Press, 2000.

56. Feinstein AR. *Clinimetrics*. New Haven, CT and London: Yale University Press, 1987.

57. Silverman J, Kurtz S, Draper J. *Skills for Communicating with Patients*. 2nd Edition. Oxford and San Francisco, CA: Radcliffe Publishing, 2005.

58. Lloyd M, Bor R, Blanche G, Eleftheriadou Z. *Communication Skills for Medicine*. 3rd Edition. Edinburgh/London/New York: 2009.

59. Wikipedia, the free encyclopedia. *Nonverbal Communication*. 15 p. at http://en.wikipedia.org/wiki/Nonverbal_communication, retrieved Nov 22, 2011.

60. Mehrabian A. *Nonverbal Communication*. Chicago, IL: Aldine Atherton, 1972.

61. Silverman J, Kurtz S, Draper J. *Skills for Communicating with Patients*. 3rd Edition. London and New York: Radcliffe Publishing, 2013.

62. Frank MG. *Understanding Nonverbal Communication*. (Transcript Book). Chantilly, VA: The Great Courses (The Teaching Company), 2016.

63. Waitzkin H. Doctor-patient communication. Clinical implications of social scientific research. *JAMA*, 1984;252(17):2441–6.

64. *Nonverbal Behavior in Clinical Settings*. Edited by P Philippot, RS Feldman and EJ Coats. Oxford and New York: Oxford University Press, 2003.

65. Jenicek M. *Foundations of Evidence-Based Medicine*. Boca Raton, FL/London/New York/Washington, DC: The Parthenon Publishing Group/CRC Press, 2003.

66. Uzelac PS, Moon RW, Badillo AG. *SOAP for Internal Medicine*. Philadelphia, PA/Baltimore, MD/New York/London: Lippincott Williams & Wilkins (Wolters Kluwer), 2005.

67. Gonzalo JD, Chuang CH, Huang G, Smith C. The return of bedside rounds: An educational intervention. *J Gen Intern Med*, 2010;25(8):792–8.doi :10.1007/s11606-010-1344-7.

68. Greenhalgh T and Hurwitz B. *Narrative Based Medicine*. London: BMJ Books, 1998.

69. Greenhalgh T and Hurwitz B. Why study narrative? *BMJ*, 1999;318:1848–50.

70. Shapiro J and Ross V. Applications of narrative theory and therapy to the practice of family medicine. *Fam Med*, 2002;34:96–100.

71. Pearson AS, McTigue MP, Tarpley JL. Narrative medicine in surgical education. *J Surg Educ*, 2008;65(2)(March–April):99–100.

72. Jordens CFC and Little M. 'In this scenario, I do this, for these reasons': Narrative, genre and ethical reasoning in the clinic. *Soc Sci & Med*, 2004;58:1635–45.

73. Hudson Jones A. Narrative based medicine. Narrative in medical ethics. *BMJ*, 1999;318:253–6.

74. Jenicek M. *A Physician's Self-Paced Guide to Critical Thinking*. Chicago, IL: American Medical Association (AMA Press), 2006.

75. Jenicek M. *Clinical Case Reporting in Evidence-Based Medicine*. 2nd Edition. London and New York: Arnold and Oxford University Press, 2001.

76. Reis S, Hermoni D, Livingstone P, Borkan J. Integrated narrative and evidence based case report. Case report of paroxysmal atrial fibrillation and anticoagulation. *BMJ*, 2002;325:1018–20.

77. Greenhalgh T and Worrall JG. From EBM to CSM: The evolution of context-sensitive medicine. *J Eval Clin Pract*, 1997;3:105–8.

78. Greenhalgh T. Narrative based medicine in an evidence based world. *BMJ*, 1999;318:323–5.

79. Skelton JR and Hammond P. Medical narratives and the teaching of communication in context. *Med Teacher*, 1998;20(6):548–51.

80. Charon R. Narrative and medicine. *N Engl J Med*, 2004;350:862–4.

81. Kalitzkus V and Matthiessen PF. Narrative-based medicine: Potential, pitfalls, and practice. *The Permanente Journal,* Winter 2009;13(1): 8 p. at http://xnet.kp.org/permanentejournal/winter09 /narrative medicine.html, retrieved Dec 8, 2010.

82. Charon R and Wyer P. Narrative evidence based medicine. *The Lancet,* 2008;371(9609):296–7.

83. Montgomery K. *How Doctors Think. Clinical Judgment and the Practice of Medicine.* Oxford and New York: Oxford University Press, 2006.

84. Toulmin S. Knowledge and art in the practice of medicine: Clinical judgment and historical reconstruction. pp. 231–49 in: *Science, Technology, and the Art of Medicine.* Edited by C. Delkeskamp-Hayes and MA Gardell Cutter. Dordrecht: Kluwer,1993.

85. International Training & Education Center on HIV (I-TECH). *Structured Clinical Vignettes: What Are They and How They Are Used?* An I-TECH Clinical Mentoring Kit. 5 pages at The University of Texas Medical Branch (UTMB). *Clinical Vignettes.* 2 p. at http://www.utmb.edu/aim/vignettes.htm, retrieved Oct 6, 2011.

86. American College of Physicians (ACP). Presenting a clinical vignette: Deciding what to present. 3 p. at http://www.acponline.org/residents_fellows/competitions/abstract/prepare/clinvin_pres.htm, retrieved Oct 6, 2011.

87. American College of Physicians. Writing a clinical vignette (case report) abstract. 2 p. at http://www .acponline.org/residents_fellows/competitions/abstract/prepare/clinvin_abs.htm, retrieved Oct 25, 2011.

88. Jenicek M. Clinical case reports and case series research in evaluating surgery. Part II. The content and form: Uses of single clinical case reports and case series research in surgical specialties. *Med Sci Monit,* 2008;14(10):RA149–RA162.

89. Albrecht J and Bigby M. Case reports and case series. pp. 134–6 in: *Encyclopedia of Epidemiology.* Edited by S Boslaugh and L-A McNutt. Los Angeles/London/New Delhi/Singapore: SAGE Publications, 2008.

90. Society of General Internal Medicine. Clinical vignettes. *J Gen Int Med,* 2004(April);19(s1):23–83. See also 241 p. at http://www.ncbi.nlm.nih.gov/pmc/articles/PMC1492602/, retrieved Oct 6, 2011.

91. Department of Medicine, University of Ottawa. Morning report. 1 p. at http://www.med.uottawa .ca$internalmedicine/residencyprogram/eng/morning_report.html, accessed March 6, 2011.

92. Parrino TA and Villanueva AG. The principles and practice of morning report. *JAMA,* 1986;256(6):730–3.

93. Schiffman FJ. Morning report and work rounds: Opportunities for teaching and learning. *Trans Am Clin Climatol Assoc,* 1995;107:275–86.

94. Amin Z, Guajardo J, Wisniewski W, Bordage G, Tekian A, Niederman LG. Morning report: Focus and methods over the past three decades. *Acad Med,* 2000;75(10):S1–S5.

95. Kravet SJ, Howell E, Wright SM. Morbidity and mortality conference, grand rounds, and the ACGME's core competencies. *J Gen Intern Med,* 2006;21(11):1192–4.

96. Goldman S, Demaso DR, Kempler B. Psychiatry morbidity and mortality rounds: Implementation and impact. *Acad Psychiatry,* 2009;33(5):385–8.

97. Kuper A, Zur Nedden N, Etchells E, Shadowitz S, Reeves S. Teaching and learning in morbidity and mortality rounds: An ethnographic study. *Med Educ,* 2010;44:559–64.

98. Van Hoof TJ, Monson RJ, Majdalany GT, Gianotti TE, Meehan TP. A case study of medical grand rounds: Are we using effective methods? *Med Educ,* 2009;84(8):1144–51.

99. University of Oxford, Centre for Evidence-Based Medicine. *Critical Appraisal.* Variable number of p. at http://www.cebm.net/index.aspx?o=1157, retrieved May 6, 2011.

100. Ontario Public Health Libraries Association. *Critical Appraisal of Research Evidence 101.* 16 pdf p. at wwww.health.gov.on.ca/english/proviers/program/.../caore.pdf, retrieved May 6, 2011.

101. Deenadayalan Y, Grimmer-Somers K, Prior M, Kumar S. How to run an effective journal club: A systematic review. *J Eval Clin Pract,* 2008;14:898–911.

102. *ACP Journal Club.* Variable number of p. at http://www.annals.org/site/acpjc/index.xhtml, retrieved May 6, 2011.

103. McMaster University Health Information Research Unit. *ACP Journal Club Purpose and Procedure.* 4 p. at http://hiru.mcmaster.ca/acpjc/Pplong,htm, retrieved May 6, 2011.

104. Harris J, Kearley K, Heneghan C, Meats E, Roberts N, Perera R, Kearley-Shiers K. Are journal clubs effective in supporting evidence-based decision making? A systematic review. BEME Guide No. 16. *Med Teacher,* 2011;33(1):9–23.

105. Sackett DL, Richardson WS, Rosenberg W, Haynes RB. *Evidence-Based Medicine. How to Practice and Teach EBM.* New York and Edinburgh: Churchill Livingstone, 1997.

106. Straus SE, Richardson WS, Glasziou P, Haynes RB. *Evidence-Based Medicine. How to Practice and Teach EBM.* 3rd Edition. Edinburgh/London/New York: Elsevier/Churchill Livingstone, 2005.

107. Laine C, Taichman DB, Mulrow C. Trustworthy clinical guidelines. (Editorial) *Ann Intern Med,* 2011;154:774–5.

108. Hill J, Bullock I. A summary of the methods that the National Clinical Guideline Centre uses to produce clinical guidelines for the National Institute for Health and Clinical Excellence. *Ann Intern Med,* 2011;154:752–7.

109. Kripalani S, LeFevre F, Phillips CO, Williams MV, Basaviah P, Baker DW. Deficits in communication and information transfer between hospital-based and primary care physicians. *JAMA,* 2007;297(8):831–41.

110. Hayward RSA, Rockwood K, Sheehan GJ, Bass EB. A phenomenology of scut. *Ann Intern Med,* 1991;115:372–6.

111. Jenicek M. *Fallacy-Free Reasoning in Medicine. Improving Communication and Decision-Making in Research and Practice.* Chicago, IL: American Medical Association (AMA Press), 2009.

112. The Nizkor Project. *Fallacies.* Evolving number of p. at http://www.nizkor.org/features/fallacies/, retrieved March 14, 2011.

113. Thompson B. *Bruce Thompson's Fallacy Page.* Evolving p. (including other related subsites) at http://www.cuyamaca.net/bruce.thompson/Fallacies/intro_fallacies.asp, retrieved Nov 1, 2006.

114. Curtis GN. *Fallacy Files.* Evolving number of p. (including subsites) at http://www.fallacyfiles.org, retrieved March 14, 2011.

115. Wikipedia, the free encyclopedia. *List of Cognitive Biases.* 10 p. at http://en.wikipedia.org/wiki/List_of_cognitive biases, accessed March 14, 2011.

116. Wikipedia, the free encyclopedia. *List of Fallacies.* 10 p. at http://en.wikipedia.org./wiki/List_of_fallacies, retrieved March 14, 2011.

117. Downes S. *Stephen's Guide to Logical Fallacies.* Evolving number of p. at http://www.fallacies.ca/new.htm, retrieved March 14, 2011.

118. Canadian Institutes of Health Research (CIHR). *Glossary of Funding Related Terms.* 14 p. at mhtml:file://Glossary of Funding Related Terms – CIHR.mht, retrieved March 15, 2011. See also http://www.cihr-irsc.gc.ca/e/29418.html.

119. Yeoh MJ. Knowledge translation. Chapter 34, pp. 235–241 in: Croskerry P, Cosby KS, Schenkel SM, Wears RL. *Patient Safety in Emergency Medicine.* Philadelphia, PA: Wolters Kluwer/Lippincott/Williams & Wilkins, 2009.

120. Public Health Agency of Canada. *Glossary.* 19 p. at http://cbpp-pcpe.phac-aspc.gc.ca/glossary/all_terms_eng.html, retrieved Dec 17, 2009.

121. Kurtz S, Silverman J, Draper J. Foreword by J van Dalen and FW Pratt. *Teaching and Learning Communication Skills in Medicine.* 2nd Edition. Oxford and San Francisco, CA: Radcliffe Publishing, 2005.

122. Harrington A, Beverley L, Barron G, Pazderka H, Bergerman L & Cleland S for Alberta Health Services – Alberta Mental Health Board, Alberta Mental Health Research Partnership Program. *Knowledge Translation: A Synopsis of the Literature 2008.* Edmonton: Alberta Mental Health Research Partnership Program, 2009. See also 27 p. at www.mentalhealthresearch.ca/.../Knowledge%20Translation%20review_FINAL.pdf, retrieved March 15, 2011.

123. WhatisKT. *KT Terms.* Variable number of p. at http://whatiskt.wikispaces.com/KT+terms, retrieved Jan 10, 2011.

124. *Knowledge Translation in Health Care: Moving from Evidence to Practice.* Edited by S Straus, J Tetroe and ID Graham. Oxford and London: Wiley/Blackwell/BMJ Books, 2009.

125. Jenicek M. *Medical Error and Harm. Understanding, Prevention, and Control.* Boca Raton, FL/London/New York: CRC Press/Taylor & Francis/Informa/Productivity Press, 2011.

Chapter 12

Sharing Our Thinking about Clinical Cases: Clinical Case Reporting—"Getting the Best Information from Just One Case or from a Fistful of Cases or Events?"*

Executive Summary

Historically, **clinical case reports** are among the oldest ways of communicating lived clinical experience. Today, the objectives, purposes, and reasons for this kind of communication have expanded from simple descriptions and observations to a wide range of scientific activity. This range includes the challenges of diagnosis, features of error and harm, treatment effects, management and clinical care delivery and its setting, cause-effect inquiries, etiology and evidence, case study conditions, medical technologies, and particular skills.

* This chapter is based as a revised, updated, and edited version, with the permission of the publisher, of Chapter 7 in: Jenicek M. *Writing, Reading, and Understanding in Modern Health Sciences. Medical Articles and Other Forms of Communication.* Boca Raton, FL/London/New York: CRC Press/Taylor & Francis/Productivity Press, 2014.

There are three different types of clinical case reports used in medical communication and reviewed in this chapter: case reports, clinical vignettes, and case series reports.

Case reports, as fact finding tools, expand research and knowledge related to specific conditions or treatments. They use an argumentation approach to and **are powerful "generators" of new hypotheses** including etiological research. A recent trend to explore single or few clinical cases as causal proofs, beyond hypotheses generation, is still evolving. This type of exploration is a result of the need to report and examine rare cases and events like adverse effects studies in clinical pharmacology, clinimetric challenges in homeopathy, and other alternative medicines generating the notion of cognition-based medicine, which requires further evaluation and refinements. Expert judgments, algorithmic questions-answers and Bayesian management of probabilities were also proposed for this specific view of causality.

Clinical vignettes are mostly teaching tools, and thus differ from case reports. They provide a synopsis of a brief interesting or challenging patient encounter that addresses an opportunity to learn about a therapeutic encounter, patient management, or the clinician-patient relationship. They usually include a presentation and discussion component. Given the infrequency of events reported through clinical vignettes, these are not an effective way to study of medical error and harm. Lathology (domain of error and harm) must count on the causal analyses of cases like root cause analysis and other methods of inquiry.

Like case reports, **case series reports** use an argumentation report. A case series report presents a number of similar cases as a way to understand clinical experiences with a given scenario. Cases may be assembled from several different sources. Case series reports present "numerators without denominators," that is a number of cases are presented, but it is not exhaustive, thus it is not possible to determine rates or exposure.

Like other types of medical communication and argumentation, case reports continue to evolve. Experience from a broader experience in qualitative research, probability analysis, systems analysis, and other emerging fields may prove attractive to provide an even better analysis and interpretation of individual clinical case reports and case series and their uses in medical decision-making in practice and research. This chapter provides an understanding on the contributions that case reports make to medical communication and argumentation.

In This Chapter

Executive Summary: 373
Thoughts, Thinkers, and Things to Think About 375
Introductory Comments 377
What Might We Propose as a Thesis for This Chapter? 378
Content and Architecture of a Clinical Case Report Presented Orally and in Written
    Communication 380
12.1 Fundamental Considerations and Gnostic Classification of Clinical Case Reports 382
12.2 Case Reporting Topics 383

12.3 Types of Case Reporting 383
    12.3.1 The "Classical" Clinical Case Report 384
    12.3.2 A Clinical Vignette 385
    12.3.3 A Case Series Report 386
12.4 Structure and Organization of Case Reporting 386
12.5 The Message Itself and Ways to Convey It in an Argumentative Manner 386
12.6 Causal Proof: Is There a Role for Single or a Few Case Observations and Analyses
    in the Demonstration of Causality? 387
    Epidemiological Demonstration of Causality Based on Frequent Cases 388
    Considerations of Causality in Clinical Pharmacology: The Mainly
        Non-Epidemiological Study of Infrequent Cases 388
    Considerations of Causality in "Cognition-Based" Medicine: Non-Epidemiological
        Reasoning Focused on Specific Cases 388
12.7 Can We Critically Appraise Clinical Case Reports? 389
Let Us Conclude 389
References 391

Thoughts, Thinkers, and Things to Think About

The Government (clinical epidemiologists and other medical researchers alike) *is keen on amassing statistics. They collect them, add them, raise them to the power, take the cube root and prepare wonderful diagrams. But what you must never forget is that every one of those figures comes in the first instance from the village watchman* (like an experienced practicing clinician) *who just puts down* (in his or her clinical case report) *what he damn pleases.*
Sir Josiah Stamp (1929)
Quoting an anonymous English Judge
(insertions by the author)
He or she should ensure that the right stuff is put down!

Precision of communication is important, more important than ever, in our era of hair-trigger balances, when a false, or misunderstood word may create as much disaster as a sudden thoughtless act.
James Thurber (1894–1961)
"Friends, Romans, Countrymen, Lend Me Your Ear Muffs"
Lanterns and Lances (1961)
Even in clinical case reporting, Jim!

*Efficiency in clinical case reporting means
reporting clinical cases right. Effectiveness
means reporting the right cases.*
Paraphrasing
Peter F. Drucker (1909–2005)
Shouldn't we do both, Peter?

*It is more important to know what kind
of patient has the disease than what kind
of disease the patient has.*
Sir William Osler
(1849–1919)
Quoted in *Psychiatric Annals* (1983)
Francis Scott Smyth (1985–1972)
in the *Journal of Medical Education*,
37:495, 1962 disagrees to some point:
*To know what kind of person has a disease
is as essential as to know what kind of a
disease a person has.*
**Both are also important in a clinical
case report!**

*Many diseases now well recognized, with
an established pattern of symptoms and
signs started out with reporting of a single
case. ... Should we have said to these
(authors), "I am sorry your case report is
not acceptable and your description of this
unusual condition or operation has no place
in the established literature?"*
Asha Senapati
in the *Journal of the Royal
Society of Medicine* (1996)
**Shouldn't we also say "why" and
"why now?" Dr. Senapati?**

*You must acquire the ability to describe
your observations and your experience in
such language that whoever observes or
experiences similarly will be forced to the
same conclusions.*
Martin Fischer
(1879–1962)
Quoted by Howard Fabing and
Ray Marr in *Fischerisms*
Shouldn't we learn first how to do it?

Clinical case reporting is more
enriching if you have a reason for it and
if you know how.

Introductory Comments

Clinical case reports have gained a range of reputations in the past two generations, including that of a valuable tool that permits the sharing of clinical knowledge and experience. These reports are also considered quick and simple medical articles which require less research, time, and expertise than other scientific initiatives and that can enhance the author's professional profile and the clinician's professional and academic curriculum. Nonetheless, how many times have we heard that "*Clinical case reports prove nothing*"?

There are two ways to deal with clinical case reports (CCRs). One is to dismiss them instantly as a voluminous nuisance within the ever-increasing volume of health information, complicating knowledge translation in health sciences. The other is to make them more meaningful and useful for practice and research.

In the spirit of recent calls for clinical case reporting to be better focused, better structured, and more helpful for clinical understanding, decision-making and medical research,[1,2] we need to better understand the current state of medical thinking. Medical **casuistics**, the study, analysis, and reporting of clinical cases, is flourishing. Casuistics may be confused by some with **casuistry**, which means rather a specious, deceptive, or over-subtle reasoning, a bickering, fruitless and aimless debate. These two terms should not be mixed up.

About 15 years ago, the first *ad hoc* monographs devoted to clinical case reporting[3-5] were among several initiatives[6-9] that launched the current increase of interest in quality clinical case reporting and its relevance, both in medicine and surgery. This trend was also supported by an evolving number of new and old periodicals devoted exclusively to clinical case reporting. Some examples of these include the *Cambridge Medicine Journal (CMJ), International Journal of Surgery Case Reports, Journal of Surgical Case Reports, Elsevier Medical Case Reports, Journal of Medical Cases, Case Reports in Medicine* (Hindawi), *International Medical Case Reports Journal, BMJ Case Reports, Radiology Case Reports, Journal of Radiology Case Reports, Journal of Orthopaedic Case Reports, Journal of Medical Case Reports, American Journal of Case Reports* (formerly *Case Reports and Clinical Practice Review*), *Case Study and Case Report, International Journal of Clinical Case Reports, and Clinical Medicine Insights: Case Reports* (a HINARI Publisher Partner). New publications focused on case reports are constantly appearing. To support this development, *ad hoc* articles for medicine,[10-12] pharmacy,[13] nursing,[14] chiropractic medicine,[15,16] and acupuncture[17] have been published to provide basic guidance for how to write case studies.

With this trend, however, some clinicians and protagonists of evidence-based medicine view clinical case and case series reports as lowest in the hierarchy of medical evidence. But what kind of evidence and about what? This may hold true in the hierarchy of a cause-effect proof, be it the beneficial effects of treatment or the consequences of exposure to noxious factors. What should be done in situations in which there are not enough cases for clinical trials or formal case control or cohort etiological research? Single clinical case reports or case series reports of any size may not be appropriate vehicles for formal epidemiological research, but they provide important evidence nonetheless.

So far, most attention in clinical case reporting has been given to unusual and rare events (often without specifying their rarity) and to the role of interventions believed to be beneficial in these cases. There is increasing interest in medical error and harm (that fortunately have a low frequency of occurrence) and clinical errors in lathology (the study of error and harm). Analysis of clinical cases, like those addressed in clinical case reports, rely on qualitative research used in such reports. Recent methodological contributions from qualitative research are another important asset for reporting health benefits or harm through clinical case reports.

What Might We Propose as a Thesis for This Chapter?

Clinical case reports may be considered in some circumstances a "first line of evidence."[3-5] However, they are also often the only evidence available. When they are well-written, they are indispensable and powerful generators of hypotheses for further etiological research. Moreover, they can be subjects for meta-analysis of cases. Readers can search for them, as well as for their integration and systematic reviews, in numerous sources or worksites. Sometimes, unique cases are the only ones available in the world of cause-effect assessment.

The purpose of this chapter is to review the characteristics, distinct features, and methodological challenges of clinical case reporting today, how to write them, and how to report them as meaningful medical articles. Unexaggerated in their presentation, conclusions and implications, clinical case reports and case series reports are the fruit of an invaluable, rich clinical experience and are irreplaceable in the domain of clinical casuistics. They will remain necessary testimonies of lived clinical and community (field) experience of any health professional.

What does a good clinical case report worthy of publishing require today? Let us understand this through:

- some fundamental considerations;
- an ever-broadening array of subjects and topics to be reported;
- types of case reporting: "classical," clinical vignette, case series, situations, processes, and activities as "case" study;
- structure of case reporting;
- content and ways of reporting in terms of argumentation;
- frequent challenges of causal proof sought in single or limited numbers of clinical case reports;
- qualitative research and case study uses from other domains like error and harm; and
- inquiry (lathology).

Methodologically speaking, Figure 12.1 shows that the purpose of clinical case reports may be a clinical "snapshot" of the case, discussion of some kind of cause-effect relationship, philosophical aspects of the case and other, most often unspecified reasons, for reporting. The purpose of the case may be oriented toward either understanding or decision-making about this or similar cases. Such orientation may be dealt with using either the argumentative or non-argumentative approach.

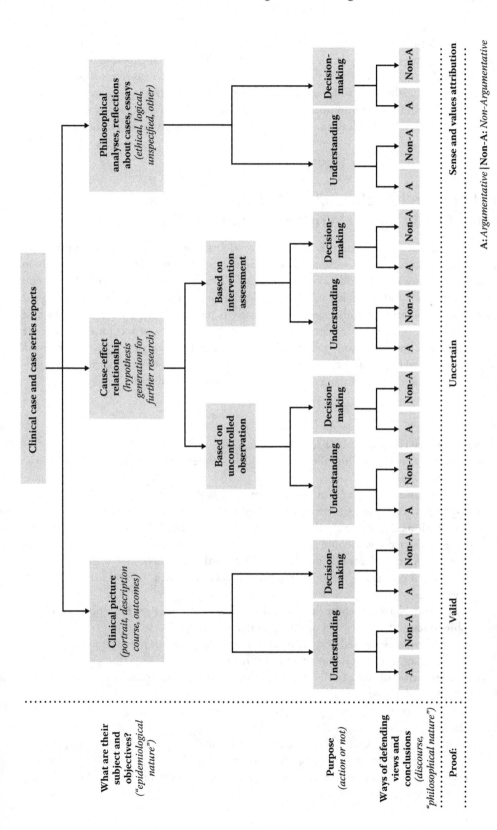

Figure 12.1 Operational and gnostic classification of clinical case reports. (Redrawn from Jenicek M. *Writing, Reading, and Understanding in Modern Health Sciences.* Boca Raton, FL: CRC Press, 2014. Reproduced with permission.)

There is no uniform thinking about clinical cases and their reporting because there are many reasons for studying and reporting them. Each may require a more specific methodology depending on the reason.[8 modified] Reasons to publish a clinical case report or case series study apply to medicine in its entirety, although some are of particular interest for surgery.[8] These are summarized in Table 12.1. Failure to communicate reasons for single clinical case or case series reports contributes to their misunderstanding and related actions underlying potential errors and eventual harm.

Content and Architecture of a Clinical Case Report Presented Orally and in Written Communication

In essence, any clinical case report is an exercise in argumentation and communication. Communicating a case report in a medical journal requires a structured presentation, usually in sections such as "Summary," "Introduction to the Case," "Presentation of the Case," "Discussion of the Case Experience," and "Conclusion" that may be drawn from such an experience. From the perspective of argumentation, claims (conclusions) made as part of the argument about the case are integrated with the other most important building blocks in the case report format. These are illustrated below. Note that while any oral or written version of a clinical case report is limited in time and page space, the following elements (which should also be part of the case research protocol) must be available and ready to share on request with any interested party.

1. The **summary** typically comprises four elements:
   - **motives** and reasons for the report, which answers the question *"Why are we reporting this?"*
   - **background** to the problem, which answers *"In what context?"*
   - **highlights** of the report, answering the question *"What have we found?"*
   - **conclusions**, summarizing the whole process be answering *"What does this mean?"*
2. In the **introduction**, we should find:
   - the definition of the **topic** (problem, disease, clinical activity);
   - the general **context** of the topic (relevant knowledge, present clinical situation and challenges);
   - a **question** that this report should answer, a gap in knowledge this report can fill;
   - **objectives** and justification of this report; and
   - what is to be **evaluated** as a result of the report—the soundness, structure, process, impact, constancy, consistency—of the claim.
3. The **presentation of the case** incorporates the grounds of an argumentation process. It includes the following:
   - **situation, context,** and **triggering factor** of the report;
   - clinical and paraclinical **initial state** of the patient;
   - **evolution** of the clinical and paraclinical spectrum and gradient of the case;
   - diagnostic and therapeutic **acts**, care, and support;
   - expected and actual **results** of actions carried out or omitted; and
   - unexpected results and events.

Table 12.1 Complementary Reasons and Phenomena of Interest in General Case Reporting and in Reporting Events More Specific to Surgery

Clinical Cases in General	Surgical Cases
• Obtaining leads as index manifestations to establish diagnostic criteria for a "new" disease • Unusual presentation of unknown etiology • Unusual natural history • Unusual natural or clinical course • Challenging differential diagnosis • Clinical failures, errors, and harm related to diagnosis and treatment • Unusual and/or unexpected effects of treatment (outcomes) or diagnostic results, whether good or bad • Diagnostic and therapeutic 'accidents' (causes, consequences, remedies) • Unusual co-morbidity (diagnosis, treatment, outcome) • Unusual setting of medical care (e.g., emergency or field conditions) • Patient compliance • Patient/doctor interaction (not only in psychiatry!) • Single case clinical trial ("*N*-of-1" study) • Clinical situations as valuable experience from an uncontrolled setting that cannot be reproduced for ethical reasons • Limited access to cases (economy, ethics, social reasons, patient choices) • Index case(s) of a potential or real outbreak (more cases expected to come) • Confirmation of something already known (only if useful for a systematic case report review and synthesis) • Solving a challenging problem in medical ethics • Economical aspects of the management of the case • Evaluation of the potential burden of the case (family, health services, work environment, social services, economy) • Detailed intimate information provided by qualitative research about the case (narratives) • Any set of cases allowing health administrators to assess and define needs and supplies in human, material, and organizational resources in order to respond adequately to individual and community needs • Operational research findings • Capture of rare cases	• New medical/surgical technology (use, outcomes, consequences) • Transfer of medical technology (from one disease, organ, or system to another) • Emergency, often heuristic management of a case with or without necessary evidence, data, and information • Technical challenges in the surgical management of the case • Operational research findings and considerations in this and other cases • Complications of surgery (adverse effects, rejections, other failures, intolerance of procedures) • Faith, cultural, and social considerations implicated in the case management and decisions • Legal aspects of the case management and its outcomes • Demonstrated or newer dexterities, ergonomics, ease, or technical and technological requirements for the surgery and management of the case • Generation and proposal of a hypothesis about biological and other mechanisms of the health problem relevant to surgery (often by way of qualitative research methodology; *vide infra*) • Presentation of "Black Swan" evidence (all swans are white, this unique black swan [a disease, its causes and interventions] proves otherwise) • Tolerance of a procedure by the patient (equiv. Phase I clinical trial) • Ancillary interventions and care, i.e., co-treatments for this and other health problems (co-morbidity) • Medical and/or surgical error and its connection to potential and real harm • Medical/surgical harm and inquiries about its potential and real causes • Operational findings (again) • Medical humor (use sparingly and with care)

4. **Discussion** and **conclusion** sections are where the exercise of modern argumentation is found, especially the warrant, qualifier, rebuttals, and the acceptance or refutation of the claim. This section includes:
   - the **discussion of observations** and results preferably through modern argumentation;
   - the **contribution** of the report to the fundamental knowledge of the problem represented by the reported case; and
   - the **proposals and recommendations** for practice (clinical decisions) and for research (new hypotheses generated by the case).
5. **References** are often a weak section of case reports. Only the most important are usually included, but they should clearly cover different elements, including:
   - the health **problem** and disease under study;
   - the most important **past experience** for comparisons;
   - clinical and paraclinical **actions**;
   - **decisions** made and under consideration; and
   - **methodology** and **techniques** specific to all the above.

Clinical case reports and case series reports have a limited role of clinical case reports and case series reports in causal proofs. When they are correctly done and interpreted in a non-exaggerated way, they are an important part of the methods and techniques used in clinical and field epidemiology.[18] Even oral presentations of clinical cases should incorporate the most relevant elements of written clinical case reporting format.

12.1 Fundamental Considerations and Gnostic Classification of Clinical Case Reports

Essentially, a clinical case report is an argumentative essay. Its purpose is to share a clinical or community medicine observation, interpretation of what has been witnessed, and offer proposals regarding what to do with the particular case next. Whether presented orally at the bedside, during various floor encounters, at hospital rounds, scientific meetings or communicated in writing, they all carry several common traits of form and content.

Clinical case reporting incorporates two different but related approaches. In one, a single case report is presented and discussed. In the case series report, several cases or events which share commonalities in either form or function, are reported. This can present some challenges.

In many case reports, the question about some cause-effect relationship may be considered. The rarity of cases implies that **epidemiological considerations of causality** are only one approach. Another approach must be **other considerations which derive causality from single or few observations**, which are subject to different and often complementary criteria of causes and considerations of consequences.

In other case reports, **individuals only** (patients as "cases") are studied or 'cases' represented by "*What's going on?*" In this circumstance, **situations**, **events**, **activities**, or **happenings** are viewed as an interactive milieu involving individuals (patients, health professionals) and their environment, whether it is within a clinical care or community health context. The latter should benefit from case studies methodology in social sciences and in the qualitative research domain.[19]

12.2 Case Reporting Topics

Choosing the topic for a clinical case report goes beyond selecting something defined as "new" and/ or "rare." The variety of topics for clinical case reporting is constantly increasing.[1,7,8] Let us reiterate that two types of case reports are worthy of attention, each implying a different, but complementary methodology: 1) physical (patient body and mind) cases and 2) clinical situations as cases. The failure to communicate reasons for single clinical case or case series reports and their nature contributes to their misunderstanding and related actions underlying potential errors and eventual harm.

Here is a sample of the ever-growing list of possible topics for clinical case reporting as Figure 12.2.

The quality and relevance of case reporting topics also depend on their structure and organization (form) and on the matter, and type of reasoning, critical thinking, and argumentation about the case(s) (content).

12.3 Types of Case Reporting

There are three major types of case reports: the classical clinical case report, the clinical vignette, and the case series report. The methodology, purpose, and objectives of these types of case reporting differ. They are reviewed in the sections that follow.

Topics for clinical case reporting

Manifestations, observations, past and present descriptions (a "classical" clinical case report): An unusual presentation of disease features, course, etiology, natural history, a rare case, or unique case.

Diagnosis: Search for diagnostic criteria for a new phenomenon, differential diagnosis experience, unusual comorbidity and its management, etc.

Features of error and harm: Clinical failures, complications, adverse effects, their causes and control.

Treatment: Unusual treatment effects (good or bad), tolerance, ancillary interventions and care, N-of-1 clinical trials, etc.

Management and clinical care delivery and their setting: Compliance, "patient/health care provider" interaction, assessment of needs, operational research information, technical, legal, sociological challenges, etc.

Cause-effect inquiries, etiology land evidence: Reporting potential index cases, burden of case(s) assessment, hypothesis generation about causes of events of interest.

Case study conditions: Burden of the case for the family and community, access to cases and care, challenging problems in medical ethics, etc.

Technology, skills: Uses, tolerance, outcomes, consequences of new technologies, transfer (new application) of medical technology, demonstration of new dexterities, technical requirements for surgery and management of the case.

Figure 12.2 Topics for clinical case reporting.

12.3.1 The "Classical" Clinical Case Report

As perhaps the oldest form of clinical communication, clinical cases are reported today for two major reasons. First, as a teaching tool, and second to expand research and knowledge. The former is the domain of the clinical vignette, the latter is the domain of single case reports and case series reports.

> A **clinical case report** (CCR) is a structured presentation of a clinical experience with a single patient according to predetermined objectives and purposes for **fact finding, rather than education**. The CCR, then, is used to exchange information about observed facts. This approach takes into account the improvement of practice in habitual clinical settings and traces possible directions in researching a health problem. In this approach, the single patient is representative of a larger experience and the case offers directions for further management of the problem and care.

Communicating a case report in a medical journal requires an increasingly structured presentation, usually in sections represented here by the acronym **SIPDiSC** as in Figure 12.3. This acronym stands for.[20]

Objectives, reasons, questions asked and ways to obtain answers to them, should be clear both to the author and the reader. We have detailed this elsewhere[3–5] because "*making it interesting*" is not enough. This structure, however, may vary slightly from one journal to another. In essence, any clinical case report and any case series study (as with any medical article, in fact) is presented in the form of a five-part essay that has its origins in classical

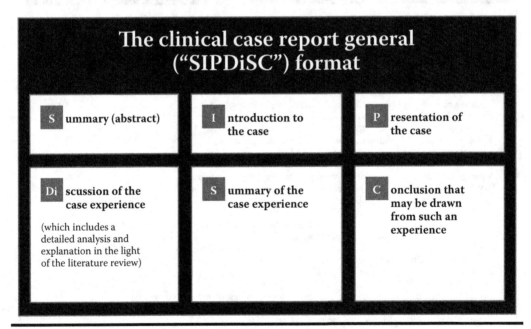

Figure 12.3   The clinical case report general ("SIPDiSC") format.

rhetoric: introduction (includes a thesis), narration (what was witnessed), affirmation (evidence and arguments in favor of the thesis), negation or refutation (evidence and arguments against the thesis), and conclusion (review and summary of the path from the thesis to the argument and its claim). Again, as is the case with any other reflective process, an essay is based on argumentation. This concept was outlined in more detail in Chapter 5 of this series.

12.3.2 A Clinical Vignette

A **clinical vignette** is a concise presentation of an interesting or challenging patient encounter.[21] Clinical vignettes are descriptions of a clinical experience, usually with one clinical case, in a simple format that includes "title and author information, introduction (preferably with teaching and learning objectives), case presentation, literature review (sometimes), discussion and summary."[22,23] At its core is a presentation of the chief complaint, history, physical examination, laboratory and radiographic studies, assessment and plan as in Figure 12.4.

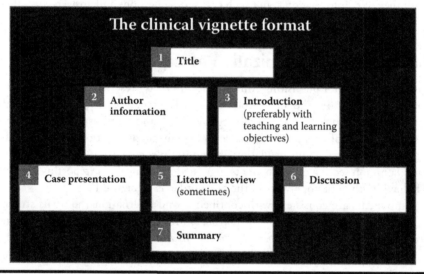

Figure 12.4 The clinical vignette format.

In encounters preceding the publication of clinical vignettes, trainees are asked a series of questions. Their answers, which should cover the core elements of the vignette, are used as a tool to measure and enrich the trainees' knowledge and clinical reasoning. The presentation and its discussion are shaped to highlight either the natural history of a given health problem, a therapeutic relationship between clinician and patient, or patient management to improve knowledge and clinical skills.[21] It is viewed primarily as a **teaching and learning experience**. A clinical vignette may or may not be published.

12.3.3 A Case Series Report

Epidemiologically speaking, clinical case series reports are sets of cases that present *"numerators without denominators."* A case series report *could* be used to determine rates of events, assessment of prevalence or incidence of cases, however to do this, denominators are required. Denominators may be considered in advance or sought after "sets"— or a series—of cases are obtained. In both cases, denominators are challenging to obtain.

In a case series, cases are not always from a single source, site or study. Thus it is important to consider how all dependent and independent variables, clinical events and maneuvers, patient and physician characteristics, and outcomes are defined. All **clinimetrics**, that is measurement, counting, quantification and classification of clinical manifestations and events, depend on **orismology**, the study, use, and evaluation of definitions, as outlined in Chapter 7. All such considerations may be even more important if some meta-analysis of single cases or case series is attempted after the original observations are made and assembled. Medical articles based on case reports or case series reports are even better if they offer information about such case series questions and answers.

12.4 Structure and Organization of Case Reporting

The structure and layout for publishing clinical case reports is prescribed by the journals in which they are published. Typically, the format follows a similar structure, listing various combinations and sequences of items including technical, legal, ethical, and administrative directions (tables, figures making, formats of additional files, style and language, publication fees in the case of open journals, rules for submission and evaluation of manuscripts, etc.).

The most common section or components suggested for clinical case reporting ideally includes all of the following, though not always in the same order as in Figure 12.5.

These components are consistent with continental and international journals structural suggestions for clinical case reporting.[21–23] The *Journal of Medical Case Reports* instructions to authors of a case report article[24] and the *European Journal of Medical Research* instructions for authors of a case report[25] are among the most detailed.

12.5 The Message Itself and Ways to Convey It in an Argumentative Manner

As with any exchange of spoken or written information and communication, a medical article is an exercise in argumentation about something, and for something: it's new, it's different, it works and never worked before, and this might cause it. Whatever the subject, it is covered by most, if not all, elements of the modern argument[26,27] as outlined in Chapter 4 of this book. These include:

- **proposal** (original or working claim),
- **grounds** (observations),
- **backing** (extended body of evidence),
- **warrant** (allowing a general rule which infers a claim based on the grounds),

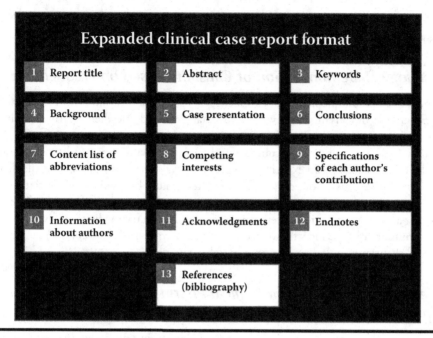

Figure 12.5   Expanded clinical case report format.

- **support** (pros and cons, balanced and weighted),
- **rebuttals** (conditions which may make the claim invalid, i.e., exclusionary conditions, states and circumstances of individuals, community, or environment),
- **qualifications** (strength of conclusions which express our certainty about the claim in light of the whole argumentative process), and
- the **final claim**.

Each of these elements requires the best and most specific and relevant evidence as the basis for its support.

Practically all subjects and claims of clinical case reports may be seen as reasoning paths for argumentation. A clinical case report, such as a medical article, is, or should most often be, a five paragraph (introduction, narration, affirmation, negation, conclusion) persuasive or argumentative essay,[28] even within the customary article structure and format (**SSIMRaD**, i.e., **s**tructured **s**ummary, **i**ntroduction, **m**aterial and methods, **r**esults, **a**nd **d**iscussion with conclusions and recommendations for further research and practice).[29] This directly or indirectly contains elements of the modern argument outlined previously. An additional list of resources regarding how to write essays may be found online[29,30] and can also be found in the introductory chapter.

12.6 Causal Proof: Is There a Role for Single or a Few Case Observations and Analyses in the Demonstration of Causality?

In case reporting, there are not a sufficient number of cases to develop inferential biostatistics and epidemiological reasoning and criteria for causality. The question is then, how do we use this reporting method to demonstrate cause-effect? Clinical pharmacology and cognition-based and anthroposophical medicines try to look at this problem.

Epidemiological Demonstration of Causality Based on Frequent Cases

Due to the rarity and unique nature of cases, clinical case reports cannot fulfill the requirements for classical criteria of causality (overviewed in Chapter 8 and elsewhere).[31] These requirements include temporality, strength, manifestation and causal specificity, biological gradient, consistency, and biological plausibility, all coherent and analogous with prevalent knowledge and supported (wherever possible) by an experimental proof and systematic review of all available relevant evidence. Alternative causal considerations and criteria must be used. Some initiatives, still to be fully developed and validated, originate from clinical pharmacology, lathology (the study of medical error and harm) and from alternative and complementary medicines. Given the inherent nature and number of case reports, we are faced with two distinct but complementary worlds, concepts and theories of causality. It cannot be otherwise.

Considerations of Causality in Clinical Pharmacology: The Mainly Non-Epidemiological Study of Infrequent Cases

Establishing a cause-effect relationship based on evidence from only a few cases is appropriate in clinical pharmacology in specific cases where required conditions are met and related to adverse drug reactions. These four conditions are related to adverse drug reactions and which stem from anecdotal reports (i.e., few cases):

1. **Extracellular or intercellular tissue deposition** of the drug or a metabolite.
2. **Specific location** or pattern of injury.
3. **Physiological dysfunction** or direct tissue **damage** demonstrable by physiochemical testing.
4. **Infection** as a result of the administration of an infective agent as the therapeutic substance or because of demonstrable **contamination**.[32]

Considerations of Causality in "Cognition-Based" Medicine: Non-Epidemiological Reasoning Focused on Specific Cases

This challenge is also covered in Chapter 8 of this book. Let us only remind ourselves here that alternative approaches to causality based on a single or a few cases are proposed by their authors from the domain of cognition-based[33–35] and anthroposophical[36,37] medicines in the literature. In those domains, the reasoning and decision-making is based on individual clinical cases, methodology varying from one medicine to another. Together with limited bibliography available, single-case considerations are covered in Sections 8.5, 8.6, and 8.7 of Chapter 8. These considerations are examined there side by side with the mainstream epidemiological considerations of causality.

12.7 Can We Critically Appraise Clinical Case Reports?

Critical appraisal questions in the case reporting domain, as proposed by Roever and Reis,[38] are very similar to the appraisal questions of other types of research and communication. According to Roever and Reis, these questions including the following.

- Did the study address a clearly focused question/issue?
- Is the study design appropriate for answering the research question?
- Was the study protocol well defined?
- Are both the setting and the subject's representative with regard to the population to which the findings will be referred?
- Is the researcher's perspective clearly described and taken into account?
- Are the methods for collecting data clearly described?
- Are the methods for analysing the data likely to be valid and reliable? Are quality control measures used?
- Was the analysis repeated by more than researcher to ensure reliability?
- Are the results credible, and if so, are they relevant for practice? Are results easy to understand?
- It was clinically relevant outcomes?
- Are the conclusions drawn justified by the results?
- Are the findings of the study transferable to other settings?[38]

This approach to the critical appraisal of case reports must be tested. Most clinical case reports are still presented as simple descriptions of a health phenomenon of interest. Appraisal and conclusions of the case report are being left to the reader, as well as the critical appraisal itself.

Let Us Conclude

Single clinical case experience and case series experience are unique and extremely valuable experiences that can lead to better understanding and decisions about health phenomena under scrutiny. To do so, however, they must have appropriate content and must be presented using appropriate structure and methods, even in situations where limitations apply. Nonetheless, challenges in understanding their role in providing clinical evidence persist. Some readers continue to question if case reports really *"prove nothing."*

The persistent low perceived value of clinical case reports is due to the fact that the cause-effect relationships in case reports are often explored there at any price. Causality itself is derived through different approaches from infrequent and frequent cases which occur and are reported. More often, other valuable information is provided by case reports.

Further development of clinical case reporting will certainly benefit from the rapidly expanding methodology of case studies in qualitative research in general as we have already commented on elsewhere.[20] Some interface between classical clinical case reporting, clinical case series reporting, and multiple case designs in case studies research in social sciences will certainly develop soon. Methodological similarities in case reporting domain, its objectives, research questions, analytic techniques, and the search for answers where control groups do not exist lie behind such converging domains.

Given particular characteristics of both, the author and reader of medical articles both make both proper distinctions between a "case study" in qualitative research at large[39] and "clinical case report" in health sciences. More merging of experience from clinical case reporting and case studies in qualitative research at large may be expected.

Correctly structuring a clinical case report is no longer a major problem. The IMRAD format and its alternatives and modifications are well rooted, known, and used across the literature. The major challenge of clinical case reporting today, as it always will be, is its data, its ideas, their analysis and interpretation. Modern argumentation and critical thinking becomes a necessity even in the clinical case domain, and not only in "scientific" research.

Obsession with causality-based case reports is often unjustified because the spectrum of reasons to report cases today goes well beyond the etiology of what we have witnessed, even when webs of causes and webs of consequences do not ease the case study and reporting. Types, subjects, and topics for case reports are widening accordingly. Developing some universal and encompassing clinical case reporting guidelines may prove itself more than challenging.

The future handling of this problem should prove interesting. It remains to be seen how such methodological considerations, real clinical situations and experiences based on interaction with patients will be used in the most beneficial way for clinical case reporting.

Clinical case studies and reports are 'scientific' research with their own focus, quality, strengths, and limitations! They all must be known, understood, and practiced. Just overselling their contributions to medical literature is always an undesirable temptation. In the light of their review, we agree with Nissen and Wynn[40] that the attitudes toward publishing case reports and case series shifted from their decline in the 1970s to their resurgence from the late 1990s. This is a well merited and positive trend.

There is an ongoing project to develop a consensus-based clinical reporting guideline.[41] Only the future will show if such over encompassing guidelines will not be too general given the diversity of objectives and related methodologies and techniques across the wide spectrum of clinical case and case series reports. Balancing the content and form of clinical case reporting in view of future adoptions and uses in research and practice will always be a challenge.

In the light of the above, it is our position that:

- the generation of new ideas and hypotheses would be much harder without clinical cases experience;
- the experience with defining clinical and community observations at early stages of understanding clinical phenomena, their measurement and classification (i.e., clinimetrics) would be impossible; so
- they must be done right both in their form and their content.

Given all these considerations, the future of clinical case reporting in all health sciences is bright.

References

1. Vandenbroucke JP. In defense of case reports and case series. *Ann Intern Med,* 2001;134:330–4.
2. Jenicek M. Clinical case reports: Sources of boredom or valuable piece of evidence? Invited Editorial. *Nat Med J India,* 2001;14:193–4.
3. Jenicek M. *Casuistique médicale. Bien présenter un cas clinique. (Medical Casuistics. Making a Good Clinical Case Report.)* St. Hyacinthe et Paris: EDISEM et Maloine Éditeurs, 1997.
4. Jenicek M. *Clinical Case Reporting in Evidence-Based Medicine.* Oxford: Butterworth Heinemann, 1999.
5. Jenicek M. *Clinical Case Reporting in Evidence-Based Medicine.* 2nd (Rewritten and Expanded) Edition. London and New York: Arnold and Oxford University Press, 2001. Followed by editions in Italian (*Casi clinici ed evidence-based medicine. Come preparare e presentare case report. Edizione italiana cura di Luigi Pagliaro.* Roma: Il Pensiero Scientifico Editore, 2001), Japanese (same title—Tokyo: Igaku Shoin, 2001), and Korean (same title—Seoul: Gyechuk Munwha Sa., 2002).
6. Jenicek M. *Étude de cas (Clinical Case Studies and Reports).* Presented at the INSERM/AFM Seminar *'Réseaux de recherche sur les maladies rares' (Rare Diseases Research Network),* Paris: Génocentre (Evry), November 20, 2001. 13 unnumbered p. in: *Proceedings from the Seminar on Rare Diseases.* Evry: INSERM/AFM/Department (Ministry) of Health (France), 2001.
7. Jenicek M. Clinical case reports and case series research in evaluating surgery. Part I. The context: General aspects of evaluation applied to surgery. *Med Sci Monit,* 2008;14(9):RA133–43.
8. Jenicek M. Clinical case reports and case series research in evaluating surgery. Part II. The content and form: Uses of single clinical case reports and case series research in surgical specialties. *Med Sci Monit,* 2008;14(10):RA149–62.
9. Agha R, Rosin RD. Time for a new approach to case reports. *Int J Surg Case Rep,* 2010;1(1):1–3.
10. McCarthy LH and Reilly EH. How to write a case report. *Fam Med,* 2000;32(3):190–5.
11. WikiHow. *How to Write a Medical Case Study Report.* 3 p. at http://www.wikihow.com/Write-a -Medical-Case-Study-Report, retrieved July 22, 2013.
12. BMJ Group. *BMJ Case Reports. Instructions for Authors.* 5 p. at http://casereports.bmj.com/site/about/guide lines.xhtml, retrieved Jan 18, 2013.
13. Cohen H. How to write a patient case report. *Am J Health-Syst Pharm,* 2006;63(Oct 1):1888–92.
14. Pasadena City College. *How to Write a Case Study Paper (with a Sample Nursing 52 Paper).* 2+7 p. at http://www.pasadena.edu/hstutoringlab/writingcasestudy,cfm, retrieved Jan 18, 2013.
15. Green BN and Johnson CD. How to write a case report for publication. *J Chiropr Med,* 2006;5:72–82.
16. Budgell B. Guidelines to the writing of case studies. *J Can Chiropr Assoc,* 2008;52(4):199–204.
17. Vinjamury SP. Writing a case report. *The American Acupuncturist,* 2008;Spring:18–19,27.
18. Albrecht J, Bigby M. Case reports and case series. Pp. 134–6 in: *Encyclopedia of Epidemiology.* Edited by S Boslaugh and I-A McNutt. Los Angeles, CA/London/New Delhi/Singapore: SAGE Publications, 2008.
19. Wikipedia, the free encyclopedia. *Case Study.* 7 p. at http://en.wikipedia.org/wiki/Case_study, retrieved Jan 28, 2013.
20. Jenicek M. *Writing, Reading, and Understanding in Modern Health Sciences. Medical Articles and Other Forms of Communication.* Boca Raton, FL/London/New York: CRC Press/Productivity Press, 2014.
21. International Training & Education Center on HIV (I-TECH). *Structured Clinical Vignettes: What Are They and How They Are Used?* An I-TECH Clinical Mentoring Kit. 5 p. at The University of Texas Medical Branch (UTMB). *Clinical Vignettes.* 2 p. at http://www.utmb.edu/aim/vignettes.htm, retrieved Oct 6, 2011.
22. American College of Physicians (ACP). Presenting a clinical vignette: Deciding what to present. 3 p. at http://www.acponline.org/residents_fellows/competitions/abstract/prepare/clinvin_pres.htm, retrieved Oct 6, 2011.
23. American College of Physicians. *Writing a Clinical Vignette (Case Report) Abstract.* 2 p. at http://www .acponline.org/residents_fellows/competitions/abstract/prepare/clinvin_abs.htm, retrieved Oct 25, 2011.

24. Journal of Medical Case Reports. Instructions for authors. Case report articles. 7 p. at http://www
    .jmedicalcasereports.com/authors/instructions/casereport, retrieved March 12, 2012.
25. European Journal of Medical Research. Instructions for authors. Case report. 6 p. at http://www
    .eurjmedres.com/authors/instructions/casereport, retrieved March 12, 2012.
26. Toulmin SE. *The Uses of Argument*. Cambridge and New York: Cambridge University Press, 1958.
    (Updated Edition 2003).
27. Jenicek M and Hitchcock DL. *Evidence-Based Practice. Logic and Critical Thinking in Medicine*.
    Chicago, IL: American Medical Association (AMA Press), 2005.
28. Wikipedia, the free encyclopedia. *Five Paragraph Essay*. 3 p. at http://en.wikipedia.org/wiki/Five
    _paragraph_essay, retrieved March 8, 2012.
29. Caprette DR. *Writing Research Papers*. (Rice University Bios 211). 8 p. at http://www.ruf.rice.edu
    /~bioslab/tools/report/reportform,html, retrieved March 3, 2012.
30. Livingston K. *Guide to Writing a Basic Essay. Find Additional Essay Resources On-Line*. 5 p. at http://
    lklivingston.tripod.com/essay/links.html, retrieved March 8, 2012.
31. Jenicek M. *Foundations of Evidence-Based Medicine*. Boca Raton, FL/London/New York/Washington,
    DC: The Parthenon Publishing Group, A CRC Press Company, 2003.
32. Hauben M and Aronson JK. Gold standards in pharmacovigilance. The use of definitive anecdotal
    reports of adverse drug reactions as pure gold and high-grade ore. *Drug Safety*, 2007;30(8):645–55.
33. Kiene H. Was ist Cognition-Based Medicine? *Z ärtzl Fortbild Qual Gesundh wes*, 2005;99:301–6.
34. Kiene H and von Schön-Angerer T. Single-case causality assessment as a basis for clinical judgment.
    Altern Ther Health Med, 1998;4(1):41–7.
35. Kiene H. *Komplementäre Methodenlehre der klinischen Forschung*. Berlin/Heidelberg/New York:
    Springer–Verlag, 2001.
36. Kiene H. Causality, anthroposophic medicine and statistics. *J Anthroposophic Med*, 1996;13(1):42–8.
37. Wikipedia, the free encyclopedia. *Anthroposophical Medicine*. 7 p. at http://en.wikipedia.org/wiki
    /Anthroposophical_medicine, retrieved March 1, 2008.
38. Roever L and Reis O. Critical appraisal of a case report. *Evidence Based Medicine and Practice*,
    2015;1(1):e103 at http://dx.doi.org/10.4172/EBMP.1000e103.
39. Yin RK. *Case Study Research. Design and Methods*. Thousand Oaks, CA/London/New Delhi/
    Singapore: SAGE Publications Inc., 2014.
40. Nissen T and Wynn R. The recent history of clinical case report: A narrative review. *J Roy Soc Med Sh
    Rep*, 2011;3:87.doi: 10.1258/shorts.2012.012046.
41. Gagnier JJ, Kienle G, Altman DG, Moher D, Sox H, Riley D; and the CARE Group. The CARE
    guidelines: Consensus-based clinical case reporting guideline development. *Global Adv Health Med*,
    2013;2(5):38–43.doi: 10,7453/gahmj.2013.008.

Chapter 13

Sharing Our Thoughts in Written Essays, Research-Based Articles, and Other Types of Written Medical Communication: "Should We Not Think about and Communicate Our Research, as Well as How We Have Done It?"*

Executive Summary

Not all articles in medicine and other health sciences are based on scientific research; an extensive array of subjects and messages in medical journals may be presented in an essay form instead. An essay is not always based on the best evidence provided by a scientific method-based research. It essentially

* This chapter is based, with permission of the publisher, on elements in Chapters 1, 2, 3, and 4 in: Jenicek M. *Writing, Reading, and Understanding in Modern Health Sciences. Medical Articles and Other Forms of Communication*. Boca Raton, FL/London/New York: CRC Press/Taylor & Francis/Productivity Press, 2014. Revised, edited, updated.

offers the author's personal, subjective point of view regardless of whether it is supported by evidence.

An **essay** must be written and understood according to the nature, purpose, and structure of its message, with all their inherent limitations to the scientific mind. In general, essays consist of several different types and natures: narrative or expository essays; persuasive, classification essays; descriptive, causation-related essays; and critical or literary essays.

The structure of essays can be quite varied. The structure may be informal, a more structured five-part or "hamburger" essay, or it can be a multi-directional "restaurant menu" set of interrelated statements, or even a more argumentative structure in terms of critical thinking. A health sciences essay may also be seen as an exercise in rhetoric, particularly an argumentative/persuasive exercise.

Medical journals are based on research articles, but they also comprise other types of articles. While these types of articles vary from one journal to another, they are often in variable essay form. Some other types of articles that may be found in journals include letters to and from the editor, review articles, position papers, book reviews, notes on personal experience, value judgments and proposals, medical humor, and sadly, obituaries. Editors do not always provide authors with guidance and leadership on how to write these articles. Some suggestions and guidance are offered in this chapter.

A medical research article presents an objective view of a health problem, studied and solved to some degree and extent by an inquiry based on the scientific method. The research which leads to a medical article may be of quantitative, qualitative, or mixed-methods nature. With some variations from one journal to another, the medical research article is written in an "IMRAD" format: **I**ntroduction (with an appropriate thesis), **M**aterial and methods (working data with methods of inquiry), **R**esults (new data obtained and ensuing findings), **and D**iscussion (meaning of findings) and conclusions (implications for practice and recommendations for further research and action). The bibliography, or references section, completes the article and situates the research within the context of existing research and expands it beyond the study itself.

In this chapter we also review several different "types" of medical research articles. In basic health sciences, a "**lab report**" **format** is close to the IMRAD format. The scientific method which underlies the research and informs the article essentially follows the thesis of the article and the observational and/or experimental methods of health inquiry. A medical article as a **business report** combines research findings and experience expressed in essay-style articles and then proposes how to see and use the new evidence in terms of organizational objectives, strategies, solutions, results, and recommendations of what to do. **Case studies**, **case reports**, and **clinical case reports** are distinct entities by subject, objectives, structure, and methodology, and are not to be confounded.

Selected important topics covered by and otherwise related to the IMRAD format are examined in other chapters. The "thesis" and "definitions" are subjects discussed separately in Chapters 6 and 7. Discussion and conclusions sections are a principal site for the argumentative and critical analysis vital to the medical article message, findings, and repercussions.

In This Chapter

Executive Summary 393

Thoughts, Thinkers, and Things to Think About 396

Introductory Comments 398

13.1 Essay-Based Medical and Other Articles 398

    13.1.1 General Types of Essays 401

    13.1.2 Nature and Purpose of Essays 401

    13.1.3 Structure of Essays 403

    13.1.4 Health Sciences Essays as an Exercise in Rhetoric: An Argumentative/

            Persuasive Essay 405

    What to Conclude about Essays? 407

13.2 Original Medical Research Articles and Other Scientific Papers 407

    13.2.1 Thinking behind Medical Articles 408

    13.2.2 The IMRAD Format 411

            13.2.2.1 Overview of the IMRAD Format 411

            13.2.2.2 Comments on Additional IMRAD Elements 413

            13.2.2.3 IMRAD Preceding Entities: Identifications 413

            13.2.2.4 IMRAD Following Entities: Contextual and Collateral Information

                    Which Follows the IMRAD Core of the Article 414

            13.2.2.5 Related to the Medical Article, the "Lab Report" Format 415

13.3 Thinking beyond Editorial Expectations for Structure, Language, and Style:

    The Scientific Method behind Research and Ensuing Medical Articles 416

Steps of the Scientific Method 417

13.4 The Business Method and Format: Medical Article as a Business Report 418

Steps in Business Reporting 418

13.5 Qualitative Research-Based and Case Studies-Based Articles and Their Format 418

    13.5.1 Clinical Case Studies vs. Clinical Case Reports 419

    13.5.2 Valuing Qualitative Research Studies and Articles 421

Let Us Conclude 422

References 425

Thoughts, Thinkers, and Things to Think About

Art is I, science is we.
Claude Bernard
(1813–1878)
An essay is I; a scientific medical article is we.

Research at the origin of a scientific medical article is much more than a simple reporting about gathering high quality data and analyzing them well, quantitatively and qualitatively, to produce the best possible evidence in the health domain.
It is a product of our thought about it!

There are three rules for writing a medical article. Unfortunately, no one knows what they are.
Paraphrasing W. Somerset Maugham
(1874–1965)

Guttenberg makes everybody a reader. Xerox makes everybody a publisher.
Marshall Herbert McLuhan
(1911–1980)
In the *Guardian Weekly*
(June 12, 1977)
Nobody still made everybody an author of a medical article!

A problem is defined and isolated, information is gathered, alternatives are set forth; an end is established, means are created to achieve that end; a choice is made.
James MacGregor Burns
(1918–2014)
On the decision-making process,
Leadership (1978, 14)
Shouldn't we find all this also in a medical article?

When you have mastered the numbers,
you will feel in fact no longer be reading
numbers, any more than you read words
when reading a book. You will be reading
meanings.
Harold Geneen
(1910–1997)
with Alwin Moscow in
Managing (1984, 9)
Shouldn't we do both when reading
medical articles?

Science is built up of facts, as a house is
built of stones, but the accumulation of facts
is no more than a heap of stones is a house.
Henri Poincaré
(1854–1912)
Science and Hypothesis (1905, 9)
Tout à fait d'accord, Monsieur
Poincaré! A medical article should be
more than an accumulation of facts.

The pen is the tongue of the mind.
Miguel de Cervantes Saavedra
(1547–1616)
El Ingenioso Hidalgo Don Quixote de la
Mancha
(1605 and 1615)
Shouldn't a medical article be one of
the tongues of the medical mind?

The essay is a literary device for saying
almost everything about almost anything.
Aldous Huxley
(1894–1963)
What about a medical article as
an essay? It should not be! There is
nothing wrong with a medical article
in the good form of an essay, and well
written as scientific articles are.

How many professional and academic careers (and the health of our patients) are not influenced by the ways we share our experiences in medical articles? Let us always try to do them right.

Introductory Comments

We wish to share our new, current, and past medical thoughts and experience to listeners and readers through the best methods possible. Chapter 11 reflects mostly the oral sharing of medical thinking and experience, and the previous chapter (Chapter 12) covers clinical case reporting, which may be either oral or written.[1] On these pages, let us review some important aspects of written communication between health professionals themselves and their wider readership as ways of sharing our thoughts.

Clinicians' ability to share experience from research and practice may be based on the existing body of work on the topic, their own painstaking of original observation, experience, and analysis. Both "medical articles," which deal with health problems, and "scientific articles," which deal with other problems, appear across all health professions and sciences. Figure 13.1 offers their classification, emphasizing their three main types: essays, research and scientific method based reports (medical articles *per se*, covering etiology, treatment, or basic health information), and directive information conveying articles (that is, reportive/prescriptive/directive messages about how things are or should be done). Each of these types may or may not be evidence-supported and presented in the argumentative or non-argumentative way.

Medical articles may be reporting disease and other health phenomena occurrence; these types of articles can be called either "**descriptive**" studies or "portraits" of disease, or "**analytical**" studies. Descriptive studies can be considered "portraits" of disease, whereas analytical studies report etiological research of cause-effect relationships between bad factors and their consequences (mostly observational) or good factors and their effects like in clinical or field trials. Given the time factor and number of observations in time, such studies may be a "single shot," that is, one observation in time studies (**cross-sectional** studies), or **longitudinal** studies (multiple observations of one or more groups) or **semi-longitudinal** (completing multiple observations of multiple groups over time) studies, that is, repeated observations in time of single or multiple groups. Figure 13.2 represents such classification of medical articles.

Essay-based articles, quantitative research-based articles ("medical articles"), qualitative research based studies, business reports, and other formats merit all attention in this chapter.

13.1 Essay-Based Medical and Other Articles

Not all medical articles are "scientific." What about literary and other kinds of essays as communication tools? Essay-type messages are devoted to general experiences while scientific-research articles present original work based mostly on facts, data, and observations gathered by researchers. These data may be blood cell counts, x-ray readings, or findings from multiple independent studies. In this section medical essays are discussed. In the next Section 13.2, original studies will be reviewed.

A medical article may be either the expression of views about some topic of interest, or the fruit of research. Medical articles are often something other than reports on the results of scientific

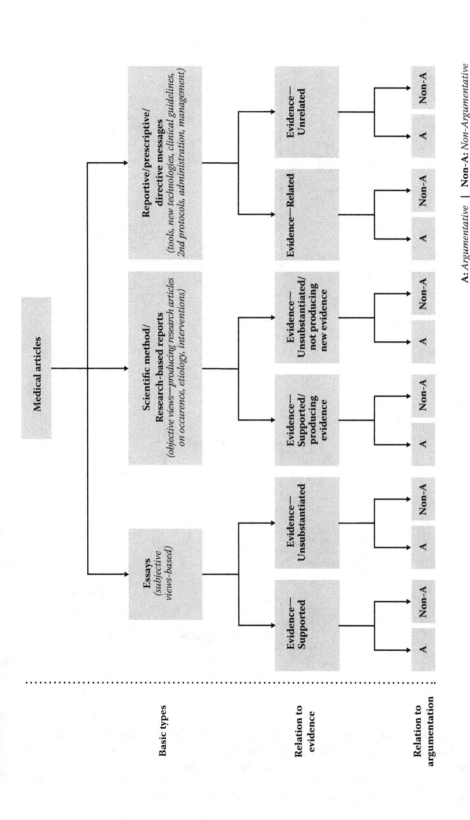

Figure 13.1 Major categories and types of medical articles. (Based on Jenicek M. *Writing, Reading, and Understanding in Modern Health Sciences. Medical Articles and Other Forms of Communication.* Boca Raton/London/New York: CRC Press/Taylor & Francis/Productivity Press, 2014.)

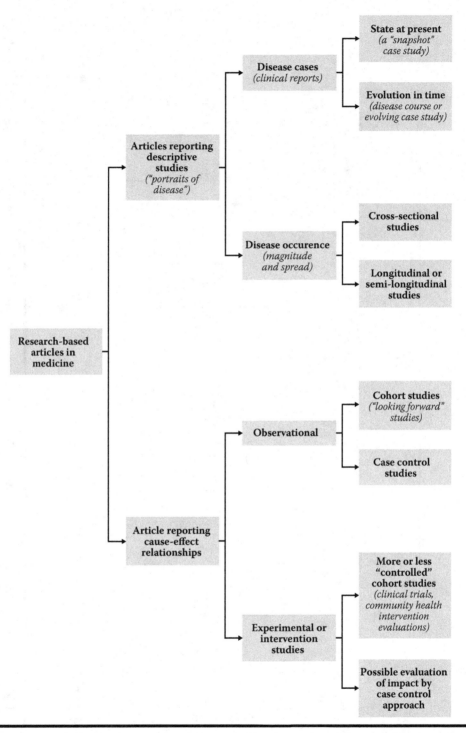

Figure 13.2 Classification of research-based articles and the type of their underlying research. (Redrawn from Jenicek M. *Writing, Reading, and Understanding in Modern Health Sciences. Medical Articles and Other Forms of Communication.* Boca Raton/London/New York: CRC Press/Taylor & Francis/Productivity Press, 2014. Reproduced with permission.)

endeavor. In medical journals, editorials, personal opinions, book reviews, and personal views that are not based on original research are an integral part of written medical communication.

An **essay in general** is broadly defined as a piece of writing based on an author's **personal point of view.**[2] In this context, an essay is a written message presenting an author's perspective based on a presumed or accepted reality. Writings that are frequently presented in an essay form include some types of criticisms, strategic declarations, learned arguments, observations, and experiences from daily life and practice, recollections, and reflections.

Specific to the world of medicine, a **medical essay** may cover a problem from basic sciences, clinical practice, community medicine, or public health. In medical journals editorials, letters to and from the editor, review articles, position papers, book reviews, personal experience, and value judgments are often reported in essay form.

13.1.1 General Types of Essays

Essays can be presented in numerous formats[3–11] which are generally defined by their purpose or intent. The type and form of essays have been described by various authors outside of the health professional community. We have identified and defined seven different essay types that are of particular interest and utility to the medical and health professional community. These are presented below from the most straightforward (narrative or expository essays including reflective or opinion-writing) to the more complex essay types that include more analysis (critical essay). There is some overlap between these types of essays.

13.1.2 Nature and Purpose of Essays

The nature and purpose of an essay depends on what message it conveys. These include:

1. A **narrative** or **expository essay** is, simply put, an essay that "tells a story." It provides readers with an understanding of *"how a situation or problem really looks"* and *"what's going on?"* A **narrative essay** in general is the simplest one. It presents a story from a certain viewpoint, having its plot(s), characters, setting, event, and climax for a specific purpose or reason. Policies and activities, experiences in clinical case reporting, or health policies and programs debates are usually "narrated" in this way. The author presents his or her subjective views as **reflective essays**, or **opinion writing**. An **expository essay** can also take a form of instruction, a how-to manual or explanation of a natural or technological process.[9]
2. A **classification essay** provides direction on *"how all this may be meaningfully organized."* This type of essay is of an observational nature to describe and organize various subjects of interest in categories, scales and other groupings for a given purpose. In the field of epidemiology, observational studies are most similar to this type of essay.
3. **Descriptive** essays are another type of essay used to provide a subjective portrait of phenomena and events. They are not as structured as occurrence (descriptive) studies in epidemiology.

4. A **cause-and-effect essay**, or a "*what's behind it?*" essay. This type of essay may be used to explore possible cause-effect relationships, mostly as a tool for generating hypotheses. In epidemiology, this type of essay is used to confirm evidence and demonstrate causality.[12] It is used in other articles based on the scientific method and experience. **Argumentative/persuasive papers** and **compare-and-contrast essays** may be supported by some evidence. When they are not, they remain in the domain of subjective opinion. A cause-and-effect essay is in essence a **persuasive essay**, however weak it may be.

5. A **critical essay** is a "*does it make sense, and how much does all this really make sense?*" essay. In a critical essay, positive and negative aspects of a given problem are gathered, weighted for coherence, completeness, and the quality of supporting data, leading to the acceptance or rejection of the essay thesis. The author seeks to create a balance between positive and negative aspects while remaining impartial. Conversely, in an argumentative essay, the author tries to convince the reader about his or her position mostly by offering positive views that support the claim.[11]

6. A subcategory of critical essays are **literary essays**. This type of essay is a look at "*how others struggle and succeed by writing about something which I also try to tackle somehow and somewhere at times and places,*" or "*an essay about other essays.*" In this type of essay, the meaning and construction of a piece of literature are reviewed and the quality and completeness of evidence is under scrutiny. It may be structured or not. Reviews of medical article manuscripts or book reviews may be presented as literary essays.

7. A **personal essay** (**personal narrative**) is an essay about its author's life, thoughts, or experiences.

8. Contrary to other types of essays, an **academic essay**[14,15,11] is built to persuade by reasoned discourse designed to advance ideas among scholars themselves, or to assist students in developing their critical thinking skills. This type of essay is related to the *critical thinking* **essay** defined here. Specifically, an academic essay falls under the definition of critical thinking related to the "*ability to read theory accurately, appropriate it meaningfully, apply it independently, generate results based on that application, analyze the results, and form a clear argument based on those results that can be defended with a specific line of reasoning.*"

Essays are structured in a variety of ways—from quite informal to those with distinctive formats.[16] The four different essay structures are described here and how the structure supports the overall purpose of the essay is explained. The structures described below may all be used in health sciences writing, however argumentative writing is strongly emphasized across the more basic literature and references.[12,13,17,18]

13.1.3 Structure of Essays

The structures below are just some of the ways that an essay may be structured. Essays in the health sciences may follow one of these formats, or they may not.

1. An **informal essay** is a *"simply, what crosses my mind"* essay. An informal essay does not have a specific structure or purpose. Medical humor may be presented in this way.

2. A more formal **five-part essay** is a *"path from some proposal to conclusions about it."* It may be written as a five-step message,[19] also called a "**hamburger essay**," "**three-one essay**," "**three tier essay**," "**five-paragraph essay**," "**five-part essay**," or "**layer cake essay**." The five-part essay follows this format:

   Step 1: The problem of interest is introduced. An "introduction" is a **general idea** about the problem, a statement of the problem in general, and an introductory thesis more specific to the matter to be presented, a "**narrative hook.**"

   Step 2: In this step, the **evidence to support the argumentation** about the problem of interest is presented. A "**narration**" follows which includes some background literature and a structural overview of the essay.

   Step 3: This step **affirms** the **evidence and arguments in favor of the thesis.**

   Step 4: Evidence and arguments against the thesis are presented. This is a "**negation**" in the form of a refutation or concession-based on this evidence.

   Step 5: A "**conclusion**" summarizes the whole argumentative process, specifically related to the thesis or narrative hook, and in relation to broader connected issues.

Hence, graphically and symbolically speaking:

Top part of the hamburger bun:	Step 1: Introduction (leading idea, topic, reason)
↓	
Tomato/lettuce layer:	Step 2: Supporting statement(s)
↓	
Bacon/cheese/mayo layer:	Step 3: Affirmation or alternative or complementary supporting statement(s)
↓	
Beef pattie(s):	Step 4: Negation or another alternative or complementary statement(s)
↓	
Bottom part of the hamburger bun:	Step 5: Conclusion, confirming, rejecting, complementing, and expanding introduction statement(s)

Steps 2–4 may also be represented by three related statements, from the strongest to the weakest idea or claim, or by three more independent ones. All steps are presented as a visually "blunt" hamburger bun with introduction and thesis about the topic as the top bun, followed by the three layers of thesis supports and topic sentences, with enough details and examples to support such sentences. The three related statements, Steps 2–4 in this model of essay are not a stringent rule or necessity. Less than three, or more than three related statements, may be used depending on the nature of the subject and problem to be solved. The bottom part of the bun, the conclusion, restates the three main reasons that support the thesis and include a statement of significance, possibly with additional general information such as predictions or recommendations for the future.

3. A **multidirectional** or "**restaurant refined menu**" **essay** has a variable number of statements which are related back, forward, and between them from the opening statement to the conclusion. Similar to expectations when opening a restaurant menu, choosing interconnecting "dishes of interest" according to what appeals to us, and leads to the conclusion about how satisfied we are with our gastronomic experience. More formally, a linear sequence of the thought sequence from the top to the bottom of the five-part essay model may then be refined and expanded by searching, analyzing and presenting other ideas and issues between the parts and relationships[17,20–22] as illustrated in the following Figure 13.3.

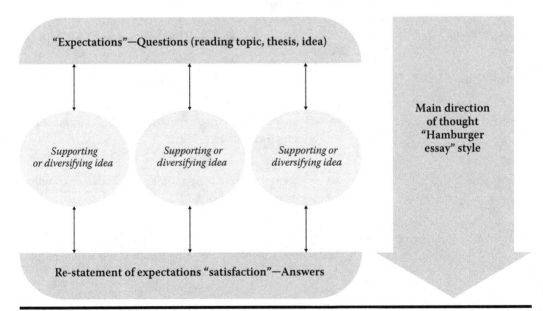

Figure 13.3 **Essay format as path from expectations and questions to answers and proponent satisfaction. From a "hamburger essay" to a "refined menu" essay. (Redrawn from Jenicek M.** *Writing, Reading, and Understanding in Modern Health Sciences.* **Boca Raton: CRC Press, 2014. Reproduced with permission.)**

4. An **argumentative essay** is a sort of argumentation-based investigation of the topic which rests on the generation and/or collection of evidence, evaluation of that evidence, and the establishment of the author's position about the topic of interest. Its purpose is to show that the author's assertion about the problem of interest (diagnosis, treatment, etc.) is correct, more truthful than others, worthy of adoption, or of further development. The underlying evidence is often limited.

The argumentative essay in this more general sense is also known as a "**reflective essay**," it presents the viewpoint of an author recognized by the journal of having something worthwhile to contribute on a specific topic. Hence, even an essay as a subjective view is an exercise in argumentation and communication. Desirable uses of the best ("objective") evidence are not, however, omnipresent. The author of an argumentative essay article uses this approach to engage the reader and gain acceptance for his or her views and rationale. Of note, in our view, the term 'argumentative essay' should be reserved for any message based on Toulmin's modern argumentation model as further discussed in Chapter 4.

For philosophers working in the domain of informal logic and argumentation, an "argumentative essay" is effectively an exercise in argumentation. Damer[21] proposes the structure for this type of essay in six steps:

1. The question and the underlying problem are stated first and made available to any other arguing person, participating in the clarification of a given problem and question.
2. An initial position about the problem is stated at the beginning of the essay.
3. Argument(s) in support of the position and responses to the anticipated criticisms of the premises are proposed and presented.
4. Objections to the argument(s) and replies to those objections follow.
5. Other argument(s) against alternative positions are included and detailed.
6. Resolution of the question by the argumentative process whose steps are outlined above closes the argumentative essay.

We may note that Steps 1 and 5 above may equate to the "buns" of a "hamburger essay" or a five-step essay as outlined above.

13.1.4 Health Sciences Essays as an Exercise in Rhetoric: An Argumentative/Persuasive Essay

From a philosophical point of view, any **medical article is an exercise in rhetoric**, or "*the use of discourse, either spoken or written, to inform or motivate an audience* (and readership in our case) *whether that audience is made up of one person or a group of persons.*"[22] It may be based on the scientific method like original research, a structured systematic review of evidence (meta-analyses), or personal opinion like some other review articles, points of view, and position papers. In all cases, modern argumentation is at the core of such endeavors.

Edward J Huth, former Editor-in-Chief of the *Annals of Internal Medicine*, reminded us in the 1980s that:

> *scientific papers are not just baskets carrying unconnected facts like telephone directory; they are instruments of persuasion. Scientific papers even if they are based on sound research, must argue you into believing what they conclude; they must be based on the principles of critical argument.*[23]

An argument must be seen in this context as a coherent series of reasons, statements, or facts intended to support or establish the conclusion of an argumentative process reproduced across any piece of scientific writing.

Any research paper is an argument that is based on individual and/or collective views justifying research and its findings. A presentation at any scientific meeting is an argument in favor of an idea and its supporting findings. Any grant application is an argument supporting a favorable decision to finance a proposed research project. Indeed, even a Master of Science or Doctor of Philosophy thesis as a dissertation (and its defense) is an argument in favor of the candidate's formulation of the research problem. The design of any experimentation or research reflects, to a variable degree, subsequent reasoning, decisions, and interpretation of the nature of reported findings. In this sense, research project formulations, applications for funding, evaluations of ongoing research progress, publications, and evaluations of results are all exercises in argumentation.

Research papers in any health science, then, can be seen as exercises in argumentation. These papers are only as good as the initial basic elements constituting the argumentative process, which itself is only as valid as the research, definition and use of all its relevant components. However, do we all know how to correctly explain and defend our ideas? Research production, reporting, and use require the mastery of a specific methodology (such as DNA analysis or magnetic resonance imaging) in order to study and solve well-defined problems. Communicating these findings must also be supported by scientific thinking throughout the research protocol and its execution, and the development and analysis of an argument about the problem to be solved.

In this context, an **argument** represents *a connected series of statements originating from past and present experience to establish a position in medical, nursing, dentistry, chiropractic and alternative and complementary medicines problem solving, understanding and decision-making.* The strength of the argument depends on the quality of the statements and the best available evaluated evidence underlying such statements. **Argumentation** in health sciences is not a dispute, it is the methodological use and presentation of arguments to solve a problem in medical practice and research. The rules for argumentation are the same for all health sciences.

Is our medical article of interest also an exercise in argumentation and critical thinking based on the best evidence available? Yes, it is! Both medical essays and medical research articles are based on modern argumentation as developed by logicians and critical thinkers over the past two generations. Elements of argumentation must be supported by the best available evidence as advanced by protagonists of "evidence-based medicine." How can we now look more specifically at medical information in this light? Chapter 4 of this book offers approaches to structure the argumentative essay.

What to Conclude about Essays?

Clinicians are interested in learning from the best possible medical articles possible, which have been traditionally considered to be those using the scientific method. However, the array of articles in biomedical sciences is much wider. Do we need for these articles, the "other" articles (those considered to be non-scientific), rules of writing and biomedical journals' editorial boards' requirements that are as well-structured as those for "scientific" ones? We are not without resources: The methodological armamentarium for essay papers has increased in recent years. An extensive array of "how to write an essay" information is available online[2–10,13–16,24,25] as well as in print.[26–28]

National and international interest groups like the International Committee of Medical Journals Editors[29] have concentrated on developing criteria, rules, and recommendations for objective articles of a scientific nature. Do we need similar criteria, rules, and recommendations for essays in health sciences? Some types of essays like cause and effect or classification essays may be overlapping with etiological research the scientific way. Do other types of articles as reviewed in this introductory essay merit a similar in-depth attention? We believe so. How we will succeed, only future initiatives will show. Let us at least try.

13.2 Original Medical Research Articles and Other Scientific Papers

A **medical research article**, sometimes called an *"original article,"* presents an **objective view** of a health problem which is studied and solved to some degree and extent by an inquiry based on the scientific method. As a matter of fact, a medical research article must reflect general considerations of scientific and professional communication. These articles report either results of **quantitative research**, **qualitative research**, or combination of the two, **mixed method research**.

In **quantitative research**, multiple observations are measured and/or counted, grouped in sets, compared, and analyzed for possible causal relationships and other contrasts. **Qualitative research** consists of findings in which unique, single, or very few cases are observed and analyzed in depth and without statistical considerations. **Mixed-methods research** is based on both quantitative and qualitative methods and experiences. The format of reporting them accommodate both the common traits and distinctions of such research methodologies which underlie a medical article about them, events and problems of interest, their results, and meaning.

In a medical article authors do more than present results of original research. Authors communicate findings and discuss them with readers. Medical article consumers judge their relevance and decide if they will put into practice what research shows. Consumers critically appraise them, that is, evaluate if a medical article 'makes sense' from a scientific standpoint and if it is in a larger sense a result of the application of the scientific method. They also must read and understand such scientific communication as an argumentative process leading to some conclusions, claims, and recommendations for practice and further research. A medical article must be 'logical' in this latter sense.

Research-based medical articles are presented in medical journals in their own special sections. In the *British Medical Journal* research-based articles are found under the section 'Original Research,' in the *Journal of the American Medical Association* they are found in "Research"/"Original Investigation," and in the *Canadian Medical Association Journal* under "Research." Other journals have their own similar sections for research articles.

13.2.1 Thinking behind Medical Articles

Most medical research articles are, or, should be seen and understood as one giant logical argument and exercise in critical thinking. They must be sound in clinical, epidemiological, and biostatistical terms. Medical research articles should also be considered as a form of an argument, and critically assessed.

A medical article reporting original research has a fairly standard form accepted by major medical journals as recommended by the International Committee of Medical Journals Editors and detailed as Uniform Requirements for Manuscripts Submitted to Biomedical Journals.[29,30] This is known as a **SIMRAD** (**S**ummary, **I**ntroduction, **M**aterial and methods, **R**esults, **a**nd **D**iscussion) format. The format is outlined here.[31,32]

- a **Summary** that reflects sections of the article to come, in an increasingly structured manner, summarizing (as they are in the *Annals of Internal Medicine*) "objective, design, setting, participants, interventions, main results, conclusions";
- an **Introduction** that defines the problem and often offers a related review of the literature (past experience);
- the **Material** and methods present a technical framework of "how it was done";
- the **Results** section is a factual presentation of findings of the study; **and**
- a **Discussion** section debates possible and real strengths and weaknesses of the study, missing information, and possible other completions and corrective measures.
- Conclusion(s), often coupled with discussion, highlight the most important findings for the understanding of the problem and further decision-making for research and practice.

The elements of modern argumentation are found in the above-mentioned article sections, to a more or less complete degree. They are somewhat obscured in the natural language of the article and are discovered by reconstructing arguments from the natural language of written or spoken medical communication. The subsequent understanding of a medical article depends on how well it is executed and presented as an occurrence or etiological study or clinical trial, as well as how the problem is defined. These following four points represent the essence of what needs to be defined to understand the argument being made. Without these clear formulations the recipient of the message cannot understand what is covered in an article. As such, it is important that the problem be defined in terms of the

■ **topic**, that is, the health problem that is being discussed, at least in part, through the intended research which includes "defining **definitions**" in the best operational terms of all entities and variables of interest;

■ research **objectives** that identify the specific (to be reached by the study itself) or general (those of the broader set of activities into which the study falls) endpoints that are desired;

■ research **hypothesis** as a proposition to be evaluated, accepted, or rejected by the research study and its results; and

■ **research question** as an expression of doubt and uncertainty about the nature and solution of a health problem in their specific context (population, setting of care, community) to be discussed, solved, and answered by an intended inquiry.

An article written in natural language that reflects an argument format (problem in context, grounds, backing and warrant, support and rebuttals, qualifier, and claim) shows:

Natural Language	Argument Building Block	Its Location
The subject of this study is... We found that...	Claim, Conclusions	Title, Conclusions
The original issue to be studied is (was)...	Problem in context	Introduction
The results of our study show... The findings indicate	Grounds	Results
The strength of these findings... The results in the context of the area of interest show...	Qualifier	Discussion
The rationale for these findings may be...	Warrant	Review of literature (Introduction, Discussion)
Considering the results in the context of past and present experience, or other evidence...		Discussion, Conclusion
The balance of evidence between the supporting and negating elements in this argument...	Adducts (findings for), Rebuttals	Discussion
Based on this evidence, the strength that can be attributed to the findings...	Qualifier (as some kind of quantification of our conviction about the Claim) and Backing	Introduction, Discussion, Conclusions
As a result of this evidence and analysis, we can determine...	Claim	Conclusions (may appear in the Title)

In summary, the problem and backing may be found in the short review of literature in the "Introduction" section of the article, the problem and possible rebuttals are in the "Methods" section, and the grounds are in by the "Results" section. The claim appears and then the backing and rebuttals reappear in the "Discussion" ("Comment") section. A detailed and concrete application of this type of analysis of modern argumentation within a medical article is detailed also elsewhere.[33–35] Reading and understanding can be expanded by reading these sources.

Medical articles are one of the fundamental components of medical education and learning. Medical articles that report original research or reviews represent not only the state of science, but they must also incorporate the highest standards of logic and critical thinking. They must reflect the former as much as the latter. A logical analysis of medical articles should consider:

- Does the message derive from simple intuition as non-inferential knowledge or is it also a structured argument?
- Is the message (description, observational analytical study, experimental study, or trial) acceptable from a clinical epidemiological and/or field epidemiology standpoint?
- If it is acceptable from a clinical epidemiological or field epidemiology standpoint, examine the title to see if it leads to what will follow as (a) logical argument(s) to support it.
- If it is not acceptable, is similar information made explicit in the introduction of the medical article? If not, is it possible to rebuild it from the available information that may eventually be spread across different sections of the article?
- Do the discussion of results focuses on the same problem as stated in the introduction? The discussion itself should reflect the process of an argument and its resolution, that is, its path from the initial proposition to backing, warrant, grounds, support, rebuttals, qualifier, and ensuing claim (conclusion).
- If it is not clear that the discussion of results follows from the same problem stated in the introduction, can you make sense of the argument? Reconstruct all relevant statements and arguments to obtain a message whose cogency would be more suitable for understanding, assessment and interpretation from a logical standpoint.
- Are the arguments cogent, with justified premises, complete information, warranted inferences, and absence of rebuttals to the warrants?
- Does the whole message make sense not only from a clinical, epidemiological, biostatistical, biological, and medical (decision-making) standpoint, but also from the point of view of logic and critical thinking?
- Can you better explain and understand what the authors did not state clearly enough? A reader may hesitate between improving the "authors' homework" (in this case, there is not enough information provided, information is missing, or incomplete building blocks of the argument at hand) or concluding that there is not enough elements of the argument available to improve the message in this sense.
- Do you accept (with or without explicit and clear reserve), adopt, or reject the message of the paper?

Horton proposes to adopt Toulmin's model in medical articles[36] and Gleischner suggests to use general journal articles as a base for learning critical thinking[37] and to improve further critical thinking in medicine and elsewhere. They are right. Beyond introductory pages, Huth's monograph on writing and publishing in medicine[23] is not only for authors. It is for readers as well.

Indeed, Greenhalgh[38] puts the reading of medical papers in the context of evidence-based medicine especially for readers. To spread and share medical knowledge and experience through effective communication remains not only a challenge, but also a subject of development, implementation, and evaluation of the new and still crystallizing domain of knowledge translation in medicine.

13.2.2 The IMRAD Format

As has already been noted, writing a research paper means providing content to complete the now conventional **IMRAD format**[31,32] recommended as *Uniform Requirements for Manuscripts Submitted to Biomedical Journals: Writing and Editing for Biomedical Publication by the International Committee of Medical Journal Editors*[29,30] and others.[39] The IMRAD format—"**I**ntroduction, **M**aterial and Methods, **R**esults or Research findings, **a**nd **D**iscussion"—can be expanded for greater clarity to "**SSIMMRaDeCaRR**." that is, "**S**tructured **S**ummary, **I**ntroduction, **M**aterials and **M**ethods, **R**esults **a**nd **D**iscussion, **e**nsuing **C**onclusions **a**nd **R**ecommendations, and **R**eferences" in order to better reflect information in a structured way.

Not included in these acronyms is that all medical articles are, of course, preceded by the title, names, and affiliations of the authors. **Acknowledgments** to individuals or organizations to whom the authors are indebted may precede the article, or follow at the end. **References** (bibliography) are included to provide appropriate attribution at the end of the article.

13.2.2.1 Overview of the IMRAD Format

In more colloquial terms, the IMRAD format categorizes the writer's thoughts, work, and findings. The IMRAD format relies heavily on information initially provided by authors in the research proposal for their original research.

Research proposals typically include:

- research problem(s) and the objectives of the study;
- rationale and location of the study;
- research questions and hypotheses;
- review of related literature and other background information;
- methodology of the study (design, variables);
- selected dependent and independent variables in causal research;
- participating subjects (health professionals, patients, population);
- data collection and analysis;
- risks of the study (balancing anticipated strengths and weaknesses of the study and its findings);
- ethical considerations; and
- administrative aspects (budget, timetable, granting agencies, administrative bodies running the research and recipients of knowledge translation including results users, recipients, and further pursuers of research and practice activities).

The structure of a research-based medical article as a whole is detailed in Figure 13.4 which follows.

The structure of a research-based medical article as a whole

IMRAD is preceded by:

Title of the article:	More than attention hook, may be problem identification, formulation, or its solution.
Author(s) of the article:	Individuals, interest groups (acronym labeled), organizations or professional, academic, or social institutions.
Structured abstract:	Follows more or less closely the IMRAD format itself.

Message within the IMRAD Format:

I ntroduction:	What are the reasons of our doing, what we mean to do and why, in which context and in which setting of persons, time, and place. Research, population, and health policies, present and possibly future state in which the proposed research sets in.
M aterial and Methods:	What are the individuals subjects of the study, what larger group they represent, which methods and techniques of data collection will be used, how they will be analyzed and interpreted.
R esults:	What did we find in quantitative and qualitative terms.
A nd D iscussion:	What all this means and what are the strengths and weaknesses of our findings.
Conclusions and recommendations:	What all this means for the advancement of the theory, what is relevant, and further usable for research and practice, and what are the further steps in research and practice based on this topic and findings as well as what evaluation needed of the impact of this study and its implementation in further research and practice?
References:	References to other work and publications covering the topic, target populations), methodology of data collection, analysis, and interpretation, as well as works and situation in related and comparable domains.

IMRAD is followed by:

Contextual / collateral information:	Sponsors and funding, acknowledgments, conflict of interest disclosure (including authors' affiliations), contact information (postal and electronic), registration of the underlying research (trials), other related contributions and contributors.

Figure 13.4 **The structure of a research-based medical article as a whole. (Redrawn from Jenicek M.** *Writing, Reading, and Understanding in Modern Health Sciences.* **Boca Raton: CRC Press, 2014. Reproduced with permission.)**

13.2.2.2 Comments on Additional IMRAD Elements

In this section, an overview of the standard elements of the IMRAD format which precede and follow the actual article are provided. These elements include the title, the authors, and following the article, the references and the contextual and collateral information. The sections below provide information on how to prepare these important elements required for publication of a research-based article.

13.2.2.3 IMRAD Preceding Entities: Identifications

Entities that precede the IMRAD format include the Title, Authors, or Abstract. They deserve as much attention as the IMRAD itself.

Title

The **title** is the core of the IMRAD format. Typically, the title is proposed by the author, discussed, and then mutually agreed upon with the editors of medical articles. To date, there is no known preference for style among editors. The title of a medical article may be:

- any formulation of the proposal or some strategies to consider that catches the attention of the reader (*"Should we pay more attention to the effectiveness and adverse effects of statins in elderly patients suffering from high low-density lipoprotein cholesterol level?"*);
- a working hypothesis of the research under consideration, often devised as a research question (*"Do treatment by statins in elderly patients suffering from high low-density lipoprotein cholesterol levels cause rhabdomyolysis in some patients and which ones?"*);
- an initial claim that is the main theme of the argumentation process regarding the subject of interest (*"Statins are a potential cause of rhabdomyolysis in patients suffering from X and treated by Y"*).
- conclusions reached through the causal research and argumentation about the problem of interest (*"Statins cause rhabdomyolysis in particular patients suffering from X"*);
- any kind of political or strategic statement (*"Statins as a subject of concern in treatment of patients suffering from X in our community and the impact of such initiatives on policies of fighting the Y"*); and
- any parable to catch the attention of the reader or show how imaginative the author(s) are (*"The pain reigns, the sufferer thrives!"*).

Authors

The **authors** to be named also precede the IMRAD format. More authors do not always mean greater quality or authority! Again, what is preferred by the editors of a medical journal is not always known. Authors who are named may include those who have written the article and/or those who have made, formulated, and/or initiated the research study or who have collected the material, analyzed, and interpreted it. Authors may also include individuals and organizations that have made the study possible by offering means to human and other resources. This should include identification of groups of authors or other groups of interest, whether loose or well-defined, behind the reported activity. For example, the group identified by the acronym GRADE[40]

(Grades of Recommendations, Assessment, Development, and Evaluation) includes members and interested contributors from different parts of the world.

Naming the group alone is not enough. Multiple authors within the group must also be specified. Does it give enough authority to the reported facts? Not always. In extremis, the Author of this book is a leader of an *N-of-1* interest group, a thinktank entitled *Fostering Argumentation, Reasoning, and Thinking in Medicine*. Would its appropriate acronym give more credibility to such endeavor, an acronym like FosART in Medicine? Likely not.

Structured Abstract

Medical article abstracts which summarize the article's message now have a more and more structured format. This format is now preferred by many leading medical journals like *The New England Journal of Medicine*, *The Lancet*, *British Medical Journal*, *JAMA*, *The Canadian Medical Association Journal* and many others. Abstract sections may include:

- **background** (and include **importance** and **objectives**);
- **methods** (and include **design**, **setting**, and **participants**, **study subjects**);
- **results (findings)**;
- **interpretation** offering authors' proposed meaning of results and findings; and
- **conclusions** (and include **relevance**, ideally specifying relevance for research, teaching, practice or any combination of the above, and **limitations** of the message as well).

13.2.2.4 IMRAD Following Entities: Contextual and Collateral Information Which Follows the IMRAD Core of the Article

These entities may vary from one article to another and from one periodical to another. References and acknowledgements of funding and other supports, conflicts of interests, and other affiliations, are included. Some of these are outlined here.

References (bibliography) are found at the end of an article. They are high level information (authors, title, periodical, date, and page numbers) that identify the source of the content that is covered in the article. This information allows a reader to, should they wish, find the original research articles, review articles, books and other monographs, publications of administrative, legal, or managerial nature produced by governing bodies and other interested parties that were used to develop the article.

Other contextual and collateral information that should be included in the publication of a research-based article. This parenthetical information provides some of the autobiographical-type material that can inform readers about the author's perspectives and context. This information includes:

- **funding and other support** of underlying research (grants for public and private sources, agencies, and organizations);
- **the role of the sponsor;**

- **acknowledgments**, that is, words of appreciation to individuals and bodies which did not contribute directly to the article and its underlying research, but who were vital in realizing the research. Typically this includes granting agencies and their contribution in means and resources, civic and administrative bodies in the health sector, and general community or various levels of government;
- **technical assistance appreciation** to individuals for laboratory work, review and editing, administrative and secretarial assistance, and other research and reporting activities;
- **conflict of interest disclosure**, in which both potential and real conflicts are reported;
- **contact information** which provides the where, how, and by what means the authors may be reached in view of the additional article and research related information which may be requested by readers;
- **registration**, in the case of clinical trials, surveillance, or record linkage studies;
- **additional information available online**;
- **authors' affiliations**; and
- other related contributions and contributors.

13.2.2.5 Related to the Medical Article, the "Lab Report" Format

The "lab (short for laboratory) report," a term drawn from the current literature, is the primary means of communication among scientists and researchers, and its format is slightly different than the typical IMRAD. The lab report may or may not end up as a research paper. In experimental biosciences, a "**research paper**" is also largely synonymous to the "medical" IMRAD format and structure. The lab report format is very similar to the IMRAD format.[32,33] As Figure 13.5 shows, this format consists of a title, abstract, introduction, material and methods, results, discussion, tables and figures, and references (no acronym proposed).

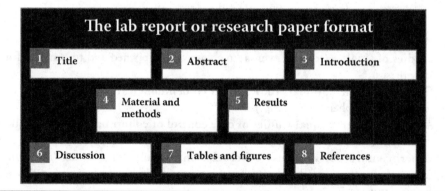

Figure 13.5 The lab report or research paper format. (Redrawn from Jenicek M. *Writing, Reading, and Understanding in Modern Health Sciences*. Boca Raton: CRC Press, 2014. Reproduced with permission.)

13.3 Thinking beyond Editorial Expectations for Structure, Language, and Style: The Scientific Method behind Research and Ensuing Medical Articles

The products of clinical communication (medical articles, lab reports) are the sum of some type of research method. In this section, we describe how clinicians *think* in developing communications and the content of the scientific method process. The scientific method is the type of thinking that leads to communication vehicles like research articles.

Scientific thinking as a form of investigation, and the argumentation about it, is used throughout all the steps of the **scientific method**. Both modern argument structure and components of medical article sections (as outlined further in Chapter 4) reflect various elements of the scientific method. Schafersman reminds us that:

> *the scientific method has proven to be the most reliable and successful method of thinking in human history and it is quite possible to use scientific thinking in other human endeavors. For this reason, critical thinking—the application of scientific thinking to all areas of study and topics of investigation—is being taught throughout the U.S., and its teaching is being encouraged as a universal ideal.*[42]

Medical research is undertaken for three main reasons:

1. To obtain the best possible **description** (picture, portrait) of the health phenomenon of interest.
2. To **explain** the health phenomenon relationships, such as the cause-effect one.
3. To evaluate the **impact of interventions**, health phenomenon related actions such as preventive or curative measures, community interventions.

Seven major types of studies (including the above three) are used to address the rationale for medical research. These seven types of studies are

1. **Basic biomedical research** (biological and other plausibility)
2. **Studies of single cases and events** (to show what happened and to generate further hypotheses)
3. **Descriptive observational studies of an epidemiological nature** about the occurrence of health phenomena (the "*portrait*")
4. **Analytical observational studies of case control or cohort nature** to find causes of health phenomena
5. **Experimental studies of cause-effect relationships** like clinical trials (the "*whys*")
6. **Research synthesis** of the above ("*epidemiology of results and findings*" or "*to which extent is it true*")
7. **Managerial studies and health administration experience** ("*what does it mean in terms of human and material resources and functioning?*"), and what can and should be done as a result.

In these studies, the scientific method loosely follows the Socratic method, or "dissent" (discussed also in part in Chapter 3). This method is a structured and rigorous path leading to health problem understanding and/or its solving. It consists of the steps outlined here (see also Chapter 3).

Steps of the Scientific Method

1. Identify **characterizations, define** the **domain of interest** in its current situation and state, and the **thesis**, which describes the research and how it will be presented.
2. Pose the **research question** (the approach leading to the solution of the problem is defined).
3. Formulate a **hypothesis** about the problem as a testable proposition to be accepted or rejected in light of the proposed research (study) finding(s).
4. Develop operational **definitions** of phenomena to observe (domain, problem itself, dependent, independent variables, settings, etc.) that make further steps practicable.
5. Form the **prediction** as a formal way to test a hypothesis.
6. Develop a properly designed **experiment** or some other kind of study to study **cause-effect relationships**. It is frequently the center of interest.
7. Account for and address **errors, biases,** and **fallacies**.
8. Consider the **falsifiability** of findings by identifying conditions and circumstances where findings do not apply.
9. **Replicate** the study. Execute the study more than once to confirm the findings, increase precision, and to obtain a closer estimation of sampling error. In the biological and behavioral sciences, the consistency of results on replication is perhaps the most important criterion in judgments of causality.
10. Make a **decision**. The hypothesis is accepted, or rejected. If rejected, other testing(s), similar, different, or complementary, is (are) required.
11. Prove the **action** (corrective, strengthening, or other) to further confirm or revise the new understanding of the problem.
12. **Evaluate the identified action(s)** for their effects and contributions to general and specific experience with the problem. Rational directions for further actions are proposed, justified by past and present experience, and rational anticipation of evidence-based trends.

The scientific experience is to some degree reflected in the general IMRAD format outlined in Section 13.2.2. But is scientific thinking and the method underlying its reporting enough to make scientific reporting meaningful? Something more is needed: building a medical paper as a way of, and a tool for, reasoning, decision-making, and communication of a health problem and question.

13.4 The Business Method and Format: Medical Article as a Business Report

Thompson defines a business report as a **medium presenting information to assist in business decision-making**.[43] Medical decision-making can be seen as a kind of "decision-making" in the "business of health and care." A medical report is a kind of business report that provides a proposal to solve a business problem based on the record of past business information that is useful for action and future business planning.

Where essays and research reports are most often searching for ways to understand and provide care, business reports offer straightforward directions of what to do. The development and presentation of clinical guidelines are one kind of business report in medicine, but it is not the only one. The steps for developing a business report are outlined here.

Steps in Business Reporting

1. Determine the **scope** of the report in terms of organizational objectives, strategies, solutions, findings, and recommendations of what to do.
2. Specify the **target readership** or audience.
3. Gather and organize **supporting information**.
4. **Analyze and weigh** the supporting information. Grading of evidence in health sciences is a good example of this.
5. Present **solutions, findings** and/or **recommendations**.

An example of a business report is Jackson, Pitkin, and Kington's *Evidence-Based Decision-making for Community Health Programs*.[44] This report is longer than a customary medical article and analyzes how scientific evidence can help persons and organizations that fund or implement community-based health programs. This particular report demonstrates how community-based health interventions can be evaluated and the information used to make program decisions.

When compared to essays or research reports, the space for polemics in a business report is limited, and sometimes does not exist at all. One approach for organizing the components of a finalized and presented business report is as in Figure 13.6.

13.5 Qualitative Research-Based and Case Studies-Based Articles and Their Format

Not all research is based on a series or sets of observations which are described, compared, and analyzed in the classical scientific method. From the social sciences, qualitative research[45–49] is finding its right place in nursing, medicine, and other health sciences.[50,51] Qualitative research has its own focus, purposes, and objectives, organization, observational base, and analysis, and consequently a corresponding "look" for an article in which qualitative data is reported.

We have already defined qualitative research and commented on it as a method of inquiry which aims to gather an in-depth understanding of human behavior and the reasons which govern such behavior without using statistical descriptions and analyses.[52] Qualitative methods are

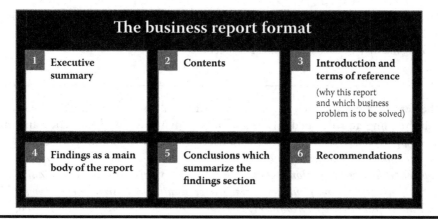

Figure 13.6 The business report format. (Redrawn from Jenicek M. *Writing, Reading, and Understanding in Modern Health Sciences.* Boca Raton: CRC Press, 2014. Reproduced with permission.)

typically based on an in-depth study of cases which may focus on either individuals or situations (events). Using these methods seek answers to questions in understanding and decision-making like why and how. Conversely, quantitative methods seek answers to what, where, and when questions.

In medicine, the subject of qualitative research may be professional practice, environmental issues affecting health, treatments, or healthcare economics, among others.[53] Making sense of cases, interpretation, and discovery of meanings are emphasized in qualitative research. Any kind of research that produces findings not arrived at by means of statistical procedures or other means of quantification about persons' lived experience with health events and problems and related behaviors is produced via qualitative research. It also includes research on organizational, functional, social, or interactional relationships between health professionals and their patients and community.

13.5.1 Clinical Case Studies vs. Clinical Case Reports

Across the current literature, "cases" and "case studies" or "case reports" may mean different things, although they are sometimes confounded. As demonstrated in Chapter 12, **clinical case report in medicine** is most often a detailed description of a single patient state (present or evolving), his or her unusual manifestations, etiology, and/or treatment success or failure. Case studies are reported in special *ad hoc* sections or under special identification in medical journals like "Original Investigation" (*JAMA*), "Original Research" (*Ann Int Med*), "Research" (*BMJ*), or in special periodicals devoted more or exclusively to clinical case reports like *Clinical Medicine Insights Case Reports* (online).

A **case study** is rather "*a detailed analysis of the occurrence, development, and outcome of as particular problem or innovation, often over a period of time.*"[54] It may focus at a person, an event or situation, an action and its remedy, a program, a time period, a critical incident, a small group, a department within an organization, an organization itself, or a community.

As for a differentiating example from daily life, describing and analyzing the sinking of the *Titanic* may be a case study. A multiple trauma and drowning in a *Titanic* passenger, its happening, and outcome may be seen as a clinical case report.

The term "case study" comes from a traditional research in health sciences and beyond, focusing at a detailed analysis of a case, dynamics, and normalcy and abnormalcy of a given state, disease, organization, structure, or functioning. In other general terms, "*an intensive analysis of an individual unit (as a person or community) stressing developmental factors in relation to environment.*"[55] It can also be defined as "*a study of an individual unit as a person, family, or social group, usually emphasizing developmental issues and relationships with the environment, especially in order to compare a larger group to the individual unit.*"[56]

Case studies are most frequently found in sociology research.[57–59] They typically focus on single or few unique events, often without expanding comparisons as subjects. In this type of study, events, situations, or happenings are most often studied, rather than individuals as "cases" which are usually of interest in health sciences. These fall mostly into the domain of qualitative research.[45–49]

In health sciences, clinical case reports and clinical case series reports (see Chapter 12), and studies of infrequent occurrences of medical error and harm, also share many characteristics of qualitative research and case study inquiries from the social sciences and elsewhere.[39] The structure and content of a medical article that uses qualitative research must then be then adapted accordingly. Giustini[61] suggests that there are six different types of case studies in health sciences. These include:

- ■ *explanatory* studies that sharing observations and findings with others;
- ■ *exploratory* studies that serve as a prelude to further in-depth research;
- ■ *descriptive* studies that offer observations about an issue of interest;
- ■ *intrinsic* studies which explore a researcher's personal interest in the subject;
- ■ *collective* studies where a group of individuals is studied; or
- ■ *instrumental* studies of individuals or groups allow researchers to understand more than what is obvious.

The article that is the result of a qualitative study reflects a qualitative research protocol. While a case study differs in terms of its components from a medical article, it logically follows several elements of the IMRAD format. Methodology for how to conduct case studies[53–59] is now also increasingly available online[60,61] and in print as well.[62–65]

> The five important components of a research design for a case study are
>
> ■ the study **question**;
> ■ the study's **propositions** (if any);
> ■ its **units (data)** of analysis;
> ■ **linking data to propositions**; and
> ■ **criteria for interpreting** the findings.[47]

Yin[62 modified] offers an overview of a case study format. It consists of eight elements, and is similar to a medical report. The eight elements are:

■ purpose of the study and research question(s);
■ literature review;
■ review of case study variables, entities, and their definitions;
■ review of the quality and completeness of the protocol;
■ methodological reminders (procedures and evidence used, tools and techniques of inquiry);
■ data collection procedures;
■ analysis and evaluation of findings as results of the study; and
■ references

How do we value a qualitative research-based article or a case study? They differ in their direction from hypothesis formulation and related research (induction and deduction in epidemiology) and in the qualities of argumentation they generate (deductive validity and inductive strength).[66–70] In the next section a valuation of these are offered.

13.5.2 Valuing Qualitative Research Studies and Articles

Quantitative research-based studies, and articles about them, are based more often (and preferably!) on a deductive intellectual process. This process leads the reader from an *a priori* formulated hypothesis, to data collection, analysis, and hypothesis confirmation or rebuttal, leading to and depending on, the study result. This approach offers better chances that the resulting argumentation will be deductively valid, that is, offering conclusions which necessarily (without exception) follow from the initial premises.

Qualitative research-based studies and case studies in this domain proceed rather in the direction of induction. That is, through an intellectual process in which hypotheses are generated, confirmed, or refuted on the basis of previously observed phenomena and gathered data. Hypotheses are generated on the basis of observations which have not been pre-selected in view of some *a priori* idea about the problem under study. Qualitative research, by virtue of its detailed scrutiny of situations and cases, generates a more granular understanding of the issue. This follows an inductive way of reasoning and argumentation where conclusions that follow from those premises with some degree of probability are reported. These conclusions may be inductively strong or weak, but not deductively valid.

Medical articles should provide enough information to the reader that will allow them to understand the deductive value and inductive strength of reported research findings. This information should primarily be found in the "results and discussion" sections of the article. If differences between the deductive value and inductive strength of the research findings exist (as they often do), the author should specify and provide enough information in the "discussion and conclusions" sections outlining how the argumentation in the article is deductively valid or inductively strong or weak. The reader should be able to assess the inductive or deductive qualities of the message on the basis of the information provided by the author. Both should share a common understanding in these matters.

Qualitative research-based studies should not be blamed for their frequent lack of deductive value. They have not been conceived with this purpose in mind. They should be, however, as inductively strong as possible.

Let Us Conclude

Whatever type and format, a medical article is one of the crucial communication tools of what is new, tried, tested, proposed, and shared in clinical learning and practice. As with any other communication method, writing and reading medical articles are processes by which findings and their meaning are conveyed to create shared understanding between the author and readers. Misunderstandings can be avoided and solved through formulations, questions and answers, paraphrasing, examples, and other vehicles of the article's message.

Editorial boards as well as reviewers have a challenging task to evaluate the message of the article itself (what is communicated), their author(s) as communicator, sender and encoder of the message, and potential readers as the receivers, targets, or decoders of the message. Receivers may be either individuals or groups of individuals (interest groups, professional, academic, or civic bodies), or both. In this view, any oral or written communication must be seen as a multifaceted activity appropriate for multiple disciplines and targeted at multiple targets (readers).

As with any other skill, communication in health sciences and elsewhere is a learned process. It does not come "out of the blue." It is supported now by both undergraduate programs (such as Biomedical Communications Minor (HBSc) at the University of Toronto) and graduate programs like the Master of Science in Health Communication at the Tufts University School of Medicine.

As a communication tool, medical articles are an important vehicle of information in the process of knowledge translation. Though defined in many ways,[70,71] **knowledge translation** is understood in our context as a process of synthesis, dissemination, exchange, and ethically sound application of acquired knowledge, attitudes, and skills. This is done with the aim of improving the health of individuals and communities and providing more effective health services through a strengthened health system. As authors, we are interested not only if a medical article conveying knowledge is good, but also if its message brings something to all who will use it in their understanding, decision-making, and ensuing actions in health sciences and practices. So far, we often are unsure or ignore the impact of medical writing and its message.

Medical articles as vehicles of thought and information are among the most important tools of knowledge translation in the health professional community. Recent initiatives pay attention to books as knowledge translation mechanisms.[72] Thus medical books are currently better known than medical articles as vehicles of knowledge translation, its adoption and impact. Different paradigms of medical articles exist. Writing the best article and gaining the greatest benefit from reading them requires that we see them as a multifaceted endeavor.

A medical article serves both as a communication tool, and a reporting tool. As a **communication tool**, the medical article has an important role in the developing domain of knowledge translation. The introduction to this chapter deals with some of its aspects. A medical report also serves as a **reporting tool**. The medical article reports experience acquired by using the scientific method of inquiry to examine health, disease, and care. The introduction to this chapter focuses on distinctions between medical articles as essays and scientific articles, those reporting original research and research synthesis from such multiple sources, meta-analysis, and research synthesis. An article's research thesis, specifying the article's objectives, purposes, hypotheses, research questions, and ways to solve the problem remains one of the founding cornerstones of research inquiry.

So far we have been accustomed to viewing good medical articles as those which report some experience based on quantitative research. This current experience stems from three methodologically and conceptually different domains:

1. The prevalence in medical literature of **quantitative research** means that the field is ruled by the traditional classical scientific method. It relies heavily on calculating frequencies, measurements, quantifications and their comparisons and interpretations to which biostatistics, field and clinical epidemiology, and other "metrics" contribute so much.

2. **Qualitative research** enriches knowledge through deep scrutiny, producing better understanding of the nature of events and phenomena of interest. Quantitative research may follow later. **Case study** (syn. **instrumental case study, intrinsic case study**) research, which originates from sociology and social studies experience, may further expand our valuable understanding. In case studies, individual patients and their experiences are "cases" or events that can be explored to better understand the experience. The current methodology will soon adapt itself to problems of interest in health sciences and professions.

3. **Mixed methods**[73–77] research offers an opportunity to combine both quantitative and qualitative methodologies to enrich our understanding and decision-making, typically about infrequently occurring phenomena.

The characteristics of qualitative research alone, or as part of mixed methods research, include:[47 modified]

- studying the meaning of the target populations' lives and experiences under real-world conditions;
- representing the views, valuing and other perspectives of participants in a study (patients, health professionals, health and social organizations, community);
- studying and reporting the contextual conditions within which study participants and target populations of the study live;
- producing new insights for existing and emerging concepts that may help explain human, professional, or social behavior; and
- using multiple sources of evidence rather than relying on a single source alone.

Will the format and structure of medical articles follow and make distinctions between these three trends? All three types of research rely on a different perception of what scientific research is and what are its objectives. Such objectives are defined by the nature of phenomena of interest which thus generated the quantitative, qualitative, and mixed approaches to health problems solving. Medical articles may further diversify if need and consensus deem it appropriate.

As was already emphasized in the chapter's introduction, several elements underlying the content of medical articles assure the quality, understanding, and relevance of medical articles communication and reporting quality. Choosing, presenting, evaluating, and understanding **definitions** (domain of *orismology*) largely defines the quality and success of communication and understanding of scientific inquiry literature. It is the focus of Chapter 7 of this book. Any sharing of reflections about a health problem (essays) or proposals and claims resulting from research are, and must be, **exercises in meaningful argumentation and critical thinking**[44] as practiced in many domains of human endeavor and presented logically.

This book explores a medical article as a tool of argumentation between the article's authors and their readers. A mutual understanding of requirements and rules of valid article claims, proposals, and conclusions must be shared by all involved parties, authors and readers as well. Articles reporting **single clinical cases** and **case series** must reflect the requirements of both qualitative research, especially if presented in an essay form, and those of quantitative research, even if their demonstrations of cause and effect relationships remains limited. For these reasons, they are discussed separately in Chapter 12 of this book. When working with individual patients and communities, all health professionals follow and respect healthcare ethics; medical articles authors are subject to **medical and other health disciplines publication ethics.** This is consistent with the case of human and laboratory research as well.

Medical articles must communicate their intended message well, be scientifically sound, include convincing argumentations, respond to the requirements of both qualitative and quantitative research, and reflect strong research ethics. Hence, while this chapter has focused on the form and function of a medical article, it is clear that the challenge is much broader than presenting an article of whatever specific type in a generally required, adopted, and tested IMRAD structure and form. Elements of all the above must be found in any orientation, structure and form of the message conveyed by medical writing. Let us not be discouraged.

Importantly, medical communication is frequently reported by journalists and other media players. Guidelines for both health professionals and media specialists, such as print and broadcast journalists and other laic bodies and interest groups, require another mutual understanding and establishment of guidelines, which are currently under development.[76] Journalists and members of the media wanting to report on medical and clinical issues need to have a strong understanding of how medical findings are conducted in order to best communicate this information.

In other domains, such as psychology, natural sciences, philosophy, and other liberal arts and humanities, writing scientific articles is a subject to rules, requirements and recommendations reviewed in this chapter for health sciences and professions. These recommendations are comparable in form and content, and consistent with those of the Modern Language Association (MLA) and the American Psychological Association (APA). Shuttleworth et al.'s[77] website can provide complementary reading for some research reporters and readers in the health domain.

Excellent medical research merits, and requires, an equally excellent way to communicate research and practice the lived experience of clinicians and researchers. In these chapters, let us argue and claim in favor of the best way to share our experience with others. For the best impact, ways of thinking, decision-making, and communication must be common for all interacting health sciences, the writers of medical articles, their readers, and other stakeholders in clinical and community health.

References

1. Jenicek M. *Writing, Reading, and Understanding in Modern Health Sciences. Medical Articles and Other Forms of Communication*. Boca Raton, FL/London/New York: CRC Press/Taylor & Francis/ Productivity Press, 2014.
2. Wikipedia, the free encyclopedia. *Essay*. 10 p. at http://en.wikipedia.org/wiki/Essay retrieved Nov 23, 2012.
3. Actden.com. *Writing Tips. Essay Builder – Writing DEN. Essays*. Variable number of p. at http://www2.actden.com/writ_den/tips/essay/, retrieved Nov 9, 2012.
4. Essay Info. *Essay Types*. Variable number of p. at http://essayinfo.com/essays/, retrieved Nov 9, 2012.
5. PrivateWriting.com. *Types of Essay*. Variable number of p. at http://www.privatewriting.com/types-of -essays.html, retrieved Nov 9, 2012.
6. Livingston K. Guide to writing a basic essay: Essay links. Find additional essay resources on-line. 5 p. at http://lklivingston.tripod.com/essay/links.html, retrieved March 8, 2012.
7. Gallaudet University. *Guide to Different Kinds of Essays*. 8 p. at http://www.galaudet.edu/tip/english _works/writing/essays/different_kinds_of_essays.html, retrieved Nov 9, 2012.
8. Fleming G. Essay types – Find one to fit your personality. Variable number of p. by type at http://homeworktips.about.com/od/essaywriting/a/howtoessay.htm, retrieved Feb 23, 2017.
9. ThesisLand.com. *Types of Essays*. 3 p. at http://www.thesisland.com/types-of-essays.htm, retrieved Nov 23, 2012.
10. Daily Writing Tips. *3 Types of Essays are Models for Professional Writing Forms*. 7 p. at http://www .dailywritingtips.com/3-types-of-essays-are-mdoels-for-professional-writing-for..., retrieved Nov 23, 2012.
11. Page M and Winstanley C. *Writing Essays for Dummies*. Chichester: John Wiley & Sons Ltd, 2009.
12. Jenicek M. *Foundations of Evidence-Based Medicine*. Boca Raton, FL/London/New York/Washington, DC: The Parthenon Publishing Group/CRC Press, 2003.
13. Privatewriting.com. *Critical Essay*. 2 p. at http://www.privatewriting.com/critical-essay.html, retrieved Nov 11, 2012.
14. Ho T. The academic essay. 5 p. at http://www.darthmouth.edu/-eng|5vr/guidelines.htm, retrieved Feb 21, 2017.
15. University of Edinburgh English Language Teaching Centre. *Academic Essay Writing for Postgraduates*. 51 pdf p. at www.ed.ac.uk/atoms/files//aewpg_ismaterials.pdf, retrieved Feb 21, 2017.
16. Wikipedia, the free encyclopedia. *Essay*. 10 p. at https://en.wikipedia.org/wiki/Essay, retrieved Feb 2, 2017.
17. Greene L. *Writing in the Life Sciences. A Critical Thinking Approach*. New York and Oxford: Oxford University Press, 2010.
18. Friedman S and Steinberg S. *Writing and Thinking in the Social Sciences*. Englewood Cliffs, NJ: Prentice Hall, 1989.
19. Wikipedia, the free encyclopedia. *Five Paragraph Essay*. 3 p. at http://en.wikipedia.org/wiki/Five_para graph_essay, retrieved Nov 4, 2012.
20. Good S and Jensen B. *The Student's Only Survival Guide to Essay Writing*. Victoria, BC and Custer, WA: Orca Book, 1995.
21. Writing an argumentative essay. Chapter X, pp. 194–205 in: Damer ET. *Attacking Faulty Reasoning. A Practical Guide to Fallacy-Free Arguments*. 5th Edition. Belmont/Singapore/Victoria/Toronto/ London/Mexico/Madrid: Thomson/Wadsworth, 2005.
22. Corbett EPJ. *Classic Rhetoric for the Modern Student*. 3rd Edition. New York and Oxford: Oxford University Press, 1990.
23. Huth EJ. *Writing and Publishing in Medicine*. 3rd Edition. Previously titled *How to Write and Publish Papers in Medical Sciences* (1982, 1990). Baltimore, MD/Philadelphia, PA/London: Williams & Wilkins, 1999.

24. Livingston K. Guide to writing a basic essay: Essay links. Find additional essay resources on-line. 5 p. at http://lklivingston.tripod.com/essay/links.html, retrieved March 8, 2012.

25. University of Guelph Writing Services. *Writing Lab Reports or Research Reports.* Learning Commons Fastfacts Series, 2004. 5 p. at http://www.learningcommons.uoguelph.ca, retrieved Sept 10, 2012.

26. Writing an essay. Chapter 2, pp. 8–38 in: Northey M and McKibbin J. *Making Sense. A Student's Guide to Research and Writing.* 7th Edition. Oxford/New York/Don Mills: Oxford University Press Canada, 2012.

27. Warburton N. *The Basics of Essay Writing.* London and New York: Routledge/Taylor & Francis, 2006.

28. Vaughn L and Scott McIntosh J. *Writing Philosophy. A Guide for Canadian Students.* Don Mills, ON/Oxford/New York: Oxford University Press, 2013.

29. International Committee of Medical Journal Editors. Uniform requirements for manuscripts submitted to biomedical journals. *Ann Intern Med,*1997;126(1):36–47.

30. International Committee of Medical Journal Editors. *Uniform Requirements for Manuscripts Submitted to Medical Journals: Writing and Editing for Biomedical Publication.* (Section *IV.A.1.a. Preparing a Manuscript for Submission to a Biomedical Journal*). 17 pdf p. at http://www.icmje.org.urm_full.pdf, retrieved Nov 28, 2012.

31. Wikipedia, the free encyclopedia. *IMRAD.* 3 p. at http://en.wikipedia.org.wiki/IMRAD, retrieved November 26, 2012.

32. Sollaci LB and Pereira MG. The introduction, methods, results, and discussion (IMRAD) structure: A fifty-year survey. *J Med Libr Assoc,*2004,92(3):364–71.

33. Writing and talking about experiences and research. Medical articles and scientific communications as arguments. Chapter 2, pp. 43–99 in: Jenicek M. *A Physician's Self-Paced Guide to Critical Thinking.* Chicago, IL: American Medical Association (AMA Press), 2006.

34. Fallacies in medical research and articles. Chapter 2, pp. 35–70 in: Jenicek M. *Fallacy-Free Reasoning in Medicine. Improving Communication and Decision-Making in Research and Practice.* Chicago, IL: American Medical Association (AMA Press), 2009.

35. Logic in research: Critical writing and reading of medical articles. Chapter 5, pp. 147–78 in: Jenicek M and Hitchcock DL. *Evidence-Based Practice. Logic and Critical Thinking in Medicine.* Chicago, IL: American Medical Association (AMA Press), 2005.

36. Horton R. The grammar of interpretive medicine. *CMAJ,*1998,159:245.

37. Gleischner JA. Using journal articles to integrate critical thinking with computer and writing skills. *NTCA J,*1994;38(Dec 4):34–5.

38. Greenhalgh T. *How to Read a Paper. The Basics of Evidence-Based Medicine.* 4th Edition. Oxford and Hoboken, NJ: John Wiley & Sons Ltd and BMJ Books, 2010.

39. American Psychological Association. *Publication Manual of the American Psychological Association.* 65th Edition. Washington, DC: American Psychological Association, 2010.

40. GRADE Guidelines. Straus S., Shepperd S., Guest Editors. First article: *J Clin Epidemiol,* 2011;64:380–2. Last article of this series: *J Clin Epidemiol,*2013;66:124–131. (This reference abridged.)

41. Caprette DR and Rice University. *Writing Research Papers.* 10 p. at http://www.ruf.rice.edu/~bioslabs/tools/report/reportform.html, retrieved November 23, 2012.

42. Schafersman SD. An introduction to science. Scientific thinking and the scientific method. 8 p. at http://www.geo.sunysb.edu/esp/files/scientific-method.html, retrieved Sept 3, 2017.

43. Thompson A. Guide to business report writing. Appendix G, pp. 103–73 in: *Entrepreneurship and Business Innovation. The Art of Successful Business Start-Ups and Business Planning.* At: http://bestentre preneur.murdoch.edu.au/Guide_to_Report_Writing.pdf, retrieved Sept 12, 2012.

44. Jackson CA, Pitkin K, Kington R. *Evidence-Based Decision-Making for Community Health Programs. Prepared for the Main Line Health System.* Santa Monica, CA and Washington, DC: RAND, 1998.

45. Creswell JW. *Qualitative Inquiry and Research Design. Choosing among Five Traditions.* Thousand Oaks/London/New Delhi: SAGE Publications, Inc., 1998.

46. *The SAGE Encyclopedia of Qualitative Research Methods.* Edited by LM Given. Los Angeles, CA/London/New Delhi/Singapore: SAGE Publications Inc., 2008.

47. Yin RK. *Qualitative Research from Start to Finish.* New York and London: The Guilford Press, 2011.

48. *The SAGE Handbook of Qualitative Research*. Edited by NK Denzin and YS Lincoln. Los Angeles, CA/London/New Delhi/Singapore/Washington, DC: SAGE Publications, Inc., 2011.
49. Bazeley P. *Qualitative Data Analysis. Practical Strategies*. Los Angeles, CA/London/New York/Singapore/Washington, DC: SAGE Publications Ltd., 2013.
50. *Qualitative Research in Health Care*. 3rd Edition. Edited by C Pope and N Mays. Oxford and London: Blackwell Publishing and BMJ Publishing Group Ltd., 2006.
51. Boffa J, Moules N, Mayan M, Cowie RL. More than just great quotes: An introduction to the Canadian Tri-Council's qualitative requirements. *Can J Infect Dis Med Microbiol,*2013;24(2):103–8.
52. Jenicek M. *A Primer on Clinical Experience in Medicine. Reasoning, Decision-Making, and Communication in Health Sciences*. Boca Raton, FL/London/New York: CRC Press/Taylor&Francis/Productivity Press, 2013.
53. *Case Study Research (Volumes I – IV)*. Edited by M David. London/Thousand Oaks, CA/New Delhi: SAGE Publications, 2006.
54. *A Dictionary of Epidemiology*. 5th Edition. Edited by M. Porta, S Greenland, and JM Last, Associate Editors. A Handbook Sponsored by the I.E.A. Oxford and New York: 2008.
55. *Merriam Webster's Collegiate Dictionary*. 11th Edition. Springfield, MA: Meriam-Webster, Inc., 2007.
56. *Random House Webster's Unabridged Dictionary*. V.22 and V.30 Electronic Edition. Springfield, MA: Merriam Webster, Inc./Lernout & Houspie, 1998.
57. Yin RK. *Case Study Research. Design and Methods*. Newbury Park, CA: SAGE Publications, 1988.
58. Rothe JP. *Qualitative Research. A Practical Guide*. Heidelberg and Toronto: RCI/PDE Publications, 1993.
59. Gary T. *How to Do your Case Study. A Guide for Students and Researchers*. Thousand Oaks, CA: SAGE Publications, 2011.
60. Wikipedia, the free encyclopedia. *Case Study*. 6 p. at https://en.wikipedia.org/wiki/Case_study, retrieved Feb 25, 2017.
61. HLWIKI Canada. Giustini D. *How to Write a Case Study*. 4 p. at http://hlwiki.slais.ubc.ca/index.php/How_to_write_a_case_study, retrieved Feb 25, 2017.
62. Yin RK. *Case Study Research. Design and Methods*. 4th Edition. *Applied Social Research Methods Series, Volume 5*. Los Angeles, CA/London/New Delhi/Singapore/Washington, DC: SAGE Publications, Inc., 2009.
63. Swanborn P. *Case Study Research What, Why and How?* Los Angeles, CA/London/New Delhi/Singapore/Washington, DC: SAGE Publications Inc., 2010.
64. *Encyclopedia of Case Study Research*. Edited by AJ Mills, G Durepos, and E Wiebe. Los Angeles, CA/London/New Delhi/Singapore/Washington, DC: SAGE Publications Inc., 2010.
65. Murphy TF. *Case Studies in Biomedical Research Ethics*. Cambridge, MA and London: The Massachusetts Institute of Technology (MIT Press), 2004.
66. Jenicek M. *Epidemiology. The Logic of Modern Medicine*. Montréal: EPIMED International, 1995.
67. Jenicek M. *Foundations of Evidence-Based Medicine*. Boca Raton, FL/London/New York/Washington, D.C.: The Parthenon Publishing Group/CRC Press, 2003.
68. Jenicek M, Hitchcock DL. *Evidence-Based Practice. Logic and Critical Thinking in Medicine*. Chicago, IL: American Medical Association (AMA Press), 2005.
69. Jenicek M. *A Physician's Self-Paced Guide to Critical Thinking*. Chicago, IL: American Medical Association (AMA Press), 2006.
70. What is KT? *KT Terms*. Variable number of p. at http://whatiskt.wikispaces.com/KT+terms, retrieved Jan 10, 2011.
71. Serenko A, Bontis N, Moshonski M. Books as a knowledge translation mechanism: Citation analysis and author survey. *J Knowledge Management,*16(3):495–511.
72. *Handbook of Mixed Methods in Social and Behavioral Research*. Edited by A Tashakkori and C Teddlie. Thousand Oaks, CA/London/New Delhi: SAGE Publications, Inc., 2003.
73. Creswell JW. *Research Design. Qualitative, Quantitative, and Mixed Methods Approaches*. 3rd Edition. Los Angeles, CA/London/New Delhi/Singapore: SAGE Publications, Inc., 2009.
74. Creswell JW and Plano Clark VL. *Designing and Conducting Mixed Methods Research*. 2nd Edition. Los Angeles, CA/London/New Delhi/Singapore/Washington, DC: SAGE Publications, Inc., 2011.

75. Creswell JW, Klassen AC, Plano Clark VL, Clegg Smith K. *Best Practices for Mixed Methods Research in Health Sciences*. Bethesda, MD/Washington DC: NIH Office of Behavioral and Social Sciences Research (OBSSR), 2011. At: obssr.od.nih.gov/.../methodology/mixed_methods_research/section2 .aspx, retrieved June 21, 2013.

76. SIRC, Social Issues Research Centre. *Guidelines on Science and Health Communication*. Oxford: Social Issues Research Centre (SIRC), November 2001 – ISBN 0 85403 570 2. See also 17 p. at http:// www.sirc.org/publik/revised_guidelines.shtml, retrieved Aug 7, 2012.

77. Shuttleworth M et al. *Writing a Research Paper. A Guide on How to Write Academic Papers*. Evolving number of p. and links at http://explorable.com, retrieved Aug 21, 2013.

An Epilogue: What Did You Read in This Book?

As summary, let us return to *A Word from the Author* at the beginning of this book and see if we have succeeded in building knowledge and understanding among readers in thinking about medicine, reasoning, decision-making, and communication in our practice and experiences in healthcare.

Thoughts, Thinkers, and Things to Think About

> *Learn in order to teach and to practice.*
> Talmud (1st–6th centuries)
> **Shouldn't we then try now to teach**
> **and practice our ways, subjects, and**
> **methods of thinking in health sciences?**

> *The physician ought to know literature ...*
> *to be able to understand or to explain what*
> *he reads. Likewise also rhetoric, that he*
> *may delineate in true arguments the things*
> *which he discusses; dialectic also so that he*
> *may study the causes and cures of infirmities*
> *in light of reason.*
> Isidore of Seville
> (570–636)
> **Isn't this book somehow justified**
> **one and half of millennium ago?**

It is necessary that a surgeon should have a temperate and moderate disposition. That he should have well formed hands, long slender fingers, a strong body, not inclined to tremble, and with all his members trained to the capable fulfillment of the wishes of his mind. He should be well grounded in natural science, and should know logic well, as to able to understand what is written; to talk properly, and to support what he has to say by good reasons.
Lanfranc of Milan
(Guido Lanfranchi)
(1250–1306)
Hence, isn't this book also for surgeons?

I am still learning.
Michelangelo
(1475–1564)
So is the author of this book.

An able and dextrous Chirurgion is a great Treasure in the Army, and cannot be valued enough, especially if he consults in all dangerous cases with the understanding Physitian. These two, Physitians and Chirurgions, are to be intimate friends together, assisting one another without envy and pride, for the better relief and the greater safety of their Patients.
Raymund Mindererus
(1570–1621)
Yes, the Author of this book is a "Physitian," an intimate friend of the "Chirurgions"!

The foundations of medicine are reason and observation.
Duro Armano Bagliavi
(1668–1707)
Definitely! Reasoning, decision making and communication of the above belong to the foundations of medicine even today, if not more than half a millennium ago!

*One of the chief defects in our country's
education plan is that we give too much
attention to developing the mind; we place too
much stress on acquiring knowledge and too
little on the wide application of knowledge.*

William James Mayo
(1861–1939), 1933
Are you still sure, Dr. Mayo?

*Knowledge is acquired when we succeed
in fitting a new experience into a system of
concepts based upon our old experiences.
Understanding comes when we liberate
ourselves from the old and make possible a
direct, unmediated contact with the new, the
mystery, moment by moment, of our experience.*

Aldous Huxley
(1894–1963), 1956
**We can do it if we know "how" to do
it, and "why" to do it?**

*Get the facts, or the facts will get you. And you
get'em, get'em right, or they will get you wrong.*

Thomas Fuller
British Physician
(1654–1734)
Gnomonologia (1723)
**Thinking right about them will
also help!**

*To think justly, we must understand what
others mean: to know the value of our thoughts,
we must try their effect on other minds.*

William Hazlitt
(1778–1830)
"On People of Sense"
The Plain Speaker (1826)
**Aren't we doing it reciprocally with our
patients and readers as well?**

*Mastering good reasoning, decision making,
or communication do not come by themselves,
They are a learned and practiced experience.
Shouldn't we all try?*

The introductory and illustrative quotations to this Epilogue show us that efforts to understand and achieve the best possible reasoning and understanding are nothing new. They have been in development over the past and present millennia. Only their scope, methodology, and uses expand and improve.

Practicing and researching medicine is much more than the accumulation of facts and evidence. This book offers a contribution to what is needed for improving clinical practice and knowledge. It includes more conventional areas of medical knowledge and practice:

- **knowledge** based on what we have read, heard, and seen;
- **experience**, ours and that of our peers; and
- best **sensory** and **motor skills** learned and acquired through an often long practice.

However, this book also explores the application of broader considerations and learnings in philosophy and thinking in the world of medicine. This includes:

- our ways of **thinking**, **reasoning**, and **understanding** about health problems and management;
- making **decisions** based on knowledge, experience, and skills outlined above about what to do;
- **acting** or **not acting** in a given case, under established conditions, and settings;
- **evaluating** how useful our actions were, are or might be; and
- **sharing our experience** with others through the best possible oral or written communication.

Building on practice and research, this text provides an argument that medical reasoning, decision-making, and communication are three distinct entities both in their philosophical underpinnings and execution (methods). To enhance medical effectiveness and patient safety, they should be implemented as free of fallacies as possible. For the best patient outcomes and medical practice, medical reasoning, decision-making and communication should be integrated and used in conjunction with other clinical skills.

In today's world, it may be easy to see electronic tools as a kind of salve or solution for better communication. Over-reliance on the use of electronic communication media is not a sign of a physician being up-to-date or modern. In some cases, those uncomfortable with in-person communication may hide and isolate himself or herself behind Bluetooth devices, smartphones, earphones, or earplugs. This is not a sign of sophisticated communication skills.

Some electronic communication tools and processes are useful. Electronic communication can enhance activities in emergency medicine and surgical specialties. Newer educational techniques ("simulation-based") such as using standardized patients or mannequins ("patient dolls") may also be useful. However, limitations of these developing electronic devices and tools are noticeable. Patients talk (and argue if they are trained for it), and mannequins don't (yet). Communication with patients and health professionals is more than passing words from one person's mouth to someone else's ears electronically. Indeed, communication is far more complex. Tone, body language, medium, setting, and so many other contextual factors impact on comprehension and understanding.

Let us emphasize again: Simply absorbing the largest possible volume of knowledge and information and successfully learning necessary sensorimotor clinical skills is not enough. Reasoning well, developing some clinical judgment skills or mastering of evidence-based and structured decision-making is not enough either. Integrating all of the above is—that may be why the medicine education and training process is so long.

Even the most straightforward and simple clinical procedures are preceded and followed by important medical thinking, reasoning, and communication. For example, a new or clinician-in-training may use a clinical decision tree to determine whether or not to insert a catheter in a patient. The decision to use the catheter precedes its successful execution. Once it is completed, then the clinician may correctly ask, '*Did I do it right?*' and '*What led me to do it?*' and '*What will it give?*' These types of evaluation questions are an integral part of the process. Asking good questions, and getting good answers, is a critical part of ongoing learning.

Clinician reasoning, decision-making rules, and communication may seem overwhelming at first, but learning them has important rewards. Medical technologies, drugs, management of care, and health administration will change with time. Essential approaches to handling them intellectually will not. In health sciences and professions, clinicians mostly live not only in a world of uncertainties and probabilities, with wrong, missing, and in never complete, but always required information. We also live in a world of errors which may lead to harm for patients. We should make every effort to eliminate mistakes in reasoning, decision-making, and communication that may contribute to these often dramatic events for patients and their physicians.

Evidence-based medicine has gained a high profile in medicine in many parts of the world. Clinical epidemiology remains at its core. It is not enough, however, to produce, grade, and otherwise evaluate the best evidence available. We must also *use* it in the best way possible. Critical thinking, structured reasoning and argumentation, and their major topics and subjects are essential for this purpose. Modern argumentation is the foundation for acceptance of any criterion of cause-effect relationships, whether negative (for example, generating disease) or beneficial (for example, treatment supporting cure and recovery). Let us reiterate that modern argumentation is a learned experience like other more traditional health-related skill.

Assessing evidence and making decisions about clinical issues relies first on often forgotten and rigorous semantics, pragmatic understanding, and decision-oriented taxonomy for health problems of interest as well as their beneficial or noxious causes. Presented with a healthcare phenomenon of interest, physicians need first to accurately define and categorize the issue before deciding what to do about it, and to whom it applies. Our strategies regarding cardiovascular disease, cancer, psychiatric problems, social well-being, and even a newly emerging domain of 'spiritual health' depend on it. Chapter 7 details the importance and process for understanding and developing definitions of our observed phenomena, thoughts, and actions.

Rational medical thinking through argumentation is not limited to cause-effect relationships (as outlined in Chapter 8), no matter how prevalent they are in medicine. It also supports, as we saw in Chapter 5, every step of clinical work. Modern argumentation is a meaningful way to answer questions raised in the Socratic dialogue. Any discussion of a clinical problem or reviewing specific patient care benefits from it. The learning process itself requires that learners understand how their teachers reason; and conversely, teachers must know how and why learners react and interact to a variety of teaching processes and methods.

Understanding clinical problems faced by practitioners is just the first part of the challenge. Chapter 10 considers medical decision-making as the process used to resolve clinical challenges. Reasoning in this domain requires the mastery of additional methodology in the gnostic domain. Whatever the transition and interface may be between knowing and deciding, these two distinct entities remain complementary.

Mutual understanding, based on the use of best evidence in rational argumentation and decision-making relies on a third element, communication and is explored in Chapters 11, 12, and 13.

There are many more types of communication than person-to-person exchanges within the patient–physician world. Rounds, reviews, bedside or hallway discussions, consults, administrative and other operational summaries, journal articles, lab essays, and case and clinical reports are all subjects of rational thinking, judgment, and decision-making. Oral and written communication are supplemented by nonverbal communication—all essential for sharing thoughts, knowledge, and ideas.

Even the simplest *"Why?"* question raised by any learner should be answered in an argumentative way, grounded in the best available evidence. The learner should recognize elements and good building blocks of argumentation as proposed by the teacher.

These chapters define and expand on our fundamental thesis: Health problems, whatever their genus, must be defined and presented first as an argument. This process requires that clinicians define topics, objectives, and research questions from the beginning, and uses methodologies to explore the problems that reflect their nature—epidemiological, biostatistical, operational, administrative, qualitative or quantitative research, or other. Once results or outcomes are presented, they too must be assessed through an argumentation process to determine their worth and relevance. This is one way to help prevent and avoid the unrelated "techno-babble" that often seeps into medical articles.

Understanding the reasoning process in argumentation will further serve the younger learner when exposed (sooner or later) to larger scale health policy and program development, making, and evaluation. The general rules in reasoning and argumentation in these broader areas are similar to those used in individual or group patient care. The productivity of health professionals should not be limited in a single sphere. On the contrary!

Clinicians enter the medical field to do good. However, a medical degree and desire to do good in and of itself is simply not enough. Using a more deliberate, purposeful, and methodological approach to reasoning and decision-making will ensure that our good intentions to arrive at meaningful results will succeed: our patients and communities will be healthier, safer, and unharmed; research money, energies, and human resources will be well invested. Adopting the message presented in the pages of this introductory reading provides a roadmap to ensure these better outcomes.

And what about the future of teaching and learning clinical reasoning and decision-making? Certainly these approaches are already being taught in a selective and scattered way in courses on epidemiology, clinical epidemiology, biostatistics, preventive medicine, and public health; through formal and clinical teaching in family medicine and clinical specialties; and in other forms of sharing clinical and community medicine expertise. The next quest may be, sooner or later, to integrate, absorb, and harmonize all these crucial contributions to the development of professional knowledge and competency into a framework of understanding, decision-making, and communication in health professions as outlined in the broadest of terms in the preceding pages.

Would it be opportune to add some new specialty courses, above and beyond more traditional ones, in health professional graduate or undergraduate teaching and programmes to address these integrated areas? Perhaps a single semester course based on the 13 chapters of this book with applications to help students develop integrated reasoning, decision-making, and communication skills that could assist their very practical efforts in developing, writing, and presenting their research projects, grant applications, and oral communications of research to their peers. This course can also help them to share their practical experiences more broadly, writing articles or case studies, or even just to best review existing health and medical literature. Over the last decade, the integration of reasoned approaches in medicine have increased with the addition of elements in health and medical training that include "reasoned medicine," "best-backing evidence and argument-based medicine," "evidence-grounded argument-based medicine," "reasoned medicine," "evidence-based critical thinking medicine," "cognitive medicine and medical thinking," "iatrology," and other labels for medical thinking.[1–5] Will this trend continue and grow? The author looks forward to these potential developments.

The *Oxford Dictionary*'s lexical definition of cognition is "*the mental action of process of acquiring knowledge and understanding through thought, experience, and the senses.*" It encompasses processes such as knowledge, attention, memory and working memory, judgment, and evaluation, reasoning and "computation," problem solving and decision-making, comprehensions, and production of language. Research in, and the practiced of medicine, then, are cognitive processes. In the light of this monograph, are we not moving toward **Evidence-Based Cognitive Medicine**? The forthcoming years will tell.

Last but not least, consider what medical ethicists think: Is it ethical not to produce the best evidence if we can? Is it ethical or not to evaluate evidence? Is it ethical to not *use* the best evidence if we can? Is it ethical to not use the best evidence, in an appropriate way, for reasoning, decision-making and communication if we can?

The experiences and contributions of past and present generations clinicians, epidemiologists, biostatisticians, and philosophers, as well as ethicists, have made tremendous advances in the way modern health sciences "makes sense." The well-being of our communities and patients would benefit from so much more from even more development in this area.

Our journey to discover how the clinical environment works is now over. Let us hope that readers enjoyed it and found it useful. Welcome now to the hospital wards, offices, labs, and managerial and administrative starting gates! The race is about to begin.

References

1. Jenicek M. The hard art of soft science: Evidence-Based Medicine, Reasoned Medicine or both? *J Eval Clin Pract*, 2006;12(4):410–9.
2. Jenicek M. Towards evidence-based critical thinking medicine? Uses of best evidence in flawless argumentations. *Med Sci Monit*, 2006;12(8):RA149–53.
3. Jenicek M. Evidence-based medicine: Fifteen years later. Golem the good, the bad, and the ugly in need of a review? *Med Sci Monit*, 2006;12(11):RA241–RA251.
4. Jenicek M, Croskerry P, Hitchcock DL. Evidence and its uses in health care and research: The role of critical thinking. *Med Sci Monit*, 2011;17(1):RA12–RA17.
5. Jenicek M. Do we need another discipline in medicine? From epidemiology and evidence-based medicine to cognitive medicine and medical thinking. *J Eval Clin Pract*, 2015;21(ISSN 1365-2753): 1028–34.

Glossary: Preferred Terms and Their Definitions in the Context of This Book

Definitions of terms in this glossary primarily reflect the meaning attributed to them in this reading. The author has attempted to establish a delicate balance between meanings in philosophy, medicine, and law. The following definitions also closely follow meanings ascribed to them in current major general, medical, epidemiological, and legal dictionaries as well as in textbooks of epidemiology, clinical epidemiology, and evidence-based medicine. Some additional terms from the philosophy domain, and which the reader might find elsewhere in health-related literature, complete this glossary. The glossary is not intended to replace the above-mentioned sources, but rather complements them, and are consistent with the message of this book.

If a term is composed of two or more words, it may be presented as it is already in the literature as a gnostic entity, such as "informal logic" or "critical thinking," not always as "logic (informal)" or "thinking (critical)" or "evidence-based medicine" instead of "medicine (evidence-based)." This is how many readers may read and understand them better.

This glossary defines terms as they are used and understood in the spirit, context, and content of this reading. The universal and official validity of these definitions in medicine and the health sciences may vary or be limited. However, in our modest opinion, they represent, an optimal selection from human and medical literature and experiences.

How did we compile this glossary? We followed several defined steps, outlined here.

1. To decide what terms to include, two criteria were used. First, operational quality or adequacy for practical uses (inclusion/exclusion criteria, measurability, and taxonomy suitability) was used as a criterion. Second, the term's compatibility with prevailing meaning and terminology in mainstream clinical epidemiology, evidence-based medicine, and their uses of evidence in reasoning, critical thinking, understanding, and decision-making in medicine and allied health sciences were considered.
2. Additional attention was paid to overlapping of various definitions (like between an incident and error or adverse event). Such instances were avoided as much as possible.
3. Some basic epidemiological, logic, critical thinking, evaluation, and medical terms were excluded since they would have unnecessarily encumbered the glossary. Only definitions of terms less well known to health professionals at large, and more specific to lathology, were retained in this selection.

4. Some terminology of law pertaining to error and harm has been included and is detailed in Chapter 9.
5. Whenever more than one definition is quoted, it is because the definitions are complementary and their inclusion builds a comprehensive understanding of the terms.
6. Anything else besides the above that could help readers who may not be health professionals to consult these pages with more ease.

In the first section of this glossary, general sources are provided for some basic terms used in this book. Most of them come from epidemiology, biostatistics, evidence-based medicine, and modern argumentation and critical thinking from philosophy. They have been used to generate the definitions for terms in this book and might prove of interest for some readers.

In the second section, we provide definitions for specific terms used in this book, in alphabetical order. These terms are referenced and a list of citations is offered at the end of the section.

A. Sources for Definitions, by Domain

1. For health sciences and medical research in general:

Medical Dictionary, the Free Dictionary. Variable number of p. at http://medical-dictionary .thefreedictionary.com

Stedman's Medical Dictionary. 28th Edition. Philadelphia/Baltimore/New York/London: Lippincott Williams & Wilkins, 2006.

Taber's Cyclopedic Medical Dictionary. 22nd Edition. Edited by D Venes. Philadelphia: F.A. Davis Company, 2009.

Dorland WA Newman. *Dorland's Illustrated Medical Dictionary.* 30th Edition. DM Anderson, Chief Lexicographer. Philadelphia, PA: Saunders/Elsevier, 2003.

2. For epidemiology and biostatistics:

Encyclopedia of Epidemiology. Edited by S Boslaugh and L-A McNutt. Los Angeles/London /New Delhi/Singapore: SAGE Publications, 2008.

Encyclopedia of Biostatistics. Edited by P Armitage and T Colton. Chichester, NY: J Wiley, 1998.

A Dictionary of Public Health. Edited by JM Last. Oxford and New York: Oxford University Press, 2007.

A Dictionary of Epidemiology. 5th Edition. Edited by M Porta, S Greenland, and JM Last, Associate Editors. A Handbook sponsored by the I.E.A. Oxford and New York: Oxford University Press, 2008.

Encyclopedia of Biostatistics. 2nd Edition in 8 Vol. Edited by P Armitage and T Colton. Chichester, West Sussex, UK: John Wiley & Sons, 2005.

Encyclopedia of Epidemiologic Methods. Edited by MH Gail and J Bénichoux. Chichester, West Sussex, UK: John Wiley & Sons, 2000.

Feinstein AR. *Clinical Epidemiology. The Architecture of Clinical Research.* Philadelphia, PA: W.B. Saunders Company, 1985.

3. For logic, critical thinking, and argumentation with applications to health sciences:

Jenicek M and Hitchcock DL. *Evidence-Based Practice. Logic and Critical Thinking in Medicine.* Chicago, IL: American Medical Association (AMA Press), 2005. See the Glossary in this book, pp. 259–78.

Elder L and Paul R. *A Glossary of Critical Thinking Terms and Concepts. The Critical Analytic Vocabulary of the English Language. With Commentary for Students, Educators, and Citizens.* Dillon Beach, CA: The Foundation for Critical Thinking, 2009.

Glossary: Preferred terms and definitions in the context of this book. Pp. 279–314 in: Jenicek M. *A Primer on Clinical Experience in Medicine. Reasoning, Decision-making, and Communication in Health Sciences.* Boca Raton, London, New York: CRC Press/ Taylor & Francis/Productivity Press, 2013.

Jenicek M. *Foundations of Evidence-Based Medicine.* Boca Raton/London/New York/ Washington: Parthenon/CRC Press, 2003.

Jenicek M. *Medical Error and Harm. Understanding, Prevention, and Control.* A Productivity Press Book. Boca Raton, FLA/London/New York: CRC Press/Taylor & Francis, 2011. See its lathology-related glossary, pp. 289–308.

4. **To expand the knowledge of some other terms which might escape to attention of some mainstream health professionals:**

Encyclopedia of Research Design. Edited by JN Salkind. Los Angeles/London/New Delhi/ Singapore: SAGE Publications, Inc., 2010.

The SAGE Encyclopedia of Qualitative Research Methods. Edited by LM Given. Los Angeles/ London/New Delhi/Singapore: SAGE Publications, Inc., 2008.

Encyclopedia of Case Study Research. Edited by AJ Mills, G Durepos, and E Wiebe. Los Angeles/ London/New Delhi/Singapore/Washington DC: SAGE Publications, Inc., 2010.

Reese WL. *Dictionary of Philosophy and Religion. Eastern and Western Thought.* Expanded Edition. Amherst, NY: Humanity Books/Prometheus Books, 1999.

The Cambridge Dictionary of Philosophy. Second Edition. R Audi, General Editor. Cambridge and New York: Cambridge University Press, 1999.

Everitt BS. *The Cambridge Dictionary of Statistics in the Medical Sciences.* Cambridge/New York/Melbourne: Cambridge University Press, 1995.

Vogt WP. *Dictionary of Statistics and Methodology. A Nontechnical Guide for the Social Sciences.* Newbury Park/London/New Delhi: SAGE Publications, 1993.

Wikipedia, the free encyclopedia. Various entries in the current electronic version.

Clapp JE. *Radom House Webster's Dictionary of Law.* New York: Random House, 2000.

Notes on these sources: References for other terms are provided directly in the main body of the text. Readers are encouraged to use the index to navigate through the chapters.

B. Glossary

This Glossary does not contain exhaustively biostatistical and epidemiological terms and their definitions. Authors or readers of medical articles should already be familiar with terms such as odds, relative risk, multivariate analysis or correlation, and others.

Wherever appropriate, entries in this Glossary include: definition, its synonym(s), examples, and comments.

Abduction: A form of reasoning in which one reasons from observed phenomena to a hypothesis which would explain them. Usually, abductive reasoning shows only that the hypothesis is a possible explanation, and further observation or experiment and reasoning is required to determine whether the hypothesis is justified.

Accident (in general): A specific, identifiable, unexpected, unusual, and unintended event that occurs in a particular time and place, without apparent or deliberate cause, but with marked effects. It implies a generally negative probabilistic outcome that may have been avoided or prevented had circumstances leading up to the accident been recognized and acted upon, prior to its occurrence.[1] It is an event that was neither planned, nor expected.

Accident (in medicine):

■ An unexpected, specific, identifiable, unusual, and unintended (unplanned) event that occurs at a particular time and place of medical care, originally without an apparent or deliberate cause, but with marked effects.

■ An adverse outcome that was NOT caused by chance or fate. Most accidents and their contributing factors are predictable and the probability of their occurrence may be reduced through system improvements.[2]

■ An unexpected, specific, identifiable, unusual, and unintended (unplanned) event that occurs in a particular time and place of medical care, originally without an apparent or deliberate cause, but with marked effects.

Action-based error (slip, in medicine): Attentional or perceptual failure of an action.[3]

Example: Dispensing an excessively elevated dose of medication.

Active error (human, medical): An error or failure resulting from human reasoning, or decision-making resulting in an active behavior, that is made by a health professional (operating surgeon, prescribing internist, consulting psychiatrist, nurse at floors or in the operating room, etc.) who, in a health establishment, provides direct clinical or community care, acts, or services. The active error may be knowledge-based, rule-based, or skill-based.

Active failure (Syn. patent failure, salient failure, proximate failure):

■ An event/action/process that is undertaken, or takes place, during the provision of direct patient care and fails to achieve its expected claims. While some active failures may contribute to patient injury, not all do.[2]

■ Failure of reasoning, judgment, and ensuing decision made by the operator, that is, executing health professional responsible for directly delivering healthcare to its recipient (patient or community).

■ A failure that immediately precedes error and its consequences. (N.B. What is immediate and what is not?)

Additive effect: An arithmetic sum of the effects of a set of factors (like drugs or pollutants).

Adduct: A common term for rebuttals and all supporting elements related to conclusions (claims) of an argument.

Adverse drug reaction:

■ An undesirable effect expected or not, produced by the use of medication, regardless of whether the medication was used as recommended. Its mechanisms may be known or still unknown given its newness.

■ A medication-related adverse event.[6]

Adverse effect: An unfavorable, undesirable, and harmful result of a correct process or action.[7] modified

Adverse event in health sciences and professions (in one of the following ways):

■ An unexpected and undesired incident directly associated with the care and services provided to the patient.[2]

■ An incident that occurs during the process of providing healthcare and that results in patient injury or death. (N.B. See *Incident and Critical Incident* definitions.)[2]

■ An adverse outcome for a patient, including injury or complication.[2]

- An untoward incident, therapeutic misadventure, iatrogenic injury, or other adverse occurrence directly associated with care or services provided within the jurisdiction of a medical center, outpatient clinic, or other (health) facility.[8]
- An injury related to medical management, in contrast to complications of disease. Medical management includes here all aspects of care. Adverse events may be preventable or non-preventable.[6]

Algorithm (clinical): A step-by-step written protocol or flowchart drawn for management of a health problem. Each step (consideration, decision) depends unequivocally on the preceding one. It is often confused with a decision tree. See *Decision tree* entry.

Algorithm in medicine: A graphical representation (flowchart) of a set of rules to solve a clinical problem by setting down individual steps in a sequence of actions and their results; each action step depends on the result of the preceding one. Therefore, as opposed to a decision tree, an algorithm is an unequivocal *direction giving* tool.

Alternative medicine: A label for a heterogeneous collection of clinical maneuvers, whose efficacy and safety are generally not necessarily scientifically tested, which are not used in mainstream medicine, and which are intended to replace conventional medical treatments. See also *Complementary medicine*, a label for maneuvers intended to supplement conventional medical treatments.

Analytical study (in fundamental and clinical epidemiology): Study of cause-effect relationships between health phenomena, based on single or multiple observations of multiple sets of data or observations. Exposure (cause) may be single or multiple over persons, place, or time. Incidence, prevalence, duration, and other consequences (effects) are *comparisons* of the above. Exposure may be to noxious factors (most often by observational studies) or to beneficial factors (by arbitrary, often at random) assignment. Study of the exposure is conducted to understand analysis of an experimental group(s), factor of interest exposed, and control group(s) compared to other factors, or to none exposed, or factor of interest unexposed. Without such assignments, the study is **analytical observational**. With such assignments, the study is **analytical experimental**, like clinical trials.

Argument (in general):

- A connected series of statements or reasons intended to establish one position, that leads to another statement as a conclusion. A position or conclusion may be the diagnosis, patient admission or treatment decision or that an error and/or harm occurred, etc.
- As a vehicle of reasoning, an argument consists of various statements or propositions (premises) from which we infer an understanding to another statement or conclusion.
- As vehicle of reasoning, a set of statements, some of whose premises are offered as reasons for another statement, the conclusion. *Example:* You have a streptococcal infection, so you must start taking antibiotics. *Premise:* You have a streptococcal infection. *Conclusion:* You must start taking antibiotics.

Argument (in medicine): A connected series of statements originating from a lived situation, experience, or research in medicine intended to establish a position (another statement as conclusion) in medical problem solving, understanding, and decision-making. In a medical argument, a position or conclusion may be the diagnosis, patient admission, treatment decision, or an error and/or harm that occurred, and so on. As an exchange of ideas, views or opinions, it may focus on problem solving in a specific patient (should the patient undergo surgery or not?), or it may be directed toward finding the best solution to a more encompassing problem to find the best way to manage it (for example, nosocomial infections or medical errors in a hospital or in a broader medical care system).

Argument-based error: Misusing or omitting valid argument components (grounds, backing, warrant, qualifier, rebuttals, conclusions, or claims) or using inappropriate arguments and linking them poorly in medical decision-making.

Argument-based medicine: The research and practice of medicine in which understanding and decisions in patient and population care are supported by, and based on, flawless arguments using the best research and practice evidence and experience as argument and argumentation building blocks in a structured and fallacy-free manner.

Argumentation (in general):
■ A discussion between two or more people in which at least one advances an argument.
■ The methodological use or presentation of arguments.

Argumentation (medical): The methodological use or presentation of medical arguments to solve a problem in medical practice or research.

Argumentation and critical decision-making in clinical decision-making: The process by which interested parties, physicians, nurses, their patients, and other stakeholders in health seek the best choices and decisions under uncertain and ambiguous conditions.

Argumentative essay: Presentation of an argument-based investigation of the topic which rests on the generation and/or collection of evidence, evaluation of evidence, and the establishment of the author's position about the topic of interest.

Art (in general):
■ Skills directed toward the work of imagination, imitation, or design, or gratification of the aesthetic senses.
■ The application or the principles of application, of skill, knowledge, and so on, in a creative effort to produce something. The art of medicine, for example, contributes to producing (or preserving) health. Fine art in particular produces works that have a form of beauty, aesthetic expression of feeling, and so on, as in music, painting, sculpture, literature, architecture, and the dance. Beyond its scientific basis, a good part of plastic and reconstructive surgery is fine art.

Art of medicine:
■ The systematic application of sensory skills, creative imagination, faithful imitation, innovation, intuition, and knowledge in speech, reasoning, or motion in the care of the health of patients and communities.
■ A mastery of dealing with human interactions, feelings and sensations, ideas, and making meaningful lateral and holistic connections between and among them, and thus contributing to the body of medical knowledge, attitudes, and skills.

Association: A tendency of two variables to be systematically related in a group of individuals. As defined, association is not the same as causation. 'Association' is one of the most nebulous terms in medicine and epidemiology. Across the literature and in medical talk, it may mean a statistical (probabilistic) association (as defined here), a causal association, or any other parallel observation of two or more phenomena. Readers beware!

Atomization of a problem: Bringing a problem to its manageable parts.

Attending:
■ A health professional, most often a physician, who as authorized and plenipotentionary decision-maker by their position in an accredited hospital, has primary responsibility and authority for a patient and their care.

- A form of "***attending function***" may be found in any other health profession: nursing, respirology, re-adaptation, physiotherapy, and others.

Attitude(s):

- A part of the affective domain that can be viewed in this context as learned tendencies to act and decide in a consistent manner with regard to a particular object and situation.
- It means also having in the decision-making process the capacity to sense and recognize the situation, and to act in a controlled and predictable and consistent manner, relevant to the problem requiring a decision. The decision-maker's attitudes must be appropriate for the task to avoid errors in decision-making.
- A learned tendency to act and decide in a consistent manner toward a particular object and situation.
- A capacity to sense and recognize the situation, act in a controlled, predictable, and consistent manner, relevant to the problem at hand.

Attributable fraction: Same as attributable risk percent (see below).

Attributable risk (in epidemiology):

- In cohort studies, the difference between the risk of an outcome of interest in subjects exposed to a suspected causal factor, and the risk in unexposed subjects. Both groups compared share presumably the same web of causes except the factor under study. Also called *risk difference.*
- The difference between the rate of events in a group of interest (subjects exposed to a factor) and a control group (non-exposed group).

Attributable risk percent (in epidemiology): In etiological studies, it is the proportion of all observations (morbid events) which may be explained by the causal factor under study (from the whole web of causes). Syn. *etiological fraction, attributable fraction.*

Backing (in modern argument): The body of experience and evidence that supports the warrant and grounds in modern argument and argumentation. One of the six elements in the contemporary layout of arguments due to Toulmin. See also *Warrant.*

Belief:

- A dispositional psychological state in virtue of which a person will assent to a proposition under certain conditions.
- More narrowly, the acknowledgment that a proposition is true in the absence of demonstrable proof as required by scientific method. As such, it is a rather primary cognitive state as a precursor for reasoning toward evidence.

Best research evidence: The most valid clinically relevant research from the available options.

Bias in medicine: A non-random, <u>systematic</u> deviation from truth, or a well-defined "reality." Caveat: Bias, cognitive error, or cognitive bias are often considered synonyms.

Blunt end (in lathology): Layers of healthcare actions and processes that precede direct contact with patients and where error-related events occur at a site of latent error. These errors might be made by health policy makers, managers, technology designers, and so on, rather than direct clinical providers of care. An error in programming an intravenous pump is a sharp end (see this entry) or active error. Designing and manufacturing a defective pump is a blunt end (latent) error.[9 modified]

Business report: A presentation of information necessary for, and leading to, business decision-making.

CAM: Abbreviation for *complementary* and *alternative medicine* (for each, see separate entries).

Case control study (in epidemiology): A type of study of cause-effect relationships based on a single comparison of (often past) exposure to a potentially causal factor in groups of potentially factor-produced diseased individuals (cases of disease) and non-cases.

Case fatality rate: The occurrence of death in individuals suffering from a specific disease. Used as an expression of disease severity.

Case series report or case series study (clinical): A detailed description and analysis of a series of cases that explain the dynamics, pathology, management, and/or outcome of a given disease (or of harm or error in our context).

Case series study (clinical): A detailed description and analysis of series of cases that explains the dynamics, pathology, management, and/or outcome of a given disease (or of harm or error in our context).[10]

Case study (in qualitative research): An in-depth examination, analysis, and interpretation of a single instance or event such as the occurrence of error or harm.

■ An in-depth examination, analysis, and interpretation of a single instance or event such as the occurrence of error or harm.

■ A detailed analysis of the occurrence, development, and outcome of a particular problem or innovation, often over a period of time.

Categorical statement: A statement which affirms or denies that some predicate belongs to all or some members of some subject class. Simple affirmative or negative statements about an individual ("Mrs. Fitzpatrick is critically ill") can also be regarded as categorical statements by treating them as statements about all members of the class consisting just of that individual.

Examples of categorical statements:

"All patients in our intensive care unit require continuous monitoring of their vital signs," or "Mrs. Fitzpatrick requires continuous monitoring of her vital signs." (universal affirmative or A statement—*affirmo*)

"None of the patients in our intensive care unit should be transferred to another ward without a thorough assessment of their needs, risks, and prognosis," or "Mrs. Jones does not require continuous monitoring of her vital signs." (universal negative or E statement—*nego*)

"Some patients in the coronary care unit can be transferred to other wards without a thorough assessment of their prognosis and needs." (particular affirmative or I statement—*affirmo*)

"Some patients with a respiratory distress syndrome should not be transferred to other wards without a thorough assessment of their care needs and prognosis." (particular negative or O statement—*nego*)

Categorical syllogism: A classical, Aristotelian form of argument consisting of three elements (building blocks): a general statement (major premise), a specific (about a particular case) statement, and an inference indicators-related conclusion.

Categorical syllogism (medical application): Reasoning or argument consisting of two premises and a conclusion, all of which are *categorical statements* (see above). The predicate of the conclusion occurs in one premise, the subject of the conclusion in the other, and a common middle term occurs in both premises.

Examples:

All patients in the intensive care unit are critically ill; all critically ill patients require continuous monitoring of their vital signs; therefore, all patients in the intensive care unit require continuous monitoring of their vital signs. In this example, which is deductively **valid**, the subject of the conclusion, *"patients in the intensive care unit,"* occurs in the first premise; the predicate of the conclusion, *"require continuous monitoring of their vital signs,"* occurs in the second premise; and the middle term, *"critically ill patients,"* occurs in both premises.

Not all patients in Ward 17 require continuous monitoring of their vital signs; Mrs. Fitzpatrick is a patient in Ward 17; therefore, Mrs. Fitzpatrick does not require monitoring of her vital signs. In this example, which is deductively invalid, the subject of the conclusion, *"Mrs. Fitzpatrick,"* occurs in the second premise; the predicate of the conclusion, *"require continuous monitoring of vital signs,"* occurs in the first premise; and the middle term, *"patients in Ward 17,"* occurs in both premises.

Causal tree (in root cause analysis in lathology):

■ A linear sequence of events established to trace flaws in the process of healthcare or practice.

■ An investigation and analysis technique used to record and display, in a logical, tree-structured hierarchy, all the actions and conditions that were necessary and sufficient for a given sequence to have occurred.[11]

Causality:

■ Relationship between a presumed cause and its effect.

■ Path from a cause to an effect.

In this book, causation is a preferred term to causality. See *Causation.*

Causation: A relationship between two events that holds when, given that one occurs, it produces, brings forth, determines, or necessitates, a second. See *Causality.*

Causation in civil law: Demonstration that a particular agent or act is a more probable than improbable cause of a given state of affairs (e.g., a health problem).

Causation in criminal law: Proof beyond a reasonable doubt that a given state of affairs (e.g., a health problem) is due to and only to a given factor.

Cause:

■ **In general:** An event without which some subsequent event would not have occurred, or because of which, it occurred. An agent or act (a cause) that produces some phenomenon (the effect).[12]

■ **In the error domain:** An antecedent set of actions, circumstances, or conditions that produce an event, or phenomenon (that is, error and its consequences).[2]

■ **At courts of law:** Each separate antecedent of an event that, in some manner, is accountable for a condition that brings about an effect, or that produces a cause, for the resultant action or state.[12]

■ **In clinical medicine and public health:** Contextual factors which produce changes such as the occurrence of disease or its cure.

Chain of causes: A sequence of events in time in which each possibly related event follows (and may be caused by) another.

Chance:

■ An uncalculated, and possible, incalculable element, of existence.

■ The contingent, as opposed to the necessary, aspects of existence.

■ Also, a probability of an event.

Chaos (chaos theory, chaotic behavior in biological systems): An aperiodic, seemingly random and unpredictable behavior in systems governed by deterministic laws that exhibits a sensitive dependence on initial conditions.

Claim: A conclusion to which we arrive through our reasoning and supported by the argument at hand.

Claim (in modern argument):

■ As one of the six elements in the contemporary layout of arguments due to Toulmin: The claim or conclusion is the proposition at which we arrive as a result of our reasoning, or which we defend in an argument by citing our supporting grounds and inference from them.

■ Conclusion of the argument; proposition as a result of reasoning based on supporting grounds and inference from them.

Clinical: Pertaining to the care of the individual patient both in the hospital and in outside-hospital settings (e.g., medical practice office). See *Paraclinical.*

Clinical algorithms:

■ Step-by-step written protocols for health management, and descriptions of steps to be taken in patient care, in specified circumstances.

■ A set of rules for approaching a solution to a complex clinical problem by setting down individual steps and delineating how each step follows from the preceding one.

Clinical care: See *Healthcare.*

Clinical case report: A structured form of scientific and professional communication normally focused on an unusual single event (patient or clinical situation) to provide a better understanding of a case and of its effects on improved clinical decision-making.[10]

Clinical clerk: A medical or other health sciences undergraduate (nursing, dentistry, physiotherapy, imaging technology, etc.) working with patients under the supervision and control of an instructor. Clerkship is usually scheduled in the second part of the medical undergraduate curriculum and is an unpaid activity. See *Extern.*

Clinical context: A set of case-related established clinical practices, healthcare providers, patients and physical environments (technologies included), which apply to a particular case such as a patient, strategies of care, or teamwork and which influence meaning, understanding, and decision-making about the case.

Clinical decision analysis:

■ An application of decision analysis in a clinical setting. It has three main components: choices available either to the patient, his or her physician or both; chances as probabilities of outcome for each choice; and values of treatment options and their outcomes for interested parties.

■ It represents any activity, systematizes (organizes) decision-making, clarifies decision-making, and leads to the 'correctness' of decisions.

Clinical decision tree: Temporal and spatial representation, in a proper clinical sequence of options, offered to the clinician so that they may make a specific decision at clearly defined moments of clinical work. Decisions may include (add) a diagnostic method or not, to treat or not to treat, to choose different treatments, and so on.

Clinical epidemiology:

■ The science and method of studying and making optimal decisions in clinical medicine, while taking into account the epidemiological characteristics of the patient, the patient's external clinical environment, the pathology concerned, and the factors and maneuvers to which the patient is exposed in their clinical environment, especially medical actions.

■ The application of epidemiological knowledge, reasoning, and methods to study clinical issues and improve medical and other decisions when dealing with individual patients and groups of patients, and to improve overall clinical care (N.B. and its outcomes).[13 modified]

■ Also, using the experience acquired in groups in reasoning and decision-making in the care of individuals.[14]

Clinical expertise: The ability to use clinical skills and past experience at any and all stages of clinical work with the patient.

Clinical guidelines: A standardized set of information describing the best practices for addressing health problems commonly encountered either in clinical or public health practice.

Clinical judgment: The capacity to make and choose data and information to produce useful (true or false) claims in clinical practice and research. It also means critical thinking in the research and practice of clinical medicine based on the 'patient/evidence/setting' fit.

Together with elements of knowledge and experience, it relies on the process of integrating meanings and values of clinical and paraclinical observation and data into the making of conclusions and decisions derived from such an integration.

Clinical practice guidelines: A set of systematically developed evidence and other elements-based statements to assist practitioners' and patients' decisions about the best possible healthcare for specific clinical and community medicine circumstances. As opposed to clinical protocols, clinical practice guidelines are not prescriptive; they are proposals for what to do.

Clinical protocols: Structured and organized step-by-step activities to be followed in a given health structure, setting, and situation. As opposed to clinical practice guidelines, critical protocols are prescriptive; they must be followed in the framework of a given clinical activity.

Clinical reasoning: A context-dependent way of thinking and decision-making in professional practice to guide practice actions. It involves the construction of narratives to make sense of multiple factors and interests pertaining to the current reasoning task. It occurs within a set of problem spaces informed by the practitioner's unique frames of reference, workplace context, and practice models, as well as by the patient or client contexts. It utilizes core dimensions of practice knowledge, reasoning, and decision-making.

Clinical sign: See *Sign (clinical)*.

Clinical symptom: See *Symptom (of disease)*.

Clinical trial:

■ A cause-effect study based on a random and otherwise controlled assignment of patients and groups of patients to a clinical event of interest (medical treatment, surgery, or other alternative event). Short- or long-term effects (improvement in health) are most frequent outcome measures, but adverse effect occurrences may be added to the study, if ethical.

■ An experimental procedure based on the scientific method to evaluate if some health interventions like drug treatment, surgery, or other types of patient or community care produce expected results. Randomization of patients into groups that are compared, blinding of patients and of clinical trialists, i.e., the clinicians who are running a clinical trial are also blinded themselves and other methods of arriving at unbiased information are just some of the ways to make a trial as objective as possible.

Clinical vignette: A concise presentation of an interesting or challenging patient encounter as clinical experience of present and future interest.

Clinimetrics:
- The domain of observation, measurement, classification, and categorization of clinical phenomena. A medical equivalent to biometrics, econometrics, and other "–metrics" in their respective domains.
- The domain concerned with qualification, counting, measurement, and categorization of clinical observations, data, and information.
- The definition, measurement, classification, validation, and evaluation of clinical observations such as symptoms and signs, indices and scales, and other distinct clinical phenomena to make them as reproducible and meaningful as possible.

Close call (in lathology): An event or situation that did not produce patient injury, but which might have, given the patient's condition, a lack of rapid corrective intervention by the care provider, or other circumstances. See also *Near miss incident*.[9 modified]

Closed (closed-ended) questions: Questions requiring direct answers. They initiate inductive reasoning, and serve to confirm hypotheses as hypotheses testers.

Cogent argument:
- A compelling argument.
- An argument that justifies its conclusion to its addressee(s). Both the argument's author and the addressee(s) must be justified in accepting the premises, the premises must include all good relevant information obtainable by either the author or addressee, the conclusion must follow in virtue of a general warrant which both author and addressee(s) are justified in using, and if the warrant is not universal both author and addressee(s) must be justified in assuming that in the particular case there are no exceptional circumstances (rebuttals) which rule out the application of the warrant.

  Example: "This patient has Group A streptococcal pharyngitis, so she should take penicillin for 10 days. She informed me that she is not allergic to penicillin." The *premise* that the patient has Group A streptococcal pharyngitis, is assumed to be justified by laboratory test of a throat culture. Given what is already stated in the premises, no further practically obtainable information is relevant to the conclusion. The *warrant* is that penicillin is the drug of choice for the treatment of group A streptococcal pharyngitis (GAS), except in individuals with a history of penicillin allergy; this warrant is justified by the best available evidence as of June 2003. The statement of the patient is taken to justify the belief that there is no contraindication in this case to treatment by penicillin.

Cognition:
- Human faculty of processing information, creating, changing, and applying knowledge and preferences.
- Mental functions and processes (thought, comprehension, inference, decision-making, planning and learning, abstraction, generalization, concretization, specialization, meta-reasoning, beliefs, desires, knowledge, preferences, intentions of individuals, objects, agents, and systems)[15,16 modified] in view of the development of knowledge and concepts culminating in both thought and action.

Cognitive error (bias): Pattern of deviation in judgment that occurs in particular (in our context) in medical and clinical situations or in medical research reasoning and conclusions.

Cognitive science: An amalgamation of disciplines including artificial intelligence, neuroscience, philosophy, and psychology. Within cognitive science, cognitive psychology is an umbrella discipline for those interested in cognitive activities such as perception, learning, memory, language, concept formation, problem solving, and thinking.[17]

Cohort study: A study of two or more groups (cohorts) of individuals over a defined period of time allowing the description of a health event over time, the establishment of a causal association between exposure to a factor of interest and the occurrence of disease, its good or bad outcomes over time, or its prevention.

Colophon (in medical and other publishing): A brief statement at the end of a printed message containing the information about the publication of the book (or other printed matter), the place of publication, the publisher, and the date of publication. It may be also presented at the verso of the title-leaf or at the back-cover of the book.

Common knowledge: A shared knowledge between individuals.

Common sense: Both sensation and certain intuitively known general truths or principles that together yield knowledge of external objects. In the layperson's mind, common sense means logic. It does not! It is a mental faculty which all people are supposed to possess 'in common' for knowledge of basic everyday truths.

Communication in medicine:
- The imparting or interchanging of thoughts, opinions, or information about a health problem through speech, writing, or signs. It is a process by which information is exchanged between health professionals, patients, and other stakeholders in health through a common system of symbols, signs, or behavior.
- Transactional process in which messages are filtered through the perceptions, emotions, and experiences of those involved. Interpersonal communication remains the linchpin of medical practice.

Communicology: The science of human communication between individuals and communities (groups). It is based on the critical study of discourse and uses the logic-based research methods of semiotics and phenomenology to explain human consciousness and practice in the context of other people and their environment. Communicology is currently developing in medicine, psychiatry, and nursing.

Community: A group of patients bearing particular characteristics (demographic, hospitals setting where they are treated, requiring similar clinical care), including sometimes all other individuals from the same environment such as residents of an area, a socio-economic and/or ethnic group or a group of faith. It is important that a community in clinical research, practice, and research, always be well defined.

Community medicine: Practice of medicine at the community (beyond individual) level and setting, having as a purpose to identify health problems and needs, and the means by which these needs may be met, and to evaluate the extent to which health services meet these needs.[13 modified]

Co-morbidity: A clinical condition (disease, state requiring additional care) existing simultaneously and most often independently with another condition, that is the main subject of ongoing attention and care, and that alters and/or expands current understanding and care decisions regarding a patient.

Competent layperson: A non-expert who has generic intellectual abilities to delve into areas of specialization. In medicine, a patient who is able, due to his or her intellectual abilities, experience and judgment broader than the medical field, to assist the physician by proper questions and other information to direct even better clinical decisions in his or her case.

Complementary medicine: A heterogeneous ensemble of often poorly defined traditional, popular, or new health trends parallel to mainstream medicine. It includes proven and mostly unproven clinical maneuvers to add to accepted mainstream medical practices.

Complete information (condition of): The premises include all practically obtainable good information relevant to the question.

Complication: A disease or injury resulting from another disease, health state and/or healthcare intervention related to them.[2 modified]

Composite definitions (in health sciences): Definitions stemming from more than one entity meaning often different things from one understanding to another and different uses.

Concept map: A visualized time-space drawing of interrelationships of causes, consequences, interventions, outcomes, and other person/time/space characteristics of both patients and their caregivers.

Conclusion (in argumentation): The ending-point of reasoning or argument, that which is drawn from the premise or premises. For examples, see entries for *Argument* and *Reasoning*.

Conclusion (of any medical information): An ending section of the oral or written message which states the ideas and concepts based on a given experience. It follows the body of the message and may be also followed by an additional information and statement such as an epilogue (often a synonym of a conclusion), postscript, appendix, addendum, glossary, bibliography, index, errata, or a colophon.

Conclusion indicator: A word or phrase which indicates that an immediately following phrase, clause, or sentence is the conclusion of an argument or piece of reasoning.
Examples: Therefore, thus, so, hence, shows that, accordingly, it can be concluded that.
Warning: Most of these words and phrases can also be used to indicate other roles of the immediately following phrase, clause, or sentence—especially the role of being an effect. Attention to context is needed to determine whether a word or phrase is actually functioning to indicate a conclusion.

Connectives (connectors): Expressions (words) connecting various parts of statements.
Examples: if, or, and, only if

Connotation (Syn. *"intension," "comprehension," "sense"*):
■ One of two dimensions of meaning.
■ A single set of characteristics which a person grasps who understands what a term means. See *Denotation*.

Consult: Conferring with another physician about a case.

Contributing factor:
■ Any factor that increases the risk of error besides the factors considered to be a principal cause. (N.B. Nowhere did we find a clear distinction between what is a principal cause and a contributing factor.)
■ An external, organizational, staff and/or patient-related circumstance, action, or influence thought to have played a part in the origin or development of an incident or to have increased the risk of an incident.[18]

Contributing factor (in lathology):
■ Any factor that increases the risk of error besides the factors considered to be a principal cause. (N.B. Nowhere did we find a clear distinction between what is a principal cause and a contributing factor.)
■ An external, organizational, staff and/or patient-related circumstance, action, or influence thought to have played a part in the origin or development of an incident or to have increased the risk of an incident.[18]

Copula: A connector between subject and predicate terms. It binds together subject (S) and predicate (P) terms, most often by some form of the verb 'to be' (with 'not' in negative propositions). *Example*: This psychiatric patient (S) is suicidal (P).

Correct reasoning: See *Good reasoning.*

Craft (in general): A practical and utilitarian art, trade, or occupation requiring special manual skill and dexterity.

Craft (medical): Not only medical sensorimotor skills, but also history taking, physical examination, case presentation, communication, learning skills, nonverbal communication, and specialty evaluations represent the craft of medicine.

Critical appraisal:

■ More generally, the systematic evaluation of a process, service, research design, and so on, consisting of the detailed scrutiny and logical analysis of all phases of the process with the aim of ensuring that it conforms to acceptable standards, or, if it does not, identifying the shortcomings of the service, process, research design, and procedures.[58]

■ More specifically, critical appraisal is the application of rules of evidence to a study to assess the validity of the data, completeness of reporting, methods and procedures, conclusions, and compliance with ethical standards, and so on. The rules of evidence vary with the circumstances.[13]

Critical incident: An incident leading to, or resulting in, serious harm (loss of life, limb, or vital organ) to the patient, or the significant risk thereof, requiring an immediate investigation and response and subsequent actions to reduce the likelihood of recurrence.[2 modified]

Critical thinking:

■ Reasonable reflective thinking that is focused on deciding what to do or believe.[20]

■ The intellectually disciplined process of actively and skillfully conceptualizing, applying, synthetizing, and/or evaluating information gathered from, or generated by observation, experience, reflection, reasoning, or communication as a guide to belief and action.[19]

■ A 'purposeful, self-regulatory judgment' which results in interpretation, analysis, evaluation, and inference, as well as in the explanation of the evidential, conceptual, methodological, criteriological, or contextual considerations upon which that judgment is based.

■ Reasonable reflective thinking that is focused on deciding what to do or believe.[20] By contrast, dogmatic or unreflective thinking.

■ Thinking correctly for oneself that successfully leads to the most reliable answers to questions and solutions to problems.[59]

Critical thinking has several components, whose sequencing varies with the situation. (1) *Identify* and if necessary *analyze* the problem. (2) *Clarify* meaning. (3) *Gather* evidence. (4) *Assess* evidence. (5) *Infer* conclusions. (6) *Consider* other relevant information. (7) *Judge* how to solve the problem.

Critical thinking requires both abilities and dispositions, the latter combining attitudes and inclinations.

Cross-sectional study: A single observation of a single set or multiple sets, or ensembles of populations, focusing most often at health phenomena *prevalence* and its characteristics distributed by persons, place, and time.

Data:

■ Facts or figures from which conclusions may be drawn.

■ Rough quantitative (measured and quantified) and qualitative 'first line' observations, which enter the reasoning process.

Example: Blood pressure of 120/80 mm Hg, blood sugar, or any cell count. See *Information.*

Decision analysis:

■ A systematic approach to decision-making under conditions of uncertainty.

■ A derivative of operations research and game theory to identify all available choices, and potential outcomes of each, in a series of decisions that have to be made (e.g., about aspects of patient care such as diagnostic procedures, preventive and therapeutic regimens, and prognosis). Epidemiological data play a large part in determining the probabilities of outcomes following each potential choice.

Decision analysis (in medicine): A method to find the best solution among available multiple options (choices, actions, outcomes, and their values) derived from operations research and game theory. Risks, diagnoses, treatments, disease outcomes, burdens, and costs may represent components of decision analysis.

Decision-making in medicine:

■ A process of reasoning and judgment in the path from recognition of the health problem to be solved to its formulation, generation of alternatives, information and evidence search, selection, and action.

■ The process of selecting what to do in preventive and curative care from among various options already understood, while also taking into account the problem as a whole.

Decision theory in medicine: A set of quantitative methods for reaching optimal decisions in medical and healthcare.

Decision tree (in decision analysis): A space-time organized structure (flowchart) of clinical options, decisions, actions, their outcomes, probabilities, and values used to assess the choice of the best possible clinical care and public health actions which are most beneficial for the patient and other involved parties. As opposed to an algorithm, a decision tree is a *direction searching* tool.

Decision tree (in medicine): A graphical representation of various options in health and disease evolution and management. Their analysis leads to the best option (most beneficial, most effective, etc.) between multiple choices. Hence, a decision tree is not direction-giving; algorithms are (see above). It is device that is used to seek direction.

Deduction: A form of reasoning in which one reaches a conclusion by a deductively valid inference. It often proceeds from the general to the particular.

Deduction (in epidemiology): Intellectual process from an *a priori* formulated hypothesis leading to data collection, analysis, and hypothesis confirmation or rebuttal, leading to, and depending on, the result of the study. Hypothesis precedes its ground. Deduction is used to accept or refute generalizations through observations (data).

Deductive reasoning: A type of reasoning in which the conclusion (findings) is *definitely true* if the premises presented are true.

Deductive research: A type of research in which a general principle or hypothesis is used as a starting point for data collection, analysis, and interpretation in order to confirm or refute a pre-established hypothesis. Deductive research often leads to deductive reasoning in which the conclusion (findings) is definitely true if premises are true. Deductive research provides (at least theoretically) *absolute support* for study findings and their conclusions.

Deductively valid inference: An inference in which it is impossible for the premises to be true and the conclusion false, because of their meaning. Typically one premise will be an unqualified warrant.

Example: My patient has a streptococcal infection. Patients with streptococcal infections must be treated with antibiotics. Therefore, my patient must be treated with antibiotics.

Defeasible warrant (in argumentation): A warrant with a modal qualifier other than 'necessarily', which can be defeated by a rebuttal, an exceptional circumstance in which the conclusion is false.

Example: In general, an antibiotic may be prescribed for treatment of a bacterial infection. But not if the patient is allergic to it.

Definitions: Formal statements of the conceptual content, meaning, and significance of entities (expressions) of interest (domains, individuals and communities, subjects of interest, interacting variables and their relationships, tools, conditions, target populations, settings, and what is or has to be done, etc.).

Delphi method:
- A method for reaching a consensus about a given clinical or other problem based on the progressive repetitive exclusion of the least important opinions from an array of choices to solve the problem.
- An iterative circulation of the problem discussion by a panel of expert health professionals (ideally mutually anonymous) during which questions and responses are refined in light of responses to each preceding round of questions. The number of viable options and solutions is reduced to ultimately arrive at a consensus judgment preventing any participant from dominating the process.

Delusion: A false belief, which cannot be corrected by reason. It is logically unfounded and cannot be corrected by argument or persuasion or even by the evidence of the patient's own senses.

Denotation: Synonym for "extension" or "reference." One of two dimensions of meaning. The denotation of a term means the individual objects to which the term applies. See *Connotation*.

Diagram (circle diagram): An outline figure using circles intended to represent sets. The relative arrangement or marking of the circles indicates relationships (overlap, proper inclusion, or non-overlap) between the sets. See *Venn diagrams* and *Euler diagrams*.

Differential diagnosis: Making choices between various diagnostic options that might apply to the same patient or clinical situation.

Discourse: A continuous stretch of language containing more than one sentence: conversations, narratives, arguments, or speeches.

Discussion (section in medical articles): A section of a medical research paper in which the author(s) explain the nature, meaning, strengths, weaknesses, possible remedies for errors, and directions for the future, pertaining to the raw findings as reported in the "results" section which precedes the discussion.

Disease gradient: A directional expression of different grades of disease according to the severity of disease manifestations and outcomes.

Disease prevention: Policies and actions to eliminate a disease or minimize its effect.

Disease spectrum: The range of different systematic manifestations of the disease.

Disposition:
- A right state of mind and inclination regarding something.
- The natural or prevailing aspect of one's mind as manifested in behavior and relationships with patients and peers.
- A disposition is an acquired state, a habit, a preparation, a state of readiness, or a tendency to act in a specific way.

Dispositional reasoning (in fuzzy logic): Reasoning based on propositions which are fuzzy and hence not always true.

Example: Heavy alcohol drinking is a *leading cause* of liver cirrhosis.

Distilled clinical judgment (in clinical epidemiology): A judgment which encompasses and integrates knowledge of facts, evidence, experience, intuition, common sense, and gut feeling in medical problem understanding, solving, and related decision-making.

Doing nothing: One of the conclusions available in decision-making processes which must be equally justified by all available factual and evidence-based means as a decision to do something, like operate or not, prescribe or not, admit a patient or not, and so on.

Effectiveness: Beneficial and other results under "ordinary," prevailing, or customary conditions and for "ordinary," prevailing, or customary patients. An answer to the *"Does it work?"* question.

Effectiveness/efficiency/efficacy triad: An evaluation of the impact of medical, clinical, or community interventions (error and harm control included) in habitual conditions (*effectiveness*), in ideal conditions (*efficacy*), and in relation to the cost (material and human means) invested in health interventions (*efficiency*).[14]

Efficacy: In health economics, a beneficial result under ideal conditions. An answer to the *"Can it work?"* question.

Efficiency: Effects of the end results in proportion to the effort (human and material resources, time) invested in the healthcare activity. An answer to the *"What does it cost for what it gives?"* question.

Empathy:

■ The ability to understand and share the feelings of another individual.

■ The capacity to understand or feel what another person is experiencing from the other person's frame of reference, that is, the capacity to place oneself in another's position. Types of empathy include cognitive empathy, emotional empathy, and somatic empathy.[Wikipedia]

Enthymeme:

■ The simplest form of argument consisting of one reason (statement, proposition, and premise) leading to (connected to) a claim (argument conclusion, recommendation, and orders).

■ Reasoning or argument which is not deductively valid but which can be made deductively valid by adding one or more premises. Typically the added premise will be a warrant which licenses the original inference.

Example: The sphygmomanometer shows a reading of 200/120 mm Hg, so the patient has high blood pressure. This piece of reasoning would become deductively valid if one added as a premise the warrant: Anyone with a sphygmomanometer reading of 200/120 mm Hg has high blood pressure.

Epidemiological forecasting: Estimation of what may happen in the future of a health phenomenon that relies on the extrapolation of existing trends.

Epidemiology:

■ The study of the occurrence and distribution of health-related states or events in specified populations, including the study of determinants influencing such states (causes), the ensuing decisions and the impact of such intervention decisions on individuals, groups of individuals, communities, diseases of interest, their treatment, and the health of those under scrutiny. The direction of reasoning in epidemiology is from multiple observations of individuals to the applications to communities and the health problem as a whole.

■ Epidemiology may be subdivided into clinical epidemiology, field epidemiology, and fundamental epidemiology. (See separate entries for these terms.)

Epistemology: The theory of knowledge.

Equity: In health economics, the fairness and impartiality of healthcare activities like access to healthcare as a possible cause or effect of a healthcare activity. Equity seeks to answer the *"How well are costs and benefits distributed?"* question.

Error (human):

- The failure to complete a planned action as it was intended, or when an incorrect plan is used in an attempt to achieve a given aim.[2]
- All those occasions in which a planned sequence of mental and physical activities fails to achieve an intended outcome, and when these failures cannot be attributed to the intervention of some chance agency.[36]
- Failures committed either by an individual or a team of individuals.

Error (in general):

- An act of commission (doing something wrong) or omission (failing to do the right thing) that leads to an undesirable outcome or significant potential for such an outcome.
- An act that through ignorance, deficiency, or accident, departs from or fails to, achieve what should be done.

Error (medical): An inaccurate or incomplete assessment of a patient's risks and diagnosis, conservative or radical treatment, prognosis, follow-up and care, including disease, injury, syndrome, behavior, infection, and other subjects of care. It usually reflects a deficiency in the system of care.

Error chain: Sequence of latent and active errors and other events leading to a harming outcome. Root case analysis helps in the understanding of an error chain.

Error creators: Latent error-generating individuals at the "blunt end." These may include new medical technologies engineers, developers of clinical guidelines and work protocols, and organizers of clinical care.

Error outcomes: Incidents, accidents, and their physical, mental, and social consequences for the patient, health professional, and community. They may be negative (that is, causing harm) or, less frequently, positive (changing health for the better).

Essay (in general): A piece of writing based on an author's personal point of view, presenting his or her perspective based on a presumed or accepted reality.

Etiological fraction (in epidemiology): The proportion of events in exposed subjects which is due to the factor of interest from the web of potential causes of the health problem under study. See also *Attributable risk percent.*

Euler diagram: A diagram which represents the relation between sets by the spatial relationship of circles representing the sets. Two partially intersecting circles represent partial overlap between the sets; for example, a partial intersection of circles for melancholia and delusional depression indicates that some people have both conditions, that some have melancholia but not delusional depression, and that some have delusional depression but not melancholia. One circle completely inside another indicates that the set represented by the first circle is a proper subset of the set represented by the second one. For example, a circle for persons with AIDS inside a circle for persons infected by HIV indicates that all persons with AIDS have been infected by HIV, but not all persons infected by HIV have AIDS at a given moment. Sometimes the extent of overlap or inclusion indicates proportional relationships. For example, a diagram with 60% of the delusional depression circle inside the melancholia circle indicates that 60% of people with delusional depression have melancholia.

Evaluation (in medical lathology):

■ A process that attempts to determine as systematically and objectively as possible the relevance, effectiveness and other characteristics of activities, programs, and policies to prevent and control medical error and its consequences as well as the impact of such activities, programs, and policies in light of their objectives.[13 modified]

■ The systematic assessment of the activity (medical or other) and/or the outcomes of such an activity, program, or policy, compared to a set of implicit or explicit standards as a means of contributing to the improvement of the activity.

Event (in lathology):

■ In this context (as in the case of "error" in lathology), anything that leads to injury of the patient or poses a risk of harm.[6]

Event (medical):

■ Something that happens to, or with, a patient and/or a health professional, or any other person involved in healthcare.

Evidence (in general): Any piece of information or data needed, required, and used either to understand a problem or to make a decision about it.

Evidence (in law):

■ Any species of proof or probative matter legally presented for the purpose of inducing belief in the minds of court or jury as to their content.

■ An assertion of fact, opinion, belief, or knowledge, whether material or not and whether admissible or not. It includes judgments, decisions, opinion, speeches, and all other matters done and said before the court, including matters relating to the procedure. This definition is much broader than the definition of evidence in medicine and philosophy by including as "evidence" procedural matters at courts.

Evidence (in law, in relation to medicine): Any type of proof of facts in court:

■ *real evidence* (defective medical instruments);

■ *direct evidence* (photographs, prescriptions, patient records, oral testimonies);

■ *circumstantial evidence* (circumstances in which the medical error occurred);

■ *hearsay* (third party information quoted by the health professional);

■ *confession* by the defendant;

■ *dying declarations* (made prior to death by a patient);

■ *other statements that prove to be relevant at the hearing* (records of some routine observations);

■ *declarations against interest* (information showing the motive of a health professional's actions);

■ *connected events proving design or intent* (repeated past events contradicting an isolated happening); and

■ *evidence as to the character of the defendant* (health professional or patient).

The admissibility of various types of evidence is decided by the court. The term 'evidence' in this context has a broader meaning than in medicine.[22]

Evidence (in medicine): Any data or information, whether solid or weak, obtained through experience, observational research, or experimental work (trials) to understand and/or solve a health phenomenon. This data or information must be relevant and convincing to some (best possible) degree to enable understanding of the problem (case) or the diagnostic, therapeutic, or otherwise care oriented clinical decisions made about the case. 'Evidence' is not automatically correct, complete, satisfactory, and useful. It must first be evaluated, graded, and used based on its own merit.

Examples: Clinical case observations as proof of effectiveness of treatment (weak evidence) or randomized double-blind controlled clinical trials (strong evidence that the treatment works, that is, that there is a cause-effect relationship between treatment and cure). Other types of evidence may concern disease history and course, disease occurrence, its causes, prognosis, and other topics of interest in health sciences.

Evidence-based community medicine, healthcare, and public health:

■ The application of best available evidence in setting public health policies and priorities.

■ The process of systematically finding, appraising, and using contemporaneous clinical and community research findings and other experience as the basis for decisions about the care of communities in the domain of health protection, disease prevention, and health maintenance and improvement (health promotion).

Evidence-based error: Using poor or inappropriate evidence in argumentation and decision-making in clinical practice and research.

Evidence-based medicine:

■ *Original definition*: The process of systematically finding, appraising, and using contemporaneous research findings as the basis of clinical decisions.

■ *Current definition*: Practice of medicine based on the integration of best research evidence with clinical expertise and patient values. Comment: It is an application of critical thinking in medical practice.

Its components are (1) Formulation of the question concerning the patient which has to be answered (*identifying need for evidence*); (2) Search for the evidence (*producing the evidence*); (3) Appraisal of evidence (*evaluating the evidence*); (4) Selection of the best evidence available for clinical decision-making (*using the evidence*); (5) Linking evidence with clinical knowledge, experience and practice and with the patient's values and preferences (*integrated uses of evidence*); (6) Using evidence in clinical care to solve the patient's problem (*uses of evidence in specific settings*); (7) Evaluation of the effectiveness of the uses of evidence in this case (*weighing the impact*); (8) Teaching and expanding EBM practice and research (*going beyond what was already achieved*).

Evidence-based public health (community medicine): Three definitions currently prevail:

■ The process of systematically finding, appraising, and using contemporaneous clinical and community research findings as the basis for decisions in public health.

■ The conscientious, explicit, and judicious use of current best evidence in making decisions about the care of communities and populations in the areas of health protection, disease prevention, and health maintenance and improvement (health promotion).

■ The integration of best research evidence with public health (community medicine) expertise and community (population) values.

Exclusion criteria: Present (diagnosis, etc.) and future (prognosis, etc.) characteristics of persons, work methods, and techniques which make them ineligible as health phenomena of interest for practice or research.

Expertise: Special skills and knowledge acquired by a person (a health professional in the context) through education, training and experience.

Extern (medical):

■ A medical student or graduate in medicine who assists in patient care in the hospital but does not reside there.

■ Undergraduate medical student (in the third or fourth year of medical school (in North America)), who attends ward rounds of a teaching hospital, ands learns clinical medicine by example and quasi-active participation in patient management.

Definition may vary from one health system to another.

Factoid: An apparent fact that is not a fact.

Failure (in lathology): Non-performance or inability of the system or component (human included) to perform an intended function in a specific person/time/place/context and specific conditions to reach an intended objective. Therefore, not all faults are failures.

Failure mode (in lathology):

■ Any manifestation of error such as a precocious change in care, stopping, or replacing ongoing care, or a reporting decision in this sense.

■ Any error or defect in a process, design, or item, especially those that affect the customer (the patient in our case), and that can be potential or actual.[25]

■ The characteristic manner in which a failure occurs. Within a failure mode diagnostic model, failure modes represent specific ways in which a system, device, or process can fail.[26]

■ The physical or functional manifestation of a failure. For example, a system in failure mode may be characterized by a slow operation, change of operation, addition of a new operation, incorrect outputs, or incomplete (or precociously completed) termination of execution. Any surgical, obstetrical, or gynecologic operation fits the activity as quoted above.[27 modified]

Failure mode and effect analysis (FMEA) in lathology:

■ A procedure for analysis of potential failure modes, that is, descriptions of the way the failure occurs and the manner by which a failure is observed.[28]

■ A step-by-step approach for reviewing and identifying all possible failures in organizational process, policies, and procedures, design, manufacturing, or assembly process, or product or service.[29]

Failure mode and effect analysis applies also clinical and community medicine activities and practices.

Fallacy (in general):

■ A mistake or flaw in reasoning, argument or argumentation. In the broadest of terms, it is a violation of the norms of good reasoning, rules of critical discussion, dispute resolution, and adequate communication.

Medical example: In diagnostic reasoning, ignoring possible diagnoses consistent with the patient's observed symptoms. For example, ignoring the possibility of more than one fracture consistent with swelling in the wrist, the patient's report of soreness after a recent fall, and an X-ray in which only one fracture is visible.

Fallacy (in medicine): Any error in reasoning pertaining to a health problem and its supporting evidence(s) and pertaining to the handling of evidence in our reasoning, and throughout the process of argumentation interfering with the best possible understanding and decision-making in the task of health problem solving.[24]

Fallacy in medical communication: Error in reasoning and/or decision-making by a health professional, or produced through a health professional's communication with another health interested party, or in the interaction with another party in the understanding and/or solving of a health problem.

Falsity: The opposite of truth. The property of a statement (belief, proposition) of asserting what is not really the case.

Field epidemiology:

- Using experience gathered from individuals when dealing with health and disease at the community level.[14]
- The practice of epidemiology in the community, commonly in a public health service. Sometimes termed 'shoe-leather epidemiology' given its "on foot, door-to-door" practice of inquiry and services delivery.
- Using experience gathered from individuals when dealing with health and disease at the community level by ways of epidemiological surveillance, disease outbreak investigations, etc.

Flaw (in lathology): Any characteristic, deficiency, or inadequacy in technology, operation, human reasoning, and decision-making contrary to expectations from the expected function, task, and outcomes of a healthcare event. This term denotes any variable that may be considered a possible (often yet to be proven) causal factor or marker related to domains of risk and prognosis in the domain of medical error and its consequences.

Flowchart in health sciences: A graphical representation of the progress of a system for the definition, analysis, and solution of healthcare problem. Algorithms and decision trees are both flowcharts.

Force of morbidity: See *Incidence density.*

Forcing function: An aspect of the design of a clinical tool or procedure that prevents a potentially harming target action from being performed or that allows its performance only if another specific action is performed first.
Examples: Security caps on medications, and authorization and supervision of medical care actions.

Formal logic: A branch of logic which builds a formalized system of reasoning, using abstract symbols for the various aspects of natural language.

Fraction (relative frequency): Two related numerical entities (frequencies) as expressions between them. Rates, ratios, or odds are fractions.

Frequency (absolute frequency): A simple number of events or entities of interest.

Fundamental epidemiology: The development and testing of basic manners of reasoning and decision-making in epidemiology through various domains such as philosophy, epistemology, logic and critical thinking, quantitative methods (biostatistics), and/or qualitative research in dealing with health and disease at the group of individuals and community levels.

Fuzziness: Data which is imprecise or has uncertain boundaries.

Fuzzy: An adjective identifying any phenomenon without clear and well-specified borders and distinctions between its presence and absence.

Fuzzy decision-making: Decision-making based on fuzzy premises.

Fuzzy logic: A kind of formal logic based on fuzzy set theory.

Fuzzy predicates, probabilities, or quantifiers: Semi-quantitative identifiers of a degree in fuzzy set theory. *Example:* "Moderately" elevated blood pressure, "advanced" atherosclerosis.

Fuzzy set theory: A kind of set theory which replaces the two-valued set-membership function with a real-valued function; that is, membership is treated as a probability, or as a degree of truthfulness. Likewise one assigns a real value to assertions as an indication of their degree of truthfulness; 0 is definitely false, 1 definitely true, 0.6666 (repeating) is two-thirds true. The theory reflects the view that phenomena around us are not necessarily dichotomous and that many things are a matter of degree. *Example:* Blood pressure is a matter of degree rather than being either normotensive or hypertensive.

Fuzzy syllogism: A syllogism based on one or more fuzzy premises. Its conclusion will necessarily be fuzzy.

Fuzzy theory (logic): A paradigm of perceiving phenomena without precise borders; everything is a matter of degree like obesity, being conscious, being dehydrated, and such situations where bivalent thinking (it is/it is not) corresponds to the multivalent reality of the phenomena under consideration.

Gestalt: A German term meaning "pattern" or "configuration." See *Pattern recognition.*

Good argument:

- An argument which serves its function well. If the function of the argument is to justify the conclusion to one or more addressees, then
    - both the argument's author and the addressee(s) must be justified in accepting the premises;
    - the premises must include all good relevant information obtainable by either;
    - the conclusion must follow in virtue of a general warrant which both author and addressee(s) are justified in using; and
    - if the warrant is not universal, both author and addressee(s) must be justified in assuming that in the particular case, there are no exceptional circumstances (rebuttals) which rule out application of the warrant. If an expert in some field addresses an argument to a non-expert (for example, physician to patient, automobile mechanic to customer), then the non-expert's justification may be acceptance of the authority of the expert. See *Cogent argument.*

Good argumentation: Argumentation which serves its function well. If the function is to resolve rationally a conflict of opinion, then argumentation must be addressed to the issue in dispute and any argument advanced must justify its conclusion to all parties in the discussion.

Good reasoning:

- Reasoning which justifies the conclusion to the reasoner. The reasoner must be justified in accepting the premises; that is, they must be evidence-based. This means that the:
    - the premises must include all good practically obtainable relevant information;
    - the conclusion must follow in virtue of a justified general warrant; and
    - if the warrant is not universal, the reasoner must be justified in assuming that in the particular case there are no exceptional circumstances (rebuttals) that rule out application of the warrant.

Example: This patient has a pulsating abdominal mass, so she may have an aneurysm of her abdominal aorta. It is assumed that the reasoner has felt the pulsating abdominal mass, thus justifying the premise by direct observation, and that no other practically obtainable information is relevant to the conclusion that the patient *may* have an aneurysm of her abdominal aorta. The warrant is that a pulsating abdominal mass may indicate an aneurysm of the abdominal aorta. Since the warrant is qualified by the word 'may', the conclusion is quite weak and there are no rebuttals. Further investigation is needed to arrive at a definite diagnosis.

Gradient of disease: See *Disease gradient*.

Grading of evidence: Evaluating the degree of relevance of evidence for its uses, based on its quality, strength, absence of bias and relevance for systematic and summarized reviews, health technology assessment, and clinical practice guidelines.

Grounds:
- One of the six elements in the contemporary layout of arguments due to Toulmin: The basis from which we reason and argue.
- They are the specific facts relied on to support a given claim or conclusion.

Grounds (in modern argument):
- Specific facts, data and information from research and/or practice, as a basis for a claim.
- The basis from which we reason. In medicine, they are most often fundamental data, information from various sources, and/or our own findings.

Groupthink (originally a construct of social psychology): In a desire for harmony and conformity in the group results of dealing with a problem (clinical or other), minimizing conflict by reaching a consensus decision without critical evaluation of alternative viewpoints by actively suppressing dissenting viewpoints, and by insolating themselves (as a group) from outside influences. The health domain is not free of the groupthink phenomenon either.

Guidelines: See *Clinical guidelines*.

Gut feeling (in medicine): A sudden awareness of a clinical problem through thoughts that come to one's mind without apparently effort as something potentially serious, important, and worthy of solution. Based on the wealth of evidence, experience, and knowledge; it is not "blind."

Hard data: Any data which can be well defined in operational terms and/or measured. *Example:* Body weight, blood sugar, EKG reading. See *Soft data*.

Hardening of soft data (in clinical epidemiology): Defining in more operational terms and giving a certain dimension to clinical and paraclinical observations.

Harm (in general): Injury or damage to people, property, or environment.[30]

Harm (in lathology): Unintended physical injury resulting from, or contributed to, by medical care (including the absence of indicated medical treatment) that requires additional monitoring, treatment, or hospitalization, or that results in death. Such injury is considered medical harm whether or not it occurred within the hospital. Some errors do indeed result in medical harm, but many errors do not; conversely, many incidents of medical harm are not the result of any errors. See also *Medical harm (vide infra)*.

Harm (medical): A temporary or permanent physical impairment in body functions (including sensory functions, pain, disease, injury, disability, and death) and structures, as well as suffering and other deleterious effects due to a disruption of the patient's mental and social well-being.

Hazard (in health sciences):
- A set of circumstances or a situation that could harm a person's interests, such as their health or welfare.[2]
- In epidemiology, the inherent capability of an agent or a situation to have an adverse effect.[13]

- Risk is the probability of disease occurrence, in terms of incidence or mortality densities, whereas hazard refers to probability in the field of prognosis, usually as a function of mortality, although any outcome other than death can also apply.[14]
- An error capable of causing harm; a potential source of harm.[30]
- Any threat to safety, e.g., unsafe practices, conduct, equipment, labels, names.[6]

Hazard (in epidemiology): The inherent capability of an agent or a situation to have an adverse effect. *Risk* is the probability of disease occurrence, in terms of incidence or mortality densities, whereas *hazard* refers to probability in the field of prognosis, usually as a function of mortality, although any outcome other than death can also apply.

Hazard (in lathology): An error capable of causing harm; a potential source of harm. Any threat to safety, e.g., unsafe practices, conduct, equipment, labels, naming and names.

Hazard (in medicine, epidemiology, biostatistics, lathology):

- A biostatistical, broader term for probabilities studied in the domain of prognosis.
- A theoretical measure of the probability of occurrence of an event per unit time of risk.
- Elsewhere, a factor or exposure that may adversely affect health or disease. Used sometimes this way as a synonym of risk.

Health promotion: Policies and processes, mostly at the community level, that enable people to increase control over and improve their health. Communities' behaviors and their environment are generally highlighted.

Health protection: Steps taken to eliminate as much as possible the risk of adverse consequences for health attributable (most often) to environmental and other hazards.

Healthcare (health-care, health care):

- Services provided to individuals or communities to promote, maintain, monitor, or restore health, including self-care. Those services may be provided by physicians (medical care), all other health professionals (clinical care or community care), and/ or civic bodies (in public health) either in hospitals, clinics, medical/health offices, or communities at large. The term is sometimes extended to include health-related self-care.
- Services provided to individuals or communities by agents of the health services or professionals to promote, maintain, monitor, or restore health. Healthcare is not limited to medical care, which implies action by or under supervision of a physician. The term is sometimes extended to include health-related self-care.[13]

Hermeneutics:

- The practice or theory of interpretation. Once closely associated with the interpretation of the Bible, it is now used more generally as a methodology, art, or technique of understanding and interpretation.
- In medicine, taking a patient history may be seen as falling into the domain of hermeneutics.

Heuristics: Quick and dirty mental shortcuts to discovery, which sometimes err. A heuristic approach uses heuristics to simplify our thinking in arriving at the solution of a problem, reduce the complexity of the task, save time, memory, attention, and other requirements of problem solving. It can also be used in artificial intelligence to reduce the complexity of computational tasks. Such an approach is expected to save time, memory, attention, and other requirements for a given mental or computational process.

Making a diagnosis at the bedside or in a medical office is often a heuristic process (for example, reducing the number of diagnostic options in differential diagnosis). Making decisions in an emergency setting or clinical decision-making regarding what to do under the pressure of the conditions of the clinical workplace are often heuristic processes. So is computer-assisted diagnosis.

Hindsight: A way of reasoning and drawing conclusions about an event *after* it has happened.

Hindsight bias: The tendency to judge events leading up to an accident as errors because the bad outcome is known; the more severe the outcome, the more likely that decisions leading up to this outcome will be considered errors. Judging the antecedent decisions as errors implies that the outcome was preventable.[9]

Human error (in general): The failure to complete a planned action as it was intended, or when an incorrect plan is used in an attempt to achieve a given aim. All those occasions in which a planned sequence of mental and physical activities fails to achieve an intended outcome, and when these failures cannot be attributed to the intervention of some chance agency. Failures committed either by an individual or a team of individuals.

Human error (in medicine): An operator's error in reasoning, understanding, and decision-making about the solution of the health problem and/or in the ensuing sensory and physical execution of a task in clinical and/or community care, including its consequences.

Humanities (medical): An interdisciplinary field which includes humanities (literature, philosophy, ethics, history, and religion), social science (anthropology, cultural studies, psychology, and sociology) and the arts (literature, theatre, film and visual arts) and their application to medical education, research, and practice.

Hypothesis: A proposition to be confirmed or rejected by scientific inquiry.

Hypothesis(es) in medicine: Propositions to be evaluated, accepted or refuted in light of clinical or community medicine experience with the case or problem or by a research study.

Iatrogenic illness: The adverse effect of preventive, diagnostic, therapeutic, surgical, and other medical, sanitary and health procedure(s), interventions, or programs attributable as resulting from the activity of a health professional. It also includes other harmful occurrences that were not natural occurrences of the patient's disease. It does not automatically imply the culpability or responsibility of the physician or hospital, or that the illness was necessarily preventable.

IMRAD format: Presentation of medical information consisting of **I**ntroduction of the subject, **M**aterial and methods by which it is presented and analyzed, **R**esults and research findings, **a**nd **D**iscussion containing clarifications of the above.

Incidence: The frequency of *new* cases of disease or other health event occurring over a defined period of time and community. It is usually presented as a rate by adding an appropriate denominator.

Incidence density: An incidence rate that uses as a denominator, not only the number of individuals of interest, but also the duration of observation, follow-up, or exposure of each of those individuals one by one. An average of person-period of time is obtained which is also called *force of morbidity*. For example, 10 new cases of disease over a five-year period per 100,000 persons-years of risk is an expression of incidence density or force of morbidity. Used if periods of time of interest vary considerably from one individual to another.

Incident (in general): Event, process, practice, or outcome that is noteworthy by virtue of the hazards it creates for, or the harm it causes, subjects. All accidents are incidents, but not all incidents are accidents.[38,39 modified]

Incident (in medicine and lathology):

■ Event, process, practice or outcome that is noteworthy by virtue of the hazards it creates for, or the harm it causes, patients.[2]

■ An event or circumstance that could have resulted, or did result in unintended or unnecessary harm to a person and/or in a complaint, loss, or damage.[7]

■ Adverse events, critical incidents, sentinel events, and near misses in clinical and community care. See separate entries for these terms in this Glossary. Incident means any of them.[40]

Incident reporting: Identification of occurrences that could have led, or did lead, to an undesirable outcome.[9] Incident reporting is a part of the epidemiological surveillance of medical error and harm.

Inclusion criteria: Characteristics of a health phenomenon which designate them to be a part of an entity (diagnostic entity, eligibility for a trial, group of subjects of interest, etc.).

Induction (in epidemiology):

■ Any method of logical analysis that proceeds from particular to the general. Intellectual process in which hypotheses are generated, confirmed, or refuted on the basis of previously gathered data. Hypothesis follows its ground.

■ Generalization from observations.

Inductive generalization: A form of reasoning in which one concludes that all cases of a specified kind have a specified property on the basis of observation that all examined cases of that kind have the property. The strength of support for the conclusion, assuming that the examined cases have been correctly observed to have the property, depends on the qualification of the justified warrant that applies.

Example: The sphygmomanometer shows a reading of 135/90 mm Hg. So the patient's blood pressure is approximately 135/90 mm Hg. Here the generalization is from one instance to all instances over an unspecified time interval. The word 'approximately' is an appropriate qualification, since blood pressure fluctuates according to time of day, stress, exercise, and other factors. A series of readings under different conditions gives a better estimate of blood pressure than a single reading.

Inductive reasoning: In philosophy, research producing premises which bring only *some degree* of support to conclusions (findings from the study).

Inductive research: A type of research based on using existing information and data (whatever the purpose of their collection might be) to generate and/or confirm a hypothesis. A hypothesis is generated by pre-established fact(s), data, and information.

Inductive strength: The probability that the conclusion of an inference is true given that the premises are true. Often of qualitative or comparative nature rather than a quantitative one. The probability is relative to the information in the premises; it can change with additional relevant information.

Example: A patient in the emergency department reports that he fell recently, landing on his right hand, and that his wrist has been feeling sore. This provides somewhat strong support for the conclusion that there is a broken bone in the wrist. Examination of the wrist showing swelling and painfulness to the touch gives stronger support for this conclusion. An x-ray for a definitive diagnosis is indicated. See *Inductively strong inference*.

Inductively strong inference: An inference whose conclusion is probable (in the absence of further information) given that the premises are true. Typically, one premise will be a warrant with a modal qualifier like 'probably' or 'generally.'

Example: This patient's nodular melanoma is 5 mm thick (in depth). Patients with melanoma tumors more than 4 mm in depth have a high risk of developing melanoma elsewhere in the body. So probably, this patient will develop melanoma elsewhere in the body. Here the second premise is the warrant, which could also have been expressed as the statement, "Most patients with melanoma tumors more than 4 mm in depth develop melanoma elsewhere in the body."

Inference (causal): Most often, the thought process and methods that assess or test whether a relation of cause to effect does or does not exist.

Inference (in general):
- The process of logical reasoning that combines observed phenomena with accepted truths or axioms in order to formulate generalizable statements.
- The drawing of a conclusion from one or more premises. In reasoning, inference is a mental activity, which may or may not be verbalized, either to oneself or to others. In argument, inference is a linguistic activity expressed in speaking or writing.

Inference (statistical): Statistical inference applies a process of inference to series of observations and calculates degrees of uncertainty in comparisons of various data sets.

Inference indicators: Words in natural language which identify premises and conclusions in reasoning and arguments. See *Premise indicator* and *Conclusion indicator.*

Informal logic: A branch of logic which uses methods and techniques to identify, analyze, interpret, and evaluate reasoning and argument as it happens in the context of natural language used in everyday life. Contrary to formal, symbolic or "mathematical" logic, informal logic deals directly with reasoning and argument in natural (everyday) language. It is non-symbolic and non-mathematical. Contrary to formal logic, it is non-symbolic and non-mathematical.

Information:
- Knowledge acquired or derived.
- Some conclusion drawn from raw data as a "second line" subject to reason about.
  Example: Hypertension and diabetes are conclusions drawn from blood pressure or blood sugar observations respectively for the purposes of treatment and prognostic considerations.

Integrative medicine:
- Restoring and maintaining patient's health and wellness across his or her lifespan by understanding patient's unique set of circumstances and addressing in this way the full range of physical, emotional, social, spiritual, and environmental influences that affect health.
- An attempt to make a coherent ensemble from various trends in traditional, complementary, and alternative medicine.

Intern: A graduate of a medical school serving and usually rotating in a hospital in order to be eligible for a license to practice medicine. Depending on the health system, the intern may or may not reside at the hospital.

Intervening cause (in law): An action or event that alters the course of a chain of events leading to the injury or loss that is the subject of a tort case. If the intervening event was foreseeable, it does not relieve a person who set the chain of events in motion from liability.

Intervening efficient cause (in occupational health and law): A new and independent force which breaks (positively or negatively) the causal connection between the original wrong and injury and itself becomes the direct and immediate cause of injury.

Intuition: A product of a subconscious mind, searching through our experiences, and finding a good match for what we are facing.

Journal club: A periodic interactive meeting of learners (clinical clerks, interns, and residents) and elders (professional and academic staff) to critically review selected topics or arrays of topics of the day communicated by medical periodicals and other electronic media.

Judgment (clinical):

- The capacity to make and choose data and information to produce useful (true or false) claims in clinical practice and research.
- It also means critical thinking in the practice of medicine based on the 'patient/evidence/setting' fit.
- Together with elements of knowledge and experience, it relies on the process of integrating meanings and values of clinical and paraclinical observation and data into the making of conclusions and decisions derived from such integration.

Judgment (in general):

- The act or faculty of affirming or denying a proposition, whether based on a direct comparison of objects or ideas or derived by a process of reasoning.
- The mental process of making an assertion.
- Thinking of a proposition.
- The ability to make realistic appraisals of matters of facts.
- The evaluation of the nature and soundness of some information, giving it a value for subsequent decision-making.
- The act or faculty of affirming or denying a proposition, whether based upon a direct comparison of objects or ideas, or derived by a process of reasoning.
- The evaluation of the nature and soundness of some information, giving it a value for subsequent decision-making.

Knowledge (in general):

- Justified true belief.
- Alternatively, true belief which has been acquired by a generally reliable process.
- A part of the cognitive domain that encompasses both retention of data and information about the subject and the capacity to apply them to specific tasks.

Knowledge (in the context of knowledge translation):

- A fluid mix of framed experience, values, contextual information, evidence interpretation, and expert insight that provides a framework for decision-making, evaluating and incorporating new experiences and information. It may be explicit and tacit, and individual or collective. In organizations, it often becomes embedded not only in documents or repositories, but also in organizational routines, processes, practices, and norms.
- More generally, it is the range of one's information or understanding of facts or ideas acquired by study, investigation, observation, or experience.

Knowledge translation: A dynamic and iterative process that includes synthesis, dissemination, exchange, and ethically sound application of knowledge to improve the health of a defined community, provide more effective health services and products, and strengthen the healthcare system.

Knowledge translation implies a multidirectional, multilateral, and multiparty continuous communication between researchers, practicing physicians, other health professionals, patients, community, and policy makers, pharmaceutical and other technology producers, and stakeholders regarding the health of individuals and whole communities.

Lapse: Failures of memory that do not necessarily manifest themselves in actual behavior and may only be apparent to the person who experiences them.[36]

Lapse (in lathology): Failures of memory that do not necessarily manifest themselves in actual behavior and may only be apparent to the person who experiences them.

Lapse (in medicine): A memory-based error, a memory generated failure. For example: Forgetting a patient's allergy to an antibiotic.

Latent error (medical) or latent failure:

■ Error that results from underlying system failure(s).[4,5]

■ Less apparent failure(s) of organization or design that contributed to the occurrence of errors or allowed them to cause harm to patients. [9,36]

■ Any part in a chain of flawed more or less remote events that precede (and may lead to) the active error and harmful action.

■ A defect in design, organization, training, or maintenance in the system that leads to operator errors and whose effects are typically delayed.[6]

■ Latent error or failure may then be human, technical, external, and/or design-construction-material related.

Latent or remote event (cause, event, condition):

■ A factor that, in the past, might have contributed to a predisposition to the event, effect, or phenomenon such as error.[2 modified]

■ In lathology, a "***blunt end***" event (also see above).

Lathology: Our definition as *the study and management of error and harm* (medical error and harm in the context of this book). From the Greek "lathos," that is, error, and "logos," that is, study.

Layout of arguments: Graphical representation of components of arguments and their inter-relationships.

Learning curve: The description of the development and acquisition of a new surgical or medical skill in the search for moments, levels, or stages of reaching a potential for lower-than-expected success rates or higher-than-expected error, complication, and/or harm rates. Learning curve study and analysis is used increasingly in the evaluation of health professional training progress.

Likelihood: A state of being likely or probable or the probability that an event that has already occurred would yield a specific outcome. It differs from ***probability*** which refers to the occurrence of future events.

Likelihood ratio (in the domain of diagnosis): The probability that a given test result would occur in a person with the target disorder divided by the probability that the same result would occur in a person without that disorder.

Logic: The normative science which investigates the principles of valid reasoning and correct inference.

Logic in medicine: A system of thought and reasoning that governs understanding and decisions in clinical and community care, research, and communication. It defines valid reasoning, which helps us to understand the meaning of medical phenomena and leads us to the justification of the choice of clinical and paraclinical decisions on how to act upon such phenomena.

Logical operators: Words or phrases that indicate logical properties or relations. They include *qualifiers* ("some," "all," "no," "at least two"), *sentence connectives* ("and," "or," "if"), *indicators of identity* or *negotiations* ("equals," "not"), and *modal qualifiers* ("necessarily," "possibly").

Logical positivism: A position in philosophy, advocated by the Vienna Circle in the 1920s and 1930s. Its central doctrine was the verification principle, that a sentence is meaningful if and only if it is either "analytic" or empirically verifiable. The verification principle is self-refuting and has been discredited as anything more than a prejudice.

Major term (in categorical syllogisms): The predicate of the conclusion.

Malpractice: Improper or unskillful conduct on the part of a medical practitioner that results in injury to the patient. It generally describes professional misconduct or negligence on the part of a person delivering professional services.

Measurement (in clinimetrics): Processing of raw data, not only to give them (signs, symptoms, etc.) some dimension like severity, but also labelling them qualitatively through classification, group formation, and validation as syndromes and other diagnostic entities indicative of further specific attention and care.

Medical business report: A business report presenting a direct proposition to solve a business problem based on the record of past business information, which is useful for action and future business planning.

Medical care: See *Healthcare*.

Medical decision: The choice of the best option in assessing risk (explanatory decisions), in treating patients (managerial decisions), or in making prognosis (both explanatory and managerial, if treatment decisions are involved).

Medical decision-making: A process by which one arrives at a given medical decision, the latter being the result or endpoint of such a process.

Medical error:

- An individual and/or system failure resulting from human behavior made by a health professional (for example, operating surgeon, prescribing internist, consulting psychiatrist, nurse at floors, or surgical or office setting) who, in a health establishment or community setting provides direct clinical or community care, acts, or services. It may be knowledge-based, rule-based, or skill (execution)-based.
- Unintentionally being wrong in conduct or judgment in medical care.
- Human or system error (as defined already in this book) in healthcare and community medicine and medicine-related public health.
- Unintentionally being wrong in conduct or judgment in medical care.[7 modified]
- Medical error leads often (but not always) to medical harm; these two entities, however, must not be confused. In other words, medical error is reasoning and decision-making-based. It is an inaccurate or incomplete assessment and management of a patient's risks and diagnosis, or choosing and executing radical or conservative treatment, or making prognosis and extending and widening patient and community care. Such faults fall into the category of fallacies, biases, and cognitive errors.

Medical ethics:

- Rules of conduct for a health professional to distinguish between right and wrong. They serve as moral basis in medical, nursing and other care, research, and administration.
- Study of values of health, disease, and care and the morality of physicians' actions, behavior, and conduct.

Medical harm: A temporary or permanent physical impairment in body functions (including sensory functions, mental functioning, social and occupational functioning, pain, disease, injury, disability, or death) and structures as well as suffering which disrupt a patient's physical, mental and/or social well-being.

Some errors result in medical harm, but many errors do not. Conversely, many incidents of medical harm are not the results of any errors. Reasoning, deciding, or acting poorly lead to medical errors and harm.

Medical humanities: See *Humanities (medical).*

Medical logic: See *Logic in medicine.*

Medical philosophy: Any informal reflection on the practice of medicine—usually by physicians on clinical medicine, based in their reflections on their own clinical experiences.

Medical propedeutics: A preliminary instruction, introductory course, or preparatory teaching preceding and pertaining to clinical training and care. See *Propedeutics (medical)* for the preferred term.

Medical research article: An article presenting an objective view of a health problem, studied and solved to some degree and extent by an inquiry based on the scientific method and most often presented in a corresponding format (IMRAD).

Medication error:

■ Human error as defined in the process of providing medications to patients.[2] It may be due to an omission, an incorrect dose, a failure to order a particular procedure, an incorrect form, an incorrect time, an incorrect route, a deteriorated drug, an incorrect rate of administration, an incorrect administration technique, or an incorrect dose preparation related to the dispensing a pharmacological agent (drug).[42 modified]

■ Any preventable event that may cause or lead to inappropriate medication use or patient harm when the medication is in the control of the health professional, patient, or consumer.[43]

Medicine:

■ The art and science of diagnosis, treatment, and prevention of disease, and the maintenance of good health. This definition applies both to the care of individual patients and to the care of individual patients and the care of the community.

■ The profession and calling concerned with the care of the sick, including care by skilled professional staff, lay healers, and family members. Medicine is a wide-ranging field of human activity, not confined to the profession that requires a university education.

Mensuration (in clinimetrics): Production of raw individual data from medical history, physical examination, paraclinical explorations, and other primary sources of information (like simple observation and others).

Meta-analysis in medicine: A mostly statistical integration of original research studies focusing on a similar problem and question, leading to a largely quantitative summary of pooled results. Looking across studies in this way helps us to better understand whether health interventions work or if other causal relationships exist beyond an original study. It is a quantitative component of research synthesis; systematic review is its qualitative one. See *Systematic review.*

Meta-cognition (in general and in medicine):

■ Thinking about our own thinking.

■ Reflection about the thought processes that led to a particular diagnosis or other clinical or scientific decisions in order to consider whether biases or cognitive shortcuts may have had a detrimental effect.[9 modified]

Meta-evaluation: An evaluation of evaluations.

Meta-language: A language used to talk about another language, which is known correlatively as the "*object language.*"

Example: If you explain in English the meaning of a French word, English is your meta-language and French your object language. Discourse in English about the meaning of English words (*hypertensive, schizophrenia,* or *diabetic*) takes place in a meta-language with respect to the statements that use those words to describe reality.

Metaphysics: Any inquiry that raises questions about reality that lie beyond or behind those capable of being tackled by the method of science.

Middle term (in categorical syllogisms): The term that appears in each premise but not in the conclusion.

Minor term (in categorical syllogisms): The subject of the conclusion.

Mistake (in general): Deficiency or failure in the judgmental and/or inferential processes involved in the selection of an objective or in the specification of means to achieve it, irrespective of whether or not the actions directed by this decision-scheme run according to plan.[36]

Mistake (medical):

■ An incorrect reasoning, problem solving, and/or decision-making or sensory-motor action in clinical care.

■ Inappropriate planning of knowledge-based and rule-based actions resulting in errors in clinical care or in medical research.

■ A commission or omission with potentially negative consequences for the patient that would be judged wrong by skilled and knowledgeable peers at the time it occurred, independent of whether there were any negative consequences.

Mitigating factor: An action or circumstance that prevents or moderates the progression of an incident toward harming the patient.[4] (N.B. Mitigating factors have a different meaning in law.)

Mixed methods research: Any kind of research which uses and combines methodology and findings usually obtained separately by quantitative or qualitative research. Such method of research should bring additional information and insight as opposed to information produced either by isolated quantitative or qualitative research only.

Modal logic: A branch of logic that focuses on logical operators which are modal qualifiers, principally "necessarily" and "possibly."

Modal qualifier: An adverb indicating the scope of a warrant, and thus the degree to which the conclusion of some reasoning or argument is supported by the premises, if they are true. Examples: probably, presumably, necessarily, possibly.

Modern (Toulmin's) argument: An argument consisting of six elements (building blocks) such as grounds, backing, warrant, qualifier, rebuttals, and conclusion.

Morbidity: The occurrence of disease in a defined community. Usually presented as a rate.

Morbidity and mortality reports and rounds: Conferences and meetings representing a forum for faculty and trainees to explore the management details of particular cases and expand such details into the broader understanding of problems they reflect. They are expected to contribute to the improvement of patient care, medical knowledge, communication skills, professionalism, and problem-based learning and improvement.

Morning report: A summary of events that happened at the hospital floor, service, or department to the individuals and teams in charge during the working period (shift) and that is communicated to the individuals and teams who take over.

Mortality: The occurrence of deaths caused by a specific health problem in a defined community.

Narrative: An orderly, continuous account of an event or series of events by the patient or by a health professional. Clinical care reports and case series reports are often narratives or preceded by narratives.

Narrative competence: The set of skills required to reorganize, absorb, interpret, and be moved by the stories one hears or reads.

Necessary cause: Within a web of causes, a causal factor whose presence is required for the occurrence of some effect. See also *Necessary condition* and *Sufficient cause.*

Necessary condition: A condition that is required for something else to occur. If the necessary condition is not present, then the other thing does not occur. A contrasting concept is *sufficient condition*. A necessary condition need not be a sufficient condition.

Example: The tuberculosis bacillus is not a sufficient condition for getting tuberculosis; many people infected by this bacterium do not get clinically manifested tuberculosis. On the other hand, it is a necessary condition: A person who has not been infected by the bacterium will not have tuberculosis. Many necessary conditions are necessary causes, but not all are.

Example: Pain in the chest is a necessary condition for a diagnosis of angina pectoris, but this is a necessity of definition; the pain does not cause the angina pectoris, but is part of the condition. See *Necessary cause* and *Sufficient condition.*

Nocebo effect: Any negative effect like causation of sickness or death by a pill, potion, or procedure, but not due to its pharmacodynamic or specific properties. Harm due to the power of suggestion.

Example: Voodoo in Caribbean health culture.

Nomogram: A graphical representation that enables its users to establish the value of a variable of interest at its scale from an intersection of the values of two other determining variables read on their respective scales. Two variable scales used to predict a third one.

Nonverbal communication (in health professions): Sending and receiving of messages by ways other than speech between health professionals and their patients and communities.

Nursing:

- A health profession based on assisting individuals and groups of individuals under medical or other health professional care, whether sick or well, in the performance of those activities which he or she could not accomplish independently, contributing thus to health and its recovery and gaining independence. This is a North American perspective.

- Nursing is the use of clinical judgment in the provision of care to enable people to improve, maintain, or recover health, to cope with health problems, and to achieve the best possible quality of life, whatever their disease or disability, until death. This is a British paradigm. Medical, surgical, pediatric, psychiatric, or public health nursing are among its specialties.

Object language: A language used to talk directly about (non-linguistic) reality, as contrasted to the "meta-language" used to talk about an object language. See *Meta-language.*

Objectives: Points to be reached in practical clinical problem solving or in research, either *specific* to the problem or in *general*, encompassing a broader context into which the problem belongs.

Ockham's razor: See *Parsimony* (the *principle of parsimony*).

Odds: The ratio of the probability of occurrence of an event to that of non-occurrence of that same event in another set of observations. Odds are fractions having an event in the nominator and a non-event in the denominator. It is the ratio of the probability that something is one way to the probability that it is another way.

Odds ratio (Syn. cross-product ratio, relative odds):
- A ratio of two odds.
- In case control studies, the ratio of the odds in favor of exposure to a supposed causal factor among cases of a disease to the odds in favor of exposure among non-cases.
- Like relative risk from cohort studies, the odds ratio is a useful estimation of the strength of cause-effect relationships.

Open-ended questions: Questions offered to multiple answers, like "How does it feel?" They reflect deductive reasoning from which hypotheses are derived.

Operations (Syn. operational research, decision science, management science) research in medicine: A multidisciplinary science based on mathematics, probability and statistics, computer science, modeling, simulation, path exploration, optimization, and other approaches which is devoted to the analysis of a process of operation used in making decisions.

A maximum profit for the price of a minimum loss decision is sought. Not to be confused with surgical operations which may be or not the subject of operational research as defined above.

Operational research: A research encompassing a wide range of problem-solving techniques and methods applied in the pursuit of improved decision-making and efficiency. Used often synonymously with operations research (*vide infra*).

Orismology (in medicine and health sciences): Study, use, and evaluation of definitions pertaining to medical practice and research. (From Greek *orismos,* meaning *definition* and *logos,* meaning *study.*

Outcome:
- Product, result or practical effect of healthcare in terms of patient health and associated costs.[2 modified]
- "What happens" when acting on patient (or community) health and disease.
- The health status of an individual, a group of people, or a population that is wholly or partially attributable to an action, agent, or circumstance.[7]

Outcomes research in health sciences: Research that seeks to understand end results of particular healthcare practices and interventions; effectiveness, better ways to monitor and improve the quality of care are its objectives. The ability to function, quality of life, mortality and other clinical events serve as "outcomes."

***P* value:** In biostatistics, the probability of obtaining a result as extreme as, or more extreme, than the one observed if the dissimilarity is entirely due to variation in measurement or in subject response—that is, if it is the result of chance alone.

Paraclinical: Activities and services beyond bedside care but related to it and most often vital for it.
Examples: Clinical laboratory, diagnostic imaging sites and technology. See *Clinical.*

Paradigm: A theoretical framework for scientific or philosophical endeavors and investigations of problems. A way in which we look at things.
Example: Medicine is probabilistic. The universe is infinite.

Paradigm (medical):
- A way we see a health phenomenon, state, context, or care.
- A distinct set of concepts of thought patterns, including theories, research methods, postulates, and standards for what constitutes legitimate contributions to a field and domain of medicine.

Parsimony (principle of ...; Ockham's razor): Keeping things (hypotheses, studies, data, ana-lyzes or interpretations) as simple as possible. Not complicating things beyond a strict necessity. Parsimony, or Ockham's razor, is a useful rule of thumb in formulating hypoth-eses for investigation, whether in general causal research or in diagnosis of individual patients. But it is not an infallible guide; sometimes the truth is complicated. Diagnosis relies often, sometimes too often, on pattern-recognition.

Patient-centered care:
■ A way of doing things that sees the people using health and social services as equal partners in planning, developing, and monitoring care to ensure it means their needs.
■ Putting people and their families at the center of decisions and setting them as experts, asking alongside professionals in view of getting the best outcome.

Patient safety: The reduction and mitigation of unsafe acts (and of their undesirable conse-quences) within the healthcare system, as well as through the use of best practices shown to lead to optimal patient outcomes.

Patient values: Each individual's unique preferences, concerns, and expectations related to clini-cal decisions.

Pattern-recognition of a health problem: A mental process of finding characteristics of a health problem corresponding or identical to a previously lived and/or learned experience. Diagnosis relies often (sometimes too often) on pattern recognition. Particular not only to diagnosis, but also important in surgery and execution and evaluation of sensorimotor skills.

Personalized medicine: Medical practice in which the clinical, genetic, genomic, and environ-mental features of the patient determine the intervention of choice to prevent or treat a disease.

Philosophy in general:
■ A systematic analysis and critical examination of fundamental problems and the nature of being, reality and thinking, perception, values, causes, and choices under-lying principles of physical and ethical phenomena. Its fundamental branches are metaphysics, epistemology, logic, and ethics.
■ Thinking about thinking.

Philosophy *in* medicine:
■ Use and application of philosophy to health, disease, and medical care. It examines the methods used by medicine to formulate hypotheses (like questions about diag-nosis and treatment) and directions on the basis of evidence (what to do), as well as the grounds on which claims (diagnoses, treatment decisions and effects, prognoses made), about patients and health problems may be justified. Its aim is to study and understand general principles and ideas that lie behind views, understanding, and decisions about health, disease, and care.
■ Use of the formal tools of philosophical inquiry to examine the matter of medicine itself as a subject of study, the place of patients and health professionals within it, and establishment of the rule of their conduct in the domain of health, disease, and care.
■ Thinking about medical thinking.

Philosophy *of* medicine:
■ Formal inquiry into the structure of medical thought.
■ Philosophical inquiry on the nature of medicine as medicine and subsequent devel-opment of some general theory of medicine and its activities. It pays a lot of attention

to medicine's own contributions to philosophy, such as clinical trials or the methodology of observational analytical studies in the domain of cause-effect proof.

■ Philosophical considerations of the nature of medicine's own additional contributions to philosophy in general such as the experience from clinical trials or other studies of cause-effect relationships; the focus is on the advancement of the theory of medicine.

■ Critical reflection on the matter of medicine—on the content, method, concepts, and presuppositions peculiar to medicine as medicine.

Philosophy of science: Systematic philosophical study of the workings and functioning of science, of the extent of its ability to gain access to the truth about the material world, and of concepts used in scientific inquiry, such as laws of nature, causality, probability, and explanation.

Phronesis (in medicine):

■ A label given by some authors to the process of knowing and doing, experiencing and acting, undertaken by a physician on behalf of a particular patient in a specific clinical situation and setting.

■ Practical wisdom in dealing with particular individuals, specific problems, and the details of particular cases or actual situations.

Pimpee: A junior clinical clerk who is the unfortunate target and recipient of pimping (*vide infra*).

Pimper: An attending or resident quizzing subordinates on minutiae and medical trivia during rounds or class as a questionable test of a junior's knowledge.

Pimping:

■ A clinical practice where persons in power and entitled to decision-making (attending, seniors) ask questions of their junior colleagues (medical students, residents) with often blurred and infrequent expectations in order to correctly execute assigned tasks.

■ It is the quizzing of juniors with objectives ranging from knowledge acquisition to embarrassment and humiliation; it may be positive or negative.

■ Pimping is done by barraging juniors with seemingly random and topic/problem unrelated or unanswerable questions to which the juniors most often do not have answers leading to humiliation regardless of the conscious intention of the attending or resident asking the questions. Thus, it creates a feeling of "I do not know" in the face of peers and those who know better.

Placebo effect:

■ Any healing, suffering alleviating or comforting effect attributable to a pill, potion, or procedure but not to its pharmacodynamic or specific properties.

■ Effect due to the power of suggestion.

PoCICOST: An acronym for a research question in medicine which includes "**Po**pulation targeted, **C**ondition of interest, **I**ntervention, **C**ontrols, **O**utcomes, **S**etting, **T**imeframe."

Post hoc ergo propter hoc:

■ A Latin term for "After this, therefore because of this."

■ The fallacy of inferring a causal relationship from mere temporal sequence of a presumed cause and its expected effect instead of from its plausible causal proof.

Example: After more storks arrived, more babies were born; therefore storks bring babies.

Postulate:

■ *In philosophy and mathematics*, a proposition which forms a starting point of inquiry but which is neither definition, nor provisional assumption, nor so certain that it can be taken as axiomatic. Such postulates are laid down as true, and used without demonstration.

■ An absolutely necessary assumption in contrast to the conjectural nature of hypothesis.

■ Often, an equivalent of **posit**, as something put forward as a useful assumption or starting point, but not necessarily regarded as known to be true.

■ However, postulates **in medicine** bear often many of these above-mentioned properties.

Examples: A working diagnosis of a new phenomenon like SARS—sudden acute respiratory syndrome. "Gastric ulcer is a stress-produced disease" before the demonstration of its infectious etiology.

Potentiation of effect: The combined effect of multiple causal factors (drugs, pollutants, etc.) which is more than the arithmetic sum of the effects of each.

Practice (in general): The action or process of performing or doing something.

Practice of medicine:

■ An action, sensorimotor or other, in the domain of health and disease resulting from critical thinking about a problem and decisions regarding what to do to reach a solution of a health problem. Recognition, treatment, and prevention of disease are emphasized.

■ Utilization and exercise of knowledge in the practical recognition, treatment, and prevention of disease and maintenance of physical, mental, and social health in an individual patient and community.

Predictive value of a negative test result: The probability that an individual who tested negative really does not have the disease of interest. It shows how many individuals from among all who tested negative really do not have the disease in question.

Predictive value of a positive test result: The probability that an individual who tested positive for a disease really has it. It shows how many individuals from among all who tested positive really do have the disease of interest. The clinician's certainty before action is sought.

Premise:

■ A statement or proposition which leads (most often with other premises) to the conclusion of an argument. An argument is drawn from such premise or premises.

■ A starting point of reasoning or argument, that from which the conclusion is drawn, possibly in combination with other premises.

Examples: See entries for *Argument* and *Reasoning*.

Premise indicator: A word or phrase which indicates that an immediately following phrase, clause, or sentence is the premise of an argument or piece of reasoning.

Examples: since, as, because, given that, given.

Warning: Most of these words and phrases can also be used to indicate other roles of the immediately following phrase, clause, or sentence—especially the role of being a cause. Attention to context is needed to determine whether a word and phrase is actually functioning to indicate a premise.

Presumptive evidence (in law):

■ *Prima facie evidence* or evidence which is not conclusive and admits of explanation or contradiction.

■ Evidence which must be received and treated as true and sufficient until and unless rebutted by other evidence.

■ Evidence deemed true and sufficient unless discredited by other evidence.

Prevalence: The frequency of disease or other health event in a defined community (patients, community at large) at a given moment (point prevalence) or over some time interval (period prevalence). Usually presented as a rate.

Prevention (disease prevention):
- Policies and actions to eliminate a disease or minimize its effect.
- Actions that control disease occurrence either by preventing new cases (primary prevention), lowering disease prevalence, usually by shortening the duration of cases (secondary prevention), minimizing the severity and sequellae of cases beyond primary and secondary control (tertiary prevention), or actions to limit iatrogenesis (quaternary prevention).

Primary prevention: Actions and measures to reduce the incidence of disease by personal and community factors.

Primordial prevention: Actions and measures to minimize hazards to health and that hence inhibit the emergence and establishment of processes and factors (environmental, economic, social, behavioral, and cultural) known to increase the risk of disease. In this context, there is an obvious overlap with the definition of health protection.

Probability: Quantification of uncertainty.

Probable cause (in law):
- A "*reasonable cause*"; having more evidence for than against.
- A set of probabilities grounded in the factual and practical considerations that govern the decisions of reasonable and prudent persons and is more than mere suspicion but less than the quantum of evidence required for conviction in a criminal case.

Problem (topic) in focus: The health problem to be solved in practice or research.

Process (in healthcare evaluation):
- A course of action or sequence of steps, including "*what is done*" and "*how it is done.*"
- A "*how does it work*" characteristic of an activity or system within which errors occur.
- All that is done to patients in terms of diagnosis, treatment, monitoring, and counseling.

Producing cause (in law and occupational health): That cause which, in a natural and continuous sequence, produces an effect (e.g., a death), and without which the effect (e.g., death) would not have occurred. See *Necessary cause.*

Prognosis:
- The art of foretelling the course of disease, or the application of this art to a particular case, or the result of such an application.
- The prospect of survival and recovery from a disease as anticipated from the usual course of that disease and indicated by special features of the case in question.

Prognosis (in medicine): An assessment of the patient's future (based on probabilistic considerations of various beneficial and detrimental clinical outcomes as causally or otherwise determined by various clinical factors, biological and social characteristics of the patient), and of the pathology under study (disease course) itself.

Prognostic factors: Causally related characteristics or health events once the individual has the disease of interest and *which can be modified*, then possibly the outcomes of the disease of interest.

Prognostic markers: Causally or otherwise related characteristics or health events once the individual has the disease of interest and *which cannot be modified*, however related they might be to the outcomes of the disease of interest.

Progress notes (clinical): Written or verbal recording of patient state and evolution which includes subjective and objective observations and findings, their assessment, as well as a plan of further care based on such an updated evaluation of individual clinical course.

Propedeutics (in general): The knowledge which is necessary or useful for understanding or practicing an art or science, or which explains its nature and extent, and the method of learning it.

Propedeutics (medical): A way of acquiring the basic preparatory knowledge, attitudes, and skills required for further full learning and training, but which is not enough itself for necessary and sufficient proficiency in understanding, decision-making, and actions and their evaluation in a particular clinical or community medicine setting and domain.

Proposition (in critical thinking and argumentation): An assertion (affirmation or denial) of something which is capable of being judged true or false.

Example: Diagnosis: An error is the cause of harm in this patient.

Proximate cause (in law):
■ That which in natural and continuous sequence, unbroken by any new independent cause, produces an event, and without which the injury would not have occurred.
■ In tort cases, it is a wrongful conduct by a defendant leading to an injury complained of in a sufficiently direct way to justify holding the defendant liable for the plaintiff's damages.

Public health: A society's organized efforts, structures, policies and programs to protect, promote, restore, and improve health and prolong the life of the community.

Qualifier (in modern argument and argumentation):
■ An expression in argumentation, often a single word or number, somehow quantifying our certainty about our claim in light of the preceding argument blocks and the links between them.
■ One of the six components in the modern layout of arguments due to Toulmin: A word or phrase that indicates the strength conferred by the warrant on the inference from grounds to claim, and thus the strength of support given to our conclusion by the grounds we offer (assuming those grounds are true). See *Warrant, Grounds, Claim.*

Qualitative reasoning (in fuzzy logic): Reasoning based on fuzzy "if-then" rules where premises and conclusions involve linguistic variables, which may themselves be fuzzy.

Qualitative research (in error and harm domain): Any kind of research on error and harm that produces findings not arrived at by means of statistical procedures or other means of quantification about persons' lived experience with error and harm, and behavior facing them, and also on organizational, functional, social or interactional relationships between health professionals and their patients and community.[46 modified]

Qualitative research (in general):
■ A research which focuses and consists of findings in which unique, single, or very few cases are observed and analyzed in depth and without statistical considerations.
■ A method of inquiry, without statistical descriptions and analyses, which aims to gather an in-depth understanding of human behavior and the reasons which govern such behavior.
■ Qualitative methods, based on an in-depth study of cases which may be either individuals or situations (events), focus on the why and how of understanding and decision-making. Quantitative methods focus instead on what, where, and when.
■ In medicine, its subject may be professional practice, environmental issues affecting health, treatments, healthcare economics among others. Making sense of cases, interpretation and discovery of meanings are emphasized.

■ A method of inquiry, without statistical descriptions and analyses, which aims to gather an in-depth understanding of human behavior and the reasons which govern such behavior.

Quality of healthcare: Degree to which health services for individuals and populations increase the likelihood of desired health outcomes and are consistent with current professional knowledge.[9] The extent to which a healthcare service or product produces a desired outcome or outcomes.[7]

Quantifiers: Words that indicate the quantity of some phenomenon: how often, how much, how many, and so on. They give dimension to our observations and statements, even when given in fuzzy terms. See *Fuzzy logic, Fuzzy set theory.*
Example: An "*occasional*" dyspnea; "*profuse*" bleeding; "*frequent*" hemoptysis; "*all*" patients with streptococcal pharyngitis; "*some*" pulsating abdominal masses.

Quantiles: Divisions of a directional (from smallest to biggest, etc.) distribution into equal, ordered subgroups. Deciles are tenths, quartiles are quarters, and centiles (percentiles) are hundredths.

Quantitative research:
■ A mainstream type of research referring to the systematic empirical investigation of quantitative properties and phenomena and their relationship. Biostatistical and epidemiological methods focus most often on cause-effect relationships such as phenomena related to disease occurrence or its cure.
■ A research in which multiple observations are measured and/or counted, grouped in sets, compared, and analyzed for possible causal relationships and other contrasts.

Quaternary prevention: Actions that identify patients at risk of over-diagnosis or over-medication and that protect them from excessive medical intervention.

Rate: Events related to both events and non-events (other events). The coupling of a set of observations in the numerator like disease cases (a) with a set in the denominator which includes those same observations (a) and some additional ones such as non-cases (b), with two sets creating a community: a/a+b.

Ratio:
■ A relationship between two different entities (sets of observations) in the numerator (a) and the denominator (b) in a fraction: a/b.
■ The value obtained by dividing one quantity by another. It is a relationship between two separate and distinct quantities, neither of which is included in the other.

Rational: Conformable to reason; judicious; sensible.
Example: This patient is rational, and that one is irrational.

Rational medicine: A precursor of evidence-based medicine defined in the 1960s as "the practice of medicine based upon actual knowledge" without making distinctions between actual *knowledge* and *evidence.*

Rational thought: According to Henrik Wulff, an analysis of reasons given for different statements and a determination how these reasons are related in justifying and/or understanding other statements.

Reasoning (clinical): See *Clinical reasoning.*

Reasoning (in general):
■ Thinking leading to a conclusion.
■ Thinking leading to conclusions, making judgments or inferences from facts, observations, and/or hypotheses.

▪ A tool to form conclusions, judgments, or inferences from facts or premises. It is a methodological employment or presentation of arguments.

▪ Ideally, thinking enlightened by logic.

Example: (Said to oneself) This patient of mine has a streptococcal infection, so he must be treated with antibiotics immediately. *Premise*: This patient of mine has a streptococcal infection. *Conclusion*: He must start taking antibiotics.

Rebuttals (in modern argument and argumentation):

▪ Exceptional (exclusionary) circumstances undermining or weakening or nullifying final conclusions (claim) of an argument.

▪ One of the six elements in the contemporary layout of arguments identified by Toulmin. Exceptional circumstances which show that a warrant does not apply in the particular case.

Example: A patient's allergy to penicillin, which rebuts the conclusion that the patient, who has a bacterial infection, may be treated with penicillin. Rebuttals may or may not be specified in the warrant.

Example: Patients with a bacterial infection may be treated with penicillin, unless they are allergic to penicillin or there is reason to believe that the bacterium is resistant to penicillin. Patients with a bacterial infection may generally be treated with penicillin.

▪ Conditions or circumstances under which a claim stemming from an argument do not apply. In medicine, differential diagnosis and/or exclusion criteria in diagnosis and/or decision-making are often used as rebuttals.

Reconstruction of an argument: A process giving a structured, analyzable, interpretable, and evaluable argument on the basis of its conversion from natural language into a standard form with clearly identified premise(s) and conclusion.

Reflective thinking (in law): Solving a problem in the law by pondering a given set of facts in order to perceive their connection.

Relative risk:

▪ A ratio of two risks. A fraction relating the incidence of events in one group to the incidence of events in another group.

▪ In cohort studies, the ratio of risk of an outcome in exposed subjects to its risk in unexposed subjects to a factor of interest (smoking, drug abuse, etc.). It is a measure of the strength of a cause-effect relationship.

Research objectives (in medicine): Points we want to reach in a study, such as clinical trial, diagnostic test evaluation, or cost-effectiveness assessment of medical care and intervention, community health program, or some kind of research synthesis and interpretation of the above.

Research question: An expression of doubt and uncertainty about the nature and solution of a health problem in its specific context (population, setting of care, or community) to be discussed and solved by an intended inquiry.

Research questions: Questions regarding a health problem to be solved which specify (in various combinations and completeness from case to case) the population under consideration, condition of interest, intervention, controls when comparisons are made, outcomes, setting, and timeframe.

Research synthesis: Answering, confirming, or rejecting research questions and findings through the linking and integration of scientific information available from multiple sources, activities, and experience. It has a quantitative component (*meta-analysis of findings*) and a qualitative component (*systematic review of evidence*).

It is '*an epidemiology of research findings.*'

Resident: A graduate and licensed physician residing in a hospital, usually pursuing training in a specialty of his or her choice.

Rhetorical ploy: A non-argumentative deficiency in reasoning, containing misdirecting premises, proposals, or claims to reach their proponent's goals (often unrelated to the question) as the art of mental trickery and manipulation to a variable degree.

Rhetorical ploys (in law): Non-argumentative deficiencies in reasoning.

Examples: Appeals to novelty or to fear.

Risk:

■ The probability of danger, loss, or injury within the healthcare system.[2]

■ In epidemiology, it is the probability that a health event will occur, for example, that an individual will become ill or die within a stated period of time or by a certain age.[16,30]

■ Usually, an unfavorable outcome or event is in focus, but probabilities of other events (even beneficial ones) may be quantified as risk.

■ To be at risk is often not limited to noxious factors. Most often related to persons who still do not have a disease of interest.

Risk (in medicine and epidemiology): Absolute or relative probability of the occurrence of an event (e.g., disease occurrence or its cure) over a specified period of time in relation to its determining factors.

Risk difference: See *Attributable risk*.

Risk factors: Causally related characteristics which *can be modified* (for example, overeating in obesity).

Risk management: Organizational activities in healthcare designed to prevent patient injury or moderate actual financial losses following an adverse outcome.[2]

Risk markers: Causally related characteristics which *cannot be modified* in their possible causal relationship such as age or gender (for example, age or sex in disease etiology).

Root cause (in lathology): A causal factor that, if corrected, would prevent recurrence of the incident, encompassing and derived from several contributing causes such as system deficiencies, management failures, performance errors, and inadequate organizational communication.[47]

Root cause analysis:

■ A structured retrospective and already acquired knowledge-based process for identifying the causal or contributing factors underlying adverse events or other critical incidents.[9] modified Primarily of descriptive value.

■ A systematic iterative process whereby the factors that contribute to an incident are identified by reconstructing the sequence of events and repeatedly asking "Why?" until the underlying initial ('root') causes have been elucidated.[29]

■ An analytic tool that can be used to perform a comprehensive, system-based review of critical incidents. It includes the identification of root and contributory factors, identification of risk reduction strategies, and development of action plans along with measurement strategies to evaluate the effectiveness of the plans.[38]

Rounds (clinical, floor rounds):

■ Bedside, floor, or formal classroom meetings, or other less formal encounters between health professionals, often including patients, to discuss the cases under current care, and expanded further into a learning experience about broader clinical problems underlying patients (cases) under current care.

- Reviewing cases with other physicians and health professionals focusing on laying out elements of arguments and defending them.
- Analysis and consensus for plans for care at any getting together clinical opportunity.

Rule-based error: Error due to the misapplication of or the failure to apply a good rule, or a bad rule.

Science (in general):
- The study of the material universe or physical reality in order to understand it.
- A method of investigating nature—way of knowing about nature—that discovers reliable knowledge about it. "Reliable knowledge" in this definition is "knowledge that has a high probability of being true because its veracity has been justified by a reliable method."

Science of medicine:
- Organized reasoning, discovery, implementation, use, and evaluation of evidence in understanding human health, disease, and care decisions, and their evaluation which are based on the scientific method.
- A structured and organized way of using probability, uncertainty, and facts in preventive medicine and clinical care to best benefit the patient and the community. It is a logical and systematic approach to the exploration, organization, and interpretation of data from initial observations to clinical decisions and final conclusions concerning problems of interest. The latter are defined, measured, analyzed, and interpreted with a satisfactory degree of reproducibility.
- Discovery, implementation, and evaluation of evidence in understanding human health, disease, and care.

Scientific method:
- A way and direction of conducting research from currently available experience and evidence, formulating hypotheses and research questions, conducting observational and experimental studies, to analyzing results, driving conclusions, and reporting the entire experience.
- Method of study of nature involving problem definition, hypothesis formulation, observation, measurement, analysis, and interpretation of findings, as well as subsequent generation of new hypotheses. This "hypothetico-deductive" method is one of many methods used in science as scientific method.
- A body of techniques for investigating phenomena, acquiring the new knowledge, or correcting and integrating previous knowledge. Characterizations of observations, definitions, and measurements as subjects of inquiry, hypotheses, predictions, and experiments are behind the practice of the scientific method and research.[60]

Scientific theory: A plausible and consistent explanation for observable phenomena. In the sciences, it comprises a collection of concepts, including abstractions of observable phenomena expressed as quantifiable properties, together with rules (that is, scientific laws) expressing relationships between observations of such concepts. Such a proposed explanation of empiric phenomena is made in a way consistent with the scientific method.

Scientific thinking: A mental tool (a thought process) that uses the scientific method to study or investigate the nature of the universe.[59]

Screening: A presumptive diagnostic test, technique, or procedure whose purpose is not to establish a definitive diagnosis and prescribe treatment, but to lead patients with positive results to a more complete diagnostic workup, evaluation, and treatment, as required.

Scut work: A daily hospital and floor chore of clinical trainees that consists of the repeated execution of necessary basic and general clinical care acts such as the establishment and maintenance of patient charts, vital functions surveillance, or providing medications or wound care.

Secondary prevention: Actions and measures to reduce the prevalence of disease by shortening its duration. Most clinical medicine falls into this domain.

Semiotics, semeiotic or semiotic (in general and in medicine):
■ The science or study of the relationship of signification between three concepts: sign, object, and mind. In health sciences, communication with patients, peers are subjects of semiotics.
■ The general study of symbolic systems, including signs and language.
■ Study of the interpretation of signs, as a part of hermeneutics.
■ General science of signs and languages. The subject is divided into three areas: syntax, or the abstract study of the signs and their interrelationships; semantics or the study of the relation between the signs and those objects to which they apply; and pragmatics as the relationship between users and the system.
■ Pertaining to the signs or symptoms of disease: pathognomonic.

Sensitivity: The property of a diagnostic test to detect cases of disease from all cases existing in a given clinical and community setting. It shows how a test works in diseased subjects. The clinician does not want to miss cases that should be treated.

Sensitivity analysis (in the decision-making domain): Looking at how a clinical decision would change if probabilities, reference values, and/or probabilities of outcomes and their own value (utility) were to change.

Sentinel event (in lathology):
■ An adverse event in which death or serious harm to a patient or community has occurred.[9 modified] All sentinel events are not expected and they may be unacceptable, such as wrong side or wrong organ operations.
■ Egregiousness of the harm and the likelihood that its investigation will reveal serious problems in current policies and procedures.[9 modified]
■ Unexpected incident related to the system or process deficiencies and/or human error, which leads to death or major and enduring loss of function (and/or anatomy) for a recipient of healthcare services.[40]

Set:
■ A defined, categorized, and enumerated group of observations such as patients, exposure to noxious or beneficial factors, and otherwise related to other events which is distinguishable from another group.
■ A collection of defined, distinct, or somehow related items.
Examples: Human races, ethnic groups, types of blood cells, series of measurements in an experiment.

Set of causes: A defined, categorized, and enumerated set of observations *with no* specific time, space, and any other *interrelationships* between them.

Side effect (in general):
■ An effect, other than that intended, produced by an agent. See *Adverse effect* or *Reaction*.[7]
■ Any effect that occurs besides the main, expected, and desired one.

Side effect (in medicine): An effect, other than that intended, produced by a preventive, diagnostic, or therapeutic procedure or regimen. It is not necessarily harmful.

Sign (clinical): Objective and definable manifestations of disease. Those disease manifestations that are perceived by a third person.

Example: Exanthem, external bleeding, diarrhea.

Significance: Something that is meaningful from a clinical standpoint and/or from public health, scientific, statistical, social, emotional, or political view(s). It may abide by probability, judgment, anecdotes, emotions, and other considerations that, depending on the context may be as important (significant, see *Significance in biostatistics*), or more so, that associations unlikely to occur by chance.

Significance (clinical):

■ The importance, relevance, or meaning for individuals involved in clinical care, patients, health professionals, and specified others.

■ The importance of medical decisions and other considerations does not mean the degree of statistical significance. Statistical significance may sometimes be a prerequisite for other considerations of significance.

Significance (in biostatistics):

■ A significance which follows the laws of probability.

■ A characteristic of a health phenomenon or an observation that is unlikely to have occurred by chance. In biological sciences, an event is often considered as significant if it is unlikely to occur by chance more often than one time in 20, that is, with a probability $p<0.05$ or less than 1 in 100 ($p<0.01$). See *P value*.

Skill-based errors: Slips and lapses; errors in execution of correctly planned actions, encompassing both action-based errors (slips) and memory-based errors (lapses).[3]

Skills:

■ A part of the psychomotor domain, defined in general as expertness, practical ability, facility in doing something, dexterity, and tact.

■ In the decision-making domain, they are abilities to apply structured decision-making methodology to the solution of problems in practice. Errors may occur if the decision-maker's skills are inadequate for the successful execution of the task.

■ An expertness, practical ability, dexterity, tact, and facility in doing something.

Slip (in general): An action not in accord with the actor's intention, the result of a good plan, but a poor execution,[49] hence physical, sensory/motor failure.[50]

Slip (medical):

■ An inappropriate action and execution, the incorrect execution of a correct action sequence, due also to competing sensory or emotional distractions, fatigue, or stress.

■ Failure in schematic (often learned and mastered) behavior due to distractions rather than to professional qualification and experience. May be related to execution (goals, intention, action specification, and execution itself) and/or evaluation (perception, interpretation, and action evaluation).

■ Action-based error centered on attention or perceptual failure of an action, like the dispensing of an elevated dose of medication, and other failures.

Socratic dissent, debate, dialogue: A negative method of hypotheses elimination, in that better hypotheses are found by steadily identifying and eliminating those leading to contradictions. Its form consists of the following:

■ statement of the question;

■ answer to the question;

- exploration of objections to the answer;
- revised answer that avoids these objections; and
- exploration of objections to the revised answer.

The successful dialogue reaches its end when the answer stands up against all objections.

Soft data: Any observation that cannot be adequately defined in precise operational terms and/or measured.

Example: Sorrow, anger, nausea. See *Hard data*.

Specificity (in diagnostic testing): The property of a diagnostic test to confirm, by its negative result, that healthy individuals effectively do not have the disease of interest. It shows how the test works in non-diseased individuals. A clinician's measure of certainty to do nothing (needlessly treating a non-diseased patient) is sought.

Specificity of an association: Magnitude of how a particular suspected causal factor of interest prevails among other possible causes. See *Attributable risk* and *Attributable risk percent*.

Spectrum of disease: See *Disease spectrum*.

Standard of care: A set of steps that would be followed or an outcome that would be expected. A level of measure, rather than a rule or policy.

Stochastic process: A process that incorporates some degree of randomness.

Strength of association: The distance between two or more series of observations. This is appropriately expressed by *relative risk* in cohort studies and by the *odds ratio* in case control studies.

Structure (of a health activity or system):

- The supporting framework of essential parts including all elements of the healthcare system that exist before any actions or activities take place. The "consisting of what," and "how is it organized" characteristic of an activity or system within which errors occur.
- The setting in which care occurs and the capacity of that setting to produce quality.
- Structural measures such as credentials, patient volume, and academic affiliation.

"Structure-Process-Outcome" triad: The triangular evaluation of the quality of clinical and community care. Such a view of quality depends on what is part of care, how the care is delivered, and what is its impact, that is, favorable outcomes in patients or members of the community.

Structured abstract (of a medical article): An abstract consisting in the presentation of the background of the selected topic, methods used in the research, results (findings), their interpretation, and conclusions including the relevance of the research experience and its limitations.

Sufficient cause: In a web of causes, a set of conditions, factors or events which will produce a given outcome, regardless of what other conditions are present or absent. It is a complete causal mechanism that does not require the presence of any other determinant in order for the outcome, such as disease, to occur. See *Sufficient condition* and *Necessary cause*.

Sufficient condition:

- A condition which is enough by itself for something else to occur. If the sufficient condition is present, then the other thing occurs. *Contrasting concept*: "necessary condition." See *Necessary condition* and *Sufficient cause*.

Example: Irreversible cessation of heartbeat and respiration is a sufficient condition for death.

- A sufficient condition need not be a necessary condition.

Example: Irreversible cessation of heartbeat and respiration is not a necessary condition for death, in many legal jurisdictions. In New York State, for example, a person may be declared dead if their heartbeat and respiration are being maintained by "extraordinary mechanical means," provided that there is "an irreversible cessation of all functions of the entire brain, including the brain stem."[1]

■ Many sufficient conditions are sufficient causes, but not all are.
Example: Angina pectoris is a sufficient condition for pain in the chest, but this is a matter of definition; angina pectoris *is* a certain sort of pain in the chest.

Sufficient evidence (in law): That which is satisfactory for the purpose.

Superseding or supervening cause (in tort law): An action or event that intervenes so dramatically and unexpectedly in a chain of causation, and changes its course so significantly, that the law regard it as a proximate cause of the injury or of the damage complaint. See *Proximate cause.*

Survival:

■ In epidemiology, it does not mean merely 'avoiding death,' when death represents the disease outcome of interest.

■ It is a broader term for a state inception until the occurrence of some event or outcome of interest.

■ It can be any discrete event such as a relapse, recovery, disease spell (well-defined), or any other change of disease course. The term 'survival' is chosen here because of its persisting use, although it represents time-to-event, survival time, or any prognostic function of interest.

Survival curve: A curve that starts at 100% of the population and shows by time increments or intervals the percentage of the population surviving as long as the information is available. *Survival* used here is a misnomer of sorts, because phenomena other than death can be illustrated and studied this way: disease complications, freedom from disease, and other phenomena related to treatment, prognosis, and exposure to noxious or beneficial factors and their covariates.

Syllogism: Defined by Aristotle as a discourse or argument in which certain things have been laid down (like A and B) and something other than what has been laid down (C) follows by necessity from their being so. See *Categorical syllogism.*

Symbolic logic: See *Formal logic.*

Symptom (of disease): Manifestation of disease as perceived subjectively by the patient himself. Often hidden to other people.
Example: Hot flushes, itching (unless the patient scratches himself), pain, feeling of persecution.

■ Also: Overview of qualitative characteristics of original studies of a given problem, "*epidemiology of results.*"

System (in general):

■ A set of interacting and independent entities, real or abstract, forming an integrated whole.

■ A set of relationships that are differentiated from relationships of the set to other elements, and from relationships between an element of the set and elements not part of the relational regime.

■ Systems have a structure that is defined by their parts and their composition. They have behavior that involves inputs, processing and outputs of material, information, or energy. Various parts of a system have functional as well as structural relationships between each other.

System (in healthcare): A set of interdependent components interacting to achieve a common claim. System characteristics include complexity and coupling.[2]

System analysis: Analysis of a broad system of events with a chain of contributing factors combined in the future with incident analysis and with anticipation of future problems based on current experience.[54]

System approach: Alternative, complementary, or expanded approach to errors and harm attributable to health professionals as individuals, analyzing systems (rather than the behavior of individuals only) in order to identify situations or factors likely to give rise to human error and harm and to implement 'system' changes as remedial measures, and to reduce the occurrence of errors and harms and minimize their impact on patients.[9 modified]

System error (in medicine): Error imputable to technology and end environment of medical care and its interaction with their users, that is, health professionals as operators of the system and their recipients (patients and other receivers of therapeutic and preventive care).

System failure: A fault, breakdown, or dysfunction within an organization's operational methods, processes, and infrastructure.[7]

Systematic review of evidence: The uniform application of (mostly qualitative) strategies and the qualitative overview of original studies of a given health problem to improve information, limit bias in the assembly, critical appraisal, and synthesis of available (preferably all) relevant studies of the same specific topic. It is also a kind of *epidemiology of research results* across the available information.

Systematic review of evidence (in evidence-based medicine):
- The application of strategies that limit bias in the assembly, critical appraisal, and synthesis of all relevant studies on a specific topic. Meta-analysis may be, but is not necessarily, used as a part of this process.

Taxonomy: Classification of entities of interest. Usually it covers a particular domain like error and/or harm in our case.

Team error: A human error committed by a group of individuals within their interaction while planning, performing, and evaluating a task.[15]

Technical slip in medicine (examples): Errors in writing of orders, inappropriate clinical maneuver execution, dispensing technique, recording, and information storage. (See the *Slip* entry for basic definitions of that term.)

Tertiary prevention: Measures aimed at softening the impact of long term disease and disability, and handicap; minimizing suffering, and maximizing potential years of useful life. The severity, spectrum, and gradient of the disease are emphasized rather than its duration.

Theory (in general):
- A coherent group of general propositions used as principles of explanation for a class of phenomena.
- A particular conception or view of something to be done, or of the method of doing it. It encompasses inter-related constructs (variables), definitions, and propositions that present a systematic view of phenomena by specifying relations among variables, with the purpose of explaining natural phenomena.
- A set of ideas, concepts, principles, or methods used to explain a wide set of observed facts. A theory may or may not have been confirmed by scientific inquiry, explanation, and proof.

Examples: The theory of evolution (of biological species), the germ theory of disease, the theory of special relativity, Newtonian mechanics, plate tectonics, and thermodynamics.

Theory of medicine:

- "The body of principles of the science and art of medicine as distinguished from the practice of medicine," or "the application of those principles in actual practice."
- Colloquially speaking, it is anything that happens in the head of the physician, researcher, or practitioner of medicine before orders, by word or stroke of the pen, are given and an action by hand or other technological tools are taken.

Thesis:

- Central and controlling idea behind the message.
- A proposition in medical research and practice, stated and put forward for consideration, especially one to be discussed and proved or to be maintained against objections.

Thinking: Mental action, which, if verbalized, is a matter of combining words in propositions. Not all thinking can be verbalized. Visual imaginings in daydreaming, for example, cannot be completed expressed in oral communication.

Thought experiment:

- A proposal for an experiment that would test a hypothesis or theory, but cannot actually be performed due to practical, ethical, or other limitations (cultural, value, etc.); instead its purpose is to explore the potential consequences of the principle in question.
- A device of the imagination used to investigate the nature of things.

Threshold knowledge: Core concepts that once understood, transform the perception of a given subject.

Time-to-event analysis:

- An analysis of intervals between two events and the meaning of such intervals in relation to the nature of events and relationships between them. Used in clinical trials, prognosis, survival studies, lathology, and elsewhere.
- In the broadest sense, it includes also analyses of incubation periods of diseases and generation time in the infectious disease domain.

Tort (in law): A wrongful act, other than a breach of contract, that results in injury to another person, property, reputation, or some other legally protected right of interest, and for which the injured party is entitled to a remedy of law, usually in the form of damages.[57] Tort may be intentional or non-intentional.

Tort litigation: Evaluation by courts of law of harm, its causes, responsibility, and compensation.

Translation (in the context of knowledge translation): Multiple ways of moving experience, knowledge, facts, and their meaning from their original source and transmitters to their recipients or receivers in the framework of mutual understanding. It is followed by actions to change the receivers' actions and the care and health states of their expected beneficiaries.

Tree diagram (in logic): The graphical representation of the structure of reasoning or argument from premises to conclusions in a spoken or written text.

Truth: The property of a statement (belief, proposition) of asserting what is really the case.

Uncertainty (in general):

- Any situation where probabilities of different possible phenomena or outcomes are not known due to our poor knowledge of them whatever the reason for such imperfect knowledge might be.
- Probability refers to the quantification of uncertainty.

Uncertainty (in medicine, clinical uncertainty): Incomplete knowledge (whatever its reason might be) of the clinical or community health problem as an entity, its etiology, controllability, prognosis, natural, and clinical course.

Understanding in medicine and other health sciences: The successful sense-making or accurate synthesis of health and disease-related information pertaining to an entity (a patient, a health problem, or clinical and community care) that allows a justified explanation of the characteristics, behaviors, and events (their occurrence, evolution, and changes) associated with the entity. Proper understanding is a pre-requisite for rational decision-making in health promotion, health protection, disease prevention, and clinical and community care.

Validity (of an inference): See *Deductively valid inference.*

Value (in decision analysis): A weight given to possible outcomes of clinical or community health activity which, beyond monetary terms, is represented by social, cultural, and faith value, and other weight and importance given by an individual or community to options and outcomes of any possible choice in the search of the best one for patients, health professionals, or community.

Venn diagram: A diagram which represents the relations between sets by shading out subsets which are empty (that is, with no members) and putting an "x" in subsets which are nonempty (that is, with at least one member). Venn diagrams can be used to test whether a categorical syllogism is deductively valid.

Example: Diagram the information that all patients in the intensive care unit are critically ill and that all critically ill patients need continuous monitoring of their vital signs. In this case, three sets are mentioned: patients in the intensive care unit (ICU), critically ill patients (CIP), patients who need continuous monitoring of their vital signs (CMVS). Draw three circles, one for each set, with the circles overlapping so that all possible combinations are represented by a segment. Shade out the part of the ICU circle that is *outside* the CIP circle, to represent the information that all patients in the intensive care unit are critically ill. Shade out the part of the CIP circle that is *outside* the CMVS circle, to represent the information that all critically ill patients need continuous monitoring of their vital signs. Notice that all parts of the ICU circle that are outside the CMVS circle are now shaded out, thus showing that this subset is empty; that is, all ICU patients need continuous monitoring of their vital signs. The diagram thus shows that the inference from the given information to the latter proposition is deductively valid: If the information is correct, the conclusion *must* be correct.

Warrant (in modern argument):

■ A general rule or experience, understanding of the nature of the problem under study, allowing us in argumentation to infer to the claim.

■ One of the six elements of the contemporary layout of arguments due to Toulmin: A general rule which permits us to infer a claim of the given type from grounds of the type we have adduced. See Grounds.

Example: Given that a patient has a streptococcal infection, you may conclude that the patient must be treated with antibiotics. Warrants may be expressed as general statements.

Example: Patients with streptococcal infections must be treated with antibiotics. Warrants are usually implicit (that is, unstated) in reasoning and arguments; if the warrant is added as an explicit premise, the inference becomes deductively valid, provided that any modal qualifiers are removed.

Example: My patient has a streptococcal infection. Patients with streptococcal infections must be treated with antibiotics. Therefore, my patient must be treated with antibiotics.

Warranted inference: An inference with a justified warrant.

Web of causes: An enumerated set of observations with specified time, space, and other interrelationships between causes and their consequences.

Web of causes (in epidemiology): An ensemble (set) of causes of a health phenomenon (health, disease, cure, etc.) with all their interaction and relationship in time and space.

Web of consequences (in epidemiology): An ensemble or set of outcomes (health problems) with all their interaction and relationship in time and space as produced by their cause(s).

Workers' compensation board: An organization established by a government to provide compensation to workers who suffer a work-related injury or disease. Courts of law as sites for litigation are replaced for ease of settlement by various health and civic stakeholders whose mandate is to evaluate risk, harm, prognosis of occupation-related health problems, and in particular cases financial compensation and health and social needs. These settings may vary from one country to another. Workers' compensation boards may be one of them.

Related Additional Useful References to the Glossary

1. Davies JM, Hébert P, Hoffman C. *The Canadian Patient Safety Dictionary*. Ottawa: Royal College of Physicians and Surgeons of Canada, October 2003. 58 pdf p. at http://rcpsc.medical.org/publications /PatientSafetyDictionary_c.pdf, retrieved Jan 21, 2009.
2. Wikipedia, the free encyclopedia. *Accident*. 2 p. at http://en.wikipedia/org/wiki/accident, retrieved Nov 11, 2008.
3. Ferner RE and Aronson JK. Clarification on terminology in medication errors. Definitions and classification. *Drug Safety*, 2006;29(1):1011–22.
4. White JL. *Adverse Event Reporting and Learning Systems: A Review of the Relevant Literature, June 25, 2007*. A Paper Prepared for CPSI. Edmonton and Ottawa: Canadian Patient Safety Institute (CPSI), 2007. 80 pdf p. at www.patientsafetyinstitute.ca/uploadedFiles/News/CAERLS_Consultation _Paper_*AppendixA*.pdf, retrieved Jan 26, 2009.
5. Battles JB, Kaplan HS, Van der Schaaf TW, Shea CE. The attributes of medical event-reporting systems. Experience with a prototype medical event-reporting system for transfusion medicine. *Arch Pathol & Lab Med*, 1998;122(3):231–8. (See the *Eindhoven Classification Model for Medical Domain*, p. 235).
6. World Alliance for Patient Safety. *WHO Draft Guidelines for Adverse Event Reporting and Learning Systems*. Geneva: World Health Organization (Document WHO/EIP/SPO/QPS/05.3), 2005.
7. Runciman WB. Shared meanings: Preferred terms and definitions for safety and quality concepts. *MJA*, 2006;184(10):S41–43.
8. United States Department of Veteran Affairs, National Center for Patient Safety. *Glossary of Patient Safety Terms*. 5 p. at http://www.va.gov/NCPS/glossary.html, retrieved Nov 9, 2008.
9. Agency for Healthcare Research and Quality (AHRQ), US Department of Health & Human Services. *Glossary*. 31 p. at http://www.webmm.ahrq.gov/popup_glossary.aspx, retrieved Jan 3, 2009 and 30 p. at http://www.wbmm.ahrq.gov/glossary.aspx, retrieved July 7, 2009.
10. Jenicek M. *Clinical Case Reporting in Evidence-Based Medicine*. 2nd Edition. London and New York: Arnold and Oxford University Press, 2001.
11. Wilson W. *Causal Factor Tree Analysis*. 3 p. at http://www.bill-wilson.net/b56.html, retrieved June 19, 2009.
12. Jenicek M and Hitchcock DL. *Evidence-Based Practice. Logic and Critical Thinking in Medicine*. Chicago, IL: American Medical Association (AMA Press), 2005.
13. *A Dictionary of Epidemiology*. 5th Edition. Edited for the International Epidemiological Association by M Porta. New York and Oxford: Oxford University Press, 2009.

14. Jenicek M. *Foundations of Evidence-Based Medicine.* Boca Raton, FL/London/New York/Washington, DC: The Parthenon Publishing Group Inc. (CRC Press), 2003.

15. Sasou K and Reason J. Team errors: Definition and taxonomy. *Reliability Eng Syst Safety,* 1999;65(1):1–9.

16. Answers.com™. *Cognition.* 12 p. at http://www.answers.com/topic/cognition, retrieved Nov 12, 2008.

17. Bogner MS. Introduction. Pp. 1–12 in: *Human Error in Medicine.* Edited by MS Bogner. Hillsdale, NJ: Lawrence Erlbaum Associates, 1994.

18. WHO World Alliance for Patient Safety. *The Conceptual Framework for the International Classification for Patient Safety (ICPS). Version 1.0 for Use in Field Testing 2007–2008.* Geneva: World Health Organization, July 2007. 48 pdf p. at http://www.who.int/patientsafety/taxonomy/icps_download/en/print.html, retrieved Feb 4, 2009.

19. Scriven M and Paul R. Critical Thinking Community. A working definition of *critical thinking.* Available at http://lonestar.texas.net/~mseifert/crit2.html, retrieved June 2005.

20. Ennis RH. *Critical Thinking.* Upper Saddle River, NJ: Prentice Hall, 1996.

21. Institute of Medicine, Committee on Quality of Health Care in America. *To Err is Human. Building a Safer Health System.* Edited by LT Kohn, JM Corrigan, and MS Donaldson. Washington, DC: National Academy Press, 2000.

22. Simpson K. *A Doctor's Guide to Court. A Handbook on Medical Evidence.* London: Butterworths, 1967.

23. Dowden B. *The Internet Encyclopedia of Philosophy. Fallacies.* 44 p. at http://www.iep.utm.edu/f/fallacy.htm, retrieved October 31, 2006.

24. Jenicek M. *Fallacy-Free Reasoning in Medicine. Improving Communication and Decision-Making in Research and Practice.* Chicago, IL: American Medical Association (AMA Press), 2009.

25. Wikipedia, the free encyclopedia. *Failure Mode and Effect Analysis.* 7 p. at http://en.wikipedia.org/wiki/Failure_mode_and_effects_analysis, retrieved July 11, 2009.

26. Testability.com. *Reliability Terms.* 5 p. at http://www.testability.com/reference/Glossaries.aspx?Glossary=reliability, retrieved July 11, 2009.

27. Thiyagarajan Veluchamy Blog. *Glossary.* 29 p. at http:///thiyagarajan.wordpress.com/glossary/, retrieved July 11, 2009.

28. Wikipedia, the free encyclopedia. *Failure Mode and Effect Analysis.* 4 p. at http://en.wikipedia.og/wiki/Failure_mode_and_effects_analysis, retrieved Feb 3, 2009.

29. American Society for Quality (ASQ). *Failure Modes and Effect Analysis (FMEA).* 3 p. at http://www.asq.org/learn-about-qyality/process-analysis-tools/overview/fmea.html, retrieved Feb 3, 2009.

30. Peters GA and Peters BJ. *Human Error. Causes and Control.* Boca Raton, FL/London/New York: CRC/Taylor & Francis Group, 2006.

31. Runciman W, Hibbert P, Thomson R, Van der Schaaf T, Sherman H, Lewalle P. Towards an international classification of patient safety: Key concepts and terms. *Int J Qual Health Care,* 2009;21(1):18–26.

32. WHO World Alliance for Patient Safety. *The Conceptual Framework for the International Classification for Patient Safety (ICPS). Version 1.0 for Use in Field Testing 2007–2008.* Geneva: World Health Organization, July 2007. 48 pdf p. at http://www.ismp-canada.org/definitions.htm, retrieved Feb 4, 2009.

33. Institute for Safe Medication Practices Canada; c2000–2006. *Definitions of Terms.* 3 p. at http://www.ismp-canada.org/definitions.htm, retrieved Septr 7, 2009.

34. Gold JA. The 5 million lives campaign: Preventing medical harm in Wisconsin and the nation. *Wisconsin Med J,* 2008;107(5):270–1.

35. Sheridan-Leos N, Schulmeister L, Hartfant S. Failure mode and effect analysis™. A technique to prevent chemotherapy errors. *Clin J Oncol Nurs,* 2006;10(3):393–401.

36. Reason J. *Human Error.* Cambridge and New York: Cambridge University Press, 1990.

37. Steel K, Gertman PM, Crescenzi C, Anderson J. Iatrogenic illness on a general medical service at a university hospital. *N Engl J Med,* 1981;304:838–42.

38. Croskerry P, Cosby KS, Schenkel SM, Wears RL. *Patient Safety in Emergency Medicine.* Philadelphia, PA: Wolters Kluwer | Lippincott Williams & Wilkins, 2009.

39. Busse DK. *Cognitive Error Analysis in Accident and Incident Investigation in Safety-Critical Domains.* A PhD Thesis. Glasgow: University of Glasgow, Department of Computing Science, September 2002. 288 + XIII p. at http://www.dcs.gla.ac.uk/~johnosn/papers/Phd_DBusse.pdf, retrieved Oct 25, 2008.

40. Baker R, Grosso F, Heinz C, Sharpe G, Beardwood J et al. Review of provincial, territorial and federal legislation and policy related to the reporting and review of adverse events in healthcare in Canada. Pp. 133–7 in: White JL. *Adverse Event Reporting and Learning Systems: A Review of the Relevant Literature.* Edmonton and Ottawa: Canadian Patient Safety Institute, June 25, 2007. 220 pdf p. at http://www.patientsafety institute.ca/uploadedFiles/News/CAERLS_Consultation_Paper_AppendixA.pdf, retrieved Jan 26, 2009.

41. Yogis JA and Cotter C. *Barron's Canadian Law Dictionary.* 6th Edition. Hauppauge, NY: Barron's Educational Series, Inc., 2009.

42. Thomsen CJ. *The Scope of the Medication Error Problem.* 7 html p. at http://74.125.113.132 /search?q=cache:iJ_sGynyyTWJ:www.thethomsengroup.com/TTGI..., retrieved Jan 28, 2009.

43. National Coordinating Council for Medication Error Reporting and Prevention. *What Is a Medication Error?* 1 p. at http://www.nccmerp.org/aboutMedErrors.html?USP_Print=true&frame=lowerfrm, retrieved Jan 14, 2009.

44. Wu AW, Cavanaugh TA, McPhee SJ et al. To tell the truth: Ethical and practical issues in disclosing medical mistakes to patients. *J Gen Intern Med,* 1997;12:770–5.

45. College of Licensed Practical Nurses of Nova Scotia, College of Occupational Therapists of Nova Scotia, College of Physicians & Surgeons of Nova Scotia, College of Registered Nurses of Nova Scotia, Nova Scotia College of Pharmacists, Nova Scotia College of Physiotherapists. *Joint Position Statement on Patient Safety.* 8 pdf p. at http://www.cpsns.ns.ca/2008-joint-patient-safety.pdf, retrieved Jan 27, 2009.

46. Strauss A and Corbin J. *Basics of Qualitative Research. Grounded Theory Procedures and Techniques.* Newbury Park, CA: SAGE Publications, 1990.

47. *New Technology and Human Error.* Edited by J Rasmussen, K Duncan, and J Leplat. Chichester and New York: John Wiley & Sons, 1987.

48. The Royal College of General Practitioners. *2. Significant Event Analysis.* 1 p. at http://www.org.uk /practising_as_a_gp/distance_learning/egp2_update/learning_tool..., retrieved June 19, 2009.

49. *Human Error: Cause, Prediction, and Reduction.* Analysis and Synthesis by JW Senders and NP Moray. Hillsdale, NJ/Hove/London: Lawrence Erlbaum Associates, 1991.

50. Cosby KS. Developing taxonomies for adverse events in emergency medicine. Chapter 5, pp. 58–69 in: Croskerry P, Cosby KS, Schenkel SM, Wears RL. *Patient Safety in Emergency Medicine.* Philadelphia, PA/London/Sydney/Tokyo: Wolters Kluwer | Lippincott Williams & Wilkins, 2009.

51. Zhang J, Patel VL, Johnson TR, Shortliffe EH. A cognitive taxonomy of medical errors. *J Biomed Informatics,* 2004;37:193–204.

52. Donabedian A. Evaluating quality of medical care. *Milbank Mem Fund Quarterly,* 1966;44 (Suppl.):166–206.

53. Wikipedia, the free encyclopedia. *System.* 6 p. at http://en.wikipedia.org/wiki/System, retrieved Jan 26, 2009.

54. Vincent C, Taylor-Adams S, Chapman JE, Hewett D, Prior S, Strange P, Tizzard A. How to investigate and analyze clinical incidents: Clinical risk unit and association of litigation and risk management protocol. *BMJ,* 2000;320(18 March):777–81.

55. Wikipedia, the free encyclopedia. *Thought Experiment.* 12 p. at http://en.wikipedia.org/wiki /Thought_experiment, retrieved Jan 26, 2009.

56. Stanford Encyclopedia of Philosophy. *Thought Experiments.* March 25, 2007 Revision. 14 p. at http:// plato.dstanford.edu/entries/thought-experiment/, retrieved Jan 26, 2009.

57. Cacciabue PC. *Guide to Applying Human Factors Methods. Human Error and Accident Management in Safety Critical Systems.* London/Berlin/Heidelberg: Springer Verlag, 2004.

58. *A Dictionary of Public Health.* Edited by JM Last. Oxford and New York: Oxford University Press, 2007.

59. Schafersman SD. *An Introduction to Science, Scientific Thinking and the Scientific Method.* 8 p. at http://www.geo.sunysb.edu/esp/files/scientific-method.html, retrieved Sept 3, 2017.

60. Wikipedia, the free encyclopedia. *Scientific Method.* 31 p. at https://en.wikipedia.org/wiki/Scientific _method, retrieved Sept 3, 2017.

Also see the glossaries in Milos Jenicek's books, listed in the *"About the Author"* closing document of this book and elsewhere throughout its chapters.

Appendix A: List of Cognitive Biases

Annotated *Wikipedia, The Free Encyclopedia* List

This Appendix is an author-edited version of the *List of Cognitive Biases* by *Wikipedia, the free encyclopedia* at http://en.wikipedia.org/wiki/List_of_cognitive biases, last retrieved September 25, 2017. Permission is granted under the terms of the GNU Free Documentation License, Version 1.2 or any later version published by the Free Software Foundation; with no invariant sections, with no front-cover texts, and with no back-cover texts. In terms of *Wikipedia Copyrights* (http://en.wikipedia.org/wiki/Wikipedia:Copyrights, 8 pages retrieved February 3, 2008), this appendix is licensed under the GNU Free Documentation License. It uses the material from the Wikipedia article *"List of Cognitive Biases."*

In respect and conformity with Wikipedia rules and requirements, any copy of this Appendix can be made without restrictions.

Under the name of cognitive bias, this list contains several entries which are elsewhere in this book synonymous to some entities under the name of fallacies as defined and commented in the next Appendix A: *List of fallacies*. With some overlaps, this list completes then other lists quoted and referred to in this book.

List of cognitive biases

From Wikipedia, the free encyclopedia

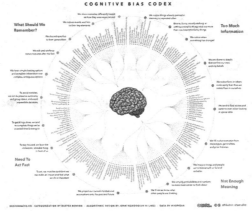

Cognitive biases can be organized into four categories: biases that arise from too much information, not enough meaning, the need to act quickly, and the limits of memory.[1]

Cognitive biases are tendencies to think in certain ways that can lead to systematic deviations from a standard of rationality or good judgment, and are often studied in psychology and behavioral economics.

Although the reality of these biases is confirmed by replicable research, there are often controversies about how to classify these biases or how to explain them.[2] Some are effects of information-processing rules (i.e., mental shortcuts), called *heuristics*, that the brain uses to produce decisions or judgments. Such effects are called *cognitive biases*.[3][4] Biases have a variety of forms and appear as cognitive ("cold") bias, such as mental noise,[5] or motivational ("hot") bias, such as when beliefs are distorted by wishful thinking. Both effects can be present at the same time.[6][7]

There are also controversies over some of these biases as to whether they count as useless or irrational, or whether they result in useful attitudes or behavior. For example, when getting to know others, people tend to ask leading questions which seem biased toward confirming their assumptions about the person. However, this kind of confirmation bias has also been argued to be an example of social skill: a way to establish a connection with the other person.[8]

Although this research overwhelmingly involves human subjects, some findings that demonstrate bias have been found in non-human animals as well. For example, hyperbolic discounting has been observed in rats, pigeons, and monkeys.[9]

Contents

- • 1. Decision-making, belief, and behavioral biases
- • 2. Social biases
- • 3. Memory errors and biases
- • 4. Common theoretical causes of some cognitive biases

- 5. Individual differences in decision making biases
- 6. Debiasing
- 7. See also
- 8. Notes
- 9. References

Decision-making, belief, and behavioral biases

Many of these biases affect belief formation, business and economic decisions, and human behavior in general. They arise as a replicable result to a specific condition. When confronted with a specific situation, the deviationfrom what is normally expected can be characterized by:

Name	Description
Ambiguity effect	The tendency to avoid options for which missing information makes the probability seems "unknown."[10]
Anchoring or focalism	The tendency to rely too heavily, or "anchor," on one trait or piece of information when making decisions (usually the first piece of information acquired on that subject)[11][12]
Anthropocentric thinking	A tendency observed in children to use human analogies as a basis for reasoning about other, less familiar biological phenomena.[13]
Anthropomorphism or personification	The tendency to characterize animals, objects, and abstract concepts as possessing human-like traits, emotions, and intentions.[14]
Attentional bias	The tendency of our perception to be affected by our recurring thoughts.[15]
Automation bias	The tendency to depend excessively on automated systems which can lead to erroneous automated information overriding correct decisions.[16]

Availability heuristic	The tendency to overestimate the likelihood of events with greater "availability" in memory, which can be influenced by how recent the memories are or how unusual or emotionally charged they may be.[17]
Availability cascade	A self-reinforcing process in which a collective belief gains more and more plausibility through its increasing repetition in public discourse (or *"repeat something long enough and it will become true"*).[18]
Backfire effect	The reaction to disconfirming evidence by strengthening one's previous beliefs.[19] cf. Continued influence effect.
Bandwagon effect	The tendency to do (or believe) things because many other people do (or believe) the same. Related to groupthink and herd behavior.[20]
Base rate fallacy or Base rate neglect	The tendency to ignore base rate information (generic, general information) and focus on specific information (information only pertaining to a certain case).[21]
Belief bias	An effect where someone's evaluation of the logical strength of an argument is biased by the believability of the conclusion.[22]
Ben Franklin effect	A person who has performed a favor for someone is more likely to do another favor for that person than they would be if they had *received* a favor from that person.
Berkson's paradox	The tendency to misinterpret statistical experiments involving conditional probabilities.
Bias blind spot	The tendency to see oneself as less biased than other people, or to be able to identify more cognitive biases in others than in oneself.[23]
Cheerleader effect	The tendency for people to appear more attractive in a group than in isolation.[24]
Choice-supportive bias	The tendency to remember one's choices as better than they actually were.[25]

<u>Clustering illusion</u>	The tendency to overestimate the importance of small runs, streaks, or clusters in large samples of random data (that is, *seeing phantom patterns*).[12]
<u>Confirmation bias</u>	The tendency to search for, interpret, focus on and remember information in a way that confirms one's preconceptions.[26]
<u>Congruence bias</u>	The tendency to test hypotheses exclusively through direct testing, instead of testing possible alternative hypotheses.[12]
<u>Conjunction fallacy</u>	The tendency to assume that specific conditions are more probable than general ones.[27]
<u>Conservatism (belief revision)</u>	The tendency to <u>revise one's belief</u> insufficiently when presented with new evidence.[5][28][29]
<u>Continued influence effect</u>	The tendency to believe previously learned misinformation even after it has been corrected. Misinformation can still influence inferences one generates after a correction has occurred.[30] cf. <u>*Backfire effect*</u>.
<u>Contrast effect</u>	The enhancement or reduction of a certain perception's stimuli when compared with a recently observed, contrasting object.[31]
<u>Courtesy bias</u>	The tendency to give an opinion that is more socially correct than one's true opinion, so as to avoid offending anyone.[32]
<u>Curse of knowledge</u>	When better-informed people find it extremely difficult to think about problems from the perspective of lesser-informed people.[33]
<u>Declinism</u>	The belief that a society or institution is tending toward decline. Particularly, it is the predisposition to view the past favorably (<u>*rosy retrospection*</u>) and future negatively.[34]
<u>Decoy effect</u>	Preferences for either option A or B change in favor of option B when option C is presented, which is similar to option B but in no way better.

Denomination effect	The tendency to spend more money when it is denominated in small amounts (e.g., coins) rather than large amounts (e.g., bills).[35]
Disposition effect	The tendency to sell an asset that has accumulated in value and to resist selling an asset that has declined in value.
Distinction bias	The tendency to view two options as more dissimilar when evaluating them simultaneously than when evaluating them separately.[36]
Dunning–Kruger effect	The tendency for unskilled individuals to overestimate their own ability and the tendency for experts to underestimate their own ability.[37]
Duration neglect	The neglect of the duration of an episode in determining its value.
Empathy gap	The tendency to underestimate the influence or strength of feelings, in either oneself or others.
Endowment effect	The tendency for people to demand much more to give up an object than they would be willing to pay to acquire it.[38]
Exaggerated expectation	Based on the estimates, real-world evidence turns out to be less extreme than our expectations (conditionally inverse of the conservatism bias).[5][39]
Experimenter's or expectation bias	The tendency for experimenters to believe, certify, and publish data that agree with their expectations for the outcome of an experiment, and to disbelieve, discard, or downgrade the corresponding weightings for data that appear to conflict with those expectations.[40]
Focusing effect	The tendency to place too much importance on one aspect of an event.[41]
Forer effect or Barnum effect	The observation that individuals will give high accuracy ratings to descriptions of their personality that supposedly are tailored specifically for them, but are in fact vague and general enough to apply to a wide range of people. This effect can provide a partial explanation for the widespread acceptance of some beliefs and

	practices, such as astrology, fortune telling, graphology, and some types of personality tests.
Framing effect	Drawing different conclusions from the same information, depending on how that information is presented
Frequency illusion	The illusion in which a word, a name, or other thing that has recently come to one's attention suddenly seems to appear with improbable frequency shortly afterward (not to be confused with the *recency illusion* or *selection bias*).[42] This illusion may explain some examples of the Baader-Meinhof Phenomenon, when someone repeatedly notices a newly learned word or phrase shortly after learning it.
Functional fixedness	Limits a person to using an object only in the way it is traditionally used.
Gambler's fallacy	The tendency to think that future probabilities are altered by past events, when in reality they are unchanged. The fallacy arises from an erroneous conceptualization of the *law of large numbers*. For example, "I've flipped heads with this coin five times consecutively, so the chance of tails coming out on the sixth flip is much greater than heads."
Hard–easy effect	Based on a specific level of task difficulty, the confidence in judgments is too conservative and not extreme enough[5][43][44][45]
Hindsight bias	Sometimes called the "I-knew-it-all-along" effect, the tendency to see past events as being predictable[46] at the time those events happened.
Hostile attribution bias	The "hostile attribution bias" is the tendency to interpret others' behaviors as having hostile intent, even when the behavior is ambiguous or benign.
Hot-hand fallacy	The *"hot-hand fallacy"* (also known as the *"hot hand phenomenon"* or *"hot hand"*) is the fallacious belief that a person who has experienced success with a random event has a greater chance of further success in additional attempts.
Hyperbolic discounting	Discounting is the tendency for people to have a stronger preference for more immediate payoffs relative to later payoffs. Hyperbolic discounting leads to choices that are inconsistent over time—people make choices today that their future selves would

	prefer not to have made, despite using the same reasoning.[47] Also known as current moment bias, present-bias, and related to *Dynamic inconsistency*.
Identifiable victim effect	The tendency to respond more strongly to a single identified person at risk than to a large group of people at risk.[48]
IKEA effect	The tendency for people to place a disproportionately high value on objects that they partially assembled themselves, such as furniture from IKEA, regardless of the quality of the end result.
Illusion of control	The tendency to overestimate one's degree of influence over other external events.[49]
Illusion of validity	Belief that furtherly acquired information generates additional relevant data for predictions, even when it evidently does not.[50]
Illusory correlation	Inaccurately perceiving a relationship between two unrelated events.[51][52]
Illusory truth effect	A tendency to believe that a statement is true if it is easier to process, or if it has been stated multiple times, regardless of its actual veracity. These are specific cases of truthiness.
Impact bias	The tendency to overestimate the length or the intensity of the impact of future feeling states.[53]
Information bias	The tendency to seek information even when it cannot affect action.[54]
Insensitivity to sample size	The tendency to under-expect variation in small samples.
Irrational escalation	The phenomenon where people justify increased investment in a decision, based on the cumulative prior investment, despite new evidence suggesting that the decision was probably wrong. Also known as the sunk cost fallacy.

Law of the instrument	An over-reliance on a familiar tool or methods, ignoring or under-valuing alternative approaches. *"If all you have is a hammer, everything looks like a nail."*
Less-is-better effect	The tendency to prefer a smaller set to a larger set judged separately, but not jointly.
Look-elsewhere effect	An apparently statistically significant observation may have actually arisen by chance because of the size of the parameter space to be searched.
Loss aversion	The disutility of giving up an object is greater than the utility associated with acquiring it.[55] (see also Sunk cost effects and endowment effect).
Mere exposure effect	The tendency to express undue liking for things merely because of familiarity with them.[56]
Money illusion	The tendency to concentrate on the nominal value (face value) of money rather than its value in terms of purchasing power.[57]
Moral credential effect	The tendency of a track record of non-prejudice to increase subsequent prejudice.
Negativity bias or Negativity effect	Psychological phenomenon by which humans have a greater recall of unpleasant memories compared with positive memories.[58][59] (see also actor-observer bias, group attribution error, positivity effect, and negativity effect).[60]
Neglect of probability	The tendency to completely disregard probability when making a decision under uncertainty.[61]
Normalcy bias	The refusal to plan for, or react to, a disaster which has never happened before.
Not invented here	Aversion to contact with or use of products, research, standards, or knowledge developed outside a group. Related to IKEA effect.

<u>Observer-expectancy effect</u>	When a researcher expects a given result and therefore unconsciously manipulates an experiment or misinterprets data in order to find it (see also <u>subject-expectancy effect</u>).
<u>Omission bias</u>	The tendency to judge harmful actions as worse or less moral, than equally harmful omissions (inactions).[62]
<u>Optimism bias</u>	The tendency to be over-optimistic, overestimating favorable and pleasing outcomes (see also <u>wishful thinking</u>, <u>valence effect</u>, <u>positive outcome bias</u>).[63][64]
<u>Ostrich effect</u>	Ignoring an obvious (negative) situation.
<u>Outcome bias</u>	The tendency to judge a decision by its eventual outcome instead of based on the quality of the decision at the time it was made.
<u>Overconfidence effect</u>	Excessive confidence in one's own answers to questions. For example, for certain types of questions, answers that people rate as "99% certain" turn out to be wrong 40% of the time. [5][65][66][67]
<u>Pareidolia</u>	A vague and random stimulus (often an image or sound) is perceived as significant, e.g., seeing images of animals or faces in clouds, the <u>man in the moon</u>, and hearing non-existent <u>hidden messages</u> on <u>records played in reverse</u>.
<u>Pessimism bias</u>	The tendency for some people, especially those suffering from <u>depression</u>, to overestimate the likelihood of negative things happening to them.
<u>Planning fallacy</u>	The tendency to underestimate task-completion times.[53]
<u>Post-purchase rationalization</u>	The tendency to persuade onese lf through rational argument that a purchase was good value.

Pro-innovation bias	The tendency to have an excessive optimism toward an invention or innovation's usefulness throughout society, while often failing to identify its limitations and weaknesses.
Projection bias	The tendency to overestimate how much our future selves share one's current preferences, thoughts and values, thus leading to sub-optimal choices.[68][69][59]
Pseudocertainty effect	The tendency to make risk-averse choices if the expected outcome is positive, but make risk-seeking choices to avoid negative outcomes.[70]
Reactance	The urge to do the opposite of what someone wants you to do out of a need to resist a perceived attempt to constrain your freedom of choice (see also Reverse psychology).
Reactive devaluation	Devaluing proposals only because they purportedly originated with an adversary.
Recency illusion	The illusion that a word or language usage is a recent innovation when it is in fact long-established (see also frequency illusion).
Regressive bias	A certain state of mind wherein high values and high likelihoods are overestimated while low values and low likelihoods are underestimated.[5][71][72]
Restraint bias	The tendency to overestimate one's ability to show restraint in the face of temptation.
Rhyme as reason effect	Rhyming statements are perceived as more truthful. A famous example being used in the O.J Simpson trial with the defense's use of the phrase *"If the gloves don't fit, then you must acquit."*
Risk compensation / Peltzman effect	The tendency to take greater risks when perceived safety increases.
Selective perception	The tendency for expectations to affect perception.

Semmelweis reflex	The tendency to reject new evidence that contradicts a paradigm.[29]
Sexual overperception bias / sexual underperception bias	The tendency to over-/underestimate sexual interest of another person in oneself.
Social comparison bias	The tendency, when making decisions, to favor potential candidates who don't compete with one's own particular strengths.[73]
Social desirability bias	The tendency to over-report socially desirable characteristics or behaviors in oneself and under-report socially undesirable characteristics or behaviors.[74]
Status quo bias	The tendency to like things to stay relatively the same (see also loss aversion, endowment effect, and system justification).[75][76]
Stereotyping	Expecting a member of a group to have certain characteristics without having actual information about that individual.
Subadditivity effect	The tendency to judge probability of the whole to be less than the probabilities of the parts.[77]
Subjective validation	Perception that something is true if a subject's belief demands it to be true. Also assigns perceived connections between coincidences.
Surrogation	Losing sight of the strategic construct that a measure is intended to represent, and subsequently acting as though the measure is the construct of interest.
Survivorship bias	Concentrating on the people or things that "survived" some process and inadvertently overlooking those that didn't because of their lack of visibility.
Time-saving bias	Underestimations of the time that could be saved (or lost) when increasing (or decreasing) from a relatively low speed and overestimations of the time that could be saved (or lost) when increasing (or decreasing) from a relatively high speed.

Third-person effect	Belief that mass communicated media messages have a greater effect on others than on themselves.
Triviality / Parkinson's Law of	The tendency to give disproportionate weight to trivial issues. Also known as bikeshedding, this bias explains why an organization may avoid specialized or complex subjects, such as the design of a nuclear reactor, and instead focus on something easy to grasp or rewarding to the average participant, such as the design of an adjacent bike shed.[78]
Unit bias	The tendency to want to finish a given unit of a task or an item. Strong effects on the consumption of food in particular.[79]
Weber–Fechner law	Difficulty in comparing small differences in large quantities.
Well travelled road effect	Underestimation of the duration taken to traverse oft-traveled routes and overestimation of the duration taken to traverse less familiar routes.
Zero-risk bias	Preference for reducing a small risk to zero over a greater reduction in a larger risk.
Zero-sum bias	A bias whereby a situation is incorrectly perceived to be like a zero-sum game (i.e., one person gains at the expense of another).

Social biases

Most of these biases are labeled as attributional biases.

Name	Description
Actor-observer bias	The tendency for explanations of other individuals' behaviors to overemphasize the influence of their personality and underemphasize the influence of their situation (see also Fundamental attribution error), and for explanations of one's own behaviors to do the opposite (that is, to overemphasize the

	influence of our situation and underemphasize the influence of our own personality).
Authority bias	The tendency to attribute greater accuracy to the opinion of an authority figure (unrelated to its content) and be more influenced by that opinion.[80]
Defensive attribution hypothesis	Attributing more blame to a harm-doer as the outcome becomes more severe or as personal or situational similarity to the victim increases.
Egocentric bias	Occurs when people claim more responsibility for themselves for the results of a joint action than an outside observer would credit them with.
Extrinsic incentives bias	An exception to the *fundamental attribution error*, when people view others as having (situational) extrinsic motivations and (dispositional) intrinsic motivations for oneself.
False consensus effect	The tendency for people to overestimate the degree to which others agree with them.[81]
Forer effect (aka Barnum effect)	The tendency to give high accuracy ratings to descriptions of their personality that supposedly are tailored specifically for them, but are in fact vague and general enough to apply to a wide range of people. For example, horoscopes.
Fundamental attribution error	The tendency for people to over-emphasize personality-based explanations for behaviors observed in others while under-emphasizing the role and power of situational influences on the same behavior[59] (see also actor-observer bias, group attribution error, positivity effect, and negativity effect).[60]
Group attribution error	The biased belief that the characteristics of an individual group member are reflective of the group as a whole or the tendency to assume that group decision outcomes reflect the preferences of group members, even when information is available that clearly suggests otherwise.
Halo effect	The tendency for a person's positive or negative traits to "spill over" from one personality area to another in others' perceptions of them (see also physical attractiveness stereotype).[82]

Illusion of asymmetric insight	People perceive their knowledge of their peers to surpass their peers' knowledge of them.[83]
Illusion of external agency	When people view self-generated preferences as instead being caused by insightful, effective and benevolent agents.
Illusion of transparency	People overestimate others' ability to know them, and they also overestimate their ability to know others.
Illusory superiority	Overestimating one's desirable qualities, and underestimating undesirable qualities, relative to other people. (Also known as "Lake Wobegon effect", "better-than-average effect", or "superiority bias".)[84]
Ingroup bias	The tendency for people to give preferential treatment to others they perceive to be members of their own groups.
Just-world hypothesis	The tendency for people to want to believe that the world is fundamentally just, causing them to rationalize an otherwise inexplicable injustice as deserved by the victim(s).
Moral luck	The tendency for people to ascribe greater or lesser moral standing based on the outcome of an event.
Naïve cynicism	Expecting more *egocentric bias* in others than in oneself.
Naïve realism	The belief that we see reality as it really is—objectively and without bias; that the facts are plain for all to see; that rational people will agree with us; and that those who don't are either uninformed, lazy, irrational, or biased.
Outgroup homogeneity bias	Individuals see members of their own group as being relatively more varied than members of other groups.[85]
Self-serving bias	The tendency to claim more responsibility for successes than failures. It may also manifest itself as a tendency for people to evaluate ambiguous information in a way beneficial to their interests (see also group-serving bias).[86]

Shared information bias	Known as the tendency for group members to spend more time and energy discussing information that all members are already familiar with (i.e., shared information), and less time and energy discussing information that only some members are aware of (i.e., unshared information).[87]
Sociability bias of language	The disproportionally higher representation of words related to social interactions, in comparison to words related to physical or mental aspects of behavior, in most languages. This bias attributed to nature of language as a tool facilitating human interactions. When verbal descriptors of human behavior are used as a source of information, sociability bias of such descriptors emerges in factor-analytic studies as a factor related to pro-social behavior (for example, of Extraversion factor in the Big Five personality traits[59]
System justification	The tendency to defend and bolster the status quo. Existing social, economic, and political arrangements tend to be preferred, and alternatives disparaged, sometimes even at the expense of individual and collective self-interest. (See also status quo bias.)
Trait ascription bias	The tendency for people to view themselves as relatively variable in terms of personality, behavior, and mood while viewing others as much more predictable.
Ultimate attribution error	Similar to the fundamental attribution error, in this error a person is likely to make an internal attribution to an entire group instead of the individuals within the group.
Worse-than-average effect	A tendency to believe ourselves to be worse than others at tasks which are difficult.[88]

Memory errors and biases

Main article: List of memory biases

In psychology *and* cognitive science, a memory bias is a cognitive bias that either enhances or impairs the recall of a memory (either the chances that the memory will be recalled at all, or the amount of time it takes for it to be recalled, or both), or that alters the content of a reported memory. There are many types of memory bias, including:

Name	Description
<u>Bizarreness effect</u>	Bizarre material is better remembered than common material.
<u>Choice-supportive bias</u>	In a self-justifying manner retroactively ascribing one's choices to be more informed than they were when they were made.
Change bias	After an investment of effort in producing change, remembering one's past performance as more difficult than it actually was.[89]
<u>Childhood amnesia</u>	The retention of few memories from before the age of four.
Conservatism or Regressive bias	Tendency to remember high values and high likelihoods/probabilities/ frequencies as lower than they actually were and low ones as higher than they actually were. Based on the evidence, memories are not extreme enough.[71][72]
Consistency bias	Incorrectly remembering one's past attitudes and behavioras resembling present attitudes and behavior.[90]
<u>Context effect</u>	That cognition and memory are dependent on context, such that out-of-context memories are more difficult to retrieve than in-context memories (e.g., recall time and accuracy for a work-related memory will be lower at home, and vice versa)
<u>Cross-race effect</u>	The tendency for people of one race to have difficulty identifying members of a race other than their own.
<u>Cryptomnesia</u>	A form of <u>*misattribution*</u> where a memory is mistaken for imagination, because there is no subjective experience of it being a memory.[89]
<u>Egocentric bias</u>	Recalling the past in a self-serving manner, e.g., remembering one's exam grades as being better than they were, or remembering a caught fish as bigger than it really was.

<u>Fading affect bias</u>	A bias in which the emotion associated with unpleasant memories fades more quickly than the emotion associated with positive events.<u>[91]</u>
<u>False memory</u>	A form of *misattribution* where imagination is mistaken for a memory.
<u>Generation effect</u> (Self-generation effect)	That self-generated information is remembered best. For instance, people are better able to recall memories of statements that they have generated than similar statements generated by others.
<u>Google effect</u>	The tendency to forget information that can be found readily online by using Internet search engines.
<u>Hindsight bias</u>	The inclination to see past events as being more predictable than they actually were; also called the "*I-knew-it-all-along*" effect.
Humor effect	That humorous items are more easily remembered than non-humorous ones, which might be explained by the distinctiveness of humor, the increased cognitive processing time to understand the humor, or the emotional arousal caused by the humor.<u>[92]</u>
<u>Illusion of truth effect</u>	That people are more likely to identify as true statements those they have previously heard (even if they cannot consciously remember having heard them), regardless of the actual validity of the statement. In other words, a person is more likely to believe a familiar statement than an unfamiliar one.
<u>Illusory correlation</u>	Inaccurately remembering a relationship between two events.<u>[51][52]</u>
Lag effect	The phenomenon whereby learning is greater when studying is spread out over time, as opposed to studying the same amount of time in a single session. See also <u>spacing effect</u>.
<u>Leveling and sharpening</u>	Memory distortions introduced by the loss of details in a recollection over time, often concurrent with sharpening or selective recollection of certain details that take on exaggerated significance in relation to the details or aspects of the experience lost through leveling. Both biases may be reinforced over time, and by repeated recollection or re-telling of a memory.<u>[93]</u>

Levels-of-processing effect	That different methods of encoding information into memory have different levels of effectiveness.[94]
List-length effect	A smaller percentage of items are remembered in a longer list, but as the length of the list increases, the absolute number of items remembered increases as well. For example, consider a list of 30 items ("L30") and a list of 100 items ("L100"). An individual may remember 15 items from L30, or 50%, whereas the individual may remember 40 items from L100, or 40%. Although the percent of L30 items remembered (50%) is greater than the percent of L100 (40%), more L100 items (40) are remembered than L30 items (15).[95]
Misinformation effect	Memory becoming less accurate because of interference from *post-event information*.[96]
Modality effect	That memory recall is higher for the last items of a list when the list items were received via speech than when they were received through writing.
Mood-congruent memory bias	The improved recall of information congruent with one's current mood.
Next-in-line effect	That a person in a group has diminished recall for the words of others who spoke immediately before himself, if they take turns speaking.[97]
Part-list cueing effect	That being shown some items from a list and later retrieving one item causes it to become harder to retrieve the other items.[98]
Peak-end rule	That people seem to perceive not the sum of an experience but the average of how it was at its peak (e.g., pleasant or unpleasant) and how it ended.
Persistence	The unwanted recurrence of memories of a traumatic event.
Picture superiority effect	The notion that concepts that are learned by viewing pictures are more easily and frequently recalled than are concepts that are learned by viewing their written word form counterparts.[99][100][101][102][103][104]
Positivity effect	That older adults favor positive over negative information in their memories.

Primacy effect, recency effect & serial position effect	That items near the end of a sequence are the easiest to recall, followed by the items at the beginning of a sequence; items in the middle are the least likely to be remembered.[105]
Processing difficulty effect	That information that takes longer to read and is thought about more (processed with more difficulty) is more easily remembered.[106]
Reminiscence bump	The recalling of more personal events from adolescence and early adulthood than personal events from other lifetime periods.[107]
Rosy retrospection	The remembering of the past as having been better than it really was.
Self-relevance effect	That memories relating to the self are better recalled than similar information relating to others.
Source confusion	Confusing episodic memories with other information, creating distorted memories.[108]
Spacing effect	That information is better recalled if exposure to it is repeated over a long span of time rather than a short one.
Spotlight effect	The tendency to overestimate the amount that other people notice your appearance or behavior.
Stereotypical bias	Memory distorted toward stereotypes (e.g., racial or gender), e.g., "*black-sounding*" names being misremembered as names of criminals.[89]
Suffix effect	Diminishment of the recency effect because a sound item is appended to the list that the subject is *not* required to recall.[109][110]
Suggestibility	A form of misattribution where ideas suggested by a questioner are mistaken for memory.

Telescoping effect	The tendency to displace recent events backward in time and remote events forward in time, so that recent events appear more remote, and remote events, more recent.
Testing effect	The fact that you more easily remember information you have read by rewriting it instead of rereading it.[111]
Tip of the tongue phenomenon	When a subject is able to recall parts of an item, or related information, but is frustratingly unable to recall the whole item. This is thought to be an instance of *"blocking"* where multiple similar memories are being recalled and interfere with each other.[89]
Travis Syndrome	Overestimating the significance of the present.[112] It is related to the enlightenment Idea of progress and chronological snobbery with possibly an appeal to noveltylogical fallacy being part of the bias.
Verbatim effect	That the *"gist"* of what someone has said is better remembered than the verbatim wording.[113] This is because memories are representations, not exact copies.
Von Restorff effect	That an item that sticks out is more likely to be remembered than other items.[114]
Zeigarnik effect	That uncompleted or interrupted tasks are remembered better than completed ones.

Common theoretical causes of some cognitive biases

- Bounded rationality—limits on optimization and rationality
  - Prospect theory
  - Mental accounting
  - Adaptive bias—basing decisions on limited information and biasing them based on the costs of being wrong.
- Attribute substitution—making a complex, difficult judgment by unconsciously substituting it by an easier judgment[115]
- Attribution theory
  - Salience
  - Naïve realism

- <u>Cognitive dissonance</u>, and related:
  - <u>Impression management</u>
  - <u>Self-perception theory</u>
- <u>Heuristics in judgment and decision making</u>, including:
  - <u>Availability heuristic</u>—estimating what is more likely by what is more available in memory, which is biased toward vivid, unusual, or emotionally charged examples[51]
  - <u>Representativeness heuristic</u>—judging probabilities on the basis of resemblance[51]
  - <u>Affect heuristic</u>—basing a decision on an emotional reaction rather than a calculation of risks and benefits[116]
- Some theories of <u>emotion</u> such as:
  - <u>Two-factor theory of emotion</u>
  - <u>Somatic markers hypothesis</u>
- <u>Introspection illusion</u>
- Misinterpretations or <u>misuse of statistics</u>; <u>innumeracy</u>.

A 2012 <u>*Psychological Bulletin*</u> article suggested that at least eight seemingly unrelated biases can be produced by the same <u>information-theoretic</u> generative mechanism that assumes noisy information processing during storage and retrieval of information in human memory.[5]

Individual differences in decision making biases

People do appear to have stable individual differences in their susceptibility to decision biases such as <u>overconfidence</u>, <u>temporal discounting</u>, and <u>bias blind spot</u>.[117] That said, these stable levels of bias within individuals are possible to change. Participants in experiments who watched training videos and played debiasing games showed medium to large reductions both immediately and up to three months later in the extent to which they exhibited susceptibility to six cognitive biases: <u>anchoring</u>, bias blind spot, <u>confirmation bias</u>, <u>fundamental attribution error</u>, <u>projection bias</u>, and <u>representativeness</u>.[118]

Debiasing

<u>Debiasing</u> is the reduction of biases in judgment and decision making through incentives, nudges, and training. <u>Cognitive bias mitigation</u> and <u>cognitive bias modification</u> are forms of debiasing specifically applicable to cognitive biases and their effects.

See also

- *Psychology portal*
- *Sociology portal*
- *Thinking portal*
- 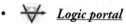 *Logic portal*

- Affective forecasting
- Anecdotal evidence
- Apophenia
- Black swan theory
- Chronostasis
- Cognitive bias in animals
- Cognitive bias mitigation
- Cognitive distortion
- Cross-race effect
- Dysrationalia
- Feedback
- Frame rate
- List of common misconceptions
- List of fallacies
- List of memory biases
- List of topics related to public relations and propaganda
- Lists of thinking-related topics
- Media bias
- Mind projection fallacy
- Pollyanna principle
- Positive feedback
- Prevalence effect
- Publication bias
- Recall bias
- Self-handicapping
- Systematic bias

Notes

Jump up⌃ retrievable

1. *"Cognitive bias cheat sheet – Better Humans"*. Better Humans. 2016-09-01. Retrieved 2017-05-27.
2. *Dougherty, M. R. P.; Gettys, C. F.; Ogden, E. E. (1999). "MINERVA-DM: A memory processes model for judgments of likelihood" (PDF). Psychological Review. 106 (1): 180–209. doi:10.1037/0033-295x.106.1.180.*
3. *Kahneman, D.; Tversky, A. (1972). "Subjective probability: A judgment of representativeness". Cognitive Psychology. 3: 430–454. doi:10.1016/0010-0285(72)90016-3.*
4. *Baron, J. (2007). Thinking and deciding (4th ed.). New York City: Cambridge University Press. ISBN 9781139466028.*
5. *Martin Hilbert (2012). "Toward a synthesis of cognitive biases: How noisy information processing can bias human decision making" (PDF). Psychological Bulletin. 138 (2): 211–237. PMID 22122235. doi:10.1037/a0025940. Lay summary.*
6. *Maccoun, Robert J. (1998). "Biases in the interpretation and use of research results" (PDF). Annual Review of Psychology. 49 (1): 259–87. PMID 15012470. doi:10.1146/annurev.psych.49.1.259.*
7. *Nickerson, Raymond S. (1998). "Confirmation Bias: A Ubiquitous Phenomenon in Many Guises" (PDF). Review of General Psychology. Educational Publishing Foundation. 2 (2): 175–220 [198]. ISSN 1089-2680. doi:10.1037/1089-2680.2.2.175.*
8. *Dardenne, Benoit; Leyens, Jacques-Philippe (1995). "Confirmation Bias as a Social Skill". Personality and Social Psychology Bulletin. Society for Personality and Social Psychology. 21 (11): 1229–1239. ISSN 1552-7433. doi:10.1177/01461672952111011.*
9. *Alexander, William H.; Brown, Joshua W. (1 June 2010). "Hyperbolically Discounted Temporal Difference Learning". Neural Computation. 22 (6): 1511–1527. PMC 3005720* ⊚
. *PMID 20100071. doi:10.1162/neco.2010.08-09-1080.*
10. Baron 1994, p. 372
11. *Zhang, Yu; Lewis, Mark; Pellon, Michael; Coleman, Phillip (2007). "A Preliminary Research on Modeling Cognitive Agents for Social Environments in Multi-Agent Systems" (PDF): 116–123.*
12. *Iverson, Grant; Brooks, Brian; Holdnack, James (2008). "Misdiagnosis of Cognitive Impairment in Forensic Neuropsychology". In Heilbronner, Robert L. Neuropsychology in the Courtroom: Expert Analysis of Reports and Testimony. New York: Guilford Press. p. 248. ISBN 9781593856342.*
13. *Coley, John D; Tanner, Kimberly D (2012). "Common Origins of Diverse Misconceptions: Cognitive Principles and the Development of Biology Thinking". CBE-Life Sciences Education. 11 (3): 209–215. ISSN 1931-7913. doi:10.1187/cbe.12-06-0074.*
14. *"The Real Reason We Dress Pets Like People"*. LiveScience.com. Retrieved 2015-11-16.
15. Bar-Haim, Y., Lamy, D., Pergamin, L., Bakermans-Kranenburg, M.J., & van IJzendoorn, M.H. (2007). "Threat-related attentional bias in anxious and non-anxious individuals: A meta-analytic study." *Psychological Bulletin.*
16. Goddard, Kate; Roudsari, Abdul; Wyatt, Jeremy C. (2011). "Automation Bias –A Hidden Issue for Clinical Decision Support System Use." *International Perspectives in Health Informatics.* Studies in Health Technology and Informatics. IOS Press. doi:10.3233/978-1-60750-709-3-17
17. *Schwarz, N.; Bless, Herbert; Strack, Fritz; Klumpp, G.; Rittenauer-Schatka, Helga; Simons, Annette (1991). "Ease of Retrieval as Information: Another Look at the Availability Heuristic" (PDF).Journal of Personality and Social Psychology. 61 (2): 195–202. doi:10.1037/0022-3514.61.2.195. Archived from the original (PDF) on 9 February 2014. Retrieved19 Oct 2014.*
18. *Kuran, Timur; Cass R Sunstein (1998). "Availability Cascades and Risk Regulation". Stanford Law Review. 51: 683. doi:10.2307/1229439.*
19. *Sanna, Lawrence J.; Schwarz, Norbert; Stocker, Shevaun L. (2002). "When debiasing backfires: Accessible content and accessibility experiences in debiasing hindsight." (PDF). Journal of Experimental Psychology: Learning, Memory, and Cognition. 28 (3): 497–502. ISSN 0278-7393. doi:10.1037/0278-7393.28.3.497.*
20. *Colman, Andrew (2003). Oxford Dictionary of Psychology. New York: Oxford University Press. p. 77. ISBN 0-19-280632-7.*
21. Baron 1994, pp. 224–228
22. *Klauer, K. C.; Musch, J; Naumer, B (2000). "On belief bias in syllogistic reasoning". Psychological Review. 107 (4): 852–884. PMID 11089409. doi:10.1037/0033-295X.107.4.852.*
23. *Pronin, Emily; Matthew B. Kugler (July 2007). "Valuing thoughts, ignoring behavior: The introspection illusion as a source of the bias blind spot". Journal of Experimental Social Psychology. Elsevier. 43 (4): 565–578. ISSN 0022-1031. doi:10.1016/j.jesp.2006.05.011.*

24. *Walker, Drew; Vul, Edward (2013-10-25). "Hierarchical Encoding Makes Individuals in a Group Seem More Attractive". Psychological Science. 25 (11): 230–235. PMID 24163333. doi:10.1177/0956797613497969.*

25. *Mather, M.; Shafir, E.; Johnson, M.K. (2000). "Misrememberance of options past: Source monitoring and choice" (PDF). Psychological Science. 11 (2): 132–138. PMID 11273420. doi:10.1111/1467-9280.00228.*

26. *Oswald, Margit E.; Grosjean, Stefan (2004). "Confirmation Bias". In Pohl, Rüdiger F. Cognitive Illusions: A Handbook on Fallacies and Biases in Thinking, Judgement and Memory. Hove, UK: Psychology Press. pp. 79–96. ISBN 978-1-84169-351-4. OCLC55124398.*

27. *Fisk, John E. (2004). "Conjunction fallacy". In Pohl, Rüdiger F.Cognitive Illusions: A Handbook on Fallacies and Biases in Thinking, Judgement and Memory. Hove, UK: Psychology Press. pp. 23–42. ISBN 978-1-84169-351-4. OCLC55124398.*

28. *DuCharme, W. M. (1970). "Response bias explanation of conservative human inference". Journal of Experimental Psychology. 85 (1): 66–74. doi:10.1037/h0029546.*

29. *Edwards, W. (1968). "Conservatism in human information processing". In Kleinmuntz, B.Formal representation of human judgment. New York: Wiley. pp. 17–52.*

30. *Johnson, Hollyn M.; Colleen M. Seifert (November 1994). "Sources of the continued influence effect: When misinformation in memory affects later inferences". Journal of Experimental Psychology: Learning, Memory, and Cognition. 20 (6): 1420–1436. doi:10.1037/0278-7393.20.6.1420.*

31. Plous 1993, pp. 38–41

32. *Ciccarelli, Saundra; White, J. (2014). Psychology (4th ed.). Pearson Education, Inc. p. 62.* ISBN0205973353.

33. *Ackerman, Mark S., ed. (2003). Sharing expertise beyond knowledge management (online ed.). Cambridge, Massachusetts: MIT Press. p. 7.* ISBN9780262011952.

34. Steven R. Quartz, *The State Of The World Isn't Nearly As Bad As You Think, Edge Foundation, Inc.,* retrieved 2016-02-17.

35. Why We Spend Coins Faster Than Bills by Chana Joffe-Walt. *All Things Considered,* 12 May 2009.

36. *Hsee, Christopher K.; Zhang, Jiao (2004). "Distinction bias: Misprediction and mischoice due to joint evaluation". Journal of Personality and Social Psychology. 86 (5): 680–695. PMID 15161394. doi:10.1037/0022-3514.86.5.680.*

37. *Kruger, Justin; Dunning, David (1999). "Unskilled and Unaware of It: How Difficulties in Recognizing One's Own Incompetence Lead to Inflated Self-Assessments". Journal of Personality and Social Psychology. 77 (6): 1121–34. CiteSeerX10.1.1.64.2655 ⓐ. PMID 10626367. doi:10.1037/0022-3514.77.6.1121.*

38. (Kahneman, Knetsch & Thaler 1991, p. 193) Richard Thaler coined the term "endowment effect."

39. *Wagenaar, W. A.; Keren, G. B. (1985). "Calibration of probability assessments by professional blackjack dealers, statistical experts, and lay people". Organizational Behavior and Human Decision Processes. 36 (3): 406–416. doi:10.1016/0749-5978(85)90008-1.*

40. *Jeng, M. (2006). "A selected history of expectation bias in physics". American Journal of Physics. 74 (7): 578–583. doi:10.1119/1.2186333.*

41. *Kahneman, Daniel; Alan B. Krueger; David Schkade; Norbert Schwarz; Arthur A. Stone (2006-06-30). "Would you be happier if you were richer? A focusing illusion" (PDF). Science. 312 (5782): 1908–10* PMID16809528. doi:10.1126/science.1129688.

42. *Zwicky, Arnold (2005-08-07). "Just Between Dr. Language and I". Language Log.*

43. *Lichtenstein, S.; Fischhoff, B. (1977). "Do those who know more also know more about how much they know?". Organizational Behavior and Human Performance. 20 (2): 159–183. doi:10.1016/0030-5073(77)90001-0.*

44. *Merkle, E. C. (2009). "The disutility of the hard-easy effect in choice confidence". Psychonomic Bulletin & Review. 16 (1): 204–213. doi:10.3758/PBR.16.1.204.*

45. *Juslin, P; Winman, A.; Olsson, H. (2000). "Naive empiricism and dogmatism in confidence research: a critical examination of the hard-easy effect". Psychological Review. 107 (2): 384–396. doi:10.1037/0033-295x.107.2.384.*

46. *Pohl, Rüdiger F. (2004). "Hindsight Bias". In Pohl, Rüdiger F. Cognitive Illusions: A Handbook on Fallacies and Biases in Thinking, Judgement and Memory. Hove, UK: Psychology Press. pp. 363–378. ISBN 978-1-84169-351-4. OCLC 55124398.*

47. *Laibson, David (1997). "Golden Eggs and Hyperbolic Discounting". Quarterly Journal of Economics. 112 (2): 443–477. doi:10.1162/003355397555253.*

48. *Kogut, Tehila; Ritov, Ilana (2005). "The 'Identified Victim' Effect: An Identified Group, or Just a Single Individual?" (PDF). Journal of Behavioral Decision Making. Wiley Inter Science. 18: 157–167. doi:10.1002/bdm.492. Retrieved August 15, 2013.*

49. *Thompson, Suzanne C. (1999). "Illusions of Control: How We Overestimate Our Personal Influence". Current Directions in Psychological Science. Association for Psychological Science. 8 (6): 187–190. ISSN0963-7214. JSTOR20182602. doi:10.1111/1467-8721.00044.*

50. *Dierkes, Meinolf; Antal, Ariane Berthoin; Child, John; Ikujiro Nonaka (2003). Handbook of Organizational Learning and Knowledge. Oxford University Press. p. 22. ISBN978-0-19-829582-2. Retrieved 9 September 2013.*

51. *Tversky, Amos; Daniel Kahneman (September 27, 1974). "Judgment under Uncertainty: Heuristics and Biases". Science. American Association for the Advancement of Science. 185 (4157): 1124–1131. PMID17835457. doi:10.1126/science.185.4157.1124.*

52. *Fiedler, K. (1991). "The tricky nature of skewed frequency tables: An information loss account of distinctiveness-based illusory correlations". Journal of Personality and Social Psychology. 60 (1): 24–36. doi:10.1037/0022-3514.60.1.24.*

53. *Sanna, Lawrence J.; Schwarz, Norbert (2004). "Integrating Temporal Biases: The Interplay of Focal Thoughts and Accessibility Experiences". Psychological Science. American Psychological Society. 15 (7): 474–481. PMID15200632. doi:10.1111/j.0956-7976.2004.00704.x.*

54. Baron 1994, pp. 258–259

55. (Kahneman, Knetsch & Thaler 1991, p. 193) Daniel Kahneman, together with Amos Tversky, coined the term "loss aversion."

56. *Bornstein, Robert F.; Crave-Lemley, Catherine (2004). "Mere exposure effect". In Pohl, Rüdiger F. Cognitive Illusions: A Handbook on Fallacies and Biases in Thinking, Judgement and Memory. Hove, UK: Psychology Press. pp. 215–234. ISBN978-1-84169-351-4.OCLC55124398.*

57. *Shafir, Eldar; Diamond, Peter; Tversky, Amos (2000). "Money Illusion". In Kahneman, Daniel; Tversky, Amos. Choices, values, and frames. Cambridge University Press. pp. 335–355. ISBN978-0-521-62749-8.*

58. *Haizlip, Julie; et al. "Perspective: The Negativity Bias, Medical Education, and the Culture of Academic Medicine: Why Culture Change Is Hard". Retrieved October 3, 2012.*

59. *Trofimova, IN (2014). "Observer bias: an interaction of temperament traits with biases in the semantic perception of lexical material". PLoS ONE.9 (1): e85677. PMC3903487 ⓐ . PMID24475048. doi:10.1371/journal.pone.0085677.*

60. Sutherland 2007, pp. 138–139

61. Baron 1994, p. 353

62. Baron 1994, p. 386

63. Baron 1994, p. 44

64. Hardman 2009, p. 104

65. *Adams, P. A.; Adams, J. K. (1960). "Confidence in the recognition and reproduction of words difficult to spell". The American Journal of Psychology.73(4): 544–552. PMID13681411. doi:10.2307/1419942.*

66. *Hoffrage, Ulrich (2004). "Overconfidence". In Rüdiger Pohl. Cognitive Illusions: a handbook on fallacies and biases in thinking, judgement and memory. Psychology Press. ISBN978-1-84169-351-4.*

67. Sutherland 2007, pp. 172–178

68. *Hsee, Christopher K.; Hastie, Reid (2006). "Decision and experience: why don't we choose what makes us happy?" (PDF). Trends in Cognitive Sciences. 10 (1): 31–37. PMID16318925. doi:10.1016/j.tics.2005.11.007. Archived from the original on 2015-04-20.*

69. *Trofimova, IN (1999). "How people of different age sex and temperament estimate the world". Psychological Reports. 85/2: 533–552. doi:10.2466/pr0.1999.85.2.533.*

70. Hardman 2009, p. 137

71. *Attneave, F. (1953). "Psychological probability as a function of experienced frequency". Journal of Experimental Psychology. 46 (2): 81–86. PMID13084849. doi:10.1037/h0057955.*

72. *Fischhoff, B.; Slovic, P.; Lichtenstein, S. (1977). "Knowing with certainty: The appropriateness of extreme confidence". Journal of Experimental Psychology: Human Perception and Performance. 3 (4): 552–564. doi:10.1037/0096-1523.3.4.552.*

73. *Garcia, Stephen M.; Song, Hyunjin; Tesser, Abraham (November 2010). "Tainted recommendations: The social comparison bias". Organizational Behavior and Human Decision Processes. 113 (2): 97–101.* ISSN0749-5978. doi:10.1016/j.obhdp.2010.06.002. Lay summary *– BPS Research Digest (2010-10-30).*

74. *Dalton, D. & Ortegren, M. (2011). "Gender differences in ethics research: The importance of controlling for the social desirability response bias". Journal of Business Ethics. 103 (1): 73–93.* doi:10.1007/s10551-011-0843-8.

75. Kahneman, Knetsch & Thaler 1991, p. 193

76. Baron 1994, p. 382

77. Baron, J. (in preparation). *Thinking and Deciding*, 4th edition. New York: Cambridge University Press.

78. *Forsyth, Donelson R (2009).* Group Dynamics *(5th ed.). Cengage Learning. p. 317.* ISBN978-0-495-59952-4.

79. "Penn Psychologists Believe 'Unit Bias' Determines The Acceptable Amount To Eat". Science Daily (Nov. 21, 2005)

80. *Milgram, Stanley (Oct 1963). "Behavioral Study of obedience". The Journal of Abnormal and Social Psychology. 67 (4).*

81. *Marks, Gary; Miller, Norman (1987). "Ten years of research on the false-consensus effect: An empirical and theoretical review". Psychological Bulletin. American Psychological Association. 102 (1): 72–90.* doi:10.1037/0033-2909.102.1.72.

82. Baron 1994, p. 275

83. *Pronin, E.; Kruger, J.; Savitsky, K.; Ross, L. (2001). "You don't know me, but I know you: the illusion of asymmetric insight". Journal of Personality and Social Psychology. 81 (4): 639–656.* PMID11642351. doi:10.1037/0022-3514.81.4.639.

84. *Hoorens, Vera (1993). "Self-enhancement and Superiority Biases in Social Comparison". European Review of Social Psychology. Psychology Press. 4 (1): 113–139.* doi:10.1080/14792779343000040.

85. Plous 2006, p. 206

86. Plous 2006, p. 185

87. *Forsyth, D. R. (2009). Group Dynamics (5th ed.). Pacific Grove, CA: Brooks/Cole.*

88. *Kruger, J. (1999). "Lake Wobegon be gone! The "below-average effect" and the egocentric nature of comparative ability judgments". Journal of Personality and Social Psychology. 77 (2): 221–32.* PMID10474208. doi:10.1037/0022-3514.77.2.221.

89. *Schacter, Daniel L. (1999). "The Seven Sins of Memory: Insights From Psychology and Cognitive Neuroscience". American Psychologist. 54 (3): 182–203.* PMID10199218. doi:10.1037/0003-066X.54.3.182.

90. *Cacioppo, John (2002). Foundations in social neuroscience. Cambridge, Mass: MIT Press. pp. 130–132.* ISBN 026253195X.

91. *Walker, W. Richard; John J. Skowronski; Charles P. Thompson (1994).* "Effects of Humor on Sentence Memory" *(PDF). Journal of Experimental Psychology: Learning, Memory, and Cognition. American Psychological Association, Inc. 20 (4): 953–967.* doi:10.1037/0278-7393.20.4.953. *Retrieved 2015-04-19.*

92. *Schmidt, Stephen R. (2003).* "Life Is Pleasant—and Memory Helps to Keep It That Way!" *(PDF). Review of General Psychology. Educational Publishing Foundation. 7 (2): 203–210.* doi:10.1037/1089-2680.7.2.203.

93. *Koriat, A.; M. Goldsmith; A. Pansky (2000). "Toward a Psychologyof Memory Accuracy". Annual Review of Psychology. 51 (1): 481–537.* PMID10751979. doi:10.1146/annurev.psych.51.1.481.

94. Craik & Lockhart, 1972

95. *Kinnell, Angela; Dennis, S. (2011). "The list length effect in recognition memory: an analysis of potential confounds". Memory & Cognition.* Adelaide, Australia: *School of Psychology,* University of Adelaide. *39 (2): 348–63.* doi:10.3758/s13421-010-0007-6.

96. *Wayne Weiten (2010).* Psychology: Themes and Variations: Themes and Variations. *Cengage Learning. p. 338.* ISBN978-0-495-60197-5.

97. *Wayne Weiten (2007).* Psychology: Themes and Variations: Themes And Variations. *Cengage Learning. p. 260.* ISBN978-0-495-09303-9.

98. *Slamecka NJ (1968). "An examination of trace storage in free recall". J Exp Psychol. 76 (4): 504–13.* PMID5650563. doi:10.1037/h0025695.

99. *Shepard, R.N. (1967). "Recognition memory for words, sentences, and pictures". Journal of Learning and Verbal Behavior. 6: 156–163. doi:10.1016/s0022-5371(67)80067-7.*

100. *McBride, D. M.; Dosher, B.A. (2002). "A comparison of conscious and automatic memory processes for picture and word stimuli: a process dissociation analysis". Consciousness and Cognition. 11: 423–460. doi:10.1016/s1053-8100(02)00007-7.*

101. *Defetyer, M. A.; Russo, R.; McPartlin, P. L. (2009). "The picture superiority effect in recognition memory: a developmental study using the response signal procedure". Cognitive Development. 24: 265–273. doi:10.1016/j.cogdev.2009.05.002.*

102. *Whitehouse, A. J.; Maybery, M.T.; Durkin, K. (2006). "The development of the picture-superiority effect". British Journal of Developmental Psychology. 24: 767–773. doi:10.1348/026151005X74153.*

103. *Ally, B. A.; Gold, C. A.; Budson, A. E. (2009). "The picture superiority effect in patients with Alzheimer's disease and mild cognitive impairment". Neuropsychologia. 47: 595–598. doi:10.1016/j.neuropsychologia.2008.10.010.*

104. *Curran, T.; Doyle, J. (2011). "Picture superiority doubly dissociates the ERP correlates of recollection and familiarity". Journal of Cognitive Neuroscience. 23 (5): 1247–1262. PMID20350169. doi:10.1162/jocn.2010.21464.*

105. *Martin, G. Neil; Neil R. Carlson; William Buskist (2007). Psychology (3rd ed.). Pearson Education. pp. 309–310. ISBN978-0-273-71086-8.*

106. *O'Brien, Edward J.; Myers, Jerome L. (1985). "When comprehension difficulty improves memory for text". Journal of Experimental Psychology: Learning, Memory, and Cognition. 11 (1): 12–21. doi:10.1037/0278-7393.11.1.12.*

107. Rubin, Wetzler & Nebes, 1986; Rubin, Rahhal & Poon, 1998.

108. *David A. Lieberman (8 December 2011). Human Learning and Memory. Cambridge University Press. p. 432. ISBN978-1-139-50253-5.*

109. Morton, Crowder & Prussin, 1971.

110. *Ian Pitt; Alistair D. N. Edwards (2003). Design of Speech-Based Devices: A Practical Guide. Springer. p. 26. ISBN978-1-85233-436-9.*

111. *E. Bruce Goldstein. Cognitive Psychology: Connecting Mind, Research and Everyday Experience. Cengage Learning. p. 231. ISBN978-1-133-00912-2.*

112. *"Not everyone is in such awe of the internet". Evening Standard. Evening Standard. Retrieved 28 October 2015.*

113. Poppenk, Walia, Joanisse, Danckert, & Köhler, 2006.

114. *Von Restorff, H (1933). "Über die Wirkung von Bereichsbildungen im Spurenfeld (The effects of field formation in the trace field)". Psychological Research. 18 (1): 299–342. doi:10.1007/bf02409636.*

115. *Kahneman, Daniel; Shane Frederick (2002). "Representativeness Revisited: Attribute Substitution in Intuitive Judgment". In Thomas Gilovich; Dale Griffin; Daniel Kahneman. Heuristics and Biases: The Psychology of Intuitive Judgment. Cambridge: Cambridge University Press. pp. 49–81. ISBN 978-0-521-79679-8.OCLC47364085.*

116. *Slovic, Paul; Melissa Finucane; Ellen Peters; Donald G. MacGregor (2002). "The Affect Heuristic". In Thomas Gilovich; Dale Griffin; Daniel Kahneman. Heuristics and Biases: The Psychology of Intuitive Judgment. Cambridge University Press. pp. 397–420. ISBN0-521-79679-2.*

117. *Scopelliti, Irene; Morewedge, Carey K.; McCormick, Erin; Min, H. Lauren; Lebrecht, Sophie; Kassam, Karim S. (2015-04-24). "Bias Blind Spot: Structure, Measurement, and Consequences". Management Science. 61: 2468–2486. doi:10.1287/mnsc.2014.2096.*

118. *Morewedge, Carey K.; Yoon, Haewon; Scopelliti, Irene; Symborski, Carl W.; Korris, James H.; Kassam, Karim S. (2015-10-01). "Debiasing Decisions Improved Decision Making With a Single Training Intervention". Policy Insights from the Behavioral and Brain Sciences. 2 (1): 129–140. ISSN 2372-7322. doi:10.1177/2372732215600886.*

References

- *Baron, Jonathan (1994). Thinking and deciding (2nd ed.). Cambridge University Press. ISBN 0-521-43732-6.*
- *Baron, Jonathan (2000). Thinking and deciding (3rd ed.). New York: Cambridge University Press. ISBN 0-521-65030-5.*
- *Bishop, Michael A.; Trout, J. D. (2004). Epistemology and the Psychology of Human Judgment. New York: Oxford University Press. ISBN 0-19-516229-3.*
- *Gilovich, Thomas (1993). "How We Know What Isn't So: The Fallibility of Human Reason in Everyday Life". New York: The Free Press. ISBN 0-02-911706-2.*
- *Gilovich, Thomas; Griffin, Dale; Kahneman, Daniel (2002). Heuristics and biases: The psychology of intuitive judgment. Cambridge, UK: Cambridge University Press. ISBN 0-521-79679-2.*
- *Greenwald, Anthony G. (1980). "The Totalitarian Ego: Fabrication and Revision of Personal History" (PDF). American Psychologist. American Psychological Association. 35 (7): 603–618. ISSN 0003-066X. doi:10.1037/0003-066x.35.7.603.*
- *Hardman, David (2009). Judgment and decision making: psychological perspectives. Wiley-Blackwell. ISBN 978-1-4051-2398-3.*
- *Kahneman, Daniel; Slovic, Paul; Tversky, Amos (1982). Judgment under Uncertainty: Heuristics and Biases. Cambridge, UK: Cambridge University Press. ISBN 0-521-28414-7.*
- *Kahneman, Daniel; Knetsch, Jack L.; Thaler, Richard H. (1991). "Anomalies: The Endowment Effect, Loss Aversion, and Status Quo Bias" (PDF). The Journal of Economic Perspectives. American Economic Association. 5 (1): 193–206. doi:10.1257/jep.5.1.193. Archived from the original (PDF) on November 24, 2012.*
- *Plous, Scott (1993). The Psychology of Judgment and Decision Making. New York: McGraw-Hill. ISBN 0-07-050477-6.*
- *Schacter, Daniel L. (1999). "The Seven Sins of Memory: Insights From Psychology and Cognitive Neuroscience" (PDF). American Psychologist. American Psychological Association. 54 (3): 182–203. ISSN 0003-066X. PMID 10199218. doi:10.1037/0003-066X.54.3.182. Archived from the original (PDF) on May 13, 2013.*
- *Sutherland, Stuart (2007). Irrationality. Pinter & Martin. ISBN 978-1-905177-07-3.*
- *Tetlock, Philip E. (2005). Expert Political Judgment: how good is it? how can we know?. Princeton: Princeton University Press. ISBN 978-0-691-12302-8.*
- *Virine, L.; Trumper, M. (2007). Project Decisions: The Art and Science. Vienna, VA: Management Concepts. ISBN 978-1-56726-217-9.*

Appendix B: List of Fallacies

Annotated *Wikipedia, the free encyclopedia* list

This Appendix is an author-edited version of the *List of Fallacies* by *Wikipedia, the free encyclopedia* at http://en.wikipedia.org/wiki/List_of_fallacies, last retrieved September 25, 2017. Permission is granted under the terms of the GNU Free Documentation License, Version 1.2 or any later version published by the Free Software Foundation; with no invariant sections, with no front-cover texts, and with no back-cover texts. In terms of *Wikipedia Copyrights* (http://en.wikipedia.org /wiki/Wikipedia:Copyrights, 8 pages retrieved February 3, 2008), this appendix is licensed under the GNU Free Documentation License. It uses the material from the Wikipedia article *"List of Fallacies."*

In respect and conformity with Wikipedia rules and requirements, any copy of this Appendix can be made without restrictions.

Under the name of fallacy, this list contains several entries which are elsewhere in this book synonymous to some entities under the name of cognitive bias as defined and commented in Appendix A: *List of Cognitive Biases*. With some overlaps, this list completes the other lists quoted and referred to in this book.

List of fallacies

From Wikipedia, the free encyclopedia
For specific popular misconceptions, see List of common misconceptions.

In reasoning to argue a claim, a fallacy is reasoning that is evaluated as logically incorrect and that vitiates the logical validity of the argument and permits its recognition as unsound. Regardless of their unsoundness, all registers and manners of speech can demonstrate fallacies.

Because of their variety of structure and application, fallacies are challenging to classify so as to satisfy all practitioners. Fallacies can be classified strictly by either their structure or content, such as classifying them as formal fallacies or informal fallacies, respectively. The classification of informal fallacies may be subdivided into categories such as linguistic, relevance through omission, relevance through intrusion, and relevance through presumption.[1] On the other hand, fallacies may be classified by the process by which they occur, such as material fallacies (content), verbal fallacies (linguistic), and again formal fallacies (error in inference). In turn, material fallacies may be placed into the more general category of informal fallacies as formal fallacies may be clearly placed into the more precise category of logical or deductive fallacies. Yet, verbal fallacies may be placed in either informal or deductive classifications; compare equivocation which is a word or phrase based ambiguity, e. g. "he is mad", which may refer to either him being angry or clinically insane, to the fallacy of composition which is premise and inference based ambiguity, e. g. "this must be a good basketball team because each of its members is an outstanding player".[2]

Faulty inferences in deductive reasoning are common formal or logical fallacies. As the nature of inductive reasoning is based in probability, a fallacious inductive argument or one that is potentially misleading, is often classified as "weak".

The conscious or habitual use of fallacies as rhetorical devices are prevalent in the desire to persuade, when the focus is more on communication and eliciting common agreement rather than the correctness of the reasoning. One may consider the effective use of a fallacy by an orator as clever but by the same token the reasoning of that orator should be recognized as unsound, and thus the orator's claim, supported by an unsound argument, will be regarded as unfounded and dismissed.[3]

Contents

- 1. Formal fallacies
  - o   1.1 Propositional fallacies
  - o   1.2 Quantification fallacies
  - o   1.3 Formal syllogistic fallacies
- 2. Informal fallacies
  - o   2.1 Faulty generalizations
  - o   2.2 Red herring fallacies
- 3. Conditional or questionable fallacies
- 4. See also
- 5. References
- 6. Further reading
- 7. External links

Formal fallacies

Main article: Formal fallacy

A formal fallacy is an error in logic that can be seen in the <u>argument's form</u>.[4] All formal fallacies are specific types of <u>non sequiturs</u>.

- <u>Appeal to probability</u> – is a statement that takes something for granted because it would probably be the case (or might be the case).[5][6]
- <u>Argument from fallacy</u> – also known as **fallacy fallacy**, assumes that if an *argument* for some conclusion is fallacious, then the *conclusion* is false.[7]
- <u>Base rate fallacy</u> – making a probability judgment based on <u>conditional probabilities</u>, without taking into account the effect of <u>prior probabilities</u>.[8]
- <u>Conjunction fallacy</u> – assumption that an outcome simultaneously satisfying multiple conditions is more probable than an outcome satisfying a single one of them.[9]
- <u>Masked-man fallacy</u> (illicit substitution of identicals) – the substitution of identical designators in a true statement can lead to a false one.[10]
- <u>Jumping to conclusions</u> – the act of taking decisions without having enough information to be sure they are right.

Propositional fallacies

A propositional fallacy is an error in logic that concerns compound propositions. For a compound proposition to be true, the truth values of its constituent parts must satisfy the relevant logical connectives that occur in it (most commonly: <and>, <or>, <not>, <only if>, <if and only if>). The following fallacies involve inferences whose correctness is not guaranteed by the behavior of those logical connectives, and hence, which are not logically guaranteed to yield true conclusions. Types of <u>propositional</u> fallacies:

- <u>Affirming a disjunct</u> – concluding that one disjunct of a <u>logical disjunction</u> must be false because the other disjunct is true; *A or B; A, therefore not B.*[11]
- <u>Affirming the consequent</u> – the <u>antecedent</u> in an indicative conditional is claimed to be true because the <u>consequent</u> is true; *if A, then B; B, therefore A.*[11]
- <u>Denying the antecedent</u> – the <u>consequent</u> in an <u>indicative conditional</u> is claimed to be false because the <u>antecedent</u> is false; *if A, then B; not A, therefore not B.*[11]

Quantification fallacies

A quantification fallacy is an error in logic where the quantifiers of the premises are in contradiction to the quantifier of the conclusion.
Types of <u>Quantification</u> fallacies:

- <u>Existential fallacy</u> – an argument that has a universal premise and a particular conclusion.[12]

Formal syllogistic fallacies

<u>Syllogistic fallacies</u> – logical fallacies that occur in <u>syllogisms</u>.

- <u>Affirmative conclusion from a negative premise</u> (illicit negative) – when a categorical <u>syllogism</u> has a positive conclusion, but at least one negative premise.[12]
- <u>Fallacy of exclusive premises</u> – a categorical syllogism that is invalid because both of its premises are negative.[12]
- <u>Fallacy of four terms</u> (*quaternio terminorum*) – a categorical syllogism that has four terms.[13]
- <u>Illicit major</u> – a categorical syllogism that is invalid because its major term is not <u>distributed</u> in the major premise but distributed in the conclusion.[12]
- <u>Illicit minor</u> – a categorical syllogism that is invalid because its minor term is not distributed in the minor premise but distributed in the conclusion.[12]
- <u>Negative conclusion from affirmative premises</u> (illicit affirmative) – when a categorical syllogism has a negative conclusion but affirmative premises.[12]
- <u>Fallacy of the undistributed middle</u> – the middle term in a categorical syllogism is not distributed.[14]
- <u>Modal fallacy</u> – confusing possibility with necessity.[15]

Informal fallacies

Main article: <u>Informal fallacy</u>

Informal fallacies – Arguments that are fallacious for reasons other than structural (formal) flaws and usually require examination of the argument's content.[16]

- <u>Appeal to the stone</u> (*argumentum ad lapidem*) – dismissing a claim as absurd without demonstrating proof for its absurdity.[17]
- <u>Argument from ignorance</u> (appeal to ignorance, *argumentum ad ignorantiam*) – assuming that a claim is true because it has not been or cannot be proven false, or vice versa.[18]
- <u>Argument from incredulity</u> (appeal to common sense) – "I cannot imagine how this could be true; therefore, it must be false."[19]
- <u>Argument from repetition</u> (*argumentum ad nauseam, argumentum ad infinitum*) – signifies that it has been discussed extensively until nobody cares to discuss it anymore;[20][21] sometimes confused with <u>proof by assertion</u>
- <u>Argument from silence</u> (*argumentum ex silentio*) – where the conclusion is based on the absence of evidence, rather than the existence of evidence.[22][23]
- <u>Argument to moderation</u> (false compromise, middle ground, fallacy of the mean, *argumentum ad temperantiam*) – assuming that the compromise between two positions is always correct.[24]
- <u>Begging the question</u> (*petitio principii*) – providing what is essentially the conclusion of the argument as a premise.[25][26][27][28]

- Shifting the burden of proof (see – *onus probandi*) – I need not prove my claim, you must prove it is false.
- Circular reasoning (*circulus in demonstrando*) – when the reasoner begins with what he or she is trying to end up with; sometimes called *assuming the conclusion*.
- Circular cause and consequence – where the consequence of the phenomenon is claimed to be its root cause.
- Continuum fallacy (fallacy of the beard, line-drawing fallacy, sorites fallacy, fallacy of the heap, bald man fallacy) – improperly rejecting a claim for being imprecise.[29]
- Correlative-based fallacies
    - Correlation proves causation (*post hoc ergo propter hoc*) – a faulty assumption that because there is a correlation between two variables that one caused the other.[30]
    - Suppressed correlative – where a correlative is redefined so that one alternative is made impossible.[31]
- Divine fallacy (argument from incredulity) – arguing that, because something is so incredible/amazing/ununderstandable, it must be the result of superior, divine, alien or paranormal agency.[32]
- Double counting – counting events or occurrences more than once in probabilistic reasoning, which leads to the sum of the probabilities of all cases exceeding unity.
- Equivocation – the misleading use of a term with more than one meaning (by glossing over which meaning is intended at a particular time).[33]
    - Ambiguous middle term – a common ambiguity in syllogisms in which the middle term is equivocated.[34]
    - Definitional retreat – changing the meaning of a word to deal with an objection raised against the original wording.[1]
- Ecological fallacy – inferences about the nature of specific individuals are based solely upon aggregate statistics collected for the group to which those individuals belong.[35]
- Etymological fallacy – which reasons that the original or historical meaning of a word or phrase is necessarily similar to its actual present-day usage.[36]
- Fallacy of accent – a specific type of ambiguity that arises when the meaning of a sentence is changed by placing an unusual prosodic stress, or when, in a written passage, it's left unclear which word the emphasis was supposed to fall on.
- Fallacy of composition – assuming that something true of part of a whole must also be true of the whole.[37]
- Fallacy of division – assuming that something true of a thing must also be true of all or some of its parts.[38]
- False attribution – an advocate appeals to an irrelevant, unqualified, unidentified, biased or fabricated source in support of an argument.
    - Fallacy of quoting out of context (contextomy, quote mining) – refers to the selective excerpting of words from their original context in a way that distorts the source's intended meaning.[39]
- False authority (single authority) – using an expert of dubious credentials or using only one opinion to sell a product or idea. Related to the appeal to authority fallacy.
- False dilemma (false dichotomy, fallacy of bifurcation, black-or-white fallacy) – two alternative statements are held to be the only possible options, when in reality there are more.[40]
- False equivalence – describing a situation of logical and apparent equivalence, when in fact there is none.
- Fallacy of many questions (complex question, fallacy of presupposition, loaded question, *plurium interrogationum*) – someone asks a question that presupposes something that has not been proven or accepted by all the people involved. This fallacy is often used rhetorically, so that the question limits direct replies to those that serve the questioner's agenda.

- Fallacy of the single cause (causal oversimplification[41]) – it is assumed that there is one, simple cause of an outcome when in reality it may have been caused by a number of only jointly sufficient causes.
- Furtive fallacy – outcomes are asserted to have been caused by the malfeasance of decision makers.
- Gambler's fallacy – the incorrect belief that separate, independent events can affect the likelihood of another random event. If a fair coin lands on heads 10 times in a row, the belief that it is "due to the number of times it had previously landed on tails" is incorrect.[42]
- Historian's fallacy – occurs when one assumes that decision makers of the past viewed events from the same perspective and having the same information as those subsequently analyzing the decision.[43] (Not to be confused with presentism, which is a mode of historical analysis in which present-day ideas, such as moral standards, are projected into the past.)
- Historical fallacy – where a set of considerations holds good only because a completed process is read into the content of the process which conditions this completed result.[44]
- Homunculus fallacy – where a "middle-man" is used for explanation, this sometimes leads to regressive middle-men. Explains without actually explaining the real nature of a function or a process. Instead, it explains the concept in terms of the concept itself, without first defining or explaining the original concept. Explaining thought as something produced by a little thinker, a sort of homunculus inside the head, merely explains it as another kind of thinking (as different but the same).[45]
- Inflation of conflict – The experts of a field of knowledge disagree on a certain point, so the scholars must know nothing, and therefore the legitimacy of their entire field is put to question.[46]
- If-by-whiskey – an argument that supports both sides of an issue by using terms that are selectively emotionally sensitive.
- Incomplete comparison – in which insufficient information is provided to make a complete comparison.
- Inconsistent comparison – where different methods of comparison are used, leaving one with a false impression of the whole comparison.
- Intentionality fallacy – the insistence that the ultimate meaning of an expression must be consistent with the intention of the person from whom the communication originated (e.g., a work of fiction that is widely received as a blatant allegory must necessarily not be regarded as such if the author intended it not to be so.)[47]
- *Ignoratio elenchi* (irrelevant conclusion, missing the point) – an argument that may in itself be valid, but does not address the issue in question.[48]
- Kettle logic – using multiple, jointly inconsistent arguments to defend a position.
- Ludic fallacy – the belief that the outcomes of non-regulated random occurrences can be encapsulated by a statistic; a failure to take into account unknown unknowns in determining the probability of events taking place.[49]
- McNamara fallacy (quantitative fallacy) – making a decision based only on quantitative observations, discounting all other considerations.
- Moralistic fallacy – inferring factual conclusions from purely evaluative premises in violation of fact–value distinction. For instance, inferring *is* from *ought* is an instance of moralistic fallacy. Moralistic fallacy is the inverse of naturalistic fallacy defined below.
- Moving the goalposts (raising the bar) – argument in which evidence presented in response to a specific claim is dismissed and some other (often greater) evidence is demanded.
- Naturalistic fallacy – inferring evaluative conclusions from purely factual premises[50] in violation of fact–value distinction. For instance, inferring *ought* from *is* (sometimes referred to as the *is-ought fallacy*) is an instance of naturalistic fallacy. Also naturalistic fallacy in a stricter sense as defined in the section "Conditional or questionable fallacies" below is an instance of naturalistic fallacy. Naturalistic fallacy is the inverse of moralistic fallacy.

- *Naturalistic fallacy* fallacy[51] (anti-naturalistic fallacy)[52] – inferring an impossibility to infer any instance of *ought* from *is* from the general invalidity of *is-ought fallacy*, mentioned above. For instance instance, *is* does imply *ought* for any proposition, although the *naturalistic fallacy* fallacy would falsely declare such an inference invalid. *Naturalistic fallacy* fallacy is an instance of <u>argument from fallacy</u>.
- <u>Nirvana fallacy</u> (perfect solution fallacy) – when solutions to problems are rejected because they are not perfect.
- *Onus probandi* – from Latin "onus probandi incumbit ei qui dicit, non ei qui negat" the burden of proof is on the person who makes the claim, not on the person who denies (or questions the claim). It is a particular case of the *argumentum ad ignorantiam* fallacy, here the burden is shifted on the person defending against the assertion.
- *Post hoc ergo propter hoc* Latin for "after this, therefore because of this" (faulty cause/effect, coincidental correlation, correlation without causation) – X happened, then Y happened; therefore X caused Y. The Loch Ness Monster has been seen in this loch. Something tipped our boat over; it's obviously the Loch Ness Monster.[53]
- <u>Proof by assertion</u> – a proposition is repeatedly restated regardless of contradiction; sometimes confused with <u>argument from repetition</u> (*argumentum ad infinitum, argumentum ad nauseam*)
- <u>Prosecutor's fallacy</u> – a low probability of false matches does not mean a low probability of *some* false match being found.
- <u>Proving too much</u> – using a form of argument that, if it were valid, could be used to reach an additional, undesirable conclusion.
- <u>Psychologist's fallacy</u> – an observer presupposes the objectivity of his own perspective when analyzing a behavioral event.
- <u>Red herring</u> – a speaker attempts to distract an audience by deviating from the topic at hand by introducing a separate argument the speaker believes is easier to speak to.[54]
- <u>Referential fallacy</u>[55] – assuming all words refer to existing things and that the meaning of words reside within the things they refer to, as opposed to words possibly referring to no real object or that the meaning of words often comes from how we use them.
- <u>Regression fallacy</u> – ascribes cause where none exists. The flaw is failing to account for natural fluctuations. It is frequently a special kind of *post hoc* fallacy.
- <u>Reification</u> (concretism, hypostatization, or the fallacy of misplaced concreteness) – a fallacy of ambiguity, when an abstraction (abstract belief or hypothetical construct) is treated as if it were a concrete, real event or physical entity. In other words, it is the error of treating as a "real thing" something that is not a real thing, but merely an idea.
- <u>Retrospective determinism</u> – the argument that because an event has occurred under some circumstance, the circumstance must have made its occurrence inevitable.
- Shotgun argumentation – the arguer offers such a large number of arguments for a position that the opponent can't possibly respond to all of them. (See "Argument by verbosity" and "<u>Gish Gallop</u>", above.)
- <u>Special pleading</u> – where a proponent of a position attempts to cite something as an exemption to a generally accepted rule or principle without justifying the exemption.
- <u>Wrong direction</u> – cause and effect are reversed. The cause is said to be the effect and vice versa.[56]

Faulty generalization

<u>Faulty generalizations</u> – reach a conclusion from weak premises. Unlike fallacies of relevance, in fallacies of defective induction, the premises are related to the conclusions yet only weakly buttress the conclusions. A faulty generalization is thus produced.

- Accident – an exception to a generalization is ignored.[57]
  - No true Scotsman – makes a generalization true by changing the generalization to exclude a counterexample.[58]
- Cherry picking (suppressed evidence, incomplete evidence) – act of pointing at individual cases or data that seem to confirm a particular position, while ignoring a significant portion of related cases or data that may contradict that position.[59]
  - Survivorship bias – when a small number of survivors of a given process are actively promoted while completely ignoring a large number of failures
- False analogy – an argument by analogy in which the analogy is poorly suited.[60]
- Hasty generalization (fallacy of insufficient statistics, fallacy of insufficient sample, fallacy of the lonely fact, leaping to a conclusion, hasty induction, *secundum quid*, converse accident) – basing a broad conclusion on a small sample.[61]
- Inductive fallacy – A more general name to some fallacies, such as hasty generalization. It happens when a conclusion is made of premises that lightly support it.
- Misleading vividness – involves describing an occurrence in vivid detail, even if it is an exceptional occurrence, to convince someone that it is a problem.
- Overwhelming exception – an accurate generalization that comes with qualifications that eliminate so many cases that what remains is much less impressive than the initial statement might have led one to assume.[62]
- Thought-terminating cliché – a commonly used phrase, sometimes passing as folk wisdom, used to quell cognitive dissonance, conceal lack of thought-entertainment, move on to other topics, etc., but in any case, end the debate with a cliché—not a point.

Red herring fallacies

A red herring fallacy, one of the main subtypes of fallacies of relevance, is an error in logic where a proposition is, or is intended to be, misleading in order to make irrelevant or false inferences. In the general case any logical inference based on fake arguments, intended to replace the lack of real arguments or to replace implicitly the subject of the discussion.[63][64][65]

Red herring – argument given in response to another argument, which is irrelevant and draws attention away from the subject of argument. *See also irrelevant conclusion*.

- *Ad hominem* – attacking the arguer instead of the argument.
  - Poisoning the well – a subtype of *ad hominem* presenting adverse information about a target person with the intention of discrediting everything that the target person says.[66]
  - Abusive fallacy – a subtype of *ad hominem* that verbally abuses the opponent rather than arguing about the originally proposed argument.[67]
  - Appeal to motive – a subtype of *ad hominem* that dismisses an idea by questioning the motives of its proposer.
  - Tone policing – a subtype of *ad hominem* focusing on emotion behind a message rather than the message itself as a discrediting tactic.
  - Traitorous critic fallacy (*ergo decedo*) – a subtype of *ad hominem* where a critic's perceived affiliation is seen as the underlying reason for the criticism and the critic is asked to stay away from the issue altogether.
- Appeal to authority (*argumentum ad verecundiam*) – where an assertion is deemed true because of the position or authority of the person asserting it.[68][69]
  - Appeal to accomplishment – where an assertion is deemed true or false based on the accomplishments of the proposer.[70]

- <u>Appeal to consequences</u> (*argumentum ad consequentiam*) – the conclusion is supported by a premise that asserts positive or negative consequences from some course of action in an attempt to distract from the initial discussion.[71]
- <u>Appeal to emotion</u> – where an argument is made due to the manipulation of emotions, rather than the use of valid reasoning.[72]
    - <u>Appeal to fear</u> – a specific type of appeal to emotion where an argument is made by increasing fear and prejudice toward the opposing side.[73][74]
    - <u>Appeal to flattery</u> – a specific type of appeal to emotion where an argument is made due to the use of flattery to gather support.[75]
    - <u>Appeal to pity</u> (*argumentum ad misericordiam*) – an argument attempts to induce pity to sway opponents.[76]
    - <u>Appeal to ridicule</u> – an argument is made by presenting the opponent's argument in a way that makes it appear ridiculous.[77][78]
    - <u>Appeal to spite</u> – a specific type of appeal to emotion where an argument is made through exploiting people's bitterness or spite toward an opposing party.[79]
    - <u>Wishful thinking</u> – a specific type of appeal to emotion where a decision is made according to what might be pleasing to imagine, rather than according to evidence or reason.[80]
- <u>Appeal to nature</u> – wherein judgment is based solely on whether the subject of judgment is 'natural' or 'unnatural'.[81] (Sometimes also called the "naturalistic fallacy", but is not to be confused with the other fallacies by that name)
- <u>Appeal to novelty</u> (*argumentum novitatis, argumentum ad antiquitatis*) – where a proposal is claimed to be superior or better solely because it is new or modern.[82]
- <u>Appeal to poverty</u> (*argumentum ad Lazarum*) – supporting a conclusion because the arguer is poor (or refuting because the arguer is wealthy). (Opposite of <u>appeal to wealth</u>.)[83]
- <u>Appeal to tradition</u> (*argumentum ad antiquitatem*) – a conclusion supported solely because it has long been held to be true.[84]
- <u>Appeal to wealth</u> (*argumentum ad crumenam*) – supporting a conclusion because the arguer is wealthy (or refuting because the arguer is poor).[85] (Sometimes taken together with the <u>appeal to poverty</u> as a general appeal to the arguer's financial situation.)
- *<u>Argumentum ad baculum</u>* (appeal to the stick, appeal to force, appeal to threat) – an argument made through coercion or threats of force to support position.[86]
- *<u>Argumentum ad populum</u>* (appeal to widespread belief, bandwagon argument, appeal to the majority, appeal to the people) – where a proposition is claimed to be true or good solely because many people believe it to be so.[87]
- <u>Association fallacy</u> (guilt by association and honor by association) – arguing that because two things share (or are implied to share) some property, they are the same.[88]
- <u>Bulverism</u> (psychogenetic fallacy) – inferring why an argument is being used, associating it to some psychological reason, then assuming it is invalid as a result. It is wrong to assume that if the origin of an idea comes from a biased mind, then the idea itself must also be a falsehood.[46]
- <u>Chronological snobbery</u> – where a thesis is deemed incorrect because it was commonly held when something else, clearly false, was also commonly held.[89][90]
- Fallacy of relative privation ("not as bad as") – dismissing an argument or complaint due to the existence of more important problems in the world, regardless of whether those problems bear relevance to the initial argument. For example, <u>First World problem</u>.
- <u>Genetic fallacy</u> – where a conclusion is suggested based solely on something or someone's origin rather than its current meaning or context.[91]
- <u>Judgmental language</u> – insulting or pejorative language to influence the recipient's judgment.
- <u>Moralistic fallacy</u> (the inverse of naturalistic fallacy) – statements about what is on the basis of claims about what ought to be.
- Motte-and-bailey fallacy: The arguer conflates two similar positions, one modest and easy to defend (the "motte") and one much more controversial (the "bailey"). The arguer advances the

controversial position, but when challenged, they insist that they are only advancing the more modest position.[92]

- Naturalistic fallacy (is–ought fallacy,[93] naturalistic fallacy[94]) – claims about what ought to be on the basis of statements about what is.
- Pooh-pooh – dismissing an argument perceived unworthy of serious consideration.[95]
- Straw man fallacy – an argument based on misrepresentation of an opponent's position.[96]
- Texas sharpshooter fallacy – improperly asserting a cause to explain a cluster of data.[97]
- *Tu quoque* ("you too", appeal to hypocrisy, I'm rubber and you're glue) – the argument states that a certain position is false or wrong or should be disregarded because its proponent fails to act consistently in accordance with that position.[98]
- Two wrongs make a right – occurs when it is assumed that if one wrong is committed, an "equal but opposite" wrong will cancel it out.[99]
- Vacuous truth – A claim that is technically true but meaningless, in the form of claiming that no *A* in *B* has *C*, when there are no *A* in *B*. For example, claiming that no mobile phones in the room are on when there are no mobile phones in the room at all.
- Appeal to self-evident truth – A claim that a proposition is self-evidently true, without being so, so needs no further supporting evidence. In many cases, there is really some kind of unstated and unexamined observation or assumption for the claim.

Conditional or questionable fallacies

- Broken window fallacy – an argument that disregards lost opportunity costs (typically non-obvious, difficult to determine or otherwise hidden) associated with destroying property of others, or other ways of externalizing costs onto others. For example, an argument that states breaking a window generates income for a window fitter, but disregards the fact that the money spent on the new window cannot now be spent on new shoes.
- Definist fallacy – involves the confusion between two notions by defining one in terms of the other.[100]
- Naturalistic fallacy – attempts to prove a claim about ethics by appealing to a definition of the term "good" in terms of either one or more claims about natural properties (sometimes also taken to mean the appeal to nature) or God's will.[81]
- Slippery slope (thin edge of the wedge, camel's nose) – asserting that a relatively small first step inevitably leads to a chain of related events culminating in some significant impact/event that should not happen, thus the first step should not happen. It is, in its essence, an appeal to probability fallacy. (e.g. if person x does y then z would [probably] occur, leading to q, leading to w, leading to e.)[101] This is also related to the reductio ad absurdum.

See also

- ∀ *Logic portal*
- *Philosophy portal*

- List of cognitive biases
- List of common misconceptions
- List of memory biases
- List of paradoxes
- List of topics related to public relations and propaganda
- Mathematical fallacy
- *Sophistical Refutations*, in which Aristotle presented thirteen fallacies
- *Straight and Crooked Thinking* (book)

References

Notes . Jump up△ retrievable

1. *Pirie, Madsen (2006). How to Win Every Argument: The Use and Abuse of Logic. A&C Black. p. 46. ISBN 978-0-8264-9006-3. Retrieved 10 September 2015.*
2. *"fallacy". Encyclopedia Brittanica. Encyclopedia Brittanica. Retrieved 13 June 2017.*
3. *Hornby, A.S. (2010). Oxford advanced learner's dictionary of current English(8th ed. ed.). Oxford [England]: Oxford University Press. ISBN 978-0194799003. sophist*
4. Bunnin & Yu 2004, "formal fallacy".
5. *Leon, Joseph (23 April 2011). "Appeal to Probability". Logical & Critical Thinking. Archived from the original on 27 September 2013.*
6. *McDonald, Simon (2009). "Appeal to probability". Toolkit For Thinking. Archived from the original on 19 February 2015.*
7. Curtis, "Fallacy Fallacy".
8. *"Base Rate Fallacy". Psychology Glossary. AlleyDog.com. Retrieved 2011-02-01.*
9. *Straker, David. "Conjunction Fallacy". ChangingMinds.org. Retrieved 2011-02-01.*
10. Curtis, "The Masked Man Fallacy".
11. Wilson 1999, p. 316.
12. Wilson 1999, p. 317.
13. Pirie 2006, pp. 133–36.
14. Wilson 1999, pp. 316–17.
15. *Bennett, Bo. "Modal (Scope) Fallacy". Logically Fallacious. Retrieved 26 August 2017.*
16. Bunnin & Yu 2004, "informal fallacy".
17. *"Johnson's Refutation of Berkeley: Kicking the Stone Again". JSTOR 2709600.*
18. Damer 2009, p. 165.
19. *"Toolkit for Thinking".*
20. *"Repetition". changingminds.org. Retrieved 2016-02-24.*
21. *"Ad nauseam – Toolkit For Thinking". toolkitforthinking.com. Retrieved 2016-02-24.*
22. *"Argument from silence – Toolkit For Thinking". toolkitforthinking.com. Retrieved 2016-02-24.*
23. *Bo Bennett. "Argument from Silence". logicallyfallacious.com. Retrieved 2016-02-24.*
24. Damer 2009, p. 150.
25. *"Your logical fallacy is begging the question". Thou shalt not commit logical fallacies. Retrieved 2016-02-24.*
26. *"Fallacy: Begging the Question". nizkor.org. Retrieved 2016-02-24.*
27. *Bo Bennett. "Begging the Question". logicallyfallacious.com. Retrieved 2016-02-24.*
28. *"Begging the Question". txstate.edu. Retrieved 2016-02-24.*
29. Dowden 2010, "Line-Drawing".
30. Pirie 2006, p. 41.
31. *Feinberg, Joel (2007). "Psychological Egoism". In Shafer-Landau, Russ. Ethical Theory: An Anthology. Blackwell Philosophy Anthologies. Wiley-Blackwell. p. 193. ISBN 978-1-4051-3320-3.*

32. *Carroll, Robert T. "divine fallacy (argument from incredulity)"*. *The Skeptic's Dictionary. Retrieved 5 April 2013.*

33. Damer 2009, p. 121.

34. Copi & Cohen 1990, p. 206.

35. Fischer 1970, p. 119.

36. Gula 2002, p. 70.

37. Pirie 2006, p. 31.

38. Pirie 2006, p. 53.

39. Gula 2002, p. 97.

40. *"Fallacy – False Dilemma". Nizkor. The Nizkor Project. Retrieved 2011-02-01.*

41. Damer 2009, p. 178.

42. Damer 2009, p. 186.

43. Fischer 1970, p. 209.

44. "The Reflex Arc Concept in Psychology", John Dewey, *The Psychological Review*, Vol. III. No. 4. July 1896. p. 367.

45. Bunnin & Yu 2004, "Homunculus".

46. *"A List Of Fallacious Arguments". Retrieved 6 October 2012.*

47. Wimsatt, William K. and Monroe C. Beardsley. "The Intentional Fallacy." *Sewanee Review*, vol. 54 (1946): 468–88. Revised and republished in *The Verbal Icon: Studies in the Meaning of Poetry*, U of Kentucky P, 1954: 3–18.

48. Copi & Cohen 1990, p. 105.

49. *Taleb, Nassim (2007). The Black Swan. Random House. p. 309. ISBN 1-4000-6351-5. Retrieved 2016-02-24.*

50. *"TheFreeDictionary". Naturalistic fallacy.*

51. John Searle, "How to Derive 'Ought' from 'Is'", *The Philosophical Review*, 73:1 (January 1964), 43–58.

52. Alex Walter, "The Anti-naturalistic Fallacy: Evolutionary Moral Psychology and the Insistence of Brute Facts", *Evolutionary Psychology*, 4 (2006), 33–48

53. Damer 2009, p. 180.

54. Damer 2009, p. 208.

55. Semiotics Glossary R, *Referential fallacy or illusion*

56. Gula 2002, p. 135.

57. Pirie 2006, p. 5.

58. Flew 1984, "No-true-Scotsman move".

59. Hurley 2007, p. 155.

60. Damer 2009, p. 151.

61. Hurley 2007, p. 134.

62. Fischer 1970, p. 127.

63. *Gary Curtis. "Logical Fallacy: Red Herring". fallacyfiles.org. Retrieved 2016-02-24.*

64. *joseph (April 17, 2011). "Red Herring Fallacy". Archived from the original on 2014-12-03.*

65. *"Logical Fallacies". logicalfallacies.info. Retrieved 2016-02-24.*

66. Walton 2008, p. 187.

67. *Bo Bennett. "Ad Hominem (Abusive)". logicallyfallacious.com. Retrieved 2016-02-24.*

68. Clark & Clark 2005, pp. 13–16.

69. Walton 1997, p. 28.

70. *Bo Bennett. "Appeal to Accomplishment". logicallyfallacious.com. Retrieved 2016-02-24.*

71. Walton 2008, p. 27.

72. Damer 2009, p. 111.

73. *Bo Bennett. "Appeal to Fear". logicallyfallacious.com.*

74. *"Appeal to Fear". changingminds.org.*

75. Gula 2002, p. 12.
76. Walton 2008, p. 128.
77. *"Appeal to Ridicule"*. *changingminds.org*.
78. *Bo Bennett. "Appeal to Ridicule". logicallyfallacious.com.*
79. *"Appeal to Spite"*. *changingminds.org*.
80. Damer 2009, p. 146.
81. *Gary Curtis. "Logical Fallacy: Appeal to Nature". fallacyfiles.org.*
82. Pirie 2006, p. 116.
83. Pirie 2006, p. 104.
84. Pirie 2006, p. 14.
85. Pirie 2006, p. 39.
86. Damer 2009, p. 106.
87. *"Appeal to Widespread Belief"*. *Retrieved 6 October 2012*.
88. *Gary Curtis. "Logical Fallacy: Guilt by Association". fallacyfiles.org.*
89. *"Encyclopedia Barfieldiana"*. *davidlavery.net*.
90. *"Archived copy"*. *Archived from the original on February 5, 2012. Retrieved February 11, 2014.*
91. Damer 2009, p. 93.
92. *Shackel, Nicholas (2005). "The Vacuity of Postmodernist Methodology". Metaphilosophy. 36 (3). For my purposes the desirable but only lightly defensible territory of the Motte and Bailey castle, that is to say, the Bailey, represents a philosophical doctrine or position with similar properties: desirable to its proponent but only lightly defensible. The Motte is the defensible but undesired position to which one retreats when hard pressed...*
93. Dowden 2010, "Is-Ought".
94. Dowden 2010, "Naturalistic".
95. *Munson, Ronald; Black, Andrew (2016). The Elements of Reasoning. Cengage Learning. p. 257. ISBN 1305886836.*
96. Walton 2008, p. 22.
97. Curtis, "The Texas Sharpshooter Fallacy".
98. Pirie 2006, p. 164.
99. Johnson & Blair 1994, p. 122.
100. *Frankena, W. K. (October 1939). "The Naturalistic Fallacy". Mind. Oxford University Press. 48 (192): 464–77. JSTOR 2250706.*
101. Walton 2008, p. 315.

Works

- *Bunnin, Nicholas; Yu, Jiyuan, eds. (2004). The Blackwell Dictionary of Western Philosophy. Blackwell. ISBN 978-1-4051-0679-5.*
- *Clark, Jef; Clark, Theo (2005). Humbug! The Skeptic's Field Guide to Spotting Fallacies in Thinking. Nifty Books. ISBN 0-646-44477-8. Also available as an ebook.*
- *Copi, Irving M.; Cohen, Carl (1990). Introduction to Logic (8th ed.). Macmillan. ISBN 978-0-02-325035-4.*
- *Curtis, Gary N. Logical Fallacies: The Fallacy Files. Retrieved 2011-04-23.*
- *Damer, T. Edward (2009). Attacking Faulty Reasoning: A Practical Guide to Fallacy-free Arguments (6th ed.). Wadsworth. ISBN 978-0-495-09506-4. Retrieved 30 November 2010.*
- *Dowden, Bradley (December 31, 2010). "Fallacy". The Internet Encyclopedia of Philosophy. ISSN 2161-0002. Retrieved 2011-04-22.*
- *Fischer, David Hackett (1970). Historians' Fallacies: Toward a Logic of Historical Thought. HarperCollins. ISBN 978-0-06-131545-9.*
- *Flew, Antony (1984). "A Dictionary of Philosophy: Revised Second Edition". A Dictionary of Philosophy. Macmillan. ISBN 978-0-312-20923-0.*
- *Gula, Robert J. (2002). Nonsense: Red Herrings, Straw Men and Sacred Cows: How We Abuse Logic in Our Everyday Language. Axios Press. ISBN 978-0-9753662-6-4.*

- *Hurley, Patrick J. (2007). A Concise Introduction to Logic (10th ed.). Cengage. ISBN 978-0-495-50383-5.*
- *Johnson, Ralph H.; Blair, J. Anthony (1994). Logical Self-Defense. IDEA. ISBN 978-1-932716-18-4.*
- *Pirie, Madsen (2006). How to Win Every Argument: The Use and Abuse of Logic. Continuum International Publishing Group. ISBN 0-8264-9006-9.*
- *Wilson, W. Kent (1999). "Formal fallacy". In Audi, Robert. The Cambridge Dictionary of Philosophy (2nd ed.). Cambridge University Press. pp. 316–17. ISBN 978-0-511-07417-2.*
- *Walton, Douglas (1997). Appeal to Expert Opinion: Arguments from Authority. Pennsylvania State University. ISBN 0-271-01694-9 Paperback ISBN 0-271-01695-7*
- *Walton, Douglas (2008). Informal Logic: A Pragmatic Approach (2nd ed.). Cambridge University Press. ISBN 978-0-511-40878-6.*

Further reading

The following is a sample of books for further reading, selected for a combination of content, ease of access via the internet, and to provide an indication of published sources that interested readers may review. The titles of some books are self-explanatory. Good books on critical thinking commonly contain sections on fallacies, and some may be listed below.

- *DiCarlo, Christopher. How to Become a Really Good Pain in the Ass: A Critical Thinker's Guide to Asking the Right Questions. Prometheus Books. ISBN 978-1-61614-397-8.*
- *Engel, S. Morris (1994). Fallacies and Pitfalls of Language: The Language Trap. Dover Publications. ISBN 0-486-28274-0. Retrieved 30 November 2010.*
- *Hamblin, C. L. (2004). Fallacies. Methuen & Co. ISBN 0-416-14570-1.*
- *Hughes, William; Lavery, Jonathan (2004). Critical Thinking: An Introduction to the Basic Skills (4th ed.). Broadview Press. ISBN 1-55111-573-5. Retrieved 30 November 2010.*
- *Paul, Richard; Elder, Linda (2006). Thinker's Guide to Fallacies: The Art of Mental Trickery. Foundation for Critical Thinking. ISBN 978-0-944583-27-2. Retrieved 30 November 2010.*
- *Sinnott-Armstrong, Walter; Fogelin, Robert (2010). Understanding Arguments: An Introduction to Informal Logic (8th ed.). Wadsworth Cengage Learning. ISBN 978-0-495-60395-5. Retrieved 30 November 2010.*
- *Thouless, Robert H (1953). Straight and Crooked Thinking (PDF). Pan Books. Retrieved 30 November 2010.*
- *Tindale, Christopher W (2007). Fallacies and Argument Appraisal. Critical Reasoning and Argumentation. Cambridge University Press. ISBN 978-0-521-84208-2. Retrieved 30 November 2010.*

External links

- Logical Fallacies, Literacy Education Online
- LogicalFallacies.info
- Informal Fallacies, Texas State University page on informal fallacies.
- Stephen's Guide to the Logical Fallacies (mirror)
- The Taxonomy of Logical Fallacies, FallacyFiles.org
- Visualization: Rhetological Fallacies, InformationIsBeautiful.net
- *Master List of Logical Fallacies* University of Texas at El Paso

Index

A

Abduction, 112
Abductive reasoning, 90, 112–113
Absent definitions, 199
Academic essay, 402
Action fallacy, 153
Active error, 257
Actor-observer bias, 505
Actuarial judgment, 165
Alethiology, 27
Allopathic medicine, 143
Alternative choice fallacy, 363
Ambiguity effect, 316, 495
Anchoring, 495
Anthropocentric thinking, 495
Anthropomorphism, 495
A posteriori–developed definitions, 201
Appeal to authority fallacy, 154
Appeal to consequences fallacy, 362
Appeal to poverty, 362
Applied ethics, 29
Arborization, diagnosis by, 135
Argumentation
    definition of, 261
    diagnosis as subject of, 139
    prognosis as subject of, 162–163
    risk as subject of, 132
    treatment as subject of, 152–153
Argumentation, tools for, 89–109
    "classical" form of reasoning (categorical syllogism or
        "three-element" reasoning), 91–94
    "modern" form of Toulmin's model of argument,
        95–109
    "naked" argument (enthymeme) ("two-element"
        reasoning), 89–91
Argumentative essay, 405–407
Argument-based medicine, 83, 88
Argumentum ad lazarum fallacy, 362
Argumentum ad numeram fallacy, 364
Argumentum ad verecundiam fallacy, 141

Art, craft, scientific method, and evidence, 37–71
    art, medicine as, 45–48
    art, craft, and science of medicine, 45–52
    challenges, 66
    chaos theory in medicine, 54
    clinical uncertainty, 53
    complexity theory, 54
    context of medicine, 45
    craft, medicine as, 48
    critical thinking, 62–63
    disease prevention, 43
    empiricism, 50
    evidence-based community medicine and public
        health, 58
    evidence-based medicine, 56–62
    falsifiability of results, 51
    fuzzy theory in medicine, 53–54
    health promotion, 43
    health protection, 43
    integrative medicine, 64
    medical crafts, 46
    medical humanities, 65
    orismology, 47
    paradigms behind the science of medicine, 52–54
    patient-centered (person-centered), personalized,
        integrative medicines, 63–65
    personalized medicine, 64
    practice of medicine, 55–56
    primary prevention, 43
    primordial prevention, 43
    probability and clinical uncertainty, 52–53
    quaternary prevention, 43
    rationalism, 50
    reflective uses of evidence, 63
    science, medicine as, 49–52
    scientific method, 49–52
    scientific theory, 49
    secondary prevention, 43
    skepticism, 50
    tertiary prevention, 43
    theory of medicine, 55

uncertainty in medicine, 52
what we should we teach, learn, and practice,
65–67
Arts and sciences, and logic and critical thinking in general
(concurrent developments in), 10–11
Ascertainment bias, 139
Attentional bias, 495
Attributable risk, 224
Authority bias, 506
Automation bias, 495
Availability bias, 315
Availability cascade, 496
Availability fallacy, 140
Availability heuristic, 496

B

Backfire effect, 496
Bandwagon effect, 496
Barnum effect, 498, 506
Base rate fallacy, 496
Base rate neglect fallacy, 140
Bayesian reasoning, 138
Belief bias, 496
Ben Franklin effect, 496
Berkson bias, 133
Berkson's paradox, 496
Bias, 265; *see also* Cognitive biases, list of
    ascertainment, 139
    availability, 315
    bias blind spot, 496
    cognitive, 265
    confirmation, 153, 315
    hindsight, 140, 266
    omission, 153
    outcome, 265
    overconfidence, 315
Biostatistics, 9
Bizarreness effect, 509
Blind conviction, 362
Blinding with science fallacy, 364
Boeotian's fallacy, 153
Bullying, 332, 334

C

Case fatality rates, 223
Casuistics, 377
Categorical syllogism, 91–94
Causal inference, 113, 234
Cause-based definitions, 200
Cause-and-effect essay, 402
Cause-effect relationships, 213–249
    analytical studies, 219
    attributable risk, 224
    case fatality rates, 223
    causal inference, 234

combining frequencies, fractions, risks, and
    proportions, 226
confidence intervals, 226
considerations of causality in "cognition-based"
    medicine, 241
criteria for accepting etiology or other cause-effect
    relationships, 235–239
criteria of causality, 235
critical thinking, communication, and decision-
    making and their connection to medical
    ethics, 243–244
descriptive studies, 219
disease or other event frequencies and fractions in
    causal reasoning, 219–226
effect of potentiation, 234
etiological fraction, 225
fallacies in medical reasoning and scientific thinking,
    239–241
incidence rates, 222
interval estimates, 226
likelihood ratio, 229
miscellaneous ways of considering causality, 243
morbidity rates, 222
mortality rates, 223
odds, 223
point estimates, 226
prevalence rates, 222
quantifying uncertainties, 226–228
range of observations, 228
relative risk, 223
role of causal reasoning in medical thinking, 241
sets, chains, webs, and concept maps of causes (single
    or multiple observations as), 228–234
single or multiple observations and findings, 234–235
single-subject research design, 241–243
statistical inference, 234
thinking about causes, 228–239
uncertainty, probabilities, disease frequency behind
    disease occurrence and its causes, 219–228
Chains of causes, 229
Change bias, 509
Chaos theory in medicine, 54
Cheerleader effect, 496
Childhood amnesia, 509
Choice-supportive bias, 496, 509
Classification essay, 401
Clinical case reporting, 373–392
    case reporting topics, 383
    case series report, 386
    casuistics, 377
    causal proof, 387–388
    "classical" clinical case report, 384–385
    clinical vignette, 385
    considerations of causality in clinical pharmacology,
        388
    considerations of causality in "cognition-based"
        medicine, 388

content and architecture of clinical case report, 380–382
critical appraisal, 389
epidemiological demonstration of causality based on frequent cases, 388
fundamental considerations and gnostic classification of clinical case reports, 382
message itself and ways to convey it in argumentative manner, 386–387
proposed thesis, 378–380
structure and organization, 386
topics, 383
types of case reporting, 383–386
Clinical and community medicine, decisions in, 287–322
    ambiguity effect fallacy, 316
    attitudes, 293
    availability bias, 315
    clinical algorithms, 305–310
    clinical practice guidelines, 310–314
    clinical practice guidelines and clinical protocols, 310–314
    clinical ritualism, 295
    closed system, 306
    collective-related fallacies (groupthink), 317
    commitment fallacy, 316
    computer-assisted decision-making, 297
    confirmation bias, 315
    control diagram, 306
    cost-benefit/effectiveness/utility analysis, 301–302
    daily life, decision-making in, 294–314
    decision analysis, 297–301
    decisions as conclusions of argumentative process, 302–305
    decision theory, decision analysis, and decision-making, 293–294
    decision tree, 306
    Delphi method, 297
    direction-giving tools in decision-making, 305–314
    disposition, 293
    distilled clinical judgment, 295
    doing nothing, 318
    ERASPEC, 310
    evidence-based clinical decision-making path, 310
    fallacies related to decisions themselves, 316–317
    flow sheet, 306
    gut feeling exploration, 295
    heuristic decision-making, 296
    hyperbolic discounting, 316
    illustrative fallacies, 314–317
    individual-related fallacies, 314–317
    intuition, 315
    knowledge, 293
    open system, 306
    outcome nodes, 300
    overconfidence bias, 315
    probability nodes, 300
    rational choice theory, 294
    reasoning-based fallacies, 314–316
    reasoning by analogy, 315
    sensitivity analysis, 300
    shortcut decisions, 296
    skills, 293
    source credibility fallacy, 316
    strategic tools, 305
    structured ways of decision-making, 297–305
    sunk cost trap, 315
    tactical tools, 305
    threshold analysis, 300
    unstructured ways of decision-making, 295–297
Clinical epidemiology, developments in, 10
Clinical life table, 161
Clinical practice guidelines (CPGs), 310–314
Clinical reasoning, 128
Clinical uncertainty, 53
Clinical work and care (step-by-step), 123–168
    actuarial judgment, 165
    analytical observational studies, 160
    appeal to authority fallacy, 154
    arborization or multiple branching, diagnosis by, 135
    argumentation, diagnosis as subject of, 139
    argumentation, prognosis as subject of, 162–163
    argumentation, risk as subject of, 132
    argumentation, treatment as subject of, 152–153
    argumentum ad verecundiam fallacy, 141
    ascertainment bias, 139
    availability fallacy, 140
    base rate neglect fallacy, 140
    Bayesian reasoning, 138
    bias, 133
    Boeotian's fallacy, 153
    cause-effect relationships, 160
    clinical life table, 161
    computer-assisted diagnosis, 136
    confirmation fallacy, 153
    criterion/criteria fallacy, 141
    decision trees, 135
    deterministic diagnostic pathway, 136
    diagnosis, 124
    diagnosis, properties of, 134–142
    diagnosis domain, thinking and reasoning in, 142
    diagnostic oversimplification fallacy, 140
    disease spectrum, 158
    exclusive exploration of data, 135
    fallacy of commission, 153
    fallacy of composition, 163
    fallacy of division, 163
    hard data, 134
    health events, clinical reasoning about, 128–129
    hindsight bias, 140
    ignoring Bayes fallacy, 140
    ignoring Ockham's razor fallacy, 141
    incidence rates, 130
    intervention studies, 160
    "is–ought" fallacy, 141
    knowledge of risk factors and markers, 132

life table, 161
misleading use of statistics, 164
omission fallacy, 153
order effect fallacy, 139
overconfidence fallacy, 153
oversimplification, 164
parallel testing, 139
patient characteristics, 151
pattern recognition, 135
primary prevention of medical error, 144
primordial prevention, 144
probability, 129
probability-based diagnosis, 135
prognosis, 124, 155–165
quality and completeness of diagnostic material, 134
quaternary prevention, 144
reasoning in the domain of treatment and preventive interventions, 154
reasoning more effectively about the future of patients, 160–162
relapse rate, 158
representativeness restraint fallacy, 139
risk, 129–134
risk assessment, 123
screening tests, 136
secondary prevention of medical error, 144
sequential testing, 139
significance of risk factors, 130–132
soft data, 134
steepest ascent method, 135
steps in making diagnosis, 135–136
survival curve, 158
survivorship study, 161
Sutton's slip, 140
tertiary prevention of medical error, 144
thinking in the domain of prognosis, 164–165
time-to-event analysis, 159
treatment, 124, 142–154
types and levels of medical therapeutic and preventive interventions, 143–147
validity of diagnostic methods and techniques, 136–139
vertical line failure fallacy, 140
what we need to know about prognostic events and outcomes, 158–159
Clustering illusion, 497
Cognition, definition of, 435
Cognitive biases, list of, 493–521
  actor-observer bias, 505
  ambiguity effect, 495
  anchoring, 495
  anthropocentric thinking, 495
  anthropomorphism, 495
  attentional bias, 495
  authority bias, 506
  automation bias, 495
  availability cascade, 496

availability heuristic, 496
backfire effect, 496
bandwagon effect, 496
Barnum effect, 498
base rate fallacy, 496
belief bias, 496
Ben Franklin effect, 496
Berkson's paradox, 496
bias blind spot, 496
bizarreness effect, 509
change bias, 509
cheerleader effect, 496
childhood amnesia, 509
choice-supportive bias, 496, 509
clustering illusion, 497
common theoretical causes of some cognitive biases, 513–514
confirmation bias, 497
congruence bias, 497
conjunction fallacy, 497
conservatism, 497, 509
consistency bias, 509
context effect, 509
continued influence effect, 497
contrast effect, 497
courtesy bias, 497
cross-race effect, 509
cryptomnesia, 509
curse of knowledge, 497
debiasing, 514
decision-making, belief, and behavioral biases, 495–505
declinism, 497
decoy effect, 497
defensive attribution hypothesis, 506
denomination effect, 498
disposition effect, 498
distinction bias, 498
Dunning–Kruger effect, 498
duration neglect, 498
egocentric bias, 506, 509
empathy gap, 498
endowment effect, 498
exaggerated expectation, 498
experimenter's bias, 498
extrinsic incentives bias, 506
fading affect bias, 510
false consensus effect, 506
false memory, 510
focusing effect, 498
Forer effect, 498, 506
framing effect, 499
frequency illusion, 499
functional fixedness, 499
fundamental attribution error, 506
gambler's fallacy, 499
generation effect, 510

Google effect, 510
group attribution error, 506
halo effect, 506
hard–easy effect, 499
hindsight bias, 499, 510
hostile attribution bias, 499
hot-hand fallacy, 499
humor effect, 510
hyperbolic discounting, 499
identifiable victim effect, 500
IKEA effect, 500
illusion of asymmetric insight, 507
illusion of control, 500
illusion of external agency, 507
illusion of transparency, 507
illusion of truth effect, 510
illusion of validity, 500
illusory correlation, 500, 510
illusory superiority, 507
illusory truth effect, 500
impact bias, 500
individual differences in decision making biases, 514
information bias, 500
ingroup bias, 507
insensitivity to sample size, 500
irrational escalation, 500
just-world hypothesis, 507
lag effect, 510
law of the instrument, 501
less-is-better effect, 501
leveling and sharpening, 510
levels-of-processing effect, 511
list-length effect, 511
look-elsewhere effect, 501
loss aversion, 501
memory errors and biases, 508–513
mere exposure effect, 501
misinformation effect, 511
modality effect, 511
money illusion, 501
mood-congruent memory bias, 511
moral credential effect, 501
moral luck, 507
naïve cynicism, 507
naïve realism, 507
negativity bias, 501
neglect of probability, 501
next-in-line effect, 511
normalcy bias, 501
not invented here, 501
observer-expectancy effect, 502
omission bias, 502
optimism bias, 502
ostrich effect, 502
outcome bias, 502
outgroup homogeneity bias, 507
overconfidence effect, 502

pareidolia, 502
Parkinson's Law of Unit bias, 505
part-list cueing effect, 511
peak-end rule, 511
Peltzman effect, 503
persistence, 511
pessimism bias, 502
picture superiority effect, 511
planning fallacy, 502
positivity effect, 511
post-purchase rationalization, 502
primacy effect, recency effect & serial position effect, 512
processing difficulty effect, 512
pro-innovation bias, 503
projection bias, 503
pseudocertainty effect, 503
reactance, 503
reactive devaluation, 503
recency illusion, 503
regressive bias, 503
reminiscence bump, 512
restraint bias, 503
rhyme as reason effect, 503
risk compensation, 503
rosy retrospection, 512
selective perception, 503
self-generation effect, 510
self-relevance effect, 512
self-serving bias, 507
Semmelweis reflex, 504
sexual overperception bias/sexual underperception bias, 504
shared information bias, 508
sociability bias of language, 508
social biases, 505–508
social comparison bias, 504
social desirability bias, 504
source confusion, 512
spacing effect, 512
spotlight effect, 512
status quo bias, 504
stereotyping, 504, 512
subadditivity effect, 504
subjective validation, 504
suffix effect, 512
suggestibility, 512
surrogation, 504
survivorship bias, 504
system justification, 508
telescoping effect, 513
testing effect, 513
third-person effect, 505
time-saving bias, 504
tip of the tongue phenomenon, 513
trait ascription bias, 508
Travis Syndrome, 513

triviality, 505
ultimate attribution error, 508
verbatim effect, 513
Von Restorff effect, 513
Weber–Fechner law, 505
well travelled road effect, 505
wishful thinking, 494
worse-than-average effect, 508
Zeigarnik effect, 513
zero-risk bias, 505
zero-sum bias, 505
Cognitive error, 87
Cognitive process, medical thinking as, 8
Commitment fallacy, 316
Communication (mostly oral), 325–372; *see also* Thesis and its seven cornerstones
    active teaching tools, 343
    alternative choice fallacy, 363
    appeal to consequences fallacy, 362
    appeal to poverty, 362
    argumentation, critical thinking-based and evidence-grounded exchange of data and information, 335–339
    blinding with science fallacy, 364
    case series reports, 354
    clinical case reports, 354
    clinical consultations as narratives, 352–353
    clinical vignettes and clinical case reports, 353–355
    commonest one-way intellectual vehicles of communication, 332
    communication errors, 360
    complementary treatment fallacy, 363
    external dialogue, 331
    eye gaze, 349
    formal (magisterial) lectures, 358–359
    gambler's fallacy, 361–362
    grand rounds, 342
    illustrative fallacies, 360–364
    intellectual vehicles of communication, 332–342
    internal dialogue, 330
    journal clubs, 356–357
    knowledge translation, 364–367
    leading questions, 346
    medical articles and scientific papers, 359
    miscellaneous forms of communication, 359
    morbidity and mortality reports and rounds, 355
    morning reports, 355
    narratives and clinical case reports, 352–355
    one-sidedness, fallacy of, 363
    one-way communication vehicles (mostly), 357–358
    oral and written exchanges of experience in clinical practice, 342–359
    passive teaching tools, 343
    patient bedside communication and progress notes (SOAPs), 351–352
    patient interviews, 345–351
    pimping (bullying), 332–334

    prejudicial language, 363
    put them all together fallacy, 363–364
    qualifiers, 347
    red herring fallacy, 335
    rhetorical ploys, 360
    rounds, miscellaneous types of, 357
    scut work, 358
    self-evidence fallacy, 362
    slippery slope fallacy, 361
    Socratic method, dissent, and dialogue, 339–342
    uttering wisdom, 335
    viewing communication, 330–332
    voice cues, 349
    wishful thinking, 362
Communication (written), 393–428; *see also* Thesis and its seven cornerstones
    academic essay, 402
    analytical studies, 398
    argumentative/persuasive essay, 402, 405–407
    business method and format, 418
    business report, 394
    Cause-and-effect essay, 402
    classification essay, 401
    clinical case studies vs. clinical case reports, 419–421
    compare-and-contrast essays, 402
    critical essay, 402
    critical thinking essay, 402
    descriptive essays, 401
    descriptive studies, 398
    essay-based medical and other articles, 398–407
    expository essay, 401
    five-part essay, 403
    IMRAD format, 411–415
    informal essay, 403
    "lab report" format, 394, 415
    literary essays, 402
    logical analysis of medical articles, 410
    medical research articles, 407–415
    mixed-methods research, 407
    multidirectional essay, 404
    narrative essay, 401
    nature and purpose of essays, 401–402
    opinion writing, 401
    personal essay, 402
    qualitative research, 407
    qualitative research-based and case studies-based articles, 418–422
    quantitative research, 407
    reflective essays, 401, 405
    "restaurant refined menu" essay, 404
    scientific method, steps of, 417
    SIMRAD, 408
    structure of essays, 403–405
    structure, language, and style, 416–417
    valuing qualitative research studies and articles, 421–422

Community medicine, *see* Clinical and community
    medicine, decisions in
Compare-and-contrast essays, 402
Complementary treatment fallacy, 363
Complexity theory, 54
Computer-assisted decision-making, 297
Concept maps, 231
Conditional fallacies, 532
Confidence intervals, 226
Confirmation bias, 153, 315, 497
Confirmation fallacy, 153
Congruence bias, 497
Conjunction fallacy, 497
Conservatism, 497, 509
Consistency bias, 509
Content-listing definitions, 200
Context effect, 509
Context-specifying definitions, 201
Continued influence effect, 497
Contrast effect, 497
Control diagram, 306
Cost-benefit analysis, 301
Courtesy bias, 497
Craft, medicine as, *see* Art, craft, scientific method, and
    evidence
Criterion/criteria fallacy, 141
Critical appraisal, 206, 356, 389
Critical essay, 402
Critical thinking and decision-making (CTDM), 75–121
    abductive reasoning, 112–113
    accumulation of evidence, 110
    argumentation, tools for, 89–109
    "classical" form of reasoning (categorical syllogism or
        "three-element" reasoning), 91–94
    clinical care and caregiver reasoning, basic
        considerations related to, 80
    cognition pathways, 110
    cognitive error, 87
    communication, 80, 81
    deductive reasoning, 112
    directionality of reasoning, 111–115
    enumerative induction, 111
    framing, 104, 118
    general medical thinking and reasoning, 79–111
    hypotheses, 105
    inductive reasoning, 111–112
    medical harm, 86
    "modern" form of Toulmin's model of argument
        ("multi-element" way of reasoning to reach
        valid conclusions), 95–109
    "naked" argument (enthymeme) ("two-element"
        reasoning), 89–91
    objectives, 106
    premise indicator, 91
    presumptions, 85
    pyramid of evidence, 118
    reasoning, 82

    statistical and causal inference, 113
    taxonomy of learning (Bloom), 81
    thesis, 103
    thinking and reasoning (essential definitions and
        meanings), 81–89
Critical thinking essay, 402
Cross-race effect, 509
Cryptomnesia, 509
Curse of knowledge, 497

D

Debiasing, 514
Decision-making, belief, and behavioral biases, 495–505;
    see also Clinical and community medicine,
    decisions in; Critical thinking and decision-
    making (CTDM)
Decision trees, 135, 306
Declinism, 497
Decoy effect, 497
Deductive reasoning, 112
Defensive attribution hypothesis, 506
Definitions, 191–211
    absent definitions, 199
    adjectives and other challenges of definitions,
        205–207
    a posteriori–developed definitions, 201
    cause-based definitions, 200
    clinical practice guidelines, 206
    composite definitions, challenge of, 203–205
    content-listing definitions, 200
    context-specifying definitions, 201
    critical appraisal, 206, 207
    definitions in medicine and health sciences and their
        subject, 196–198
    description, 195–196
    desirable qualities and attributes of definitions,
        202–203
    desirable qualities and attributes of definitions in
        medicine and other health sciences, 203
    importance of definitions, 199
    inclusion and exclusion criteria for definitions,
        204–205
    inspirational definitions, 200
    knowledge translation, 197, 205
    multiple definitions, 201
    operational definitions, 201
    patient/physician-centered definitions, 201
    persuasive definitions, 206
    purpose-missing definitions, 201
    specialty-bound definitions, 201
    strategy-motivated definitions, 200
    thesis, 195
    types of definitions in current medical research and
        practice uses, 199–202
    uncertain definitions, 201
    value (judgment)-based definitions, 200

Delphi method (decision-making), 297
Denomination effect, 498
Descriptive essays, 401
Diagnosis, properties of, 134–142
    arborization or multiple branching, diagnosis by,
        135
    argumentation, diagnosis as subject of, 139
    argumentum ad verecundiam fallacy, 141
    ascertainment bias, 139
    availability fallacy, 140
    base rate neglect fallacy, 140
    Bayesian reasoning, 138
    computer-assisted diagnosis, 136
    criterion/criteria fallacy, 141
    decision trees, 135
    deterministic diagnostic pathway, 136
    diagnosis domain, thinking and reasoning in, 142
    diagnostic oversimplification fallacy, 140
    exclusive exploration of data, 135
    hard data, 134
    hindsight bias, 140
    ignoring Bayes fallacy, 140
    ignoring Ockham's razor fallacy, 141
    illustrative fallacies, 139–141
    "is–ought" fallacy, 141
    order effect fallacy, 139
    parallel testing, 139
    pattern recognition, 135
    probability-based diagnosis, 135
    quality and completeness of diagnostic material, 134
    representativeness restraint fallacy, 139
    screening tests, 136
    sequential testing, 139
    soft data, 134
    steepest ascent method, 135
    steps in making diagnosis, 135–136
    Sutton's slip, 140
    validity of diagnostic methods and techniques,
        136–139
    vertical line failure fallacy, 140
Diagnostic oversimplification fallacy, 140
Disease prevention, 43
Disease spectrum, 158
Disposition effect, 498
Distilled clinical judgment, 295
Distinction bias, 498
Dunning–Kruger effect, 498
Duration neglect, 498

E

EBM, *see* Evidence-based medicine (EBM)
Egocentric bias, 506, 509
Electronic communication media, 432
Empathy gap, 498
Empiricism, 28, 50
Endowment effect, 498

Enthymeme, 89–91
Enumerative induction, 111
Epidemiological forecasting, 278
Epidemiological surveillance, 278
Epistemology, 13, 27–28
Error, *see* Medical error and harm
Essays, 398–407
    academic essay, 402
    argumentative/persuasive essay, 405–407
    Cause-and-effect essay, 402
    classification essay, 401
    compare-and-contrast essays, 402
    critical essay, 402
    critical thinking essay, 402
    definition of essay, 401
    descriptive essays, 401
    expository essay, 401
    five-part essay, 403
    informal essay, 403
    literary essays, 402
    multidirectional essay, 404
    narrative essay, 401
    nature and purpose of essays, 401–402
    opinion writing, 401
    personal essay, 402
    reflective essays, 401, 405
    "restaurant refined menu" essay, 404
    structure of essays, 403–405
    types of essays, 401
Esthetics, 29–30
Ethics, 13, 28–29
    applied, 29
    medical, 29
    meta-, 29
    normative, 29
Etiological fraction, 225
Evidence, *see* Art, craft, scientific method, and
        evidence
Evidence-Based Cognitive Medicine, 435
Evidence-based medicine (EBM), 56–62, 433
    composite definition, 207
    definition of, 56
    developments in, 10
    evidence-based clinical medicine, 58
    evidence-based community medicine and public
        health (EBPH), 58
    evidence-based healthcare, 59–60
    grading evidence in, 117
    grading evidence and evaluating the EBM process,
        60–62
    steps in the practice of, 56–58
Exaggerated expectation, 498
Exclusion criteria, 204
Experimenter's bias, 498
Expository essay, 401
Extrinsic incentives bias, 506
Eye gaze, 349

F

Fading affect bias, 510
Fallacies, list of, 523–536; *see also specific type*
    cause-effect relationships and, 239–241
    clinical and community medicine and, 316–317
    communication, 360–364
    conditional or questionable fallacies, 532
    faulty generalization, 529–530
    formal fallacies, 525
    formal syllogistic fallacies, 526
    informal fallacies, 526–529
    medical error and, 265–267
    propositional fallacies, 525
    quantification fallacies, 525
    red herring fallacies, 530–532
False consensus effect, 506
False memory, 510
Falsifiability of results, 51
Faulty generalization, 529–530
Five-part essay, 403
Flow sheet, 306
Focalism, 495
Focusing effect, 498
Forecasting-related errors, 278–279
Forer effect, 498, 506
Formal epistemology, 27
Formal fallacies, 525
Formal logic, 28
Formal syllogistic fallacies, 526
Framing, 104, 118, 499
Frequency illusion, 499
Functional fixedness, 499
Fundamental attribution error, 506
Fuzzy theory in medicine, 53–54

G

Gambler's fallacy, 361–362, 499
Generation effect, 510
Gestalt, 296
Glossary, 437–491
Gnostic processes, 8, 15
Google effect, 510
Grand rounds, 342
Group attribution error, 506
Groupthink, 317
Gut feeling exploration, 295

H

Halo effect, 506
Hard data, 134, 345
Hard–easy effect, 499
Health events, 128
    clinical reasoning about, 128–129
    subject to conceptually similar reasoning, 143
Health promotion, 43

Health protection, 43
Hermeneutics, 14
Heuristic decision-making, 296
Hindsight bias, 133, 140, 266, 499, 510
Historical experience, understanding of reasoning from,
    see Interactive domains
Hostile attribution bias, 499
Hot-hand fallacy, 499
Humor effect, 510
Hyperbolic discounting, 316, 499
Hypotheses, 105, 181
Hypothetical induction, 112

I

Iatrognostics, 15
Identifiable victim effect, 500
Ignoring Bayes fallacy, 140
Ignoring Ockham's razor fallacy, 141
IKEA effect, 500
Illusion of asymmetric insight, 507
Illusion of control, 500
Illusion of external agency, 507
Illusion of transparency, 507
Illusion of truth effect, 510
Illusion of validity, 500
Illusory correlation, 500, 510
Illusory superiority, 507
Illusory truth effect, 500
Impact bias, 500
IMRAD format, 411–415
Incidence rates, 130, 222
Inclusion criteria, 204
Inductive exploration, 278
Inductive reasoning, 111–112
Informal essay, 403
Informal fallacies, 526–529
Informal logic, 28, 86, 261
Information bias, 500
Ingroup bias, 507
Insensitivity to sample size, 500
Inspirational definitions, 200
Instrumental case study, 423
Integrative medicine, 64
Interactive domains, 3–19
    arts and sciences, and logic and critical thinking in
        general (concurrent developments in), 10–11
    biostatistics, 9
    clinical epidemiology and evidence-based medicine,
        developments in, 10
    clinical judgment, 11, 12
    clinical reasoning, 12
    critical thinking, 10
    epistemology, 13
    ethics, 13
    general epidemiology and biostatistics, developments
        in, 9

gnostic processes, 8, 15
hermeneutics, 14
iatrognostics, 15
judgment, 11
logic, 14
medical statistics, 9
medical thinking as cognitive process, 8
metaphysics, 13
need for another discipline for medicine and other
    health sciences, 12–15
ontology, 13
parallels between medicine and humanities, 9
philosophies, 11
phronesis, 14
qualitative research, developments in, 10
questions and proposals, 15
reasoning, 10
sciences–humanities interface, more recent
    development of, 11–12
semiotics, 14
thinking, 10
Interpretive medicine, 15
Interval estimates, 226
Intuition, 315
Irrational escalation, 500
"Is–ought" fallacy, 141

J

Journal clubs, 356–357
Judgment sentiment, 29
Just-world hypothesis, 507

K

Knowledge translation, 197, 205, 364–367

L

"Lab report" format, 394, 415
Lag effect, 510
Lapses, 264
Latent error, 257
Lathology, 111
    fallacies, biases, and cognitive errors in, 265–267
    mistakes and errors in, 264
Law of the instrument, 501
Leading questions, 346, 494
Less-is-better effect, 501
Leveling and sharpening, 510
Levels-of-processing effect, 511
Life table, 161
Likelihood ratio, 229
List-length effect, 511
Literary essays, 402

Logic, 14, 28
    formal, 28
    informal, 28, 86, 261
Look-elsewhere effect, 501
Loss aversion, 501

M

Medical error and harm, 86, 251–285
    active error, 257
    bias, 265
    clinical reasoning root cause analysis, 272
    cognitive bias, 265
    cognitive pathways as sites of error, 267–279
    defining medical error and medical harm, 257
    epidemiological forecasting, 278
    epidemiological surveillance, 278
    errors in making prognosis, 276–278
    failure, 258
    fallacies, biases, and cognitive errors in medical
        lathology, 265–267
    flawed argumentation and reasoning as sites and
        generators of error, 260–267
    follow-up, surveillance, forecasting-related errors,
        278–279
    fundamental considerations, 259–260
    getting results and their impact evaluation,
        275–276
    hindsight bias, 266
    inductive exploration, 278
    informal logic, 261
    lapses, 264
    latent error, 257
    measurement, 269
    medical harm, 257
    mensuration, 269
    meta-evaluation of human error, 279
    mistakes and errors in medical lathology, 264
    outcome bias, 265
    probabilistic risk analysis, 278
    reviewing actions as sources of error, 274–275
    reviewing decisions as sources of harm, 274
    reviewing diagnosis, 269–272
    reviewing path from diagnosis to treatment decisions
        and orders, 272
    slips, 264
    system error vs. individual human error, 257–259
Medical ethics, 29
    decision-making and, 243–244
    definition of, 244
Medical humanities, 65
Medical logic, 86
Medical research articles, 407–415
    IMRAD format, 411–415
    logical analysis of medical articles, 410

mixed-methods research, 407
    qualitative research, 407
    quantitative research, 407
    SIMRAD, 408
    thinking behind medical articles, 408–411
Medical statistics, 9
Memory errors and biases, 508–513
Mensuration, 269
Mere exposure effect, 501
Meta-epistemology, 27
Meta-ethics, 29
Metaphysics, 13, 27
Misinformation effect, 511
Mistakes, 264
Mixed-methods research, 407
Modality effect, 511
Money illusion, 501
Mood-congruent memory bias, 511
Moral credential effect, 501
Moral luck, 507
Morbidity rates, 222
Mortality rates, 223
Multidirectional essay, 404
Mystical assertion, 362

N

Naïve cynicism, 507
Naïve realism, 507
"Naked" argument (enthymeme), 89–91
Natural theology, 27
Negativity bias, 501
Neglect of probability, 501
Next-in-line effect, 511
Neyman bias, 133
Normalcy bias, 501
Normative ethics, 29
Not invented here, 501

O

Observer-expectancy effect, 502
Odds ratios, 224
Omission bias, 502
Omission fallacy, 153
One-sidedness, fallacy of, 363
Ontology, 13, 27
Operational definitions, 201
Opinion writing, 401
Optimism bias, 502
Oral communication, *see* Communication
        (mostly oral)
Order effect fallacy, 139
Orismology, 47
Ostrich effect, 502

Outcome bias, 265, 502
Outgroup homogeneity bias, 507
Overconfidence bias, 315
Overconfidence effect, 502
Overconfidence fallacy, 153

P

Pareidolia, 502
Parkinson's Law of Unit bias, 505
Part-list cueing effect, 511
Patient-centered care, 64
Patient interviews, 345–351
    nonverbal communication, 348–351
    verbal, oral, and written communication, 345–348
Patient/physician-centered definitions, 201
Pattern recognition, 296
Peak-end rule, 511
Peltzman effect, 503
Persistence, 511
Personal essay, 402
Personalized medicine, 64
Personification, 495
Persuasive definitions, 206
Persuasive essay, 405–407
Pessimism bias, 502
Philosophy for medicine (key contributions), 21–36
    alethiology, 27
    applied ethics, 29
    branches of philosophy, 26–30
    current illustrations, 33
    definition of philosopher, 30
    definition of philosophy, 25–26
    empiricism, 28
    epistemology, 27–28
    esthetics, 29–30
    ethics, 28–29
    formal epistemology, 27
    formal logic, 28
    informal logic, 28
    judgment sentiment, 29
    logic, 28
    medical philosophy, 32
    meta-epistemology, 27
    meta-ethics, 29
    metaphysics, 27
    natural theology, 27
    normative ethics, 29
    ontology, 27
    philosophy of art, 29
    philosophy and medicine, 32
    philosophy in medicine, 31–32
    philosophy of medicine, 32
    propositional knowledge, 28
    rationalism, 28

relationships, 29
social epistemology, 27
universal science, 27
Phronesis, 14
PICO (research question format), 105, 182
PICOT (research question format), 182
Picture superiority effect, 511
Pimping (bullying), 332–334
Planning fallacy, 502
PoCICOST (research question fromat), 105, 182
Point estimates, 226
Positivity effect, 511
Post-purchase rationalization, 502
Practice of medicine, 55–56
Prejudicial language, 363
Presumptions, 85
Prevalence rates, 222
Primacy effect, recency effect & serial position effect, 512
Primary prevention, 43
Primary prevention of medical error, 144
Primordial prevention, 43, 144
Probabilistic risk analysis, 278
Processing difficulty effect, 512
Prognosis, 155–165
    actuarial judgment, 165
    analytical observational studies, 160
    argumentation, prognosis as subject of, 162–163
    cause-effect relationships, 160
    clinical life table, 161
    differences between prognosis domain and risk domain, 156–158
    disease spectrum, 158
    errors in making, 276–278
    fallacy of composition, 163
    fallacy of division, 163
    illustrative fallacies, 163–164
    intervention studies, 160
    life table, 161
    misleading use of statistics, 164
    oversimplification, 164
    prognostic markers, 156
    reasoning more effectively about the future of patients, 160–162
    relapse rate, 158
    survival curve, 158
    survivorship study, 161
    thinking in the domain of prognosis, 164–165
    time-to-event analysis, 159
    what we need to know about prognostic events and outcomes, 158–159
Pro-innovation bias, 503
Projection bias, 503
Propositional fallacies, 525
Propositional knowledge, 28
Pseudocertainty effect, 503

Purpose-missing definitions, 201
Put them all together fallacy, 363–364

Q

Qualifiers, 347
Qualitative research, 407, 418–422
    developments in, 10
    research questions in, 183–185
Quantification fallacies, 525
Quantitative research, 407
Quaternary prevention, 43, 144
Questionable fallacies, 532

R

Rational choice theory, 294
Rationalism, 28, 50
Ratio of rates, 224
Reactance, 503
Reactive devaluation, 503
Reasoning
    abductive, 90, 112–113
    by analogy, 315
    Bayesian, 138
    causal, 219–226
    clinical, 128
    deductive, 112
    definition of, 82
    "three-element," 91–94
    "two-element," 89–91
    types of, 83
Reasoning, directionality of, 111–115
    abductive reasoning, 112–113
    conceptual differences, 114–115
    deductive reasoning, 112
    enumerative induction, 111
    inductive reasoning, 111–112
    statistical and causal inference, 113
Recency illusion, 503
Red herring fallacies, 335, 530–532
Reflective essay, 401, 405
Regressive bias, 503
Relative risk, 223
Reminiscence bump, 512
Reporting, *see* Clinical case reporting
Representativeness restraint fallacy, 139
Research articles, *see* Medical research articles
Research thesis, *see* Thesis and its seven cornerstones
"Restaurant refined menu" essay, 404
Restraint bias, 503
Rhetorical ploys, 360
Rhyme as reason effect, 503
Risk, 129–134
    argumentation, risk as subject of, 132
    bias, 133

characteristics, 130
compensation, 503
health sciences, risk in, 130
illustrative fallacies, 132–133
incidence rates, 130
knowledge of risk factors and markers, 132
markers, 130
probability, 129
reasoning about, 133–134
significance of risk factors, 130–132
Rosy retrospection, 512

S

Scientific method, 49–52, 417; *see also* Art, craft,
    scientific method, and evidence
Scientific theory, 49
Scut work, 358
Secondary prevention, 43
Secondary prevention of medical error, 144
Selective perception, 503
Self-evidence fallacy, 362
Self-generation effect, 510
Self-relevance effect, 512
Self-serving bias, 507
Semiotics, 14
Semmelweis reflex, 504
Sensitivity analysis, 300
Sequence of causes, 235
Sets of causes, 229, 235
Sexual overperception bias/sexual underperception bias,
    504
Shared information bias, 508
Shortcut decisions, 296
Single cause–single consequence relationship, 228
Skepticism, 50
Slippery slope fallacy, 361
Slips, 264
Sociability bias of language, 508
Social biases, 505–508
Social comparison bias, 504
Social desirability bias, 504
Social epistemology, 27
Socratic method, dissent, and dialogue, 339–342
Soft data, 134, 345
Source confusion, 512
Source credibility fallacy, 316
Spacing effect, 512
Specialty-bound definitions, 201
Spotlight effect, 512
Statistical inference, 113, 234
Status quo bias, 504
Stereotyping, 504, 512
Strategy-motivated definitions, 200
Subadditivity effect, 504
Subjective validation, 504

Suffix effect, 512
Suggestibility, 512
Sunk cost trap, 315
Surrogation, 504
Survival curve, 158
Survivorship bias, 504
Sutton's slip, 140
System justification, 508

T

Taxonomy of learning (Bloom), 81
Telescoping effect, 513
Tertiary prevention, 43
Tertiary prevention of medical error, 144
Testing effect, 513
Theory of medicine, 55
Thesis and its seven cornerstones, 171–189
    argumentative path, article in health sciences as,
        175–176
    best evidence available, critically appraised, 179
    context and setting of study, 185
    daily clinical activity, 174
    definitions used, 185
    objectives of research study, 179–181
    PICO format, 182, 183
    questions, 182
    research hypothesis, 181
    research objectives, 180
    research problem or topic of interest, 178
    research question as a formulation of research
        problem, 181–183
    research questions in qualitative research, 183–185
    task objectives, 180
    thesis statement, 178
    working thesis, 178
    written or oral communication, research and
        presentation of results defined as, 176–185
Third-person effect, 505
"Three-element" reasoning, 91–94
Threshold analysis, 300
Time-to-event analysis, 159
Time-saving bias, 504
Tip of the tongue phenomenon, 513
Toulmin's model of argument, "modern" form of,
    95–109
Trait ascription bias, 508
Travis Syndrome, 513
Treatment, 142–154
    appeal to authority fallacy, 154
    argumentation, treatment as subject of, 152–153
    Boeotian's fallacy, 153
    confirmation fallacy, 153
    critical thinking approach, 152–153
    evaluation, 147–151
    evidence-based approach, 152

fallacy of commission, 153
illustrative fallacies, 153–154
omission fallacy, 153
overconfidence fallacy, 153
patient characteristics, 151
primary prevention of medical error, 144
primordial prevention, 144
quaternary prevention, 144
reasoning in the domain of treatment and preventive
        interventions, 154
research integration, 150
secondary prevention of medical error, 144
systematic reviews, 150
tertiary prevention of medical error, 144
types and levels of medical therapeutic and
        preventive interventions, 143–147
Triage cueing, 139
Triviality, 505
"Two-element" reasoning, 89–91

U

Ultimate attribution error, 508
Uncertain definitions, 201
Uncertainty in medicine, 52
Universal science, 27

V

Value (judgment)-based definitions, 200
Verbatim effect, 513
Vertical line failure fallacy, 140
Voice cues, 349
Von Restorff effect, 513

W

Weber–Fechner law, 505
Web of outcomes, 163
Webs of causes, 231, 235
Webs of consequences, 231
Well travelled road effect, 505
Wikipedia, 493, 523
Wisdom, uttering, 335
Wishful thinking, 362, 494
Working thesis, 178
Worse-than-average effect, 508
Written communication, *see* Communication (written)

Z

Zeigarnik effect, 513
Zero-risk bias, 505
Zero-sum bias, 505

Printed in the United States
by Baker & Taylor Publisher Services